How to Get Your Child to Love Reading

BY ESMÉ RAJI CODELL

ALGONQUIN BOOKS OF CHAPEL HILL • 2003

Published by
Algonquin Books of Chapel Hill
Post Office Box 2225
Chapel Hill, North Carolina 27515-2225

a division of
Workman Publishing
708 Broadway
New York, New York 10003

Library of Congress Cataloging-in-Publication Data

Codell, Esmé Raji, 1968–
How to get your child to love reading/
by Esmé Raji Codell—1st ed.
p. cm.
Includes bibliographical references and index.
ISBN 1-56512-308-5 (pbk)
1. Children—Books and reading—United States. 2. Reading promotion
3. Reading—Parent participation. 4. Oral reading. 5. Children's literature—Bibliography
I. Title.

Z1037.A1C58 2003
028.5′5—dc21   2003040405

10 9 8 7 6 5 4 3 2 1
First Edition

How to Get Your Child to Love Reading

To Russell, my hero

Contents

Acknowledgments

A debt of gratitude to my publisher, designer, and the whole Algonquin team, and especially to Amy Gash, the world's most patient and gifted editor, who removed an ungodly number of exclamation points and had to remind me that masking tape is not a verb. Amy, the accomplishment of this book is as much yours as it is mine. This book would not have been possible without the genius of my parents, Betty and Barry Codell; thanks to both of you for your cheerleading during this project and for never letting me feel the "B" word as a child. The support of family and friends meant so much in the creation of this book. Thanks to everyone who hung on with me so patiently while I gave time and concentration to this project, with special thanks to Jim Pollock, Russell, Angelita Ballesteros, Celeste Wroblewski, the Brekke-Wasmer family, and Liza Tursky. Thanks also to Constance Roberts and Robert Storozuck (enjoy your retirements!), and the Rogers School community, to the ever intrepid Pubsters and the Teachers.net community, and the enthusiastic PlanetEsme.com gang for their encouragement and insight. Thanks to Amazon.com for their invaluable Web site, what a great research tool (sorry I didn't buy more books), to the unusually kind and enthusiastic people at the checkout and deli counter at Jewel Foods on Howard, and to the Evanston Public Library's children's department, the best in the Midwest. A hearty hat-twirl to the great state of Texas and to my favorite cowboy Dan Dailey, who publishes *The Five Owls,* where many of these essays first appeared.

Muchas gracias a Norma Gaytan, Leah Wonski, Susan Faust, and Ira Dubin for making life easier all along the way, praises to Yolanda Adams and Albertina Walker for the inspiration during the rewrites, appreciation to Patsy Oser for the dump cake recipe, and thanks to the always chivalrous UPS delivery guy Mike Hassler for carrying boxes of books up three flights of stairs. Christine, wherever you are, thank you for the circus ideas. And kisses to all the beautiful children who ever came to my home so I could read with them or helped me organize special programs in school (that means you, too, Saba and Meenaz; Cedrina Torry, future teacher, and Jane Packer, future author; and Marvelous Madame Rachel Moseberry—I know you will be a wonderful mom and I am so proud of you). Thanks, Mr. Brent, for hiring me in 1986 even though you thought my clothes were *ongepatshket.* Sincere gratitude to the children's book publishers who produce books worth writing about, with a special nod to the children's publicity departments at Candlewick, Harcourt, Henry Holt Books for Young Readers, Scholastic Inc., Houghton Mifflin, and Simon and Schuster, who cheerfully and generously supported my on-line endeavors from the very beginning. And finally, heartfelt thanks and applause to everyone whose name appears in this book. To the authors and illustrators, you are amazing magicians, you are imagination personified, you bring the world to children with your art. Even after looking at the thousands of books it took to create this one, I am still in love with you. Please send me your autographed picture for my Wall of Fame.

PART I

Beginning Your Adventure in the World of Children's Literature

Potato Power: The Art of Using What You've Got

This book started with a potato. I was sitting at my kitchen table, staring at a dimpled, wrinkling, sprouting old potato. I thought to myself, if I had a potato, nothing but a potato, how could I teach a classroom full of children?

Well, I could cut a potato in half. (I can use the paring knife from my own kitchen, right?) We could review fractions. With one half, I could cut a design and do potato prints. We could plant the eyes from the other half of the potato (it can have eyes, right?) and grow more potatoes, charting their growth. We could write a story about a potato, or write a book of potato recipes or potato poems. If we grew enough potatoes, we could make potato stamps of all the letters of the alphabet, and I could teach reading. I could go to the public library and find "The Potato with Big Ideas" from **LITTLE OLD MRS. PEPPERPOT** by Alf Proysen or **BRAVE POTATOES** by Toby Speed. We could talk about the Irish potato famine of 1845, maybe read true accounts from **FEED THE CHILDREN FIRST** by Mary E. Lyons or **BLACK POTATOES** by Susan Campbell Bartoletti. We could write letters to the executives at Frito-Lay about their potato chips, or Playskool regarding their product, Mr. Potato Head.

Perhaps I am a bit potato headed myself, wasting precious time plotting the pedagogy of potatoes, but it begs the question, how do we teach our children, using what is available to us? Moreover, is there anything available to us that is as plentiful and versatile as potatoes, ready to feed all appetites?

Yes, there *is*. Children's literature is our national potato. Thousands of studies from the U.S. Department of Education as well as findings by independent researchers here and ab—— consisten—— of ch——

Studies on the importance of lit.

can be converted into shared responsibility and success through children's literature. But the thing is, if you hand somebody a potato, or if you hand somebody a children's book, and he doesn't know how to make it cook . . . well, then.

This book is a recipe book for children's literature: how to serve it up so it's delicious and varied. Children's literature makes for a main course or a sustaining side dish, so you can use these recipes no matter what is on the menu in your child's classroom.

First, let's recognize the main ingredient: trade literature, which is the kind of books and reading material you can find readily available at bookstores and libraries. These books have clearly designated authors and illustrators, with characters that usually appear in print before they appear on a television screen. I was trained as a teacher but it was not through teacher training that I discovered there was the *whole world* in children's literature. Instead, it was during the seven years I spent in children's bookselling before I got my degree. Every genre and every subject was there in the bookstores, many at a level of quality that rivaled or exceeded that of adult literature—only specially designed with children in mind and encompassing so much energy, joy, and imagination that these elements became the criteria for excellence. This inspired me entirely. While studying to become a teacher, I could imagine nothing greater than delivering this world to the children I would teach. This dream became *my* energy and *my* joy. It was as the great Russian writer Maxim Gorky wrote about his discovery of books in *My Apprenticeship:* "I came to appreciate what good books really were and realized how much I needed them and they gradually gave me a stoical confidence in myself: I was not alone in this world and I would not perish!" By using children's literature, I had the utmost faith that when I became a teacher, I, too, would not perish or feel alone, which is a wonderful and sometimes unusual thing for a teacher to believe. But I considered myself in an even more formidable position to use exclamation points than Gorky, because not only would I not perish, not only would I not be alone in the world, I had the tool that would allow me to help children to feel the same amazing way.

As strongly as I feel about advocating for the child, I feel equally as strong about advocating for the author. If, in the course of delivering literature-based education, we can constantly remind children that authors and illustrators are real and singular people, with intentions, then we are not only giving children the books, we are giving them the people behind the books. And if you are talking about reading, you are talking about connecting the two. In facilitating this connection, the most important question we can ask about a book is, "Why did the author write this?" In other words, "What did the author want to share?" This is a very difficult question, and it is the most important question, because it connects the child across time and space with this real person, this author, who had something to share, and cared enough to share it. This is extraordinary magic, a trick that allows a child who can read the option of never being quite as alone as a child who cannot. "Why did the author write this?" is also a question that can be asked of any book on any level, thus opening up a world of picture books to older readers, because any reading is made more sophisticated when this relationship is addressed. The connection between the author or illustrator and the young reader is a particularly remarkable relationship in which an adult trusts a child with all sorts of dreams and stories and memories and confidences and explanations. For many children, this relationship with an author may be the first emotional bond shared with an adult outside her own family and community. From this perspective, it should not be taken lightly.

If your child understands that a book is an extension of an author, then your child will also understand that he may not always connect with an author's style, just like he may not always like everybody he meets. And he will understand that he can always get another book and read what someone else has to share. With the right guidance and some freedom of choice, he will find authors he likes. Most problems arise in school settings when too many mismatches have been bound into one big fat textbook that the child is assigned every day, or if the literature made available to that child is of poor quality or incongruous with the child's ability and interests. When this happens, no one can accuse a child of being unjustified if he forms negative associations with books and takes that bloodcurdling leap into the world of "I hate reading." If reading is indeed a relationship between author and reader, people in the position of matching children with books

are responsible for making informed choices so that the children are matched appropriately, so that they are most receptive to what the author or illustrator is trying to communicate. This is only difficult if you (a) don't know the body of literature available, (b) don't know the child, or (c) don't have access to books. I hope the thematic storytime adventures in this book will offer you a chance to know children's literature and to use it to connect with the children you love.

Potato Possibilities

When I figured out what I most enjoyed was sharing literature, I changed my job from "Madame Esmé, Classroom Teacher" to "Madame Esmé, School Librarian" so I could do more of what I loved. Whether working as a bookseller, storyteller, teacher, or librarian, I have discovered approaches

ALL RIGHT, ME-GENERATION-ERS. WHETHER YOU'RE READING TO YOUR OWN CHILD OR A GROUP, WHAT'S IN POTATO PEDAGOGY FOR YOU?

It's relaxing.

It's entertaining.

You will have quality time with your child.

You will laugh.

You will get to know the children your child plays with.

You will be recognized.

You get to go into classrooms when teachers' defenses are down, and to see what the dynamic is really like.

You get to *not* go into classrooms and still have confidence that you can help your child achieve in any circumstance.

Your child will be as proud of you as you are of your child.

You will get to look at good books, which you've been telling yourself you would take more time to do. (Remember New Year's Resolution #6 that you made back in 2000?)

You will have fun! (And you said you wanted to have more fun! Might I remind you of New Year's Resolution #1 that you made in 1992!)

You will get to say you kept some New Year's resolutions.

HAT TRICK

Do you look good in hats? Of course you do. You have been wearing one every day since your child was born. When you wear your Parent Hat, you encourage your child, spend time with your child, and provide for your child's basic survival. But by virtue of the fact that you are reading this book, I imagine you have another hat in your collection that you'd like to try on. When you wear the Teacher Hat, you find books and authors that your child will love to read, and you help your child find information through books. You expose your child to print, help your child learn to read, decode, comprehend, predict, question. You read aloud, integrate reading into all subject areas, model reading, show that there are real people behind the books. . . .

You see, the Teacher Hat is a big hat, more of a sombrero, and not everyone wears it well. Sometimes statements such as "literacy is the job of the school" are bandied about as a way of passing the hat. In fact, that statement is true: Literacy *is* a job of the school. In equal fact, teachers enjoy constructive parent involvement, though they may not always create opportunities for it. This book will allow you to invent those opportunities yourself, without detracting from a teacher's academic vision. Additionally, some teachers may have a lack of resources or training, or may be balancing a Parent Hat on top of their Teacher Hat, trying to instill self-esteem and create a sense of security and providing all sorts of support that used to be the business of the home. Just as it is lovely when a teacher goes that extra mile to make school a home away from home, there are things you can do to make your home a school away from school. School is just an invention, really, a place defined as a "learning zone," but it's actually quite arbitrary. There's no reason you shouldn't be empowered to make learning happen for your child wherever you see fit.

So when are you supposed to make this happen? In all your spare time? I am obviously forgetting the other hats you have hanging on your rack: the Maid Hat, the Wet-nurse Hat, The Ten-Gallon 9-to-5-Bring-Home-the-Bacon Hat, The Spouse Hat, the Chauffeur Hat. For goodness sakes! Can't the teacher just put on the Teacher Hat? *But mesdames, messieurs, ze Teacher Hat, she is ze most beautiful hat. Eet looks so good on you! You don't have to wear it all ze time, oh nonono, save it for ze special occasion.*

I'm really just trying to find a nice way of saying that when it comes to your own child's education, if you don't perform a hat dance, if you don't step outside your assigned role to do something extra exciting, don't expect that others necessarily will. With this in mind, please think big, and include as many children as you are able, because here's another scary thought: When it comes to some *other* people's children, if you don't do it, don't expect that others will, either. It's not about being a teacher, really; it's about being your brother's keeper. Or, at least, your brother's milliner.

that complement and support literature-based learning. Approaches are merely tools that allow us to present the main ingredient in delectable ways. Now, if we were talking about preparing a potato, maybe we'd approach it with a knife, a grater, a masher, a deep fryer. We'd need to come up with a lot of ways to prepare potatoes if we expected them to remain appetizing over a period of time. In this book, I discuss read-aloud, thematic, and integrated approaches to presenting literature—ways to keep books fresh, and, with a little practice, these approaches are as easy as mashing potatoes. Working with a theme, for instance, can give your child's reading a shape and can tie in to interests that will further motivate her. Nonfiction and historical fiction broaden learning's scope, and help children integrate, or see the connections between, reading and all areas of life. Read-aloud is the simple act of opening a book and reading it to a child. It can and should also be integrated into all areas of literature-based learning because read-aloud is literature-based education's gravitational force, the sun around which other planets, or literature-based approaches, revolve and maintain a forward direction.

As I was pondering potato possibilities for using what already exists, I realized that the potential for reading could reveal itself in unexpected places, too. We've all encountered the musician in the subway. Well, for a change of pace, what grown-up wouldn't enjoy a bit of read-aloud before the train arrives? Maybe an adventure serial, or a folktale for all five o'clock commuters? Wouldn't it be nice to hear the train coming and all the passengers crying, *"Aaawww,"* disappointed that they will have to wait to find out what happens—or excited to go out and buy the book for themselves?

I've also noticed children sitting on the curb in front of the Laundromat for hours, while their clothes wash, rinse, spin, wash, rinse, spin. What a perfect place for a bookshelf. Or how about the video store? How about books that were made into movies borrowed free with rental?

Then I looked at my own apartment. Couldn't I do something there?

The answer was *yes.* When I left teaching for maternity leave, and when I left again to write full-time and to run a children's literature Web site, I still had the desire to read to children. So I started to run children's literature programming out of my home. I realized how easy it was to do, and I also realized that anyone who likes children and children's books could do it, and would do it, if they knew how. People who understood the value of literacy and had the tools to instill that value in their children could create a remarkable community of readers. A country of readers. A planet of readers. Suddenly reading no longer seemed like such a solitary pursuit.

We have wonderful opportunities, all of us, to be proactive in delivering the best books for children and to work alongside educators. We aren't talking about anything exotic here. We are not talking about kiwi or rambutan or truffles or macadamias—remember, we are talking about the *potato* of education. I love when a teacher serves my child this potato. I am so thankful when she does. The great strength of our schools is that there are adults in those buildings who know what to do if they are only given a potato. But on the occasion when the schools don't deliver, I know I can. It is that freedom and empowerment that I hope to share with parents. And that is the premise and the promise of potato pedagogy. Let's not focus on worrying whether or not a child is full. Instead, let's assume a child is hungry. Let's focus on offering our children the best of what we have, knowing that if we offer it, the needs of the whole child will eventually be satisfied. All the children in this country can be fed!

Potatoes Up Close and Personal

This book is not just a book of ideas, but a book of personal experiences. These titles and suggestions have already been shared, tried, and proven with children from birth through eighth grade. I hope that they give you confidence to share, try, and innovate on your own. Some of the special features you will find in this book include:

Reading Heroes. Mentors from both the present and the past have taught me something important about reading, how to love it, and how to share it. I mention them throughout the book, in the hope that they will inspire you to consider and embrace your own reading heroes.

Dear Madame Esmé.

This "advice column" feature was inspired by the many letters and conversations I have had with teachers and parents from around the country looking for book recommendations to match their unique situations. You may find your own reading-related questions answered!

✿ Potato Picks.

No, this is not something your child pulls from his ear. Featured for excellence on the Web site PlanetEsme.com, these are suggestions for outstanding single titles, perfect for gifts or a read-aloud. Pick one with confidence whenever you need a surefire hit, or just use them to acquaint yourself as an adult with the best of children's books.

Thematic Lists. Special interests a specialty! Grab a pile of these books to create a great story-time or reading program based on the particular enthusiasms of the children you know and love. Also look for **creative cues** throughout the thematic lists. These imaginative crafts or activities serve as extensions of the ideas in the books and can help you entertain a hands-on horde.

Web sites. Log on to find resources that will further your knowledge and better your book collection.

As an author, I have personal biases that are sure to hang out like a loose hem, so I will admit to them now:

I am interested in educational theory. I like to know how children learn. There are many viable new and exciting theories and approaches out there that impact reading instruction, but I have to confess that my heart belongs to old-fashioned behaviorism, which views learning simply as a change in behavior. I have a particular interest in reading because it can be a great catalyst toward behavioral change. The changes can be subtle, such as knowing that the letter "B" goes "buh-buh-buh" when we didn't know "B" went any way at all. Or it can be more complicated: a change in the way we treat one another, such as moving from being suspicious or afraid to being at ease. Another covenant of behaviorism is that if you make people smile, they stick

around and keep trying, and if you make them frown or say "ow," they stay away. I think the changes possible through literacy are worth going to great lengths so that people smile and stick around.

Some people are of the theory that knowing theories doesn't make a doo-wah of a difference, that you can still make people smile and frown without knowing one thing about behaviorism, and that just by loving kids you will make learning happen. This may be true, but still, I don't subscribe to the theory of unilateral-theory-discard. I don't like having to operate on instinct. If you know why you are doing what you are doing, you can do a better job of advocating for your approach if it works, or understanding why it doesn't work and being more helpful next time. So I'll try not to be overbearing, but I do think it's important to acknowledge research and theoretical work now and then—to remind us that we are not reinventing the wheel here, we are trying to ride the bike.

I like read-aloud. Please assume (unless otherwise noted) that every fiction book I recommend is suitable for read-aloud and that, also in fact, I have read it out loud to a child or group of children before I recommended it here. You will find that much of the nonfiction is also right for read-aloud, but I am more circumspect about recommending it wholesale as such; cookbooks are not usually cliffhangers.

I like diversity. I take a multicultural, nonsectarian approach. Because I worked in public schools, the books I shared were centered more on holiday celebrations and less on religion or religious history. I am not an authority on sectarian literature. Nonetheless, I do believe the books I have recommended have value for character education, and I do consider literacy a worthy mission for all faiths.

I like baked goods. I fall for frosting and I'm a sucker for sprinkles. This bias makes me tend to sugarcoat things, literally. If any of my suggestions cause caloric concern, feel free to substitute granola bars, carob chips, fruit gummy-yummies, and carrot sticks for your children where you see fit.

I wish everyone could come over to my apartment so we could talk about children and I could show you some of my favorite books—but everyone is a lot of people and I don't think you'd all fit. So instead here in this book I offer the best of my bookshelves and kitchen and playroom and library and classroom. I'm going to load you down with potato stew to take to your own home and dish up to those you care about. You will, of course, add your own spice. I give you my best recipes in all self-ishness. I give to you from my own hunger for the day that all children will find the transports of reading, just as I was blessed to discover it thanks to people who cared enough.

Children's Book Basics

In folktales, the hero is given just a little advantage, some special helpful item such as an invisible cloak or magic walnut or bone or doll or needle or potion or some juicy insider advice. Since you are about to be the hero of your child's reading experience, it stands to reason that you are entitled to some special helpful item as you set out, to give you confidence that you will prevail in your efforts. Since I am low on magic bones and dolls and potions and walnuts, you will have to settle for Magic Background Knowledge, which will give you perspective on why you are doing what you are doing and help you deal with any adversaries.

Magic Piece of Background Knowledge #1
Read-Aloud Works Every Time

Literature-based learning involves maximizing the potential of what we already have in place, using our homes, libraries, and schools. All of these places have doors, and we need to hold them open in such a way that children can walk through and find a lifelong love of books. As the grown-up in charge, you will win the keys to those doors if you can answer a few simple game-show questions:

• What activity offers sixteen advantages to a child in twenty minutes?

• What helps to level the academic playing field for all children regardless of what statistical group they fall under (gender, class, race, working parents, single parents, English as a second language)?

• What approach has ten thousand research reports by the U.S. Department of Education backing it?

If you answered read-aloud to all three questions, you win a new refrigerator . . . and the key to better education. Daily read-aloud involves nothing more than reading a book out loud to a child, every day. The approach is versatile: The child may be following the text in your copy of the book, or in his or her own copy, or maybe not following the text at all, just listening to what is being read. It is unnervingly simple. It does not require any paperwork or special training, and asks nothing of the child but a little attention. In fact, it is so easy on everyone's part that it is hard to believe an activity only slightly more kinetic than television viewing could yield results that verge on the miraculous. But the results are in: Read-aloud is one of the extremely rare methods in education with positive results based not only in theory, but in reality, too. The implications and damn good reasons to read aloud are articulated in Jim Trelease's classic THE READ-ALOUD HANDBOOK.

HINTS FOR READING OUT LOUD (even to older children)

Love the book yourself before you read it to the children. Read it completely before introducing it. Then when you share it, you will be familiar with the contents and can read with more expression and anticipate questions. You will have a faith in the book's excellence that will compel you through the reading even if you have a tough audience. And when you cultivate affection for the books you read, every story you share can be a bit of a love story.

Choose a book that lends itself to reading out loud. Folktales, funny or spooky stories, stories with surprise endings, and stories in which children can join in are always fun. Unless you are dramatically gifted, books with lots of dialogue are tricky. Also, books with lots of introspection are sometimes more pleasurable to read alone.

Have high expectations. Make it clear that you expect school-age children to look, listen, and demonstrate consideration while you are sharing a book. If they falter, wait patiently while they get it together. Have high expectations of your book, too; there are too many wonderful books out there to ever share a blasé one.

Make read aloud time special. Gather around. Turn off the lights, turn on a cozy lamp or light a candle. Flop on pillows. Be comfortable, be intimate.

Be versatile in your approach. You read to them. Or, you read to them, but they all read along with their own copies. Or you read a page, then they read a page. Or . . . what else?

Introduce the artists. Always say the name of the author and illustrator before you begin reading, so children can make the connection that books are created by real people. It also sets the stage for discussion about style, creative decisions, and the all-important question, "Why did the author write this?"

Show the pictures while you read. If you are sharing a picture book, hold the book in one hand with your arm extended, with the pages facing your audience, so you are looking sideways as you read. If you are reading to a group, slowly rotate the book as you are reading so everyone can see. Use your other hand to turn pages. This all may seem obvious, but a lot of people forget. It takes a little practice to make it second nature.

Read with expression. Listen to yourself. Can your presentation be improved with dramatic pauses? Louder or softer speech? Funny voices? Don't be shy. They won't remember that you sounded silly. They'll remember an interesting book.

Don't overevaluate. The more you formally test and check, the more you kill the affective gain. That's teacher talk for "Don't take the fun out of it with tests and assignments." Use things that children can *do,* such as journaling, art projects, dramatizations, and discussion to determine whether they understand what is being shared.

Read aloud every single day. You and the children both deserve it. The more consistently you read aloud the greater the results will be. Consider it your intellectual vitamin. Read aloud from a novel, the newspaper, a poem, a diary, a play . . .

Leave them asking for more. Leave them groaning at a cliffhanger. Laughing at a joke. Crying along. Then say, "More tomorrow." And then deliver!

Applause, applause! Especially if you are reading to a group, clap when the reading is done as a way of sending thanks out to the artists, wherever they may be, and to encourage you, the reader! Good job!

Research compiled by Trelease establishes that sharing books:

1. Conditions the child to associate reading with pleasure, an association that is necessary in order to maintain reading as a lifelong activity.

2. Contributes to background knowledge for all other subject areas, including science, history, geography, math, and social studies.

3. Provides the child with a reading role model.

4. Creates empathy toward other people, because literature values humanity and celebrates the human spirit and potential, offering insight into different lifestyles while recognizing universality.

5. Increases a child's vocabulary and grammar, and has the potential to improve writing skills.

6. Improves a child's probability of staying in school.

7. Improves future probability of employment and higher quality of life.

8. Increases life span by virtue of correlated education, employment, and higher quality of life.

9. Lowers probability of imprisonment.

10. Improves problem-solving and critical-thinking skills that are fundamental and transferable to all other areas of learning.

11. Offers information.

12. Offers laughter and entertainment and an alternative to television.

13. Improves attention span.

14. Stimulates the imagination.

15. Nurtures emotional development and improves self-esteem.

And sweet 16. Reading skills are accrued skills that are bound to improve over time . . . a countdown to academic success.

Looking at this list of benefits, I see that read-aloud is kind of an education unto itself, like travel would be, which makes sense, since reading is mental travel. Older children need this trip as often as younger children do, although read-aloud tends to drop off as children age and adults become afraid to interfere in a child's reading self-sufficiency. The act of read-aloud is so easy and natural to do, and can be so enjoyable, that many parents (and teachers, too) feel it must be more appropriate and beneficial for younger children. This is a fallacy, and a very dangerous one: The fall-off of read-aloud can be correlated to the fall-off of interest in reading, with 90 percent of fifth-graders spending less than 1 percent of their time reading. Eighth-graders average a little less than two hours a week reading, including homework. While an older child may know how to decode the words, that's only the beginning of a life of reading, and without read-aloud, it could also be the end. More mature readers may need the flow of discussion to encourage prediction skills, to understand character development, to determine cause and effect. They benefit from the model of an adult reading with proper pacing and attention to dialect and punctuation, and learn to troubleshoot by watching an adult guess from context or look up an unknown word. Some adults are more comfortable taking turns reading out loud with a child, but please recognize that if the child prefers to simply listen, it is a perfectly safe indulgence. Read-aloud has the power not only to sustain but to resuscitate an interest in and affection for the printed word for children of *all* ages, and

this book will offer plenty of hooks to bring older and reluctant readers up to the same page as their more proficient peers.

Every single one of the outcomes of literature-based education is something that a child's teacher is hoping for and working toward every day, so read-aloud is the perfect home/school collaboration. Conflicts often arise between teachers and parents when they forget they are working toward the same goals. Read-aloud addresses goals that I believe everyone can agree upon, creating a beautiful bridge between school and home—in fact, making the two less distinguishable from one another. As a teacher, there was nothing I'd rather parents did with their child than read aloud on a regular basis. As a parent, there is nothing I'd rather be doing. Now that I am on the parent side of the fence, I wonder if the teacher is looking at my child with loving eyes, if she will see his potential the way that I do. Conversely, as a teacher, I have wondered if I was doing enough, recognizing enough, empowering enough. As both a parent and teacher, I have wondered which parts of my influence will dissipate over time. By reading aloud, though, I have confidence that I am giving children—my own and others—a great and lasting tool as they enter the wilderness of adulthood. A love of reading and a strong ability to read can be a compass leading children to the

information they need to survive or to live better, and leading them to a view of themselves and others that reaches toward the horizon. I don't think read-aloud will completely erase the guilt and doubt that plagues conscientious parents and teachers. I do think anyone who consistently reads aloud to a child can be assured that on some level they are giving a child the best that can be offered, whether the child attends public, private, or home school.

Magic Piece of Background Knowledge #2

Kids Have Reasons for Reading and These Reasons—or Motivations—Can Be Milked

Magazines, newspapers, picture books, comics, how-to books, novels … With the variety of print available, why is it sometimes so difficult to get children "into" reading? The simple approach I used when teaching can be modified to use at home. Think about reading in terms of motivations. I pick up a book and start scheming: "What could get a child to turn these pages?" I have found that the answer to this question falls under one of three categories: Interest, Integration, and Invention.

The Three *I*s

INTEREST

Interest-motivated reading is when a child seeks out reading materials for information and/or enjoyment. It is the motivation for pleasure reading. Maybe it's enjoying a book after seeing a related movie, wanting to read material that a

MATCHMAKER, MATCHMAKER, FIND ME A BOOK!

I hope that as a result of this book, you and your child will find not only new favorite books, but new favorite authors and illustrators. If your child likes a book I recommend, you may want to investigate what else that author or illustrator has published. I have not made any attempt to be all-inclusive (there are already several wonderful resources for that; see the start of Storytime Central, p. 341), but simply to offer credible starting points.

A single book can motivate a child in any combination of ways, provided it's the right book. Anyone actively involved in educating a child plays the role of matchmaker, taking into account all that is known about both author and reader to ensure that the matches are positive. If we are careless, we will send children on some very boring reading "dates." As parents we can vary motivators for reading and keep children engaged as they advance into intermediate and upper grades, a time in which children may already have a "history" of bad book relationships and when, unfortunately, reading scores commonly stagnate or suffer. It is less important to try to predict *how* a book will motivate a child; more important is to recognize that motivations to read really do exist and they exist for children at all ages. No child is a lost cause when it comes to reading any more than someone is a lost cause when it comes to falling in love.

new ideas and dreams. Anything we do for pleasure is also likely something we will want to repeat in the future, so even though interest is the simplest motivation, it is also the crux. Ideally it is joyful reading, indicative of will and individual taste. It is a lucky child who is allowed to choose his own books without judgment and whose parents and teachers suggest books solely to make the day more pleasant. It is through the freedom of choice that the child becomes self-actualized as a reader and is more likely to read for a lifetime.

Sample role-playing of a parent supporting a child toward interest-motivated reading:

• "You can stay up as late as you want tonight, as long as you're reading."

• "I know you like baseball. Here's a book of Hall-of-Famers."

• "Here's a flashlight. I've set a place for you in the closet/under the table/on those pillows over there, so you can have a private spot to read."

• "I've been saving this present for a rainy day. Here's a new book/my favorite book from when I was your age."

• "It is hard to wait! Here, read this, it'll make the time fly by."

• "Would you keep me company while I sort laundry by reading me an article that interests you from the newspaper?"

• "Tell me about that book you just finished. It looked interesting."

parent or teacher has shared, taking a book to camp or on vacation, reading on a rainy day, or pursuing a particular interest. Anything we do for pleasure can have visceral or emotional effects: smiles, laughter, tears; the feeling of being less alone; the sense that time is flying; the thrill of

PRETTY AS A PICTURE: INTEGRATING ART AND LITERATURE

It's nice that when talking about art, there are many ways to express a right answer. Be sure to talk about children's books from a visual perspective with children of any age who need to experience some success. If you're into it, fascinating guides such as John Warren Stewig's **Reading Pictures** series and Molly Bang's PICTURE THIS will help you help your child integrate visual arts to the fullest, but you don't need to go completely artsy-fartsy. Just a few questions like these will get you wondering alongside your child:

Where is the horizon in this picture?

Why do you think the artist chose these colors? How do they make you feel?

Why do you think the artist chose to leave all this space on the page?

What does this border or frame do to add to the picture?

What art supplies do you think the artist used to create this picture?

Isn't this artist's style realistic? Abstract? Cartoonish?

When you look at this picture, does it feel like the action is above us, next to us, or below us? How did the artist do that?

When you look at this picture, does this character/object seem near or far? Why?

What shapes do you see in this picture?

What in this picture tells us when the story happened and where the story happened?

Where does your eye want to go when you look at this picture?

Did you see how this one part of the picture is very dark, and this part is very light? Why do you think the artist chose to do that?

Show me where the artist used a line to make a shape.

Show me where the artist used a line to make texture.

What in the character's body or face shows you how he feels?

Wow! That character really seems to be moving! How did the artist make it seem like that?

Did we see that same thing on another page?

Does that look flat, or does it look like it's coming off the page? How did the artist do that?

INTEGRATION

I first learned about the power of subject integration as a bookseller in an independent bookstore. Integration was a trick used to get customers to walk away with more than they intended to buy by connecting literature to all areas of interest and learning. Integrated reading happens when a child is convinced to use reading as a springboard into other disciplines. The end product is often more tangible than interest-motivated reading, but still is directly related to the reading of a book. From an educational point of view, subject-integrated reading is extremely desirable because it affords two very special opportunities. First, it gives educators in places where arts education is undervalued a chance to incorporate the arts into basic skills: The arts are integrated every time kids are asked to create dance interpretations, dramatizations, songs, and visual art projects based on what they read. Creative interpretations are often art-integrated translations of fiction, but the *second* cool thing integrated reading does is lay out a red carpet for the reading of nonfiction. Integration takes books into the real world, where life (unlike most classroom studies) is not separated into subject areas, and where things are made and done. Your child may read a nonfiction book because of interest in the subject, but the outcome (knowing how to play a sport, measuring ingredients for a recipe, wowing friends with a yo-yo skill) may result in experiences that reach far beyond the pleasures and boundaries of the printed page.

Sample role-playing of a parent guiding a child to an integrated reading experience:

• "Why do you think the illustrator chose to put this character alone on the page, with all this space around him? Does the character seem near or far from us? How did the illustrator make it seem that way? (Reading = art.)

• "I'm so glad you enjoyed Joanna Cole's **Ms. Frizzle's Adventures in Ancient Egypt**. Let's go to the Field Museum this weekend and find out the real story about ancient Egypt." (Reading = history, social studies.)

• "I can't get this lawn mower/clock/toy to work. Would you mind going to the library to see if you can find **The Way Things Work** by David Macaulay to show us how it operates, so we can fix it?" (Reading = science.)

INVENTION

Invention-motivated reading does not only reflect the many facets of the book, it showcases the many facets of the reader. There is only a thin line between integration and invention. The best way to tell when invention-motivated reading has occurred is when the child produces something that integrates disciplines, but is unlikely or impossible to be duplicated by another child. The child departs from a formula, allowing the writing to influence his ideas, but not dictate the final product. For instance, two children can hear "The Three Bears," be given a recipe, and go home and make very similar tasting porridge. That would be integrated learning. But asked to invent a porridge that Papa Bear would enjoy, the children may come up with surprisingly different end products. That's invention . . . or, if you prefer, "inspiration," or "initiative." Reading that initiates or inspires invention may also elicit responses that have a very indirect relationship to the book, such as imitating small personal qualities of admired characters. As the young and brilliant diarist Anne Frank once wrote, "If I read a book that impresses me, I have to take myself firmly in hand before I mix with other people; otherwise they would think my mind rather queer." Reading that motivates initiative may be the most powerful of all. Such reading helps children experiment—and ultimately decide—what kind of people they want to be. Such reading helps children invent themselves.

While the other types of motivations often come into play before reading begins (attractive covers spark interest, the need to prepare a project at school leads to integration), invention is spontaneous and often determined after the reading is finished, requiring the child to not only read the book once but return to it. The decision-making and creative quality sets invention-motivated reading apart from the rest. Examples of end products might include: theatrics such as dances, puppetry, reenactments, musical interpretations; writing follow-up chapters at the end of a book, or creative writing such as in journals, letters, family newspapers; creating costumes; storytelling; creative cooking; imaginative play;

THE GLORIOUS FLIGHT
ACROSS THE CHANNEL WITH LOUIS BLÉRIOT
BY ALICE AND MARTIN PROVENSEN

social action. Adults can do less to initiate invention-motivated activities, because such reading is a very personal synthesis of the first two "I"s in order to create a sublime third "I." In other words, the book holds the child's interest, the child sees possible connections to the world beyond the book, and then the child decides to use that interest and insight to create something new. The truth is, you may usually find yourself more supportive in the *aftermath* of invention, as invention is by nature something that the child initiates, not you. If you are doing all you can to support interest and integration, you are encouraging invention. Invention-motivated children aren't just reading books. They are *doing* books, *living* books. As far as the family goes, this kind of reading can result in treasured memories and mementos.

Sample role-playing of a parent supporting a child toward invention-motivated reading:
• "Wouldn't it be fun to put together a little performance based on one of our books for a little after-dinner entertainment?"

• "Oh, what a long road trip ahead of us! What about taking this tape recorder and reading aloud a book, maybe make it into a kind of radio show that we can all listen to while we travel?"

• "Here's a pioneer lunch of johnny-cake and venison [corn bread and cold steak sandwich] to eat while you are living in the LITTLE HOUSE IN THE BIG WOODS [in the backyard]. Beware of bears!"

•"I love your collage! It looks like you got a lot of ideas from Ezra Jack Keats's THE SNOWY DAY."

• "Wow! The paper airplane you designed flies as well as the plane you read about in Alice and Martin Provensen's THE GLORIOUS FLIGHT."

"The more you read, the better you get at it; the better you get at it, the more you like it; and the more you like it, the more you do it," writes Jim Trelease. Helping children to read more is the first step to success, so one motivation is not more valid than another. But each in succession represents a heightening level of involvement with books that mirrors steps in child development: from the egocentric self-involved interest, to the world-aware integration, to the synthesizing inventive reader who ultimately creates a work of his own. In combination, they are building blocks to a lifelong love of reading and learning and a sense of competency that may translate into higher test scores and better success with other challenges. In combination, they create a fourth "I," Identity: I am a reader. I am a lover of books. I can get the information I need from words. I have the power of literacy.

YOUR JOB: CONNECT CHILDREN WITH BOOKS

I have found that it is a real minefield to ask a child with whom you are only casually acquainted, "What do you like to read?" because inevitably you will encounter the child who answers, "Nothing." And then, what are you supposed to do or say? It can be very uncomfortable. There are two better questions to ask children when trying to eke out clues to their reading motivations. One question I ask is, "Would you please empty your pockets?" The child will invariably have some little token, a toy, a button, candy, money, *some*thing to suggest an interest that can be tied to books. If the child's pockets really are empty, you can always recommend HOLES by Louis Sachar. The other tack is to ask what the child wants to be when she grows up, or what her parents do for a living. There is a book for every job in the want ads. For example:

ACCOUNTANT
ALEXANDER, WHO USED TO BE RICH LAST SUNDAY
by Judith Viorst

ARCHITECT
ROUND BUILDINGS, SQUARE BUILDINGS,
AND BUILDINGS THAT WIGGLE LIKE A FISH
by Philip M. Isaacson

BARBER
UNCLE JED'S BARBERSHOP by Margaree King Mitchell

BEAUTICIAN
RUBY'S BEAUTY SHOP by Rosemary Wells

BUS DRIVER
NEXT STOP
by Sarah Ellis

BUTCHER
LOUIS THE FISH
by Arthur Yorinks

CABDRIVER
THE ADVENTURES OF TAXI DOG
by Debra and Sal Barracca

COMPUTER PROGRAMMER
IF I HAD A ROBOT
by Dan Yaccarino

CONSTRUCTION WORKER
JOE AND THE SKYSCRAPER
by Dietrich Neumann

COSMETOLOGIST
MAKEUP MESS by Robert
Munsch

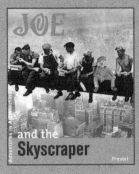

CRIMINAL
THE THREE ROBBERS by Tomi Ungerer

CURATOR
THE MOST AMAZING DINOSAUR by James Stevenson

DITCH-DIGGER
HIDDEN UNDER THE GROUND:
THE WORLD BENEATH YOUR FEET by Peter Kent

FARMER
ONCE UPON A FARM
by Marie Bradby

FIREFIGHTER
FIRE! by Joy Masoff

HOTEL MANAGEMENT
RABBIT INN
by Patience Brewster

INVENTOR
RUBE GOLDBERG: INVENTIONS by Maynard Frank Wolfe

JEWELER
A STRING OF BEADS by Margarette S. Reid

JOURNALIST
THE FURRY NEWS: HOW TO MAKE A NEWSPAPER
by Loreen Leedy

LAWYER
CHICKENS MAY NOT CROSS
THE ROAD AND OTHER
CRAZY (BUT TRUE) LAWS
by Kathy Linz

MAIL CARRIER
SPECIAL DELIVERIES
by Alexandra Day

MANUFACTURER
LITTLE FACTORY by Sarah Weeks

MILITARY
DRUMMER HOFF
by Ed Emberley

PLUMBER
THE BOY WHO HELD
BACK THE SEA
by Thomas Locker

POLICE
OFFICER BUCKLE
AND GLORIA
by Peggy Rathmann

PRESIDENT
SO YOU WANT TO
BE PRESIDENT?
by Judith St. George

REAL ESTATE AGENT
A HOUSE IS A
HOUSE FOR ME
by Mary Ann Hoberman

SALESPERSON
ON MARKET STREET
by Arnold Lobel

TAILOR
JOSEPH HAD A LITTLE OVERCOAT by Simms Taback

TELEMARKETER
TONI'S TOPSY-TURVY TELEPHONE DAY by Laura Ljungkvist

TRAIN ENGINEER
CASEY JONES by Allan Drummond

UNION ORGANIZER
CLICK, CLACK, MOO by Doreen Cronin

VET
ONE DAY AT WOOD GREEN ANIMAL
SHELTER by Patricia Casey

WAITRESS
HOPE WAS HERE by Jane Bauer
(Mature readers.)

. . . There are also books for
future artists (see Artist
Models p. 333), teachers
(see School Stories, p. 378),
doctors (see Gesundheit,
p. 408) and dentists (see Nothing but the Tooth,
p. 62), astronauts (see Far Out Space Stories, p. 405),
and environmentalists (see The Environment: Reading
for Your Great-Great-Great-Grandchildren, p. 177).

Magic Piece of Background Knowledge #3

Award Winners Are Children's Literature's Royalty and Knowing Them Is Handy

Awards are not always indicative of appeal to children, but they do call attention to distinctive writing and illustration. Awards also give publishers an impetus to continue putting out books of merit, regardless of commercial pressures, and encourage authors and illustrators to do the same. Work with children to discover, in your own opinion, which books and which book creators deserve special status.

After all, it is *your* opinion that really counts. When I see a children's book with an award, I do not automatically think, Here is a book my child should read above others. Ultimately, I have to consider what is likely to motivate my own child. Readability, personal tastes and interests will dictate children's visions of excellence, and will likely fluctuate with their development. What winning an award does mean is that a team of people in the field (usually librarians or critics) has determined that something about this book is notable. The book or the artist has met certain *criteria,* whether or not your child agrees that the book is exciting to read. The idea of standards, in general, is something all children will have to learn—or else they may be reading books featuring television cartoon characters or embossed covers for the rest of their lives. This determination of criteria by folks who give awards should be considered in the context of time; a book may have

won a prestigious award and in fact may be considered groundbreaking, but the award my have been given in 1960 when the standards of publishing were very different. The mark of a great award is one whose standards consistently reflect the highest level of excellence *for its time*—but maybe not *for all time.*

Standards, excellence, achievement—grownups love such bluster. What awards offer *children* is also the chance to applaud the achievements of somebody else. Like the World Series or the Super Bowl, awards give children's literature many of its stars, its heroes, its role models, its robberies, its victories. Awards give children's literature *drama.* There are over a hundred awards given annually, but if you were to keep up with them all, you'd go broke from renting tuxes. Keep all eyes on the following prizes if you want your finger on the pulse of children's literature.

NEWBERY AWARD AND CALDECOTT AWARD

These are the mother lodes, the awards that children's authors and illustrators stand in front of a mirror and pretend to accept. Given annually through the American Library Association (ALA), the Newbery Medal goes to the author of the most distinguished contribution to American literature for children (aka best writing), while the Caldecott Medal is given to the artist of the most distinguished picture book (aka best illustration). One gold medal in each category and several silver honors are bestowed upon the chosen few. There is a huge amazing gala ball thrown and

BIG WINNERS: WEB SITES THAT LIST AWARDS

AMAZON.COM

www.amazon.com/exec/obidos/subst/lists/awards/
awards.html

All the ALA awards plus the National Book award.

AMERICAN LIBRARY ASSOCIATION

www.ala.org/alsc/awards.html

The biggies! Awards include Newbery
(www.ala.org/alsc/newbery.html), Caldecott
(www.ala.org/alsc/caldecott.html), Laura Ingalls
Wilder, Coretta Scott King, Mildred L. Batchelder,
Robert F. Sibert, and Michael L. Printz, among others.

ASSOCIATION OF JEWISH LIBRARIES

www.jewishlibraries.org

Sydney Taylor Awards.

BOOK SENSE

www.booksense.com/readup/awards/index.jsp

Books of the year chosen by independent booksellers.

CARNEGIE AND GREENAWAY AWARDS

www.carnegiegreenaway.org.uk

British Prizes.

CATHOLIC LIBRARY ASSOCIATION

www.cathla.org/regina.html

Regina Medal.

CHILDREN'S LITERATURE WEB GUIDE

www.acs.ucalgary.ca/~dkbrown/awards.html

International awards, Children's Choice, Boston
Globe–Horn Book, Scott O'Dell, and more.

INTERNATIONAL BOARD ON BOOKS FOR YOUNG PEOPLE

www.ibby.org

Look under "IBBY Activities" to find the Hans Christian
Andersen Award.

NATIONAL BOOK FOUNDATION

www.nationalbook.org/nba.html

National Book Award.

the gold winners get to make a big speech, which is published in the *Horn Book Magazine.* Winners also receive about as much publicity as is possible for someone in the field of children's literature. The complete lists of award winners are in Appendix A, and you will probably find some very familiar and beloved titles there, such as Madeleine L'Engle's **A WRINKLE IN TIME,** Lois Lenski's **STRAWBERRY GIRL,** and Esther Forbes's **JOHNNY TREMAIN.** Outside of this list and a few references within thematic lists, you will not find a great deal of attention paid to Newbery and Caldecott winners in this book. Frankly, you would most likely encounter them without my help, and probably already have.

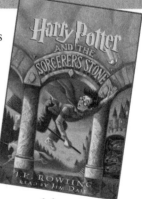

The British counterparts to these awards are the Carnegie Medal for writing, and the Kate Greenaway Medal for illustration. Though given across the Atlantic, they are well worth keeping an eye on. After all, in 1997, a Carnegie honor was given to a little book called *Harry Potter and the Philosopher's Stone* by J. K. Rowling, which proved *raw*ther popular here in the States when republished as **HARRY POTTER AND THE SORCERER'S STONE.** Beat the next British invasion by keeping abreast of their best.

LAURA INGALLS WILDER MEDAL

This prize, also given by the ALA, honors an author or illustrator whose books, published in the United States, have made a substantial and lasting contribution to literature for children over a period of years. Established in 1954 and named after the beloved author of the **Little House** series, this medal was given every five years until 1980; since 1983, it is given every three years. It's kind of a "lifetime achievement" award, and its winners indeed make up an awesome list, including legends such as Beverly Cleary, Maurice Sendak, and Dr. Seuss. The Regina Medal given by the Catholic Library Association is similar, honoring continued distinguished contribution to children's literature, but the author need not be an American.

THE NATIONAL BOOK AWARD

Traditionally an award for works aimed at adults, a National Book Award has been issued annually for "Young People's Literature" since 1996. Given for writing, this newer award is one to watch. The pool of talent reflected in the winners bodes well for these awards someday rivaling the prestige of the Newbery.

HANS CHRISTIAN ANDERSEN PRIZE

This was the first international children's book award. Given by the International Board of Books for Young People, it honors an outstanding author and illustrator every two years, sort of a "best of planet." And if you don't like subtitles but love foreign children's literature intrigue, check out the Mildred L. Batchelder Award. This ALA citation is awarded to an American publisher for the most outstanding children's book originally published in a foreign language in a foreign country, and subsequently translated into English. The award encourages American publishers to seek out

superior children's books abroad and to promote communication among the peoples of the world.

Some awards are given with special attention to genre. The Robert F. Silber Informational Books Award is awarded annually to the author of the most distinguished informational book published during the preceding year. The Michael L. Printz Award is for young adult fiction (books for mature readers). The Scott O'Dell Award honors outstanding historical fiction set in the New World, and the Edgar Allan Poe Award is for . . . what else? . . . outstanding mystery and suspense for children.

Other awards pay special attention to race, color, and creed. The Pura Belpré Awards, established in 1996 and given biennially, are presented to Latino/Latina writers and illustrators whose work best portrays, affirms, and celebrates the Latino cultural experience. The Coretta Scott King Awards are given every year to black authors and illustrators for outstanding inspirational and educational contributions to children's literature. The Sydney Taylor Awards mark what are considered the best Jewish-interest books. Such prizes acknowledge the contributions of talented artists while encouraging a strong multicultural body of children's literature—something that did not always exist.

As I have mentioned, these awards are determined by panels of "experts," but no one could be more expert than children on what children like. For the books that won children's hearts, check out the Children's Choice Awards. Each year an average of one hundred favorite books are chosen by approximately ten thousand children ages five to thirteen from different regions of the United States. Books are selected from new publications donated by North American publishers. While these books may not be as distinguished as some of the winners of awards listed above, when it comes to fun they definitely go for the gold. States

YOU LIKE ME! YOU REALLY LIKE ME! HOLD YOUR OWN AWARDS PROGRAM

"Young Authors" contests or other programs that encourage children to make their own bound books are winning ways for parents to get involved in schools. Solicit and collect student-generated books from any given year, and help a committee of children set criteria, review the books, and give an award for best writing and best illustration! Newbery and Caldecott seals are available for purchase through ALA (www.alastore.ala.org, or call to request an ALA Graphics catalog, 1-800-545-2433), although an award the committee names and designs is sure to be funkier and more personal. Have an award party or assembly and let the winners give a speech (they need the practice, in case they win a real Newbery or Caldecott down the line). Recognize all participants with a certificate or small memento. Put the books in the class or school library for check-out (if they aren't too precious), or let them be displayed for all to enjoy.

You can also hold a mock Newbery/Caldecott competition using trade books. Have children read books published in the most recent year and let them try to determine who *should* win the Newbery or Caldecott. Research the criteria and contact your local public librarian in the fall for an educated guess about which books are in the running. ALA winners are announced in January.

These contests help foster a community for reading groups, homeschoolers, and, of course, classrooms. Even if the book your children choose doesn't win, they can write that author or illustrator a letter (care of the pub-

lisher) to let the artist know the book is *still* a winner in their eyes! Of course, you can set up your own award completely separate from the criteria of the ALA and give it to the artist of your choosing. If you are lucky enough to have a school or organization with a budget, offer an honorarium and see if the winner can come to speak. Let the fanfare begin! Red carpet remnants are cheap at rug stores, and can be reused for future author visits. (See Meet a Real Live Author, p. 317.)

A word of advice: Awards programs in which children are invested can be very sportive, and as such should be very sportsmanlike. Competition should never be a popularity contest; the focus should always be on the work, not the person. Merits and strengths should be discussed more than shortcomings in making selections. Artists can be sensitive. Young artists, like old ones, sometimes need to be reminded that the goal of great art isn't to win anything, but to say something worth saying or to show a unique vision of the world. The excellence of others lays a path for our own best work.

You can order *The Newbery & Caldecott Mock Election Kit: Choosing Champions in Children's Books* directly from ALA at www.ala.org/alsc/nc_mock.html (or call 1-800-545-2433 if the computer is down), but if you simply type "mock Newbery" or "mock Caldecott" in your favorite search engine, you'll come up with all sorts of fun local competitions, such as my favorite at the Allen County Public Library, www. acpl.lib.in.us/Childrens_Services/mockawards.html.

generally have children's choice awards. Ask your local librarian for a list of past winners, and then root, root, root for the home team!

And if the book you thought would win the Literary Olympics doesn't even cross the finish line, hold on to your hope . . . for at least twenty years, when your title will be eligible for the Phoenix Award. Established in 1985 by the Children's Literature Association, it is awarded annually to a book originally published in English twenty years previously that did not receive a major award at the time of its publication.

There are also several commendations given to children's literature that can help parents distinguish notable books. You may see mentioned on front or back covers honors such as the *Boston Globe–Horn Book* Award, the *New York Times* Best Illustrated Children's Book of the Year, or the ABBY Award (given by the American Booksellers Association). A book may have received a starred review from a review source such as *Kirkus Reviews, The Horn Book Magazine, School Library Journal, Booklist, Publishers Weekly,* or *Riverbank Review.*

There are so many sources in which we can find recommendations for outstanding books—maybe too many, but maybe not. An average of four thousand new children's books are being added each year to the shelves of many thousands of children's books that have already been published, so adults who are new to juvenile treasure seeking may do well to ask for a map now and then. Periodicals like the ones mentioned above and Web sites (such as www.kidsreads.com) help provide direction. The trick is to find an award, citation, journal, or review source that reflects both your criteria for excellence and the tastes of the children with whom you plan to share.

Magic Piece of Background Knowledge #4

Levels, Shmevels! In the World of Letters, Numbers Can Be Misleading

When I was in my early twenties and working as a children's bookseller, by and large the impression customers gave me was that they thought of their children in extremes. Either they were reading prodigies ("She's in fifth grade but she can read on an eleventh-grade level!") or disappointing dullards ("She's two years behind grade level!"), and these opinions seemed rooted in numbers that were closely tied to test scores or grades. When I recommended books, before the binding was even broken, I was often asked, "What grade level is this book?" This was easy to determine, because in most cases I could just turn the book over and there it was: something written out like RL 4.8, "reading level fourth grade, eighth month." How was the reading level on the back of the book determined? The numbers and their significance were mysterious to me.

When I entered teaching school, I found that any number of formulas could have been used to create the numerical reading level. Perhaps the Kincaid Readability Formula was applied: (words

A RULE OF THUMB

The best trick I ever found for helping children choose books that won't be too frustrating is the "Rule of Thumb." Have a child choose a page in the middle of the book with a lot of text, and make a fist. Explain to the child that she should not use the fist to punch anyone in the nose. Instead, read the page silently, and if you come to a word you don't know and can't guess, put out your thumb. If you find another word, put out another finger, and so on. If you reach the end of the page and between three and five are up, that means the book will be a challenge. The child can decide if she is motivated enough to try to read it anyway (you can offer help), or she can choose to save it for the future. A pleasure read should have 0–2 fingers up. The pleasure was all mine working as a librarian, teaching the technique to classes and then watching children check on books for themselves.

I found this technique in one of my favorite education books of all time, a clever little paperback published in 1968 called HOW TO TEACH READING WITH CHILDREN'S BOOKS by Jeanette Veatch. Since sharing it with other teachers, some veterans have told me that the Rule of Thumb goes back much further than that. Grandma knows best.

per sentence $\times$ .4) + (syllables per word $\times$ 12) − 16. Or perhaps the Fry Readability Graph was used, in which a 100-word section of straight prose is chosen, and the number of sentences in the passage are counted, and then the number of syllables are counted. Are you listening? The number of sentences versus the number of syllables is compared to obtain the grade level, which is determined on the graph. Pay attention! Fry's readability graph is extremely popular, especially in textbook-land, but does not account for content, which may dramatically change how appropriate a given text is for a given age group. Dale-Chall and Spache readability tests compare texts against lists of standard vocabulary and calculate the percentage of words not on the list to determine readability. Yoo-hoo! There's the Powers-Sumner-Kearl Formula, there's the Degrees of Reading Power scale, there are the FOG and the SMOG methods of counting words and syllables. . . .

Oh, there are so, so, *so* many graphs and charts and scales to help answer the question, "What level is this?" And if you love math as much as you love reading, you can investigate them. And if you love children more than you love either math or reading, you can take all of it with a grain of salt because all the sadism that went into explaining that mumbo jumbo is the same sadism a child senses when a book has been selected with grade level as the main criterion. If reading the prior paragraph isn't enough to stop you from caring about levels, remember torture isn't the only shortcoming of numeric reading formulas.

Since there is no way of determining by the level indicated on a book which scale was used and whether that scale was most appropriate for assessing a particular text, a reading level can only be considered a suggestion. "Readability" on such scales often refers to what words a child can recognize and/or sound out, and is not necessarily an indicator of what a child comprehends. In other words, just because a child can say a word doesn't mean he knows what he's saying, and scales measure more saying than knowing.

Further, book levels assume that reading is going to be done independently, and so levels can often be ignored in cases where reading is shared. Children listen on a much higher level than they read themselves. An average first-grader, for instance, can likely understand text written for a third-grader if it is read aloud, and the same goes for a fifth-grader listening to books written on an eighth-grade level.

And finally, readability does not take into account any motivations for reading. A book written "on level" that holds no interest to a child will be much less pleasurable than a book that speaks to a child. The behavioral consequences of reading a book at grade level that holds no motivating force will be the same as that of an overly difficult book: a reading turn-off. If a child is highly motivated to experience a book that is above level, she will likely seek help in comprehension by asking another reader or by applying strategies such as guessing from context or using a dictionary. If she can successfully find that help, the book will in fact be readable and also stretch her vocabulary, word attack skills, and attention span. And if your highly capable child chooses a low-level book, perhaps she will be using it toward higher-level motivations such as integration and invention, or maybe she just needs a reading ego boost or is reading purely for entertainment. Perfectly kosher.

I am more sympathetic to adults who fear a work is "too old" for a reader or listener. Children's

books are expensive, and it is reasonable to hope that the child will be at a stage of development to receive what the artist has to offer at the time the book is shared. Optimum accessibility may begin at a certain age but does not necessarily end at any age (I'm living proof!). The danger of relying on levels occurs more often when the level indicates the book is "below" a reader. This nasty attitude separates the reader from the artist and serves the reader poorly. The process of leveling usually displaces picture books from the hands and hearts of older readers (including adults), even though an excellent picture book can model the highest forms of narrative and visual art and also offer multicultural perspectives. I hate when I am pressed to give a level. I try to start with the youngest audience I can imagine the artist would be comfortable showing his or her work to. Yet, if I say, for instance, "this book is for five and up," I know someone out there won't consider giving it to an eight-year-old because maybe the eight-year-old is above grade level anyway, so what would that eight-year-old get out of a book that would be appropriate for a five-year-old? The answer is: a laugh, a thought, an appreciation of an illustration, a connection to the author, an interest, a motivation. Maybe if I said, "This book is for five and up and up and *up*," it would help. Maybe not.

I am also sympathetic toward parents who are concerned that by ignoring book levels, they are putting their children at risk for low achievement on standardized tests. I am sympathetic, but not in agreement. You can use that energy to worry about something else, because the more exposure to print a child experiences, the more likely it is that he will be able to read well. Trust that an enjoyable quantity of quality children's books at a variety of levels should yield favorable test results.

If I have had success with a particular age group and a book, I will let you know, but for the most part, mention of numeric levels is avoided. I generally think of books as **primary** (preschool through third grade), **intermediate** (fourth through sixth) and **older readers** (seventh grade and up), again, using these stages as potential starting places to introduce books, never as ending places. Picture books predominate in the lists because of their versatility. A lot of the nonfiction titles throughout are geared toward intermediate readers because of the content. The key is basing selections on your own child's motivations. In a few cases references to adult topics such as death or sexuality warrant a **"mature readers"** notation, and I have recommended age groups in the "Potato Picks" peppered throughout to give some frame of reference and confidence to novice book-sharers.

Reading levels may indeed be useful suggestions when trying to find materials for children with special and frustrating reading challenges such as dyslexia or word recall problems. Reading levels are also useful for children in the midst of emergent literacy (see Series Books and Strategies That Support Emergent Literacy, p. 53). These children learn sight words and gain confidence from the repetitions and controlled vocabulary found in early reading books. But children who have advanced beyond emergent literacy should not have anything further to prove outside of the sustained motivation to read, which we, as adults, are in part responsible for cultivating, and which *all* books potentially can fertilize. Too much attention to book levels can create an unnecessary dependency on others to determine appropriateness of material. Nobody knows your child better than you do, except maybe your child, so there's your expert consultant.

You can encourage children to seek help as they read, you can read aloud to children, you can use reading to share in the thoughts and lives of others. When you look at reading as an experience in which there is a constant flow of support, communication, even socialization, as I have suggested, levels fall into perspective.

The bottom line is, don't let somebody else's scoring system define your child, and don't let reading levels level your child's love of reading. Make the only numbers you care about right now the number of books at your child's bedside, the number of visits to the library, the number of hours you spend reading aloud, the number of times your child asks a question about what you have read or points at a detail in a picture. You pick your numbers.

BORROWING AND LENDING: A BOOK-LOVER'S GUIDE

The adage "never a borrower or lender be" is easier said than done in the world of children's books. For one thing, picture books can be terribly expensive. A network of trustworthy parents can circulate many such treasures among their children. Grown-up book clubs may enjoy round-robin-ing children's books; the regular schedule of book club meetings is added insurance that you will ultimately get the book back, and reciprocal borrowing is nicer than one-sided borrowing. If you have a good collection, it is also a wonderful resource to lend piecemeal to your child's classroom. You may hear your friends talking about something going on in their lives or an interest that their child may have and know there's a book on your shelf just burning to be borrowed! Here are some thoughts that may help you feel more laissez-faire about lending.

LENDING

• If you like to lend books, make them last. Remove slipcovers from hardbound books before you lend them (this is a good way to keep track of what you lend out as well) or cover them with plastic book jackets sold through library suppliers. I get a 100-yard, 12″ fold-on book-jacket roll through Brodart, 1-888-820-4377, www.brodart.com. This laminate can be cut to fit and cover any size book. For paperback books, cover them with transparent ConTact paper sold at hardware and variety stores. Covering books requires some investment of time and money, but your borrowing friends will be proud to return your books in such good shape and you'll be mighty glad to have them back that way.

• Even the most responsible friend can forget where a book came from. Put bookplates in any book you lend.

Create bookplates by making a color copy of a photo of your child with a cartoon bubble, "This book belongs to me, (child's name)." Or, download plates designed by real children's book illustrators at the amazing Home Library site, www.myhomelibrary.org/home.html.

• If you are lending a book to a classroom, be sure to attach a Post-it note that clearly specifies the book is a loan, so there's no uncomfortable confusion. "Heard you were studying dinosaurs this week, thought you might like to borrow this book."

• You think you will remember what you lent, but you won't. If you write titles down in the presence of a friend, assure your friend it is a gesture not of distrust but of you keeping track of things so you won't hunt for them later.

• Consider keeping plastic bags and bookmarks handy and give them out when you lend books. Adorable ones are available through the reading promotions catalogs at Demco, 1-800-356-1200, www.demco.com and Upstart, 1-800-448-4887, www.highsmith.com, but of course you can also use whatever is handy around the house. Either way, such sidelines send a message that you care how books are treated—especially your own.

• One of my favorite scenes is in Sarah Stewart's THE LIBRARY, in which a bibliophile makes a midnight raid to retrieve a tome from the home of a delinquent borrower. Extreme? Maybe the midnight part, but if a friend does not return a book within a month or other specified time, it's fine to mention it during daylight hours. Likewise, if you are visiting a friend and notice one of yours on her shelf, it's okay to say, "Are you finished with this?"

• Do not lend books that are out of print, autographed, or otherwise precious. It is hard to say no, but a friend will understand if you explain that it is hard to replace, and if anything would happen you would hate to have any bad feelings between you. If any lending might create bad feelings, that's okay, too. Be honest and say so, and offer to write the title down for your friend.

BORROWING

• There must be some law that says, whenever you borrow a book—a book you *think* you will read and give right back—things happen, terrible, *terrible* things that rarely happen to your own books. If you do borrow a book and it is lost or damaged, don't even mention it to the person who lent it to you until you have made every effort to replace the book. Even books that are out of print are easily relocated online. If you can't replace it, offer to pay for it. In either case, apologize, of course.

• The best thing to do if your friend has a book that interests you is to write it down and buy or borrow it later from a library. If a friend notices your interest and offers to lend you the book, it's fine to accept. If it is going to take you a while to read a book, say so. If you are borrowing more than one, offer to write the titles down for your friend.

• If you borrow a book, the minute you get home write a note to yourself on a calendar a month from that day, "Did you return Jill's book?" Don't wait until your friend asks for a book back to return it. If a friend has to ask, you've waited too long.

Children, especially intermediate readers hooked on series books, often engage in book borrowing and lending. If you have book-loving children in your home, it's never too early to discuss borrowing protocol.

Magic Piece of Background Knowledge #5

You Can Locate Long-Lost Books

Children's Books go out of print relatively quickly, and so any children's book resource is doomed to have a number of outdated titles. But luckily you can still find out-of-print books in children's library collections, and *very* luckily, if you have a computer, finding an out-of-print book is nearly as easy as finding a book in print.

Check out these sites:
www.addall.com
www.alibris.com
www.bibliofind.com
www.half.com

Amazon.com lists available copies of used books—which are not necessarily out of print—whenever you look up a new title. This is kind of nefarious, because it undercuts the author's and illustrator's royalties. Sometimes books that are put up as "used" are actually advance reading copies, which were not even supposed to be for sale at all. Reviewers or industry professionals receive these "uncorrected proofs" from the publisher for free and then people get their hands on them and try to make a buck. Oh, well, I suppose all is fair in love and reading. But remember, as a reader, you are not just a consumer. You are a Patron of the Arts. If you want to be a good scout, support authors when you are able. This also helps worthwhile books stay in print.

Raise Your Hand If You Want to Volunteer in Your Child's School!

Ask not what your child's school can do for your child . . . no, I take that back. *Do* ask what your child's school can do, and then what you can do! If you are interested in joining forces with the Board of Ed, rely on this book not only for home support but to provide loads of ideas for volunteering in your child's (or grandchild's) school. I've been a teacher and so from my own experience I'll give you tips throughout the book for how you as a parent can infuse your special energy into the classroom ethers. Volunteer ideas range from easy to complicated, so how do you know what kind of volunteering is right for your time and interest level? Simple. Take the . . .

Not-So-*Cosmo* Volunteer-in-the-School Quiz!

1. The type of cookies you like to make are:

a. The ones where you have to keep the dough refrigerated overnight, roll it out, then shape with cookie cutters and decorate with a homemade frosting.

b. Slice and bake.

c. Chips Ahoy.

2. You are at a party where you realize you don't know anybody there but the hostess. You:

a. Remind yourself, "A stranger's just a friend I haven't met!" and network like it's 1999.

b. Busy yourself by helping to chop crudité and washing the odd dish, smiling at folks passing through the kitchen.

c. Whisper to the houseplant, "Somebody kill me now."

3. Your dream wedding involves:

a. A carriage ride to the church, a Vera Wang gown, a live band, and a guest list that includes your former camp counselor. Release of doves optional.

b. A trip to city hall with nearest and dearest, followed by dinner at favorite restaurant. Vegas optional.

c. An e-mail confirmation from matrimony.com: "Your marriage has been confirmed. Please print for receipt." Divorce optional.

If you answered (a) to these questions, you like to plan ahead, and you're an ebullient "people person." You're willing to put forth a lot of time and energy if you think it will pay off. As a volunteer, you are a leader. You can handle parent-run programs or special events, but anything you do will be marked by your snazzy flair.

If you answered (b), you are friendly, helpful, and down-to-earth. You can do the big stuff if the spirit moves you, but low-key fun is also just fine, especially since you've already got so much on your plate. As a volunteer, you give a warmth and humor to storytimes, bulletin boards, and simple projects.

If you answered (c), just write the school a check and back away slowly.

If you answered in combination, congratulations! You are human. You do not always have the time or inclination or hormonal balance to take on big projects, but deep down you want to make the world a better place. You look for clues, little signposts in the world to tell you *how* to do it, and you look at the calendar and the wristwatch for *when.* If you can come up with a *when,* this book will show you *how,* in the following ways.

Parent-Run Programs
(for A people)

Some of the most appreciated after-school and before-school programs are run by parents, because they are during times when teachers are trying to catch their second wind or create their first. Some programs can go year-round, such as Literature Circles (see p. 303), Cinema Club (see p. 211) and Raise-a-Reader (see p. 69). Or you can adopt a skill such as puppetry (see p. 229) or story-telling (see p. 234) and run the program workshop style over just a few weeks. This is a nice volunteer

option for parents who like to build relationships and see progress over time—and also have the time to see it. Stay-at-home parents, parents with older, more self-sufficient children, and parents with flexible work schedules may find this kind of volunteering feasible. Some schools have money, either through active Parent Teacher Associations (PTAs) or government Chapter I funds, to pay folks who run regular programs a small stipend. So if you have to decide between running a program or watching your neighbor's child for extra milk money, it doesn't hurt to ask.

Special Events and
Fund-raisers *(for A people)*

Volunteer to organize an annual event, such as a Johnny Appleseed Anniversary (see p. 80), a

A HELPFUL TACK: VOLUNTEER TO DO A BULLETIN BOARD

One of the most helpful and appreciated acts of volunteerism in the classroom (and children's library) is the decorating of the bulletin board. That innocuous bit of cork is every teacher's bane. It is supposed to be decorated regularly with cutouts that boldly booster a concept the children are learning in class or showcase the children's best work. A really nice bulletin board takes a good chunk of time to devise and decorate, time perhaps better spent on lesson planning . . . but by the same token, the children have to look at it every day, and a cheerful one does so much to brighten up the classroom. The teacher's conundrum is your big chance as a volunteer to advertise for literacy. You can create a bee-*you*-tiful bulletin board about any favorite book even if you're not a great artist. Simply take the title to a copy shop and get a transparency made of your favorite illustration (tell the guy behind the counter it's

for "one time educational use" to stay on the good side of copyright law). Then, take the transparency to the classroom and use an overhead projector to shine the image onto the bulletin board. Trace and color, and voilà! Of course, you can familiarize the children with the book through a storytime and use the board to display creative responses to the reading, such as the ones suggested in Animal Kingdom (see p. 354) and Books in Living Color (see p. 397). Bulletin-board borders, construction paper, lettering, and wonderful rolls of Fadeless Art paper that can be cut to fit any size board are staples in most teachers' pantries and should be made available to you. In a pinch, you can find what you need at teacher supply stores, office supply stores, or through www.classroomdirect.com, 1-800-248-9171; or request a catalog from The Learning Tree, www.edu mart.com/thelearningtree, 1-800-688-2959.

BOOKS MAKE PLEASANT PRESENTS

If you can't give of your time, you can still give of yourself. Tuning in to what's going on in your child's world will help you come up with thoughtful gifts. Did your child (or another child) lose his first tooth in class? Mark the occasion by donating a tooth book to your child's class library (see Nothing but the Tooth, p. 62.) Was your child out sick with strep for a week? Send him back with a book (see Gesundheit, p. 408). Couldn't chaperone on that field trip to the farm? Follow up with a good barnyard book (see Tales from the Barnyard, p. 361). How about a book basket for a teacher about to go on maternity leave (see Russell's Book Basket, p. 40), book-related dolls to decorate the school library (see Toyland Friends, p. 402), or just something great that the teacher can read aloud to your child's whole class (see Potato Picks throughout)? Most of the books included in this volume would make a wonderful gift, so use your creativity. Invent your own gift-giving occasions, or just lend books from your own family collection when they are apropos (in which case, be sure to put a bookplate with your name inside to avoid confusion (see Borrowing and Lending, p. 28). Besides showing teacher appreciation, books and book-related presents go far to incite random acts of reading! Almost anything you give is likely to be enjoyed and remembered not only by the teacher, but also by children for years to come.

Parade of Books (see p. 338) or a Poetry Performance (see p. 301). These events can be used as fund-raisers, like a Sleepover While the Sun Is Up (see p. 78), or they can just be used to create school spirit, like a Haunted House Contest (see p. 384). Sometimes schoolwide events seem overwhelming, but creating a checklist or time line of what needs to happen can ensure things go smoothly. Special events *can* be organized single-handedly, but don't get stressed. Delegate to your comfort level and be sure to enlist help for the day of the event. Besides, you can always downsize schoolwide events suggested in this book for a single classroom or grade level. If you are the sort of person who likes to make lists or throw a party, this kind of volunteering is for you.

Storytimes
(for A and B people)

This kind of volunteering is the most versatile. You can be organized and plan to read aloud regularly, or talk to the teacher and plan a story-time based on a special theme the class is studying, or simply arrange to share a book you think the children will enjoy, maybe plan an activity to match. You can do this whether you have lots of free time, or you have an odd afternoon off from work. Review the Hints for Reading Out Loud (see p. 11) to ensure a successful experience, and look to the lists in Storytime Central, including Must-Reads by the Time You're 13 (see p. 430), and Potato Picks found throughout this book for a childhood's-worth of great read-alouds.

One-on-One *(for B people)*

If you don't feel ready to "go public" with your volunteer vim and get up in front of a room full of children, don't worry, there are kids who are yearning for a little private time. Many teachers in overcrowded classrooms rarely have any stretch to give children much individualized attention. Children who need extra help will benefit from the time you spend taking dictation (see p. 57), taking turns reading aloud back and forth with a child, or simply holding a storytime with a smaller group.

Bulletin Boards and Beyond . . . Stuff You Can Make
(for B people)

There are many ways to help create a general school or classroom atmosphere that announces, "We Love Books." One of the easiest projects, and one that will earn you genuine thanks from a teacher, is that of creating a bulletin board for your child's classroom (see A Helpful Tack, p. 31). You can also build a time machine (see p. 106), organize a listening library (see p. 200), devise a gingerbread house threshold (see p. 285), or make a question board (see p. 163). While these projects vary in difficulty, they can be created at least in part at home, so this kind of volunteering is wonderful for people juggling priorities.

I have a teeny-weeny confession. Sometimes schools give me the creeps. Too many rules. The continual assertion of the nonsensical idea that if the children are having fun or making choices, they aren't learning anything. The politics. The dittos. The attitudes about food, about glitter, about open flames. *Eeeccchh.* Obviously, our brand of read-aloud sunshine is needed, so put in an appearance and do as much as you can. But may I remind you as a parent-pedagogue who knows there's more than one way to peel a potato that the school is not the *only* locale for all your fine book-sharing plans. You can do any of this stuff through a library, a house of worship, a bookstore, a park district field house, a home-schooling chapter, a scout chapter, and your home, your home, your home. The real idea behind volunteering is helping, and wherever you do it, and for whomever you do it, you deserve a hand. Good job.

THE SILENT SCREAM: ADULT ILLITERACY IN AMERICA

The National Adult Literacy survey adopted the following definition of literacy developed by Congress: "Using printed word and written information to function in society, to achieve one's goals and to develop one's knowledge and potential." Using this definition, the survey determined that more than 40 million American adults performed in the lowest level of prose literacy (which includes skills such as finding information in an article), and another 52 million Americans could barely read at all. Most current statistics can be found at the National Assessments of Adult Literacy Website at nces.ed.gov/naal. Given the numbers that you'll find there, the chances are that you know someone who can't read, even if you don't recognize it. On top of being cheated out of a tool that Congress has determined instrumental in the pursuit of happiness, people who are functionally illiterate have to go to great lengths to hide this deficit in order to survive. It is easy to forget how different life would be without the ability to read. How different would the quality of life be for your family? It's mind-boggling to consider.

You can break the cycle of illiteracy and its devastating effects on both parent and child by volunteering. Check out literacyvolunteers.org/home, or call 1-877-HELP-LVA for the chapter in your area. No experience necessary. They train, and we all gain.

CLASSROOM VOLUNTEER ETIQUETTE

• Check your school's volunteer policy. Some schools don't allow parents to volunteer in their own child's classroom because then the teachers feel scrutinized. Sometimes paperwork needs to be filled out prior to volunteering; some schools even require criminal background checks. Don't be offended; the intention is to put the children's safety first.

• Filing, copying, grading . . . there's an awful lot of grunt work that needs to get done, and that's an opportunity to volunteer in itself. Teachers will love you. But it's a very different opportunity than sharing books. If you are volunteering to do something in particular (an after-school club, a storytime, one-on-one), be sure to articulate it. Once you have, stick to your plan. You should feel free to say no when you want to say no. This may seem mean, but it's really not. If you aren't intrinsically rewarded by your volunteer work, you won't do it again, and then everybody loses.

• If you want to give a storytime, phone before you come to arrange the best time for everyone. Try to estimate how long it will take. In my years of storytimes in the library and bookstores, I have found picture books usually take about twelve minutes each, and crafts take twenty. Two or three picture books and a craft or activity make for a very nice time.

• The teacher should be willing to share what sorts of themes or topics the children will be studying so you can coordinate and integrate.

• When you volunteer, your child volunteers, too, in that he is graciously sharing your time and attention. Whenever possible, invite your own child's participation in what you're doing.

• Teachers sometimes lose their tempers, have messy desks, misplace important papers. By opening professional space to you, the teacher is trusting you. Try to resist narking on the teacher's shortcomings to other parents; things that start out as harmless gossip can snowball and damage reputations. If you see something that is a serious concern, talk directly to the teacher about it or to an appropriate administrator. By the same token, if there is something positive that you observe, praise generously.

• If you happen upon children's records or personal information (family situation, learning or behavioral differences) remember that it was supposed to be confidential. Do unto others and leave what you find in the classroom *in the classroom.*

• For protection against litigation, avoid being alone with a child or being left in charge of a class during school hours if you are not the assigned teacher, even if you are a very adept volunteer.

• If while you are volunteering the teacher is on "prep," a coveted break in which she is given time to prepare her work, don't be overly chatty. Check if it's a good time to talk, as you would on the phone.

• Don't use volunteer time to discuss your child's progress. Make a separate appointment.

• You're not in it for the thanks, but still, when you give your time a thank-you is in order. In the rare case when thanks is not forthcoming, prompt by being the first to graciously offer thanks for the opportunity to help. Why not? Many schools are so bereft of appreciation, maybe they just forgot. Just as you are a shining example of a book lover, you are a shining example of civility. Let's hope you are contagious!

PART II

Connecting Books with the Littlest Bambinos

First comes the exciting news that the stork will be making a special delivery. Then on to bottles (or boobies), diapers, and strollers. Suddenly, there's a baby on the loose. All glassware and anything with a corner must be banished, and all electrical outlets camouflaged. The finest filets are cut into pieces the size of your pinky fingernail, and you're spending your free time playing patty-cake and blowing on belly buttons. But before you know it, that little person will be waving bye-bye and marching bravely into first grade, while you are left teary and skulking about the schoolyard for one last glimpse of your star to carry you through the day. "These years are over in a blink of an eye," grandparents say. Ha, what a cliché. What a true, true cliché.

Whether you are a parent, caregiver, family member, or friend, you can honor this amazing time of early childhood by making the most of it. Use this section to start bonding with your baby through books, and watch that child's affection and ability for reading rise as steadily as the measurements on the growth chart. Please also note the suggestions to include siblings; they can play a special role in the greeting and the reading.

Great Expectations

That ninth month is a *doozy*, isn't it! A baby involves more waiting than license renewal at the DMV. While books may not speed up gestation, they sure make the wait more fun. The whole clan will enjoy Fran Manushkin's classic, **BABY, COME OUT!** depicting a stubborn infant in utero who finally finds a reason to come out and meet the family. Buy it for your own eager family, or give it to a friend approaching her due date. The laughter may induce contractions. Other good books about waiting include **PETER'S CHAIR** by Ezra Jack Keats, **WAITING FOR BABY** by Harriet Ziefert, and **HELLO BABY** by Lizzy Rockwell.

Dear Madame Esmé,

What is the perfect gift to give at a baby shower?

Dear Gentle Reader,

Diapers, of course! But if you are hoping to give a paper product that is less about waste and more about taste, Jim Trelease's **THE READ-ALOUD HANDBOOK** is always a good choice for any new parent. Collections of Mother Goose rhymes are honking-good gifts (see What's Good for the Goose, p. 44 for plenty of elegant editions). Books that anticipate the arrival are always thoughtful, like **HAPPY BIRTH DAY!** by Robie H. Harris and **THE BABIES ARE LANDING** by Joan Margalith, but if you are looking for a real keepsake, **ON THE DAY YOU WERE BORN** by Debra Frasier is a very special baby book. When the author was hospitalized due to complications in her pregnancy, things looked bleak. In a fit of hopefulness, she wrote a series of notes to herself about how the world would welcome her child. Those notes were the basis for her book, which over ten years later, her daughter and lots of other children still enjoy. Matisse-like artwork flows with gentle, informative writing to celebrate the rhythms of the natural world and a sense of global community. The author received scores of fan letters, many of which exemplify wonderful reading traditions that you can use with a book of your own choosing, too:

- Expectant parents brought the book to the hospital to be stamped with baby's footprint and signed by family members, doctors, and nurses.
- Parents read it during adoption ceremonies. (For more good books about adoption, see Family Stories, p. 347.)
- A kindergarten teacher sent the book home on the eve of each student's birthday with a journal so the parents could jot down a memory of their child's special day to be read in class.
- Grandchildren read it to their grandmother on her ninety-first birthday!

❀ *Potato Pick:*

COME ALONG, DAISY!

by Jane Simmons

Daisy is a formidable explorer, but when adventures get out of hand, Mama Duck is closer than Daisy thinks. A reassuring adventure that mirrors a child's forays into the world of independence. (Birth and up)

Sibling Arrivalry

When a new baby arrives and you are stopping by, it is always considerate to bring a small gift that big brothers or sisters ("Hel-*lo!* Remember *us?*") can enjoy. A book is a good choice because it can be shared by more than one child, and it is also useful while Mama and Daddy are occupied with the sweet, darling, little attention-vacuum. Activity and hobby books are welcome choices (see Activity and Special Interest Books in the Battle Against "B," p. 204), as are sibling books (Family Stories, p. 347); or choose from this thematic list of picture books that big brothers and sisters can also read to the new member of the family:

Allen, Jonathan	• DON'T WAKE THE BABY! AN INTERACTIVE BOOK WITH SOUNDS (Also a great gift for fathers at co-ed baby showers.)
Cowell, Cressida	• WHAT SHALL WE DO WITH THE BOO-HOO BABY?
French, Simon, and Donna Rawlins	• GUESS THE BABY
Hanson, Mary	• THE DIFFERENCE BETWEEN BABIES AND COOKIES
Harris, Robie H.	• HELLO BENNY! WHAT IT'S LIKE TO BE A BABY
Henderson, Kathy	• BABY KNOWS BEST
Henkes, Kevin	• JULIUS, THE BABY OF THE WORLD
Hindley, Judy	• THE PERFECT LITTLE MONSTER
Hines, Anna Grossnickle	• BIG LIKE ME
Hoberman, Mary Ann	• AND TO THINK THAT WE THOUGHT THAT WE'D NEVER BE FRIENDS!
Hutchins, Pat	• WHERE'S THE BABY?
King-Smith, Dick	• GEORGE SPEAKS (Short chapter book.)
L'Engle, Madeleine	• THE OTHER DOG
Leuck, Laura	• MY BABY BROTHER HAS TEN TINY TOES
Lindgren, Barbro	• BENNY AND THE BINKY
Ormerod, Jan	• 101 THINGS TO DO WITH A BABY
Pilkey, Dav	• THE ADVENTURES OF SUPER DIAPER BABY (Short chapter book.)
Stuve-Bodeen, Stephanie	• ELIZABETI'S DOLL • MAMA ELIZABETI
Wishinsky, Frieda	• OONGA BOONGA

✿ *Potato Pick:*

TOUGH BEGINNINGS: HOW BABY ANIMALS SURVIVE
by Marilyn Singer,
illustrated by Anna Vojtech

Human babies cry a lot, but it could be worse. Try being born in the sea, or on the arctic tundra! Try living in a pouch! How about having a dad that wants to eat you, or having fifty brothers and sisters? Double-page spreads and informative, clear text make for an attractive and highly readable book generously filled with plenty of "wow, I didn't know that!" moments. Animal-lovers will enjoy this book, but so will children expecting new siblings. (6 and up)

🌼 *Potato Pick:*

PAPA, PLEASE GET THE MOON FOR ME
by Eric Carle

When Monica wants the moon to play with her, Papa gets right on it, scheduling a play date. Creative paper engineering makes this book extra exciting, with pages folding open to extend long ladders (helpful in reaching the moon). A full moon opens into a sextuple page spread. Of course, check out the classic THE VERY HUNGRY CATERPILLAR by this same author. (Birth and up)

Zamarano, Ana	• LET'S EAT! (Latino family, lots of great Spanish vocabulary!)
Ziefert, Harriet	• TALK, BABY!

I remember having THE BERENSTAIN BEARS' NEW BABY read to me at four years old, in almost *explosive* anticipation of the arrival of my baby brother. Which leads me to make this point: Many children's books about expanding families focus on the rivalry and the adjustments that need to be made. Be sure to look at the books carefully so you can be sure to balance any snarky humor with the genuine joy of this fleeting time in the life of a sibling—and of a family.

Rock-a-Bye Reader

Most of the books in this list of recommendations are from my son Russell's book basket, a collection of his favorites and favorites of friends from birth through age three. Many titles are available in durable and less-expensive "board book" editions with rounded edges and thick, no-rip cardboard pages. I personally prefer the original paper-page editions. Because the pictures are so much larger, it is easier to point out details. Of course, the board books are much more fun for *baby* to hold, and laminated pages make for easy drool clean-up, so you make the call.

FAVORITES FROM RUSSELL'S BOOK BASKET:

Alborough, Jez	• HUG
Arma, Tom	• ANIMAL TIME
	• TYKEOSAURS (Babies love pictures of other babies! Check out all of Tom Arma's books along with Neil Ricklen's, below.)
Baker, Keith	• HIDE AND SNAKE
Bang, Molly	• TEN, NINE, EIGHT (I still remember when Russell's toes were the same size as the toes on the illustration . . . hold your own baby's piggies up for comparison.)
Barton, Byron	• THE WEE LITTLE WOMAN (Check out all of his boldly illustrated books!)
Bemelmans, Ludwig	• The Madeline series

Berger, Barbara Helen	• A LOT OF OTTERS
Boynton, Sandra	• OH MY OH MY OH DINOSAURS! (Check out all of Boynton's board books.)
Campbell, Rod	• DEAR ZOO
Carter, David A.	• FEELY BUGS (The exotic world of texture was Russell's first choice, but Carter also has books that focus on other concepts, such as counting, color, and the alphabet.)
Christelow, Eileen	• FIVE LITTLE MONKEYS JUMPING ON THE BED (All of Christelow's Five Little Monkeys are a barrel of . . . well, you know!)
Cousins, Lucy	• The Maisy series • NOAH'S ARK
Cowell, Cressida	• WHAT SHALL WE DO WITH THE BOO-HOO BABY?
Crews, Donald	• FREIGHT TRAIN (Check out all of Crews's books.)
Day, Alexandra	• GOOD DOG, CARL (A wordless picture book series.)
Eastman, P. D.	• ARE YOU MY MOTHER?
Falwell, Cathryn	• FEAST FOR 10
Foreman, Michael	• MICHAEL FOREMAN'S PLAYTIME RHYMES
Hill, Eric	• The Spot series
Ho, Minfong	• HUSH! A THAI LULLABY
Hughes, Shirley	• The Alfie and Annie Rose series • DOGGER
Hutchins, Pat	• CHANGES, CHANGES
Jackson, Ellen	• BROWN COW, GREEN GRASS, YELLOW MELLOW SUN
Kaye, Buddy, Fred Wise, and Sidney Lippman	• A YOU'RE ADORABLE
Keats, Ezra Jack	• THE SNOWY DAY • WHISTLE FOR WILLIE
Kirk, David	• MISS SPIDER'S TEA PARTY: THE COUNTING BOOK
Landström, Olof and Lena	• BOO AND BAA GET WET (Try the whole charming Boo and Baa series.)
Leaf, Munro	• THE STORY OF FERDINAND
Lindgren, Barbro	• SAM'S COOKIE (Check out all the books in Lindgren's Sam series.)

🌸 *Potato Pick:*

CURIOUS GEORGE'S ARE YOU CURIOUS?
illustrated by H. A. Rey

Do you ever feel happy? Are you sometimes silly? Have you ever been naughty, so you need a time out? (I mean your children . . . who did you think I meant?) Don't worry, George has, too, in this comforting book about moods. The recent **Curious George** series of abridged adventures in board book are excellent; collect 'em all! (See Yes, We Have No Bananas Today, p. 356.) (Birth and up)

🥔 *Potato Pick:*

BENNY'S HAD ENOUGH!
*by Barbro Lindgren,
illustrated by Olof Landström*

"Benny thinks everything is the pits," begins this story of a pig and his doll who runs away from the confines of his mother's rules and requests. When Benny's beloved doll is lost in a mud hole, however, Mother starts looking pretty good. Despite the modern touches (cell phones and computers abound in the illustrations), this is still a classic tale of rebellion and redemption, and I'll bet you a ham sandwich that one reading won't be enough of Benny. (3 and up, my son's favorite when he was 4! Once you and your children are done laughing, check out the companion, **BENNY AND THE BINKY.**)

Lionni, Leo	• FREDERICK'S FABLES
Martin Jr., Bill	• BROWN BEAR, BROWN BEAR, WHAT DO YOU SEE? • CHICKA CHICKA BOOM BOOM
McBratney, Sam	• GUESS HOW MUCH I LOVE YOU?
McDonnell, Flora	• GIDDY-UP! LET'S RIDE! (Read while bouncing baby on your knee.)
Merriam, Eve	• LOW SONG
Miller, Virginia	• BARTHOLOMEW BEAR: FIVE TODDLER TALES
Murphy, Mary	• HOW KIND!
Narahashi, Keiko	• IS THAT JOSIE?
Numeroff, Laura Joffe	• IF YOU GIVE A MOUSE A COOKIE
Oborne, Martine	• ONE BEAUTIFUL BABY
Oxenbury, Helen	• TICKLE, TICKLE (Beloved and prolific author—check out all her books.)
Pandell, Karen	• I LOVE YOU, SUN, I LOVE YOU, MOON
Piper, Watty	• THE LITTLE ENGINE THAT COULD
Potter, Beatrix	• THE TALE OF PETER RABBIT
Radunsky, Vladimir	• SQUARE TRIANGLE ROUND SKINNY
Rex, Michael	• THE PIE IS CHERRY
Ricklen, Neil	• BABY'S BIG AND LITTLE
Risom, Ole	• I AM A BUNNY
Roche, Denis	• OLLIE ALL OVER
Rosen, Michael	• OWL BABIES • WE'RE GOING ON A BEAR HUNT
Scarry, Richard	• RICHARD SCARRY'S PIG WILL AND PIG WON'T: A BOOK OF MANNERS (All of Scarry's books are lively and delightful.)
Sendak, Maurice	• NUTSHELL LIBRARY
Shaw, Nancy	• SHEEP IN A JEEP (Enjoy the whole series of Sheep books available.)
Weatherford, Carole	• JAZZ BABY (Snappy take-off on patty-cake.)
Wells, Rosemary	• MAX'S DRAGON SHIRT (And the whole hilarious **Max** series.)
Williams, Vera B.	• MORE, MORE, MORE SAID THE BABY
Wolff, Ashley	• STELLA & ROY

WHERE IS GOODNIGHT MOON?

Though the classic has charmed for decades, for bedtime lulling I personally preferred SUN IS FALLING, NIGHT IS CALLING by Laura Leuck. When I wanted to introduce my son to the genius of GOODNIGHT MOON's author, Margaret Wise Brown, I waited until he was an emergent reader (see Barely Beyond Baby, p. 50) and read to him from the hilarious collection FISH WITH THE DEEP SEA SMILE: STORIES AND POEMS FOR READING TO YOUNG CHILDREN, which Brown wrote especially to be read aloud to the primary students she taught. Another Brown reissue is THE DIRTY LITTLE BOY, illustrated by Steven Salerno. I imagine it was a very daunting task to find a modern illustrator who could complement the legendary Margaret Wise Brown, but

Salerno comes off squeaky clean and goes far to create a reputation of his own. In this picture book, a little boy with jam on his face, chocolate on his knee, mud between his toes, and dust in his hair asks his busy mother for a bath. She suggests he "run along, see how the animals take their baths and that way you'll learn how to get clean." Watch what happens when the little boy imitates a bird, a piggy, and a horse! This story originally appeared in *Jack and Jill* magazine in 1937 under the title "How the Animals Took a Bath," and remains as fresh as a soap bubble. Also not to be missed is Brown's collection of fifty-six poems and stories, MOUSE OF MY HEART, elegantly illustrated by Loretta Krupinski, as lovely to open as a jewelry box and just as full of gems.

Hints for Reading with Infants

• When sharing books with infants, one of the goals is looking, not reading. Talk about the pictures. Name objects and colors; count repeated images.

• Relax! Don't worry if baby turns the pages, or chews the pages. (Why won't anyone invent a zweiback-flavored book?) Choose books in board or paperback editions if it makes you feel less nervous.

• Don't be afraid to kiss and cuddle or nurse in the middle of a book. It comes with the territory. What your baby wants most is time and attention from you. If baby can make the association that books equal that time and attention, baby has made a positive association with books, regardless of what is written on the page. ▶

• Another goal is conversation. Say what you think will happen next, express your surprise, anticipation. Laugh. Ask questions. "What do you think will happen? Will the balloon pop?" All right, maybe your baby can't answer now, but someday!

• Try to find books with musical qualities, repetitions, and rhythms in the language. Mother Goose rhymes are always marvelous. Again, your baby will join in when the time is right.

• As you read, move your finger from left to right beneath the words. The fact that books in our culture are read this way, and that we turn pages in a particular direction is new information to your baby. Keep moving your finger under the words throughout your child's primary years, as it helps with word recognition.

What's Good for the Goose: Rhyme Schemes

Every gosling deserves a good collection of Mother Goose in their nest. Some folks like classic editions they remember from their own childhood such as THE REAL MOTHER GOOSE illustrated by Blanche Fisher Wright. But to me the Fabergé egg of the flock of Mother Goose editions available is the contemporary and comprehensive MY MOTHER GOOSE LIBRARY edited by Iona Opie, one of the compilers of the scholarly OXFORD NURSERY RHYMES BOOK. Mother Goose is cock-of-the-walk thanks to the generous and hilarious illustrations by Rosemary Wells, featuring her signature bunnies and other friendly animalia. The oversized books come in a boxed set, which includes both MY VERY FIRST MOTHER GOOSE and HERE COMES MOTHER GOOSE. All the greatest hits—"Humpty Dumpty," "Jack and Jill," "1, 2, Buckle My Shoe"—are here, and also the charming lesser known rhymes and clever twists on standards. I appreciate that in this edition boys are made of sugar and spice and everything nice (finally, the truth is out!). This, along with THE LUCY COUSINS BOOK OF NURSERY RHYMES and Clare Beaton's MOTHER GOOSE REMEMBERS offer the most accessible introductions to the rhythm and rock of the English language. If you are one of those lightweights who just can't abide farmers' wives chasing blind mice with carving knives and the like, well, then, try the politically correct **FATHER GANDER NURSERY RHYMES** by Douglas Larche.

Personally, I don't mind a good blackbird baked in a pie, and chances are, school-age siblings are in the mood for a slice as well. You can be very generous and give an older child **MONSTER GOOSE** by Judy Sierra or the "Surprising Sequels to Mother Goose Rhymes" found in **WHATEVER HAPPENED TO HUMPTY DUMPTY?** by David Greenberg. It's nice to have something slightly related (and slightly naughty!) to read while Mom is coddling and cooing the new arrival.

Do, Read, Mi!
Putting Books to Music

What better way to show your toddler about the musical qualities of reading than by singing them a book? There are plenty of musical theater standards and folk songs that have been illustrated, with the lyrics serving as text. Many publishers have also tried to make the visual translation with more contemporary songs such as Burt Bacharach's "I Say a Little Prayer for You," David Byrne's "Stay Up Late" and Dolly Parton's "Coat of Many Colors." The Motown Baby Love Board Book series includes abridged versions of classic R&B old-school hits such as "Ain't No Mountain High Enough," and "How Sweet It Is (To Be Loved by You)." While the illustrations for all of these books are very appealing, personally I think some of these songs are better left for wailing in the shower or dancing in the living room than for lap time; the rhythm of the music doesn't consistently match the natural pace of turning of the pages. And besides, as a grown-up you're entitled to keep your Aretha Franklin karaoke moments to yourself. Belting it over a book isn't necessarily very pleasant for baby. The lesson is, try it before you buy it, even if it means you have a slightly musical moment in the bookstore. Here are tuneful reads to get your sing-along started. The list is arranged by composer or illustrator, depending on which makes it easier to locate the title.

Adams, Pam	• OLD MACDONALD HAD A FARM (Old MacDonald also had a wood shop if you ask author Lisa Shulman, or an apartment house if you ask Judi Barrett in their Old MacDonald versions.)
Alexander, Martha	• A YOU'RE ADORABLE (Song originally written by Buddy Kaye, Fred Wise, and Sidney Lippman.)
Bryan, Ashley	• WHAT A WONDERFUL WORLD (Song by Bob Thiele.)
Carle, Eric	• TODAY IS MONDAY
Carter, David A.	• IF YOU'RE HAPPY AND YOU KNOW IT
Child, Lydia Maria	• OVER THE RIVER AND THROUGH THE WOOD (I like the version illustrated by David Catrow.)
Cooper, Floyd	• CUMBAYAH
Galdone, Paul	• CAT GOES FIDDLE-I-FEE (Or if you prefer, FIDDLE-I-FEE is also very nicely illustrated by Melissa Sweet.)
Graef, Renee	• MY FAVORITE THINGS (From the song by Richard Rodgers and Oscar Hammerstein.)
Guthrie, Woody	• BLING BLANG • HOWDI DO • MY DOLLY • THIS LAND IS YOUR LAND (Illustrated by Kathy Jakobsen.) (In the everyman spirit of Woody Guthrie, you and your child might also enjoy RISE UP SINGING: THE GROUP SINGING SONGBOOK, edited by Peter Blood and Annie Patterson.)
Hillenbrand, Will	• DOWN BY THE STATION
Hoberman, Mary Ann	• THERE ONCE WAS A MAN NAMED MICHAEL FINNEGAN
Katz, Alan	• TAKE ME OUT OF THE BATHTUB
Kellogg, Steven	• A-HUNTING WE WILL GO! • YANKEE DOODLE
Langstaff, John	• OVER IN THE MEADOW
Lass, Bonnie, and Philemon Sturges	• WHO TOOK THE COOKIES FROM THE COOKIE JAR?
Long, Sylvia	• HUSH LITTLE BABY (Or for a spacey spin on the traditional lyrics, try HUSH, LITTLE ALIEN by Daniel Kirk.)
Miller, J. Philip, and Sheppard M. Greene	• WE ALL SING WITH THE SAME VOICE

Norworth, Jack	• TAKE ME OUT TO THE BALLGAME (The version illustrated by Alec Gillman is very bold.)
Orozco, José-Luis	• FIESTAS: A YEAR OF LATIN-AMERICAN SONGS OF CELEBRATION • "DE COLORES" AND OTHER LATIN-AMERICAN FOLK SONGS FOR CHILDREN • DIEZ DEDITOS: TEN LITTLE FINGERS & OTHER PLAY RHYMES AND ACTION SONGS FROM LATIN AMERICA (Use song to help your child learn another language as well as learn to love to read!)
Peek, Merle	• MARY WORE HER RED DRESS AND HENRY WORE HIS GREEN SNEAKERS
Priceman, Marjorie	• FROGGIE WENT A-COURTING
Raffi	• DOWN BY THE BAY • BABY BELUGA • FIVE LITTLE DUCKS • SHAKE MY SILLIES OUT (Look for the Raffi's Songs to Read series. For those of you who took piano lessons, the musical notation can also be found in THE RAFFI SINGABLE SONGBOOK: A COLLECTION OF 51 SONGS FROM RAFFI'S FIRST THREE RECORDS FOR YOUNG CHILDREN.)
Rosen, Michael	• LITTLE RABBIT FOO FOO
Seeger, Pete	• ABIYOYO (A story as well as a song.)
Sendak, Maurice	• CHICKEN SOUP WITH RICE • ALLIGATORS ALL AROUND (Musical notation for both of these songs may be found in Maurice Sendak's REALLY ROSIE STARRING THE NUTSHELL KIDS. Or you can learn the songs by listening to the delightful cassette featuring Carole King.)
Taback, Simms	• THERE WAS AN OLD LADY WHO SWALLOWED A FLY
Trapani, Iza	• THE ITSY BITSY SPIDER • HOW MUCH IS THAT DOGGIE IN THE WINDOW? • OH WHERE, OH WHERE HAS MY LITTLE DOG GONE? • TWINKLE, TWINKLE, LITTLE STAR
Westcott, Nadine Bernard	• THE LADY WITH THE ALLIGATOR PURSE • MISS MARY MACK: A HAND-CLAPPING RHYME • PEANUT BUTTER AND JELLY: A PLAY RHYME • SKIP TO MY LOU

ADOPT-A-MOM

A great way to share "baby books" is to "adopt" a teenage mother and treat her to a basket of books that will encourage a love of reading for her and her baby. How about throwing in a lullaby cassette, a copy of the Hints for Reading with Infants (see pp. 43–44), and an application for a public library card? You can get the name of a deserving teenage mommy by calling your local high school counseling department, public aid, the Department of Children and Family Services, your pediatrician, or a local clinic.

Watson, Wendy	• FOX WENT OUT ON A CHILLY NIGHT
Wells, Rosemary	• GETTING TO KNOW YOU: RODGERS AND HAMMERSTEIN FAVORITES (Songs by Richard Rodgers and Oscar Hammerstein, a particularly lovely collection.)
Wimmer, Mike	• SUMMERTIME (From the song by George and Ira Gershwin.)
Zelinsky, Paul	• KNICK-KNACK PADDYWHACK (Pop-up book.) • THE WHEELS ON THE BUS (Or for a little variety, try THE SEALS ON THE BUS by Lenny Hort.)

Some of the books in Wave That Flag! (see p. 125) may also send your heart singing, and more fun for the family can be found in SING THROUGH THE DAY: EIGHTY SONGS FOR CHILDREN, edited by Marlys Swinger.

Reading Play Dates

A teacher initiated a program to ensure that young children, who one day would be attending her school, read early and read often. Using grant money, she bought multiple copies of primary picture books. She called a monthly meeting at the school for parents in the community and provided child care in the next room. Then she demonstrated to parents how to read aloud to their little ones: putting a child on a lap or right beside, showing pictures as the story is read, discussing details on each page. Afterward, all the children were brought in and parents practiced reading the book to them. At the end of each monthly meeting, each family took home a copy of the featured book to keep. The teacher bought some copies of the book in Spanish for Spanish-speaking parents, and had a translator attend the meeting to help communicate her read-aloud hints. If you have a toddler with an older sibling at school, this is a nice program to run through your older child's school library. While the particulars are perhaps best geared toward schools with high English-as-a-second-language or at-risk populations, any toddler will enjoy the chance to enter the building with big kids, and any parent enjoys the chance to get to know other parents at the school in a relaxed setting.

Outside of the school this idea can be adapted for play dates with infants. Each person can bring a few favorite books to a host's home (or you can meet at the library). It can be very informal, or you can pick a theme, such as "kitchen" or "bathtime," "animals" or "toys." Work together with your child, looking through the books for familiar objects, and then share them with the whole group. ("Whose book has a picture of a pot?" "Does anyone have a book with a picture of a green frog?" "What sound does a froggy make?") Although you are reading with your own child, you are alongside other parents and can enjoy some grown-up company. Parents can also take turns sharing with the group fine books they have found, and so every parent's book-knowledge base is broadened. Best of all, babies see from the get-go that reading can be about people.

All Wet! Books in the Bath

Don't overlook the bathtime ritual as a prime time to get in a few extra stories. Spouses or siblings can turn pages with dry hands if you're busy scrubbing, or put down the seat and keep your children company while they splash. Here are a few picture books that are especially winning in the bathroom:

Brown, Margaret Wise	• THE DIRTY LITTLE BOY
Bunting, Eve	• DUCKY
Goodman, Joan Elizabeth	• BERNARD'S BATH
Gramatky, Hardie	• LITTLE TOOT
Katz, Alan	• TAKE ME OUT OF THE BATHTUB AND OTHER SILLY DILLY SONGS
Landström, Lena	• THE LITTLE HIPPO'S ADVENTURE
Philip, Neil	• THE FISH IS ME: BATHTIME RHYMES
Puttock, Simon	• SQUEAKY CLEAN
Ripley, Catherine	• WHY IS SOAP SO SLIPPERY? AND OTHER BATHTIME QUESTIONS
Roth, Carol	• TEN DIRTY PIGS, TEN CLEAN PIGS: AN UPSIDE-DOWN, TURN-AROUND BATHTIME COUNTING BOOK
Shannon, Terry, and Timothy Warner	• TUB TOYS
Thompson, Kay	• KAY THOMPSON'S ELOISE TAKES A BAWTH
Van Laan, Nancy	• SCRUBBA DUB
Wood, Audrey	• KING BIDGOOD'S IN THE BATHTUB
Zion, Gene	• HARRY, THE DIRTY DOG

Barely Beyond Baby: Supporting Emergent Literacy

They say familiarity breeds contempt, but in the case of emergent literacy or "pre-reading," the stage in which children are just learning to read (usually between four and seven), familiarity breeds success. Here are plenty of resources that will deliver your child to the marvelous day when she shouts from the rooftop: "I can read!"

Next Time Won't You Sing with Me? Alphabet and Counting Books

One of the benchmarks of childhood literacy is learning the ABCs. There are literally hundreds of treatments of the alphabet in children's literature, and in their honor, I will list twenty-six books:

1. Aylesworth, Jim	• THE FOLKS IN THE VALLEY: A PENNSYLVANIA DUTCH ABC
2. Barker, Cecily Mary	• FLOWER FAIRY ALPHABET
3. Bowen, Betsy	• ANTLER, BEAR, CANOE: A NORTHWOODS ALPHABET YEAR
4. Doubilet, Anne	• UNDER THE SEA FROM A TO Z
5. Ehlert, Lois	• EATING THE ALPHABET: FRUITS AND VEGETABLES FROM A TO Z
6. Elting, Mary, and Michael Folsom	• Q IS FOR DUCK
7. Eschbacher, Roger	• NONSENSE! HE YELLED
8. Fleming, Denise	• ALPHABET UNDER CONSTRUCTION
9. Hobbie, Holly	• TOOT AND PUDDLE: PUDDLE'S ABC

10. Howell, Will C.   • Zooflakes ABC

11. Hubbard, Woodleigh   • C Is for Curious: An Alphabet of Feelings

12. Hyman, Trina Schart   • A Little Alphabet

13. Kitamura, Satoshi   • From Acorn to Zoo and Everything in between
                              in Alphabetical Order

14. Lobel, Anita   • Alison's Zinnia

15. Martin Jr., Bill, and   • Chicka Chicka Boom Boom
    John Archambault

16. Maurer, Donna   • Annie, Bea, and Chi-Chi Dolores

17. Rey, H. A.   • Curious George Learns the Alphabet

18. Rumford, James   • There's a Monster in the Alphabet

19. Sendak, Maurice   • Alligators All Around

20. Shannon, George   • Tomorrow's Alphabet

21. Shelby, Anne   • Potluck

22. Slate, Joseph   • Miss Bindergarten Gets Ready for Kindergarten

23. Van Allsburg, Chris   • The Z Was Zapped

24. Wildsmith, Brian   • Brian Wildsmith's ABC

25. Wood, Audrey   • Alphabet Adventure

26. Wormell, Christopher   • An Alphabet of Animals

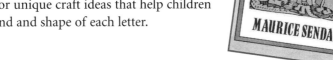

. . . And check out **Kathy Ross Crafts Letter Sounds**
and **Kathy Ross Crafts Letter Shapes**, both by
Kathy Ross, for unique craft ideas that help children
learn the sound and shape of each letter.

Most ABC books are geared specifically for young
children to simply practice and view the alphabet in an entertaining
way. Still, many authors and illustrators use the alphabet to explore a
thematic topic, or to showcase their artistic talent. Because of this,
alphabet books can be enjoyed not just through preschool but all
through childhood. Whenever your child shows interest in a particular
subject, think alphabet books. You can buy or borrow one to specifically suit your child's interest; alphabet books are included in thematic
lists throughout this book. Children can also make their own alphabet
book based on a topic they are enthused about, or as a gift for a
younger brother or sister. Or you can make one as a special gift to your
child. What an heirloom!

THE ALPHABET: NOT JUST FOR LITTLE KIDS ANYMORE

If you think alphabet books are just for learning ABCs, I'd like to introduce you to **Jerry Pallotta**. His popular and informative series of alphabet books demonstrates how a theme can carry a school-aged child's interest all the way from A to Z!

THE AIRPLANE ALPHABET BOOK

THE BOAT ALPHABET BOOK

THE BIRD ALPHABET BOOK

THE BUTTERFLY ALPHABET BOOK

THE DESERT ALPHABET BOOK

THE DINOSAUR ALPHABET BOOK

THE EXTINCT ALPHABET BOOK

THE FLOWER ALPHABET BOOK

THE FRESHWATER ALPHABET BOOK

THE FROG ALPHABET BOOK

THE FURRY ANIMAL ALPHABET BOOK

THE ICKY BUG ALPHABET BOOK

THE JET ALPHABET BOOK

THE OCEAN ALPHABET BOOK

THE SKULL ALPHABET BOOK

THE SPICE ALPHABET BOOK

THE UNDERWATER ALPHABET BOOK

THE VICTORY GARDEN VEGETABLE ALPHABET BOOK

THE YUCKY REPTILE ALPHABET BOOK

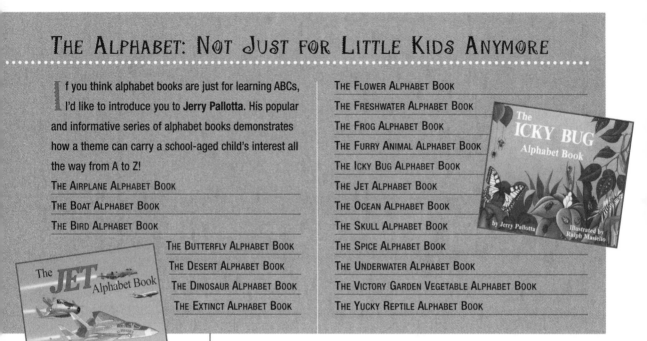

And yes, all of this goes for counting books, too. Here is one for each of your baby's piggies (on both feet):

Baker, Keith	• BIG FAT HEN
Carter, David A.	• HOW MANY BUGS IN A BOX?
Fleming, Denise	• COUNT
Falwell, Cathryn	• FEAST FOR 10
Kitamura, Satoshi	• WHEN SHEEP CANNOT SLEEP: THE COUNTING BOOK
McMillan, Bruce	• COUNTING WILDFLOWERS
Oborne, Martine	• ONE BEAUTIFUL BABY
O'Keefe, Susan Heyboer	• ONE HUNGRY MONSTER
Sheppard, Jeff	• THE RIGHT NUMBER OF ELEPHANTS
Sierra, Judy	• COUNTING CROCODILES
Ziefert, Harriet, ed.	• MOTHER GOOSE MATH

. . . Wait, wait, is that more than ten? So who's counting? When it comes to great 1-2-3 books, the more, the merrier.

Wordless Picture Books

HUG

JEZ ALBOROUGH

It may seem crazy to recommend books with only a few words for children who are just learning to read, but what a tremendous confidence booster to turn pages and tell a story! And what wonderful stories they are . . . a picture is worth a thousand words, and these stories will prove it when your child starts talking.

Alborough, Jez	• HUG
Bang, Molly	• THE GRAY LADY AND THE STRAWBERRY SNATCHER
Briggs, Raymond	• THE SNOWMAN (Beautiful, but hard to share with a group because of the small size of the illustrations; comes in a fabulous, award-winning wordless video, though!)
Day, Alexandra	• GOOD DOG, CARL (Look for the series of wordless **Carl** books.)
dePaola, Tomie	• PANCAKES FOR BREAKFAST
Hutchins, Pat	• CHANGES, CHANGES
Liu, Jae-Soo	• YELLOW UMBRELLA
Mayer, Mercer	• A BOY, A DOG AND A FROG (Look for the series of wordless **Frog** books.)
Rohmann, Eric	• TIME FLIES
Tafuri, Nancy	• HAVE YOU SEEN MY DUCKLING?
Turkle, Brinton	• DEEP IN THE FOREST
Ward, Lynd	• THE SILVER PONY
Wiesner, David	• TUESDAY

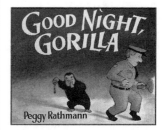

GOOD NIGHT, GORILLA

Peggy Rathmann

✿ *Potato Pick:*
GOOD NIGHT, GORILLA
by Peggy Rathmann

Gorilla releases all the animals from the zoo to join Papa Zookeeper for an unexpected slumber party. You and your children will notice how Gorilla matches the color key to the lock. Recognize any of the toys in armadillo's pen? Have fun finding the balloon in almost every picture. This wordless book can be looked at again and again; new delights await every visit to the nighttime zoo. (Birth and up)

Series Books and Strategies That Support Emergent Literacy

Repetitions in series books allow children to become acquainted with characters who appear regularly throughout a sequence of stories or books. Series books may not always contain all the same characters; they may repeat a format (length, type font, story structure, packaging) that children will find comfortable. An outstanding

JIM TRELEASE
READ-ALOUD'S LOUDEST AND PROUDEST

Inspired by observations made during volunteer visits to community classrooms, journalist Jim Trelease decided to research connections between how much a child was read to and how much a child wants to read. He found plenty of evidence linking the two in educational journals, and when he self-published his findings in layman's terms, it was the beginning of a read-aloud revolution. The book came to the attention of Penguin Publishing, and shortly after, the U.S. Department of Education's Commission of Reading cited that reading aloud to children is the single most important activity one can do to raise a reader. His READ-ALOUD HANDBOOK is now the all-time best selling guide to children's literature for parents and teachers.

Jim Trelease is my hero, and not only for his contagious enthusiasm for the subject of read-aloud. To me, he represents the power of proof. His book, above all others, is most empowering because it presents hard research alongside compelling anecdotal evidence. I was reading aloud before I read his book, but I was not fighting for read-aloud before I read his book. Jim Trelease unleashed children's literature from the contrived and sentimental nursery and brought its power into the streets. With clarity he proves a cause and effect relationship between reading to children and creating life-long readers that demands, "how can you *not* do this?" He brings his persuasive prowess off the pages and onto the podium as well: He is the most compelling speaker since Malcolm X, and a good deal friendlier.

series for pre-readers is **All Aboard Reading** published by Grosset & Dunlap. (I mention the publishers here because in most bookstores and many libraries, this is how emergent readers series are arranged, but note that many of the authors and illustrators are recognized talents in the field.) "Picture Readers" are the easiest level of the **All Aboard Reading** series and combine picture cues within the sentences, helping children develop a sight vocabulary (see Rebus Readers! p. 57 for more examples). Plus, there are fun flash cards of the pictures in the book that can be used for reading games. In this series, my family especially enjoyed SPACE KID by Roberta Edwards, BENNY'S BIG BUBBLE by Jane O'Connor, PIG OUT! by Portia Aborio, SILLY WILLY by Mary-ann Cocca-Leffler, and DON'T WAKE THE BABY! by Wendy Cheyette Lewison.

The **Brand New Readers** series published by Candlewick Press is sold with four paperback books per package; these books are preschool page turners! The brevity of the eight-page books offers new readers a sense of accomplishment, and the back page of each book offers hints to parents helping their children. I find this series consistently cheerful and frankly funny. MONKEY TROUBLE by David Martin and WELL DONE, WORM! by Kathy Caple are delightful.

Some of the books with which we parents learned to read still rate high. Many of us grew up on the **I Can Read** series, published by Harper & Row, where we met Else Holmelund Minarik's LITTLE BEAR, Arnold Lobel's FROG AND TOAD, and my favorite, Russell Hoban's Frances from **A BARGAIN FOR FRANCES.** We found other amiable reading companions in the **Beginner Books** series published by Random House, consistently printing classics such as

P. D. Eastman's **Go, Dog. Go!**, Stanley and Janice Berenstain's **The Big Honey Hunt, Bennet Cerf's Book of Riddles,** and certainly Dr. Seuss's **The Cat in the Hat.** While these books still employ the limited vocabulary with repetitions that characterize books for new readers, the more contemporary series books offer shorter stories that seem geared

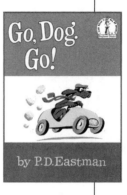

toward a slightly younger audience. Keep this in mind as you balance favorites from your own childhood with new offerings.

Children who enjoy picture-book series characters such as Madeline, Curious George, Arthur, George and Martha, Clifford, and the Berenstain Bears may enjoy graduating to chapter-book series. Series books offer emergent readers the chance to revisit favorite characters, who become like old friends. These books tend to have more realistic plots, so even though there are fewer illustrations, young readers and listeners will find the conflicts and settings recognizable. As you read these books aloud, don't forget to follow the text with your finger under the words. What you are doing is helping to create a "sight vocabulary" for your child, exposing him to words that appear repeatedly, such as "said," "the," "and," and "but."

The first read-aloud chapter books my son, Russell, ever enjoyed were—surprise!—**Russell Sprouts, Rip-Roaring Russell,** and **Russell Rides Again,** all from the **Riverside Kids** series by Johanna Hurwitz. Our affinity for the name aside, both of us enjoyed the funny, realistic stories of children living in an apartment building in New York City. These books have the same heart found in Beverly Cleary's adored **Ramona** series (see Beverly Cleary, Timeless Talent, p. 368), chronicling the everyday exploits of a young child's world. Russell then moved on to read about the adventures of Elisa and Nora, also in Hurwitz's series. By the time he entered kindergarten, we had shared twelve chapter books, and Russell had painlessly started to learn to read. He wasn't "hooked on phonics," he was hooked on Hurwitz! It just goes to show how the connection with an author can really lead to wonderful things.

WAVE BYE-BYE!
Do you have a child heading off to kindergarten? The cure for empty-nest blues can be found in "Thoughts at the Bottom of the Beanstalk" at www.geocities.com/Athens/Troy/5059/thoughts.html.

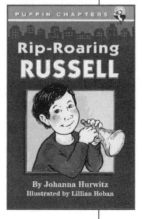

Here are some other outstanding series that will be enjoyed by children from kindergarten through the third grade or beyond:

The Tim series by Edward Ardizzone

The Biscuit series by Alyssa Satin Capucilli

The Ramona series by Beverly Cleary

The Fraser Brothers adventures by Jane Cutler

The Bailey School Kids series by Debbie Dadey

The Amber Brown series by Paula Danziger

The 26 Fairmount Avenue series by Tomie dePaola

The Jackson Friends series by Michelle Edwards

The Kids of the Polk Street School series by Patricia Reilly Giff

The Zack Files series by Dan Greenberg

The Mr. Men and Little Miss series by Roger Hargreaves

The Riverside Kids series by Johanna Hurwitz

The Horrible Harry series by Suzy Kline

The Something Queer series by Elizabeth Levy

The Judy Moody series by Megan McDonald

The Junie B. Jones series by Barbara Park

The Littles series by John Peterson

The Captain Underpants series by Dav Pilkey

The Henry and Mudge series by Cynthia Rylant

The Marvin Redpost series by Louis Sachar

The Nate the Great series by Marjorie Weinman Sharmat

The Robert series by Barbara Seuling

The Tales from Duckport series by Suzy Spafford

STILL A FAN OF DICK AND JANE?

Try OOK THE BOOK AND OTHER SILLY RHYMES by Lissa Rovetch for that old-timey phonics stuff with a fresh twist. "See kid read!"

Rebus Readers!

Mixing pictures with text in a sentence is such a clever way to put children at ease about decoding sight vocabulary (words that come up a million times such as *said, and, to*) and to encourage them to make guesses from context. Learning to read becomes a game. If your child takes to the **All Aboard Reading** series, bring home these others they are sure to love.

Banks, Kate	• THE BIRD, THE MONKEY, AND THE SNAKE IN THE JUNGLE
	• THE TURTLE AND THE HIPPOPOTAMUS
Davis, Lee	• P. B. BEAR'S BIRTHDAY PARTY
	(and the whole **P. B. Bear** Series)
Neitzel, Shirley	• THE BAG I'M TAKING TO GRANDMA'S
	• THE DRESS I'LL WEAR TO THE PARTY
	• THE JACKET I WEAR IN THE SNOW
	• I'M TAKING A TRIP ON MY TRAIN
	• OUR CLASS TOOK A TRIP TO THE ZOO
	• WE'RE MAKING BREAKFAST FOR MOTHER

In addition, consider subscribing to *Ladybug,* www.ladybugmag.com, 1-800-827-0227, and *Highlights for Children,* www.highlights.com, 1-888-876-3809. These periodicals, especially for emergent readers, often have rebus-reading features.

Take Dictation

When I work with an emergent reader, I often have that child dictate stories to me. I write them out as the child tells them, *exactly* as the child tells them. Before we begin, I usually take about four pieces of blank paper and fold them in half with a construction-paper cover. I staple the edge, for a "binding." Then I ask the child what he would like to tell a story about. When possible, I take scissors and free-hand cut the book in the shape of the subject (flower, egg, owl, etc.). I write the title and child's name on the cover, and then the child dictates the story to me. I write it down, printing very neatly and clearly, just a few words or sentences at the top of each page, leaving room on the bottom or top for illustration. When the child has finished the story, I offer to read it to him. When we're done with that, I give the child time to illustrate his work. This often entails a lot of, "What does *this* say?" When the child is finished illustrating, I ask him to read the whole story to me, or, if he requests, I read it to him again.

Dear Madame Esmé,

Now that my child is gaining reading confidence, we like to take turns reading back and forth. Are there any books specially suited to this kind of read-aloud?

Dear Gentle Reader,

There are plenty of books that give everyone a part. In **NOW WHAT CAN I DO?** *by Margaret Park Bridges and illustrated by Melissa Sweet, a mother and son raccoon are cooped up inside on a rainy day with chores to do, but Mommy knows how to make life interesting. As little raccoon uses his imagination, the pages explode with all the color of a coveted box of sixty-four crayons! The best thing about this book is that it is told solely in back-and-forth dialogue between parent and child, each part a different font, its scripted quality making it a perfect read-together. This is also a wonderful book about combating boredom, and understanding that each day is as jolly as we make it. As the last lines of the book are read son raccoon looks to the stars in the sky and says, "Oh, Mommy! There are a million things to do!" Reading this clever book is one of them.*

A great book of poetry for alternate voices is **YOU READ TO ME, I'LL READ TO YOU** *by Mary Ann Hoberman, illustrated by Michael Emberley. Inspired by the author's work with Literacy Volunteers of America, this book uses the voices of two readers, each taking turns to read a color-coded line or couplet of verse, each double-page poem ending with some variation of the heavenly mantra "You read to me, I'll read to you." Besides setting children up for reading success with controlled vocabulary and predictability, the droll narrative poetry is accented by Emberley's spot cartoons, which further help to convey the vignettes to new readers.*

And budding book lovers who enjoy this format will also find fun in **25 JUST-RIGHT PLAYS FOR EMERGENT READERS** *by Carol Pugliano, a resource that offers page after page of turn-taking pleasure.*

Do dictation with your own child and watch reading happen before your eyes. The motivation to read one's own words is formidable, and children are invariably proud of their work. The whole process usually takes about forty minutes. This is also a terrific volunteer idea, especially if you can work with one child regularly. It can make a significant academic difference for that child. I know because it worked for me; it's how I learned to read at age six.

Some people take dictation on the computer, but I don't recommend this with younger children who are learning to write and will benefit from seeing handwriting modeled. I usually save the computer for "special editions," when a child has done a number of books and has a favorite. The fonts and layout options on a desktop publishing program can make a dictated story look nearly as finished as a real trade book, which is exhilarating for a young author. And if creating fancier, longer-lasting editions appeals to the publisher in you, look to **MAKING BOOKS** by Charlotte Stowell. Whether you use technology or go the old-fashioned route, well-bound books dictated by children may be added to classroom or school library collections, to be enjoyed by other children. It is also fun to do with your own children, as such books are often treasured keepsakes.

Comic Books: My Thought Balloon

When I walk into comic-book stores around the city, there is usually one little corner set aside for what I remember as comics. The best of the rest are masterpieces that deal sensitively with the emotional landscape of adults and teem with a dark and snarky humor (for example, Art Spiegelman's **MAUS,** Chris Ware's **JIMMY CORRIGAN: THE SMARTEST KID ON EARTH,** and the Hernandez brothers' **Love and Rockets** series). The worst (and the most) read more like illustrated screenplays cast with women so staggeringly endowed that it is a wonder they are capable of standing upright, or with unfortunate aliens dripping in blood. Stereotypes, cynicism, and violence have always managed to infiltrate comics, seeping them in controversy. These objections are now being partly circumvented by marketing comics as "graphic novels," clearly intended for an adult audience and measured critically by the same yardstick as adult art and literature.

❀ *Potato Pick:*
ONCE UPON A TIME
by Nick Sharratt

Once upon a time, there was a beautiful princess who lived in a castle and met a magic fairy who helped her land a prince. Too traditional? How about this, then: Once upon a time, there was a beautiful princess who lived in a camper and met a magic toilet that helped her hook up with a space man. Still don't like it? Not a problem. This "change the story book" comes with thirty-six press-out pieces that children can easily fit into slots in the pages to create their own stories over and over again. More than the average "gimmick" book, this title is a phenomenal choice for emergent readers, introducing sight vocabulary with picture cues for building confidence. Creative, interactive fun that your child will return to more than once upon a time. (4 and up)

This new wave of comic books has managed to exclude a significant segment of the original fan base: children. This is too bad. Comic books are top choice for emergent and reluctant readers, blending visual cues with the written word and making it easier for your child to decode language using context. Comics have the same positive features as series books, in which characters recur and children can look forward to revisiting favorites in each new issue. Further, the research in G. Robert Carlsen and Anne Sherrill's dissertation VOICES OF READERS: HOW WE COME TO LOVE BOOKS (published by the National Council of Teachers of English) suggests that the comic-book reading experience is common among people who become lifelong readers. When I was a child, there was plenty of benign juvenile fare to choose from: *Archie, Richie Rich, Little Lulu, Uncle Scrooge, Peanuts, Classics Illustrated Junior.* And as I grew older I met many other children who enjoyed action comics such as *Justice League, X-Men,* and *The Shadow.* Thanks to on-line auction houses such as eBay, these comics can still be easily collected. Additionally, several picture-book authors and illustrators have stepped up and created bound books in comic-book form, ready for your children's repeated perusals.

Briggs, Raymond	• The Father Christmas series
Burton, Virginia Lee	• CALICO THE WONDER HORSE; OR THE SAGA OF STEWY STINKER
Feiffer, Jules	• I LOST MY BEAR
	• MEANWHILE . . .
	• THE GREAT COMIC BOOK HEROES
Hafner, Marylin	• A YEAR WITH MOLLY AND EMMETT
Hergé	• The Tintin series
Kitamura, Satoshi	• COMIC ADVENTURES OF BOOTS
O'Malley, Kevin	• LITTLE BUGGY
Pilkey, Dav	• The Captain Underpants series
	• The Ricky Ricotta series
Pinkney, J. Brian	• THE ADVENTURES OF SPARROWBOY
Shepard, Aaron	• MASTER MAN: A TALL TALE OF NIGERIA
Spiegelman, Art, and Françoise Mouly	• LITTLE LIT: FOLKLORE AND FAIRY TALE FUNNIES
Stevenson, James	• THE CASTAWAY
	• COULD BE WORSE!
	• WHAT'S UNDER MY BED? (Check out all of Stevenson's books about Grandpa!)

Watterson, Bill	• THE ESSENTIAL CALVIN AND HOBBES
Williams, Marcia	• CHARLES DICKENS AND FRIENDS
	• DON QUIXOTE
	• BRAVO, MR. WILLIAM SHAKESPEARE! (Check out all of Williams's comic-book takes on classics!)

Naughty, Naughty! Good Books for Bad Choices

Young children are trying all sorts of *in-ter-esting* behavior on for size (so are old children, but we'll talk about that later). Don't fret! Sometimes a bad example is the best teacher . . . and the best read-aloud for four through seven year olds.

Bemelmans, Ludwig	• MADELINE AND THE BAD HAT
Bottner, Barbara	• BOOTSIE BARKER BITES
Daly, Niki	• JAMELA'S DRESS
Donnelly, Jennifer	• HUMBLE PIE
Edwards, Pamela Duncan	• RUDE MULE
Elliot, Laura Malone	• HUNTER'S BEST FRIEND AT SCHOOL
Gantos, Jack	• The Rotten Ralph series
Gosney, Joy	• NAUGHTY PARENTS
James, Simon	• THE DAY JAKE VACUUMED (More mischief throughout the **Jake** series.)
MacDonald, Amy	• QUENTON FENTON HERTER III
Mahoney, Daniel J.	• THE SATURDAY ESCAPE
Marshall, James	• THE CUT-UPS
Murphy, Patti B.	• ELINOR AND VIOLET
Potter, Beatrix	• THE TALE OF PETER RABBIT
Preston, Edna Mitchell	• THE TEMPER TANTRUM BOOK
Rubel, Nicole	• GRODY'S NOT SO GOLDEN RULES
Schaefer, Carole Lexa	• THE LITTLE FRENCH WHISTLE
Richler, Mordecai	• JACOB TWO-TWO MEETS THE HOODED FANG (Short chapter book.)
Sendak, Maurice	• PIERRE: A CAUTIONARY TALE IN FIVE CHAPTERS AND A PROLOGUE
	• WHERE THE WILD THINGS ARE

I Read London, I Read France . . .

Children like books about underpants. If you hear so many poop jokes from the backseat during carpool that you're ready to scream, you'll know that the timing is right for this irreverent list. Also great books for reading on the potty. These are picture books unless otherwise noted.

Doyle, Roddy	• THE GIGGLER TREATMENT (Short chapter book.)
Frankel, Alona	• ONCE UPON A POTTY (Honestly, the best book for potty training. Comes in "his" and "hers" versions.)
Gomi, Taro	• EVERYONE POOPS
Grossman, Bill	• MY LITTLE SISTER ATE ONE HARE (Lighthearted look at throw-up.)
Kotzwinkle, William	• WALTER, THE FARTING DOG
Lattimore, Deborah Nourse	• I WONDER WHAT'S UNDER THERE? A BRIEF HISTORY OF UNDERWEAR
Lawrence, Michael	• THE KILLER UNDERPANTS (Chapter book.)
Levine, Deborah	• PARKER PICKS
London, Jonathan	• FROGGY GETS DRESSED
Lynch, Wayne	• THE SCOOP ON POOP (Nonfiction.)
Monsell, Mary Elise	• UNDERWEAR!
Parr, Todd	• UNDERWEAR DOS AND DON'TS
Pilkey, Dav	• ADVENTURES OF CAPTAIN UNDERPANTS (Chapter book series.) • THE ADVENTURES OF SUPER DIAPER BABY
Radunsky, Vladimir	• A SIMPLE STORY OF A BOY NAMED MANNEKEN PIS WHO PEED ON A WAR (Based on a famous Belgian legend.)
Shannon, David	• NO, DAVID! (Be mortified at all the antics in the David series!)
Wahl, Jan	• LITTLE EIGHT JOHN
Wood, Audrey	• ELBERT'S BAD WORD

. . . To be on the safe side, follow with classic books of children's etiquette: Aliki's FEELINGS and MANNERS (great for discussion, but small illustrations make these best suited for one-on-one); Caralyn Buehner's IT'S A SPOON, NOT A SHOVEL; and I DID IT, I'M SORRY; and Sesyle Joslin's WHAT DO YOU SAY, DEAR? and WHAT DO YOU DO, DEAR? (both droll and definitive).

Nothing but the Tooth: Books That Celebrate These Landmark Losses

If the tooth fairy gave me a nickel every time I was giving a storytime and a child excitedly held up a bloody bicuspid, well, I could afford braces! Let your child share the excitement of growing up by sinking his teeth into books that four out of five dentists—and teachers—recommend, and pick a few to turn into a storytime that will have everybody smiling. Maybe the tooth fairy could even be convinced to leave one of these books under the pillow from time to time?

Beeler, Selby B.	• THROW YOUR TOOTH ON THE ROOF: TOOTH TRADITIONS FROM AROUND THE WORLD
Brisson, Pat	• BERTIE'S PICTURE DAY
Brown, Marc	• ARTHUR'S TOOTH

Cleary, Beverly	• RAMONA THE PEST (Last couple of chapters about a lost tooth.)
Clement, Rod	• GRANDPA'S TEETH
Grambling, Lois	• THIS WHOLE TOOTH FAIRY THING'S NOTHING BUT A BIG RIP-OFF!
Johnson, Arden	• THE LOST TOOTH CLUB
Karlin, Nurit	• THE TOOTH WITCH
Kaye, Marilyn	• THE REAL TOOTH FAIRY
Keller, Laurie	• OPEN WIDE: TOOTH SCHOOL INSIDE!
Lasky, Kathryn	• SCIENCE FAIR BUNNIES
Middleton, Charlotte	• TABITHA'S TERRIFICALLY TOUGH TOOTH
Munsch, Robert	• ANDREW'S LOOSE TOOTH
Paxton, Tom	• THE STORY OF THE TOOTH FAIRY
Rowan, Kate	• I KNOW WHY I BRUSH MY TEETH
Simms, Laura	• ROTTEN TEETH
Sis, Peter	• MADLENKA

Reading Readiness, Learning Readiness, Living Readiness

Love, like literacy, is a great source of strength. And, like literacy, it is a gift we can give our children that never goes away.

It's all but inevitable that sooner or later our children will face the world's ruthlessness. Depression, failed relationships, financial debacles, substance abuse—these aren't part of any parents' plan for their children, and yet, they happen. Amid such challenges it can mean so much to have happy memories, to be able to think Someone has loved me. Reading with your children is one wonderful way to ensure that they will have those happy memories. But it is not the *only* way. In the words of Garrison Keillor, "Nothing you do for your children is ever wasted." *All* quality time spent with your children will foster in them the confidence to explore their world and will instill in them the security to concentrate well. Reading with them—because it is a way of spending quality time together—will help your children be receptive to all learning, including but not limited to reading. It will help them face life's challenges.

HOW WELL DO YOU KNOW YOUR KIDDIE LIT?
Take a quiz of famous first lines at Kay Vandergrift's Web site, http://scils.rutgers.edu/%7Ekvander/firstlines index.html.

THE HAPPY CHILDHOOD CHECKLIST

- Have your child dictate stories to you.

- Have a family newsletter.

- Go to the museum.

- Make positive comments about your child's teacher or caretaker in front of your child.

- Ask your child about his or her day at the end of it.

- Tell stories about grandparents and the child's family history.

- Help your child notice the alphabet and numbers in everyday situations.

- Help your child write and mail letters to people.

- Read and discuss the newspaper in front of your child.

- Switch the TV off during prime-time commercials.

- Take your child to the supermarket with you.

- Put notes in your child's lunch.

- Make music with your child.

- Bring your child on a trip.

- Bring your child to work with you one day.

- Celebrate lost teeth.

- Get your child his own library card . . . and use it.

- Take walks or bike rides together.

- Give your child unscheduled periods in which to play.

- Give thanks at mealtimes or bedtime.

- Close a book before the last page and ask your child what she thinks will happen.

- Cook with your child.

- Say you're sorry when you make a mistake.

- Say yes sometimes when your child expects you to say no.

- Stay home from work when your child is sick.

- Listen to knock-knock jokes.

- Leave a night-light on.

- Look up an answer to a question with your child.

- Take pictures and put them in an album.

- Dance with your child standing on your feet.

- Stand at the bottom of the playground slide and applaud.

- Help your child get acquainted with nursery rhymes from an early age.

- Tell your child that you're proud of him and that you love him.

- Tell your child you love him even when you're not proud.

- Read aloud to your child.

- Read aloud to your child.

- Did I mention you should read aloud to your child?

PART III

Beaucoup de Book-Coups

Life is a banquet, and some poor suckers are starving to death!" rants Rosalind Russell playing hostess in the 1958 movie *Auntie Mame*. Replace the word "life" with "reading," and unfortunately you have an apropos statement for the twenty-first century. The trick, then, is to remember that books can indeed make for a moveable feast. Let the fetes in this section serve as a formal invitation to create occasions that will entice children to step up to the book buffet and party hearty!

Reading and Eating

[As] was her habit, she had settled down with a bag of potato chips, a box of gingersnaps, a bottle of celery tonic, and her dog-eared paperback, to the happiest moments of her day. She sat in a clearing between two stacks of shoes. The top of her head was brushed by the bottoms of three plastic wardrobe bags and a selection of skirts. . . . With the greasy fingers of one hand she would turn pages and select chips and cookies, while in the other hand she held the flashlight by which she read. In the closet, Jane Eyre's woes were Franny's torments; Jane's passions, her passions; Jane's suffering, her very own despair. Her eyes moved from left to right, her jaw from north to south as she rhythmically chomped and reread . . . Mr. Rochester's first avowal of love for Jane Eyre. Ahhhhh. Chomp, chomp, chomp.

—IT ALL BEGAN WITH JANE EYRE: OR,
THE SECRET LIFE OF FRANNY DILLMAN by Sheila Greenwald

There are plenty of ways to integrate the two most satisfying activities known to humankind. We're not only talking about cookbooks here, but we'll start with the basics. If you're like me, it is easy to tell which cookbooks in your kitchen are most preferred, because they wear the war wounds of food preparation: gravy splatters, grease stains, and batter-basted bookmarks.

Good R'eating: Literature-Based Cookbooks

Sampling foods that coincide with the text is a great way to involve children in literature and bring books to life. One title that's sure to receive wear and tear is COOK-A-BOOK by Leslie Cefali, containing over a hundred children's-book recommendations and the treats to match. I had the pleasure of seeing Cefali present this delicious dissertation in person. Her book is special because it works with one child, or thirty. If Cefali's book banquet whets your child's appetite, you can expand your eating repertoire with the following literature-based cookbooks:

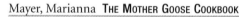

Mayer, Marianna THE MOTHER GOOSE COOKBOOK

The recipes aren't nearly so primary as the poetry, but a grown-up and child can cooperate to create Pease Porridge Hot, Humpty Dumpty's Egg Sandwiches and the Queen of Heart's Tarts.

Barchers, Suzanne I., and Peter J. Rauen STORYBOOK STEW

Offers both crafts and recipes for dozens of contemporary picture books.

Greene, Karen ONCE UPON A RECIPE: DELICIOUS, HEALTHY FOODS FOR KIDS OF ALL AGES

Exceptionally creative recipes to match classic literature. The Little Mermaid Tuna Muffins make a splash and what Wonderland tea party is complete without Curiouser and Curiouser Casserole? Greene has a refreshingly vegetarian leaning: Did you know that Peter Pan's Lost Boys prefer tofu kabobs? Out of print, but worth the hunt.

Walker, Barbara THE LITTLE HOUSE COOKBOOK

A nice companion to Laura Ingalls Wilder's **Little House** series, featuring authentic frontier fare. Children especially enjoy the molasses-on-snow candy.

Fison, Jodie, and Felicity Dahl, comps. ROALD DAHL'S REVOLTING RECIPES

At last, the recipes for Lickable Wallpaper, Frobscottle, Hansel and Gretel's Spare Ribs, and dozens of other Roald Dahl-ian delicacies that before only appeared in his fiction and in our dreams (see Roald Dahl Rules, p. 425). Compiled by his daughter, with an introduction at once affectionate and confectionate.

Waters, Alice FANNY AT CHEZ PANISSE

The author's day job is head chef at the real Chez Panisse in Berkeley, so besides choosing from almost fifty recipes, children can discover the inner workings of a restaurant by following Waters's precocious daughter, Fanny. Your child can read about other intrepid stovetop adventurers in the picture-book biographies FANNIE IN THE KITCHEN by Deborah Hopkinson and THE ADVENTUROUS CHEF: ALEXIS SOYER by Ann Arnold.

For more children's cookbooks, see Cooking Counts As Chemistry, p. 170.

Books for Breakfast

Children who arrive at school early to participate in the school breakfast program will rise and shine academically, thanks to this read-aloud boost. Many teachers need the time before school to meet with parents or prepare for the day, so this is an ideal parent-run program. Set aside a table or two in the cafeteria (you may have to negotiate a quieter place, depending on the acoustics) where you can read aloud to the children as they eat breakfast. In Colorado, children's book author Avi serialized a story in a local newspaper, which led to the creation of "Breakfast Serials." You, too, can serialize almost any good chapter book and make an exciting listening experience. Kick off the program by having children create cereal brands for their favorite book characters and decorating boxes accordingly; for example, gingerbread children cookie cereal for the witch in HANSEL AND GRETEL, dog biscuit cereal for OLD YELLER, banana cereal for CURIOUS GEORGE. Display the boxes along with the day(s) that the group will meet. This kind of program usually grows tremendously by word of mouth—it being breakfast, of course.

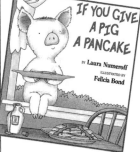

If you prefer to work on a smaller scale, you can try this at home over breakfast, or make read-aloud part of the morning carpool or public transportation routine.

Raise a Reader

Maximize the read-aloud experience by incorporating it with the timing, anticipation, and positive sensory experience of baking bread. This is a program I ran from my apartment while I was on maternity leave. I invited former students and neighborhood children over for books and baking; they ranged in age from about six to thirteen years old. A baking book group will also nourish readers in home-schooling or after-school groups who have free use of kitchens.

SHORT STACK: A FEW GREAT PANCAKE PICTURE BOOKS

Ahvander, Ingmarie	PANCAKE DREAMS
Carle, Eric	PANCAKES, PANCAKES
dePaola, Tomie	PANCAKES FOR BREAKFAST
Many, Paul	THE GREAT PANCAKE ESCAPE
McPhail, David	PIGGY'S PANCAKE PARLOR

Tired of pancakes? Try the chapter book
EVERYTHING ON A WAFFLE by Polly Horvath.

Materials

Good muffin or quick-bread recipe (for ideas, look at KNEAD IT, PUNCH IT, BAKE IT! THE ULTIMATE BREAD-MAKING BOOK FOR PARENTS AND KIDS by Judith and Evan Jones and LOAVES OF FUN: A HISTORY OF BREAD WITH ACTIVITIES AND RECIPES FROM AROUND THE WORLD by Beth Harbison) and, of course, you'll need an oven and a sink, the bread or muffin ingredients, and baking tins. And don't forget the aprons.

Procedure

1. After washing hands, children will participate in making the batter or dough by working cooperatively to measure and mix ingredients, and putting their mixture into tins to bake.

2. After cleaning up, children will gather around an adult—that's you—who will read aloud to them as a pleasant way to pass the time until the baking is completed ("storytime"). Picture books are wonderful for this, but for older children a chapter book may also be used in serial form, over a period of weekly sessions. Be very explicit about timing with the children. Describe in detail what is going to be read that day in order to help the children know when it will be appropriate to stop and check or eat the bread. It is hard to resist peeking every five minutes!

3. Once the read-aloud is finished, the bread is also finished and ready to eat, closing the experience in a gratifying and nurturing way.

GREAT BOOKS TO BAKE BREAD BY

You can read whatever you like. If you have older children, you can serialize a longer novel. My favorite baking and reading afternoon was when we made corn bread and read from FARMER BOY by Laura Ingalls Wilder. But if you want to start with a baking theme, try any of these picture books:

Brett, Jan GINGERBREAD BABY

In a twist on the traditional tale, a little boy helps his baked-good buddy escape the hordes by hiding in a gingerbread house.

Brink, Carol Ryrie GOODY O'GRUMPITY

Based on a 1937 poem set in the Plymouth Plantation, children flock when Goody O'Grumpity gets to baking. Spice-cake recipe included. Bowl-licking good fun!

Carle, Eric WALTER THE BAKER

A baker avoids punishment by inventing a roll that the sun can shine through three times. See if your children can guess what it is!

dePaola, Tomie TONY'S BREAD: AN ITALIAN FOLKTALE

A love story in which a rich young nobleman comes to an Italian town and makes the baker's—and the baker's daughter's—dreams come true.

Dragonwagon, Crescent THIS IS THE BREAD I BAKED FOR NED

Cumulative tale in which a woman sets up for a potluck, with the guest of honor bringing a surprise.

Edwards, Michelle A BAKER'S PORTRAIT

A painter cleverly creates a masterpiece featuring two homely but beloved bakers.

Forest, Heather THE WOMAN WHO FLUMMOXED THE FAIRIES

Gorgeously illustrated Scottish tale of a captured cook who manages to reunite with her family and please an insatiable band of fairies.

Galdone, Paul THE GINGERBREAD BOY

Run, run, as fast as you can. You won't catch up with the runaway cookie but maybe you'll burn some calories. For an urban flavor, try the version by Richard Egielski.

Geeslin, Campbell HOW NANITA LEARNED TO MAKE FLAN

A Mexican tale in which a little girl's magic shoes land her in the lap of a hard-driving Ranchero's wife. With the help of a parrot, she escapes with recipe in hand and shares it on the book's endpapers.

Hayes, Joe A SPOON FOR EVERY BITE

A wicked landlord is foiled when a cunning couple uses bread to outwit him.

Hennessy, B. G. THE MISSING TARTS

An expanded, illustrated version of the classic rhyme in which the Knave of Hearts can't resist pilfering the goods.

Hoban, Russell BREAD AND JAM FOR FRANCES

A mother calls the bluff of a finicky eater.

Hoopes, Lyn Littlefield THE UNBEATABLE BREAD

Uncle Jon warms his world with the baking of an "unbeatable bread" that manages to feed a whole crowd.

Hurwitz, Johanna JUST DESSERTS CLUB

A cheerful chapter book in which a group of friends always finds an occasion to cook. Each chapter ends with delightful recipes that relate to the reading.

Jackson, Kathryn PANTALOON

An enterprising poodle applies for a job at a bakery in this classic that takes the cake.

Kleven, Elisa SUN BREAD

A baker brings back the missing sunshine.

Klinting, Lars BRUNO THE BAKER

Two charming beavers bake their cake and eat it, too.

Morris, Ann BREAD, BREAD, BREAD

A photographic journey around the world, with bread at every stop.

Munson, Derek ENEMY PIE

When a boy is bullied, an ingenious father solves the problem with a little oven-baked intervention.

Polacco, Patricia THUNDERCAKE

A patient grandma teaches a girl both bravery and baking during a thunderstorm. An unusual recipe is included, chocolate cake made with tomato sauce (It's delicious, dense like a brownie!).

Scarry, Richard "The Talking Bread"
from RICHARD SCARRY'S FUNNIEST STORYBOOK EVER

What is making the bread say "mamma"? This droll vignette alone is worth the dough.

Schwartz, Ellen MR. BELINSKY'S BAGELS

When competition is the main ingredient in Belinsky's baked goods, they fall flat. Luckily, things turn out well—on the hole.

Sendak, Maurice IN THE NIGHT KITCHEN

Mickey adds milk and saves the night in his dream kitchen. While the illustrations rise to the occasion, I have to disagree with Mickey. What could be more delicious than a little boy in the batter? You knead this book in any baking collection.

Sharmat, Marjorie Weinman GETTING SOMETHING ON MAGGIE MARMELSTEIN

A wonderful chapter book describing a rivalry between a boy who likes to cook and the girl who likes to drive him crazy.

Dear Madame Esmé,

My son won't stop playing with his food. He makes smiley-faces out of ketchup and mountains out of his salt, and I won't even talk about what he does with mashed potatoes. I'm getting a bit grossed out, and scolding just doesn't help.

Dear Gentle Reader,

Don't squelch his creative spirit, simply help satiate it by serving up HOW ARE YOU PEELING? FOODS WITH MOODS *by Saxton Freymann and Joost Elffers. This title is proof that some great artists have gotten started the very same way. The wholly original photographs give fruits and vegetables a new face—in fact, many new faces: shy, bold, impatient, jealous, pouting, screaming, kissing, smiling. Thanks to its interrogative format (my favorite is "Wired? Tired? Need a kiss? / Do you know anyone like this?") and the gamut of emotions explored, this is a book that will leave readers four and up in a great mood over and over. Besides, you will never look at a salad bar quite the same way again. Break out the black-eyed peas and try making your own "foods with moods" with your child!*

And if this book creates a stir, pack Freymann and Elffers's ONE LONELY SEAHORSE *in your picnic basket and head for the beach. Again using the treasures of the produce section, this team re-creates an underwater paradise in which one lonely swimmer finds a seaful of friends he—and young listeners three and up—can count on. I especially like the octopus made of a banana peel, or is it the lobster made of gingerroot? Reading was never so delicious.*

Smith, Linda **MRS. BIDDLEBOX**
A woman bakes a bad day into a cake.

Traditional **THE LITTLE RED HEN**
Who will help work? Who will help eat? The answer is the same, if you ask hen! I like the version illustrated by Margot Zemach, also the ones illustrated by Paul Galdone and Byron Barton or Emily Bolam, but if you want to help yourself to a less traditional tale, check out Fairy Tales for Your Funnybone (see p. 266).

❀ *Potato Pick:*

YOKO
by Rosemary Wells

When Yoko brings sushi for lunch at school, the teasing begins. Well-intentioned Mrs. Jenkins tries to alleviate the situation with an International Food Day, but it's not until an epicurian classmate steps up that Yoko feels truly accepted. The story does a masterful job of resolving the conflict in a realistic way, and the cunning animal illustrations are both funny and emotionally insightful. I never thought Rosemary Wells would be able to surpass her masterpiece MAX'S DRAGON SHIRT, but she has proven me wrong. (4 and up)

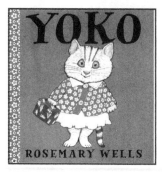

Wells, Rosemary **BUNNY CAKES**

Max knows just what he needs to add to a list of ingredients for a perfect cake for Grandma's birthday . . . if only he could write!

Willard, Nancy
THE HIGH RISE GLORIOUS SKITTLE SKAT ROARIOUS SKY PIE ANGEL FOOD CAKE
An angelic grandma comes down from on high to help with a recipe.

Wing, Natasha **JALAPEÑO BAGELS**
An ethnically diverse family cooks up something spicy for International Day at school.

Why I Hate Pizza: Some Thoughts on Rewarding Reading

I love stickers, gold stars, rubber stamps, junky prizes. I've loved them ever since I was a child. So why was I irked one day when my son came home from school and announced, before he even removed his jacket, "Read to me! Then I'll get a Pizza Hut pizza!"

I gritted my teeth. "You get pizza all the time," I reminded him. "You want a pizza? I'll make you a pizza right now."

My son looked at me with pity. Obviously, I did not understand. This was not *freezer* pizza he was after. This was *prize* pizza.

"It's nice," my husband said gently. "Three books read, a free pizza. A big company giving away stuff. Stop making a face."

I couldn't help it. My son and I had read about seventy-five books together since he had started school a month earlier. I knew this number because of another reading promotion, "Links for Literacy," in which every child made a paper chain with a link for each book read. Eventually the class would connect all the little chains and make a big chain, a lovely symbol of the kindergarten's efforts toward literacy. Okay. But now we were talking pizza. Every time I read to him now, would he be thinking of pizza? I felt violated and jealous. Pepperoni was my son's new mistress.

What was eating me? Why, in this case, didn't it feel like these two activities I love—reading and eating—were being integrated or linked in a way that supported either diet? It's always helpful to do a little research to back up one's resentment. But the findings of Teresa M. Amabile,

The Cookie Crumbles: The Death of Bake Sales

When I taught in the public schools, one of the things I really missed were the bake sales. I remember the signs from my own childhood, hung in crooked lines along the hallway about a week before the event, announcing the room number and decorated with suspicious-looking artwork: brown measled circles for chocolate chip cookies, and voluminous square cakes in pink crayon with cherries on top. I remember remembering to bring money that day, sometimes at the expense of remembering my homework (the young mind can only retain so much!), and filing into the mysterious world of another classroom, transformed into a bakery for a period or two, children waving dimes and quarters around. Anything with sprinkles and frosting went first, then anything with M&M's, then anything with marshmallow fluff. There was always some mother who insisted on making oatmeal raisin cookies, and they sagged and pouted on their plate, homely girls at a beauty pageant. There was something wonderful about shopping while at school, eating unhealthy food while at school, wondering about the cleanliness of classmates' kitchens while at school. There was something wonderful about your own mother or father getting it together long enough to bake a goody you could bring, and hopefully, be proud of.

Since those days, state and local board-of-health mandates have come down hard. Many schools do not allow any food prepared at home, and so everything sold at bake sales is store bought and prepackaged. It's not the same. Food is like an affair. If there's no danger . . . well, where's the thrill? Making money from butter and flour and eggs—things you have anyway, but are meaningless by themselves—now *that's* pretty great. What's so great about selling Hostess, Entenmann's, Little Debbie, Tastykake—products anyone could go to the strip-mall convenience store and pay for? Nobody licked the bowl. Nobody dropped the spoon. Nobody checked expiration dates (or didn't check). Nobody took turns pouring in ingredients. Nobody scared the baby with the sound of the blender. Nobody pricked the cake with a fork, or touched with a finger, or scraped with a spatula, or gloated that his mom made the best cookies in the whole school or died of embarrassment that Mom was actually going to bring them, burnt on the bottom. What's so special?

It's the end of an era. Today school administrators shake in their shoes as every scraped knee, loss of temper, lack of political correctness, or dash of food poisoning brings the threat of litigation. The reality is, there are casualties in our culture of legal conviction. Home-baked goods at school are one. We end up safe *and* sorry.

In the age of bake-sale prohibition, though, there are bound to be bootleggers. Once I saw a second-grade teacher slinking down the hall on the balls of her feet, carrying an aluminum pan. I smelled contraband.

"What's that?" I asked innocently.

She looked around to make sure the halls were empty and tried to be nonchalant, but her voice was lowered. "Brownies. I baked them myself. I told the kids I would make them brownies if they all passed the test." There was a moment of pride, and then a guilty pause. "Don't tell, okay?"

I wouldn't.

psychologist and Harvard Business School professor and author of CREATIVITY IN CONTEXT, actually helped to dissipate some of my concerns. For two decades, she collected all sorts of dirt on why extrinsic motivators (i.e., rewards like pizza) are detrimental (i.e., not good). But it turns out, in doing so, she also unearthed a few cases in which rewards *don't* hinder intrinsic motivation (i.e., doing something just for its own sake) and may in fact increase creativity and production (i.e., are fine and better than fine):

• Praise can help, writes Amabile, when it is used as "the confirmation of one's achievement by respected others." In other words, flattery won't get you anywhere but praise in the form of information might.

• Children who are operating below level may benefit by having their work evaluated. In other words, they may need a little extra incentive.

If Amabile is correct, the bottom line is that it's important to know the individual child. A child interested or proficient in say, reading, is already stimulated and will not benefit from extrinsic motivators. In fact, these may even pose a threat to this child's love of reading.

The question really isn't whether pizza can help some children read. It's why some children *need* pizza in order to motivate them to open a book. It's interesting to think how many children enter school excited to read, and by the fourth grade groan when reading is mentioned. Are schools giving enough thought to the potential harm that their grading systems and evaluations are doing by delivering them wholesale to school populations? Many children have suffered through years of what is the equivalent of late-night-television test patterns on the printed page: blasé textbooks, books without pictures, books in poor condition, tests, work sheets. Book lovers know that reading's remuneration is more reading. So the answer to appetizing reluctant readers to rise to the reading occasion, I believe, lies not in a stuffed crust, but in holding these anchovies.

I do not reward my son for every three television shows he watches or every three hours on the computer. If I did, I would be considered heaven sent by my son, but crazy to everybody else. If reading potentially offers the same entertainment as television and computers, it does seem a little crazy to reward it. I say, let's reward every three pizzas eaten with a new book. On the other hand, we should not forget that children are individuals, and for some children, *appropriate* rewards may be motivators, as Amabile's research suggests. Some children who are good readers might just fall into a slump, and can be rescued with a little recognition. If you believe your child could benefit from an extrinsic reading boost, try to keep premiums as closely linked to the reading experience as possible, choosing activities and gifts that directly complement reading content or focus on quality time rather than material dividends. Rewards could include:

• Family field trip to a museum of the child's choice

• Doll, stuffed toy, or puzzle of favorite book-related character

• Time spent together cooking a book-related dish

• Time spent together making and playing a home-made board game with a book-related theme

• Flashlight or book light

• Duplicate books read by child donated to library in child's name

• Decorated oversized cardboard box, "private reading room"

• "Stay up an extra half hour to read" or "Extra story at bed-time" coupons

• Train or bus ride

• Hobby items with related book (*Baseball Digest* magazine enclosed in glove, art supplies with drawing or craft book, telescope with star guide)

• "I'm proud of you" note, filled with glitter, sent care of your child's classroom at school, or a congratulatory e-mail (check out www.bluemountain.com for messages and family-friendly games kids love)

• Autographed picture of a favorite author (write care of the publisher)

ALTERNATIVE PRIMARY PIZZA STORIES

Barbour, Karen	• LITTLE NINO'S PIZZERIA
Khalsa, Dayal Kaur	• HOW PIZZA CAME TO QUEENS
Pelham, David	• SAM'S PIZZA
Pieńkowski, Jan	• PIZZA!
Rotner, Shelley, and Julia Pemberton Hellums	• HOLD THE ANCHOVIES!: A BOOK ABOUT PIZZA
Steig, William	• PETE'S A PIZZA
Sturges, Philemon	• THE LITTLE RED HEN (MAKES A PIZZA)
Voake, Charlotte	• PIZZA KITTENS
Walter, Virginia	• "HI, PIZZA MAN!"

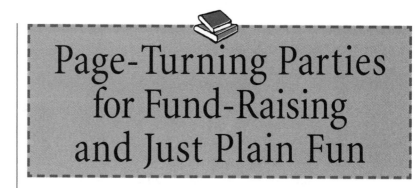

Page-Turning Parties for Fund-Raising and Just Plain Fun

I t's your party and you'll read if you want to! Professional librarians call it "programming," but you can call it a celebration. Books can be the basis of special events that give guests a reason to gather, and sometimes, to give. Unless otherwise noted, these are picture books.

Sleep-Over While the Sun Is Up

B esides being great bedtime reading for one-on-one, use these books to style a storytime program. You can have a daytime sleep-over party at your home or try it at your child's school. Arrange with your child's teachers to have children come in pajamas. Bring pillows and flashlights. Teddy bears optional. The storyteller should be costumed, too—so break out those bunny slippers and make sure the backside of your union suit is buttoned!

Read a selection of sleepytime stories:

Andersen, Hans Christian	• THE PRINCESS AND THE PEA (I like the edition illustrated by Paul Galdone.)
Bang, Molly	• TEN, NINE, EIGHT
Berger, Barbara Helen	• A LOT OF OTTERS
Branford, Henrietta	• LITTLE PIG FIGWORT CAN'T GET TO SLEEP
Brooks, Erik	• PRACTICALLY PERFECT PAJAMAS
Buller, Jon, and Susan Schade	• I LOVE YOU, GOOD NIGHT
Carle, Eric	• THE VERY LONELY FIREFLY (Turn off the lights and watch the fireflies sparkle on the last page!)
Child, Lauren	• MY DREAM BED
Corentin, Philippe	• PAPA!

Cushman, Doug	• PORCUPINE'S PAJAMA PARTY
Griffin, Adele	• OVERNIGHT
Hest, Amy	• PAJAMA PARTY (Short chapter book.)
Ho, Minfong	• HUSH! A THAI LULLABY
Hutchins, Pat	• GOOD-NIGHT, OWL!
Irving, Washington, retold by Will Moses	• RIP VAN WINKLE
Kirk, Daniel	• HUSH, LITTLE ALIEN
Kitamura, Satoshi	• WHEN SHEEP CANNOT SLEEP
Leuck, Laura	• SUN IS FALLING, NIGHT IS CALLING
Mayer, Mercer	• THERE'S A NIGHTMARE IN MY CLOSET
McBratney, Sam	• THE CATERPILLOW FIGHT
Murphy, Stuart J.	• RABBIT'S PAJAMA PARTY
Paul, Ann Whitford	• EVERYTHING TO SPEND THE NIGHT FROM A TO Z
Raschka, Chris	• CAN'T SLEEP
Rathmann, Peggy	• GOOD NIGHT, GORILLA
Rogers, Jacqueline	• BEST FRIENDS SLEEP OVER
Sendak, Maurice	• IN THE NIGHT KITCHEN
Sierra, Judy	• GOOD NIGHT, DINOSAURS
Simmons, Jane	• THE DREAMTIME FAIRIES
Spohn, Kate	• THE MERMAIDS' LULLABY
Swain, Ruth Freeman	• BEDTIME!
Waber, Bernard	• BEARSIE BEAR AND THE SURPRISE SLEEPOVER PARTY • IRA SLEEPS OVER
Waddell, Martin	• CAN'T YOU SLEEP, LITTLE BEAR?
Wood, Audrey	• SWEET DREAM PIE • THE NAPPING HOUSE

🌼 *Potato Pick:*

CLOCKWORK
by Philip Pullman

A storyteller is gifted at telling spine-tingling tales, but in the midst of telling one at a local tavern, the evil main character walks through the door to present the local clockmaker with a dreadful gift. Spellbinding stories within stories abound in CLOCKWORK, and they all wind down to a satisfying conclusion. Sixth- to eighth-graders (who may be familiar with Pullman's wildly successful fantasy series **His Dark Materials** trilogy) gladly suffer goosebumps during this read-aloud. (10 and up)

To keep older children's eyes wide open during a read-aloud slumber party, share spooky stories. Teacher Cindy Robinson of Anne Arundel County, Maryland, made a faux campfire by putting flashlights in a bucket, shining up into red and orange cellophane. Very atmospheric! I especially like the collections SHORT AND SHIVERY retold by Robert D. San Souci, SPOOKY STORIES FOR A DARK AND STORMY NIGHT compiled by Alice Low, and SCARY STORIES FOR SLEEP-OVERS by R. C. Welch. The children always love SCARY STORIES TO TELL IN THE DARK retold by Alvin

CHAPTER BOOK BONE-RATTLERS

Chill to a chapter at a preteen slumber party, or get copies to use as door prizes or raffle items for readers 9 and up.

Boston, L. M.	THE CHILDREN OF GREEN KNOWE (First title in the Green Knowe Chronicles.)
DeFelice, Cynthia	THE GHOST OF FOSSIL GLEN
Gaiman, Neil	CORALINE
Hahn, Mary Downing	WAIT TILL HELEN COMES · TIME FOR ANDREW (Good ghost story author, thrill to all of her books!)
Ibbotson, Eva	DIAL-A-GHOST
Pearce, Philippa	TOM'S MIDNIGHT GARDEN
Peck, Richard	GHOSTS I HAVE BEEN
Vande Velde, Vivian	NEVER TRUST A DEAD MAN

Younger children may prefer the Not TOO Scary Stories on p. 382.

Schwartz, but that's too scary for me! I never read from that book without making a nightmare disclaimer first. A sleep-over story doesn't *have* to be scary to keep the attention of older children, though, as long as it's surprising; for instance, IRA SLEEPS OVER by Bernard Waber, read with expression, is a hilarious read-aloud hit with *all* ages.

You can also adapt the reading pajama party to make an evening PTA event. For a fund-raiser, add the following options:

• Charge admission, and serve pizza. You've gotta have pizza at a slumber party!

• Raffle off sleep-over stuff: an oversized teddy bear, pillows or bedspreads donated by local department stores, or children's books.

• Put on a pajama fashion show.

• Have a lullaby sing-a-long, or feature lullaby perfomers. "The Seal's Lullaby" by Rudyard Kipling, "The Huntsmen" by Walter de la Mare, and the traditional "All the Pretty Little Horses" are just a few of the beautiful arrangements on the cassette LULLABIES AND NIGHTSONGS by Eric Wilder and William Engvick.

Johnny Appleseed Anniversary

Anyone can count the seeds in an apple. Who can count the apples in a seed?
                                                           —Steven R. Covey

September 26 is my favorite American's birthday: John Chapman, better known as the legendary Johnny Appleseed, who traveled all over the Ohio River Valley planting apple seeds. Johnny Appleseed was the first frontier librarian, ripping apart valuable copies of books by his favorite author, a scientist and theologian named Emanuel Swedenborg, and rotating the chapters among the settlers—kind of a one-man-one-book walking bookmobile. But the reason I am completely enamored of him is because he did one small thing every day, planting seeds, and it changed the landscape of our whole country. In a way, it is a beautiful metaphor for read-aloud (which he was also known to do); reading is one small thing we can do every day that could change our country.

A yearly tradition in my family is to mark the occasion of Chapman's birth by sitting under a tree and reading aloud from some of these books:

Aliki	• THE STORY OF JOHNNY APPLESEED
Glass, Andrew	• FOLKS CALL ME APPLESEED JOHN
Hall, Zoe	• THE APPLE PIE TREE
Harrison, David L.	• JOHNNY APPLESEED: MY STORY
Hutchins, Pat	• TEN RED APPLES
Kellogg, Steven	• JOHNNY APPLESEED
Lerner, Harriet, and Susan Goldhor	• WHAT'S SO TERRIBLE ABOUT SWALLOWING AN APPLE SEED?
Lindbergh, Reeve	• JOHNNY APPLESEED
Priceman, Marjorie	• HOW TO MAKE AN APPLE PIE AND SEE THE WORLD
Scheer, Julian	• RAIN MAKES APPLESAUCE
Tryon, Leslie	• ALBERT'S FIELD TRIP
Wallace, Nancy Elizabeth	• APPLES, APPLES, APPLES
Wellington, Monica	• APPLE FARMER ANNIE
Zagwyn, Deborah Turney	• APPLE BATTER

Consider playing a recording of the "William Tell Overture" by Rossini followed by a reading of **WILLIAM TELL** by Margaret Early. It's a great read-aloud that third-graders love as much as eighth-graders.

It is easy to tie a Johnny Appleseed–tribute storytime into a whole "Apple Afternoon" fund-raising event, complete with games and crafts:

• Sell taffy apples, apple-butter sandwiches, and apple-juice boxes.

• Sell apple seeds in kid-designed seed packets.

• Bob for apples.

• Have an apple-in-the-bucket toss.

• Play "hot apple" instead of "hot potato." Sitting in a circle, pass around an apple while the music plays, and when the music stops, whoever is

---

🍀 *Potato Pick:*

THE QUILTMAKER'S GIFT

by Jeff Brumbeau, illustrated by Gail de Marcken

A king who likes to receive presents so much that he decrees his birthday be celebrated twice a year is rebuffed by a grandmotherly quiltmaker who only makes gifts for the poor and needy. Finally she agrees to make the king a quilt if he gives away all the things he owns: "With each gift that you give, I'll add another piece to your quilt." While the parable is timely in a world of rampant consumerism and corporate greed, the story does not read as a morality play. Instead, the writing is as compulsively cliffhanging as a good fairy tale complete with peacock plumes gracing the soldiers' hats and a merry-go-round with horses that every child would want to ride. The only difficulty is that the illustrations are small and detailed, making them hard to share with a large group. So do as the king and the quiltmaker do—seek out who you want to share with one at a time until everyone has received THE QUILTMAKER'S GIFT. Visit the king and the quiltmaker online and learn to quilt at www.quiltmakersgift.com, or visit www.nmt.edu/~breynold/quiltfiction.html for a comprehensive list of quilt-related books. May inspire an old-fashioned quilting bee! (All ages)

JOANNIE APPLESEED?

For a good female Johnny Appleseed model, try MISS RUMPHIUS by Barbara Cooney, in which a girl is told by her grandfather to "do something to make the world more beautiful," and so she grows up and plants lupines everywhere. After I read this to children I taught, I set out great burgeoning bouquets of blue and purple flowers, and all afternoon the children created still-life paintings that were hung all around the library. You can also decorate homemade seed packets with the grandfather's quote to be distributed to friends, or just plant seeds in honor of Miss Rumphius's efforts. Children who like Miss Rumphius will also enjoy her cousins MY GREAT-AUNT ARIZONA by Gloria Houston and SUNFLOWER SAL by Janet S. Anderson.

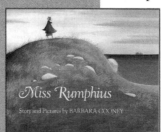

holding the apple leaves the circle. Last person in the circle wins.

• Create apple prints. These make nice cards for teachers. In my classes, we printed out apples on parchment and produced a "Johnny Appleseed's Birthday Resolution," writing out what small action we would try to take consistently for a year that would help our country be a better place. Apple-print bookmarks are nice, too.

• Make pink tissue-paper apple blossoms.

• Have an apple dunk. Rent a dunking machine from a carnival supply store, and use apples instead of baseballs. Or, let children knock down cans using apples.

• Offer up a tall-tale open mike. Give a prize to the best liar . . . *ahem* . . . I mean tale spinner.

• March in a pot-banging parade in honor of Chapman, who is said to have worn a pot on his head. How about a pot-and-pan band?

• Make paper apple wreaths by cutting out the middle of large paper plates and decorating the circumference of the plate with apple cutouts and glitter.

• Make simple bee puppets out of construction paper, with pipe cleaner antennae and popsicle sticks as handles. Or, make headbands with antennae; bees looove apples! In fact, you may want to set out citronella candles to keep the real ones away. If they come, just read to them—check out the bee stories in Buggy for Books (p. 406).

There are some children's books that will substantially increase your adult background knowledge before an apple event, and children will like them, too. Read THE REAL JOHNNY APPLESEED by Laurie Lawlor, THE LIFE AND TIMES OF THE APPLE by Charles Micucci, and THE AMAZING APPLE BOOK by Paulette Bourgeois and be ready to field any apple-related query. For more inspiration be sure to visit Appleseed Alley, the Johnny Appleseed Web site, www.johnny-appleseed.net.

A Very Merry Unbirthday!

When I was a little girl, my mother threw me the greatest birthday parties! I remember watching my mother fill out each of the invitations with her graceful, rounded handwriting. Weeks in advance, my mother would take me to the local party store, the "Ha-lo Gift Shop," where the saleswoman would ceremoniously turn on a basement light to reveal an Aladdin's cave of plastic "goody bag" treats. My mother would indulge me by letting me select absolutely every prize that caught my fancy: rings, plastic magnifying glasses, opalescent strings of beads, bubbles, pencils, pads of paper. Then, with the bag so full of booty it would pinch our fingers to carry it, we would go next door to Davidson's Bakery to order a cake: invariably chocolate and with a doll on top that had eyes that could open and close, perched on a plastic, heart-shaped stand.

My mother would be up late the night before, draping the dining room with twisted streamers and rubbing balloons on her hair so the static would make them stick to the walls.

The day of my birthday, I had a present served on my breakfast plate: my father dressed as Toot-Toot the Clown, complete with face makeup and a sequined satin top. We all played Pin the Tail on the Donkey and Hot Potato, and my cake always had one more candle on it than the number of years I was turning, "one for good luck." During the party my mother was mostly in the kitchen, preparing and serving tons of food to all the relatives and friends. I'm sure she was exhausted by the day's end.

Twenty years later, when my son was turning three years old, I read advice in the parenting books: "Have the number of guests match the age the child is turning. Birthday parties can be overwhelming." I listened while fellow parents told me, "They don't remember it anyway." "Give 'em a cupcake and they're fine." "All those prizes are an expensive waste." "You don't really want all those people in your home, do you?" So I did what anyone raised by my mother would do. I IGNORED IT! My son had fifty people at his third birthday party, which had a Curious George theme, thematic games, thematic cake, a banana-shaped piñata,

❀ *Potato Pick:*

HENRY'S FIRST-MOON BIRTHDAY
by Lenore Look

This author has the skill of a hundred birthdays! Take, for instance, GninGnin, who is cooking in the kitchen amid pots and bowls of food, "touching this one here and that one there, like a gardener tending her plants." Baby Henry smiles, "eyes like commas." Or, looking in a mirror alongside her grandmother, "I see we are a pair, like favorite shoes, side by side." Told from the viewpoint of a mischievous little girl, there is a profound immediacy to the prose, and we are as immersed in Jenny's world as Jenny is immersed in the red-as-a-firecracker dye of the lucky eggs she is coloring. Nothing is overexplained in this book; rather, we are simply privy to the homey confidence of a family preparing for a special day. A glossary of Korean words is included. (5 and up)

and a guest appearance by Curious George himself, courtesy of a costumed Daddy (who nearly fainted underneath all that fur). During his entire third year, not a day went by that my son didn't make a suggestion in regard to his fourth birthday. I never felt so appreciated in my life. I may not be able to top his third birthday, but I know we'll always remember, as a family, that we celebrated the day he was born with all of our might.

I noticed, when I became a teacher, that some primary-school-aged children had never been to an old-fashioned birthday party, with Pin the Tail on the Donkey and Musical Chairs, goody bags and party hats. Nowadays many children celebrate their birthday at restaurants, museums, and "Fun Zones," which are terrifically electric and exciting, but I still wanted my students to experience an "at home"–style party. I also noticed, sadly, that children who came from other countries and didn't speak English well, had a physical disability, or were bused from far-off neighborhoods were often excluded from birthday celebrations. Consider volunteering to make an "Unbirthday Storytime" that everyone in your child's class can partake in. Of course, you could just hold a birthday party for your own child, but, as she will remind you, that has the excruciating drawback of coming only once a year. The other plus for unbirthdays is that the focus is not on one lucky child: It's everybody's birthday at once, and nobody has to buy gifts or find a way to get to an unfamiliar location. And best of all, for the lead grown-up an Unbirthday Party is just plain jolly, sans the stress and expense riding on the once-a-year birthday.

Some things should stay the same. Don't forget to arrange to have invitations distributed in class at least a week before, because getting an invitation is so exciting. Start the Unbirthday with some read-aloud. Gift wrap a few of these books, and unwrap them as you read.

Unbirthday Stories

Barrett, Judi	• Benjamin's 365 Birthdays
Best, Cari	• Three Cheers for Catherine the Great
Bornstein, Ruth	• Little Gorilla
Carle, Eric	• The Secret Birthday Message
Carlstrom, Nancy White	• Happy Birthday, Jesse Bear!
Cohen, Carol Lee	• Happy to You!
Davis, Katie	• Party Animals

Freeman, Don	• DANDELION
Griffith, Helen V.	• HOW MANY CANDLES?
Hughes, Shirley	• ALFIE GIVES A HAND
Hutchins, Pat	• IT'S MY BIRTHDAY!
Keats, Ezra Jack	• A LETTER TO AMY
Kirk, David	• MISS SPIDER'S TEA PARTY
Kleven, Elisa	• HOORAY, A PIÑATA!
Pomerantz, Charlotte	• THE BIRTHDAY LETTERS
Ryan, Pam Muñoz	• MICE AND BEANS (A Spanish bilingual birthday.)
Stewart, Paul	• THE BIRTHDAY PRESENTS
Richardson, Judith Benét	• COME TO MY PARTY
Rose, Deborah Lee	• BIRTHDAY ZOO
Schenk de Regniers, Beatrice	• MAY I BRING A FRIEND?
Seuss, Dr.	• HAPPY BIRTHDAY TO YOU!
Theroux, Phyllis	• SEREFINA UNDER THE CIRCUMSTANCES
Tryon, Leslie	• ALBERT'S BIRTHDAY
Waber, Bernard	• LYLE AND THE BIRTHDAY PARTY
Wells, Rosemary	• BUNNY CAKES
Wormell, Mary	• HILDA HEN'S HAPPY BIRTHDAY

Follow storytime with:

Games: Pin the Tail on the Donkey, Hot Potato, Musical Chairs, or the Grand Prize Game. (For more ideas, see PIN THE TAIL ON THE DONKEY AND OTHER GAMES by Joanna Cole and Stephanie Calmenson, and BIRTHDAYS AROUND THE WORLD by Mary D. Lankford for international inspiration.) I've found that the British version of Hot Potato is very popular. Take a single prize and wrap it in many layers of wrapping paper. Children sit in a circle and pass the package around while music is played. When the music stops, the child holding the package may unwrap a single layer. If the prize is not revealed, play continues. The child who unwraps the last layer gets the prize. Or, make the prize a box of candy or stickers . . . one for everybody! (Old fashioned penny candy is sold at www.hometownfavorites.com.)

Noise: Don't forget party blowers. For more noise, you can write fortunes and tuck them inside balloons, then blow them up. Give each child a balloon, everyone covers their ears, counts to three, and . . . get your fortune!

Hats: Zany party hats are easy to make by creating crowns out of corrugated bulletin-board border and tucking brightly colored pipe cleaners into the corrugation.

Cake: If you host this party at home or are lucky enough to have a school that lets you bring baked goods in, here are a few of my favorite unbirthday desserts:

CAKE IN A CONE

Prepare your favorite cake mix as directed. Pour batter into plain, flat-bottom ice cream cones filling each a little less than half full. Bake according to package directions, but not too far in advance of the party—they get soggy after a day. Children like to ice and decorate these themselves, but you can also crown with a scoop of ice cream, or for a "soft serve" style, swirl canned whipped cream on top.

DUMP CAKE
Ingredients
1 can cherry pie filling in heavy syrup
1 can crushed pineapple in heavy syrup
1 box yellow cake mix
2 sticks melted butter (yes, I *know*!)
½ cup shredded coconut
½ cup chopped walnuts

Layer each item one on top of the other in the order above. (Do not prepare the cake mix; just empty the box on to the pile.) Drizzle the butter over the cake mix. Bake at 350 degrees for an hour. Serve warm in bowls with vanilla ice cream. Absolutely scrumptious!

DO-IT-YOURSELF ICE CREAM
Ingredients
1 cup half and half
2 tablespoons sugar
1 teaspoon vanilla
½ cup kosher or rock salt
Ice cubes
1 pint-size Ziploc bag
1 gallon-size Ziploc bag

BEST BIRTHDAY PARTY WEB SITES
www.birthdaypartyideas.com
http://family.go.com
www.birthdayexpress.com

Making this ice cream is as fun as eating it! Mix the half and half, sugar, and vanilla in the pint-sized bag (I like the "zipper" sandwich bags because they stay closed). In the gallon-sized bag, put the salt and enough ice to fill it half way. Put the small bag inside the larger bag, and seal. Then, shake shake shake! In about ten minutes, the ingredients in the smaller bag will become creamy dreamy. Add sprinkles, and eat it right from the bag with a spoon. The cost of rock salt and gallon bags really adds up if you're doing this with a large group, so if you want to make a few batches with the same bags, children can take turns shaking it. Everyone has a taste and takes home the recipe.

Song: Try "The Unbirthday Song" from Disney's *Alice in Wonderland* or a little variation I wrote on the traditional birthday song:

Happy birthday not mine,
Happy birthday not mine!
Happy birthday, someone else's,
Happy birthday not mine!

Videotape: Part of the fun of a party is watching the whole thing five minutes after it's over.

Holding a Candle to Authors and Illustrators

Celebrate the birthdays of the people behind the books. Ask your child's teacher if you can put up a permanent bulletin-board display (see A Helpful Tack, p. 31) to feature author/illustrator birthdays. Then throw a birthday party (or an Unbirthday Party) in the author/illustrator's honor. If your schedule doesn't allow for a school visit, you can send in homemade bookmarks or candy to commemorate the occasion. Or just make a point on that day (or sometime that month) of paying a visit with your child to the bookstore or library to check out the books; and eat a cupcake or healthy muffin in tribute! This is a festive way to get to know lots of classic literature. On the next page are the birthdays of many popular authors and illustrators, and you can also look up the dates for your personal favorites in THE TEACHER'S CALENDAR, compiled by Sandy Whiteley or in the reference series **Something About the Author,** available at libraries or at http://school.discovery.com/schrockguide/authorname.html.

An Author/Illustrator Birthday Calendar

JANUARY
3—J. OTTO SEIBOLD
4—JAKOB GRIMM
7—KAY CHORAO
8—MARJORIE PRICEMAN
12—CLEMENT HURD
18—RAYMOND BRIGGS
22—BRIAN WILDSMITH
26—ASHLEY WOLFF
28—VERA B. WILLIAMS
29—BILL PEET
   ROSEMARY WELLS
31—DENISE FLEMING

FEBRUARY
2—JUDITH VIORST
5—DAVID WIESNER
7—LAURA INGALLS WILDER
8—ANNE ROCKWELL
10—E.L. KONIGSBURG
   LUCY COUSINS
11—JANE YOLEN
12—DAVID SMALL
   JUDY BLUME
14—PAUL ZELINSKY
15—NORMAN BRIDWELL
17—ROBERT NEWTON PECK
25—CYNTHIA VOIGT

MARCH
2—DR. SEUSS
4—MEINDERT DEJONG
   DAV PILKEY
   PEGGY RATHMANN
6—THACHER HURD
   CHRIS RASCHKA
7—JANE DYER
11—EZRA JACK KEATS
13—DIANE DILLON
   ELLEN RASKIN
20—LOIS LOWRY
21—DAVID WISNIEWSKI
22—RANDOLPH CALDECOTT
25—PETRA MATHERS
31—ANDREW LANG

APRIL
2—HANS CHRISTIAN ANDERSEN
8—TRINA SCHART HYMAN
12—BEVERLY CLEARY
   HARDIE GRAMATKY
14—FRANK REMKIEWICZ
16—GARTH WILLIAMS
25—ALVIN SCHWARTZ
27—LUDWIG BEMELMANS

MAY
5—LEO LIONNI
8—MILTON MELTZER
9—ELEANOR ESTES
   WILLIAM PENE DU BOIS
11—PETER SIS
   ZILPHA KEATLEY SNYDER
15—L. FRANK BAUM
16—MARGRET REY
17—GARY PAULSEN
18—LILLIAN HOBAN
22—ARNOLD LOBEL
23—SCOTT O'DELL
26—LISBETH ZWERGER

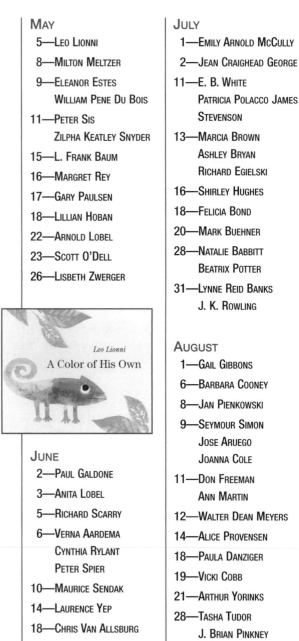

Leo Lionni
A Color of His Own

JUNE
2—PAUL GALDONE
3—ANITA LOBEL
5—RICHARD SCARRY
6—VERNA AARDEMA
   CYNTHIA RYLANT
   PETER SPIER
10—MAURICE SENDAK
14—LAURENCE YEP
18—CHRIS VAN ALLSBURG
25—ERIC CARLE
26—CHARLOTTE ZOLOTOW
30—DAVID MCPHAIL

JULY
1—EMILY ARNOLD MCCULLY
2—JEAN CRAIGHEAD GEORGE
11—E. B. WHITE
   PATRICIA POLACCO JAMES STEVENSON
13—MARCIA BROWN
   ASHLEY BRYAN
   RICHARD EGIELSKI
16—SHIRLEY HUGHES
18—FELICIA BOND
20—MARK BUEHNER
28—NATALIE BABBITT
   BEATRIX POTTER
31—LYNNE REID BANKS
   J. K. ROWLING

AUGUST
1—GAIL GIBBONS
6—BARBARA COONEY
8—JAN PIENKOWSKI
9—SEYMOUR SIMON
   JOSE ARUEGO
   JOANNA COLE
11—DON FREEMAN
   ANN MARTIN
12—WALTER DEAN MEYERS
14—ALICE PROVENSEN
18—PAULA DANZIGER
19—VICKI COBB
21—ARTHUR YORINKS
28—TASHA TUDOR
   J. BRIAN PINKNEY
30—VIRGINIA LEE BURTON
   LAURENT DE BRUNHOFF

SEPTEMBER

3—Aliki
5—Paul Fleischman
7—Eric Hill
8—Byron Barton
   Jack Prelutsky
11—Anthony Browne
13—Roald Dahl
14—Diane Goode
15—Tomie dePaola
   Robert McCloskey
16—H. A. Rey
17—Paul Goble
27—G. Brian Karas
   Bernard Waber

OCTOBER

4—Donald Sobol
6—Susan Meddaugh
7—Susan Jeffers
9—Johanna Hurwitz
10—James Marshall
14—Elisa Kleven
16—Edward Ardizzone
19—Ed Emberley
22—N. C. Wyeth
24—Barbara Robinson
25—Fred Marcellino
26—Steven Kellogg
31—Holly Hobbie
   Katherine
   Paterson

NOVEMBER

1—Hilary Knight
3—Janell Cannon
4—Gail E. Haley
9—Lois Ehlert
14—William Steig
   Astrid Lindgren
15—Daniel Pinkwater
16—Jean Fritz
23—Marc Simont
25—Marc Brown
   Jim LaMarche
27—Kevin Henkes
28—Ed Young
   Tomi Ungerer
29—C. S. Lewis
   Madeleine L'Engle
   Rosemary Wells
30—Margot Zemach

DECEMBER

2—David Macaulay
9—Jean de Brunhoff
11—William Joyce
15—Henrik Drescher
16—Quentin Blake
27—Diane Stanley

AGNES ROYER
STORY LADY

It started forty years ago, when a young mother, who baked the best birthday cakes in town and collected dolls, wanted to read a story over the radio for her daughter. What began as an act of love for her own family has been expanded widely enough to include everyone in her community in an embrace. Now Agnes Royer has the longest-running children's radio show in Alaska. Her show comes over AM 930 KTKN as part of the Fun for Kids program, serving the city of Ketchikan, as well as a Native American reservation and a logging camp. Children tucked away in the northernmost corners can tune in to possibly the best Saturday-morning entertainment in the country. Her hour has become an institution. "We don't want to think about what would happen if her show didn't come on one Saturday," sweats the station's general manager, Jeff Seifert. "Nothing—and I mean *nothing*—preempts 'The Story Lady.'"

It's inspiring (and potato-pedagogical) to think of someone using a resource such as local radio to share the best of children's literature—and to have been committed to doing it for so long. Over the airwaves, Agnes gives children her time—the greatest and most lasting gift anyone can give to a child—and she fills that time by sharing her favorite stories. Agnes's calm, sunny voice is ageless, reading aloud from book after wonderful book interspersed with classic storytelling recordings and lively music. The highlight for me, though, is that part of the show when she wishes a Happy Birthday to a particular young listener and then plays a vintage rendition of the birthday song. Every time I hear the earnest wishes and the song, I can't help but cry buckets. Agnes's show is sentimental, but not saccharine. It's a weekly reminder of the preciousness of traditions.

🌸 *Potato Pick:*

WHERE DO BALLOONS GO?
AN UPLIFTING MYSTERY

*by Jamie Lee Curtis, illustrated
by Laura Cornell*

Has your child ever lost a balloon and wondered where it
went? "Where do they go when
they float far away? Do they ever
catch cold and need somewhere
to stay?" The merry musings
are paired with brightly colored
illustrations that are as bouncy
as the rhymes, and children will
cheer for the double-page fold-
out spread of the "balloon
dance." The mystery of lost
balloons is never quite solved,
but that's part of the fun—and
part of the reason balloons are
cherished by children for as
long as they can hold on. The
question in the title is also a
great creative-writing activity.
(5 and up and up and up!)

Birthday Book Donation Program

When a school librarian blows out the candles on a birthday cake, chances are the secret wish is for more books in the school's collection. With this simple and joyful donation program, it's easy as pie (or cake) to make that wish come true. At the start of the school year, ask parents to make a donation to the Birthday Book program and fill out a form (see the prototype, Appendix B1) that includes their child's name, homeroom, and birthday (or half-birthday, if it's in the summer). When I instituted this program as a school librarian, I suggested a $10, $15, or $20 contribution per child—$10 covered paperbacks plus library processing and the higher contributions paid for hardcovers. On the child's special day, a certificate (see appendix B2) is placed in the child's homeroom mailbox with salutations. A special bookplate (see Appendix B3) is placed inside the book that was purchased using the donated funds, commemorating the child's birthday. Perhaps a display can also be placed in or near the office, naming monthly Birthday Book students.

For this kind of program it's important to be organized. I kept the forms, arranged chronologically by month, in a folder, and starred dates on a calendar so nobody would be forgotten. I set a September deadline for birthday-club membership and made up all the certificates at once, so for the rest of the year, my only job was distribution. (I made certificates with a blank space to fill in the name for students who transferred in midyear.) I also visited the classrooms of the birthday children with a colorfully decorated tambourine, and treated them to my bad singing (and a lollipop, to make up for it) before personally presenting them with a certificate commemorating their special day. This club is a great opportunity for parent involvement, especially since some librarians' schedules don't allow them to travel the school hallways as a birthday troubadour. But do make sure you coordinate the Birthday Book Club with the school librarian, who will know which books to purchase. (Of course, a birthday book club can be adapted to enhance classroom collections as well, if parents donate directly to the teacher.)

In the end, I could credit this funny little program with major library revitalization, since the hundreds-of-dollars'-worth of books went far to update the collection, and children loved coming to the library and seeing books with their names inside.

PART IV

Have Book, Will Travel: History, Social Studies, and Geography

While the territory of fiction is often what comes to mind when one imagines being "lost in a book," nonfiction can provide a substantive middle ground between legend and real life. History and historical fiction allow children to see the world in the context of a time line and, better yet, see *themselves* in the context of that time line, where they play a part in a bigger story, and where the possibility of adventure still looms. Readers are vicarious exchange students traveling all the corners of both time and space, and narrators are waiting in the bindings to give children the grand tour.

A Crash Course in Time Travel Safety Procedures

Time travel (aka history) is one of the most exciting and enlightening adventures possible through print—and potentially the most violent. Young readers may find themselves, for instance, in a Japanese internment camp or a Nazi concentration camp, in South Africa during apartheid or in the fracas of a Viking raid. They might witness a Wild West hanging or a witch-burning in Salem, or even people buried alive in Pompeii. How do we present history honestly to children through literature without desensitizing them to atrocities or giving them nightmares? The complexity and gravity of history naturally makes a parent feel protective. Many of us instinctively seek to control the intake of such mature subject matter. The answer to responsible sharing, though, is not in censorship of material but in finding material that is handled sensitively, presenting it when it is most appropriate in terms of child development, and offering meaningful support as the material is shared and absorbed.

Hey, try to open up
your heart
To beauty; go to the woods
some day
And weave a wreath of
memory there.
Then if the tears obscure
your way
You'll know how
wonderful it is
To be alive.

—From "Birdsong," by an anonymous child author in the Terezin concentration camp, 1941, in I NEVER SAW ANOTHER BUTTERFLY, edited by Hana Volavková

History Hypothesis: Gauging Your Child's Developmental Stage

Child development offers a compass for presenting history. Especially applicable is the psychosocial development theory of Erik Erikson. Erikson believed that a child's social and emotional development involves a series of stages, and at each stage, a child faces what he calls a "developmental crisis." The successful resolution of each crisis contributes to the child's ability to meet future crises. And so, sharing history should correlate with a child's psychosocial stage. Present all of history, but don't rush. Present it when children can respond to the literature in a way that is socially and emotionally positive—in other words, at the time of the child's psychosocial readiness.

What are these psychosocial stages? Early childhood is a time when children develop confidence. They learn to take initiative, but at the same time, they learn what sorts of behaviors are not acceptable. It is a stage where children trust adults to set limits and look to adults to confirm—and value—their good choices and family contributions. They use imaginative play to envision what the future might hold for them. Probably not the best time to introduce a mushroom cloud. Better choices are straightforward biographies of historical figures or books that give details about what daily life was like long ago.

As parents, we can give young children the time and opportunity to create their own stories in historical contexts. Lego, Playmobil sets, and costumes are a few store-bought toys that inspire children to pretend. It is also fun to make things; buildings can be built from boxes, mountains from pillows and blankets, people from clay or clothespins or puppets. Imaginative play helps children explore points of view, apply facts and vocabulary painlessly, and develop a sense of narrative. It also helps some children brave history when they have control over the roles they play, and the intensity of the narrative and its closure. I would not dare introduce history to younger children without offering this kind of control.

I especially love sharing more candid history with middle elementary-aged children because they are at a psychosocial stage in which their challenge is to discover their own industriousness. Children at this stage are problem-solvers, interested in communities and how conflicts in their communities might be resolved, and so, the conflicts and achievements of history are often naturally interesting to them. Not only are they capable of following first-person historical narratives, they find reading a kind of abstract imaginative play. Details and perspectives that would have once disturbed or confused them now add a thrilling texture to their vicarious experience. This is the perfect age for reading time travel, because lucky children are for the first time becoming "lost" in reading. In other words, they may have already experienced that odd out-of-body sensation (that comes with complete, engaged independent reading or a great read-aloud) of not knowing where they are or what time it is or even who they are. These children are old enough to notice disparities and ask questions, and are able to communicate feelings more articulately so an adult can feel safer in knowing that when troubling information is encountered, they can successfully support the child. Additionally, children can seek out information on their own to enrich, dispute, or confirm information discovered during their reading adventures.

Early adolescence is also a fine time for a frank revelation of history. As young teens begin a conscious search for identity, history books offer a cast of role models and examples of others who have undergone a similar search. These readers "decenter," or begin to understand that they are part of the world and that their actions affect other people. (Notice that the operative word is "begin," for those of you parenting teens who still consider themselves central in the universe.) Reading

New Readers Like Olden Times

Remember that if you have a young child who is just learning to read, history can be a lively alternative to fiction. Virtually all of the emergent readers series have some history titles, such as **Step into Reading's** Moonwalk: The First Trip to the Moon by Judy Donnelly, **Puffin Easy-to-Read's** I Am Rosa Parks by Rosa Parks, and **I Can Read's** The Josefina Story Quilt by Eleanor Coerr. Visit the "easy reader" sections in the bookstore to see the topics that will titilize your time traveler; in libraries, these books tend to be dispersed throughout the entire children's collection.

The **If You Lived** series from Scholastic Books is also accessible and appealing to the youngest history buff, with plenty of fodder for imaginative play.

If You Lived at the Time of Martin Luther King

If You Lived at the Time of the Civil War

If You Lived With the Hopi

If You Sailed on The Mayflower in 1620

If You Traveled on the Underground Railroad

If You Traveled West in a Covered Wagon

If You Were There When They Signed the Constitution

If Your Name Was Changed at Ellis Island

at this psychosocial stage can help children feel less alone and become more empathetic. As cynicism creeps in and they just don't believe in Santa Claus any more, it is nice to be able to offer the lasting magic found in books.

Helpful History: How to Get the Most Today Out of Books about Yesterday

Choose Your Format

The most popular historical books for children are often straight information. Children largely enjoy "catalog" style books, which allow them to browse freely rather than read chronologically. They like garnering details about life long ago: what people wore, what they ate, 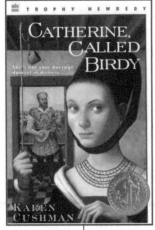 where they went to school, and the ever important question of where they went to the bathroom. Some books engage children further by offering crafts and recipes from the period. **Eyewitness, Usborne, Living History, . . . If You Lived**—there are a wealth of series that serve as guided tours to past eras. Other books offer information in clever formats: time lines, ghost stories, poems, journals, photo collections, comics, crafts, and activities (many good examples of these may be found in the Reading Time Travel lists, pp. 108 to 118). Publishers and authors have worked exceedingly hard and effectively to take the kind of information your child might ignore on a museum plaque and package it cleverly in a book that your child will enthusiastically pore over again and again.

Another type of book I find effective in sharing history with children is that of narratives in which the history is incidental to the life of the character in the story—a character with whom children can easily identify. This is a very versatile device. It can be employed through picture books, historical fiction, or even nonfiction. In the Newbery-winning novel CATHERINE, CALLED BIRDY by Karen Cushman, the main character could be any girl who loves animals, who has a sense of humor, who has a strong will. How many daughters have I just described? It just so happens that Catherine was born at the end of the twelfth century and is about to be married off by her parents, a British lord and lady. LEON'S STORY by Leon Walter Tillage is an outstanding book taken from a real speech given by a school custodian, someone just like so many working people we simply pass by and don't give much thought to. Leon's words show that this common man was in fact a witness to history. Sustained by family love, Leon survived hard years of sharecropping and abuses from the Ku Klux Klan and eventually joined the protest movement of Martin Luther King Jr. In THE WATSONS GO TO BIRMINGHAM—1963, by Christopher Paul Curtis, it is not until the last two chapters of the novel that a tragic historical event is introduced. The other thirteen chapters are spent developing characters, so that when a bomb goes off in a church, we care tremendously about the impact of the explosion on a particular family, so much more than if reported by the drone of a television. By focusing on characters, the reader realizes that in the course of simply living, each person becomes a vessel of history. This knowledge helps children value each individual person they come across, fictional or real.

Point Out Point of View

Through historical literature, we can show our children that history changes depending on who is telling it. Recognizing point of view leads to critical thinking skills that will help children in all subject areas and in all phases of life. For instance, children can read real entries from Columbus's diary in Peter and Connie Roop's **I, COLUMBUS,** then compare this perspective of Columbus's discovery/ invasion with that of a Taino boy's in ENCOUNTER by Jane Yolen. Or, your children can read any of the **Little House** series by Laura Ingalls Wilder, told from a pioneer settler girl's point of view, and compare it with THE BIRCHBARK HOUSE by Louise Erdrich, from the point of view of an Ojibwa girl whose land is being encroached upon. Was the American Revolution the same to Benedict Arnold as it was to George Washington, or the Civil War the same to slaves as soldiers? How were the 1950s different for men and women? Were the 1960s the same to older folks as they were to young ones? Discuss with your child whether point of view affects credibility. History is composed of many stories, and the more perspectives that are shared, the more complete the story becomes.

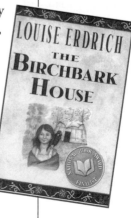

THE PACK HORSE LIBRARIANS
KENTUCKY'S RUGGED RIDERS

Kentucky in the 1930s was in rough shape. The stock market had crashed, and this already poor state was feeling the fallout. With factories closing down across the nation, the demand for coal decreased, and hundreds of mines closed, which meant unemployment and desperation for thousands of mountain families. And if that wasn't enough, in 1930 the Ohio River flooded. Besides killing over a hundred people, it washed away topsoil, making agriculture practically impossible. Shantytowns appeared and, lacking any sanitation, became breeding grounds for disease and death.

Along came Franklin Roosevelt and his New Deal and Work Projects Administration (WPA), creating jobs to get America back on its feet and off the dole. Special efforts were made to place women in positions that would not be unseemly for the "fairer sex," and the Pack Horse Library Project was born.

Pack horse librarians regularly traveled extremely rugged and isolated mountain terrain that could only be traversed by horse. Along an eighteen-mile route, they would exchange and deliver donated print material (books, magazines, pamphlets, church bulletins) to one-room schoolhouses, post offices, and private homes. In all weather, pack horse librarians covered between fifty and eighty miles a week, through treacherous routes and along creeks with names such as "Troublesome," "Hell-for-Sartin," and "Cut Shin." The carriers were in effect delivering free public library service to rural areas for the first time. The librarians' familiarity with the people along the routes and what materials they would enjoy was crucial to the success of the program, because many ▶

Talk the Talk and Walk the Walk: Taking History (and Literacy) Personally

If one of the purposes of learning history is trying not to repeat the worst of it, we have to also give children the tools to change the course of their own time in history when they see negative patterns emerging. The first of those tools is the ability to question and discuss. Use a book as a springboard to a conversation about how times have changed or stayed the same; discuss cause and effect (another critical-thinking skill applicable to all areas of learning and life). Imagine out loud, together. Encourage your children's questions, and address them as best you can. Don't be afraid to say, "I don't know," and then model seeking an answer by going on-line or to an encyclopedia, for example. Don't be afraid to be sad or angry or sorry, and then model doing something that helps, so we have less to be sad or angry or sorry about in the future.

Children can also be encouraged to take action. It is initiative, not age, that seems to yield results, as documented regularly in the "Kids Did It!" feature of *National Geographic Kids* magazine (formerly known as *World*). Subscribe to this Parents' Choice Gold Medal winner by calling 1-800-647-5463. The most valuable book I have found to help give intermediate and older children direction is THE KID'S GUIDE TO SOCIAL ACTION by Barbara A. Lewis. Children can act on their responses to history by making things happen through letter writing, speech writing, play writing, debate, interviews, further research, museum visits—all of which broaden their base of information and give history a sense of immediacy.

Keep in mind that this progression from possessing information to taking action, even when it means that your child is defying the status quo, represents the link between literacy and an informed citizenry. Reading and writing is the pragmatic basis of that often vague concept of "citizenship" that schools in a democratic society exist to serve. When schools fail to empower children in this way, it is a subversion of the principles upon which America—and public education—was founded. So step in and do your duty. Page turning is every bit as American as flag waving, or, at least, it ought to be.

History and Heritage

Sometimes children's literature is used to inform children of their own history. How wonderful! My only recommendation is that as parents we help children balance historical readings pertaining to their own culture with literature that addresses the cultures of others. While you may consider it important that your child have a cultural, racial, or ethnic identity, the fact is he is part of the human race *first*. As human beings, our children are dealing with the psychosocial challenges of carving out an identity, finding security, being productive and esteemed. It can backfire to inundate your child with the message that because of race, creed, or ethnicity certain people have hated the likes of them or found it useful to treat them badly. The fact of the matter is, there is hardly a race, creed, or ethnicity that cannot make that claim, and that is reflected in the body of historical children's literature as a whole. So why not use the whole?

Each book that describes a child's own group as persecuted can be a rock, weighing heavily on a child and making him feel isolated or guilty. But when used in conjunction with books about the burdens of others, a mountain of universal understanding and empathy can be built. This understanding seems organic to children, who more often than not respond to hate or oppression against any group first with sur-

▶ rural residents were wary of worldly "book learning," and librarians had to be careful to choose appropriately conservative materials. In fact, the librarians won the people over so completely that some patrons along the routes shared highly prized family recipes and quilt patterns in reciprocation for borrowing books. The librarians took to compiling these in scrapbooks that were circulated as well. Since the government paid only the salaries, collections consisted mainly of used books, which started out ragged and then went on to more battering through hard travel and frequent handling. The librarians had the difficult task of maintaining these worn materials and transforming them into viable collections.

Kentucky's pack horse library program is often cited as a paragon of the WPA. From 1935 to its dismantling in 1943, over 100,000 people were served. The librarians not only deserve to be remembered for a resiliency and resourcefulness that inspires all Americans to yank up those bootstraps and get to steppin' (or ridin'), but moreover, they were beacons of light to so many in that isolated part of our country. Their efforts, matched historically only by the U.S. Post Office, gave significance to the words, *wherever you are, whoever you are, you deserve to read*—and may, in fact, have influenced the establishment of the Library Services Act, in which libraries are supported through government today.

Your whole family can join a pack horse librarian en route by reading DOWN CUT SHIN CREEK: THE PACK HORSE LIBRARIANS OF KENTUCKY by Kathi Appelt and Jeanne Cannella Schmitzer. This remarkable tribute includes priceless photos and breathtaking descriptions that will carry you into the mountains of Kentucky.

ONCE UPON A TIME LINE

Good authors of historical fiction meticulously research a time period. They use their findings to tell a story incorporating enough detail to transport their readers back in time, creating characters the readers care about while informing them of accurate historical information. Take time out of your time line to share books with your children that took decades—even centuries—to write. There are thousands of volumes of historical fiction available. Here are a few stunning ones to start with:

Anderson, Laurie Halse	FEVER, 1793
Auch, Mary Jane	ASHES OF ROSES
Barrett, Tracy	ANNA OF BYZANTIUM
Blackwood, Gary	THE SHAKESPEARE STEALER
Bulla, Clyde Robert	A LION TO GUARD US
Cannon, A. E.	CHARLOTTE'S ROSE
Clements, Bruce	I TELL A LIE EVERY SO OFTEN
Curtis, Christopher Paul	BUD, NOT BUDDY
Cushman, Karen	RODZINA
Cuyler, Margery	THE BATTLEFIELD GHOST
Giff, Patricia Reilly	LILY'S CROSSING
	NORY RYAN'S SONG
Gilson, Jamie	STINK ALLEY
Hobbs, Valerie	SONNY'S WAR
Holt, Kimberly Willis	WHEN ZACHARY BEAVER CAME TO TOWN (Mature readers.)
Karr, Kathleen	GILBERT AND SULLIVAN SET ME FREE
	THE GREAT TURKEY WALK
Kinsey-Warnock, Natalie	LUMBER CAMP LIBRARY
Levine, Gail Carson	DAVE AT NIGHT
Lisle, Janet Taylor	THE ART OF KEEPING COOL
Lowry, Lois	NUMBER THE STARS
Meyer, Carolyn	MARY, BLOODY MARY (Mature readers.)
Myers, Anna	TULSA BURNING
Park, Linda Sue	A SINGLE SHARD
Pearsall, Shelley	TROUBLE DON'T LAST
Peck, Richard	FAIR WEATHER
Rinaldi, Ann	THE COFFIN QUILT (Read all of Rinaldi's books!)
Robinet, Harriette Gillem	CHILDREN OF THE FIRE
Scurzynski, Gloria	ROCKBUSTER (Mature readers.)
Speare, Elizabeth George	THE WITCH OF BLACKBIRD POND
Whelan, Gloria	ANGEL ON THE SQUARE
Wolff, Virginia Euwer	BAT 6

prise and then with indignation. These reactions can and should be fostered through literature—not discouraged. A multicultural view of literature-based education still seeks to support individual racial or ethnic pride. To really set one group apart in the world of literature, the focus must be on achievement, not suffering.

History's Horrors

As we look at historical books for children, we need to first separate feelings of what is appropriate for children with what is embarrassing to us. And history really can be shameful. The literature tells on us, the same dreadful stories again and again: how innocents pay dearly for the ambitions of others, and how adults continuously fail to create a peaceful world for the children they claim to love. But these stories from history can also tell great tales of bravery and protection, victory and discovery, survival and redemption, and above all, remembrance, which is a primary function of writing and storytelling itself, and which no child should be denied.

Some history is made more palpable by distance. Books about the terrors of the American Revolution, for instance, seem more benign because we are comfortable at this point in history assuring our children that the Redcoats *aren't* coming and that the last big British invasion involved men with music, not muskets. About two hundred years gives a "rocket's red glare" the romantic glow of a distant star. Contrast that with more recent history as depicted in THE WHISPERING CLOTH: A REFUGEE'S STORY by Pegi Deitz Shea, a picture book in which a small Hmong girl remembers lying in bed between her parents, who have been killed by soldiers, and later uses this experience to create art. This story is written with language that is accessible to a child in grade school, a child likely to ask the reasonable questions of When? Why? Could it happen *here*? And further, Is it happening to someone *else*? These are questions of a responsible, informed citizen of the world, and questions that, when answered frankly, leave very little room for the blunt reassurances that thwart big bad wolves and bogeymen. Again, as adults, we are made uncomfortable and helpless, unsure how to package a passionate world and sell it as sane. In this way, talking to a young person about history can be more daunting than talking to a young person about sex. I know I would much rather explain to a child how a condom is used than how napalm was used any day of the week. Maybe this is why so many kids know a lot about sex and only a little about history. Thank goodness for authors who are willing to speak loudly and clearly about what makes others hem and haw.

To share historical literature responsibly, it is imperative to look carefully at the content and not just the subject matter. What most often concerns me in the body of historical books is the picture books. Most books about history are geared toward older readers who hopefully have had prior experience with literature. By the intermediate grades children are

I am Mary.

I am a witch. Or so some would call me. "Spawn of the Devil," "Witch child," they hiss in the street, although I know neither father nor mother. I know only my grandmother. . . . We live in a small cottage on the very edge of the forest; Grandmother, me and her cat and my rabbit.

Lived. Live there no more. . . .

They decided to "float" her. They had plenty of evidence against her, you see. Plenty. All week folk had been coming to them with accusations. How she had overlooked them, bringing sickness to their livestock and families; how she had used magic, sticking pins in a wax figure to bring on affliction; how she transformed herself and roamed the country for miles around as a great hare and how she did this through the use of an ointment made from melted corpse fat. They questioned me, demanding, "Is this so?"

She slept in the bed next to me every night, but how do I know where she went when sleep took her?

—WITCH CHILD by Celia Rees

beginning to determine point of view, place events in the context of a time period, and have some experience in solving problems. These kinds of skills are necessary to safely indulge in historical literature. **MY HIROSHIMA** by Junko Morimoto is a book that requires such skill, though it is hard to tell at first glance. The book's format is clearly aimed at primary-school-aged children: thirty-two pages with illustrations on every page, simple vocabulary, few words. It begins with the image of a mushroom cloud on the cover, looming over two school children. A child with no prior knowledge of atomic bombs will have no understanding of the implications of such a juxtaposition. The mushroom cloud has been rendered a meaningless curiosity, and the child is immediately desensitized to its import. Then comes the story, with perfunctory descriptions of friends, family, school, and a passing mention that a war is being fought. Then, in graphic detail, the author tells of an explosion in which the world seems to disappear. There is an illustration of a screaming child trying to rouse her dead mother. Then follows another image of the mushroom cloud with no words on the page. Then, several pages of illustrated horror. A child may read this book and come away with the idea that you can be walking along, minding your own business, and then a bomb drops and hell opens up. Which is true. It could happen. It does happen. However, of all the functions of a children's author, informing very young children of their lack of control in the world seems among the least noble—and least necessary.

It is a delicate thing to criticize such books. Many of them bear witness and share extremely personal and devastating stories, no easy feat for any author. It is not my desire to call a victim into question. Everyone has a right to say, "This happened to me." The problem comes when a children's book author is so caught up in relating the experience from a child's point of view that the author actually succeeds in sharing the experience from a child's point of view, which is often an especially horrific perspective without any sense of context or control. Children's book authors have a special responsibility to insert that control and context. Use that most important question, "What is the author trying to say?" to determine whether a book is meeting the needs of a child. If it is merely meeting the needs of the grown-up, it isn't suitable history for young audiences.

GIVE PEACE A CHANCE

Teaching Tolerance
www.tolerance.org/teach/index.jsp

Eugene Peace Academy
www.eugenepeaceacademy.org

Celebrating Peace
www.celebratingpeace.com

Seeds of Peace
www.seedsofpeace.org

Hiroshima Peace Memorial Museum
www.pcf.city.hiroshima.jp/index_e2.html

LET THE CELEBRATIONS BEGIN! by Margaret Wild and Julie Vivas is another example of a picture book that is about children, written from the point of view of a child, and placed on the shelves of young children's literature at the bookstore; but it is not, in my opinion, for young children. It relates the true story of women who, while being held in the concentration camp Bergen-Belsen, made toys for the children there in anticipation of liberation. Though based on a very moving and humane episode, I can't help but wonder how a young child would perceive the illustrations of women and children in rags, heads shaved, and the allusions to no toys, no food, no mothers. What is a camp? Why are they there? It is unclear. To its intended audience, it is science fiction, surreal and bleak, probably true to the experience and to the childhood perspective. But it is not an experience young readers are prepared to handle vicariously anymore than young people in history were prepared to handle it in life.

I suggest that the best way to honor an author's witness testimony is to help present that literature at a time in a child's life when it will be most meaningful. Share MY HIROSHIMA alongside the upper-grade or high-school introduction of John Hersey's HIROSHIMA. Likewise, LET THE CELEBRATIONS BEGIN! is a hopeful postscript to Elie Wiesel's NIGHT or Anne Frank's THE DIARY OF A YOUNG GIRL, again, usually assigned in the upper grades or high school. Bottom line: Use content first, format second, in the context of psychosocial readiness, to judge whether or not to share a book. If the author or publisher in his or her eagerness has misjudged the mark of age appropriateness, don't necessarily discard the book . . . just add that bit of time travel once a child has traveled in time a bit.

I bring up works that make me uncomfortable so that if you are of the same mind, you will not balk when you encounter them. But they are exceptions. The bulk of children's historical literature is excellent and appropriately reflects children's resilience in the darkest circumstances. For instance, the classic SADAKO AND THE THOUSAND PAPER CRANES by Eleanor Coerr is about a girl who is slowly dying of cancer as a result of radiation poisoning at Hiroshima. She hopes to fold a thousand origami cranes so that she might have her magic wish granted: to be well again. Sadako folded 644 cranes. Her classmates folded the rest. The book is based on a true story, and a heartbreaking one for its intended third-to-fifth-grade audience, but it is positive and enduring and adds more to than it subtracts from a child's spirit. When it comes to great historical literature for children, it's not the dying that makes a story worth reading. It's the living.

Reading Time Travel: History and Social Studies

January 6

The time machine! Really, an old refrigerator box covered with aluminum foil, with a flashing police-car light rigged at the top and various knobs and keyboards screwed and glue-gunned on. Inside, a comfortable pillow for sitting and a flashlight attached to a curly phone cord. Maya helped me install a bookshelf inside the box with a power drill. . . .

The idea: time travel through books.

I left the machine in the classroom, buckled and locked closed with lots of signs all over it: "Top secret!" "Under construction!" "No peeking, this means YOU!" "Danger! Highly radioactive!" and the like, to build anticipation. The big question buzzing: Is it real? Does it really work?

A tricky question. I recollect clambering over laundry bags in the back of my parents' closet, eyes clamped closed, one hand groping, praying that I might enter C. S. Lewis's Narnia. Or, moving forward delicately, eyes closed once again, toward the mirror in our dining room, in the hopes that I might go through like Alice managed in THROUGH THE LOOKING GLASS. *Alas, my head bumped the back of the closet, my fingers could not penetrate the glass. This did not negate that such adventures were possible, only that I was not among the lucky ones to be so enchanted.*

"Yes, it really works," I offered, acting slightly perturbed that they would ever doubt me.

In the weeks before winter break, children from other classrooms have popped in to deliver messages or borrow things, and they stared bug-eyed. "Is it real? Does it really work?"

"Yes, of course," the children sniffed, now annoyed at the skepticism.

Then, the next biggest question: Who would be the first daring hero to risk his or her life in the contraption? In the interest of fairness, this seemed best left to chance, even at the risk some terrible realist like B. B. was chosen, who I imagined would announce, "It's nothing but a box full of books! It's a fake!"

It turned out that JoEllen was chosen. We sent her off with much fanfare, with me pressing buttons and turning knobs fever-ishly, double-checking for accuracy that the medieval period was properly set, making her promise that her mother would not sue me should something . . . unexpected . . . occur.

"Like what?" asked JoEllen.

"Being eaten," I ventured.

"Oooooh!" The class crooned enviously.

"Yes, I hear that dragons possibly existed," I began, "though people may have believed that due to the inexplicable presence of dinosaur remnants found during the period. Still, if you'd rather give up your spot . . ."

"I'll risk it," JoEllen said quickly.

"You're on school time," I reminded her. "In the event that you return in one piece, I expect a full report on what you saw."

In she went. The doors closed. On went the police-car light. "Back to work!" Silent reading time.

In a half hour, I retrieved her. She came out, breathless. "What did you see?" Everybody wanted to know. JoEllen paused. For thought? For effect? I'll never know.

"A joust."

"A what?"

"Two guys. Fighting on horses. Their armor clanging as they rode. Even the horses wore armor, on their heads. The guys car-ried two big sticks. Everyone was watching and cheering, like a sport. One of the guys died, ran through with a stick . . ."

The class was impressed. "Write it in your journal, before you forget," I suggested. "Who's next?"

For the rest of the day, the kids took turns in the time machine. So far, nobody has said, "It's just a box full of books!"

After school, I turned off the lights to leave and saw the machine with its red light still carouseling around. "Their armor clanging as they rode," I remembered. The words, the detail, they seemed peculiar to what JoEllen regularly produces. I couldn't help squinting suspiciously at the silver box before turning it off.

—Educating Esmé: Diary of a Teacher's First Year
by Esmé Raji Codell

This entry from the diary I kept during my first year as a public schoolteacher is a testament to the transports of reading. I worked with fifth-graders and intermediate readers, who are especially receptive to reading time travel because of their developmental stage (see History Hypothesis: Gauging Your Child's Developmental Stage, p. 94).

Building a Time Machine

You can make your own time machine—for your child's classroom or for home—using a box that once held a refrigerator or wide-screen TV: any very large box. Really a glorified closet, what makes it a time machine is the decision to use it for traveling through time. Where to go? World War II? Jurassic Period? Queen Victoria's England? Joan of Arc's France? The Ming Dynasty? The Groovy Sixties? The Great Depression? The Gold Rush? Does your child want to march for Civil Rights? Ride on a ship full of Vikings, or pirates, or with Christopher Columbus? Would she like to survive reading about the Great Chicago fire, the sinking of the *Titanic*, the San Francisco earthquake? Would she prefer the music and art of the Italian Renaissance, or the Harlem Renaissance? Or, rather than visiting a single period in time, what about exploring a theme through big blocks of history: Sports through the Ages, Medicine in the Nineteenth Century, Immigration, Women's Rights? Nothing is impossible when you combine books with the magic box! Create it for your child's classroom or your local library, or just keep it at home for your own child as a secret, special place to read. One caveat: Building a time machine is not an easy project. But come on, it's time travel; it's not supposed to be easy. And, all said and done, it's cheaper than Disney World.

On the Outside

Decorate the outside with aluminum foil, knobs, old keyboards, old telephone and computer guts, Christmas lights, doorknobs, drawer pulls, calculators, mirrors, steering wheels, gears, washers, broken watches . . . anything shiny and/or mechanical. In my classroom, we had a police-car light on the top of the box with a wire running into the box where it could be turned on, so when the light was flashing, the Time Machine was occupied. We cut out large posterboard shapes to represent the phases of the moon, covered them with aluminum foil, and staked them on each corner of the top of the machine. It looked cool, if I do say so myself. Almost any item can be attached with the help of a power drill, glue gun, and silver duct or packing tape. In my classroom, the door was made of cardboard; if yours is, too, send the child in with an egg timer because the time machine can be pretty hot when you close the door; it takes about twenty minutes before the child is well done! You can also cut some slits a few inches wide and long near the top of the box for ventilation, or place a hand-held fan inside. Students at the College of Education at the University of South Florida greatly improved my design by simply attaching silver material that could be pulled back and forth like a shower curtain, which made for improved ventilation. Breathing is good.

On the Inside

I suggest doing this part yourself, in secret, to maintain some of the mystery of the machine. Measure the length of the inside of the box, and find a piece of light-weight wood or very heavy-duty corrugated cardboard of the same length—if necessary tape together several pieces of cardboard—to create a shelf strong enough to hold books. If you're like me, you won't measure at all, you'll just squint and "eye" it. Wedge the shelf in; drill from the outside. I drilled a couple of very long bolts right underneath the shelf for extra support; or, you could do the smarter thing and use shelf holders or window-box holders to support the shelf. Another more sensible option is rain gutters, which are very light, reinforced-plastic pieces sold at hardware stores for about three dollars per ten-foot strip. These can be held in place by brackets that are screwed into the walls of the time machine, and are used so as to allow books to face out. (In fact, you can use rain gutters for this purpose anywhere, not just in the Time Machine; check out www.trelease-on-reading.com/whats_nu_raingutters.html#pagetop for photographs of how rain gutters have been used to promote reading.) Put pillows on the floor and attach a high-beam flashlight from the ceiling.

Once you have decided on your destination, wallpaper the interior accordingly, with old newspaper clippings, book illustrations, photographs, magazine articles, and pre-made, die-cut, history bulletin-board decorators found at teacher supply stores. The public library is an outstanding resource for finding and xeroxing the visual "wallpaper," as well as the books you will need. The decorations should be removable. You can attach decorations to the inside of the machine with looped tape or, better yet, use StikkiClips with wax adhesive (a great removable and reusable product sold at office- and teacher-supply stores) or good old Velcro—both of which make the materials on display very easy to take

"Name?" He asked Tante, who was, of course, first in line.

"Feindele Schmukler," she answered.

"Um, Schmukler means jeweler, right? You'll be Mrs. Jewel here," he declared.

Tante took a very deep breath, puffed up, and turned purple, proclaiming, "Mistuh, my brother-in-law is already American. Name? Schmukler. One family, one name. We are not now and never will be Jewels!"

"A Jewel you ain't," he retorted, glaring at tubby Tante, then winked. "So welcome, Fanny Schmukler."

—My Name Is Not Gussie by Mikki Machlin

The townsfolk looked hard at us. All they had left for us was mean looks and a heap of hate. We jarred to a stop in front of gates that marked the entrance to a stockade.

"It says Andersonville," Pink whispered.

My heart stopped. I had heard of this place. It was one of the worst of the Confederate camps.

When we were pulled from the buckboard, we fell hard to the ground.

"No, no," I begged as they pulled us both along.

Because of his fever, Pink stumbled and fell. They dragged him along with such meanness. He did not protest until they forced us in different directions.

Then he reached for me and said, "Let me touch the hand that touched Mr. Lincoln, Say, just one last time."

—PINK AND SAY by Patricia Polacco

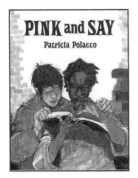

off and change as needed. If the machine is going to be visited by many children, I recommend laminating the decorations with clear Con-Tact paper before hanging them. Then, fill the shelf with books from the desired time period. There is a wealth of nonfiction available for almost any time period you can come up with. Get books on many levels, regardless of the level at which you think your child (or group of children) is reading; get books that feature photographs, reenactments, illustrations, straight text, easy readers, diary entries, fiction and nonfiction. That way, whatever your child's mood or ability, she will come away with some information. The *choice* is what really gives the Time Machine that extra magic, along with the privacy; there is no one in the box to judge selection, so your child can genuinely act on his motivation.

To get you started, here are some lists of books of all sorts and at all different levels for several popular historical topics. Enjoy the trips!

Civil War

Archer, Jules	• A HOUSE DIVIDED: THE LIVES OF ULYSSES S. GRANT AND ROBERT E. LEE
Alcott, Louisa May	• HOSPITAL SKETCHES
Beatty, Patricia	• CHARLEY SKEDADDLE • TURN HOMEWARD, HANALEE • WHO COMES WITH CANNONS?
Bolotin, Norman	• CIVIL WAR A TO Z
Chang, Ina	• A SEPARATE BATTLE: WOMEN AND THE CIVIL WAR
Clinton, Catherine	• SCHOLASTIC ENCYCLOPEDIA OF THE CIVIL WAR
Cohen, Daniel	• CIVIL WAR GHOSTS
Denenberg, Barry	• WHEN WILL THIS CRUEL WAR BE OVER? THE CIVIL WAR DIARY OF EMMA SIMPSON, GORDONSVILLE, VIRGINIA, 1864
Egger-Bovet, Howard, and Marlene Smith-Baranzini	• BOOK OF THE AMERICAN CIVIL WAR (Brown Paper School US Kids History)
Fleischman, Paul	• BULL RUN
Freedman, Russell	• LINCOLN: A PHOTOBIOGRAPHY
Fritz, Jean	• JUST A FEW WORDS, MR. LINCOLN: THE STORY OF THE GETTYSBURG ADDRESS
Haskins, Jim	• THE DAY FORT SUMTER WAS FIRED ON • BLACK, BLUE AND GRAY: AFRICAN AMERICANS IN THE CIVIL WAR

Herbert, Janis	• THE CIVIL WAR FOR KIDS: A HISTORY WITH 21 ACTIVITIES
Kiger, Fred W.	• CIVIL WAR (Fandex Family Field Guides)
Lyons, Mary E., and Muriel Branch	• DEAR ELLEN BEE: A CIVIL WAR SCRAPBOOK OF TWO UNION SPIES
Moore, Kay	• IF YOU LIVED AT THE TIME OF THE CIVIL WAR
Murphy, Jim	• THE BOYS' WAR
Polacco, Patricia	• PINK AND SAY
Ransom, Candice F.	• THE PROMISE QUILT
Ray, Delia	• BEHIND THE BLUE AND GRAY: THE SOLDIER'S LIFE IN THE CIVIL WAR
Reeder, Carolyn	• SHADES OF GRAY
Reit, Seymour	• BEHIND REBEL LINES: THE INCREDIBLE STORY OF EMMA EDMONDS, CIVIL WAR SPY
Sandler, Martin W.	• CIVIL WAR (Library of Congress Books)
Shura, Mary Francis	• GENTLE ANNIE: THE TRUE STORY OF A CIVIL WAR NURSE
Stanchak, John	• CIVIL WAR (Eyewitness Books)
Turner, Ann	• ABE LINCOLN REMEMBERS
Wisler, G. Clifton	• WHEN JOHNNY WENT MARCHING HOME: YOUNG AMERICANS FIGHT THE CIVIL WAR

Another Perspective: Slavery

The African American perspective on slavery and reconstruction has its own body of children's literature. The unique insight can (and should) be incorporated into the context of a Civil War Time Machine, but there is also enough outstanding material to warrant a session of its own.

Berry, James	• AJEEMA AND HIS SON
Bial, Raymond	• THE STRENGTH OF THESE ARMS: LIFE IN THE SLAVE QUARTERS • THE UNDERGROUND RAILROAD
Feelings, Tom	• THE MIDDLE PASSAGE: WHITE SHIPS/ BLACK CARGO
Fox, Paula	• THE SLAVE DANCER

❧ *Potato Pick:*

ONLY PASSING THROUGH:
THE STORY OF
SOJOURNER TRUTH

by Anne Rockwell, illustrated
by R. Gregory Christie

In a strong, straightforward
voice, the author chronicles the
life and hardships of Sojourner
Truth—former slave, great ora-
tor, abolitionist, and role model.
Once grown and freed, she
returned to the plantation to
find that her five-year-old son
had been sold. She bravely took
the master to court ... and won!
The illustrations are profound
and compelling with
Sojourner's strength conveyed
by huge, powerful hands and a
proud expression. Although this
book deals with very powerful
subject matter, thanks to the
sensitivity and dedication of the
book's creators, it is presented
in an accessible way, even for
children in the primary grades.
It's impressive enough to be
worthy of the woman to whom
it is a tribute. (6 and up; great
for 12-year-olds, too!)

Fradin, Dennis Brindell	• BOUND FOR THE NORTH STAR: TRUE STORIES OF FUGITIVE SLAVES
Grifalconi, Ann	• THE VILLAGE THAT VANISHED
Hamilton, Virginia	• THE PEOPLE COULD FLY
Hansen, Joyce	• I THOUGHT MY SOUL WOULD RISE AND FLY: THE DIARY OF PATSY, A FREED GIRL, MARS BLUFF, SOUTH CAROLINA, 1865
Hopkinson, Deborah	• SWEET CLARA AND THE FREEDOM QUILT
Howard, Elizabeth Fitzgerald	• VIRGIE GOES TO SCHOOL WITH US BOYS
Hurmence, Belinda, ed.	• MY FOLKS DON'T WANT ME TO TALK ABOUT SLAVERY
Lyons, Mary E.	• LETTERS FROM A SLAVE GIRL: THE STORY OF HARRIET JACOBS
McGill, Alice	• IN THE HOLLOW OF YOUR HAND: SLAVE LULLABIES
McKissack, Patricia C. and Frederick L.	• DAYS OF JUBILEE: THE END OF SLAVERY IN THE UNITED STATES • REBELS AGAINST SLAVERY: SLAVE REVOLTS
Miller, William	• FREDERICK DOUGLASS: THE LAST DAY OF SLAVERY
Nolen, Jerdine	• BIG JABE
Pearsall, Shelley	• TROUBLE DON'T LAST
Porter, Connie	• MEET ADDY: AN AMERICAN GIRL
Rappaport, Doreen	• FREEDOM RIVER NO MORE! STORIES AND SONGS OF SLAVE RESISTANCE
Robinett, Harriette Gillem	• FORTY ACRES AND MAYBE A MULE
Rockwell, Anne	• ONLY PASSING THROUGH: THE STORY OF SOJOURNER TRUTH
Rosen, Michael J.	• A SCHOOL FOR POMPEY WALKER
Schroeder, Alan	• MINTY: A STORY OF YOUNG HARRIET TUBMAN
Wesley, Valerie	• FREEDOM'S GIFTS: A JUNETEENTH STORY
Williams, Sherley Anne	• WORKING COTTON
Winter, Jeanette	• FOLLOW THE DRINKING GOURD

World War II: The Holocaust

Abells, Chana Byers	• THE CHILDREN WE REMEMBER
Anne Frank House, The	• ANNE FRANK IN THE WORLD
Auerbacher, Inge	• I AM A STAR: CHILD OF THE HOLOCAUST
Ayer, Eleanor	• PARALLEL JOURNEYS
Bachrach, Susan D.	• TELL THEM WE REMEMBER
Bishop, Claire Huchet	• TWENTY AND TEN
Chaikin, Miriam	• A NIGHTMARE IN HISTORY
Deedy, Carmen Agra	• THE YELLOW STAR: THE LEGEND OF KING CHRISTIAN X OF DENMARK
Frank, Anne	• THE DIARY OF A YOUNG GIRL
Gold, Alison Leslie	• A SPECIAL FATE: CHIUNE SUGIHARA, HERO OF THE HOLOCAUST
Greenfeld, Howard	• AFTER THE HOLOCAUST
Hautzig, Esther	• THE ENDLESS STEPPE: GROWING UP IN SIBERIA
Innocenti, Roberto	• ROSE BLANCHE
Kerr, Judith	• WHEN HITLER STOLE PINK RABBIT
Lakin, Patricia	• DON'T FORGET
Levoy, Myron	• ALAN AND NAOMI
Lobel, Anita	• NO PRETTY PICTURES
Lowry, Lois	• NUMBER THE STARS
Meltzer, Milton	• RESCUE • NEVER TO FORGET
Napoli, Donna Jo	• STONES IN WATER
Orgel, Doris	• THE DEVIL IN VIENNA
Polacco, Patricia	• THE BUTTERFLY
Reiss, Johanna	• THE UPSTAIRS ROOM
Richter, Hans Peter	• FRIEDRICH
Shemin, Margaretha	• THE LITTLE RIDERS
Siegal, Aranka	• UPON THE HEAD OF THE GOAT
Toll, Nelly S.	• BEHIND THE SECRET WINDOW: A MEMOIR OF A HIDDEN CHILDHOOD
van der Rol, Ruud, and Rian Verhoeven	• ANNE FRANK: BEYOND THE DIARY
Volavková, Hana, ed.	• I NEVER SAW ANOTHER BUTTERFLY
Warren, Andrea	• SURVIVING HITLER

Dear Madame Esmé,

Why do little boys seem to like dinosaur books so much?

Dear Gentle Reader,

I have a theory that as little boys grow and sense the onus soci-ety puts on them to become brave and strong, tearless and fearless, it feels good to imagine monsters that have long gone the way of the tar pit. Lucky for us, wonderful dinosaur books are never extinct, and both *boys and girls enjoy them.* Patrick O'Brien begins his true tale of a dinosaur as awesome and fearsome as Tyrannosaurus rex—only larger, the terror of the Cenozoic sea: "It was ten million years ago. Mysterious beasts swam the oceans. Strange creatures walked the earth." Here is MEGATOOTH, the story of Jaw's bigger brother. Accessible text combined with exciting and thoughtful illus-tration create an absolutely thrilling book for brave children five and up. Wait until your child sees the actual size of a Megaladon's tooth! Encourage him to show it to his dentist!

THE DINOSAURS OF WATERHOUSE HAWKINS by Barbara Kerley, illustrated by Brian Selznick, is a good choice for children seven and over. This book is a tour de force—the biggest thing to hit children's lit since the Brontosaurus. In 1853 nobody knew what a dinosaur looked like but thanks to Benjamin Waterhouse Hawkins that was about to change. Using his imaginative genius, he pieced together the puzzling fossils to create the first life-sized models of dinosaurs. To unveil his masterpieces, Waterhouse sent out invitations in-scribed on a pterodactyl wing for a dinner party on New Year's Eve. A feast was served inside a gigantic model iguanodon. You'd think everyone would want to be friends with a guy who could throw a party like this, but alas, when the great artist crossed both the Atlantic and the corrupt New York politician Boss Tweed, some of Waterhouse's Paleozoic pals come to harm. The truth is stranger than fiction in this fabulous picture-book biography, paying homage to the life of a man who brought imagination to life and integrated art and science. If you can't physically visit Waterhouse's creations at the Crystal Palace in Sydenham, England, Selznick's magical and meticulously researched illustrations will take your child there.

Jurassic Period

Aliki	• Fossils Tell of Long Ago
	• My Visit to the Dinosaurs
Arnold, Caroline	• Dinosaurs with Feathers: The Ancestors of Modern Birds
Barner, Bob	• Dinosaur Bones
Benton, Michael	• The Encyclopedia of Awesome Dinosaurs
Birney, Betty G.	• Tyrannosaurus Tex
Brooke, William J.	• A Is for Aarrgh!
Burton, Virginia Lee	• Life Story
Camper, Cathy	• Bugs Before Time: Prehistoric Insects and Their Relatives
Carrick, Carol	• Patrick's Dinosaurs
Cole, Joanna	• The Magic School Bus in the Time of the Dinosaurs
Conrad, Pam	• My Daniel
Dodson, Peter	• An Alphabet of Dinosaurs
Donnelly, Lisa	• Dinosaur Garden
Gillette, J. Lynett	• Dinosaur Ghosts: The Mystery of Coelophysis
Grambling, Lois G.	• Can I Have a Stegosaurus, Mom? Can I? Please!?
Henderson, Douglas	• Asteroid Impact
Hoff, Syd	• Danny and the Dinosaur
Joyce, William	• Dinosaur Bob and His Adventures with the Family Lazardo
Kerley, Barbara	• The Dinosaurs of Waterhouse Hawkins
Lambert, David, et al.	• Dinosaur Encyclopedia (Dorling Kindersley)
Lauber, Patricia	• Living with Dinosaurs
Lessem, Don	• Raptors! The Nastiest Dinosaurs
	• Supergiants! The Biggest Dinosaurs
Markle, Sandra	• Outside and Inside Dinosaurs
Most, Bernard	• Dinosaur Cousins?
Nolan, Dennis	• Dinosaur Dream
Norman, David, and Angele Milner	• Dinosaur (Eyewitness Books)
O'Brien, Patrick	• Mammoth

Rohmann, Eric	• TIME FLIES
Wahl, Jan	• THE FIELD MOUSE AND THE DINOSAUR NAMED SUE
Yolen, Jane	• HOW DO DINOSAURS SAY GOODNIGHT?
Zimmerman, Howard	• BEYOND THE DINOSAURS • DINOSAURS! THE BIGGEST, BADDEST, STRANGEST, FASTEST
Zoehfeld, Kathleen Weidner	• DINOSAUR PARENTS, DINOSAUR YOUNG

Medieval England

Aliki	• A MEDIEVAL FEAST
Anno, Mitsumasa	• ANNO'S MEDIEVAL WORLD
Cushman, Karen	• CATHERINE, CALLED BIRDY THE MIDWIFE'S APPRENTICE
Crossley-Holland, Kevin	• THE WORLD OF KING ARTHUR AND HIS COURT: PEOPLE, PLACES, LEGEND, AND LORE • THE SEEING STONE (Arthur Trilogy, Book One)
Deary, Terry	• THE MEASLY MIDDLE AGES
Gibbons, Gail	• KNIGHTS IN SHINING ARMOR
Gravett, Christopher	• KNIGHT (Eyewitness Books) • CASTLE (Eyewitness Books)
Hastings, Selina	• SIR GAWAIN AND THE LOATHLY LADY
Hazen, Barbara Shook	• THE KNIGHT WHO WAS AFRAID OF THE DARK
Hodges, Margaret	• THE KITCHEN KNIGHT: A TALE OF KING ARTHUR • SAINT GEORGE AND THE DRAGON
Hunt, Jonathan	• BESTIARY: AN ILLUMINATED ALPHABET OF MEDIEVAL BEASTS • ILLUMINATIONS
Konigsburg, E. L.	• A PROUD TASTE FOR SCARLET AND MINIVER
Langley, Andrew, et al.	• MEDIEVAL LIFE
Mitgutsch, Ali	• A KNIGHT'S BOOK
Olofsson, Helena	• THE LITTLE JESTER
Sabuda, Robert	• ARTHUR AND THE SWORD
San Souci, Robert D.	• YOUNG ARTHUR • YOUNG GUINEVERE • YOUNG LANCELOT • YOUNG MERLIN
Talbott, Hudson	• LANCELOT

Tomlinson, Theresa	• THE FOREST WIFE
Winthrop, Elizabeth	• THE CASTLE IN THE ATTIC
Wrede, Patricia C.	• DEALING WITH DRAGONS

Ancient Egypt

Adronik, Catherine M.	• HATSHEPSUT: HIS MAJESTY, HERSELF
Aliki	• MUMMIES MADE IN EGYPT
Bower, Tamara	• THE SHIPWRECKED SAILOR: AN EGYPTIAN TALE OF HIEROGLYPHS
Clements, Andrew	• TEMPLE CAT
Climo, Shirley	• THE EGYPTIAN CINDERELLA
Cole, Joanna, and Bruce Degen	• ANCIENT EGYPT (Ms. Frizzle's Adventures)
Delafosse, Claude	• PYRAMIDS (First Discovery Books)
dePaola, Tomie	• BILL AND PETE GO DOWN THE NILE
Donnelly, Judy	• TUT'S MUMMY LOST . . . AND FOUND
Frank, John	• THE TOMB OF THE BOY KING
Gantos, Jack	• ROTTEN RALPH HELPS OUT
Gerrard, Roy	• CROCO'NILE
Hart, George	• ANCIENT EGYPT (Eyewitness Books)
Hawcock, David	• AMAZING POP-UP, PULL-OUT MUMMY BOOK
Hofmeyr, Dianne	• THE STAR BEARER: A CREATION MYTH FROM ANCIENT EGYPT
Hooper, Meredith	• WHO BUILT THE PYRAMID?
Lattimore, Deborah Nourse	• THE WINGED CAT: A TALE OF ANCIENT EGYPT
Logan, Claudia	• THE 5,000-YEAR-OLD PUZZLE: SOLVING A MYSTERY OF ANCIENT EGYPT
Macaulay, David	• PYRAMID
McGraw, Eloise	• MARA, DAUGHTER OF THE NILE
Perl, Lila	• MUMMIES, TOMBS, AND TREASURE: SECRETS OF ANCIENT EGYPT
Petras, Kathryn and Ross	• MUMMIES, GODS, AND PHARAOHS (Fandex Family Field Guides)
Sabuda, Robert	• TUTANKHAMEN'S GIFT
Snyder, Zilpha Keatley	• THE EGYPT GAME
Stanley, Diane	• CLEOPATRA

🍀 *Potato Pick:*

NINE FOR CALIFORNIA

*by Sonia Levitin, illustrated by
Cat Bowman Smith*

"What good is gold, without my family?" That's what Pa says in a letter, in which he encloses all the money he has in the world, sending Mama and five "young 'uns" on a twenty-one-day journey by stagecoach to California. In Mama's mysterious flour sack are all the necessities for the long ride, and whenever young Amanda wishes something would happen, it does, with adventurous results. The rustic cartoons are full of action and humor, and the earth-toned watercolors effectively carry across the dusty frontier.
(6 and up)

Steedman, Scott	• THE EGYPTIAN NEWS
Steele, Philip	• I WONDER WHY PYRAMIDS WERE BUILT? AND OTHER QUESTIONS ABOUT ANCIENT EGYPT
Trumble, Kelly	• CAT MUMMIES

The Gold Rush

Cooper, Michael	• KLONDIKE FEVER: THE FAMOUS GOLD RUSH OF 1898
Dahlberg, Maurine F.	• THE SPIRIT AND GILLY BUCKET
Gregory, Kristiana	• SEEDS OF HOPE: THE GOLD RUSH DIARY OF SUSANNA FAIRCHILD, CALIFORNIA TERRITORY, 1849
Hurst, Carol Otis	• IN PLAIN SIGHT
Klein, James	• GOLD RUSH! THE YOUNG PROSPECTOR'S GUIDE TO STRIKING IT RICH
Krensky, Stephen	• STRIKING IT RICH: THE STORY OF THE CALIFORNIA GOLD RUSH
Levitin, Sonia	• NINE FOR CALIFORNIA
Murphy, Claire Rudolf, and Jane G. Haihj	• CHILDREN OF THE GOLD RUSH
Rau, Margaret	• THE WELLS FARGO BOOK OF THE GOLD RUSH
Sonneborn, Liz	• THE AMERICAN WEST: AN ILLUSTRATED HISTORY
Schanzer, Rosalyn	• GOLD FEVER! TALES FROM THE CALIFORNIA GOLD RUSH
Stanley, Jerry	• HURRY FREEDOM: AFRICAN AMERICANS IN GOLD RUSH CALIFORNIA

Child Labor

Auch, Mary Jane	• ASHES OF ROSES
Bartoletti, Susan Campbell	• GROWING UP IN COAL COUNTRY • KIDS ON STRIKE!
Brill, Marlene Targ	• MARGARET KNIGHT: GIRL INVENTOR
Dickens, Charles	• OLIVER TWIST
Freedman, Russell	• KIDS AT WORK: LEWIS HINE AND THE CRUSADE AGAINST CHILD LABOR
Greenberg, Polly	• OH, LORD, I WISH I WAS A BUZZARD

Jiménez, Francisco	• THE CIRCUIT
Kuklin, Susan	• IQBAL MASIH AND THE CRUSADERS AGAINST CHILD SLAVERY
McCully, Emily Arnold	• THE BOBBIN GIRL
Paterson, Katherine	• LYDDIE
Robinet, Harriette Gillem	• MISSING FROM HAYMARKET SQUARE
Williams, Sherley Anne	• WORKING COTTON

Immigration: Coming to America Then and Now

Ada, Alma Flor	• MY NAME IS MARIA ISABEL
Aliki	• MARIANTHE'S STORY: PAINTED WORDS, SPOKEN MEMORIES
Bartone, Elisa	• PEPPE THE LAMPLIGHTER
Bial, Raymond	• TENEMENT: IMMIGRANT LIFE ON THE LOWER EAST SIDE
Bode, Janet	• NEW KIDS IN TOWN: ORAL HISTORIES OF IMMIGRANT TEENS
Bunting, Eve	• GOING HOME • HOW MANY DAYS TO AMERICA?: A THANKSGIVING STORY
Cohen, Barbara	• MOLLY'S PILGRIM
Danticat, Edwidge	• BEHIND THE MOUNTAINS (Part of the excellent **First Person Fiction** series of immigrant stories.)
Freedman, Russell	• IMMIGRANT KIDS
Garland, Sherry	• THE LOTUS SEED
Gerstein, Mordicai	• SPARROW JACK
Gilmore, Rachna	• LIGHTS FOR GITA
Gilson, Jamie	• HELLO, MY NAME IS SCRAMBLED EGGS
Hest, Amy	• WHEN JESSIE CAME ACROSS THE SEA
Jiménez, Francisco	• LA MARIPOSA
Joosse, Barbara M.	• THE MORNING CHAIR
Knight, Margy Burns	• WHO BELONGS HERE? AN AMERICAN STORY
Lawlor, Veronica	• I WAS DREAMING TO COME TO AMERICA: MEMORIES FROM THE ELLIS ISLAND ORAL HISTORY PROJECT
Levinson, Riki	• WATCH THE STARS COME OUT

🌼 *Potato Pick:*

KIDS ON STRIKE!
by Susan Campbell Bartoletti

A must-read for any intermediate-aged student who ever claimed to "hate school," this is a well-researched, smooth-reading chronicle of the efforts by and for the 2 million children struggling under child labor at the turn of the century. This book offers great role models for leadership, a history of industry, as well as a perspective of school as a great and hard-won opportunity. It's brimming with poignant black-and-white photos, a comprehensive bibliography, and a time line of federal child labor laws. (9 and up)

Lord, Bette Bao	• In the Year of the Boar and Jackie Robinson
Machlin, Mikki	• My Name Is *Not* Gussie
Maestro, Betsy	• Coming to America: The Story of Immigration
Moran, Pat	• The Rainbow Tulip
Pak, Soyung	• A Place to Grow
Perl, Lila	• The Great Ancestor Hunt: The Fun of Finding Out Who You Are
Polacco, Patricia	• The Keeping Quilt
Say, Allen	• Grandfather's Journey
Stevens, Carla	• Lily and Miss Liberty
Wolfman, Ira	• Do People Grow on Family Trees? Genealogy for Kids and Other Beginners
Wong, Janet S.	• Apple Pie 4th of July
Ziefert, Harriet	• When I First Came to This Land

Time Travel: Forward and Reverse

Alexander, Lloyd	• Time Cat
Bellairs, John	• Trolley to Yesterday
Cart, Michael, comp.	• Tomorrowland: Ten Stories about the Future
Haddix, Margaret Peterson	• Running Out of Time
Krull, Kathleen	• They Saw the Future: Oracles, Psychics, Scientists, Great Thinkers and Pretty Good Guessers
Lasky, Kathryn	• The Man Who Made Time Travel
MacGrory, Yvonne	• The Secret of the Ruby Ring
Osborne, Mary Pope	• The Magic Tree House series
Peck, Richard	• Lost in Cyberspace
Rupp, Rebecca	• The Dragon of Lonely Island
Sadler, Marilyn	• Alistair's Time Machine
Scieszka, Jon	• The Time Warp Trio series
Tambini, Michael	• Future (Eyewitness Books)
Thomas, Jane Resh	• The Princess in the Pigpen

. . . Decorate the inside of this Time Machine with pictures of robots, computers, and newspaper and magazine articles about progress and new discoveries, or use a variety of decorations from all different periods and mark the centuries they depict on labels.

BETTER THAN AN ENCYCLOPEDIA

Rather than splurging on a set of World Books or saving for a Funk & Wagnall's, consider ordering a complete set of back issues of *Cobblestone* (American history) and *Calliope* (world history) magazines. These periodicals are the most useful resource available for historical information for kids. The sets come with an index, and every issue is generously illustrated and loaded with articles written in a straightforward, friendly way that children will understand *and* find interesting. Hundreds of topics are covered, and as a school librarian, I can attest to the fact that there was never a report assigned by a teacher that was not addressed in these sets. The company also offers "theme packs," or sets of back issues for commonly assigned topics. Request a catalog from Cobblestone Publishing Company, 1-800-821-0115 or www.cobblestonepub.com.

Little Footprints in the Sands of Time: Children in History

Textbooks getting tired? Children marched along every step of the time line, so try history from a young person's perspective and breathe new life into old days.

Bartoletti, Susan Campbell	• KIDS ON STRIKE!
Freedman, Russell	• CHILDREN OF THE WILD WEST
	• KIDS AT WORK
Hazell, Rebecca	• THE BAREFOOT BOOK OF HEROIC CHILDREN
Hoose, Phillip	• WE WERE THERE, TOO! YOUNG PEOPLE IN U.S. HISTORY
Murphy, Jim	• THE BOYS' WAR
Spedden, Daisy Corning Stone	• POLAR THE TITANIC BEAR
Stanley, Jerry	• CHILDREN OF THE DUST BOWL
Tanaka, Shelley	• ANASTASIA'S ALBUM
Wisler, G. Clifton	• WHEN JOHNNY WENT MARCHING HOME: YOUNG AMERICANS FIGHT THE CIVIL WAR

... Also, you can painlessly present an entire American history curriculum in your own home simply by using Scholastic's accessible historical fiction series, **Dear America** (focusing on female characters) and **My Name Is America** (focusing on males). Each book, told in journal form

🥔 *Potato Pick:*

FAIR WEATHER
by Richard Peck

This book is a ticket to the 1893 World Columbian Exposition. Mysterious Aunt Euterpe has sent for her country kin to come and get an education in the pavilions set up along Chicago's lakefront, and all of their lives are changed as a result. From the low-down dance halls to the tippy-top of the Ferris wheel, readers will feel transported alongside these marvelous characters. It's too bad Frank Capra isn't still around. He's the only movie producer fit to bring this book to the screen. And it's too bad Mark Twain isn't around. He would have loved this, as well. (10 and up)

from the perspective of a child of the time, is extensively researched by some of the most distinguished authors in the business. The series creates windows into the world of the past and validates the importance of children's own experiences.

DEAR AMERICA AND MY NAME IS AMERICA TIME LINE

1609 OUR STRANGE NEW LAND: ELIZABETH'S DIARY, JAMESTOWN, VIRGINIA by Patricia Hermes

1609 THE STARVING TIME: ELIZABETH'S DIARY, BOOK TWO, JAMESTOWN, VIRGINIA by Patricia Hermes

1620 A JOURNEY TO THE NEW WORLD: THE DIARY OF REMEMBER PATIENCE WHIPPLE, MAYFLOWER by Kathryn Lasky

1620 THE JOURNAL OF JASPER JONATHAN PIERCE: A PILGRIM BOY, PLYMOUTH by Ann Rinaldi

1763 STANDING IN THE LIGHT: THE CAPTIVE DIARY OF CATHARINE CAREY LOGAN, DELAWARE VALLEY, PENNSYLVANIA by Mary Pope Osborne

1774 THE JOURNAL OF WILLIAM THOMAS EMERSON: A REVOLUTIONARY WAR PATRIOT by Barry Denenberg

1774 LOVE THY NEIGHBOR: THE TORY DIARY OF PRUDENCE EMERSON, GREENMARSH, MASSACHUSETTS by Ann Turner

1776 FIVE SMOOTH STONES, HOPE'S DIARY, REVOLUTIONARY WAR by Kristiana Gregory

1777 THE WINTER OF RED SNOW: THE REVOLUTIONARY WAR DIARY OF ABIGAIL JANE STEWART, VALLEY FORGE, PENNSYLVANIA by Kristiana Gregory

1804 THE JOURNAL OF AUGUSTUS PELLETIER: THE LEWIS AND CLARK EXPEDITION by Kathryn Lasky

1836 A LINE IN THE SAND: THE ALAMO DIARY OF LUCINDA LAWRENCE, GONZALES, TEXAS by Sherry Garland

1838 THE JOURNAL OF JESSE SMOKE: A CHEROKEE BOY, TRAIL OF TEARS by Joseph Bruchac

1845 THE JOURNAL OF JEDEDIAH BARSTOW: AN EMIGRANT ON THE OREGON TRAIL, OVERLAND by Ellen Levine

1846 THE VALLEY OF THE MOON: THE DIARY OF MARÍA ROSALIA DE MILAGROS, SONOMA VALLEY, ALTA, CALIFORNIA by Sherry Garland

1846 THE JOURNAL OF DOUGLAS ALLEN DEEDS: THE DONNER PARTY EXPEDITION by Rodman Philbrick

1847 ACROSS THE WIDE AND LONESOME PRAIRIE: THE OREGON TRAIL DIARY OF HATTIE CAMPBELL by Kristiana Gregory

1847 SO FAR FROM HOME: THE DIARY OF MARY DRISCOLL, AN IRISH MILL GIRL, LOWELL, MASSACHUSETTS by Barry Denenberg

1848 WESTWARD TO HOME: JOSHUA'S DIARY, THE OREGON TRAIL by Patricia Hermes

1849 SEEDS OF HOPE: THE GOLD RUSH DIARY OF SUSANNA FAIRCHILD, CALIFORNIA TERRITORY by Kristiana Gregory

1852 THE JOURNAL OF WONG MING-CHUNG: A CHINESE MINER, CALIFORNIA by Laurence Yep

1856 AS FAR AS I CAN SEE: MEG'S PRAIRIE DIARY, BOOK ONE by Kate McMullan

1857 FREEDOM'S WINGS: COREY'S DIARY, KENTUCKY TO OHIO by Sharon Dennis Wyeth

1859 A PICTURE OF FREEDOM: THE DIARY OF CLOTEE, A SLAVE GIRL, BELMONT PLANTATION, VIRGINIA by Patricia C. McKissack

1861 A LIGHT IN THE STORM: THE CIVIL WAR DIARY OF AMELIA MARTIN, FENWICK ISLAND, DELAWARE by Karen Hesse

1863 MY BROTHER'S KEEPER: VIRGINIA'S DIARY, GETTYSBURG, PENNSYLVANIA by Mary Pope Osborne

1863 THE JOURNAL OF JAMES EDMOND PEASE: A CIVIL WAR UNION SOLDIER, VIRGINIA by Jim Murphy

1864 THE GIRL WHO CHASED AWAY SORROW: THE DIARY OF SARAH NITA, A NAVAJO GIRL, NEW MEXICO by Ann Turner

1864 WHEN WILL THIS CRUEL WAR BE OVER?: THE CIVIL WAR DIARY OF EMMA SIMPSON, GORDONSVILLE, VIRGINIA by Barry Denenberg

1864 AFTER THE RAIN: VIRGINIA'S CIVIL WAR DIARY, BOOK TWO by Mary Pope Osborne

1865 I THOUGHT MY SOUL WOULD RISE AND FLY: THE DIARY OF PATSY, A FREED GIRL, MARS BLUFF, SOUTH CAROLINA by Joyce Hansen

1867 THE JOURNAL OF SEAN SULLIVAN: A TRANSCONTINENTAL RAILROAD WORKER, NEBRASKA AND POINTS WEST by William Durbin

1868 THE GREAT RAILROAD RACE: THE DIARY OF LIBBY WEST, UTAH TERRITORY by Kristiana Gregory

1871 THE JOURNAL OF JOSHUA LOPER: A BLACK COWBOY, THE CHISHOLM TRAIL by Walter Dean Myers

1873 LAND OF THE BUFFALO BONES: THE DIARY OF MARY ELIZABETH RODGERS, AN ENGLISH GIRL IN MINNESOTA, NEW YEOVIL, MINNESOTA by Marion Dane Bower

1880 MY HEART IS ON THE GROUND: THE DIARY OF NANNIE LITTLE ROSE, A SIOUX GIRL, CARLISLE INDIAN SCHOOL, PENNSYLVANIA by Ann Rinaldi

READING HEROES

EDWARD THORNDIKE
MY BOYFRIEND IN THEORY

Wanna hear something smart my ex told me? "The intellectual value of studies should be determined largely by the special information, habits, interests, attitudes, and ideals that they demonstrably produce." This was said in 1924 by my boyfriend in another life, Edward L. Thorndike. What I'm pretty sure he meant was that interest in the subject is more important than the subject itself, because from that interest comes the desire and thus the ability to learn. So don't freak out thinking one subject is more important than another. "Learning," said my smart ex-boyfriend, "is . . . a process of forming a series of connections or tendencies between situations or responses." Thorndike's arguments were used as a theoretical basis for moving away from the assumed value of the classics, the viewpoint that was so dominant during the time we were dating. Thorndike's ideas, called "connectivist theory," were used to show the value of introducing to children subjects such as social studies and shop, which had not been introduced before, and helped to contribute to the variety of subjects that can be studied and enjoyed today.

YESTERDAY'S NEWS

Ever had your newspaper delivered late? How about a century late? Your children can get yesterday's news today with **History News,** a series of books from Candlewick Press in which the past is portrayed via sensational newspaper articles from the time period.

THE AZTEC NEWS

THE EGYPTIAN NEWS

EXPLORERS NEWS

THE GREEK NEWS

THE HISTORY NEWS: MEDICINE

THE HISTORY NEWS: REVOLUTION

THE HISTORY NEWS: IN SPACE

THE ROMAN NEWS

THE STONE AGE NEWS

THE VIKING NEWS

Reluctant readers and ticklish time travelers will also enjoy exploring the highs and lows of the not-so-good-old-days with the **Horrible Histories** collection published by Scholastic, which includes plenty of jokes, cartoons, and fun facts.

ARE WE THERE YET? EUROPEANS MEET THE AMERICANS

AWESOME ANCIENT ANCESTORS

THE AWESOME EGYPTIANS

THE GROOVY GREEKS

THE MEASLY MIDDLE AGES

THE ROTTEN ROMANS

THE VICIOUS VIKINGS

WHO ARE YOU CALLING A WOOLLY MAMMOTH?

1881 MY FACE TO THE WIND: THE DIARY OF SARAH JANE PRICE, PRAIRIE TEACHER, BROKEN BOW, NEBRASKA by Jim Murphy

1883 WEST TO A LAND OF PLENTY: THE DIARY OF TERESA ANGELINO VISCARDI, NEW YORK TO IDAHO TERRITORY by Jim Murphy

1896 A COAL MINER'S BRIDE: THE DIARY OF ANETKA KAMINSKA, LATTIMER, PENNSYLVANIA by Susan Campbell Bartoletti

1899 THE JOURNAL OF FINN REARDON, NEWSIE, NEW YORK CITY by Susan Campbell Bartoletti

1903 DREAMS IN THE GOLDEN COUNTRY: THE DIARY OF ZIPPORAH FELDMAN, A JEWISH IMMIGRANT GIRL, NEW YORK CITY by Kathryn Lasky

1905 THE JOURNAL OF OTTO PELTONEN: A FINNISH IMMIGRANT, HIBBING, MINNESOTA by William Durbin,

1912 VOYAGE ON THE GREAT TITANIC: THE DIARY OF MARGARET ANN BRADY, *RMS TITANIC* by Ellen Emerson White

1919 COLOR ME DARK: THE DIARY OF NELLIE LEE LOVE, THE GREAT MIGRATION NORTH, CHICAGO, ILLINOIS by Patricia C. McKissack

1932 CHRISTMAS AFTER ALL: THE GREAT DEPRESSION DIARY OF MINNIE SWIFT, INDIANAPOLIS, INDIANA by Kathryn Lasky

1932 MIRROR, MIRROR ON THE WALL: THE DIARY OF BESS BRENNAN, THE PERKINS SCHOOL FOR THE BLIND by Barry Denenberg

1938 ONE EYE LAUGHING, THE OTHER WEEPING: THE DIARY OF JULIE WEISS, VIENNA, AUSTRIA, TO NEW YORK by Barry Denenberg

1941 MY SECRET WAR: THE WORLD WAR II DIARY OF MADELINE BECK, LONG ISLAND, NEW YORK by Mary Pope Osborne

1941 EARLY SUNDAY MORNING: THE PEARL HARBOR DIARY OF AMBER BILLOWS, HAWAII by Barry Denenberg

1942 THE JOURNAL OF BEN UCHIDA: CITIZEN 13559, MIRROR LAKE INTERNMENT CAMP by Barry Denenberg 1942

1944 THE JOURNAL OF SCOTT PENDLETON COLLINS: A WORLD WAR II SOLDIER, NORMANDY, FRANCE by Walter Dean Myers

1948 THE JOURNAL OF BIDDY OWENS: THE NEGRO LEAGUES, BIRMINGHAM, ALABAMA by Walter Dean Myers

Dear Madame Esme,

Our family so enjoyed the **Little House** series by Laura Ingalls Wilder. What's a good follow-up?

Dear Gentle Reader,

I approached THE BIRCHBARK HOUSE by Louise Erdrich somewhat skeptically. A Native American perspective of Laura Ingalls Wilder's **Little House** series? Sounded gimmicky to me. But in fact, it is a book Erdrich was born to write. A year in the life of an Ojibwa girl is told from the point of view of Omakayas, or "Little Frog," named so because her first step was a hop. She is the sole smallpox survivor on Madeline Island, rescued by a strange and strong old woman named Tallow, and given to a loving family. Then smallpox strikes Omakayas's new village. Besides a plot that screams for read-aloud (complete with ghost stories!), the book is rich with authentic detail of daily living, and memorable characters. The book offers to readers of all ages and genders a long overdue perspective on frontier life. A stellar family and coming-of-age story, exemplary research, and writing that stands independently from frontier stories that have gone before it make this an important addition to children's literature.

Who's Who?
Children's Biography

Children's biography is burgeoning, and there are a few picture-book authors in particular I would recommend for intermediate readers.

DIANE STANLEY

BARD OF AVON: THE STORY OF WILLIAM SHAKESPEARE (with Peter Vennema)

CHARLES DICKENS: THE MAN WHO HAD GREAT EXPECTATIONS (with Peter Vennema)

CLEOPATRA (with Peter Vennema)

GOOD QUEEN BESS: THE STORY OF ELIZABETH I OF ENGLAND (with Peter Vennema)

❁ *Potato Pick:*
DAVE AT NIGHT
by Gail Carson Levine

Using her own father's life as inspiration, Levine creates a gripping story of a Jewish boy sent to a bleak orphanage after the death of his father, escaping nightly to accompany an old fortune-teller who attends parties amid the backdrop of the Harlem Renaissance. Conflicts arise as Dave must determine whether to leave the orphanage for good, or stay with the friends he has come to know as family. At once funny and sad, DAVE AT NIGHT is a superior read-aloud and a great tie-in to black history. (8 and up)

...And after finishing this novel, you and your child can make invitations to the Harlem Renaissance. Celebrate with an afternoon of period music (How about a Cab Calloway recording or a little Duke Ellington?), dancing (Learn the lindy hop at www.savoystyle.com), poetry (LOVE TO LANGSTON by Tony Medina or WORDS WITH WINGS selected by Belinda Rochelle), dress-up (Get inspired by Sarah Breedlove Walker, Harlem Renaissance glam-gal and entrepreneur, exalted in VISION OF BEAUTY by Kathryn Lasky), and food (Check out THE AFRICAN-AMERICAN CHILD'S HERITAGE COOKBOOK by Vanessa Roberts Parham).

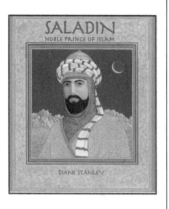

JOAN OF ARC

THE LAST PRINCESS: THE STORY OF PRINCESS
   KA'LULANI OF HAWAII (by Fay Stanley)

LEONARDO DA VINCI

MICHELANGELO

PETER THE GREAT

SALADIN: NOBLE PRINCE OF ISLAM

SHAKA: KING OF THE ZULUS (with Peter Vennema)

THE TRUE ADVENTURE OF DANIEL HALL

JEAN FRITZ

AND THEN WHAT HAPPENED, PAUL REVERE?

CAN'T YOU MAKE THEM BEHAVE, KING GEORGE?

WHERE WAS PATRICK HENRY ON THE 29TH OF MAY?

WILL YOU SIGN HERE, JOHN HANCOCK?

WHY DON'T YOU GET A HORSE, SAM ADAMS?

WHAT'S THE BIG IDEA, BEN FRANKLIN?

WHERE DO YOU THINK YOU'RE GOING,
   CHRISTOPHER COLUMBUS?

DAVID A. ADLER
A PICTURE BOOK OF . . .

. . . ABRAHAM LINCOLN	. . . JESSIE OWENS
. . . AMELIA EARHART	. . . JOHN F. KENNEDY
. . . ANNE FRANK	. . . LOUIS BRAILLE
. . . BENJAMIN FRANKLIN	. . . MARTIN LUTHER KING JR.
. . . CHRISTOPHER COLUMBUS	. . . PATRICK HENRY
. . . DAVY CROCKETT	. . . PAUL REVERE
. . . ELEANOR ROOSEVELT	. . . ROBERT E. LEE
. . . FLORENCE NIGHTINGALE	. . . ROSA PARKS
. . . FREDERICK DOUGLASS	. . . SACAJAWEA
. . . GEORGE WASHINGTON	. . . SOJOURNER TRUTH
. . . GEORGE WASHINGTON CARVER	. . . THOMAS ALVA EDISON
. . . HARRIET TUBMAN	. . . THOMAS JEFFERSON
. . . HELEN KELLER	. . . THURGOOD MARSHALL
. . . JACKIE ROBINSON	

Dear Madame Esmé,

My daughter is on the phone for hours talking to her friends about her classmates, who likes who and who did what. Nothing is quite as interesting to her as other people's business. Is there any way I can turn this preadolescent preoccupation to her academic advantage?

Dear Gentle Reader,

Containing all the dirt of a gossip column, your preteen paparazzi will dig into Kathleen Krull's **Lives of** series, which humanizes portraits of famous figures and still manages to not spare any scandal.

Lives of the Artists: Masterpieces, Messes

    (And What the Neighbors Thought)

Lives of the Athletes: Thrills, Spills (And What the Neighbors Thought)

Lives of Extraordinary Women: Rulers, Rebels

    (And What the Neighbors Thought)

Lives of the Musicians: Good Times, Bad Times

    (And What the Neighbors Thought)

Lives of the Presidents: Fame, Shame (And What the Neighbors Thought)

Lives of the Writers: Comedies, Tragedies

    (And What the Neighbors Thought)

Wave That Flag!

These titles go far to celebrate some of America's historical foundations and principles. These are also excellent gifts for young friends overseas who want to learn more about our country.

PATRIOTIC PLUMS:

Bateman, Teresa	• Red, White, Blue and Uncle Who? The Stories Behind Some of America's Patriotic Symbols
Berlin, Irving	• God Bless America (Comes with a musical CD recording by Barbra Streisand.)
Borden, Louise	• America Is . . .
Catrow, David	• We the Kids: The Preamble to the Constitution of the United States
Cohn, Amy L., compiler	• From Sea to Shining Sea: A Treasury of American Folklore and Folk Songs

❀ *Potato Pick:*

A BIG CHEESE FOR
THE WHITE HOUSE:
THE TRUE TALE
OF A TREMENDOUS CHEDDAR

by Candace Fleming

Jefferson wasn't the only big
cheese in the White House in
1801, thanks to the town of
Cheshire, Massachusetts, which
created a ridiculously enormous
cheese weighing 1,235 pounds.
The persistent undertone of the
town "downer," Phineas Dobbs
("It can never be done!" "I told
you it could never be done!"),
makes for a good read-aloud
chant. The success of the
endeavor suggests that diligence
is all that's really necessary to
overcome cynicism—and make
ideas come to fruition. Or is it
cheesition? Your child will melt
over this funny, exciting, and
true story. (5 and up)

Curlee, Lynn	• LIBERTY • RUSHMORE
Dalgliesh, Alice	• THE FOURTH OF JULY STORY (An oldie but goodie.)
Drummond, Allan	• LIBERTY!
Fradin, Dennis Brindell	• THE SIGNERS: THE FIFTY-SIX STORIES BEHIND THE DECLARATION OF INDEPENDENCE
Guthrie, Woody	• THIS LAND IS YOUR LAND (Illustrated by Kathy Jakobsen, comes with a musical CD recording by Woody and Arlo Guthrie.)
Hopkins, Lee Bennett, comp.	• MY AMERICA: A POETRY ATLAS OF THE UNITED STATES • HOME TO ME: POEMS ACROSS AMERICA • HAND IN HAND: AN AMERICAN HISTORY THROUGH POETRY
Longfellow, Henry Wadsworth	• THE MIDNIGHT RIDE OF PAUL REVERE (The version illustrated by Christopher Bing is spectacular.)
Martin Jr., Bill, and Michael Sampson	• I PLEDGE ALLEGIANCE
Miller, Millie, and Cyndi Nelson	• THE UNITED STATES OF AMERICA: A STATE-BY-STATE GUIDE (Great for reports, too!)
Ryan, Pam Muñoz	• THE FLAG WE LOVE
West, Delno C. and Jean M.	• UNCLE SAM AND OLD GLORY: SYMBOLS OF AMERICA
Younger, Barbara	• PURPLE MOUNTAIN MAJESTIES: THE STORY OF KATHARINE LEE BATES AND "AMERICA THE BEAUTIFUL"

. . . .Also, try Jean Fritz titles (see Who's Who? p. 123) and the **Dear America** series (Little Footprints in the Sands of Time, p. 119)

HAIL TO THE CHIEF!

Aronson, Steven	• PRESIDENTS (Fandex Family Field Guides)
Chandra, Deborah, and Madeleine Comora	• GEORGE WASHINGTON'S TEETH
Edwards, Susan	• WHITE HOUSE KIDS
Garland, Michael	• THE PRESIDENT AND MOM'S APPLE PIE
Harness, Cheryl	• GHOSTS OF THE WHITE HOUSE
Provensen, Alice	• THE BUCK STOPS HERE
Sharmat, Marjorie Weinman	• MAGGIE MARMELSTEIN FOR PRESIDENT (Author of the classic **Nate the Great** series!)
St. George, Judith	• SO YOU WANT TO BE PRESIDENT?

PRUDENCE CRANDALL
BRAVE TEACHER

In 1832, at the request of local citizens, teacher Prudence Crandall opened a private boarding school in Canterbury, Connecticut. These same citizens withdrew support and turned ugly when Crandall admitted her first black student, Sarah Harris, to the school. After conferring with abolitionists, Crandall reopened the school for the purpose of instructing "young ladies and little missus of color," and so established New England's first academy for black girls. Soon she had twenty students. Crandall became a pariah in the town, and her school was consistently vandalized. Crandall was jailed for breaking a law barring "the teaching of colored people." When Crandall was convicted and released on a technicality, this so enraged a mob that it tried unsuccessfully to set the school ablaze. Crandall persisted until some months later when another mob broke ninety windows. Fearing for her students' safety, Crandall closed the school. For the rest of her life, she traveled through Massachusetts, Rhode Island, New York, Illinois, and Kansas, teaching whoever wanted to learn and advocating for reforms.

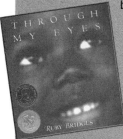

Prudence Crandall's persistence in the face of such monstrous indignity and danger underscores her conviction that all people are entitled to an equal opportunity to learn. I wonder if she could have imagined the far-reaching effects of her conviction; arguments from her trials were used in the U.S. Supreme Court's desegregation decision of 1954. This decision, along with the courage of civil rights pioneers, helped lay the groundwork not only for opportunity for all Americans, but ultimately the multicultural educational approach that is reflected in the gorgeous rainbow of children's literature available today.

FOR STORIES OF INTEREST:

Bridges, Ruby	• THROUGH MY EYES
Dingle, Derek T.	• FIRST IN THE FIELD: BASEBALL HERO JACKIE ROBINSON
English, Karen	• FRANCIE
Farris, Christine King	• MY BROTHER MARTIN: A SISTER REMEMBERS
Haskins, Jim	• SEPARATE BUT NOT EQUAL: THE DREAM AND THE STRUGGLE (Outstanding nonfiction, a must-read for grown-ups, too!)
Hesse, Karen	• WITNESS
Martin, Ann M.	• BELLE TEAL
McKissack, Patricia C.	• GOIN' SOMEPLACE SPECIAL
Miller, William	• RICHARD WRIGHT AND THE LIBRARY CARD
Pinkney, Andrea Davis	• LET IT SHINE: STORIES OF BLACK WOMEN FREEDOM FIGHTERS
Polacco, Patricia	• MR. LINCOLN'S WAY
Rappaport, Doreen	• MARTIN'S BIG WORDS
Ringgold, Faith	• IF A BUS COULD TALK: THE STORY OF ROSA PARKS • TAR BEACH
Rosen, Michael J.	• A SCHOOL FOR POMPEY WALKER
Sebestyen, Ouida	• WORDS BY HEART
Taylor, Mildred D.	• ROLL OF THUNDER, HEAR MY CRY
Wiles, Deborah	• FREEDOM SUMMER
Woodson, Jacqueline	• THE OTHER SIDE

GIFT HORSE:
A LAKOTA STTORY
by S. D. Nelson

The story of this young Lakota's coming of age is told with the pacing of a horse's smooth canter. Whether Storm is taking his horse, Flying Cloud, through a blizzard, doing a Buffalo Dance around a fire, or reeling under the constellations on a vision quest, every page absolutely glows with action and color. While this book is sophisticated in many ways, it can be enjoyed on many levels. Children as young as six or as old as twelve will be captivated. (6 and up)

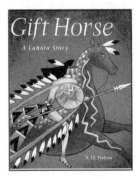

Location, Location, Location

No lost luggage. No suspicious airline food. No jet lag. Your child's library card is the only ticket he will need to book a trip around the world!

Reading: A Passport to Geography

With your child you can make a "passport" by stapling together a small booklet of blank paper; if possible, color copy the cover of a real passport for a more authentic look. Rubber-stamp a page in the booklet with every new destination, and mark it on a world map with a pushpin. Who at home or in your child's classroom is the most "well traveled"?

All American	
Ata, Te	• BABY RATTLESNAKE
Bierhorst, John	• IS MY FRIEND AT HOME? PUEBLO FIRESIDE TALES
Bruchac, Joseph	• THE GREAT BALL GAME: A MUSKOGEE STORY • A BOY CALLED SLOW: THE TRUE STORY OF SITTING BULL
Cates, Karin	• A FAR-FETCHED STORY
Cohn, Amy L., comp.	• FROM SEA TO SHINING SEA: A TREASURY OF AMERICAN FOLKLORE AND FOLK SONGS
dePaola, Tomie	• THE LEGEND OF THE BLUEBONNET
Esbensen, Barbara Juster	• THE STAR MAIDEN: AN OJIBWAY TALE
Goble, Paul	• STORM MAKER'S TIPI (Try all of Goble's exquisite Native American legends!)
Harris, Joel Chandler	• THE COMPLETE TALES OF UNCLE REMUS

THE LEGEND OF
☆ THE BLUEBONNET ☆

AN OLD TALE OF TEXAS
RETOLD AND ILLUSTRATED BY
TOMIE dePAOLA

Dear Madame Esmé,

My child likes to exaggerate when he tells a story. Is this normal?

Dear Gentle Reader,

If your child is an American, exaggeration is not only normal, it is his cultural inheritance. Hyperbole is part of our country's proud storytelling heritage. So when you share stories, think big, as Peter Selgin did in **"S.S." GIGANTIC ACROSS THE ATLANTIC.** This is a tall tale, or rather, a tremendous one, of a ship that is so gigantic that "you can't fit it in a picture," so gigantic that it can travel around the world without moving, so gigantic it has a swimming pool for other ships. The most gigantic aspect of this book, however, is the pure imagination that went into it, perfectly conveyed through the eyes of Pipsqueak, the S.S. Gigantic's tiny lookout. This is an unsinkable choice for reluctant readers five and up.

Another book that extols a little youthful embellishment is **OLIVIA SAVES THE CIRCUS** by Ian Falconer. Precocious piggy Olivia goes to school and is asked what she did over vacation. She went to the circus, but since all the performers had ear infections, Olivia takes over, becoming tattooed lady, lion tamer, and Queen of the Trampoline, to name a few. The expression on the teacher's face after Olivia relates the adventure is worth the price of the book, as is the realistic and hilarious banter: "'Was that true?'" Olivia's teacher asks. "'Pretty true,'" says Olivia. "All true?" "Pretty all true." Falconer's sophisticated line illustrations are the funniest, loveliest artwork to grace children's lit since Hilary Knight's drawings for Kay Thompson's **ELOISE.** Many clever little girls in the over-six crowd will see themselves in Olivia, but during read-alouds, it's always the boys who laugh the hardest and beg for second readings. This story is even better than Falconer's Caldecott Honor book **OLIVIA.** And I'm not exaggerating!

❀ *Potato Pick:*

WISH YOU WERE HERE (AND I WASN'T): A BOOK OF POEMS AND PICTURES FOR GLOBE TROTTERS
by Colin McNaughton

Every cross-country traveler will want to read "Are We Nearly There Yet?" "If You're Traveling in Transylvania," "I Just Don't Believe in Aeroplanes," and, of course, "Aliens on Vacation." With a generous fifty-eight pages of irreverent cartoons and poetry, this book also makes a perfect send-off gift for summer campers. (7 and up)

❧ *Potato Pick:*

BURIED BLUEPRINTS:
MAPS AND SKETCHES
OF LOST WORLDS AND
MYSTERIOUS PLACES
*by Albert Lorenz with
Joy Schleh*

Maps are often used to find treasure, but in this case, the maps *are* the treasure. Gorgeous fold-open oversized pages offer imaginative, detailed explorations into the Garden of Eden, the Tower of Babel, Ancient Egypt, King Solomon's Mines, Homer's Odyssey, Dracula's Castle, King Arthur's Camelot, the Great Wall of China (complete with Genghis Khan), and many other places. Besides being a great traveling read, no child studying map skills or classic literature should miss this exciting volume. It will inspire intermediate children to design their own maps and look at the world in new and imaginative ways. It also happens to be an out-of-the-ordinary gift for the adult who has everything. Also of interest to young navigators: Karen Romano Young's SMALL WORLDS: MAPS AND MAPMAKERS. (8 and up)

Isaacs, Anne	• SWAMP ANGEL
Jones, Jennifer Berry	• HEETUNKA'S HARVEST: A TALE OF THE PLAINS INDIANS
Keller, Laurie	• THE SCRAMBLED STATES OF AMERICA
Kellogg, Steven	• I WAS BORN ABOUT 10,000 YEARS AGO • SALLY ANN THUNDER ANN WHIRLWIND CROCKETT • MIKE FINK • PAUL BUNYAN • PECOS BILL
Lewis, Paul Owen	• FROG GIRL
Martin, Rafe	• THE WORLD BEFORE THIS ONE: A NOVEL TOLD IN LEGEND (Chapter book.)
McDermott, Gerald	• ARROW TO THE SUN: A PUEBLO INDIAN TALE
Osborne, Mary Pope	• AMERICAN TALL TALES
Paul, Frances Lackey	• KAHTAHAH: A TLINGIT GIRL (Chapter book.)
Philip, Neil, ed.	• STOCKINGS OF BUTTERMILK: AMERICAN FOLKTALES
Rappaport, Doreen	• WE ARE THE MANY: A PICTURE BOOK OF AMERICAN INDIANS (Exciting stories from real biographies)
Robbins, Ken	• THUNDER ON THE PLAINS: THE STORY OF THE AMERICAN BUFFALO
Rodanas, Kristina	• DRAGONFLY'S TALE
Sawyer, Ruth	• JOURNEY CAKE, HO!
Schwartz, Alvin	• WHOPPERS: TALL TALES AND OTHER LIES COLLECTED FROM AMERICAN FOLKLORE
Seeger, Pete	• ABIYOYO
Shannon, David	• HOW GEORGIE RADBOURN SAVED BASEBALL
Smith, Cynthia Leitich	• JINGLE DANCER (Nice Native American and other multicultural reading suggestions at the author's Web site, www.cynthialeitichsmith.com.) • INDIAN SHOES (Short chapter book.)
Spradlin, Michael P.	• THE LEGEND OF BLUE JACKET
Steptoe, John	• THE STORY OF JUMPING MOUSE
Stroud, Virginia	• DOESN'T FALL OFF HIS HORSE
Vaughan, Marcia	• NIGHT DANCER

Pete Seeger's Storysong
ABIYOYO
illustrations by Michael Hays

GETTING TO KNOW YOU

Another way to explore the world is through celebrations of faith and culture.

• Ramadan, a holy Muslim month, may fall anywhere between November and February, depending on the ninth moon of the lunar calendar. It culminates with *Eid ul Fitr*, the "Celebration of Charity." To find out more, read RAMADAN by Suhaib Hamid Ghazi with your child.

• *Diwali* is primarily celebrated in the Eastern Indian community, marking the beginning of the Hindu New Year, falling around October or November every year. To find out more, read HERE COMES DIWALI: THE FESTIVAL OF LIGHTS by Meenal Pandya.

• *Día de los Muertos,* or Day of the Dead, is a Mexican celebration that honors ancestors each November 1st and 2nd. To find out more, read DAY OF THE DEAD by Tony Johnston.

• Chinese New Year is celebrated on the new moon nearest to February 5th. To find out more, read HAPPY NEW YEAR! KUNG-HSI FA-TS'AI! by Demi.

Other international holidays and holy days can be found at the Encyclopedia of Days Web site, www.shag town.com/days. Buddhism suggests that kindness is the greatest wisdom, Christianity advises us to love thy neighbor, and the Jewish faith reminds us that in the beginning of it all, there is the word. Tie belief systems together for your child through books. Broad theological themes foster a worldly knowledge and tolerance that complements *all* faiths.

Stack, Peggy Fletcher	A WORLD OF FAITH
Osborne, Mary Pope	ONE WORLD, MANY RELIGIONS: THE WAYS WE WORSHIP
Ward, Hiley H.	MY FRIENDS' BELIEFS

Van Laan, Nancy	SHINGEBISS: AN OJIBWE LEGEND
	RAINBOW CROW: A LENAPE TALE
Vaughn, Marcia	NIGHT DANCER: MYTHICAL PIPER OF THE NATIVE AMERICAN SOUTHWEST
Wargin, Kathy-jo	THE LEGEND OF SLEEPING BEAR
Wisniewski, David	THE WAVE OF THE SEA-WOLF
Wood, Audrey	THE BUNYANS

Qué Bueno! The Spanish-Speaking World of Stories

These books are all in English, or bilingual and accessible to English speakers. *Para libros en español* or for more bilingual books, check out www.littlechiles.com and www.bilingualbooks.com. Many popular and award-winning books that are written in English are also available in Spanish translations. Studies suggest that learning to read well in a native language helps children learn to read in a second language, so don't be shy, *lee en la lengua que te gusta!*

Aardema, Verna	• Borreguita and the Coyote
Ada, Alma Flor	• I Love Saturdays y domingos
Anaya, Rudolfo	• My Land Sings
Andrews-Goebel, Nancy	• The Pot That Juan Built
Castañeda, Omar S.	• Abuela's Weave
Delacre, Lulu	• Salsa Stories (Short chapter book.)
Dorros, Arthur	• Abuela
	• Isla
Ehlert, Lois	• Moon Rope
Elya, Susan Middleton	• Eight Animals on the Town
Fine, Edith Hope	• Under the Lemon Moon
Gerson, Mary-Joan	• Fiesta Femenina: Celebrating Women in Mexican Folktale
Hayes, Joe	• Juan Verdades: The Man Who Couldn't Tell a Lie
	• A Spoon for Every Bite
Jaffe, Nina	• Sing, Little Sack: ¡Canta Saquito!
Johnston, Tony	• The Iguana Brothers
	• The Tale of Rabbit and Coyote
	• The Ancestors Are Singing
Lattimore, Deborah Nourse	• Frida Maria
Leiner, Katherine	• Mama Does the Mambo
Levy, Janice	• The Spirit of Tío Fernando
Lewis, Thomas P.	• Hill of Fire
Montes, Marisa	• Juan Bobo Goes to Work
Mora, Pat	• A Birthday Basket for Tía
Moretón, Daniel	• La Cucaracha Martina
Rohmer, Harriet	• Uncle Nacho's Hat
Ryan, Pam Muñoz	• Mice and Beans
Soto, Gary	• Too Many Tamales
	• Chato's Kitchen
Velasquez, Eric	• Grandma's Records
Wisniewski, David	• Rain Player

Dear Madame Esmé,

I'm a volunteer in a position to help kids from disadvantaged socioeconomic backgrounds. I would like these children to recognize themselves in literature, to see themselves portrayed in a positive and successful light. Any book ideas?

Dear Gentle Reader,

These books may help children turn difficult circumstances to their advantage. In SOMETHING BEAUTIFUL by Sharon Dennis Wyeth, a girl in a poor neighborhood looks through her window and sees homelessness, graffiti, danger, and decay. One day at school, her teacher spells out the word "beautiful," or "something that when you have it, your heart is happy." Inspired, the girl goes on a treasure hunt to find what is beautiful in her neighborhood. She finds plenty, and best of all, she finds the ability within herself to make a difference. There is plenty that is beautiful in this book as well: the realistic watercolors by Chris K. Soentpiet, the author's note at the end, and the empowering message that there is hope for urban America.

There is precious little available for Spanish-speaking migrant children to relate to in American children's literature, but BREAKING THROUGH fits that niche. A continuation of Francisco Jiménez's memoirs through middle school and high school, this sequel to THE CIRCUIT: STORIES FROM THE LIFE OF A MIGRANT CHILD stands solidly on its own. Jiménez's voice has an unusual dignity as he candidly reveals his own innocence and growing ambition in the face of the American Dream. In Jiménez's world, school is not a right but a privilege, and in a straightforward, matter-of-fact manner, he describes a heroic effort working as a teenager both in the fields and cleaning offices to help his family while trying to succeed at school. Jiménez's frustrated relationship with his unhappy father is surprisingly tender. Jiménez is a model for all children who have obstacles to overcome, and a great champion of mutual respect between races and classes. I can't imagine a better book to share with someone who sees high school on the horizon, or to give as a gift to English-as-a-second-language teachers. Viva Jiménez!

NEED A TOUR GUIDE?

Author Eric A. Kimmel is a one-man-trip-around-the-world! While his great strengths are his retellings of African Anansi trickster tales and his Ukrainian and Jewish folktales (he is the author of the classic HERSHEL AND THE HANUKKAH GOBLINS, which you don't have to be Jewish to love), all of his books have the mark of his storytelling background: just the right language and pacing for read-aloud. Besides an eclectic mix of settings, his work has been marked by diversity in the ethnicity of his illustrators. Don't hesitate to present his picture books to intermediate children; they will fall right in line to join his world clique.

THE ADVENTURES OF HERSHEL OF OSTROPOL (Ukraine.)

BEARHEAD: A RUSSIAN FOLKTALE

BERNAL AND FLORINDA: A SPANISH TALE

THE BIRDS' GIFT: A UKRAINIAN EASTER STORY

BOOTS AND HIS BROTHERS: A NORWEGIAN TALE

THE CASTLE OF CATS: A STORY FROM UKRAINE

A CLOAK FOR THE MOON (Israel.)

COUNT SILVERNOSE: A STORY FROM ITALY

EASY WORK! AN OLD TALE (America.)

GERSHON'S MONSTER: A STORY FOR THE JEWISH NEW YEAR

THE GREATEST OF ALL: A JAPANESE FOLKTALE

I-KNOW-NOT-WHAT, I-KNOW-NOT-WHERE: A RUSSIAN TALE

ONE EYE, TWO EYES, THREE EYES: A HUTZUL TALE (Ukraine.)

THE ROOSTER'S ANTLERS: A STORY OF THE CHINESE ZODIAC

SQUASH IT: A TRUE AND RIDICULOUS TALE (Spain.)

SWORD OF THE SAMURAI: ADVENTURE STORIES FROM JAPAN

TEN SUNS: A CHINESE LEGEND

THE THREE PRINCES: A TALE FROM THE MIDDLE EAST

THREE SACKS OF TRUTH: A STORY FROM FRANCE

THREE SAMURAI CATS (Japan.)

THE TWO MOUNTAINS: AN AZTEC LEGEND

THE WITCH'S FACE: A MEXICAN TALE

. . . Also, see December Holidays (p. 388) and Anansi: Master Trickster (p. 264).

Africa: The Storytelling Continent

Aardema, Verna	• BIMWILI AND THE ZIMWI
	• BRINGING THE RAIN TO KAPITI PLAIN
	• MISOSO: ONCE UPON A TIME TALES FROM AFRICA
	• WHAT'S SO FUNNY, KETU?
	• WHY MOSQUITOS BUZZ IN PEOPLE'S EARS
	(Aardema is the master of the African story.)
Alexander, Lloyd	• THE FORTUNE-TELLERS
Burns, Khephra	• MANSA MUSA: THE LION OF MALI
Daly, Niki	• THE MAGIC GOURD
	• JAMELA'S DRESS
	• WHAT'S COOKING, JAMELA?
Dayrell, Elphinstone	• WHY THE SUN AND THE MOON LIVE IN THE SKY
Diakité, Baba Wagué	• THE HUNTERMAN AND THE CROCODILE

Catherine Stock
Gugu's House

Diouf, Sylviane	• BINTOU'S BRAIDS
Fairman, Tony	• BURY MY BONES BUT KEEP MY WORDS: AFRICAN TALES FOR RETELLING
Feelings, Muriel	• JAMBO MEANS HELLO: SWAHILI ALPHABET BOOK • MOJA MEANS ONE: A SWAHILI COUNTING BOOK
Gershator, Phillis	• ZZZNG! ZZZNG! ZZZNG! A YORUBA TALE
Gerson, Mary-Joan	• WHY THE SKY IS FAR AWAY
Grifalconi, Ann	• DARKNESS AND THE BUTTERFLY • THE VILLAGE OF ROUND AND SQUARE HOUSES
Haley, Gail E.	• A STORY, A STORY
Hamilton, Virginia	• THE GIRL WHO SPUN GOLD
Ichikawa, Satomi	• THE FIRST BEAR IN AFRICA!
Kimmel, Eric A.	• ANANSI AND THE TALKING MELON (For more marvelous Anansi stories, see Anansi: Master Trickster, p. 264)
London, Jonathan	• WHAT THE ANIMALS WERE WAITING FOR
McDermott, Gerald	• ZOMO THE RABBIT: A TRICKSTER TALE FROM WEST AFRICA
McDonough, Yona Zeldis	• PEACEFUL PROTEST: THE LIFE OF NELSON MANDELA
Mollel, Tololwa M.	• RHINOS FOR LUNCH AND ELEPHANTS FOR SUPPER! A MAASAI TALE • THE ORPHAN BOY • MY ROWS AND PILES OF COINS
Musgrove, Margaret	• THE SPIDER WEAVER: A LEGEND OF KENTE CLOTH
Paye, Won-Ldy, and Margaret H. Lippert	• HEAD, BODY, LEGS: A STORY FROM LIBERIA
Shepard, Aaron	• MASTER MAN: A TALL TALE OF NIGERIA
Stock, Catherine	• GUGU'S HOUSE
Stuve-Bodeen, Stephanie	• ELIZABETI'S DOLL (Several sweet books about Elizabeti are available.)
Tchana, Katrin	• SENSE PASS KING: A STORY FROM CAMEROON
Unobagha, Uzo	• OFF TO THE SWEET SHORES OF AFRICA AND OTHER TALKING DRUM RHYMES

Tropical Reading Paradise

Agard, John, and Grace Nichols, eds.	• UNDER THE MOON AND OVER THE SEA: A COLLECTION OF CARIBBEAN POEMS
Bontemps, Arna, and Langston Hughes	• POPO AND FIFINA: CHILDREN OF HAITI

❀❀ *Potato Pick:*

WHAT'S COOKING, JAMELA?
by Niki Daly

"When our chicken is nice and fat, then it will be Christmas."

Between now and then, Jamela becomes extremely attached to the chicken, whom she has fittingly named "Christmas," while Jamela's grandmother increasingly looks forward to a fine holiday dinner. When Mrs. Zibi, the butcher, finally pays a house call, wearing a comical scowl and rubbing hands "that looked ready for business," Jamela abducts her pet, only to lose her in a crowd. The story climaxes with a fabulously wild scene in a ladies' hair salon and resolves in an alternative treat for Grandma. Set in a South African township, this story is energetic, funny, and masterful. Niki Daly's treatment of figures is expressive and alive. Marvel at the double-page spread of an African nativity play, with Joseph wearing a Basuto hat and wise men sporting flamboyant Madiba shirts, while "Away in a Manger" is played on marimba! A glossary is included in the back, but the text flows as naturally as water to tell a universal story of mischief and affection. I'm afraid I can't write any more about it; I must go stare at this book with my family for the sixth time. (6 and up)

GONG XI FA CAI (GUNG-HAY-FAT-CHOI)

My son and I can't wait for Chinese New Year to enjoy this unusual baked rice cake that goes along with Ying Chang Compestine's lively story about generosity, THE RUNAWAY RICE CAKE. We leave out the raisins and nuts and eat it plain, as little children sometimes like their food that way.

BAKED NÍAN-GĀO

Dry ingredients

1 pound glutinous rice flour
(also called sweet rice flour)
1¼ cups sugar
1 tablespoon baking powder
½ cup raisins
½ cup nuts

Wet ingredients

3 eggs
¾ cup canola or vegetable oil
1½ cups water

Preheat oven to 375°. Combine all the dry ingredients in a large bowl. Mix thoroughly. In a separate bowl, beat the eggs. Add other wet ingredients to the eggs and stir. Pour the wet ingredients into the dry ingredients and mix well. Pour the batter into a greased 9-inch round pan. Bake for 40 minutes; a knife poked into the center will come out clean when it is done.

For further ideas for celebrating Chinese New Year and many other Chinese events, be sure to check out MOONBEAMS, DUMPLINGS, AND DRAGON BOATS: A TREASURY OF CHINESE HOLIDAY TALES, ACTIVITIES, AND RECIPES by Nina Simonds, Leslie Swartz, and the Children's Museum, Boston. This book is lavishly illustrated by Meilo So and makes an exquisite gift.

Burgie, Irving	• CARIBBEAN CARNIVAL: SONGS OF THE WEST INDIES
Campoy, F. Isabel	• ROSA RAPOSA (Rainforest.)
DeSpain, Pleasant	• THE DANCING TURTLE: A FOLKTALE FROM BRAZIL
Dobrin, Arnold	• JOSEPHINE'S 'MAGINATION (Haiti.)
Geraghty, Paul	• STOP THAT NOISE! (Rainforest.)
Gottlieb, Dale	• WHERE JAMAICA GO?
Gunning, Monica	• NOT A COPPER PENNY IN ME HOUSE: POEMS FROM THE CARIBBEAN
Lessac, Frané	• MY LITTLE ISLAND (Caribbean.)
Martin, Rafe	• THE SHARK GOD (Hawaii.)
Olaleye, Isaac	• BITTER BANANAS (Rainforest.)
Pomerantz, Charlotte	• THE CHALK DOLL (Jamaica.)
Raouf, Mama	• THE BAREFOOT BOOK OF TROPICAL TALES
Sierra, Judy	• THE DANCING PIG (Bali.)
Williams, Karen Lynn	• PAINTED DREAMS (Haiti.)

A Great Wall of Asian Books

CHINA . . .

Bateson-Hill, Margaret	• LAO LAO OF DRAGON MOUNTAIN
Brett, Jan	• DAISY COMES HOME
Compestine, Ying Chang	• THE RUNAWAY RICE CAKE • THE STORY OF CHOPSTICKS • THE STORY OF NOODLES
Demi	• THE EMPTY POT
	• LIANG AND THE MAGIC PAINTBRUSH (Speaking of a "magic paintbrush," Demi, who writes and illustrates marvelous books that take place throughout all of Asia, has been known to paint with a mouse's whisker!)
Freedman, Russell	• CONFUCIUS: THE GOLDEN RULE (Great intermediate-level biography.)

Ginsburg, Mirra	• THE CHINESE MIRROR
Heyer, Marilee	• THE WEAVING OF A DREAM: A CHINESE FOLKTALE
Hong, Lily Toy	• TWO OF EVERYTHING
McCully, Emily Arnold	• BEAUTIFUL WARRIOR: THE LEGEND OF THE NUN'S KUNG FU
Mak, Kam	• MY CHINATOWN: ONE YEAR IN POEMS
Mosel, Arlene	• THE FUNNY LITTLE WOMAN
	• TIKKI TIKKI TEMBO
Provensen, Alice	• THE MASTER SWORDSMAN AND THE MAGIC DOORWAY
Rappaport, Doreen	• THE LONG-HAIRED GIRL
Schaefer, Carole Lexa	• THE SQUIGGLE
Yolen, Jane	• THE EMPEROR AND THE KITE

INDIA . . .

Atkins, Jeannine	• AANI AND THE TREE HUGGERS
Bannerman, Helen	• THE STORY OF LITTLE BABAJI
Brown, Marcia	• ONCE A MOUSE
Demi	• ONE GRAIN OF RICE
Galdone, Paul	• THE MONKEY AND THE CROCODILE: A JATAKA TALE FROM INDIA
Jaffrey, Madhur	• SEASONS OF SPLENDOUR: TALES, MYTHS, AND LEGENDS OF INDIA
Martin, Rafe	• THE BRAVE LITTLE PARROT
Nagda, Ann Whitehead	• SNAKE CHARMER
Shepard, Aaron	• SAVITRI : A TALE OF ANCIENT INDIA

JAPAN . . .

Davol, Marguerite W.	• THE PAPER DRAGON (Exceptional fold-out illustrations by Robert Sabuda.)
Esterl, Arnica	• OKINO AND THE WHALES
Kajikawa, Kimiko	• YOSHI'S FEAST
Kalman, Maira	• SAYONARA, MRS. KACKLEMAN
Mayer, Mercer	• SHIBUMI AND THE KITEMAKER
Morimoto, Junko	• THE TWO BULLIES
Paterson, Katherine	• THE TALE OF THE MANDARIN DUCKS
Sierra, Judy	• TASTY BABY BELLY BUTTONS
Snyder, Dianne	• THE BOY OF THE THREE-YEAR NAP
Takabayashi, Mari	• I LIVE IN TOKYO

❀ *Potato Pick:*

TASTY BABY BELLY BUTTONS
by Judy Sierra, illustrated by Meilo So

Moms and Dads all know how delicious baby belly buttons are. Unfortunately, the terrible oni have also discovered this scrumptious delicacy and steal all the babies away! Uriko-hime, or "melon princess," is born inside a watermelon (notice her pink-and-black kimono!) and grows up to rescue the toddlers in trouble. Featuring a strong female lead, this Japanese folktale-adventure is paced just right for a lively storytime with lots of good chanting ("Belly buttons/Belly buttons/Tasty Baby Belly Buttons!"). Serve butterscotch candies or some other small round treat at the end and call them belly buttons! Or, crack open a watermelon and see what's inside (probably seeds, but you never know). (5 and up)

PARISIAN PIG-OUT

When I was a teenager, I got a D– in French class, but I did manage to come away with a fake accent and a recipe for crepes that is so *magnifique,* a stomachache is the only thing that will stop me from eating them. I'll translate for you, so you can make them while your children read stories from France to you.

Ingredients:

1 cup flour
3 tablespoons white sugar
3 eggs
2 cups milk
Pinch of salt
1 tablespoon oil
Butter
Sugar, jam, or chocolate spread for decorating

In a big bowl, mix a cup of flour, three tablespoons of white sugar, and a pinch of salt. In a small bowl, beat three eggs. Add two cups of milk and mix. Put the contents of the small bowl in the big bowl, and mix some more. Add one tablespoon of oil, and give it one last good stir. Let it sit in the fridge two hours, or overnight (it will be ready for breakfast, or a midnight snack if you can't wait).

When the batter has set, heat up a wide frying pan nice and hot, and put as much butter in that hot pan as you imagine a French person would. Pour a couple tablespoons of the batter in the hot buttered pan, and move the pan around so as to cover it thinly and completely, like one big pancake. It should be so thin that you don't need to turn it; it will cook through in about a minute or less. The first one never turns out, but don't worry, the second one will be fine. Flip it on a plate, and get started on the next one. Hurry, hurry, everyone's hungry, and they go so fast! They are good drenched in white sugar, raspberry jam, or better yet, Nutella chocolate hazelnut spread drizzled all over.

ASIA FOR EVERYONE!
An invaluable resource is the Asia for Kids catalog, www.asiaforkids.com, 1-800-888-9681. Besides offering the finest children's trade literature, you'll find related music, books on tape, crafts, cookbooks, multicultural dolls, storytelling aids, and an especially nice selection for parents with adopted children.

Wells, Ruth	• A TO ZEN: A BOOK OF JAPANESE CULTURE
AND BEYOND . . .	
Aruego, Jose, and Ariane Dewey	• ROCKABYE CROCODILE: A FOLKTALE FROM THE PHILIPPINES
Brown, Don	• FAR BEYOND THE GARDEN GATE: ALEXANDRA DAVID-NEEL'S JOURNEY TO LHASA (Tibet.)
Chin-Lee, Cynthia	• A IS FOR ASIA (General Asia.)
Garland, Sherry	• CHILDREN OF THE DRAGON: SELECTED TALES FROM VIETNAM
Gerstein, Mordicai	• THE MOUNTAINS OF TIBET
Ho, Minfong	• HUSH! A THAI LULLABY
Xiong, Blia	• NINE-IN-ONE, GRR! GRR! (Laos.)
Yep, Laurence	• THE KHAN'S DAUGHTER: A MONGOLIAN FOLKTALE

Western Europe

Aliki	• THREE GOLD PIECES (Greece.)
Baker, Leslie	• PARIS CAT (France.)
Bemelmans, Ludwig	• MADELINE SERIES (France.)
Brett, Jan	• THE TROUBLE WITH TROLLS (Scandinavia.)
dePaola, Tomie	• STREGA NONA (Italy.)
Duncan, Olivia	• THE TALE OF HILDA LOUISE (France.)
Fern, Eugene	• PEPITO'S STORY (Spain.)
Fleming, Candace	• GABRIELLA'S SONG (Italy.)
Forest, Heather	• THE WOMAN WHO FLUMMOXED THE FAIRIES (Scotland.)
Hughes, Shirley	• THE BIG ALFIE AND ANNIE ROSE STORYBOOK (England.)
Kirby, David K., and Allen Woodmen	• THE COWS ARE GOING TO PARIS
Lamorisse, A.	• THE RED BALLOON (France.)
Leaf, Munro	• THE STORY OF FERDINAND (Spain.)
Locker, Thomas	• THE BOY WHO HELD BACK THE SEA (Holland.)
Macaulay, David	• ANGELO (Italy.)
McLaren, Chesley	• ZAT CAT! (France.)
Perrault, Charles	• PUSS IN BOOTS (France.)
Potter, Giselle	• THE YEAR I DIDN'T GO TO SCHOOL (Italy.)
Radunsky, Vladimir	• A SIMPLE STORY OF A BOY NAMED MANNEKEN PIS WHO PEED ON A WAR (Belgium.)
Shepard, Aaron	• THE PRINCESS MOUSE (Finland.)
Sierra, Judy	• THE BEAUTIFUL BUTTERFLY (Spain.)
Spyri, Johanna	• HEIDI (Switzerland; chapter book.)
Talbott, Hudson	• O'SULLIVAN STEW (Ireland.)
Talley, Carol	• PAPA PICCÓLO (Italy.)
Tarbescu, Edith	• THE BOY WHO STUCK OUT HIS TONGUE (Hungary.)
Titus, Eve	• The Anatole series (France.)
Vittorini, Domenico	• THE THREAD OF LIFE: TWELVE OLD ITALIAN TALES
Woelfle, Gretchen	• KATJE THE WINDMILL CAT (Holland.)

. . . See the fairy tales in Inside the Gingerbread House, p. 249, for more stories from Western Europe.

✿ *Potato Pick:*
THE DREAM STEALER
by Gregory Maguire, illustrated by Diana Bryan

The Blood Prince stalks the forests of Russia, frightening gentlefolk out of traveling to their vacation homes, which means empty supper bowls for the unfortunate villagers of Miersk who sell food to train passengers. Is the bloodthirsty wolf who preys on both bodies and souls a legend, or does he really exist? A young boy and girl take it upon themselves to seek out the answer from the fearsome witch Baba Yaga and save their modest town. Gregory Maguire weaves together many different Russian folktales to make an enchanting tapestry of both horror and beauty, and one of the most memorable reads of a childhood. (9 and up)

❀ *Potato Pick:*

THE GIRL WHO LOST HER SMILE

by Karim Alrawi, illustrated by Stefan Czernecki

When Jehan wakes up one morning to find she has lost her beautiful smile, the people of Baghdad join forces to see that she gets it back, inviting all the greatest artists in the world to come and paint pictures for her. From Italy to China, Tibet to Egypt, no one can succeed until a young man from Persia subtly shows Jehan that helping others and working hard is the way to feel better. This simply told tale, accented by bold, angular illustrations, was inspired by a story from a collection called THE MATHNAWI by the Turkish poet and mystic Jalal al-Din Rumi (who is also the founder of the Order of the Whirling Dervish). An especially exciting book since we have so little available in children's literature that focuses on the Middle East, THE GIRL WHO LOST HER SMILE also stands on its own as a quality picture book. (5 and up)

Russia, Ukraine, and Eastern Europe

Bliss, Corinne Demas	• THE LITTLEST MATRYOSHKA
Dillon, Jana	• SASHA'S MATRIOSHKA DOLLS
Ginsburg, Mirra	• CLAY BOY
Heins, Ethel	• THE CAT AND THE COOK AND OTHER FABLES OF KRYLOV
Mayer, Marianna	• BABA YAGA AND VASILISA THE BRAVE
Mayhew, James	• THE KINGFISHER BOOK OF TALES FROM RUSSIA
Ogburn, Jacqueline K.	• THE MAGIC NESTING DOLL
Oram, Hiawyn	• BABA YAGA AND THE WISE DOLL
Ransome, Arthur	• THE FOOL OF THE WORLD AND THE FLYING SHIP
Sanderson, Ruth	• THE GOLDEN MARE, THE FIREBIRD, AND THE MAGIC RING (Look for other resplendent retellings of THE FIREBIRD from Gennady Spirin, Jane Yolen, and Ruth Sanderson.)
Shepard, Aaron	• THE SEA KING'S DAUGHTER: A RUSSIAN LEGEND
Small, Ernest	• BABA YAGA
Winthrop, Elizabeth	• THE LITTLE HUMPBACKED HORSE

The Middle East

Alexander, Sue	• BEHOLD THE TREES (Israel.)
Heide, Florence Parry, and Judith Heide Gilliland	• THE DAY OF AHMED'S SECRET (Egypt.) • THE HOUSE OF WISDOM (Iraq.)
Kherdian, David	• THE GOLDEN BRACELET (Armenia.) • A WEAVE OF WORDS (Armenia.)
Lewin, Betsy	• WHAT'S THE MATTER, HABIBI?
McKay Jr., Lawrence	• CARAVAN (Afghanistan.)
Nye, Naomi Shihab	• SITTI'S SECRETS (Palestine.) • THE SPACE BETWEEN OUR FOOTSTEPS: POEMS AND PAINTINGS FROM THE MIDDLE EAST (Mature readers.)
Rumford, James	• TRAVELING MAN: THE JOURNEY OF IBN BATTUTA, 1325–1354
Shah, Indries	• THE BOY WITHOUT A NAME
Shepard, Aaron	• FORTY FORTUNES (Iran.)

Down Under

Bonnett-Rampersaud, Louise	• POLLY HOPPER'S POUCH
Czernecki, Stefan, and Timothy Rhodes	• THE SINGING SNAKE
Fox, Mem	• KOALA LOU • POSSUM MAGIC
Germein, Katrina	• BIG RAIN COMING
Lattimore, Deborah Nourse	• PUNGA THE GODDESS OF UGLY
Lester, Alison	• ERNIE DANCES TO THE DIDGERIDOO
Morpurgo, Michael	• WOMBAT GOES WALKABOUT
Payne, Emmy	• KATY NO-POCKET
Scarry, Patricia	• HOP, LITTLE KANGAROO!
Trinca, Rod	• ONE WOOLLY WOMBAT
Vaughan, Marcia K.	• WOMBAT STEW
Viorst, Judith	• ALEXANDER AND THE TERRIBLE, HORRIBLE, NO GOOD, VERY BAD DAY (Not set in Australia, but features a boy who really wants to go there!)

Chilly Willy: Stories from Antarctica and Other Cool Places

Ashman, Linda	• SAILING OFF TO SLEEP
Atwater, Richard and Florence	• MR. POPPER'S PENGUINS (Chapter book.)
Blake, Robert J.	• AKIAK
Carlstrom, Nancy White	• NORTHERN LULLABY
Dupre, Kelly	• THE RAVEN'S GIFT (Greenland.)
George, Jean Craighead	• SNOW BEAR
Joosse, Barbara M.	• MAMA, DO YOU LOVE ME?
Lester, Helen	• TACKY, THE PENGUIN (There's a whole series.)
Normandin, Christine, ed.	• ECHOES OF THE ELDERS: THE STORIES AND PAINTINGS OF CHIEF LELOOSKA (Mature readers.)
Rey, Margret and H. A.	• WHITEBACK THE PENGUIN SEES THE WORLD
Sierra, Judy	• ANTARCTIC ANTICS: A BOOK OF PENGUIN POEMS
Sloat, Terri	• THERE WAS AN OLD LADY WHO SWALLOWED A TROUT
Stafford, Liliana	• THE SNOW BEAR
Webb, Sophie	• MY SEASON WITH PENGUINS: AN ANTARCTIC JOURNAL
Wood, Audrey	• LITTLE PENGUIN'S TALE
Wood, Ted	• IDITAROD DREAM

❀ *Potato Pick:*

ERNIE DANCES TO THE DIDGERIDOO
by Alison Lester

A great tale about Australia that doesn't feature some cuddly koala or wheedling wombat, this book celebrates the real continent and the real children who live there. The author visited the community of Gunbalanya twice to create this book, and it shows in its detail and authenticity. In the story, Ernie travels to live in an Aboriginal community for a year while his parents work in a hospital, but he promises to write his classmates a letter for each of the six seasons there. Lucky readers are treated to double-page cartoon spreads describing the fun activities that take place throughout the year. The text is simple yet manages to instill a sense of newness and discovery from a child's perspective. The helpful pronunciation guide and glossary give the book special educational value. Whether or not your child—or you— can correctly pronounce "Kurnumeleng!" don't miss this trip in a book! (7 and up)

ADDRESS BOOK

Using picture books and primary-school-age nonfiction, children will be right at home imagining all the places people live. Follow up by encouraging children to illustrate and write about their dream homes, or to build models using cardboard boxes or clay. Or, they may enjoy having their own address books and collecting information from friends. To add more exotic addresses, team up with pen pals (see And Speaking of Snail Mail, p. 321).

Anholt, Catherine and Laurence	• HARRY'S HOME
Bial, Raymond	• AMISH HOME
	• CAJUN HOME
	• FRONTIER HOME
Bode, Achim, Michael Frey, and Andreas Linke	• WHERE WE LIVE
Brutschy, Jennifer	• JUST ONE MORE STORY
Buchanan, Ken	• THIS HOUSE IS MADE OF MUD
Delafosse, Claude, and Gallimard Jeunesse	• HOUSES (First Discovery Books)
Feder, Paula Kurzband	• WHERE DOES THE TEACHER LIVE?

Grifalconi, Ann	• THE VILLAGE OF ROUND AND SQUARE HOUSES
Hoberman, Mary Ann	• A HOUSE IS A HOUSE FOR ME
Kalman, Bobbie	• HOMES AROUND THE WORLD
McDonald, Megan	• MY HOUSE HAS STARS
Pinkwater, Daniel Manus	• THE BIG ORANGE SPLOT
Skorpen, Liesel Moak	• WE WERE TIRED OF LIVING IN A HOUSE
Stock, Catherine	• GUGU'S HOUSE

. . . These are all about human dwellings, but for an animal open house (and a chance to integrate science into social studies), visit **A HOUSE FOR HERMIT CRAB** by Eric Carle, **ANIMAL HOMES** by Tammy Everts and Bobbie Kalman, and the **Animal Architects** series by W. Wright Robinson:

- HOW BIRDS BUILD THEIR AMAZING HOMES
- HOW INSECTS BUILD THEIR AMAZING HOMES
- HOW MAMMALS BUILD THEIR AMAZING HOMES
- HOW SHELLMAKERS BUILD THEIR AMAZING HOMES
- HOW SPIDERS AND OTHER SILKMAKERS BUILD THEIR AMAZING HOMES

Festivals, carnivals, and feast days from around the world
BARNABAS AND ANABEL KINDERSLEY

International

Alrawi, Karim	• THE GIRL WHO LOST HER SMILE
Hergé	• The Tintin series
Kindersley, Barnabas and Anabel	• CELEBRATIONS! CHILDREN JUST LIKE ME
Lewis, J. Patrick	• A WORLD OF WONDERS: GEOGRAPHIC TRAVELS IN VERSE AND RHYME
Lobel, Anita	• AWAY FROM HOME
Mayo, Margaret	• MAGICAL TALES FROM MANY LANDS
Priceman, Marjorie	• HOW TO MAKE AN APPLE PIE AND SEE THE WORLD

Scullard, Sue	• THE GREAT ROUND-THE-WORLD BALLOON RACE (Out of print, but whenever I read it aloud, it's met with cheers from the children. Worth the hunt!)
Sierra, Judy	• NURSERY TALES AROUND THE WORLD
Singer, Marilyn	• NINE O' CLOCK LULLABY
Smith, David J.	• IF THE WORLD WERE A VILLAGE
Walker, Barbara, K., comp.	• LAUGHING TOGETHER: GIGGLES AND GRINS FROM AROUND THE GLOBE
Weiss, Nicki	• THE WORLD TURNS ROUND AND ROUND

. . . Not ready to go home quite yet? There are many more globe-trotting tales in April Fools, Tricksters, and Simpletons, p. 262.

Survival Stories

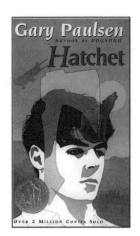

I read **HATCHET** by Gary Paulsen aloud to a group of about thirty eighth-graders. When we finished, I gave the students the option of writing their own survival stories. Afterward, I read through paragraph after paragraph of shipwrecks, plane crashes, desert wanderings . . . but one girl chose the realistic route:

> *Everyone has a survival story. Mine is living without my parents. They are alive and we live in the same house, but they are very busy. They work late so I am asleep when they come home. They don't wake up with me in the morning. And they are leaving for work when I come home from school. I have almost raised myself and I survived. I also think I did a good job of raising myself.*

She did, indeed. I kept this paragraph and I look at it from time to time, her lead sentence ringing true as a bell: *Everyone* has a survival story, and as was the case with this girl, it can be hard to recognize survivors at first glance. What difficult terrain are children navigating? These books acknowledge the spoken and unspoken struggles of adolescence and serve as emotional support—especially for teens and 'tweens—by modeling perseverance, self-reliance, and critical thinking. One of the strengths of a great survival story is graphic—even gory—detail, another fact that makes the genre more suited to mature readers. The characters themselves are usually older and their life experiences are often a crucial part of their survival. It can be empowering to read tales in which people prove bigger and better than anything that comes their way.

WHERE DID THAT COME FROM?

Remember being in fourth or fifth grade, trying to reword information about climate, geography, and the economy for reports, even though you could barely understand what you were reading? I wish I had the **Look What Came From** series, published by Franklin Watts back then! The double-page spreads featuring child-friendly headers, such as fashion, music, sports, and holidays, help youngsters appreciate that the things they encounter every day in America actually came from other countries. The last page of each book in the series debunks a misconception—something that the reader may have thought came from one place but in fact originated somewhere else. Your child may still need an encyclopedia for population facts and economic statistics, but the recipes, pronunciation guide, and relevant Web sites in each book will definitely go far to give your child a global perspective. Books in the series:

LOOK WHAT CAME FROM . . .	. . . IRELAND
. . . AFRICA	. . . ITALY
. . . AUSTRALIA	. . . JAPAN
. . . AUSTRIA	. . . MEXICO
. . . CHINA	. . . THE NETHERLANDS
. . . EGYPT	. . . RUSSIA
. . . ENGLAND	. . . SPAIN
. . . FRANCE	. . . SWITZERLAND
. . . GERMANY	. . . THE UNITED STATES
. . . GREECE	
. . . INDIA	

Besides all that, the stories are just plain great adventure. Is it because the characters are at the mercy of nature, because the exploits often have a basis in real history, or because the rugged and well-researched details in these narratives bring the settings to life? It would seem that such gripping tales would make exciting read-alouds, and I know that many classroom teachers love their cliff-hanging quality. When I am faced with the choice of reading a survival story aloud or the child not reading the story at all, I have done it. When I have my druthers, though, I prefer children to read these books on their own when they are entering adolescence. Why? First, I find them hard to read aloud. Survival stories are often told in first-person narratives or contain long descriptive passages, both of which can be difficult to lumber through out loud. The detail that characterizes great survival stories can also be rather intimate and psychological, revealing the unspoken, inner thoughts and conflicts of the characters, and some children seem to need personal space to react to such confidences. Also, *because* survival stories are such cliff-hangers, even reluctant readers find themselves flipping pages, achieving a sense of ease and accomplishment, not to mention reading's magical transport. You can read these books out loud, of course, and many do so successfully but I strongly suggest reading the title yourself first to make the determination.

Another workable option with a reluctant intermediate or older reader is to read aloud through all the straightforward set-up that is usually at the beginning of a survival story until the point of no return. You can tell when you are at that point because the child begins to make impatient noises when you stop. At that point, turn the book over to the newly motivated reader.

In the course of a good survival story, both the character and the reader are changed. The reader emerges more equipped to believe, "I can get through this." No one will have any trouble getting through these:

Cole, Brock	• THE GOATS (Mature readers.)
Eckert, Allan W.	• INCIDENT AT HAWK'S HILL
Farmer, Nancy	• A GIRL NAMED DISASTER
George, Jean Craighead	• JULIE OF THE WOLVES
	• MY SIDE OF THE MOUNTAIN
Hautzig, Esther	• THE ENDLESS STEPPE
Holm, Jennifer L.	• BOSTON JANE: AN ADVENTURE
Holman, Felice	• SLAKE'S LIMBO
Martin, Jacqueline Briggs	• THE LAMP, THE ICE, AND THE BOAT CALLED FISH
O'Dell, Scott	• ISLAND OF THE BLUE DOLPHINS
Paulsen, Gary	• HATCHET
Sachar, Louis	• HOLES
Taylor, Theodore	• THE CAY
Ullman, James Ramsey	• BANNER IN THE SKY
Voigt, Cynthia	• HOMECOMING

Water, Water Everywhere: Sea Voyages

Some of the most exciting adventures take place in the middle of the ocean. This motley crew of books for not-so-ancient mariners is sure to float your child's boat (and grown-ups thrill to them, too!). Because these adventures can really run the gamut, I have noted the picture books so readers who are still wet behind the ears can join in hoisting jibs and singing chanties.

Ardizzone, Edward	• The Tim series (Picture books.)
Avi	• THE TRUE CONFESSIONS OF CHARLOTTE DOYLE
Blumberg, Rhoda	• SHIPWRECKED! THE TRUE ADVENTURES OF A JAPANESE BOY
Brown, Margaret Wise	• THE SAILOR DOG (Picture book.)
Buzzeo, Toni	• THE SEA CHEST
Creech, Sharon	• THE WANDERER
Dash, Joan	• THE LONGITUDE PRIZE

✿ *Potato Pick:*

THE *TIM* SERIES

by Edward Ardizzone

I love this series so much, I gave my son the middle name "Edward," after the author/illustrator. I could just as well have named him "Excitement." Ardizzone delivers adventure on the high seas, complete with twists of fate, captains both good and evil, and plenty of close-call rescues. What child could wish for a better group of friends to travel with than Tim and Charlotte, always so resourceful and courageous and kind, and their comically impulsive friend Ginger? From five-year-olds to fifth-graders, I have never met a child who didn't like these stories! So let your child stow away with some of the best children's books of the last century. (5 and up)

Fritz, Jean	• AROUND THE WORLD IN A HUNDRED YEARS: FROM HENRY THE NAVIGATOR TO MAGELLAN
Hesse, Karen	• STOWAWAY
Hopkinson, Deborah	• BIRDIE'S LIGHTHOUSE (Picture book.)
Lawrence, Iain	• THE SMUGGLERS • THE WRECKERS
Masefield, John	• JIM DAVIS: A HIGH-SEA ADVENTURE
Meyer, L. A.	• BLOODY JACK
Mikaelsen, Ben	• RED MIDNIGHT
Montgomery, Hugh	• THE VOYAGE OF THE ARCTIC TERN
Moore, Robin	• THE MAN WITH THE SILVER OAR
Neale, Jonathan	• LOST AT SEA
Rand, Gloria	• SAILING HOME: A STORY OF A CHILDHOOD AT SEA (Picture book.)
Roop, Peter and Connie	• TAKE COMMAND, CAPTAIN FARRAGUT!
Smith, Sherri L.	• LUCY THE GIANT (Mature readers.)
Van Allsburg, Chris	• THE WRETCHED STONE (Picture book.) • THE WRECK OF THE ZEPHYR (Picture book.)

Since sailing is a very old occupation, the literature goes back a ways. If your child shows interest in the nautical theme, there's buried treasure to be found in some classic books. The language can be extremely archaic and challenging, so your enthusiasm and read-aloud support will help your child experience these books in a positive way.

Colum, Padraic	• THE CHILDREN'S HOMER (Also try Rosemary Sutcliff's THE WANDERINGS OF ODYSSEUS: THE STORY OF THE ODYSSEY and BLACK SHIPS BEFORE TROY: THE STORY OF THE ILIAD, and Mary Pope Osborne's series, TALES FROM THE ODYSSEY.)

DR. CAROLINE FELLER BAUER
READING'S GREAT ADVENTURER

Dubbed the "Pied Piper of Books," Caroline Feller Bauer says "basically what I do is run around speaking to librarians, teachers, and parents about how to get children and books together." And this speaker does get around, sharing her book-loving gospel. She has traveled to all of the fifty states and to sixty-five countries including Russia, Saudi Arabia, Indonesia, Iraq, and Togo. I'm sure if there are any literacy initiatives on Mars, she will be the first one in a space suit. And those lucky Martians! While an associate professor at the University of Oregon, she became the first woman to receive the Ersted Award for Distinguished Teaching. In 1986, Bauer was awarded the Dorothy C. McKenzie Award for Distinguished Contribution to the Field of Children's Literature. She writes children's books herself, has produced a children's storytelling program for educational television, and is an active member of the international brotherhood of magicians.

In her *spare* time, Bauer pursues her other interests. One of her main hobbies seems to be winning. She won the woman's slalom and downriver races in Colorado. She won a gold medal in New York at an open-speed skate meet, wins local tennis tournaments, and took first place in the Benihana Chef contest. But when it comes to interests, it's reading that takes the gold. "In a book you can do anything. Reading is a lifetime sport." Bauer leaves no stone unturned when it comes to life, and so she speaks with authority when she says that reading is one of the finest pleasures life has to offer. In this way, she bade a bon voyage to the image of reader as armchair traveler; I can only imagine her sitting in an armchair if it were in a hot-air balloon. In demonstrating that the world is a reader's oyster, Caroline Feller Bauer has proven herself to be the pearl. Visit www.ber.org to see if her seminars are coming to your town.

Defoe, Daniel	• ROBINSON CRUSOE
Stevenson, Robert Louis	• TREASURE ISLAND (I like the editions illustrated by N.C. Wyeth or Robert Ingpen.)
Verne, Jules	• **20,000 LEAGUES UNDER THE SEA** (I like the edition illustrated by Leo and Diane Dillon.)
Kipling, Rudyard	• CAPTAINS COURAGEOUS
Windham, Sophie, ed.	• THE MERMAID AND OTHER SEA POEMS (Classic poetry in a glowing, illustrated picture book!)

THE MERMAID and Other Sea Poems

Compiled and Illustrated by SOPHIE WINDHAM

Dear Madame Esmé,

School, office, lessons, sport practices, homework . . . Our lives are one big routine. We want to schedule in some reading thrills. Give me adventures from the edge that I can serialize for my children at bedtime.

Dear Gentle Reader,

Grab your bungee cord and skateboard and head to the library for ADVENTURES OF THE LITTLE WOODEN HORSE by Ursula Moray Williams. The little wooden horse is devoted to Uncle Peder, but when the toymaker is overcome by poverty and then illness, the little wooden horse sets out to seek his fortune on his friend's behalf. His journey takes him into coal mines, onto circus high wires, across ocean waves brimming with hostile sea horses, into the gentle hands of royal princesses and the clutches of pirates. The villains on his journey are memorable and terrible. The manic Farmer Max rivals Robert Mitchum's performance in The Night of the Hunter, and the quarrelsome nursery children match Sid from Toy Story blow for blow. In the end, the twists of fate endured by the dear little wooden horse are exponentially more compelling than anything your child could find on screen today. This is one of the greatest adventure stories of all time and also a moving testament to unflinching devotion that Pinocchio himself could take a lesson from. I have used the edition illustrated by Peggy Fortnum as a read-aloud for hundreds of children of all ages, and hope you will read it aloud to hundreds more.

BLACK JACK by Leon Garfield is another great book for serial read-alouds. Pulitzer prize-winner Alison Lurie wrote, "If James Bond were a twelve-year-old boy living in eighteenth-century England, his life of surprise and danger and self-discovery might have been recorded by Leon Garfield." Indeed, surprise and danger are the operative words when the seven-foot Black Jack seems to rise from the dead and then takes on an unwitting boy as his companion through madhouses, circuses, and the underbelly of the dirty city. Garfield is fearless, taking intermediate children on the romantic adventures they only dream of experiencing.

PART V

The Math
and Science of
Reading

Which is more important, the sun or the moon? That's the question that comes to mind whenever I hear school honchos argue over where the academic concentration should fall. In our frenzied race to keep up with the future, it is easy to lose a focus on reading for fear that children won't accrue the skills they need to succeed in our industrial, high-tech rat-race. This short-shrift is short-sighted. While the content of reading may be as whimsical as we choose, the *skill* of reading is one that will bolster any child's ability in the more hard-boiled subjects of math, science, and technology.

The use of a computer assumes literacy. Nearly all of the information conveyed on the World Wide Web is in the form of written language, so anything from research to receiving e-mail requires the ability to read. Reading can make the difference between harmony and homicide when troubleshooting software glitches. The skills of prediction, critical thinking, and writing cultivated by reading are indispensable in creating even the simplest computer codes, such as HTML, used in Web-page design. And all the codes in the world won't help a Web site without viable content, which readers and writers have an edge in creating. If you expect your child to someday compete in a job market mobilized by computers and technology, let her know that reading is a major component of her mental hard drive, not a peripheral.

Reading adds up to math success as well. Abstract concepts are made more concrete through written stories. Stories put math problems into real-life contexts and help to motivate problem-solving. How many word problems do you remember doing? Can you remember a standardized test that didn't have them? So many children who are good at math have grades and scores that don't fully reflect that ability because they are not good readers. The task of reading well and carefully is a hurdle that comes before the task of solving the math problem.

Simply being a skilled reader enables a child to answer a million questions when it comes to science, which is good, because most children have at *least* that many to ask. What are all the names of the dinosaurs? Who

The Earth and I

FRANK ASCH

lives in the rain forest's canopy? What would it be like to live on other planets? Where does my hamburger go once I've eaten it? What makes thunder? How are babies made? An appreciation of science involves introducing a body of background knowledge that is truly astounding in size. Sharing with children the vocabulary and explanations behind the natural world can be a bit overwhelming, but somebody's got to do it. Let some of those somebodies be willing authors and illustrators.

Applied science requires a good deal of written communication, and according to the Nation's Report Card from the National Assessment of Educational Progress (NAEP), good writers read even more than they write. The same children who read to find the answer to a question, perform a science experiment, or create content for a science fair display may grow up to be researchers, doctors, pharmacists, environmental watchdogs—or even folks on the space station waving down to the folks pointing telescopes up at them! Science-related jobs are jobs for *readers*, readers who comprehend the research of other scientists, make predictions, note and describe details, distinguish between cause and effect, and are able to clearly communicate their own findings . . . all skills that began in the petri dish of their elementary-school reading experiences.

Corporations already understand the connection between math and science and reading. Every year industry spends billions of dollars on employees who require reading remediation. Meanwhile, corporations send thousands of jobs out of the country to nations such as India and Ireland, seemingly less powerful or wealthy but with a workforce matching or exceeding ours in literacy and the abilities that come with it. Even the army has stopped accepting a General Equivalency Diploma (GED). These are just a few painful indicators suggesting that literacy is an American Achilles' heel, affecting our economy and our security.

Creating readers is a part of creating professionals who are in demand. I found out the hard way. I remember going to a dentist when I was in college. I was nervous about trying someone new, but his rates were affordable, and he had the same name as one of my professors, which I thought was a sign of good luck. Later in class, I heard this same professor joke about his son, how he didn't like to read and never did a lick of homework and still grew up to be a dentist. I rushed to a more reputable professional who noticed in an X ray that the first dentist had broken off parts of instruments in my mouth and left them there! Two root canals later . . . well, I'm here to tell the tale. Okay, maybe you don't need to read to know that leaving dental instruments in a patient's mouth is bad dentistry, but for me it was telling. I just don't *want* someone who didn't read what they were supposed to read to fix my teeth. I don't want someone who doesn't read to process my insurance claim (though I think this has happened before, too). Now, imagine someone who doesn't read flying a plane or operating on your grandmother or trying to keep an innocent man out of jail.

Reading is a helpful thing to like, in that people who read are often in a better position to be helpful. They simply have more information at their disposal. What's more, reading provides children with a healthy and necessary combination of the pragmatic (knowing *how* to do things) and the philanthropic (knowing how to use that knowledge to assist others). We have seen, historically, what happens when industry and algorithms are left to feed off of themselves without the interest, empathy, and humor that reading serves to nurture. That's why I think of reading and math/science as like the sun and the moon. They must always be in the sky together, full force, shining light, and pulling tides in equal turn. When the study of math and science eclipses reading skills, everyone ends up in the dark.

Science Magic Show

When I was in training to become a teacher, my brilliant "Methods of Teaching Science" professor, Dr. Barrett, told us something very important about turning kids on to science. He said, whenever possible, an experiment should have a lot of "wow" in it. Some of the experiments found in children's books are loaded with "wow" and worthy of an audience. Publishers capitalize on this, and you will come across many science-related tomes with the word "magic" in the title. "Science" is really a synonym for "magic" from a kid's perspective, and you can make a magic show using almost any good science experiment book. Pick a few to perform as a model, and then encourage your child to discover the "wows" in science books and put on his own show. A few excellent experiment books to get you started:

Ardley, Neil	• **101 GREAT SCIENCE EXPERIMENTS**
Chahrour, Janet Parks	• **FLASH! BANG! POP! FIZZ! EXCITING SCIENCE FOR CURIOUS MINDS**

Cobb, Vicki, and Kathy Darling	• BET YOU CAN! SCIENCE POSSIBILITIES TO FOOL YOU • BET YOU CAN'T! SCIENCE IMPOSSIBILITIES TO FOOL YOU • WANNA BET? SCIENCE CHALLENGES TO FOOL YOU (I'll bet that you'll love Vicki Cobb, an original and dependable science author.)
Green, Joey	• THE MAD SCIENTIST HANDBOOK
Smith, Alistair	• THE USBORNE BIG BOOK OF EXPERIMENTS
Walpole, Brenda	• 175 SCIENCE EXPERIMENTS TO AMUSE AND AMAZE YOUR FRIENDS
Wiese, Jim	• MAGIC SCIENCE: 50 JAW-DROPPING, MIND-BOGGLING, HEAD-SCRATCHING ACTIVITIES FOR KIDS (Another prolific author; I love all of his books.)

Getting Your Hands on Experiments

Part of the fun of science is the hands-on experimenting. Finding a book to suit the scientific occasion is as easy as finding a Bunsen burner in Dr. Frankenstein's lab. Your children can do experiments in a restaurant (using WHILE YOU'RE WAITING FOR THE FOOD TO COME: EXPERIMENTS AND TRICKS THAT CAN BE DONE AT A RESTAURANT, THE DINING ROOM TABLE, OR WHEREVER FOOD IS SERVED by Eric Muller); the bathtub (SCIENCE MAGIC IN THE BATHROOM by Richard Robinson, part of the **Science Magic** series, which offers experiments for every room in the house); the movie theater (MOVIE SCIENCE: OVER 40 MIND-EXPANDING, REALITY-BENDING, STARSTRUCK ACTIVITIES FOR KIDS by Jim Wiese, a great tie-in for Cinema Club, p. 211); or even the backseat of a car (I don't know what nastiness *you're* thinking of, but perfectly *wholesome* experiments may be found in Vicki Cobb and Kathy Darling's DON'T TRY THIS AT HOME! SCIENCE FUN FOR KIDS ON THE GO).

Must-Haves: Criteria for Experiment Book Selection

There are so many science books available that there are a few criteria you might want to keep in mind. The packaging of science experiment books for children can be especially zany and gimmicky, but when I pick one up, I better be able to see past the neon and find a few things right away:

A list of materials. Do the experiments require items easily found around the neighborhood, or are you going to be hunting down potassium hydroxide on the net? Some of the most memorable experiments require exotic materials, but that may be too much trouble. Experiments are like recipes; you need to see what you're getting into.

Illustrations. Pictures that show procedures step by step are heaven sent, but there should always be *some* illustration depicting what it will look like when the experiment is done correctly. Beware: Some science experiment books are brimming with spot illustrations that are *soooo* cute but do nothing to help your child along.

Clear Warnings. Points in an experiment at which particular danger is present or when a parent's assistance is recommended should be clearly marked in bold print, a different color type or some other attention-getting symbol. In this day and age when aspiring scientists may also be latchkey kids, it is especially important that authors help keep their readers safe.

Explanations. Some experiment books can go through a whole experiment and never even explain what occurred and why, which sort of undermines the whole point of doing science. Look for an answer to a question at the end of the experiment, a "what happened," "why," or "how it works."

And Watch Those Repetitive Redundancies

If you pursue enough children's experiment books, you'll notice that it is actually hard to find a truly original science experiment. The same concoctions are repackaged over and over again: vinegar-soaked "rubber" eggs, the good old electric-lemon-that-can-run-a-clock, Ping-Pong balls hovering over blow dryers, chromatography capers, and the ever popular hole-in-the-hand optical illusion are a few standards you're sure to come across. This is fine as the experiments you see repeated usually demonstrate sound scientific concepts and actually work. The frustration comes when you are spending the big bucks for books with experiments in them, only to discover that if you com-

DANGER, WILL ROBINSON

Something to keep in mind if you do wows with children who aren't your own: When demonstrating science with an element of danger involved, such as heat or chemicals, call the parents to let them know you're playing Poindexter. If you don't know the parents well, make a copy of the experiment for the children and have them write a bright-colored note to their folks, "We did a cool experiment . . . help me do it again!" You can warn and warn and warn some children not to mess around, but if they are left unsupervised, sometimes a devil on their shoulder makes them forget. Children who mischievously try an experiment without supervision and *don't do it correctly* are in even more danger.

OLDIES AND GOODIES

Some of the best experiments come from books published by Dover Publications. Visit Dover on-line at www.doverpublications.com to request the unique children's catalog by writing to 31 East 2nd Street, Mineola, New York, 11501. Requests or orders over the phone are not accepted. Dover books are old-fashioned, ranging in feel from the Victorian age to the filmstrip era. Whatever you think of the style, the substance is uncompromising. For instance, I would not be willing to go without my SPORTS SCIENCE FOR YOUNG PEOPLE by George Barr, or Eugene F. and Asterie Baker PROVENZO'S 47 EASY-TO-DO CLASSIC SCIENCE EXPERIMENTS. Luckily, Dover seems to have maintained the prices of the eras it represents; all of the many titles offered in the catalog are available for a song.

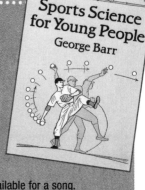

Sports Science for Young People
George Barr

piled all the experiments from half a dozen books, you'd maybe end up with enough different experiments to fill *one*. I solve this problem by using the library whenever possible and creating a file of the best science experiments from all the books. If I find a book that I keep returning to or that has *enough* original experiments in an attractive format for children, I then decide to make a purchase. After all, you need to save your pennies for all that vinegar and baking powder!

There's no better way to learn the meaning of science "wow" than to *try* a science wow. So here is my favorite wow experiment:

47 EASY-TO-DO CLASSIC SCIENCE EXPERIMENTS

Eugene F. Provenzo, Jr. and Asterie Baker Provenzo
With 69 Illustrations Prepared by Peter A. Zorn, Jr.

THE EGG IN THE BOTTLE TRICK (adapted from Don Herbert's MR. WIZARD'S SUPERMARKET SCIENCE)

Materials
A hard-boiled egg
An 8-ounce glass nursing bottle or milk jug
Cooking oil, butter, or margarine
A match
A small piece of paper, folded lengthwise
A fire extinguisher or bucket of water

Procedure
1. Remove shell of the hard-boiled egg.
2. Smear oil, butter, or margarine around the mouth of the bottle. See that the opening of the bottle is not so big that the egg will just fall through. The idea is that the egg will be sucked into an opening that is too small for it.

3. Give a long speech about fire safety to kids. Frown and make them swear that they will not try this next step without an adult present, and if they do, they should not sue you when their house burns down, because it will. Point out the fire extinguisher and/or water for added seriousness and safety.

4. Light the match and set a small piece of paper on fire. BE CAREFUL! Immediately plunge the lit piece of paper into the bottle, putting the egg over the opening right away.

5. The egg starts dropping into the mouth of the bottle and POP! It plops to the bottom.

6. Listen for the WOOOOW!

Explanation

The gases inside the bottle (both the air and the gases produced by the burning) are heated by the flame and expand. Some of the gasses are forced out past the egg, which acts as a one-way valve. When the flame goes out, the gasses in the bottle contract, forming a partial vacuum. The air pressure around the bottle and the egg do the rest.

Getting the egg out of the bottle is even easier than getting it in. Fill the bottle with water, and with your finger holding the egg away from the bottle's mouth, pour out the water and what's left of the burned paper. Then turn the bottle upside down so that the egg falls into the neck and blocks the opening from the inside just as it did when it was on the outside. Continuing to hold the bottle upside down, blow as hard as you can into the bottle. The air flows past the egg. When you stop blowing, the egg again acts as a one-way valve. The air pressure behind the egg slowly forces it out of the bottle's mouth and *pop!* It's in your hand!

Anyone care for egg à la Bernoulli's Principle? That's what was just demonstrated: Rapidly moving air creates a low-pressure situation.

Two wows in one chapter? Well, all right, why not? I like you!

ERUPTING COLORS (adapted from MaryAnn Kohl and Jean Potter's SCIENCE ARTS)

Materials

Cake pan with edges or custard cup

Milk

Food coloring

Liquid dishwashing detergent

Janice VanCleave This, Janice VanCleave That!

If you want to see what a good children's science experiment book should look like, turn to the master, Janice VanCleave. I don't think there is an elementary science teacher out there who hasn't sent up a silent word of thanks for VanCleave's amazing contribution to the science shelves. Her books can be relied on for originality, dependability, and clarity and cover virtually any scientific concept that can be conjured (or if not, you can bet she's working on it). Entire hands-on science curriculums have been constructed using her books, but why should schools have all the fun? Don't let another science fair go by without her helping hand.

For the little ones, preschool through first grade, explore the **Play and Find Out** series ("Easy Activities for Young Children"):

JANICE VANCLEAVE'S PLAY AND FIND OUT ABOUT . . .

. . . BUGS
. . . THE HUMAN BODY
. . . MATH
. . . NATURE
. . . SCIENCE

For grade-school children, the series I like for everyday demontrations and experiments is the **Science for Every Kid** series ("Easy Activities That Make Learning Science Fun"):

JANICE VANCLEAVE'S . . .

. . . CHEMISTRY FOR EVERY KID
. . . CONSTELLATIONS FOR EVERY KID
. . . EARTH SCIENCE FOR EVERY KID
. . . ECOLOGY FOR EVERY KID
. . . FOOD AND NUTRITION FOR EVERY KID
. . . GEOGRAPHY FOR EVERY KID
. . . GEOMETRY FOR EVERY KID
. . . THE HUMAN BODY FOR EVERY KID
. . . MATH FOR EVERY KID
. . . OCEANS FOR EVERY KID

Older children can put science on display using Janice VanCleave's **Spectacular Science Projects** series ("Mind-Boggling Experiments You Can Turn into Science Fair Projects"):

JANICE VANCLEAVE'S . . .

. . . ANIMALS
. . . EARTHQUAKES
. . . GRAVITY
. . . INSECTS AND SPIDERS
. . . MOLECULES
. . . PLANTS
. . . ROCKS AND MINERALS
. . . SOLAR SYSTEM
. . . VOLCANOES
. . . WEATHER

And for everyday science fun:
JANICE VANCLEAVE'S . . .

. . . SCIENCE AROUND THE YEAR
. . . SCIENCE THROUGH THE AGES
. . . 202 OOZING, BUBBLING, DRIPPING, AND BOUNCING EXPERIMENTS
. . . 203 ICY, FREEZING, FROSTY, COOL, AND WILD EXPERIMENTS

Janice even has a fan club, which your children can join for free. Help your child send name, address, and favorite Janice VanCleave experiment to: Science for Every Kid Club, Fan Club Headquarters/F. Nachbaur, John Wiley & Sons, 605 Third Avenue, New York, New York 10158. It's like the AAA for young scientists!

Procedure

1. Pour milk into the cake pan or cup until the bottom is covered.

2. Sprinkle several drops of food coloring on the milk.

3. Add a few drops of dishwashing detergent in the centers of the largest drops of coloring.

4. Watch the resulting eruption of colors. WOOOW!

Make combinations of colors for fun. Did you ever think milk could be so trippy?

Explanation

Milk contains water and fat, which don't actually mix. So even though milk looks like one substance, it is really separate water and fat. Detergent is a substance that will mix with water *or* fat. When detergent is dropped into milk, one end of the detergent molecule attaches to the fat in the milk and the other end of the detergent molecule attaches to the water, which causes a boiling effect. It's a solubility/emulsion shake!

Snotty Science

Another vocabulary word in the world of children's science literature is "gross." "Gross" is a much more definitive and honest word than "magic." Magic can mean almost anything, but gross means *exactly* what it says. You would be wise to recognize "gross" at once as a warning to parents and an invitation to kids. The one who really turned disgust into a science, aptly named "Grossology," is Sylvia Branzei, who had a strong enough stomach to articulate instructions for making fake snot and measuring urine capacity and has a section in one book titled "Barf." My favorite in Branzei's series of books is HANDS-ON GROSSOLOGY: THE SCIENCE OF REALLY GROSS EXPERIMENTS, admittedly not only because it has the most activities but because I can hardly get past the covers of her other books. You can visit her on-line at www.grossology.org. Children with a taste for waste may also enjoy OH, YUCK! THE ENCYCLOPEDIA OF EVERYTHING NASTY by Joy Masoff. I have to give the authors this: Gross is a definite wow.

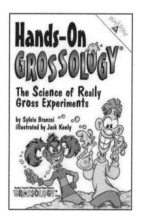

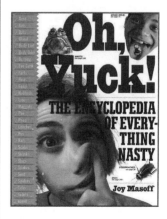

After experimenting with science, drive home the reading and science connection. Make it a point to explain to children that reading has a lot to do with science. Ask them how they could do an experiment without reading the directions? Tell them that if they intend to do even more interesting and complicated experiments, they will need to keep honing their reading skills. Reading may be something we take for granted, but it's hard to find all the wows in life without it!

Inventions

Some schools are foregoing traditional science fairs for invention fairs, and why not? Inventions give children a great opportunity to apply the principles of science and build a better mousetrap in the process. And as far as reading goes, it's the very definition of a motivation (see The Three Is, p. 13). Here are some titles both informational and inspirational:

Brinley, Bertrand R.	• THE MAD SCIENTISTS' CLUB (Chapter book.)
Caney, Steven	• STEVEN CANEY'S INVENTION BOOK
Erlbach, Arlene	• THE KIDS' INVENTION BOOK
Harper, Charise Mericle	• IMAGINATIVE INVENTIONS
Jones, Charlotte Foltz	• ACCIDENTS MAY HAPPEN • MISTAKES THAT WORKED
Kassinger, Ruth	• REINVENT THE WHEEL: MAKE CLASSIC INVENTIONS, DISCOVER YOUR PROBLEM-SOLVING GENIUS, AND TAKE THE INVENTOR'S CHALLENGE
McCloskey, Robert	• HOMER PRICE (Chapter book must-read for young inventors.)
Pène du Bois, William	• THE TWENTY-ONE BALLOONS (Another chapter-book must-read.)

REAL PEOPLE, REAL SCIENCE

Houghton Mifflin's **Scientists in the Field** series does an impressive job of showing intermediate and older children that there are individuals behind scientific inquiry. Each attractive photo essay brings children on the job and is sure to get many readers psyched about a career in science.

Batten, Mary	• ANTHROPOLOGIST: SCIENTIST OF THE PEOPLE
Bishop, Nic	• DIGGING FOR BIRD-DINOSAURS
Jackson, Donna M.	• THE BUG SCIENTISTS • THE WILDLIFE DETECTIVES
Jackson, Ellen	• LOOKING FOR LIFE IN THE UNIVERSE
Kramer, Stephen	• HIDDEN WORLDS: LOOKING THROUGH A SCIENTIST'S MICROSCOPE
Mallory, Kenneth	• SWIMMING WITH HAMMERHEAD SHARKS
Montgomery, Sy	• THE SNAKE SCIENTIST
Osborn, Elinor	• PROJECT ULTRASWAN
Sayre, April Pulley	• SECRETS OF SOUND: STUDYING THE CALLS OF WHALES, ELEPHANTS, AND BIRDS
Swinburne, Stephen R.	• ONCE A WOLF: HOW WILDLIFE BIOLOGISTS FOUGHT TO BRING BACK THE GRAY WOLF

Perry, Andrea	• HERE'S WHAT YOU DO WHEN YOU CAN'T FIND YOUR SHOE: INGENIOUS INVENTIONS FOR PESKY PROBLEMS
St. George, Judith	• SO YOU WANT TO BE AN INVENTOR?
Sullivan, Otha	• AFRICAN AMERICAN INVENTORS
Tomecki, Stephen M.	• WHAT A GREAT IDEA! INVENTIONS THAT CHANGED THE WORLD
Thimmesh, Catherine	• GIRLS THINK OF EVERYTHING: STORIES OF INGENIOUS INVENTIONS BY WOMEN • THE SKY'S THE LIMIT: STORIES OF DISCOVERY BY WOMEN AND GIRLS
Tucker, Tom	• BRAINSTORM! THE STORIES OF TWENTY AMERICAN KID INVENTORS
Wulffson, Don L.	• THE KID WHO INVENTED THE POPSICLE: AND OTHER EXTRAORDINARY STORIES BEHIND EVERYDAY THINGS • THE KID WHO INVENTED THE TRAMPOLINE: MORE SURPRISING STORIES ABOUT INVENTIONS • TOYS! AMAZING STORIES BEHIND SOME GREAT INVENTIONS
Zaunders, Bo	• FEATHERS, FLAPS, AND FLOPS: FABULOUS EARLY FLIERS (Children interested in flight might also enjoy THE AMAZING AIR BALLOON by Jean Van Leeuwen and THE GLORIOUS FLIGHT: ACROSS THE CHANNEL WITH LOUIS BLÉRIOT by Alice and Martin Provensen.)

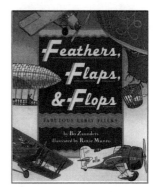

Museum Science Books

I know when I used to take students on field trips, it felt more like gym than science, chasing as they raced from display to display. Luckily, some of the most outstanding and comprehensive science books containing both experiments and explanations are inspired by museums, giving families ideas they can *really* run with.

Cassidy, John	• EXPLORABOOK: A KIDS' SCIENCE MUSEUM IN A BOOK
Murphy, Pat	• THE SCIENCE EXPLORER: FAMILY EXPERIMENTS FROM THE WORLD'S FAVORITE HANDS-ON SCIENCE MUSEUM (The Exploratorium in San Francisco put together this awesome volume.)
Ontario Science Centre	• SPORTWORKS • FOODWORKS • SCIENCE EXPRESS (These are hard to find but worth the hunt.)

Rudy, Lisa Jo, ed.	• THE BEN FRANKLIN BOOK OF EASY AND INCREDIBLE EXPERIMENTS (The Franklin Institute in Philadelphia)
Zubrowski, Bernie	• SHADOW PLAY: MAKING PICTURES WITH LIGHT AND LENSES (This Boston Children's Museum book is fun to tie in to shadow puppetry.)

Reading any of the books in the **Eyewitness** series feels like a field trip through a museum exhibit (without the chasing). Its photographic approach revolutionized children's publishing. You will be astounded by the number of science and natural history topics covered.

After reading any of the museum science books or the **Eyewitness** series, children may be inspired to create their own museum-style exhibits. For a nice twist on that tired science-fair display and a great project for a rainy day, intermediate and older children may appreciate the structure suggested in Robert Gardner's MAKE AN INTERACTIVE SCIENCE MUSEUM. But really, your children's own creativity is the only guide needed.

EYEWITNESS BOOKS

AFRICA	CIVIL WAR	FIRST LADIES	MEDIEVAL LIFE	SHIPWRECK
AMPHIBIAN	COSTUME	FISH	MONEY	SKELETON
ANCIENT CHINA	COWBOY	FLAG	MUMMY	SOCCER
ANCIENT EGYPT	CRIME & DETECTION	FLYING MACHINE	MUSIC	SPACE EXPLORATION
ANCIENT GREECE	CRYSTAL & GEM	FOOTBALL	MYTHOLOGY	SPORTS
ANCIENT ROME	DANCE	FORCE & MOTION	NORTH AMERICAN INDIAN	SPY
ARCHEOLOGY	DESERT	FOSSIL	OCEAN	SUPERBOWL
ARCTIC & ANTARCTIC	DINOSAUR	FUTURE	OLYMPICS	TECHNOLOGY
ARMS AND ARMOR	DOG	GORILLA, MONKEY, & APE	PIRATE	TIME & SPACE
ASTRONOMY	EAGLE & BIRDS OF PREY	HORSE	PLANT	TITANIC
AZTEC, INCA, & MAYA	EARLY HUMANS	HUMAN BODY	POND & RIVER	TRAIN
BASEBALL	EARTH	HURRICANE & TORNADO	PREHISTORIC LIFE	TREE
BATTLE	ECOLOGY	INSECT	PRESIDENTS	VIKING
BIBLE LANDS	ELECTRICITY	INVENTION	PYRAMID	VOLCANO &
BIRD	ELECTRONICS	JUNGLE	RELIGION	EARTHQUAKE
BOAT	ELEPHANT	KNIGHT	RENAISSANCE	WEATHER
BOOK	ENERGY	LEONARDO & HIS TIMES	REPTILE	WHALE
BUILDING	EPIDEMIC	LIFE	RESCUE	WITCHES &
BUTTERFLY & MOTH	EVEREST	LIGHT	ROCKS & MINERALS	MAGIC-MAKERS
CAR	EVOLUTION	MAMMAL	RUSSIA	WORLD WAR II
CASTLE	EXPLORER	MATTER	SEASHORE	
CAT	FARM	MEDIA & COMMUNICATION	SHARK	
CHEMISTRY	FILM	MEDICINE	SHELL	

The Question Board

The first step in the scientific method of problem-solving is inquiry, or asking a question, so most children are natural scientists. To encourage children to pursue their curiosity, hang up a small, attractive bulletin board in your home. You can make it more decorative by painting the cork, and by lopping the tops off small silk flowers and collecting shells and acorns and other natural things, then with a hot glue-gun attach them to the flat heads of thumbtacks. (Martha Stewart is watching you!) Attach a pen on some pretty ribbon, and keep a pad nearby. Underneath or near the board, make available a shelf of question-and-answer books. When someone in the family comes up with a question, write it down and tack it to the board. See if another family member can find the answer at her leisure, and tack it to the board with the question. If it doesn't ruin your decor, keep the board as close as possible to the . . . *ahem* . . . facilities; question-and-answer books make great bathroom reading. Who asks the most challenging questions in the family? Who is the best answer detective? Watch as your child's curiosity, knowledge, and scientific confidence grow with every solved science puzzle. You can also make a question board and book collection for your child's classroom. Given the number of questions a teacher is called upon to answer, it's a gift that any teacher will appreciate for years.

For Your Question Board Bookshelf:

Catherine Ripley's **WHY: THE BEST EVER QUESTION AND ANSWER BOOK ABOUT NATURE, SCIENCE, AND THE WORLD AROUND YOU.** The big question Catherine Ripley had was "What questions do children have?" As a former editor of the award-winning *Chickadee* magazine for young children, Catherine collected questions submitted by curious readers, and visited schools and libraries to ask, ask, ask. Her book is where children will find answers, answers, answers.

One of my favorite primary series is the Kingfisher Books **I Wonder Why** series. Do you wonder why it is my favorite? It has an extremely accessible, heavily illustrated format just right for young answer-seekers, and even the list of titles addresses more questions than I could even think of asking.

🌼 *Potato Pick:*

FANDEX FAMILY FIELD GUIDES

What an innovative series of reference guides from Workman Publishing. Long attached cards "fan out" to reveal attractive photographs and a wealth of information. Leaves, mythology, presidents, the Civil War, dogs, cats, and birds . . . name your pleasure! They are perfect for reluctant readers, and their "flash card" style tilts these unconventional books toward self-testing and expertise. Every classroom should have a set, and they are great for browsing at home, too. Try 'em, you'll like 'em! (All ages)

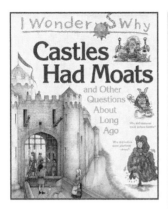

I Wonder Why . . .

. . . Camels Have Humps and Other Questions About Animals

. . . Castles Had Moats and Other Questions About Long Ago

. . . the Dodo Is Dead and Other Questions About Extinct and Endangered Animals

. . . Flutes Have Holes and Other Questions About Music

. . . I Blink and Other Questions About My Body

. . . Mountains Have Snow on Top and Other Questions About Mountains

. . . Planes Have Wings and Other Questions About Transportation

. . . Snakes Shed Their Skin and Other Questions About Reptiles

. . . Soap Makes Bubbles and Other Questions About Science

. . . Stars Twinkle and Other Questions About Space

. . . the Sea Is Salty and Other Questions About the Oceans

. . . the Sun Rises and Other Questions About Time and Seasons

. . . the Telephone Rings and Other Questions About Communication

. . . Trees Have Leaves and Other Questions About Plants

. . . Triceratops Had Horns and Other Questions About Dinosaurs

. . . Tunnels Are Round and Other Questions About Building

. . . Vultures Are Bald and Other Questions About Birds

. . . the Wind Blows and Other Questions About Our Planet

. . . Zippers Have Teeth and Other Questions About Inventions

Kingfisher also has books with slightly different formats for intermediate readers; the differences are very subtle, so explore to see which is right for your child. The **Questions and Answers** series has a "Quick Fire Quiz" on each page (not so bad if you're not getting graded). The **Question Time** series is similar in format to the **I Wonder Why** series but with just a little more text and a fun game on each double-page spread in which the reader is asked to find something in the illustration. And the **I Didn't Know That** series is also in the same vein with a less interrogative and more exclamatory approach.

I Didn't Know That . . .

... Chimps Use Tools

... Crocodiles Yawn to Keep Cool

... Dinosaurs Laid Eggs

... Giant Pandas Eat All Day Long

... Mountains Gush Lava and Ash

... Only Some Big Cats Can Roar

... People Chase Twisters

... Sharks Keep Losing Their Teeth

... Some Birds Hang Upside Down

... Some Boats Have Wings

... Some Bugs Glow in the Dark

... Some Cars Can Swim

... Some Planes Hover

... Some Plants Grow in Midair

... Some Snakes Spit Poison

... Some Trains Run on Water

... Spiders Have Fangs

... the Sun Is a Star

... Tidal Waves Wash Away Cities

... Whales Sing

... Wolves Howl at the Moon

... You Can Jump Higher on the Moon

Dear Madame Esmé,

What is the most wonderful children's book in the world?

Dear Gentle Reader,

I don't know, but here is a wonderful children's book that is definitely the most. THINGS THAT ARE MOST IN THE WORLD by Judi Barrett, illustrated by John Nickle, asks the questions: What is the silliest thing in the world? The quietest? The smelliest? What is the funniest book in the world? It may very well be this one! The book is superlative, lending itself beautifully to creative writing and language-arts integration. Your child can make his own book of "mosts"! For more "mosts," turn to author Robert E. Wells, who really measures up to questions about size, weight, time, and quantity:

HOW DO YOU KNOW WHAT TIME IT IS?

CAN YOU COUNT TO A GOOGOL?

HOW DO YOU LIFT A LION?

IS A BLUE WHALE THE BIGGEST THING THERE IS?

WHAT'S FASTER THAN A SPEEDING CHEETAH?

WHAT'S SMALLER THAN A PYGMY SHREW?

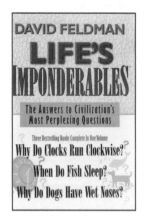

David Feldman's LIFE'S IMPONDERABLES: THE ANSWERS TO CIVILIZA-TION'S MOST PERPLEXING QUESTIONS is a compilation of the author's three bestsellers WHY DO CLOCKS RUN CLOCKWISE?, WHEN DO FISH SLEEP?, and WHY DO DOGS HAVE WET NOSES? in one economical volume. The format may be a little wordy for some younger readers, but intermediate and older children will definitely find answers to everything under the sun, including why doughnuts have holes, why all dentist offices smell the same and why hot dogs come ten to a package while hot dog buns come eight.

David Macaulay's illustrated accomplishment THE NEW WAY THINGS WORK explains the principles of every kind of machine you could imagine in plain English. I have used his book to fix toilets and toasters, and to answer dozens of questions. Great for future engineers and their parents.

HOW COME? and HOW COME? PLANET EARTH by Kathy Wollard are nice chunky volumes full of questions about natural wonders, with a highly biological bent.

The Scholastic **Question and Answer** series by Melvin and Gilda Berger works well for both primary and intermediate readers (note the same series title as Kingfisher Books, but different publisher) includes:

ARE MOUNTAINS GETTING TALLER? QUESTIONS AND ANSWERS ABOUT THE CHANGING EARTH

CAN IT RAIN CATS AND DOGS? QUESTIONS AND ANSWERS ABOUT WEATHER

CAN SNAKES CRAWL BACKWARDS? QUESTIONS AND ANSWERS ABOUT REPTILES

CAN YOU HEAR A SHOUT IN SPACE? QUESTIONS AND ANSWERS ABOUT SPACE EXPLORATION

DID DINOSAURS LIVE IN YOUR BACKYARD? QUESTIONS AND ANSWERS ABOUT DINOSAURS

DO ALL SPIDERS SPIN WEBS? QUESTIONS AND ANSWERS ABOUT SPIDERS

DO BEARS SLEEP ALL WINTER? QUESTIONS AND ANSWERS ABOUT BEARS

DOES IT ALWAYS RAIN IN THE RAIN FOREST? QUESTIONS AND ANSWERS ABOUT RAIN FORESTS

DO PENGUINS GET FROSTBITE? QUESTIONS AND ANSWERS ABOUT POLAR ANIMALS

DO STARS HAVE POINTS? QUESTIONS AND ANSWERS ABOUT STARS AND PLANETS

DO TARANTULAS HAVE TEETH? QUESTIONS AND ANSWERS ABOUT POISONOUS CREATURES

DO TORNADOES REALLY TWIST? QUESTIONS AND ANSWERS ABOUT TORNADOES AND HURRICANES

DO WHALES HAVE BELLY BUTTONS? QUESTIONS AND ANSWERS ABOUT WHALES AND DOLPHINS

How Do Bats See in the Dark? Questions and Answers About Night Creatures

How Do Flies Walk Upside Down? Question and Answers About Insects

How Do Frogs Swallow with Their Eyes? Questions and Answers About Amphibians

Is a Dolphin a Fish? Questions and Answers About Dolphins

What Makes an Ocean Wave? Questions and Answers About Oceans and Ocean Life

Where Did the Butterfly Get Its Name? Questions and Answers About Butterflies and Moths

Where Have All the Pandas Gone? Questions and Answers About Endangered Species

Why Do Wolves Howl? Questions and Answers About Wolves

Why Do Volcanoes Blow Their Tops? Questions and Answers About Volcanoes and Earthquakes

Why Don't Haircuts Hurt? Questions and Answers About the Human Body

It's not strictly scientific, but everyone needs the current year of **Guinness World Records** on hand to answer all those biggest-strongest-fastest-slowest-type questions.

And when inquiry sparks interest, turn to the nonfiction picturebook series **Let's-Read-and-Find-Out Science** published by HarperCollins, which lends itself nicely to primary read-aloud:

Air Is All Around You by Franklyn M. Branley

American Alligators by Anne F. Rockwell

Animals in Winter by Henrietta Bancroft and Richard G. Van Gelder

Ant Cities by Arthur Dorros

Archaeologists Dig for Clues by Kate Duke

Baby Whales Drink Milk by Barbara Juster Esbensen

Be a Friend to Trees by Patricia Lauber

The Big Dipper by Franklyn M. Branley

Big Tracks, Little Tracks: Following Animal Prints by Millicent E. Selsam

Bugs Are Insects by Anne F. Rockwell

Chirping Crickets by Melvin Berger

Corn Is Maize: The Gift of the Indians by Aliki

Day Light, Night Light: Where Light Comes From by Franklyn M. Branley

Digging Up Dinosaurs by Aliki

Dinosaur Babies by Kathleen Weidner Zoehfeld

DINOSAURS BIG AND SMALL by Kathleen Weidner Zoehfeld

DOWN COMES THE RAIN by Franklyn M. Branley

EARTHQUAKES by Franklyn M. Branley

FEEL THE WIND by Arthur Dorros

FLASH, CRASH, RUMBLE, AND ROLL by Franklyn M. Branley

FLOATING IN SPACE by Franklyn M. Branley

FROM CATERPILLAR TO BUTTERFLY by Deborah Heiligman

FROM SEED TO PUMPKIN by Wendy Pfeffer

FROM TADPOLE TO FROG by Wendy Pfeffer

GERMS MAKE ME SICK! by Melvin Berger

HEAR YOUR HEART by Paul Showers

HOW ANIMAL BABIES STAY SAFE by Mary Ann Fraser

HOW A SEED GROWS by Helene J. Jordan

HOW DO APPLES GROW? by Betsy Maestro

HOW DO BIRDS FIND THEIR WAY? by Roma Gans

HOW MANY TEETH? by Paul Showers

HOW MOUNTAINS ARE MADE by Kathleen Weidner Zoehfeld

THE INTERNATIONAL SPACE STATION by Franklyn M. Branley

IS THERE LIFE IN OUTER SPACE? by Franklyn M. Branley

LET'S GO ROCK COLLECTING by Roma Gans

LOOK OUT FOR TURTLES by Melvin Berger

MISSION TO MARS by Franklyn M. Branley

THE MOON SEEMS TO CHANGE by Franklyn M. Branley

MY FEET by Aliki

MY FIVE SENSES by Aliki

MY HANDS by Aliki

MY VISIT TO THE DINOSAURS by Aliki

A NEST FULL OF EGGS by Priscilla Belz Jenkins

AN OCTOPUS IS AMAZING by Patricia Lauber

OIL SPILL! by Melvin Berger

OUR PUPPIES ARE GROWING by Carolyn Otto

PENGUIN CHICK by Betty Tatham

THE PLANETS IN OUR SOLAR SYSTEM by Franklyn M. Branley

POP: A BOOK ABOUT BUBBLES by Kimberly Brubaker Bradley

A SAFE HOME FOR MANATEES by Priscilla Belz Jenkins

THE SKELETON INSIDE YOU by Philip Balestrino

SLEEP IS FOR EVERYONE by Paul Showers

SNAKES ARE HUNTERS by Patricia Lauber

SNOW IS FALLING by Franklyn M. Branley

SOUNDS ALL AROUND by Wendy Pfeffer

SPONGES ARE SKELETONS by Barbara Juster Esbensen

STARFISH by Edith Thacher Hurd

THE SUN: OUR NEAREST STAR by Franklyn M. Branley

SUNSHINE MAKES THE SEASONS by Franklyn M. Branley

SWITCH ON, SWITCH OFF by Melvin Berger

TERRIBLE TYRANNOSAURS by Kathleen Weidner Zoehfeld

A TREE IS A PLANT by Clyde Robert Bulla

VOLCANOES by Franklyn M. Branley

WHAT COLOR IS CAMOUFLAGE? by Carolyn Otto

WHAT HAPPENS TO A HAMBURGER? by Paul Showers

WHAT IS THE WORLD MADE OF? ALL ABOUT SOLIDS, LIQUIDS, AND GASES by Kathleen Weidner Zoehfeld

WHAT LIVES IN A SHELL? by Kathleen Weidner Zoehfeld

WHAT MAKES A MAGNET? by Franklyn M. Branley

WHAT MAKES A SHADOW? by Clyde Robert Bulla

WHAT THE MOON IS LIKE by Franklyn M. Branley

WHAT'S ALIVE? by Kathleen Weidner Zoehfeld

WHAT'S IT LIKE TO BE A FISH? by Wendy Pfeffer

WHAT WILL THE WEATHER BE? by Lynda DeWitt

WHERE ARE THE NIGHT ANIMALS? by Mary Ann Fraser

WHERE DOES THE GARBAGE GO? by Paul Showers

WHO EATS WHAT? FOOD CHAINS AND FOOD WEBS by Patricia Lauber

WHY DO LEAVES CHANGE COLOR? by Betsy Maestro

WHY FROGS ARE WET by Judy Hawes

WHY I SNEEZE, SHIVER, HICCUP, AND YAWN by Melvin Berger

YOU'RE ABOARD SPACESHIP EARTH by Patricia Lauber

ZIPPING, ZAPPING, ZOOMING BATS by Ann Earle

You can also get answers in the children's question-and-answer magazine *Ask*, available by calling 1-800-827-0227 or visiting www.cricketmag.com.

Finally, you and your child can log on to Ask Jeeves for Kids, www.ajkids.com, and search cyberspace for the answer to your question.

Cooking Counts As Chemistry!

Children's cookbooks are an invaluable source for learning math and science. Through cooking, children read and follow directions, measure, tell time, predict, observe, and consider variables. Some titles are sold as special "science in the kitchen" books, but the two I've come across that are actually focused on science experiments are SIMPLE KITCHEN EXPERIMENTS by Muriel Mandell and SCIENCE EXPERIMENTS YOU CAN EAT by Vicki Cobb. Other books are collections of recipes with a little scientific commentary sprinkled here and there like spice. The bottom line: You can use any simple cookbook and achieve the same results as these specially marketed volumes (see Good R'eating, p. 68). You can even come up with your own culinary footnotes as needed with the help of Howard Hillman's KITCHEN SCIENCE: A GUIDE TO KNOWING THE HOWS AND WHYS FOR FUN AND SUCCESS IN THE KITCHEN, which is a book for grown-ups that will help you field questions while you cook, such as why potatoes turn a funny color if they are not put in water and why onions make you cry. (This is also a nice book for your "Question Board" collection, see Question Board, p. 163).

Twenty years later, I am *still* using my Betty Crocker's COOKBOOK FOR BOYS AND GIRLS but if you are looking for some more contemporary sources for culinary adventures you can share with your children, grab a book and let learning come to a boiling point.

Brennan, Georgeanne and Ethel
THE CHILDREN'S KITCHEN GARDEN: A BOOK OF GARDENING, COOKING, AND LEARNING
Based on a curriculum implemented at the East Bay French-American School in Berkeley, this book helps children establish a connection with the food they eat and the world in which they live by showing children how to grow their own ingredients. An excellent science tie-in to cooking.

COOKING ON THE COMPUTER

If you like Mollie Katzen's style, check out BRY-BACK MANOR www.bry-backmanor.org/picture recipes.html and WHAT'S COOKING? at http://members.cox.net/tinsnips/pages/cooking.html. Both of these Web sites offer easy-to-print recipes for children told in pictures as well as words. If your children invent their own great recipes, they can post them online at Kids: Kings of the Kitchen, www.scoreone.com/kids_kitchen, and try munchies other children have made!

Buck-Murray, Marian

THE MASH AND SMASH COOKBOOK: FUN AND YUMMY RECIPES EVERY KID CAN MAKE!

One of the zanier children's cookbooks, this definitely offers a hands-on approach. Spaghetti soup and bubbling yo-yo, anyone?

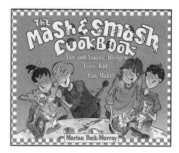

Cunningham, Marion

COOKING WITH CHILDREN: 15 LESSONS FOR CHILDREN, AGE 7 AND UP, WHO REALLY WANT TO LEARN TO COOK

Cunningham creates a children's cooking school in one of the absolute best books available for teaching children basic culinary skills. Since the author earned fame as a compiler of the adult classic **FANNIE FARMER'S COOKBOOK**, be sure to offer Deborah Hopkinson's lovely picture book tribute to Farmer, **FANNIE IN THE KITCHEN,** as a side dish.

Enderle, Judith Ross and Stephanie Jacob Gordon

SOMETHING'S HAPPENING ON CALABASH STREET

It's the Calabash street fair, and your children can follow along in the story, sampling all the flavors of a multicultural neighborhood.

Goss, Gary **BLUE MOON SOUP: A FAMILY COOKBOOK**

An African saying goes, "a good soup attracts chairs," and so it stands to reason a good soup cookbook will attract readers. The challenging recipes will introduce children to more sophisticated ingredients, and the whimsical illustrations are sure to charm. Follow up with the picture book **ALVIE EATS SOUP** by Ross Collins.

Katzen, Mollie and Ann Henderson

PRETEND SOUP AND OTHER REAL RECIPES: A COOKBOOK FOR PRESCHOOLERS & UP

Katzen sets a new standard for clarity by creating a cookbook that even very young children can follow easily, with colorful and simply drawn illustrations of every step. While I find the recipes themselves a little bland, I always enjoy using this book with children because they are in control and really learn to follow a recipe. Older children can graduate to Katzen's **HONEST PRETZELS AND 64 OTHER AMAZING RECIPES FOR COOKS AGES 8 & UP.**

Kohl, MaryAnn F., and Jean Potter

COOKING ART: EASY EDIBLE ART FOR YOUNG CHILDREN

Legendary chef Julia Child once exclaimed, "Oh, look how beautiful that is! Somebody must have had their

A POEM TO SING WHILE YOU COOK

Beautiful Soup, so rich and green,
Waiting in a hot tureen!
Who for such dainties would not stoop?
Soup of the evening, beautiful Soup!
Soup of the evening, beautiful Soup!
Beau-ootifil Soo-oop!
Beau-ootifil Soo-oop!
Soo-oop of the e-e-evening,
Beautiful, beautiful soup!

—Lewis Carroll,
ALICE'S ADVENTURES IN WONDERLAND

fingers all over it!" Such a comment might apply to the cooking capers in this book. It includes 89 recipes that require no baking, 64 recipes that use 5 ingredients or less, 25 recipes that take fifteen minutes or less to prepare, child-readable icons and thematic chapters . . . Now, *this* is a cookbook with primary children in mind.

Robins, Deri THE KIDS' AROUND THE WORLD COOKBOOK

A passport for your child's palate! Families will enjoy travelling through both science and geography using this heavily illustrated, step-by-step tasting tour of the world. Integrate treats into Reading: A Passport to Geography, p. 128.

. . . Some other general cookbooks seasoned to children's tastes are KIDS COOKING by the editors of Klutz Press (laminated to withstand spills) and COOKING WIZARDRY FOR KIDS by Margaret Kenda and Phyllis S. Williams.

For more cookbooks see Good R'eating, p. 68.

And if in the end your child is simply the type to burn water, don't worry. Just tell her to save her dinner scraps. Good eaters have the same chance to learn science as good cooks if they use MAKE YOUR OWN DINOSAUR OUT OF CHICKEN BONES: FOOLPROOF INSTRUCTIONS FOR BUDDING PALEONTOLOGISTS by Chris McGowan. Another option for children who can't cook is simply to spoil everyone else's appetite; they can read aloud from IT'S DISGUSTING AND WE ATE IT: TRUE FOOD FACTS FROM AROUND THE WORLD AND THROUGHOUT HISTORY by James Solheim or HOW TO EAT FRIED WORMS by Thomas Rockwell.

Mythology and Science . . . Pourquoi Pas?

What makes the seasons? What causes a rainbow to stretch across the sky? Why do spiders spin webs? These questions about our natural world intrigue children today, as they have for thousands of years. Nowadays, we can find very concrete scientific explanations for phenomena but long ago such questions were answered with imaginative stories that explained *why*. These stories once reflected systems of belief, but now that we are privy to more scientific rationales, they have been removed from the religion shelves and placed under the heading "mythology." A child's interest in science is a great opportunity to present this classical literature. There are lots of books available about mythologies from all cultures worldwide (GODDESSES, HEROES, AND SHAMANS: THE YOUNG PEOPLE'S GUIDE TO WORLD MYTHOLOGY, for example). But to me, the granddaddy of them all is D'AULAIRES' BOOK OF GREEK MYTHS.

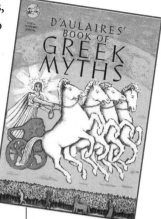

As Edith Hamilton's MYTHOLOGY was a definitive collection for adults, Ingri and Edgar Parin D'Aulaires's book is the definitive collection for introducing mythology to children. I have been sharing this book since I appropriated my brother's copy when I was ten years old, and I have yet to meet a child of any ethnic background who was not entranced with this violent, passionate, and imaginative history. This book is as necessary to a children's collection as a Phillips head screwdriver is to a toolbox. Use the stories to do a double dive into both left- and right-brain activities. For instance, use the reference to Iris, the messenger of the gods who runs on a rainbow path from Olympus to earth, as an opportunity to study light and color and prisms. Marvel with new respect at the weavings of real spiders after reading about the come-uppance of Arachne. Mourn with poor mother Demeter as her daughter is kidnapped to the land of Hades, then explore the earth's rotation that causes the seasons. As Phaethon seeks to ride alongside his father, the firey Helios, you and your child can measure earth's distance to the sun. Examine the science of human behavior as beautiful Pandora, seduced into opening her forbidden box, unleashes all the miseries that plague mankind.

After reading any of these myths and thinking about them from scientific angles, children can construct their own myths to explain why we have rainbows, why spiders spin webs, why the seasons change, why the sun moves across the sky, and why bad things happen to good people. And through it all, children can look to the skies (and books about the skies) to explore the universe that may contain the real answers to all these mysteries, along with the constellations that twinkle in immortal tribute to the Greeks' speculation.

Mythology is the first cousin to a type of folktale called a *pourquoi* tale, French for "why." Some of the strongest samples of pourquoi tales come from cultures that have historically valued storytelling. African and Native American nations have made notable contribu-

THE SKY'S THE LIMIT! CONSTELLATION COMPILATIONS

Burke, Juliet Sharman	STORIES FROM THE STARS: GREEK MYTHS OF THE ZODIAC
Hatchett, Clint	THE GLOW-IN-THE-DARK NIGHT SKY BOOK
Klutz, the editors of	BACKYARD STARS: A GUIDE FOR HOME AND THE ROAD BEDROOM ASTRONOMY
McCaughrean, Geraldine	STARRY TALES
Mitton, Jacqueline	ZOO IN THE SKY
Rey, H. A.	FIND THE CONSTELLATIONS

tions to the genre, but just like myths, *pourquoi* tales exist wherever there are storytellers and children who ask questions. In fact, the line differentiating mythology from *pourquoi* tradition is tenuous. As far as I can tell, mythology explains things in nature as occurring through the forces of deities, while *pourquoi* tales usually offer more folksy interpretations of cause and effect. "A *pourquoi* tale is in the eye of the beholder," one librarian explained to me. "One person's *pourquoi* tale can be someone else's mythology, and one person's mythology can be another person's religion. It all depends on where you put it on the shelf." Librarians wield such power!

For the purposes of integrating science and literature, mythology and *pourquoi* tales both uphold Einstein's statement, "Imagination is more important than knowledge." Or at least, one encourages the other.

Dear Madame Esmé,

Guess what my child does? He tattles! He tattles on his brothers and sisters. He tattles on his classmates. And worst of all, he tattled on me and told my mother-in-law that I order out and say it's really my cooking whenever she comes to visit. Enough is enough! Do you have a story to end this stage?

Dear Gentle Reader,

You just tattled on your own child, but I'll let it pass if you try to do better next time. The cautionary tale ARMADILLO TATTLETALE by Helen Ketteman will likely squelch the squealing in primary-aged people. Armadillo overhears everything with his preposterously large ears and takes it upon himself to repeat everything that is said, even if he doesn't remember the words exactly. Armadillo finally meets his comeuppance when he tattles on Alligator. The illustrations are just plain goofy, and the twists that Armadillo's tattling take are laugh-out-loud with the read-aloud crowd. Children respond to the drama of this pourquoi tale and the story offers an earful about the Golden Rule as well as why the armadillo runs so fast. A nice story with a similar theme is Patricia C. McKissack's THE HONEST-TO-GOODNESS TRUTH.

POUR UN PETIT PEU DE POURQUOI, CHECK OUT:

Aardema, Verna	• WHY MOSQUITOS BUZZ IN PEOPLE'S EARS
Bryan, Ashley	• ASHLEY BRYAN'S AFRICAN TALES, UH-HUH
Bruchac, Joseph	• THE FIRST STRAWBERRIES: A CHEROKEE STORY
	• THE GREAT BALL GAME: A MUSKOGEE STORY
	• HOW CHIPMUNK GOT HIS STRIPES: A TALE OF BRAGGING AND TEASING
Dayrell, Elphinstone	• WHY THE SUN AND THE MOON LIVE IN THE SKY
Gerson, Mary-Joan	• WHY THE SKY IS FAR AWAY
Goble, Paul	• THE GIFT OF THE SACRED DOG
Haley, Gail E.	• A STORY, A STORY
Hamilton, Martha, and Mitch Weiss	• HOW & WHY STORIES: WORLD TALES KIDS CAN READ & TELL
Kipling, Rudyard	• JUST SO STORIES
Martin Jr., Bill	• THE LITTLE SQUEEGY BUG
Oughton, Jerrie	• HOW THE STARS FELL INTO THE SKY: A NAVAJO LEGEND
Philip, Neil	• NOAH AND THE DEVIL
Poole, Amy Lowry	• HOW THE ROOSTER GOT HIS CROWN
Root, Phyllis	• BIG MOMMA MAKES THE WORLD

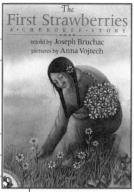

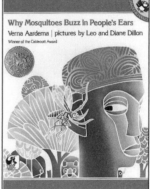

Mother Nature's Library

If you want to get your child deeply rooted in reading, hike to the library and fill your backpack with books on a subject that matters to all readers great and small. Trade literature about the natural world offers a compelling combination of information and imagination. Children, for instance, can weather natural disasters or revel in the seasons, climb Mount Everest without a sherpa, wonder at the biodiversity of the rain forest, stare at phosphorescent monsters at the bottom of the ocean, and even contemplate how they will protect the physical marvels described in these books.

✿ *Potato Pick:*

RIVER FRIENDLY,
RIVER WILD

*by Jane Kurtz, illustrated by
Neil Brennan*

Based on memories of living
through the flood in Grand
Forks, North Dakota, the author
uses free verse to carry the
reader through the confusion,
horror, and hope of a community in the throes of survival.
The dramatic story is complemented with muted paintings
of fire and water, submerged
homes, rescued Christmas
ornaments, and Red Cross
trucks. This realistic, haunting
book succeeds in being sensitive without saccharine and
will move empathetic readers.
Teachers and home-schoolers
will find an easy connection
with natural disaster studies
and weather units. (7 and up)

Weather-Beaten Books

Growing up in the Midwest had a huge impact on my appreciation of the forces of nature. We had tornado drills in school,
all of us crouching down with our heads covered, visualizing
the twister scene from *The Wizard of Oz* and windows exploding out
into a million sharp needles (as my imaginative teachers liked to
describe). We had bellowing thunderstorms that would wake the whole
family in the night, rattling the windowpanes and lighting up the sky in
blinding silver. We had blizzards with snow so deep it buried cars and
came up to the necks of stop signs; we had to hold the tops of fences as
we walked so that we would not disappear under the drifts. Weather
made my childhood extra exciting, and it also taught me that Mother
Nature might even be a tougher cookie than my own mama. Stories
about extreme weather are stories with drama and these picture books
and nonfiction titles will widen the eyes and quicken the hearts of children in any geographic location.

WACKY AND WHIMSICAL WEATHER READ-ALOUDS

Barrett, Judi	• CLOUDY WITH A CHANCE OF MEATBALLS
Darrow, Sharon	• OLD THUNDER AND MISS RANEY
Huntington, Amy	• ONE MONDAY
Krupp, E. C.	• THE RAINBOW AND YOU
McKissack, Patricia C.	• MIRANDY AND BROTHER WIND
Prigger, Mary Skillings	• AUNT MINNIE AND THE TWISTER
Seuss, Dr.	• BARTHOLOMEW AND THE OOBLECK
Tresselt, Alvin	• HIDE AND SEEK FOG
White, Linda Arms	• COMES A WIND
Wiesner, David	• SECTOR 7

WICKED AND WANTON WEATHER READ-ALOUDS

Beard, Darleen Bailey	• TWISTER
Doyle, Malachy	• STORM CATS
Henderson, Kathy	• THE STORM
Kurtz, Jane	• RIVER FRIENDLY, RIVER WILD
London, Jonathan	• HURRICANE!
Lyon, George Ella	• ONE LUCKY GIRL
Myers, Anna	• STOLEN BY THE SEA (Chapter book.)

| Steig, William | • BRAVE IRENE |
| Wiesner, David | • HURRICANE |

FOLLOW UP WITH SOME WILD WEATHER NONFICTION!

Berger, Melvin and Gilda	• CAN IT RAIN CATS AND DOGS? QUESTIONS AND ANSWERS ABOUT WEATHER
Bortz, Fred	• DR. FRED'S WEATHER WATCH: CREATE AND RUN YOUR OWN WEATHER STATION
Breen, Mark, and Kathleen Friestad	• THE KIDS' BOOK OF WEATHER FORECASTING
Klutz, the editors of	• DISASTER SCIENCE
Murphy, Jim	• BLIZZARD: THE STORM THAT CHANGED AMERICA
Simon, Seymour	• STORMS (See Simon Says Science, p. 182.)
Singer, Marilyn	• ON THE SAME DAY IN MARCH: A TOUR OF THE WORLD'S WEATHER

. . . Also, for wet weather, check out Stories for a Rainy Day, p. 346.

The Environment: Reading for Your Great-Great-Great-Grandchildren

Scientific reading is potent in promoting environmental responsibility and inquiry. Sharing science from this perspective can, for some people, create a lot of the same uncomfortable feelings that sharing history creates. Just as we may feel defensive about our failures to have protected children in the past, it is hard to talk about environmental science without admitting that the way we behave now is not truly supportive of our children's future. The fact of the matter is, most of us grown-ups in industrialized nations developed some pretty bad habits because we assumed we had unlimited resources. We know now that our children can't afford to be as flippant. Since we helped to create so many of the problems that our children will have to solve, it seems only reasonable that we preen them to be more Earth-conscious than we have been. You can begin to accomplish this by offering your child a basic appreciation for the natural world. Learning about ecosystems, water cycles, and wildlife can help your child develop a concern

❀ *Potato Pick:*

LOST! A STORY IN STRING

by Paul Fleischman, illustrated by C. B. Mordan

A lightning storm hits, and knocks out the power. No TV! No VCR! No radio! No computer! "I'll die!" moans a nine-year-old girl. But Grandmother has the perfect remedy for a night without electricity: a story, told with a loop of yarn and a stretch of memory. Grandmother tells a story of a poor mountain girl who "didn't own one store-bought toy," but instead twisted and turned a piece of string and used her imagination until the string resembled items in her everyday life. When the girl's beloved dog runs away, she hunts for it in the woods, only to find herself lost and dependent on her own resourcefulness. The bold ink-on-clayboard illustrations give this compelling adventure an old-fashioned feel. Detailed directions about how to create the string figures depicted throughout are included in the back of the book, so the next time the power is out, your children will be able to look to their own powers to spin an exciting "yarn." (7 and up)

about the issues of pollution, allocation of resources, and species endangerment. Reading about science helps children value our planet and understand that in the end we need it more than it needs us. The purpose is not necessarily to get children to take a stand on global warming or some such issue. It is simply to guide them toward a healthy respect for the environment so that they can make responsible choices about what is right for our planet. Reading science-related material trains future doctors of the environment to "do no harm" by giving them information and cultivating awe.

Unfortunately, at this juncture in publishing, a number of children's books about the environment have too much awe and not enough information. They can be a bit "New Age-y" or schmaltzy for some comfort levels, including mine. When I read some of these books, I get a flashback of the old commercial featuring a Native American man observing someone littering while a tear slowly falls from his eye. I was surprised to discover many books carrying this cliché into print. Beware of stories that end with a slow tear falling. There is enough real information that is tear worthy without emotionally manipulating children.

Speaking of tears, we want children to be aware, not frightened. The urgency some authors convey about an environmental agenda sometimes backfires and becomes dogma. As a result, certain well-intentioned children's books on environmental subject matter are not in line with the emotional development of their intended audience. Holes in the ozone, acid rain, contaminated water, the felling of the forests that create most of the air we breathe . . . these are scary concepts for anyone, let alone children. It is not fair to present children with material that suggests their environment is being poisoned or desecrated without offering them some sense of control or reasonable chance to participate in making improvements. This control and opportunity will vary based on your child's individual maturity and your own willingness to support his decisions to live in an earth-friendly way (for suggestions for social action, see Earth Friendly Deeds = Earth Friendly Reads, p. 184).

TRASHY READING FOR KIDS

Invite the garbage man . . . *ahem* . . . sanitation engineer to deliver a storytime with this messy mix of fiction and nonfiction.

Asch, Frank	THE EARTH AND I
Gibbons, Gail	RECYCLE: A HANDBOOK FOR KIDS
Leedy, Loreen	THE GREAT TRASH BASH
McMullan, Kate	I STINK!
Sharmat, Mitchell	GREGORY, THE TERRIBLE EATER
Showers, Paul	WHERE DOES THE GARBAGE GO?
Zimmerman, Andrea, and David Clemesha	TRASHY TOWN
Zion, Gene	DEAR GARBAGE MAN

There are, in fact, some excellent books about the problems in our environment and what can be done about them, but if you want children's books to help even the youngest child value the living world, the first step, as I have suggested, is to offer books *about* the living world. Offer books that show beauty, metamorphosis, growth: books about animals and insects, trees and flowers. Offer books that show process: cause and effect, how things are made, science experiments that demonstrate real concepts. Offer books that show variety and diversity, such as field guides. Offer books that show our relationship to nature: books about weather, gardening, creatures living in a variety of climates and natural environments. Offer books that give children real-life science heroes and mentors, such as biography. Books with clear, accurate, non-fiction content are what will give children background information, problem-solving skills, and the genuine desire to get involved. Show children *what* is worth saving, and they will grow up to make meaningful efforts. Two titles that can help us grown-ups with our eco-show-and-tell are **THE SENSE OF WONDER** by Rachel Carson and **EARTH CHILD 2000: EARTH SCIENCE FOR YOUNG CHILDREN** by Kathryn Sheehan and Mary Waidner. Also, be sure to experience **EARTHSEARCH: A KIDS' GEOGRAPHY MUSEUM IN A BOOK** by John Cassidy alongside your child. If you want to use reading to help the planet, follow the Earth's lead and don't drill too deep. Just act natural.

WORK THESE NATURE-SMOOCHING READ-ALOUDS INTO YOUR CHILD'S READING ENVIRONMENT . . .

. . . Along with books in Far Out Space Stories, p. 405; Animal Kingdom, p. 354; Buggy for Books, p. 406; Rainy Day, p. 346; Plant the Seed to Read, p. 413; and Stories for All Seasons, p. 374:

Allen, Judy, and Tudor Humphries	**Backyard Books series** (Terrific primary series.)

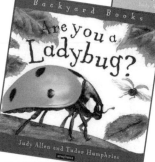

- ARE YOU AN ANT?
- ARE YOU A BEE?
- ARE YOU A BUTTERFLY?
- ARE YOU A DRAGONFLY?
- ARE YOU A GRASSHOPPER?
- ARE YOU A LADYBUG?
- ARE YOU A SNAIL?
- ARE YOU A SPIDER?

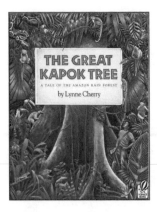

Arnosky, Jim	• FIELD TRIPS: BUG HUNTING, ANIMAL TRACKING, BIRD-WATCHING, SHORE WALKING, WITH JIM ARNOSKY (Wonderful author of about a hundred nature guides for children and the popular **Crinkleroot** series.)
Aruego, Jose, and Ariane Dewey	• WEIRD FRIENDS: UNLIKELY ALLIES IN THE ANIMAL KINGDOM
Bang, Molly	• NOBODY PARTICULAR: ONE WOMAN'S FIGHT TO SAVE THE BAYS (Comic-book style makes it a tricky read-aloud with large groups but worthwhile one-on-one.)
Baylor, Byrd	• HAWK, I'M YOUR BROTHER
Best, Cari	• GOOSE'S STORY
Bortz, Fred	• COLLISION COURSE: COSMIC IMPACTS AND LIFE ON EARTH
Cannon, Janell	• STELLALUNA • VERDI
Carle, Eric	• SLOWLY, SLOWLY, SLOWLY, SAID THE SLOTH
Cherry, Lynne	• THE GREAT KAPOK TREE: A TALE OF THE AMAZON RAIN FOREST • A RIVER RAN WILD: AN ENVIRONMENTAL HISTORY (Cherry is a formidable environmental reading force; check out all her books. Detailed illustrations, though, are better for small groups.)
Cobb, Vicki	Imagine Living Here series: • THIS PLACE IS COLD • THIS PLACE IS CROWDED • THIS PLACE IS DRY • THIS PLACE IS LONELY • THIS PLACE IS WET
DuQuette, Keith	• THEY CALL ME WOOLLY: WHAT ANIMAL NAMES CAN TELL US
Dyer, Sarah	• FIVE LITTLE FIENDS
Dorling Kindersley, publisher	Look Closer series: • CORAL REEF • DESERT LIFE • FOREST LIFE • MEADOW • POND LIFE • RAIN FOREST • RIVER LIFE • SWAMP LIFE • TIDE POOL • TREE LIFE
Fleming, Denise	• WHERE ONCE THERE WAS A WOOD

Frasier, Debra	• ON THE DAY YOU WERE BORN
Fyleman, Rose	• A FAIRY WENT A-MARKETING
George, Jean Craighead	• JULIE OF THE WOLVES (Chapter book.) • THE MISSING 'GATOR OF GUMBO LIMBO: AN ECO MYSTERY (Chapter book.) • MY SIDE OF THE MOUNTAIN (Chapter book. A prolific and gifted author; check out all of her work.)
Geraghty, Paul	• STOP THAT NOISE!
Hiaasen, Carl	• HOOT
Hurwitz, Johanna	• MUCH ADO ABOUT ALDO (Chapter book, vegetarianism.)
Jeffers, Susan, illus.	• BROTHER EAGLE, SISTER SKY: A MESSAGE FROM CHIEF SEATTLE
Jenkins, Steve	• LIFE ON EARTH: THE STORY OF EVOLUTION • THE TOP OF THE WORLD: CLIMBING MOUNT EVEREST • WHAT DO YOU DO WHEN SOMETHING WANTS TO EAT YOU? (Steve Jenkins is an accomplished nature author; check out all his books.)
Johnson, D. B.	• HENRY HIKES TO FITCHBURG (Based on Thoreau.)
Johnson, Tony	• BIGFOOT CINDERRRRELLA
Karas, G. Brian	• ATLANTIC
Kleven, Elisa	• THE DANCING DEER AND THE FOOLISH HUNTER
Lasky, Kathryn	• SHE'S WEARING A DEAD BIRD ON HER HEAD!
Lewis, Richard	• IN THE SPACE OF THE SKY
Locker, Thomas	• CLOUD DANCE • MOUNTAIN DANCE • WATER DANCE
McDonald, Megan	• JUDY MOODY SAVES THE WORLD! (Short chapter book.)
Nicholls, Judith, ed.	• EARTHWAYS, EARTHWISE: POEMS ON CONSERVATION
Paulus, Trina	• HOPE FOR THE FLOWERS
Peet, Bill	• FAREWELL TO SHADY GLADE
Pratt, Kristin Joy	• A WALK IN THE RAINFOREST
Pringle, Laurence	• SCHOLASTIC ENCYCLOPEDIA OF ANIMALS

LIFE ON EARTH
THE STORY OF EVOLUTION
BY STEVE JENKINS

I THINK THAT I SHALL NEVER SEE . . .

Oxygen for breathing, brought to us by trees. Timber for our homes, brought to us by trees. Paper for our books, brought to us by trees! The least we can do is hug a tree. Or if that's a bit too crunchy-granola for you, harbor the arbor in these picture books.

George, Kristine O'Connell	OLD ELM SPEAKS: TREE POEMS
Gibbons, Gail	• TELL ME, TREE: ALL ABOUT TREES FOR KIDS
Hiscock, Bruce	• THE BIG TREE
Kelley, Marty	• FALL IS NOT EASY
Robbins, Ken	• AUTUMN LEAVES
Romanova, Natalia	ONCE THERE WAS A TREE
Silverstein, Shel	• THE GIVING TREE
Udry, Janice May	• A TREE IS NICE

SIMON SAYS SCIENCE!

Seymour Simon is the author of two hundred informational children's books, half of which have been named Outstanding Science Trade Books for Children by the National Science Teachers Association. Inspired by the lack of good science books available when he began teaching in the New York City public schools in 1955, he continues to teach intermediate children to this day through his straightforward and enlightening writing style encompassing both facts and a healthy dose of marvel ("If the sun were hollow, it could hold 1.3 *million* Earths."). There is hardly a scientific topic he hasn't covered—dinosaurs, paper airplanes, pets in a jar, optical illusions, animal migration—in his astonishingly beautiful photo essays. OUT OF SIGHT: PICTURES OF HIDDEN WORLDS and ANIMALS NOBODY LOVES are two examples of his style but his works fall under wide themes:

EARTH SCIENCE

DESERTS
EARTHQUAKES
ICEBERGS AND GLACIERS
LIGHTNING
MOUNTAINS
OCEANS
STORMS
TORNADOES
VOLCANOES
WEATHER
WILDFIRES

OUTER SPACE

COMETS, METEORS, AND ASTEROIDS
DESTINATION: JUPITER
DESTINATION: SPACE

EARTH: OUR PLANET IN SPACE
EXPLORING SPACE
GALAXIES
JUPITER
MARS
MERCURY
NEPTUNE
OUR SOLAR SYSTEM
SATURN
SPACE WORDS
STAR WALK
  (THE POETRY OF SPACE)
STARS
THE SUN
URANUS
THE UNIVERSE

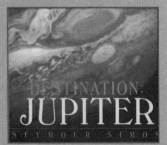

THE HUMAN BODY

BONES: OUR SKELETAL SYSTEM
THE BRAIN: OUR NERVOUS SYSTEM
THE HEART: OUR CIRCULATORY SYSTEM
MUSCLES: OUR MUSCULAR SYSTEM

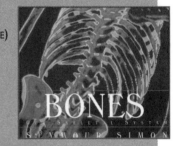

To make sure children of every age can enjoy science, Simon has also come out with the **SeeMore** series of science books for emergent readers, also using photographs, with such compelling topics as FIGHTING FIRES, WILD BEARS, BABY ANIMALS, and GIANT MACHINES. And if your child is more a fiction fan, you will still be able to squeeze in some science facts with Simon's intermediate mystery series, **Einstein Anderson, Science Detective.** Check out Simon's Web site, www.seymoursimon.com, to be scintillated both by science and by the latest in the career of a great children's book creator.

Rockwell, Anne	• BECOMING BUTTERFLIES • GROWING LIKE ME
Ryder, Joanne	• EACH LIVING THING • EARTHDANCE
Sandved, Kjell B.	• THE BUTTERFLY ALPHABET
Schaefer, Lola M.	• THIS IS THE RAIN
Schlein, Miriam	• HELLO, HELLO!
Dr. Seuss	• THE LORAX
Silverstein, Shel	• LAFCADIO: THE LION WHO SHOT BACK (Short chapter book; an interesting parable about assimilation.)
Van Allsburg, Chris	• JUST A DREAM
Walsh, Ellen Stoll	• DOT & JABBER AND THE MYSTERY OF THE MISSING STREAM • DOT & JABBER AND THE GREAT ACORN MYSTERY

A FEW GOOD "HOW-TO" BOOKS TO GET YOUNG ONES GO-ING AND HOE-ING:

Banck, Yvette Santiago	• GARDENING WIZARDRY FOR KIDS
Bjork, Christina, and Lena Anderson	• LINNEA'S WINDOWSILL GARDEN
Brennan, Georgeanne and Ethel	• THE CHILDREN'S KITCHEN GARDEN: A BOOK OF GARDENING, COOKING, AND LEARNING
Carlson, Laurie	• GREEN THUMBS! A KID'S ACTIVITY GUIDE TO INDOOR AND OUTDOOR GARDENING
Clausen, Ruth Rogers	• WILDFLOWER (Fandex Family Field Guides)
Fausch, Karen	• THE WINDOW BOX BOOK
Glaser, Linda	• COMPOST! GROWING GARDENS FROM YOUR GARBAGE
Herck, Alice	• THE ENCHANTED GARDENING BOOK
Lovejoy, Sharon	• ROOTS, SHOOTS, BUCKETS & BOOTS • SUNFLOWER HOUSES
Raftery, Kevin, and Kim Gilbert	• KIDS GARDENING: A KID'S GUIDE TO MESSING AROUND IN THE DIRT
Rhoades, Diane	• GARDEN CRAFTS FOR KIDS: 50 GREAT REASONS TO GET YOUR HANDS DIRTY
Rosen, Michael J., ed.	• DOWN TO EARTH: GARDEN SECRETS! GARDEN STORIES! GARDEN PROJECTS YOU CAN DO!
Ryden, Hope	• WILDFLOWERS AROUND THE YEAR (Flower identification.)

Going, Going, Almost Gone: A Nonfiction Menagerie

Charman, Andy	• I Wonder Why the Dodo Is Dead and Other Questions About Extinct and Endangered Animals
Cohen, Daniel	• The Modern Ark: Saving Endangered Species
Facklam, Margery	• And Then There Was One: The Mysteries of Extinction
Fowler, Allan	• It Could Still Be Endangered
Lessem, Don	• Dinosaurs to Dodos: An Encyclopedia of Extinct Animals
Markle, Sandra and William	• Gone Forever: An Alphabet of Extinct Animals
McCully, Emily Arnold	• Hurry!
Pallotta, Jerry	• The Extinct Alphabet Book
Robbins, Ken	• Thunder on the Plains: The Story of the American Buffalo (Beautiful book, great read-aloud.)
Wright, Alexandra	• Will We Miss Them? Endangered Species (Written by a sixth-grader!)

Earth Friendly Deeds = Earth Friendly Reads! A Planet-a-Thon

A Planet-A-Thon is something you can do in your own family or with your child's class. Children take pledges for every Earth-friendly act they can accomplish in a week. Record acts in a seven-day log. Money collected can go to the library for science books, or for seeds and supplies to start a garden in front of the library to make it more inviting! The Planet-A-Thon also encourages reading because children will be reading in order to research Earth-friendly acts they can perform. Finished logs can be displayed at the school or public library. While of course children could donate the money to a worthy environmental organization instead of the library, using the money to buy books or promote reading is also perfectly legitimate because children with the resources to learn about the earth may be inspired to take care of it. Try this fund-raiser the week before Earth Day in April, and culminate with a bike parade and treats. I suggest Land and Sea cups: blue Jell-O with gummi fish suspended throughout, or chocolate pudding topped with chocolate wafer crumbs and gummi worms.

Grown-ups can learn, too: When I started researching environmental books for children, I discovered that some of the ways in which I could care for the earth were so easy that I couldn't believe I hadn't been doing them all along! Go over these Earth-friendly suggestions with your children to get them started.

Twenty-five Planet-a-Thon Prompts

1. Reuse or recycle tinfoil.
2. Buy eggs in a cardboard carton instead of a Styrofoam carton.
3. Use beeswax crayons or make your own art supplies using KIDS' CRAZY ART CONCOCTIONS by Jill Frankel Hauser.
4. Compost.
5. Help your family prepare a tofu or tempeh recipe.
6. Turn off the tap when you aren't using the water while you brush your teeth (save about four gallons each time).
7. Conserve water by taking a shower instead of a bath (save about twenty-five gallons).
8. Pick up litter on the beach or at the park.
9. Make a bird feeder. (I like to cut toast with cookie cutters, spread peanut butter on the shapes, and dip them in bird seed. Poke a hole in the top and add a loop of string through the hole. They are so pretty, hanging on a tree!)
10. Plant a butterfly garden, a window-box garden, or a tree.
11. Move a bug out of your home without killing it.
12. Buy tuna that's labeled "dolphin friendly."
13. Avoid fast food. . . . Make a home-cooked meal.
14. Donate your used toys to a worthy cause.
15. Snip plastic "six-pack rings," the little plastic circles that hold together six-packs of canned drinks, so animals don't get caught in them.
16. Bring your own bag to the grocery store.
17. Use both sides of the paper for homework.
18. Dust your light bulbs (dusty bulbs use more energy).
19. Ride a bike or walk instead of asking your parents to drive (skipping a single car trip each week can prevent the emission of up to 950 pounds of carbon dioxide each year).
20. Remind cooks to put the lid on a pot when bringing water to a boil.
21. Write to a textbook company and ask them to print on recycled and tree-free paper. Ask your classmates to sign the letter.

22. Remind your family to unplug appliances when not using them.

23. Hang your family's clothes out to dry.

24. Buy fewer greeting cards to save trees. . . . Make your own from recycled paper or send your special messages via e-mail (www.bluemountain.com has greetings 4 U 2 send).

25. Flush one less time a day! Gross, maybe, but worth it; if everyone did it, our country would save about a billion gallons every day.

Dear Madame Esmé,

In the face of petroleum shortages, are there any good books for kids about alternative energy?

Dear Gentle Reader,

These picture books are a gas, and will get you and your family thinking about alternative everything. WESLANDIA *by Paul Fleischman is a tale about young renegade Wesley, who plans his own civilization using a mysterious crop that he has cultivated in his backyard. In the process, Wesley changes his community's perspective of the world and of himself. This book can be a springboard for other projects, whether real research about the impact and potential of natural resources or more creative assignments similar to the one Wesley gives himself: starting a society of one's own, complete with languages and sports. Kevin Hawkes's bold and imaginative artwork, with colors as lush as any farmers market, is the perfect accompaniment to this inspired and inspiring story of how individuality can ultimately make you the leader of your team.*

Slow and steady wins the race and enjoys a good stroll in D. B. Johnson's HENRY HIKES TO FITCHBURG, *inspired by a passage from Henry David Thoreau's* WALDEN. *Young readers will root for the two bears as they make their way to Fitchburg: one by working for the money to buy a train ticket, one by walking and delighting in the world around him. Contemporary, angular illustrations with matte blues, greens, and mustards enhance the text and will please children page after page.*

Math Magic

Thesese books are wonderful for coaxing children who respond to art and narrative into the math-loving equation. Where were these books when I was a kid? Maybe then I wouldn't have had to look over and see Carlo D'Agostino's answers all the time. (Sorry, Mr. Porok, my high school algebra teacher. You tried.) These books focus on math *concepts* rather than *counting*, and if you add them up you'll have children with improved math skills *and* reading comprehension.

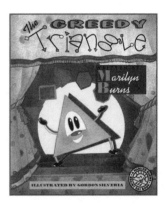

Adler, David A.	• SHAPE UP! (Polygons.)
Anno, Mitsumasa and Masaichiro	• ANNO'S MYSTERIOUS MULTIPLYING JAR (Factoring.)
Appelt, Kathi	• BATS AROUND THE CLOCK (Time.) • BATS ON PARADE (Multiplication.)
Burns, Marilyn	• THE GREEDY TRIANGLE (Geometry.) • THE I HATE MATHEMATICS! BOOK (Math anxiety, problem-solving games, and strategies.)
Clemson, Wendy	• TIMES TABLES! (Not a story, but a good concrete visual explanation of times tables.)
D'Amico, Joan, and Karen Eich Drummond	• THE MATH CHEF: OVER 60 MATH ACTIVITIES AND RECIPES FOR KIDS (Mucho math in the kitchen.)
Daniels, Teri	• MATH MAN (Real-world math situations.)
Demi	• ONE GRAIN OF RICE: A MATHEMATICAL FOLKTALE (Exponential theory.)
Enzensberger, Hans Magnus	• THE NUMBER DEVIL: A MATHEMATICAL ADVENTURE (Math anxiety chapter book, plus tons of fun math puzzles.)
Friedman, Aileen	• THE KING'S COMMISSIONERS (Place value.)
Geisert, Arthur	• ROMAN NUMERALS I TO MM (Roman numerals.)
Greene, Rhonda Gowler	• WHEN A LINE BENDS . . . A SHAPE BEGINS (Shapes.)
Hightower, Susan	• TWELVE SNAILS TO ONE LIZARD: A TALE OF MISCHIEF AND MEASUREMENT (Measurement.)
Hopkins, Lee Bennett, ed.	• MARVELOUS MATH: A BOOK OF POEMS (Math poems.)

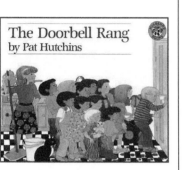

Hutchins, Pat	• THE DOORBELL RANG (Division.)
Julius, Edward H.	• ARITHMETRICKS: 50 EASY WAYS TO ADD, SUBTRACT, MULTIPLY, AND DIVIDE WITHOUT A CALCULATOR (Math shortcuts.)
Lasky, Kathryn	• THE LIBRARIAN WHO MEASURED THE EARTH (Measurement and history!)
Ledwon, Peter	• MIDNIGHT MATH: TWELVE TERRIFIC MATH GAMES
Leedy, Loreen	• 2 × 2 = BOO! A SET OF SPOOKY MULTIPLICATION STORIES (Multiplication.) • FRACTION ACTION (Fractions.) • MISSION: ADDITION (Addition.) • THE MONSTER MONEY BOOK (Money.) • SUBTRACTION ACTION (Subtraction.)
Lewis, J. Patrick	• ARITHME-TICKLE: AN EVEN NUMBER OF ODD RIDDLE-RHYMES (Simple operation riddles.)
Maganzini, Christy	• COOL MATH: MATH TRICKS, AMAZING MATH ACTIVITIES, COOL CALCULATIONS, AWESOME FACTOIDS, AND MORE
Markle, Sandra	• MATH MINI MYSTERIES (Investigative math.)
McMillan, Bruce	• EATING FRACTIONS (Fractions.) • JELLY BEANS FOR SALE (Money.) • ONE, TWO, ONE PAIR! (Pairs.)
Mills, Claudia	• 7 × 9 = TROUBLE! (Short chapter book; math anxiety, multiplication tables.)
Myller, Rolf	• HOW BIG IS A FOOT? (Measurement.)
Nagda, Ann Whitehead, and Cindy Bickel	• CHIMP MATH: LEARNING ABOUT TIME FROM A BABY CHIMPANZEE (Time.) • TIGER MATH: LEARNING TO GRAPH FROM A BABY TIGER (Graphing.)
Neuschwander, Cindy	• AMANDA BEAN'S AMAZING DREAM: A MATHEMATICAL STORY (Multiplication.) • SIR CUMFERENCE AND THE FIRST ROUND TABLE: A MATH ADVENTURE (Circumference and diameter.)
Peterson, Ivars, and Nancy Henderson	• MATH TREK: ADVENTURES IN THE MATHZONE (Advanced math concepts.)
Pinczes, Elinor J.	• INCHWORM AND A HALF (Measurement with fractions.) • ONE HUNDRED HUNGRY ANTS (Division, grouping.) • A REMAINDER OF ONE (Division with remainders.)

Schwartz, David M.
- **G Is for Googol**
  (Math vocabulary; great book!)
- **How Much Is a Million?** (Large numbers.)
- **If You Hopped Like a Frog** (Ratio and proportion.)
- **On Beyond a Million: An Amazing Math Journey**
  (Counting by powers of 10.)

Scieszka, Jon
- **Math Curse** (Math anxiety.)

Tang, Greg
- **The Best of Times** (Strategies for multiplication.)
- **The Grapes of Math** (Math riddles, visual problem-solving strategies.)
- **Math for All Seasons** (More math riddles.)

Dear Madame Esmé,

My child is ahead in reading, but the report card tells another story when it comes to math. Can reading skills help math skills?

Dear Gentle Reader,

If you add the skills together in one book and divide by two (you and your child spending time with each other), you'll find the answer to your problem. **The Grapes of Math** by Greg Tang, illustrated by Harry Briggs is a fun book to read together. Visual puzzles challenge children simply to count "how many," which is harder than it looks. With a few simple problem-solving techniques, though, the answers can be found faster than you can count to ten! Children will look at numbers in a whole new way, thanks to this combination of visual learning and verbal verve. A book to inspire critical thinking and for which the only criticism I found is that it's hard to share with a large group; you may want to make overhead transparencies of the illustrations if you take it to your child's classroom. Am I suggesting copyright infringement? Qui, moi? I am merely suggesting that you do what you need to do to share this wonderful book, as this team has gone far to effectively promote a love of math. Absolutely grape for intermediate and upper mathematicians! Count on the sequels **Math for All Seasons, Math Appeal,** and the multiplication strategy book **The Best of Times** to be just as mind-bending.

Thompson, Lauren	• ONE RIDDLE, ONE ANSWER (Value of zero.)
Tompert, Ann	• GRANDFATHER TANG'S STORY (Tangrams.)
Walters, Virginia	• ARE WE THERE YET, DADDY? (Map skills.)
Zaslavsky, Claudia	• MATH GAMES & ACTIVITIES FROM AROUND THE WORLD (Math games.)

Stuart J. Murphy: An Author You Can Count On

You may notice from the list above that many authors like to "do" math books: Loreen Leedy, Elinor Pinczes, Bruce McMillan, Mitsumasa Anno, David Schwartz, Kathi Appelt . . . but one guy has them all outnumbered! Stuart Murphy's books are complemented with artwork by a wide variety of talented illustrators, and I can't think of many authors who are so prolific and have maintained such a high standard of excellence. Exposure to these books increases exponentially the probability of loving math. Also, I can't think of a primary teacher who wouldn't love a complete set of his **Mathstart** series, which present early math concepts, making it a great end-of-the-year class gift from all the parents. The collection is also a valuable addition to the family bookshelves, but if that involves a little too much subtraction from the old bank account, use this list below (yes, ALL by the Murphymeister!) to match the books to the concepts you need.

ANIMALS ON BOARD (Addition.)

BEEP BEEP, VROOM VROOM! (Patterns.)

THE BEST BUG PARADE (Size comparison.)

THE BEST VACATION EVER (Data collecting.)

BETCHA! (Estimating.)

BIGGER, BETTER, BEST! (Area.)

CIRCUS SHAPES (Shape recognition.)

DAVE'S DOWN-TO-EARTH ROCK SHOP (Classifying.)

DIVIDE AND RIDE (Division.)

ELEVATOR MAGIC (Subtraction.)

EVERY BUDDY COUNTS (Counting.)

A FAIR BEAR SHARE (Regrouping.)

GAME TIME! (Time measurement.)

GET UP AND GO! (Time lines.)

GIVE ME HALF! (Halves.)

THE GREATEST GYMNAST OF ALL (Opposites.)

HENRY THE FOURTH (Ordinals.)

JUMP, KANGAROO, JUMP! (Fractions and division.)

JUST ENOUGH CARROTS (Comparing amounts.)

LEMONADE FOR SALE (Bar graphs.)

LET'S FLY A KITE (Symmetry.)

MISSING MITTENS (Odds and evens.)

MONSTER MUSICAL CHAIRS (Subtracting one.)

ONE . . . TWO . . . THREE . . . SASSAFRAS! (Number order.)

A PAIR OF SOCKS (Matching.)

THE PENNY POT (Counting coins.)

PEPPER'S JOURNAL: A KITTEN'S FIRST YEAR (Calendar.)

PROBABLY PISTACHIO (Probability.)

RABBIT'S PAJAMA PARTY (Sequencing.)

RACING AROUND (Measuring distance.)

READY, SET, HOP! (Addition and subtraction.)

ROOM FOR RIPLEY (Capacity.)

SEAWEED SOUP (Matching sets.)

SHARK SWIMATHON (Subtracting 2-digit numbers.)

SLUGGERS' CAR WASH (Money.)

SPUNKY MONKEYS ON PARADE (Counting by 2s, 3s, and 4s.)

SUPER SAND CASTLE SATURDAY (Measuring.)

TOO MANY KANGAROO THINGS TO DO! (Multiplication.)

. . . Stuart J. Murphy keeps adding to his collection, and he's putting 'em out faster than I can count 'em. Keep up with new releases on-line at www.harperchildrens.com.

Another talented math team: Amy Axelrod, whose work is consistently illustrated by Sharon McGinley-Nally. Their series shows children how math is used in real-world situations in the most porcine way possible!

PIGS AT ODDS: FUN WITH MATH AND GAMES

PIGS IN THE PANTRY: FUN WITH MATH AND COOKING

PIGS GO TO MARKET: HALLOWEEN FUN WITH MATH AND SHOPPING

PIGS ON A BLANKET: FUN WITH MATH AND TIME

PIGS ON THE BALL: FUN WITH MATH AND SPORTS

PIGS ON THE MOVE: FUN WITH MATH AND TRAVEL

PIGS WILL BE PIGS: FUN WITH MATH AND MONEY

And for one last hurrah that covers both readin' and 'rithmetic, try MATH TOGETHER: HELP YOUR CHILD LEARN TO LOVE MATH AGES 5+. Published by Candlewick, this slipcased set contains six . . . count 'em, six! . . . paperbacks all integrating math. Storybooks, a puzzle book, poems, and folktales make this a number-one pick for aspiring mathematicians.

Penny Power

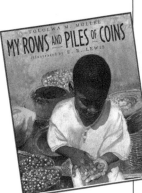

Here's your chance to turn the root of all evil into the root of all reading. A money storytime is great during February, the month in which Lincoln and Washington—those stars of pennies and dollar bills—have birthdays. Read a money book every allowance payday, read aloud at a fund-raising PTA meeting, deliver the storytime to your child's class, or volunteer to arrange for a finance-related guest reader: bond traders, stockbrokers, bank tellers, or bank robbers. Both grown-ups and children enjoy this wealth of stories about money, so use this list whenever you want reading to pay off.

The Purse

Kathy Caple

Brisson, Pat	• BENNY'S PENNIES
Caple, Kathy	• THE PURSE
Craft, Charlotte	• KING MIDAS AND THE GOLDEN TOUCH
Demi	• THE GREATEST TREASURE
Hoban, Russell	• A BARGAIN FOR FRANCES
Mollel, Tololwa M.	• MY ROWS AND PILES OF COINS
O'Neill, Alexis	• ESTELA'S SWAP
Schenck de Regniers, Beatrice	• WAS IT A GOOD TRADE?
Schwartz, David M.	• IF YOU MADE A MILLION
Stanley, Sanna	• MONKEY FOR SALE
Stewart, Sarah	• THE MONEY TREE

READING RUNGS:
CLIMBING THE CORPORATE LADDER

If your child keeps her allowance in an IRA and invests profits from lemonade sales in the NASDAQ, if more trades go on in her room than on the stock-market floor, there are several outstanding intermediate titles that belong in your child's portfolio. For starters, no money-minded child should go without a financial consultation with THE GREAT BRAIN by John D. Fitzgerald. The Great Brain is John's con-artist older brother Tom, who finagles his way through chapter after chapter, conspiring to retire cruel schoolteachers, save children lost in caves, offer a Greek immigrant boy a crash course

in naturalization, teach a peg-legged friend how to win a running race, and always turning a dime in the end. The story takes place in Utah at the turn of the century, but the seamlessness of the anecdotes and the vivacity of the dialogue make this book timeless and deserving of its classic status. This first of a series is the book to give a child that never knew he could like books.

Likewise, the **Owen Foote** stories by Stephanie Greene are tales about incentive. A good one to start with is OWEN FOOTE, MONEY MAN. There is just so much stuff that sends Owen's heart a-flutterin', especially in the "Junk You Never Knew About" catalog. Since allowance is slow in coming, Owen schemes with the vim that suggests perhaps he is the distant cousin of Fitzgerald's Great Brain. This book is chock full of sassy dialogue and ambition, and children will just love integrating it into any learning they do about money.

Two other books that work for budding capitalists are Sheila Greenwald's THE MARIAH DELANY LENDING LIBRARY DISASTER and MARIAH DELANY'S AUTHOR-OF-THE-MONTH CLUB. Mariah Delany is a little bit of a book lover and a whole lot of businesswoman. She's an exciting character who takes a contagious amount of initiative, even though her best-laid plans often go hilariously awry. Whether lending out valuable books from her parent's collection in the hopes of collecting overdue fines or inviting real live authors to her apartment for a celebrity show-and-tell, the conundrums are always creative. Written in the spirit of authors Constance Greene and Beverly Cleary, these reissues are perfect picks for mother-daughter book clubs. Anyone who has had an idea that has spun a bit out of control will delight in these well-written books.

Finally, Howie Fingerhut runs the "Boy for All Seasons" lawn-care service and is ambitiously competing for the H. Marion Muckley Junior Business Person of the Year Award. In the meantime, he has also decided to write this book, published as THE CONFE$$ION$ AND $ECRET$ OF HOWARD J. FINGERHUT by Esther Hershenhorn. After all, Howie reasons, authors make lots of money for books with confessions and how-to secrets, so it seems like a good safety net. Howie's strong ego and even a little id come through in his earnest account, and the humor of it all will keep your child's interest growing steadily.

Viorst, Judith	• ALEXANDER, WHO USED TO BE RICH LAST SUNDAY
Wells, Rosemary	• BUNNY MONEY
Williams, Vera B.	• A CHAIR FOR MY MOTHER
Zemach, Harve and Margot	• A PENNY A LOOK
Zimelman, Nathan	• HOW THE SECOND GRADE GOT $8,205.50 TO VISIT THE STATUE OF LIBERTY

There are many more marvelous money poems and activities in one of the greatest reading resource books of all time, THIS WAY TO BOOKS by Caroline Feller Bauer (see Reading Hero, p. 147). In it, Bauer suggests a fund-raising idea that a parent can organize: Children bring their penny collections and are given large pieces of posterboard, upon which the children work together to design pictures with their pennies.

The penny art remains on the floor the following day to be admired by the community. The pennies are then brought to a collection agency for counting, where they are transformed into cash to purchase print material for the school or classroom library. The school Bauer described, consisting of four hundred inner-city kids, collected about $600. Cha-*ching*!

PART VI

Now Playing in a Book Near You: Broadcast and Performance

Besides garbage, entertainment is our nation's biggest export. Granted, sometimes it is hard to differentiate between the two. Children are inundated with so many sounds and messages and scintillating displays that we adults may find ourselves either marveling or mortified at their precociousness. The lure of performance—the glow of the television in a dark room, the dial of the radio, or the footlight on the stage—is one of great light, both literally and figuratively.

Alternate reality is convincing. Fact and fiction can become mixed up and even when we explain to children that most of what they see on the screen is "pretend," this just adds to its appeal. After all, most children also love to pretend; it's fascinating to discover that grown-ups pretend, too.

Believing and pretending and escaping into the imagination are qualities that make books absorbing as well, so I don't see why one art form should necessarily be elevated above the other. Rather, the thing that makes print or performance successful for children is, again, a matter of what the artist is trying to communicate (whether the artist is a screenwriter, scriptwriter, lyricist, illustrator, performer, cinematographer) and whether that artist has given thought to how that message may be interpreted by a child. Television and movies, which potentially reach large audiences quickly, are a bit slack on this last point. Casting its broad fishing net, the entertainment industry often snags children with material that is not appropriate or not intended for them. (Any child with a television in her home or who sits through movie trailers will have this experience at some point.)

What a shame that teaching media literacy, the understanding of mass market messages, is not considered a bigger deal in American education. It's inevitable that children are going to see and hear things that inform them, confuse them, excite them, pressure them, insult them, or are simply not intended for them, and it seems that the very least we could do is try to help them sort it all out. Children who possess more information about mass media might grow up to improve it. If children are old enough to watch MTV, they are old enough to make choices.

I admit it's fun
To smear my face
 with paint,
Causing ev'ryone
To think I'm what
 I ain't . . .
Yet when once the
 curtain's down
My life is pure,
And how I dread it!

—from "Life Upon The Wicked Stage," *Showboat,* lyrics by Oscar Hammerstein II, music by Jerome Kern

❧ *Potato Pick:*

WHITEBLACK THE PENGUIN SEES THE WORLD

by Margret and H. A. Rey

Yes, it's the creators of Curious George, and this time the hero is the Chief Storyteller on station WONS, the radio station for all of Penguinland. When he runs out of stories, he does what any good journalist would do: He travels the world in search of more. Join Whiteblack as he traverses desert and sea; then break out the old tape recorder and produce your own "radio show" with the family. After all, as this entertaining book goes to show, adventure is where you make it. (4 and up)

Visit www.medialit.org or www.med.sc.edu:1081 for resources that will help you show children how to differentiate the cream from the . . . well, you know.

There is something definitely creamy-dreamy about the curtain parting, so in this chapter you'll find alternatives that will help you use the media as a dramatic overture or a thrilling climax, and even make it more of a family affair. If you carefully combine the energy of performance with the insights of literature, you can make the passive activity of viewing a movie an active attempt at seeking the truth or discovering history. Conversely, children can make the solitary activity of reading a book a chance to translate a story into a new art, such as puppetry, or have the transcendental experience of hearing their own voices carry out over an audience. Such *divertissements* will help children appreciate that they do not need to look outward for light; it is within them.

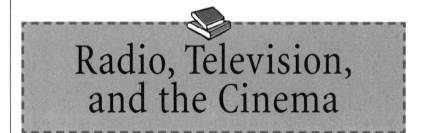

Radio, Television, and the Cinema

"It's not a contest! You're each wonderful in your own way." No, I'm not talking about sibling rivals. I'm talking about books and broadcasts. So often screens, signals, and print are pitted against each other when it would be so much nicer if they could play together, or better yet, if our children could join in. Use these activities to find multimedia's happy medium.

Radio Days

I still remember being ten years old and watching my uncles, just a few years older, try to put together a radio using aluminum foil, wire, and an oatmeal box. The reception was about as good as you could expect from aluminum foil, wire, and an oatmeal box, but I still remember their contraption making a sound, an amazing, mysterious electrostatic scratching that eerily suggested voices were invisibly hanging in the air all around me. At ten, I was an especial fan of all things eerie, amazing, and mysterious. An audiophile was born.

BING! BANG! BOOM! SOUND EFFECT SOURCES

Every so often children will play your eardrums like bongos, mirroring characters from Charlotte Zolotow's THE QUIET MOTHER AND THE NOISY LITTLE BOY, Alexis O'Neill's LOUD EMILY, or Dr. Seuss's GERALD MCBOING BOING. Check out these Web sites to make homemade radio sound effects, and make sure things never get too quiet around your house.

• www.mtn.org/~jstearns/Sound_Effects.html

• home.sprynet.com/~palermo/mtr_rad4.htm

Created by Tony Palermo, who has done creative work for the Museum of Television and Radio in both Los Angeles and New York, how-to's for dozens of sound effects, plus how to build sound-effect devices.

• www.pbs.org/ktca/newtons/12/movisnd.html
From a PBS *Newton's Apple* show, movie sound-effect hints that can be applied to radio.

• Also, order "The Magic of Radio, October 1988" back issue from *Cobblestone* magazine (www.cobblestone pub.com or 1-800-821-0115), which includes lots of great articles about the history of radio as well as sound-effect suggestions.

In this day and age of screens and pictures, storytelling without visuals is an archaic prospect. It seems natural to want to "see" a story. It always strikes me as funny that in so many vintage photographs, families gathered around the radio seem to be *looking* at it, even though there was nothing really to see. Actually, they were forming the necessary visuals in their imaginations. I understand (though it was a bit before my time) that kids used to race home to decode messages during *Little Orphan Annie*. I hear they reveled in the adventures of *The Green Hornet*, were chilled by *The Shadow* and *Suspense*, laughed along with their parents to *Fibber McGee and Molly*. Often, late at night, I find myself listening for the echo of this laughter, turning my dial over the lonely tundra of AM radio in search of the miracle of a little *Jack Benny*.

Radio is a major contributor to the cultural literacy of the twentieth century. Why shouldn't every child be acquainted with Orson Welles's marvelous "War of the Worlds" mischief, with Charlie McCarthy and Edgar Bergen's banter, Abbott and Costello's "Who's on First" debacle? Why shouldn't every child recognize the Lone Ranger's cry of "Hi ho, Silver," the *Dragnet* theme, or the horn section of Benny Goodman's orchestra? These benchmarks of American entertainment are

MAKING RADIO WAVES WITH READING

The *Loose Leaf Book Company* was a weekly hour-long public radio series for adults that celebrated children's literature. The on-line archive offers great opportunities to listen to the voices of talented book creators and hear about great new books that fall under compelling themes. You can tune in at www.looseleaf.org.

alluded to throughout our culture, certainly in print, and children's familiarity with the references only adds to their enjoyment and sense of accomplishment as they read. Radio broadcasts also can help instill an interest in history and nonfiction, and the vocabulary of radio broadcasts can be expanding and challenging, not unlike read-aloud. Your family can gather 'round and hear for yourselves with Joe Garner's book and CD heavily narrated combinations, WE INTERRUPT THIS BROADCAST: THE EVENTS THAT STOPPED OUR LIVES ... FROM THE HINDENBURG EXPLOSION TO THE ATTACKS OF SEPTEMBER 11 and AND THE CROWD GOES WILD: RELIVE THE MOST CELEBRATED SPORTING EVENTS EVER BROADCAST.

Aside from news items, most children today don't think of finding a story when they turn on a radio. With a flick of the switch, they are inundated by the vocal gyrations of the musical flavors of the month. These days, enticing children to ride the radio wave has to be done subtly. Try the White Noise Ploy: Buy or borrow narrative tapes, either of vintage shows or books on tape, and play them in the background of low-key activities such as school commutes, cleaning the house, fixing dinner, or bedtime. Do it consistently, and see if your child tunes in. You'll know you've turned her on if she misses it when it's gone. If she doesn't, *you* surely will.

And remember my uncles? To this day, I still think of them as geniuses of the same caliber as Edison, but in fact anyone can repeat and improve upon their wondrous feat with radio-building kits purchased at electronics stores, educational toy stores, and science supply stores.

READ ALOUD THE RADIO

Avi	• "WHO WAS THAT MASKED MAN, ANYWAY?"
Barasch, Lynne	• RADIO RESCUE
Birch, Beverley, and Robin Bell Corfield	• MARCONI'S BATTLE FOR RADIO
Dorros, Arthur	• RADIO MAN/DON RADIO
Sorel, Edward	• JOHNNY ON THE SPOT

Being a listener isn't the only fun part. You and your children can create your own "books on tape" by reading aloud into a simple tape recorder. Or if your PTA has the funds, a tape recorder can be sent home

A BEAR NECESSITY OF CHILDREN'S RADIO

One of the most famous children's radio programs ever produced was the 1937 *Cinnamon Bear* Christmas serial, in which twins Jimmy and Judy join Paddy O'Cinnamon in a search for the elusive silver star that belongs on top of the family tree. If the school your child attends isn't too concerned about separating church and state or is a parochial school, ask if the *Cinnamon Bear* can be played over the intercom with morning announcements, perhaps in conjunction with a holiday teddy-bear drive for needy children. The tapes can also be brought out in the summer for an icy "Christmas in July" for your family. For green and red popsicles, pour lime juice or green-colored soda into ice trays, half full, cover with plastic wrap, and poke in frilly matching toothpicks. Freeze. Remove the plastic wrap, fill the trays the rest of the way with cranberry juice or pink lemonade, and freeze again. When the popsicles are ready, lick and lounge around with fans and clan while listening as our hear-oes search for their cool silver star.

Another favorite vintage radio series to share with children is *Let's Pretend*, full cast dramatizations of classic fairy tales. All those voices really bring them to life! Additionally, these tapes are an entertaining change of pace if your child is sick in bed, or if a friend has the flu. Children love to make their own radio dramatizations à la tape recorder after listening to a few shows. To own great radio broadcasts from yesteryear, such as the *Cinnamon Bear* and *Let's Pretend*, contact Metro Golden Memories, www.mgmemories.com, 1-773-736-4133.

with each child "round robin" style. Parents and children will have a chance to read and record a favorite children's book, and then may choose to purchase and donate the corresponding book as well. In this way, your school can build a substantial collection of books with read-aloud counterparts for use in classrooms or the library. Parents may also want to purchase copies of the tape for a keepsake from the child's classroom. Resist the temptation to read aloud only picture books; older children often benefit from hearing chapter books read aloud, sometimes even hearing only the first chapter is enough to stimulate interest and bolster the confidence that gets a reluctant reader through an entire book. How about a "first chapter" collection of tapes of Newbery winners, or a specific genre (first chapters of science fiction, animal stories, etc.)?

Homemade books on tape can be used in many ways. Share them with the blind or dyslexic (contact the Radio Reading Service in your area for information). Donate them to the children's ward at a hospital. Play them on intercoms at schools. Let children listen during long school-bus rides or carpools. Mail them to distant friends and relatives. Make family recordings of readings that will be heard for generations!

Television: The Bad Guest

My teacher friend has a good rule of thumb. "We don't consider television a member of the family," she explains. "We consider it a guest in our house. When it is a bad guest, we ask it to leave. I don't allow any behavior from the people on television that I wouldn't accept from people in my house." While I enjoy zonking out in front of the set as much as the next person, when I get tired of counting shoot-outs or insults or women's navels, I decide television has been a bad guest and turn it off. If you live in a home where your guest is putting a strain on your hospitality but the addiction is strong, get group help at www.tvturnoff.org or check out Lynn Gordon's deck of activity cards, **52 ALTERNATIVES TO TV**.

Another friend cleverly paid her children in checker pieces for chores done. These checkers could be "spent" on television or computer time, fifteen minutes per checker, to help control the in-front-of-the-screen-scene. Remember, Buddha says everything in moderation.

If your children start showing symptoms of withdrawal, you can at least read picture books *about* television to them (as they may have wearied of stories about how when you were a kid they didn't even *have* cable and how you traveled ten miles barefoot in the snow to school, uphill both ways!).

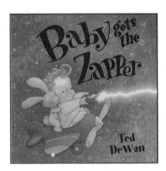

TELEVISION TITLES

Brown, Marc	• THE BIONIC BUNNY SHOW
Dewan, Ted	• BABY GETS THE ZAPPER
Heilbroner, Joan	• TOM THE TV CAT
McCoy, Glenn	• PENNY LEE AND HER TV
Nickle, John	• TV REX
Novak, Matt	• MOUSE TV
Polacco, Patricia	• AUNT CHIP AND THE GREAT TRIPLE CREEK DAM AFFAIR
Van Allsburg, Chris	• THE WRETCHED STONE
Ziefert, Harriet	• WHEN THE TV BROKE

Reading Commercials Beat Book Reports

My favorite part of the popular PBS series *Reading Rainbow* has always been when those cute real-live children come on and plug a book. When I became a teacher, we had great fun following the show's example and producing reading "commercials" using a home video

FRED ROGERS

AMERICA'S SWEETHEART

One of my favorite songs by Fred Rogers is "There Are Many Ways to Say I Love You." But Mr. Rogers, how can I count the ways? We could start with the number seven million, which is about how many families watch his reruns every week. If you have a television, chances are you too have tuned in to *Mister Rogers' Neighborhood,* where the kind, cardigan-clad gentleman reaches through the set to encourage the healthy emotional growth of children. Don't underestimate him by his measured speech and mild manner, his songs and his puppets. He was a Clark Kent with the brave heart of a Superman.

To say he had an accomplished career is an understatement. In 1968, he was appointed Chairman of the Forum on Mass Media and Child Development of the White House Conference on Youth and continually lobbied for excellence in children's television. He set the standard, receiving every major award in television, and appeared on PBS for more than thirty years, producing over a thousand episodes. He was awarded honorary degrees at no fewer than thirty-five colleges and universities. He was an ordained Presbyterian minister. He chaired the nonprofit Family Communications, Inc., www.familycommunications.org, which diversified the "Neighborhood" into nonbroadcast materials that continue to support families. For all his successes, I think he could be proudest of the way he was able to create an unparalleled connection with his fans.

In teacher training, Rogers's ideas influenced me. He debunked the prevailing assumption of young children as empty vessels that we fill, or blank slates that we write upon. Rogers maintained that the day children are born, they come to us with a full vessel, a full emotional life. He believed everyone has the resources not only all around them, but *within* them, to do and share wonderful things. So much of what Rogers stood for on screen is reflected in the best of children's books: variety, imagination, enthusiasm, an authentic voice, an empathetic and thoughtful view of child development, and an empathetic and thoughtful view of our own ability to care for one another.

I think of Fred Rogers the same way as I think of a great children's author or illustrator: an artist with something to say—in his case, "love thy neighbor." He used television as the medium for his message, but Fred Rogers raised the bar for all material presented for young audiences, including children's literature. Rogers consistently modeled reading, and encouraged children to ask questions, make predictions, and seek information, all behaviors of good readers. But he was even more subtle than that in opening up children to books. Rogers explained in song, "When your heart can sing another's gladness, / then your heart is full of love. / When your heart can cry another's sadness, / then your heart is full of love." A great book helps fill hearts in this way and brings us closer to these profound feelings.

Fred Rogers died in 2003. He was a most remarkable man, and his influence is such that I think he should be considered one of the great models of peace in our time.

camera. The children each wrote out a short script, starting with a "lead" (a question, description, or strong statement that caught the viewer's interest), followed by the child introducing himself, the title and author of the book, a short synopsis that didn't give away the ending and a "hook," or statement that left the viewer wanting more. (Hook: "So if you want to find out how to escape when cornered by a dinosaur, read this book . . . before it's too late!") I proofread the scripts, and then the children wrote them out in big letters on big pieces of construction paper. These were used as "cue cards," and the children practiced reading aloud from them. When the tape was rolling, the children held up their books, smiled, and read the cue cards. You can use a tripod for more professional results. The tape was a great hit on parent night, and then it was donated to the library where the commercials kept rolling to entertain and entice young patrons. This is a wonderful undertaking for scout troops and home-schoolers, as well as a parent-run classroom project. It's also handy to have a tape of family-produced commercials loaded in the VCR; press "play" on your remote during breaks in favorite prime-time shows, sports events, or news for a painless way to block material your children just don't need to see.

Activity and Special Interest Books in the Battle Against "B"

I don't like to be a total language dictator, but there's one word I simply can't abide from children. It's the "B" word: "boring." It's as unacceptable to me as the "F" word (gasp!). What a joy to never hear it in my home and what a joy see my son raise his eyebrows and giggle when he hears another child toss it off. He knows that to use the word "boring" is to insult yourself. To say "I'm bored" is to say "I'm boring," because it is each our own job to keep ourselves interested in the world, a notion that is not always supported in a culture in which so much time, energy, and money is spent trying to entertain us. As long as we have our free will and imagination, what should we know from "boring?"

I tell my own son, when you love to read, you will never be bored, and you will never be lonely, and I believe it. Next time you hear the "B" word, offer your child Peter Spier's BORED—NOTHING TO DO! and OH, WERE THEY EVER HAPPY!, two hilarious and inspiring picture books about children's boredom and their more powerful potential for initiative.

Another naughty word is "weird," because it's usually used to judge somebody else's interests or style, instead of its more correct meaning of "uncanny, unearthly, or eerie." In my home, we try to only use "weird"

Dear Madame Esmé,

Help! I am running out of ideas, and the rain keeps coming down. The kids are starting to whine. When I was young (in the old days), we had the **Childcraft** series to turn to for indoor fun. Any great to-do books today?

Dear Gentle Reader,

A phenomenal book that is an umbrella against boredom is CRAFTS FOR ALL SEASONS by Kathy Ross, with page after page of art projects both children and grown-ups can get excited about doing. When testing this book, I asked children to please put a Post-it note on a page with something to do that would interest them—and the kids ran out of Post-it notes. I myself couldn't resist the projects: Spring-Cleaning Apron, Necktie Windsock, Huffing and Puffing Mr. Wind Puppet, Columbus Hat, Teddy Bear Cave, Pitter-Patter Rain Stick, Plastic Bag

Butterflies, a Pop-Up Groundhog Puppet, and an Ice Skater that skates on real ice. I have never come across a craft book with more original ideas. Every project has helpful illustrations by Vicky Enright and each double-page spread is decorated with a charming and cheerful border. The materials are easy to find, the directions are clear, and best of all the projects really come out. Parents and primary teachers take special note: This craft book will get you through a whole year. Also try Kathy Ross's other books, such as CRAFTS FROM YOUR FAVORITE FAIRY TALES (Mermaid Mobile, Lunchbag Gingerbread House) and MAKE YOURSELF A MONSTER! A BOOK OF CREEPY CRAFTS (Blob in a Bottle Necklace, Throbbing Brain Puppet). This woman is the children's craft master, deserving of a 21-glue-gun salute.

COLLECT BOOKS ABOUT COLLECTORS & COLLECTIONS

when talking about ghosts or coincidences, not people with feelings who are trying something new or doing something differently.

Knowing that we will never be bored and never be weird in our house frees us up to pursue a lot. And there is a lot to pursue, more than any of us could master in a lifetime. But why not try? A book a day keeps "boringitis" away, considering there's a children's book for nearly every interest you and your child can name. For instance:

chess • magic equestrian • knitting • quilting • sewing • stargazing • birdwatching • calligraphy • sports • playing an instrument • drawing • printmaking • papier-mâché • journaling • cartography • gardening • fishing • cooking • juggling • photography • jewelry making • genealogy • pen-palling • pets • making miniatures • rubber stamping • yo-yoing • videography • model trains • puppetry • pottery • string games • storytelling • scrapbooking • inventing • treasure hunting • martial arts • jump roping • web design • origami • short wave radio • hair and makeup • kite flying • dance • learning a language • playing cards • puzzles and mazes • skateboarding • mad science • entertaining • Legos • flower pressing • fortune telling • racing cars • weather tracking • volunteerism and activism

. . . Plus, your child can take up collecting as a hobby, and there are books available about any assortment of treasures:

stamps • bugs • shells • bottlecaps • beads • buttons • postcards • magnets • marbles • coins • dolls • rocks, crystals, and minerals • trading cards • comics • beanie babies • key chains • Christmas ornaments • autographs • tropical fish • matchbox cars • music • video • leaves • sports memorabilia • stickers • a glass menagerie

. . . And don't forget books as a prized collection! Children commonly collect books by series, but some of the best book collections are by genre:

pop-ups • poetry • historical fiction • sports biographies • environmental science • folktales from a particular part of the world • books by a particular author • miniature books • books about airplanes or bears or outer space or whatever interests your child!

You'll have a baby bibliophile in no time!

You may be investigating books that reflect your child's interests, anyway, but if you point out that it's a real specific thematic collection she is building and that you are willing to make purchases, she may be more eager to follow you into the bookstore. While she is in there, notice other sparks of interest that you can fan into flames.

If after all is said and done your child still is using the "B" word, collect some of these great activity books:

Caney, Steven	• STEVEN CANEY'S KIDS' AMERICA
Gibson, Ray	• WHAT SHALL I DO TODAY?
Hetzer, Linda	• RAINY DAYS & SATURDAYS
Manning, Mick	• SUPER SCHOOL
Metropolitan Museum of Art	• WHAT CAN YOU DO WITH A PAPER BAG?
Moss, Marissa	• DR. AMELIA'S BOREDOM SURVIVAL GUIDE
Roche, Denis	• OODLES TO DO WITH LOO-LOO AND BOO

Condition, Read, Repeat: Creating Reading Routines As Regular As the TV Schedule

Children know that dessert comes after dinner, what time their favorite TV show comes on, and that a fire drill means line up and file out in an orderly fashion. Our senses are trained and served through stimulus and routine. This same combination can help children anticipate literature just as they anticipate ice cream when that white truck rolls down the street playing "Pop Goes the Weasel."

Music is a potential reading signal. A toot of a kazoo, a ting of a triangle, a few chords on piano or guitar can signal a storytime as sure as the first tuneful bars signal a favorite television show. You can use any musical instruments you have around or create makeshift ones. My favorite signal has always been the bleat that comes from blowing through a sawed-off garden hose (Wynton Marsalis has nothing to fear!). A pot-and-pan parade to a storytime spot is cute if you can stand the cacophony, or perhaps just fill a few water glasses partway and knock gently to create signature "chimes." Grandfather or cuckoo clocks can announce family story sharing and have the added benefit of being set for the same time every day.

"Call and Response" works well, too. In Haiti, the storyteller queries "krik?" which means, "want to hear a story?" and a receptive audience

❀ *Potato Pick:*

ROCKS IN HIS HEAD

by Carol Otis Hurst,
illustrated by James Stevenson

The author recollects the life of her father, an avid rock collector. People teased him for having "rocks in his pockets and rocks in his head," and someone warns him, "There's no money in rocks." Nonetheless, even as he grew up and ran a filling station, he collected rocks. Even as he dealt parts for Model T Fords, he collected rocks. Even when the Great Depression hit, he collected rocks. And one rainy day, his rock collecting leads him to meet someone who will change his life, proving that this father was no rock-head but a diamond in the rough. This story embraces learning and sharing without pretension and demonstrates the importance of following where your heart leads and living the life you were meant to live. Stevenson's plain, muddy illustrations give this book a homey warmth. (6 and up)

replies with an enthusiastic "krak!" which is shorthand for "we're ready for your story, sock it to us!" The question and response "Krik? Krak!" may go on for some time, building anticipation both to tell and to hear. A whistle is another call and response that can be exchanged, like two birds calling. If you can't manage to put your lips together and just blow, many toy stores sell great wooden train whistles that you can use to call "all aboard for reading!"

Of course, the call of the choo-choo may have older children rolling their eyes right out of their sockets and pronouncing you the new mayor of Dorkville. I found the greatest success in signaling preadolescents when I surrendered to their opinion of me and donned a "television helmet." Simply take a box the size of your head and cut out a "screen" for your face to peek through. Paint the box black, add knobs and silver pipe-cleaner antennae. This device was useful at school when I needed seventh- and eighth-graders to give me their undivided attention. Although they laughed, they were so conditioned to stare at anything that looked like a TV set that they listened to me read to them at great length. In an extensive U.S. Department of Education study of eighth-graders, it was discovered that kids spend 21.2 hours a week watching TV and about 2 hours a week reading outside of school, and that includes homework. The helmet is also handy at home when I need to interrupt scheduled viewing for a Test of the Emergency Read-Aloud System.

Children also respond to more subtle visual cues. Children's literature lecturer Caroline Feller Bauer suggests lighting a candle at the start of storytime and blowing it out at the end. As a public school teacher, I was not keen on open flames. I substituted a small stained-glass lamp, and when I turned off those awful fluorescent fixtures and turned on that tiny light, all ages gathered round for what they knew would be a cozy storytime. A special "reading lamp" can become a family treasure as well. Use it to signal a time to connect through stories.

Mealtimes are another delicious opportunity for conditioning. How about books for breakfast? Just think, when your child grows up, every time he scrambles an egg or toasts a bagel, he will have the strange urge to go to the library! If mealtimes are too hectic at your house, just pick a time each week to have a favorite treat and share a favorite book. My friends gave me some training in this. When I was a young girl, a Parisian *amie* used to fix cocoa served in a large bowl with lots of whipped cream, kind of a "hot chocolate soup." When I was in my twenties, a pregnant friend introduced me to the ambrosia-like combination of hot buttered popcorn sprinkled with M&M's. Now I love sharing these fragrant, tasty

Shankar's Third "I"
THE CHILDREN'S BOOK TRUST

Keshav Shankar Pillai, known internationally as "Shankar," was an extremely popular political cartoonist in India. In 1957 Shankar founded the Children's Book Trust with the mission to promote and produce well-written, well-illustrated, and well-designed children's books that would be subsidized to keep prices within the reach of the average Indian family. The publishing arm of the Trust, Indraprastha Press, has been winning India's National Award for printing and designing since its inception in 1965 and publishes *Children's World* magazine, linking children worldwide through the common bond of creativity. But the Trust's enthusiasm is not limited to its own publications: The Dr. B. C. Roy Children's Reading Room and Library houses a collection of over 35,000 books.

The Trust also is in charge of Shankar's International Children's Competition for writing and painting, which includes Shankar's On-the-Spot Painting competition held in Delhi every November with about ten thousand young contestants. Talk about encouraging future authors and illustrators! Shankar died in 1989, but his Academy of Art and Book Publishing ensures the perpetuation of his vision through its diploma programs.

One of the quirkier features of the Trust is the International Dolls Museum, which houses one of the largest collections of costumed dolls in the world. Inspired by the gift of a single doll received from a Hungarian ambassador in the 1950s, Shankar began to acquire dolls when he traveled abroad, and he soon had a collection of five hundred. The dolls were frequently exhibited with the paintings done by children but when Shankar became chagrined with the wear and tear these traveling exhibits caused, Indira Gandhi suggested a solution: a permanent museum for dolls. Today the collection consists of 6,500 exhibits from eighty-five countries. While at first a doll collection may seem incongruous with the Trust's literary mission, there is precedent. In the 1920s American philanthropist Jane Addams employed a similar draw. Her children's reading room at Hull House contained a small museum of toys from around the world, "to induce a wider range of interest." Similarly, by integrating his own pursuits, Shankar invented something the whole world could enjoy.

The latest chapter in the Trust's initiative is the astoundingly ambitious International Centre for Children. Shankar's mantra, "Children deserve nothing but the best," will serve the cause of peace here. Using land allotted in the Diplomatic Enclave of New Delhi, the Centre will house and display the Trust's painting gallery, library, and Dolls Museum; provide hobby rooms where arts and skills such as pottery, carpentry, puppet- and toy-making, classical and folk dance will be taught; and establish programs for children with special needs. One other important offering will be that of lodging facilities for young visitors from around the globe, which is important because the Centre is intended to serve as a meeting ground for children from everywhere, "a visible symbol of goodwill and the sense of togetherness among children of the world."

With the help of those dedicated to his literature-based Trust, Shankar's dream continues to bear fruit for children throughout the world. You can visit and support the Children's Book Trust at www.childrensbooktrust.com.

PROTECT THE BABIES FROM BOREDOM

Immunize primary children against "boringitis" with these picture books:

de Regniers, Beatrice Schenk
WHAT CAN YOU DO WITH A SHOE?

What do you do with a book like this? Read it twice, as my primary classes always insisted! In this colorful re-issue of a 1955 book, follow two exuberant children through their ridiculous explorations of shoes, hats, cups, chairs, and brooms. The dedication page of this book says it all: "for fun."

Heap, Sue WHAT SHALL WE PLAY?

What a joyful book! Three friends decide, page after page, what to pretend to be next. Trees? Cars? Fairies? Wibbly-wobbly Jell-O? The dynamic of the children is true to the best of children, as one boy, one girl, and one child littler than the other two cheerfully negotiate the difficult deci-sion by making sure everyone's idea gets a turn. The multimedia illustrations are absolutely magical, fun, and big and smiley and silly, and very, very pretty. Naturally, any listener will want to play what the children in the story are playing, making for a sensational interactive read-aloud. Another fun tie-in is to have your children make their own illustrated "what shall we play" cards. Throw them in a bag and pick one to see what everyone can play next. In many ways, this is a perfect picture book. It belongs in every early childhood collection.

Ryan, Pam Muñoz,
MUD IS CAKE

When is mud cake? When is juice tea? When is a tub a boat? When you use your imagination, of course! This book has no shortage of that commodity. Page after page of gentle watercolors show children whose merry mindset changes the world around them. The verse sways and lilts in a pleasing sing-song, just right for read-aloud. An inspired book that will further inspire some great pretending in little ones. Let them read cake!

treats with children in my home, and I happily read as they crunch, munch, or slurp. Let the smell and taste of popcorn, chocolate, or any favorite treat remind them of days spent hearing stories but consider keeping the edible conditionings down to once a week, or you'll all be reading to the tastes and smells of defrosted Weight Watchers dinners.

Call it manipulative Skinnerian deviance. Call it Pavlovian pander-ing. Call it conniving advertising tactics. Call it what you will, but the Pied Piper wasn't just whistling "Dixie." Signal the children that you want to take them to a land where all things are possible, the land of books. Whistle your happy tune, pop some corn, put a box on your head, and the children will follow.

Schachner, Judith Byron Yo, Vikings!

A little girl who loves to pretend is assigned Erik the Red for World Discovery Day at school. She quickly becomes enamored with the romantic legends of the Vikings, inventing fabulous homemade costumes for herself and her little brother, who warns her father, "Emma wants a Biking ship for her birthday. You can buy it at the Biking store." Imagine Emma's surprise when her friend, the local children's librarian, shows her an advertisement in the newspaper for a real Viking ship for $7000 or best offer. Not having the cash, Emma makes her best offer, with surprising results. Based on a true story, the characters are so individually conceived that there is no one like them in any other book, and they are sure to be remembered lovingly well into adulthood. This tale is likely to induce terrific interest in Viking history and encourage an enthusiasm for learning in general, and goes far to affirm the outlook that anything can happen!

AND MORE PICTURE BOOKS THAT CELEBRATE IMAGINATION:

Avi	• Things That Sometimes Happen: Very Short Stories for Little Listeners
Drescher, Henrik	• Simon's Book
Ets, Marie Hall	• In the Forest
Gray, Libba Moore	• Miss Tizzy
Haas, Irene	• The Maggie B.
Henkes, Kevin	• Jessica
Hindley, Judy	• Rosy's Visitors
Jones, Elizabeth Orton	• Twig (Chapter book.)
Krauss, Ruth	• The Carrot Seed
Lester, Alison	• Imagine
Marzollo, Jean	• Pretend You're a Cat
McLerran, Alice	• Roxaboxen
Narahashi, Keiko	• Is That Josie?
Pennypacker, Sara	• Stuart's Cape (Short chapter book.)
Shaw, Charles G.	• It Looked Like Spilt Milk
Seuss, Dr.	• And to Think That I Saw It on Mulberry Street
Thompson, Kay	• Eloise

Couch-Potato Pedagogy: Cinema Club

Shhh! Don't tell anybody, but when I was a kid I was a terrible truant. Thirty-three days absent here, forty-two days absent there, I don't even think it's legal to be that absent anymore. A number of those days missed I can blame on technology, or the lack of it. I grew up before VCRs and cable, so if a movie was scheduled on television and I missed it, well, who knew when it would come on again? That's why my kind and intelligent father decided to prioritize cultural literacy in my education and suggested I stay home. I wasn't *really* truant. I was home-schooled. By Spencer Tracy. By Leslie Caron. By Shirley Jones and Katherine Hepburn, by Judy Holliday and Ann Miller. By Gene Kelly and Judy Garland and Cyd Charisse and Cary Grant. Excellent teachers all.

Once when I was teaching, I made reference to "Somewhere Over the Rainbow" and was met with blank stares and the sound of crickets. I asked how many children had seen *The Wizard of Oz*, and only half of the class raised a hand. I began to realize I was dealing with a lot of kids who thought Peter Pan was a brand of peanut butter and that the *Hunchback of Notre Dame* and *Tarzan* were written by Walt Disney. I decided that since they didn't know history, I would doom them to repeat it, and started a Cinema Club. Friday afternoons the classroom was transformed into a movie theater, complete with popcorn. We sent tickets to other classrooms and teachers gave them to deserving students who came as our special guests. Permission slips were signed so children could stay until the end of the movie, which sometimes ran close to two hours past the last school bell. We always had a full house, and many parents joined us.

A big hurdle in the children's initial enjoyment was that many of the movies were black-and-white. This proved traumatic for a couple of shows, but then the audience got used to it. Watching Anne Bancroft fist-fight with Patty Duke over the dining room table in *The Miracle Worker*, well, you just didn't need Ted Turner's colorization to keep your eyes glued to the screen. The other hurdle was that movies were sometimes black-and-white in other ways; racial stereotypes were rampant, even in movies that were otherwise wonderful and sophisticated. This afforded a great opportunity to discuss what we were watching and to put it into historical context. I loved showing the movies, warts and all, because nearly all of them could be integrated into both American and world history, geography and social studies. Musicals were painful, especially for the boys, until I showed *Oliver!* and *West Side Story,* and then at least they saw that if singing and dancing was cool enough for the Artful Dodger and the Sharks and the Jets, it was palatable enough to sit through.

Some of the movies had strong language, some had mild violence or romance. I was concerned until I started watching the prime-time television shows that my students recommended. I noticed there was more sexual innuendo and violence in the commercial breaks than there was in any one of the movies I was showing. I always made myself

HINTS FOR CINEMA CLUB

1. Have tickets, serve popcorn.

2. Expand horizons by showing movies that the children may be less likely to see or choose on their own.

3. Watch the movie yourself first, to anticipate ways you may support your audience and to determine appropriateness for that particular group.

4. Offer incentives for itchy kids to make it through movies; for instance, get your ticket stub punched at the end of the show, and turn in five stubs for a homemade award/T-shirt/gift certificate to the local movie theater (which might be willing to make a donation).

5. Discuss historical context every time.

6. Point out and discuss racial and gender stereotypes before and after every showing.

7. If you show the film in a school, take care to notify families beforehand what movies are going to be shown and what their ratings are, and collect signed permission slips so you are less likely to get an earful about content later.

8. Be sure to use the pitch, "you've seen the movie, now read the book!" and have the title available. Reluctant readers, especially, rush to rediscover familiar plots.

available to discuss or clarify what we were watching during Cinema Club. Characters who made poor choices or said or did inappropriate things did so in a developed story rather than in a show in the midst of a ratings war or an advertisement desperately trying to soak the viewer for money.

Cinema Club was about narrative and dramatization, and proved to be a natural extension of our literature-based learning. Many children took an interest in reading the book after seeing the movie based on it. Further, the older movies tend to have more challenging vocabulary and fast-paced dialogue, which I believe contributed to increased attention spans and listening skills . . . to say nothing for sense of humor and timing. Through the movies, low-achieving students were introduced to the timeless plots, characters, and language of classic literature without excessive frustration. I also found that the movies helped immigrant children feel affection for their new country; children who were struggling to read or write in English did not have to struggle to be entertained, and filmic knowledge seemed to usher them into the culture.

Start a Cinema Club at your child's school or do it in your home. When I left the classroom, I had an equally fun time having children in my apartment for movies. It made for perfect dark afternoons in Chicago's snowy winters.

A Few Good Ancient Movies for Kids

Ancient, by kid standards, means before 1980, or BC (before cable)! I guess that makes us ancient, too, huh! If the movie was a book first the title is noted.

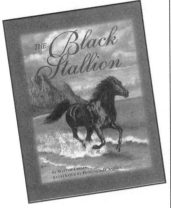

- *The Adventures of Robin Hood* (with Errol Flynn) (1938) THE MERRY ADVENTURES OF ROBIN HOOD by Howard Pyle, or THE SONG OF ROBIN HOOD, edited by Anne Malcolmson.

- *Around the World in 80 Days* (1956) AROUND THE WORLD IN 80 DAYS by Jules Verne.

- *Auntie Mame* (1958)

- *The Black Stallion* (1979) THE BLACK STALLION by Walter Farley.

- *Boys Town* (1938)

- *Bringing Up Baby* (1938)

- *Bugsy Malone* (1976)

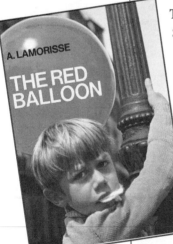

- *Camelot* (1967) KING ARTHUR AND HIS KNIGHTS OF THE ROUND TABLE, from Sir Thomas Malory's LE MORTE D'ARTHUR, edited by Sidney Lanier; also, try THE WORLD OF KING ARTHUR and HIS COURT: PEOPLE, PLACES, LEGEND, AND LORE by Kevin Crossley-Holland and the picture books about young Genevieve, Arthur, Lancelot, and Merlin by Robert D. San Souci.

- *Captains Courageous* (1937) CAPTAINS COURAGEOUS by Rudyard Kipling.

- *Chitty Chitty Bang Bang* (1968) CHITTY CHITTY BANG BANG by Ian Fleming.

- *Conrack* (1974) THE WATER IS WIDE by Pat Conroy.

- *Damn Yankees* (1958) THE YEAR THE YANKEES LOST THE PENNANT by Douglass Wallop.

- *Duck Soup* (1933) The children's choice, though I personally prefer *A Night at the Opera*, 1935, for my Marx Brothers nickel.

- *The 5,000 Fingers of Dr. T* (1953) Screenplay by Dr. Seuss . . . break out all of his books!

- *Goodbye, Mister Chips* (1939) GOOD-BYE, MISTER CHIPS by James Hilton.

• *Hans Christian Andersen* (1952) A fictionalized account of the author's life. For his books, see Hans Christian Andersen, p. 274.

• *How Green Was My Valley* (1941) **HOW GREEN WAS MY VALLEY** by Richard Llewellyn.

• *The Hunchback of Notre Dame* (You can't beat the one with Charles Laughton, 1939.) **THE HUNCHBACK OF NOTRE DAME** by Victor Hugo, **THE BOY OF A THOUSAND FACES** by Brian Selznick

• *I Remember Mama* (1948)

• *It Happened One Night* (1934)

• *The King and I* (1956) **ANNA AND THE KING OF SIAM** by Margaret Landon.

• *Lili* (1952)

• *Meet Me in St. Louis* (1944)

• *The Miracle Worker* (1962) **THE MIRACLE WORKER** by William Gibson; also, **THE STORY OF MY LIFE** by Helen Keller and **THE WORLD AT HER FINGERTIPS** by Joan Dash.

• *Oliver!* (1968) **OLIVER TWIST** by Charles Dickens; I like the edition illustrated by Don Freeman.

• *Paper Moon* (1973)

• *Peter Pan* (1960. Not the Disney version, the Mary Martin version.) **PETER PAN** by J. M. Barrie; I like the versions illustrated by Trina Schart Hyman and Jan Ormerod. Don't forget to prepare children for politically incorrect material in both the book and the movie.

• *Pocket Full of Miracles* (1961) **CINDERELLA** by Charles Perrault; I like the ones illustrated by K. Y. Craft or Marcia Brown.

• *The Red Balloon* (1955) **THE RED BALLOON** by Albert Lamorisse.

• *The Red Shoes* (1948) **THE RED SHOES** by Hans Christian Andersen (also, see Dance book list, p. 335, and Hans Christian Andersen book list, p. 277). This movie is a little long and suited very much to particular tastes (i.e., ballet fanatics), so I sometimes cheat and just show children the "Red Shoes Ballet" sequence, which is about a half hour long and more universally entertaining.

- *Rikki Tikki Tavi* (1975) **Rikki-Tikki-Tavi** by Rudyard Kipling.

- *The Secret Life of Walter Mitty* (1947) **The Secret Life of Walter Mitty** by James Thurber.

- *Singin' in the Rain* (1952)

- *Some Like It Hot* (1959)

- *Tarzan, the Ape Man* (1932) **Tarzan of the Apes** by Edgar Rice Burroughs.

- *Treasure Island* (I like the 1934 version with Wallace Beery and Jackie Cooper.) **Treasure Island** by Robert Louis Stevenson; I like the editions illustrated by Robert Ingpen or N. C. Wyeth.

- *West Side Story* (1961) **Romeo and Juliet** by William Shakespeare.

- *Willy Wonka & the Chocolate Factory* (1971) **Charlie and the Chocolate Factory** and **Charlie and the Great Glass Elevator** by Roald Dahl.

- *The Wizard of Oz* (1939) **The Wonderful Wizard of Oz** by L. Frank Baum; make sure you also look at the one-hundredth anniversary commemorative pop-up illustrated by Robert Sabuda.

- *The World of Henry Orient* (1964)

Film Festivals

Have a Frank Capra film festival! All of his movies are fine family fare. Just as an author has something to share, so does a director. Can your children answer the question: Why did the director make this? What themes do Frank Capra's movies have in common? How does his style change over time? Comparing and contrasting the body of work of a creative artist is great for critical thinking and critical viewing habits.

- *Lost Horizon* (1937)

- *You Can't Take It with You* (1938)

- *Mr. Smith Goes to Washington* (1939)

- *It's a Wonderful Life* (1946)

Have a *silent* film festival featuring Charlie Chaplin. Whenever possible, try to find video versions in which the music matches the content. Some cheaper video dubs play *any* old-timey recording, and when the mood of the music doesn't match the action it's surprisingly noticeable and annoying. Where's an organ player when you need one! Maybe you know a child who can do piano accompaniments?

- *The Kid* (1921)
- *The Sheik* (1921) (Rudolph Valentino.)
- *Safety Last* (1923) (Harold Lloyd.)
- *The Gold Rush* (1925) (See The Gold Rush, p. 116, for book suggestions.)
- *The General* (1927) (Buster Keaton.)
- *Modern Times* (1936)

If you *must,* have a Disney film festival, featuring a few of his finest and the literature that goes along:

- *Mary Poppins* (1964) **Mary Poppins** series by P. L. Travers; prepare children for racially inappropriate and gender stereotypical material in the book. Also, make available other fine governess stories: IDA EARLY COMES OVER THE MOUNTAIN by Robert Burch, the **Mrs. Piggle-Wiggle** series by Betty B. MacDonald (does anyone know what ever happened to *Mr.* Piggle-Wiggle?) and of course the classic JANE EYRE by Charlotte Brontë for older readers.

- *Dumbo* (1941) One of the animators of this feature was Bill Peet, who went on to write and illustrate dozens of outstanding children's books. He received a Caldecott Honor for BILL PEET: AN AUTOBIOGRAPHY, in which he writes at length about what it was like to work for Disney; a wonderful, eye-opening read for both children and adults. Besides his bio, check out all of Peet's picture books, and why not throw in a few elephant titles from the Animal Kingdom, p. 354, while you're at it?

- *Snow White and the Seven Dwarfs* (1937) Straightaway, read aloud chapter three of Tomie dePaola's **26 FAIRMOUNT AVENUE**, in which he remembers his childhood experience of seeing *Snow White* in the movie theater for the first time. Then it's on to print renditions of the classic tale. There are so many beautiful picture-book editions available of almost any fairy tale you can name, so shop around for a few versions to suit your tastes and to tell the story in different ways. Personally, I like the Snow White versions illustrated by Josephine Poole, Nancy Buckert, Trina Schart Hyman, and the version in Berlie Doherty's FAIRY TALES

HEY, ESMÉ!
WHERE'S THE SOUND OF
MUSIC ON YOUR LIST
OF MOVIES? EVERYBODY
LOVES THE SOUND
OF MUSIC!

I happen to hate *The Sound of Music*. That's okay—if you love it, you show it. Build a collection that reflects *your* tastes, movies that *you* are excited to share. Children won't always like what you share, but they will always like that you tried to share.

illustrated by Jane Ray. Introduce children to the lesser known SNOW WHITE AND ROSE RED; I cherish my edition illustrated by Barbara Cooney (I have hunted for years in thrift shops for dresses like the ones on the next-to-last pages). Now's a great time to look at the Dover FAIRY TALE books (see Dover information in Oldies and Goodies, p. 156) such as THE BLUE FAIRY BOOK, THE RED FAIRY BOOK, THE GREEN, THE YELLOW, . . . a whole rainbow of fairy-tale magic!)

• Look for Disney's **Favorite Stories** series on videotape, including *The Legend of Sleepy Hollow* (1949). This animated version holds to the original text very nicely and can be supplemented with the book by Washington Irving. Wake up, don't miss Irving's other classic in book form, RIP VAN WINKLE; I like the editions illustrated by N. C. Wyeth and Will Moses. Also in the **Favorite Stories** videotape series is *The Three Little Pigs* (1933). After watching, read Paul Galdone's version or Jon Scieszka's parody from the wolf's point of view, THE TRUE STORY OF THE 3 LITTLE PIGS!

Of course, some more recent children's movie releases have been of a high caliber. If your children have been trained by commercials and video games to expect visually sophisticated images on screen, they may be comfortable with these more flashy and fast-paced pictures. Mix the old and new to keep everyone happy and to affirm your children's modern tastes.

• *Anne of Green Gables* (1985) ANNE OF GREEN GABLES by Lucy Maud Montgomery.

• *Babe* (1995) BABE: THE GALLANT PIG by Dick King-Smith.

• *The Borrowers* (1998) My students and I liked the newer one with John Goodman, despite shameless and distracting brand-name plugs at the beginning, which should be pointed out. THE BORROWERS by Mary Norton.

• *Dinotopia* (2002) DINOTOPIA by James Gurney.

• *The Fool of the World and the Flying Ship* (1991) THE FOOL OF THE WORLD AND THE FLYING SHIP retold by Arthur Ransome.

• *Gulliver's Travels* (The 1995 Hallmark production with Ted Danson is long but excellent and keeps to the book, or you can show Max Fleischer's 1939 animated version released by Paramount, the second feature-length animated movie after Disney's *Snow White and the Seven Dwarfs.*) GULLIVER'S TRAVELS by Jonathan Swift. For younger children, I like the one retold by Ann Keay Beneduce and illustrated by Gennady Spirin, GULLIVER'S ADVENTURES IN LILLIPUT.

▶

HEY AGAIN, ESMÉ! I LIVE ON A FARM/ON TOP OF A MOUNTAIN/IN A DESERT/IN A TREE, SO WHERE AM I SUPPOSED TO FIND THESE OBSCURE OLD MOVIES YOU RECOMMEND?

In your mailbox! You can rent or buy them via post through what I consider the greatest movie store in the world, Facets Multi-media, Inc., www.facets.org, 1-800-331-6197. Ask about receiving a complete video catalog, with a collection of about 35,000 tapes, including many beautiful foreign films that are suitable for children. Subtitles count as reading!

While not offering rentals, a great selection of hard-to-find children's videos can be purchased through Library Video Company, www.libraryvideo.com, 1-800-843-3620. While more expensive than renting, its selection of family fare puts movie rental places to shame, offering hundreds of quality productions as well as wonderful children's shorts that you would be hard pressed to find anywhere else, including the celebrated Weston Woods award-winning animation productions of picture books. Many of the children's videos have shorter playing times, which may prove more manageable for younger audiences. Library Video Company also offers children's programming from PBS and cable on video. Most of the selections have the potential for literature tie-ins, and the catalog is arranged thematically. The company is also an excellent source for literature-based CD-roms, if you are that multimedia minded.

It's sometimes hard to keep up with history, but Chuck Schaden's Nostalgia Digest, Box 421, Morton Grove, Illinois, 60053, has lots of fun-to-read information about the screen and radio stars of the golden age, providing useful background when presenting vintage programming with children. E-mail TWTDchuck @aol.com for current subscription information.

And finally, take your family on a road trip to Chicago, Illlinois, for the Cannes for kids. The International Children's Film Festival takes place every fall at Facet's Multi-media Center and is every young movie-lover's dream come true. Visit www.cicff.org or call 1-800-331-6197 to sign up for the festival mailing list and to find out how your child can audition as a critic.

Your child might be president of the AV club yet!

• *The Incredible Adventures of Wallace & Gromit* (containing *A Grand Day Out*, 1990; *The Wrong Trousers*, 1993; and *A Close Shave*, 1995). Also, by the same director, *Chicken Run* (2000)

• *The Iron Giant* (1999) **THE IRON GIANT** by Ted Hughes, published originally in England as **THE IRON MAN**

• *The Little Princess* (Shirley Temple did the 1939 original, which is terrific, but *A Little Princess*, the one produced in 1995 starring Eleanor Bron, is actually even more exciting and beautiful!) **A LITTLE PRINCESS** by Frances Hodgson Burnett. Abridged picture book version illustrated by Barbara McClintock.

• *Matilda* (1996) **MATILDA** by Roald Dahl.

• *The Nightmare Before Christmas* (1993) The opening is a little scary for younger children.

• *Pee-Wee's Big Adventure* (1985)

• *The Princess Bride* (1987) **THE PRINCESS BRIDE** by William Goldman.

• *Shrek* (2001) **SHREK!** by William Steig.

• *The Snowman* (1982) **THE SNOWMAN** by Raymond Briggs.

Lure Mystery Lovers into the Cinema Club Mix

Start with any mystery movie, such as *The Thin Man* (1934), *Murder by Death* (1976), *It's a Mad, Mad, Mad, Mad World* (1963), or *A Shot in the Dark* (1964). The **Ghostwriter** series of children's videos is also excellent. Older children who love mysteries may be ready for Alfred Hitchcock's works or film noir classics such as *D.O.A.* (1949), *The Manchurian Candidate* (1962), or *Double Indemnity* (1944). I am always somewhat surprised at how engaging these movies can be to audiences in their early teens. Personally, I think adolescence has enough mystery, intrigue, paranoia, and crime in it to choke a horse, but I guess it's fun for the children to see it on the screen instead of in the mirror for a change. Take your "film noir" lovers to the library to locate some "reading noir," as suggested in the mystery reading section that follows.

Unlocking Sherlock: An Investigation into Children's Mystery Reading

I was sitting behind my desk at the bookstore minding my own business when she came in. I had seen her type before. Legs long and strong as tree trunks from walks to the library. Beautiful eyes that glanced into every corner of the room, searching for some detail that may prove useful down the pike. "What can I do for you, doll-face?" I asked.

"Lenny sent me," she paced the room. "Lenny the Librarian."

I felt my stomach drop, like I was on an elevator going down to a floor with a negative number.

"He said you might be able to help me. You see, I need you to find something," she said in a voice so deep it sounded like Dorothy Lamour talking from the bottom of a well.

"I'll see what I can do." I lit a chocolate cigarette.

"I'm looking for . . . a mystery." She adjusted her fur stole and turned away, her face turning a shade of red to match her ruby rings.

"Now, what's a nice girl like you want to get mixed up in all that for?" I asked. "Come on, sister, move on. There's other fish in the sea. Science fiction. Romance. Settle down with a nice respectable cookbook."

"A cookbook!" She reared her head back and laughed a throaty laugh. "Once I've had mystery, do you think I could ever go back to cookbooks? Listen to me, and listen good. I was born a mystery reader, and . . . and . . . I'll die a mystery reader, if I have to, do you hear me! With or without your help!"

I hoped it wouldn't come to that, but every now and then there comes a horse race where you're not sure where to lay your bet. "I didn't say I wouldn't help you." I adjusted my fedora. "I just wanted to make sure you understood the risks."

"Nothing ventured, nothing gained." She smiled a sophisticated smile, a Mona Lisa smile, a smile that smiled like trouble smiles, and pushed the glasses up the bridge of her nose.

I led her to the stacks . . .

Truth be told, I find that mystery readers actually *are* a bit of trouble, because many are remarkably faithful to their genre. While they may appease a friend or teacher by reading something else, they are secretly just waiting for the next stumper to solve. If mystery readers were a zodiac sign, they might be described as enigmatic, observant, with out-standing recall, good judges of character, dry wits, but sometimes ruthless and not especially versatile in their tastes. There are many children who fall under this description, and so there are many children destined to don a detective's hat. When it's to the exclusion of other material, their passion may be frustrating to their parents and teachers, but in the long run it is really no matter, because children's mysteries run the gamut from delicious dime-store drivel to some of the most accomplished works in young people's literature.

I was never a great fan of mysteries as a child, though I tried desperately, because everyone knows that solving crimes is cool. My

mother had a collection of all the **Trixie Belden** and **Nancy Drew** mysteries in the back of a closet. I would go sit there with a flashlight, preparing myself to gasp and "a-ha!" my way through the plots, but within an hour I would come crawling out, yawning, in search of my comic books. As I grew older, though, I discovered that there are really *two* kinds of children's mysteries. One invites the reader quite explicitly to look at the clues and try to solve the puzzle, as in the classic **Encyclopedia Brown** series or in Ellen Raskin's award-winning WESTING GAME.

Then there is another, more subtle kind of mystery that occurs in a few books not always categorized as mysteries. In these stories the denouement reveals a kind of a secret, something that pulls everything in the plot together. For instance, the endings of the masterpieces Louis Sachar's HOLES and Sharon Creech's WALK TWO MOONS leave readers audibly groaning "OoooOOOOOHHHhh!" as all loose threads are as skillfully and startlingly interlaced together as if Arachne herself were doing the weaving. It is also possible that the reader/sleuth may have already deduced the logical conclusion (all the clues are there, after all) but the child has the *choice* to solve it or not. The story is equally satisfying whether or not the reader has participated in this way. What makes a great mystery for children, then, is not necessarily the device of crimes or clues, but the painstaking formalistic attention the author gives to the story's complicated line. The talent that allows them to do it so seamlessly is the most mysterious thing of all.

A Few Likely Suspects for Intermediate Mystery Read-Aloud Capers

Avi	• The True Confessions of Charlotte Doyle • Who Stole the Wizard of Oz?
Bellairs, John	• The House with a Clock in Its Walls (Read all of Bellairs's books)
Blackwood, Gary L.	• Shakespeare's Scribe • The Shakespeare Stealer
Cameron, Ann	• Julian, Secret Agent (Quickie read!)
DeFelice, Cynthia	• The Ghost of Fossil Glen (Some mature themes.)
Fitzhugh, Louise	• Harriet the Spy
Hahn, Mary Downing	• Wait Till Helen Comes (A bit scary for me, but the kids love it.)
Hilgartner, Beth	• A Murder for Her Majesty
Hoeye, Michael	• Time Stops for No Mouse: A Hermux Tantamoq Adventure
Hoobler, Dorothy	• The Ghost in the Tokaido Inn
Howe, Deborah and James	• Bunnicula
Jackson, Donna	• The Wildlife Detectives: How Forensic Scientists Fight Crimes Against Nature (Nonfiction mystery.)
Klise, Kate	• Trial by Journal
Konisburg, E. L.	• From the Mixed-Up Files of Mrs. Basil E. Frankweiler
Kotzwinkle, William	• Trouble in Bugland: A Collection of Inspector Mantis Mysteries
Newman, Robert	• The Case of the Baker Street Irregular
Nickerson, Sara	• How to Disappear Completely and Never Be Found
Raskin, Ellen	• The Strange Disappearance of Leon (I Mean Noel) • The Westing Game
Schlein, Miriam	• The Year of the Panda
Shannon, George	• Stories to Solve: Fifteen Folktales from Around the World

Research Skills? Elementary, My Dear Watson.

The Mysteries of Research by Sharron Cohen offers cases in which middle-school detectives can eliminate suspects by checking the facts in the almanac, atlas, biographical dictionary, dictionary, encyclopedia, and Guinness World Records. Solving these mysteries also solves the problem of teaching children how to use print references instead of just relying on the Internet, and how to apply research skills in an interesting way. The book can be ordered from Highsmith Press, 1-800-558-2110.

Stanley, Diane	THE MYSTERIOUS MATTER OF I. M. FINE
Van Draanen, Wendelin	SAMMY KEYES AND THE HOTEL THIEF
Vande Velde, Vivian	NEVER TRUST A DEAD MAN
Yep, Laurence	THE CASE OF THE FIRECRACKERS

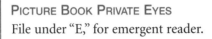

PICTURE BOOK PRIVATE EYES
File under "E," for emergent reader.

Bonsall, Crosby Newell	THE CASE OF THE CAT'S MEOW
Christelow, Eileen	WHERE'S THE BIG BAD WOLF?
Cushman, Doug	AUNT EATER LOVES A MYSTERY
Hurd, Thacher	MYSTERY ON THE DOCKS
Palatini, Margie	THE WEB FILES
Wisniewski, David	TOUGH COOKIE
Yolen, Jane	PIGGINS

GUMSHOES GALORE!

There's been a series of crimes—when parents don't pair up their children with these literary private-eye series! The other charge is that in most mystery series available, you are more likely to find an animal solving cases than a child of color. Hopefully, someday that case will be closed. In the meantime, introduce your children to:

The Bernie Magruder series by Phyllis Reynolds Naylor

The Boxcar Children series by Gertrude Chandler Warner

The Cam Jansen series by David A. Adler

The Chet Gecko series by Bruce Hale

The Einstein Anderson series by Seymour Simon

The Encyclopedia Brown series by David J. Sobol

The Flatfoot Fox series by Eth Clifford

The Hank the Cowdog series by John R. Erickson

The Jigsaw Jones series by James Preller

The Nate the Great series by Marjorie Weinman Sharmat

The Tintin series by Hergé

. . . The **Something Queer** and **Invisible Inc.** mysteries by Elizabeth Levy are also full of likable sleuths, and of course you can always track down the **Hardy Boys**, **Nancy Drew** and . . . gulp! . . . **Trixie Belden**!

The World Is a Stage: Literature-Based Performances Starring Your Children

Don't just watch, listen, or read children's literature . . . get into the act.

Reader's Theater

I have to confess, I don't usually like listening to children read aloud in a group setting at school. Typically, it's the textbook "round-robin" torture where the teacher calls on child after child to read a section. The teacher may "jolt" a child to attention by calling on him, or worse, the teacher calls on children in some kind of predictable order. There is always one child who . . . reeeeaaaads . . . liiiiiiike . . . thiiiiis, and is dreading his turn, embarrassed about stumbling over words and discouraged by the eye-rolling of his cohorts. But don't worry. If you know of a child who is burned out by the "round-robin" or lacks confidence in oral reading, reader's theater is a tonic as much as an approach.

Reader's theater is a form of read-aloud where every child looks forward to their turn and gets a chance in the limelight. And while the technique proves Shakespeare's theory that all the world's a stage, it's not a big production for the grown-ups. In fact, rather than a list of what you will need to do reader's theater, it's easier to create a list of what you will *not* need:

You will not need costumes.
You will not need a set.
You will not need props.
You will not need makeup.
You will not need anybody to memorize anything.
You will not need a stage.
And most of the time, you will not even need to get *up*!

What you do need is a script for each player, and some chairs to sit on. That's it! Bind the scripts, so papers don't fall all over the place. (If you bind them all with the same cover, it looks very fancy when everyone sits down to read.) Show the children how to highlight their lines in accordance with their assigned parts so they can recognize when to speak, and explain that they shouldn't read the character names or stage directions aloud. The children should first read the script silently to themselves, then practice their lines together with the other readers, to make the reading fluid and tight, to decode the pronunciation of challenging words, and to gain confidence in reading with expression.

There are some reader's theater scripts available in print, but they can be hard to find because most scripts of this sort are derived from existing children's literature, and copyrights are a sticky wicket. So scripts are often somewhat underground endeavors shared among teachers. A few kind and canny authors have taken their own writings and transcribed them into reader's theater form (see Looking for the Right Words, p. 227). PRESENTING READER'S THEATER by Caroline Feller Bauer unabashedly lifts material from poetry, classics, and funny stories. She has a series of playful warm-ups and also provides a nice prototype in which the characters all introduce themselves before the reading begins. The scripts are indexed by length and number of roles.

You can write a reader's theater script yourself, which is not hard, because all you have to do is take a trade book or other literary piece that the children already love, and has plenty of characters and dialogue, and break it into parts. Take this poem, for instance, "Jug and Mug" by David McCord:

"Jug, aren't you fond of Mug?"
"Him I could hug," said Jug.
"Mug, aren't you fond of Jug?"
"Him I could almost slug!"
"Humph," said Jug with a shrug.
"When he pours, he goes Glug!*" said Mug.*
"Well, I don't spill on the rug," said Jug.
"Smug old Jug," said Mug.
"I'll fill you, Mug," said Jug.
"Will, will you, Jug!" said Mug.
"Don't be ugly," said Jug juggly.
"Big lug," said Mug.
Glug.

To make this into a script, separate out the voices into parts, and add a narrator. Put a few simple stage directions in parenthesis. Then read it aloud. Try reading it right now! Yes, this very minute! Get three other people. Perhaps they live in your home with you? If you are all alone, go out and find three other people on the sidewalk or at the corner store. Give every person a part, except the grouchiest person, who can be the audience. Everybody first reads their part quietly, to get used to the words and think how to say them with the most feeling. Then, when everyone has seen their lines, go for it.

JUG AND MUG
From the poem "Jug and Mug," by David McCord

Characters:
Jug
Mug
Narrator

Narrator: Juuuug? Aren't you fond of Mug?
Jug: Him I could hug.
Narrator: Oh, Muuuug! Aren't you fond of Jug?
Mug: *Him*! *Him* I could almost *slug*!
Jug: *Hummmph!*
Mug: (*disgusted*) When he pours, he goes "glug!"
Jug: Well, *I* don't spill on the rug.
Mug: Smug old Jug.
Jug: (*shaking a fist*) I'll fill you, Mug!
Mug: (*chin out, growling*) *Will*, will you Jug!
Jug: Oh, don't be ugly.
Narrator: Said Jug juggly.
Mug: Big lug.
All: *Glug.*

Take a bow.

Now, that was very silly. Was it reader's theater? Nearly. To make it official you would need three copies of the script, one for each character. You would have more time to read and practice your lines. Then you would sit in three chairs, in front of an audience, and you would read your parts.

LOOKING FOR THE RIGHT WORDS?

SCRIPTS IN PRINT:

Blau, Lisa	• SUPER SCIENCE! READER'S THEATRE SCRIPTS AND EXTENDED ACTIVITIES (A subject-integrated approach to reader's theater, very cool!)
Fleischman, Paul	• BIG TALK: POEMS FOR FOUR VOICES
Pugliano-Martin, Carol	• 25 JUST-RIGHT PLAYS FOR EMERGENT READERS (Great for very young children.)

SCRIPTS ON LINE:

www.aaronshep.com/rt/
A definition of readers' theater, tips, and scripts, and information on obtaining Aaron Shepard's helpful book STORIES ON STAGE: SCRIPTS FOR READER'S THEATER.

www.teachingheart.net/readerstheater.htm
From one of my all-time favorite sites, Teaching Is a Work of Heart, tons of scripts and great links.

www.geocities.com/EnchantedForest/Tower/3235/index.html
Downloadable ready-to-read scripts from some of the best children's literature, including multicultural folktales.

www.suzykline.com
Reader's theater scripts from a popular children's author, adapted from her own work.

"Jug and Mug" is about as short and simple as you can get. Usually when you create a reader's theater script of your own, it will be quite a bit longer, especially if it's developed directly from prose. Select stories with plenty of dialogue. Be cognizant of how many characters are in the story relative to how many children you expect to participate. Know that you don't have to hold faithfully to original texts. If you are feeling creative, you can create parodies, or change the story to reflect a different setting or perspective. You can add or subtract characters, or change endings. Or,

TO READ OR NOT TO READ . . .

That is *not* the question! Share these stage-struck read-alouds, and watch your young thespians applaud.

PICTURE BOOK FICTION:

Aliki	• WILLIAM SHAKESPEARE & THE GLOBE
Bond, Felicia	• THE HALLOWEEN PLAY
Conford, Ellen	• The Annabel the Actress series (Chapter book.)
Daly, Niki	• BRAVO, ZAN ANGELO! A COMEDIA DELL'ARTE TALE
Davidson, Rebecca Piatt	• ALL THE WORLD'S A STAGE
Garfield, Leon	• SHAKESPEARE STORIES (Short stories.)
Hoffman, Mary	• AMAZING GRACE
Marshall, James	• FOX ON STAGE
Patterson, Nancy Ruth	• A SIMPLE GIFT (Chapter book.)
Robinson, Barbara	• THE BEST CHRISTMAS PAGEANT EVER (Chapter book.)
Sendak, Maurice	• MAURICE SENDAK'S REALLY ROSIE (A play. Listen to the audio-tape by Carole King!)
Stadler, Alexander	• BEVERLY BILLINGSLY TAKES A BOW
Wasserstein, Wendy	• PAMELA'S FIRST MUSICAL

NON-FICTION:

Bany-Winters, Lisa	• FUNNY BONES: COMEDY GAMES AND ACTIVITIES FOR KIDS • ON STAGE: THEATER GAMES AND ACTIVITIES FOR KIDS
Burdett, Lois	• Shakespeare Can Be Fun! series
Friedman, Lise	• BREAK A LEG! THE KID'S GUIDE TO ACTING AND STAGECRAFT
Hayes, Ann	• ONSTAGE & BACKSTAGE: AT THE NIGHT OWL THEATER
Muir, Kerry, ed.	• CHILDSPLAY: A COLLECTION OF SCENES AND MONOLOGUES FOR CHILDREN
Thee, Christian	• BEHIND THE CURTAIN
Turner, Glennette Tilley	• TAKE A WALK IN THEIR SHOES
Vennema, Peter	• BARD OF AVON: THE STORY OF WILLIAM SHAKESPEARE

rather than work from a book at all, you can create your very own original story in the form of a script. The thing that makes it "reader's theater" is not the derivation from literature, but the straight reading of the script. The derivation from literature is a bonus, just another great opportunity to give children a chance to listen and read. Reader's theater can be original pieces created exclusively for the purpose of reading aloud, but the reason reader's theater is usually taken from literature is because the story and dialogue are already in place, making it a relative piece of cake to turn into a script. In fact, once children learn the format, many will be capable of creating sensational reader's theater scripts on their own.

I like reader's theater because even though it requires a little more effort and forethought, it's so mellow. It's like the round-robin read-aloud, but all fun. Everybody gets a turn to read, and the listener gets to hear this concert of voices all working together to tell the same story. Children really love it because it's like being in a play without the pressure of forgetting one's lines. After your children get the hang of it, consider performing in nursing homes, hospitals, libraries, at PTA meetings, at the Laundromat, the bus stop, a coffee shop, a dinner party, a park bench, a Books for Breakfast program (see p. 69) . . . and bask in the applause.

Yackety-Yack to Yesterday and Back: Reader's Theater Interviews

After reading a biography about a historical figure (see Who's Who? Children's Biography, p. 123), children can use the information to create a script in the form of a talk-show interview. The facts will be made more memorable to both readers and audience through the performance. Basically, children are creating comprehension questions and answering them on their own, but don't spoil the fun by telling your child how educational it all is. These interviews are fun to "do up" a bit with fake accents, some simple costuming, and a videotape rolling.

Puppetry

Puppetry, to me, is the creating of personalities for otherwise inanimate objects. Anthropomorphizing. That means it's a little on the crazy side. Which also means, children can't get enough of it. This is good because from puppetry, children can learn about characterization and plot and practice reading comprehension. While children are playing with puppets, they are working as a team, listening for cues, improvising, and creating mood.

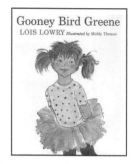

✿ *Potato Pick:*

GOONEY BIRD GREENE

by Lois Lowry, illustrated by Middy Thomas

When the teacher explains that the class is learning about what makes a good story, Gooney Bird grabs the baton and obliges the class with a series of tales such as "How Gooney Bird Came from China on a Flying Carpet" and "Beloved Catman is Consumed by a Cow." While seemingly outlandish, they all prove to be, as Gooney Bird puts it, "absolutely true." What's more, Gooney Bird manages to impart several pearls of wisdom about what makes a good story to her class, and to all who read this book. Lowry writes classroom banter that is impeccably accurate, and Gooney Bird is irresistible with her grade-school glamour, accessorizing with tutus, flip-flops, and black opera gloves. A very funny read in the tradition of PIPPI LONGSTOCKING, this is a pragmatic introduction to storytelling. Hopefully there will be Gooney Bird sightings in every second grade classroom in the nation. (7 and up)

Making Puppets

Puppetry is a rich and ancient tradition. There are so many different kinds of puppets: marionettes, rod puppets, Bunraku style. Be impressed at www.sagecraft.com/puppetry. Using a few simple objects from around the house, you, too, can have puppets.

You can make a finger puppet by drawing two eyes and a mouth on your finger with a felt-tip pen. You can make a finger puppet by cutting off a finger on an old glove and painting a face on it. You can make a hand puppet by decorating a paper bag. You can make a hand puppet by sewing buttons on a sock. You can make a puppet on a rod, or a straw, or a branch, or a chopstick. Just design a figure on posterboard, cut it out, and attach the back of it to the rod. You can create moving parts by attaching limbs with brass brads. Such simple puppets can be attractive, and while less expressive, they can still be very effective in telling a simple folktale. I have a memory of watching *Mister Rogers' Neighborhood* when I was about three years old. Fred Rogers used homemade rod puppets to tell the story of *King Midas and the Golden Touch.* When King Midas kissed his daughter, Mr. Rogers turned the cut-out figure of the princess around and revealed that the other side was covered entirely with gold glitter. It's all in the delivery, folks.

My favorite puppets to create are papier-mâché: a little harder and more time consuming, but a lot fancier. To make papier-mâché, mix three cups of water with one cup of flour in a saucepan, stirring constantly until it forms a thick paste, about twenty minutes. The paste stores well in the refrigerator in an airtight container for about three days, if you get called away from the project. I like to shape a head out of wire first, but I know that many teachers use small balloons for head shapes, or shape the head out of clay. With masking tape, attach a toilet-paper tube where you want the neck to be. Cover the shape smoothly and evenly with newsprint dipped generously in papier-mâché paste, and let the head and neck dry for a couple of days. If you are using a balloon for a head shape, pop it and remove once the papier-mâché has dried. If you are using clay, cut the head in half with an X-Acto knife once the papier-mâché has dried, remove the clay, secure the head back together with masking tape, and add one new layer of papier-mâché. When the head is complete, paint with acrylics; it's fun to attach beads, yarn hair, button eyes, faux fur with a glue gun. Cut and sew simple felt bodies using the shape of your hand or a child's hand as a guide, and then use a glue-gun to attach the body to the neck. Voilà! Children delight in the gooky mud-puddle feel of papier-mâché and the chance to decorate with all the baubles and frills, so let them in on every step possible.

Shadow puppets are always a huge hit. These are simply silhouettes of people and objects cut out of firm paper, such as poster board. (Don't use construction paper; it's too floppy.) The idea is to capture the silhouette—just the shape, or the outline. Nothing your child draws within the outline will be seen. Attach a stiff wire (or soda straw or chopstick) to the bottom of the puppet; your child will hold the puppet from below. For shadow-puppet plays, you need a special screen. To make that screen, attach a piece of blank newsprint or white butcher paper across a cardboard frame with masking tape so it is flat and taut. Attach to the stage of your puppet theater (Don't have one? See Making a Puppet Theater, p. 232), using bulldog clips (available at office supply stores). Take a plant "grow light" or a clamp-on desk lamp and clip it to the top of your puppet theater, so the light shines onto the screen from behind. Take care to keep the light bulb far from the paper and cardboard; it should not touch either or it could cause a fire. Remind children not to touch the hot bulb. Hold the puppet flush against the screen. If you want to visit a classroom and give a really easy shadow-puppet show, you can lay puppets on an overhead projector screen and use the same stiff wire (or soda straw or chopstick) to move them. Your fingers will also work, in a pinch.

Shadow-puppet shows can be exciting and mysterious. For my birthday one year, my husband created for me all the puppets for a telling of Gerald McDermott's **ANANSI THE SPIDER**. I presented this show to all the children at my school, first through eighth grades, and then invited them to create their own literature-based shows. The older children gave some very impressive performances. A group of four boys created magnificent shadow puppets for **TIME FLIES** by Eric Rohmann, a wordless picture book about a bird who flies back in time to meet dinosaur ancestors. They played Wagner in the background and used colored transparent film to simulate red lava flowing from the volcano. Another group of eighth-grade girls created a chilling recreation of the poem "We Organized" from **THE DARK-THIRTY: SOUTHERN TALES OF THE**

GIVE CHILDREN'S PUPPET-MAKING BOOKS A HAND

Lade, Roger	• THE MOST EXCELLENT BOOK OF HOW TO BE A PUPPETEER
Philpott, Violet, and Mary Jean McNeil	• KNOWHOW BOOK OF PUPPETS
Wallace, Mary	• I CAN MAKE THAT

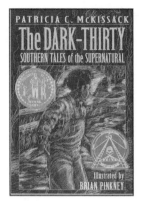

SUPERNATURAL by Patricia C. McKissack, about an abusive slave master whose charges use conjuring power to free themselves from his tyranny. These were not "gifted" children who accomplished these feats, not great test-takers or verbal hotshots. These were inspired children who had access to books. Children's books? Perhaps. Children's books *below grade level*? Arguably. But the sophisticated interpretation of one art form into another left us all breathless, and not a one of us debated whether or not we were working from "baby" books or if puppetry was "kid stuff" or at what level we were working. The children were doing what true artists do: seeing something in a way nobody else had seen it before, and then sharing their vision in a style all their own.

Making a Puppet Theater

To make a simple puppet theater, turn a large cardboard box upside down. The best size for children is always refrigerator size, but a box large enough to hold diapers or a TV will do. Using an X-Acto knife, cut a large screenlike rectangle out of the front of the box, starting about three inches from the top and ending at about the middle of the box. Then, use the X-Acto knife to cut out the entire back panel of the box. You will be left with three panels and a top. It should be free standing. From the inside of the box, attach curtain-rod holders above the rectangle you cut. (You can attach the rod holders with nuts and bolts, strong tape or Velcro, or a glue gun should do the trick.) It is hard to find a curtain rod short enough to fit, so use a wooden dowel rod from a home-improvement store and trim it to fit the holders. If you are the sewing sort, you can make curtains. If you are not the sewing sort, like me, you can drape scarves or sari material around the rod to create a curtain effect. Decorate the outside; if you use poster paint, be sure to apply fixative or the paint will crumble and fall off; I prefer acrylics. If you want to get elaborate, cut a "shelf" a few inches wide from the extra piece of cardboard you cut off and using a glue gun attach it to the bottom side of the rectangle, so puppets have a place to lay props. Other simple puppet theaters can be made by attaching curtain-rod holders low on a doorway threshold allowing the curtain to be hung during shows and removed when not in use. Or, try a tipped-on-its side card table or a broomstick across two chairs with a cloth draped over it.

A broomstick across two chairs . . .

For more formal presentations, I have children script out the show like a play, noting stage directions and parts (for hints, see Reader's

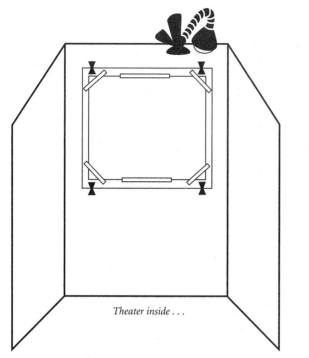

Theater inside . . .

And theater outside . . .

In a doorway . . .

A card table tipped on its side . . .

Theater, p. 225) and then read their lines into a tape recorder. They can include music for mood or transitions. When it is time for the show, they play the tape and concentrate on the movements of the puppets. I try to warn children not to show that the puppet is talking by shaking it. We practice jumping up and down every time we speak to see how silly that really is. Puppets should have nuances and gestures, just like people. Sometimes children like to give impromptu shows. These can be side-splittingly funny, but can also deteriorate quickly into bathroom humor and puppet fights. These are the qualities that made Punch and Judy legendary (and also that make puppetry a winner for children with behavioral disorders), so tolerate the buffoonery for as long as you can, and then gently encourage children toward more structured performances.

You don't need to be fancy to have fun. When my son was four, he had the best attitude about puppetry. He would stick inanimate objects in my face and order, "Make him talk to me." Hamburgers could talk. Teakettles could talk. Cars could talk. Shoes could talk. As soon as the object could talk, my son asked the question, the same question over and over. "So, do you like me? Are you my friend?" It's the question we all want answered, and we want it answered in the same way over and over: "*Like* you! I *love* you! You're terrific! Great! Stupendous!" Sometimes this is an easier question to ask of a hamburger or a shoe than it is of a person. Thankfully, the answer through puppetry is a little more predictable.

Storytelling: The Tell-Tale Art

What are Americans most scared of? In second place is death. In first place is public speaking. Let's nip neurosis in the bud! What I like about empowering children to tell stories is that it gives those with a dramatic flair some time in the limelight, but the process of learning to tell a story is so filled with incremental successes that even children who are terribly shy will ultimately find the skills to sparkle.

Children of all ages are natural storytellers. Ask why the chores aren't done for a sample of this inborn talent! But for the kind of story *re*-telling that this section is about, which is a little more formal, generally children ages eight and up perform most successfully. And while you can certainly and absolutely show a single child how to tell a story, I always like working with groups, large or small. Then there are plenty of listeners as well as tellers handy, and the sound of laughter is so encouraging. Best of all, you can culminate the acquisition of storytelling skills with a festival the whole community can enjoy and the children will always remember.

Storytelling has all the benefits of read-aloud. It improves language skills such as vocabulary, prediction skills, sequencing, comprehension, story structure, and recall. These skills will also help children become better writers. Children who engage in storytelling learn about history and culture, develop emotionally, and have better self-esteem. Stimulating imagination to the *nth* degree, storytelling also creates a love of narrative that can translate into a lifelong love of books.

The difference between storytelling (or story re-telling, as is the case here, since we are working from children's trade literature and less from original work or family history) and read-aloud is that storytelling is always inventive. To execute a performance, the storytelling child needs to synthesize all sorts of cognitive operations with gross motor skills and emotional interpretations. Because of this synthesis, every performance is unique to the teller. The other difference is the connection with the audience. The eye contact alone makes storytelling a different animal than read-aloud. When you try it, you'll see.

Before You Start Teaching Kids How to Tell a Story

Learn to tell a story yourself, because you are the grown-up and you are the model. So go through all the steps before teaching others. Then the children will not feel you are, how you say, "bogus." Model your ability immediately to the children you are teaching, not to show off but so that your performance can be a frame of reference for skills such as voice projection, eye contact, characterization, and expression. As an added bonus, your storytelling ability will give you greater confidence to work in front of a group of children, making you a more helpful asset whenever you visit your child's classroom.

Offer children a choice of which story they want to tell. If *they* choose the book, they will be invested in the story and do a better job. You can use your library card to get a nice pile to choose from. If you are a teacher or running a workshop, you may be able to get a grant. (Check out The Foundation Center at www.fdncenter.org for leads.) Preferably, let the children choose a story from a selection to which you have already applied criteria so all choices are suitable. When determining whether or not a book will work well, keep these measures in mind:

A good book for storytelling will . . .

• have a clear beginning, middle, and end (folktales often fit this bill)

• have text that stands independently from the illustrations

• have places where the audience can join in (repeated verses, or cumulative tales in which the plot is built on repetitions of lines that came before)

• make you laugh or cry or feel scared—in other words, play on basic emotions

A tricky book for storytelling will . . .

• depend on the illustrations to help tell the story

• have a lot of dialogue

• have flowery, literary language that makes it hard for the teller to re-tell in her own way

Also consider dialect and first-person voice. Sometimes these can be well matched to a child; at other times the voices can seem forced and uncomfortable, making listeners uncomfortable as well. Some stories include bouts of singing. This may be a hurdle for children who are tone deaf and don't care to prove it publicly. Ensure a successful experience by helping children find a tale that fits their comfort level. Stories should also be brief. Ten minutes is enough time for novice storytellers. Each child should have her own story to tell. A list of tried-and-true "good books" is included at the end of this section.

Resort to an anthology if you are really broke or you owe the library money or your library stinks. Copy stories for the children to choose and

use. This is initially much less exciting than selecting an illustrated book and may be detrimental to children who are visual learners, but I will begrudgingly admit that children can still learn stories from them. My favorite publisher of storytelling anthologies is August House, 1-501-372-5450, www.augusthouse.com. Other excellent resources for tellable tales are PETE SEEGER'S STORYTELLING BOOK by Pete Seeger and Paul DuBois Jacobs and STORIES IN MY POCKET by Martha Hamilton and Mitch Weiss.

Get your hands on a copy of CHILDREN TELL STORIES: A TEACHING GUIDE by Martha Hamilton and Mitch Weiss, the best and most straightforward book I know on the subject. It includes lots of clever games such as "Pass the Face" and "Walk the Walk" for fostering expressive performances, and there is also a generous collection of stories at the end that are suitable for telling. Much of my teaching approach was adapted and modified from the activities and ideas in their book. You can order the book through their Web site, www.beautyandthebeaststorytellers.com.

Discuss why storytelling is a good thing to know. When talking about storytelling with children, I tell them that in Africa, there is a saying: Every man dies two deaths. The first, when his body dies. The second, when the last person remembers him dies. Stories, too, die when the last person who knows the story dies. So the trick is not only to know the story, but to make people remember the story, so it will live on and on. Body language and facial expressions are part of making the story memorable, keeping it alive, which is why it is important to be expressive, even if it seems extreme or embarrassing at first. The audience will most likely not remember how silly you acted or looked. They will remember enjoying the story. And that means you did your job as a storyteller.

I also tell children that storytelling is an actual career that some people choose, and that professional storytellers earn money. (This usually takes care of the less sentimental kids in the audience.) If they are willing to practice, they can be assured that they will learn something they can use for their whole life. (And earn money. Say it twice. Children these days can be very pragmatic.)

The Steps to Learning a Story

1. Read the book to yourself twice.
No pressure; just get familiar with it.

2. Introduce voice projection.
Teach children to get loud. Ask children to turn to their neighbor and say hello in the way that they normally do. Ask them to put their hands

on their throats when they say it. Do they feel anything? Ask them to put their hands right over their rib cage and say "hi." Do they feel anything? Discuss the physiological process of speaking, only don't use the word "physiological," it's too long. Maybe instead share the picture book **How You Talk** by Paul Showers (by the way, you are integrating science, in case you haven't noticed).

Have children lie on the floor with a book on their diaphragm. (Wait a number of minutes while savvy children with older siblings laugh contagiously at the word "diaphragm." At this point you may choose to integrate health and family education or you may let the moment pass.) Instruct them to breathe normally. The books will rise and fall slowly as they breathe. Tell them to feel the movements of their diaphragms and rise slowly from the floor, working for the same movement. Have children keep their hand over the diaphragm and breathe in and out more markedly. Have children say "hi" when exhaling. Then let the children say "hi" like they did in the beginning. With hands on diaphragms and throats let them feel the difference. Tell them that with storytelling, they

What if I looked at someone and they made me laugh and I start cracking up? What if I tell the story messed up? Like I put the ending first then the starting then the middle?

—from the journal of Jamian, fourth-grader

Recorders to the Rescue

Tape recorders are very useful in helping children become storytellers. Children can read aloud the story into the tape recorder, and then once the story has been learned, they can tell the story and compare. Tapes are also a useful tool, especially if you are trying to help many children at once; listen to the children's tapes at your convenience and jot down suggestions about pacing, speaking more loudly, characterization, and so forth, tailored to the individual child. Children themselves can also listen to the tape to determine what is needed. You might also consider compiling a single tape of their recorded performances to donate to the library (and for sentimental reasons, too, of course).

If you are lucky enough to live where cultural events abound, you can take a field trip to watch some of the professionals who regularly perform at museums, libraries, festivals, bookstores, and community centers.

Or, if you can get the funds, consider hiring a storyteller to come to you. You can find one through the National Storytelling Directory which is part of the amazing National Storytelling Network home page, www.story net.org/. If a live performance is over your budget, however, videotapes afford a great opportunity to watch professional storytellers. Many storytellers have videotaped performances available. Borrow them at libraries, or order direct from the storytellers themselves. A few videos are widely distributed and may be ordered through book chains and video stores. Videos and live performances allow children to see all the subtle body movements, facial expressions, eye contact, and other nuances that make the storytelling tradition so electric. Videotaping the children themselves can be informative, but can also make sensitive children self-conscious, so I suggest sticking with low-end technology when practicing.

At first it kind of scary but then I was getting exciting then it felt very good and I said to my self I am going to tell this hole book! I felt happy because they gathered around me and I knew that they wanted to hear my story and I really wanted to be a basketball player but storytelling is better.

—from the journal of Frank, fifth-grader

should use that energy and strength of exhaling to carry their words. Practice saying words and sentences while exhaling. Make sure you take deep breaths in between the exercise (or have smelling salts available!).

This may seem like a goofy exercise and will probably get a lot of giggles. But it is a very important first exercise, because it helps assure the children that they will be heard. It's horrible to imagine telling a story and having listeners yell at you, "I can't hear!" Children need to know immediately that voice projection is part of telling the story. For a child who has a difficult time getting the idea, I hang a drawing of a child's head on the opposite far wall, and tell that child that "your brother can't hear you." Children get used to yelling at their "brother" on the far wall. It is also helpful for listeners to give a silent "thumbs-up" sign when the storyteller is forgetting to project during practice. This is much less distracting than children yelling, "Louder!"

Encourage children to watch music videos (yes, you read right!) and try to observe who is singing from the diaphragm by the rise and fall of the chest cavity, and who is lip-synching or has a weak voice. (Who's bogus *now*?) Invite children to try singing along with a favorite CD. Ask them if they can sing louder than the performer, using the air in their diaphragms.

Eye contact is another attention-holding device that you should introduce early on. Just for fun, stare at each person in the room; have the children do the same. Tell them they must try to make each listener feel as if the story is being told just for him, and eye contact helps the listeners feel that way. If the storytellers-in-training are too shy for eye contact, they can look at the tops of people's heads.

3. Memorize first and last lines.

Some children may want also to memorize particular lines that have beautiful language or refrains that help to carry the story, but for the most part stories are best told in a spontaneous, anecdotal fashion, as if the story happened to the child personally or to someone they knew. Storytelling is not about memorizing. In fact, memorizing too much and recalling too little can make children "blank out," freeze, and forget what's been memorized if nerves get bad enough. Memorizing first and last lines, though, offers a sense of confidence. It assures the child that she knows how to start and how to end, so that she can at least get on and off the stage.

4. Make character webs.

A character web is a drawing of a circle with a single character's name in the middle and rays around the circle. The unique qualities of the character are written along the rays (one trait per ray). When finished, the web looks like a spider or a sun covered with words. For instance, a character web of Baby Bear from "Goldilocks and the Three Bears" might have statements written on the rays such as "likes to go on walks," "had chair broken by intruder," "won't eat porridge when it is too hot," "observant." Demonstrate making a web in front of the children with their help, using a character from a familiar story so they see how it's done. The point of a character map is to really reflect on and get to know the characters in a story, so when the time comes to dramatize the characters, the children will have insight into them.

This is a nice place to start introducing some of the games from Hamilton and Weiss's CHILDREN TELL STORIES, because from here on out children should work on adding expression to their stories. What facial expressions would a character wear? How would a character hold his body if he was happy? Frightened? Angry?

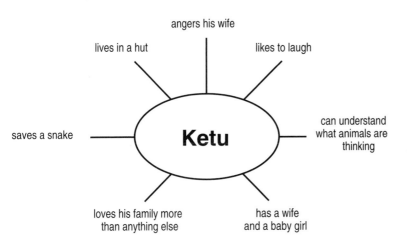

I practiced a hole hour yesterday.

—from the journal of Funsho, fifth-grader

Character web for Ketu from What's So Funny, Ketu? *by Verna Aardema*

5. Make a picture map.

A picture map is an invaluable way of learning the sequence of a story. Even as a grown-up, I never learn a story without making a set. A picture map is a bunch of index cards that are doodled on, each card depicting an important event in the story. Picture maps help familiarize children with the order of events in the story. A picture map shouldn't be a work of art. It can consist of stick figures, just so long as the person telling the story can understand what's going on. The cards should really not have words, just pictures, like a caveman might use if preparing for a storytelling. Children throw the cards up in the air, putting them out of order, and then try to get the cards back in order. They repeat this for practice as many times as necessary.

STORYTELLING IS SERIOUS BUSINESS!

As real live storytellers, children will need business cards, of course. Have children give you the information they would like to appear on their cards. When I ran this program from schools, the children included their full name, room number, and the name of the story they could tell. If you run this program out of your home or community center, take care to be discreet about children's addresses for the children's safety. Before computers, I made elegant business cards for the children using copy machines and rubber stamps (wonderful literature-based rubber stamps are available through Kidstamps, www.kidstamps.com, 1-800-727-5437), and with the advent of computers, printing up business cards became a breeze. The cards are terrific affirmations of the children's status as storytellers, and were useful to teachers who later invited my students to come and present.

6. Read the book aloud, twice.

This time, it's not just for fun. These are reflective readings. When is a good time to speak extra slowly? To hold a facial expression? To speak more loudly? To pause? To use a stage whisper? To suggest people join in? Ask the children at which place in their story one of these devices could be employed. (Except, don't say, "When will you employ these devices?" Say, "So, where exactly will you use this stuff to make your storytelling unbelievably super terrific?")

7. Practice telling the story.

Practice equals fluency, so the more practice, the better. Children should:

• Tell the story to a mirror.

• Tell the story to a doll or toy or pet goldfish or appliance (toasters are *excellent* listeners).

• Tell the story to a friend or family member.

This progression is not accidental. Moving from nonjudgmental and inanimate audiences to a loving, interested audience provides the practice that earns the confidence, and the ability, to tell a story well.

Now that your child can tell a story by heart—and *with* heart!—it's time to "take some elsewhere, and let some come back to me." This is the storyteller's mandate from Gail Haley's **A STORY, A STORY**. Stories are meant not only to be learned but to be passed around and around, so the child's next step is to take that story and deliver it to as much of the world as possible.

The Storytelling Festival

For some children, telling the story to a friend is enough. For others, performing for a small, familiar group is perfectly gratifying, maybe branching out to entertaining sibling's friends in a day care center, visiting a few children in a pediatric ward or wowing a parent's book club. But there are always a few Broadway babies who aren't satisfied until they hit the big time. All stars need to shine to their fullest potential. A festival allows young storytelling supernovas to blind a larger audience with their brilliance while bringing satisfying closure to the accomplishment of learning to tell a story.

Places to hold a storytelling festival:

Library (my first choice because if you can make it there, you'll make it anywhere!)

Classroom (invite another class as guests)

Bookstore (tie it in with a PTA fund-raiser)

City park field house (or in the park itself)

Church, temple, other place of worship

Nursing home

Party room or lobby of an apartment complex

Basement, backyard, or garage of somebody's house

Auditoriums tend to be somewhat cold and make performers feel Carnegie Hall amounts of pressure. If possible, keep the space cozy and folksy, or take it outdoors. Storytelling performances are also a nice tradition to add to your annual neighborhood block party or family reunion. More performance ideas can be found in Performing Poetry, p. 301.

If they laugh I don't care I got to tell a story that I worked hard on and I'm happy.

—from the journal of Suhela, fifth-grader

Storytelling Festival Sidelines

What are the components of the festival? Try food, fund-raising, and fun. For the festivals I have organized, we've had games that were tied into the literary folktale theme, such as Teddy Bear Cake Walks;

HAVE WE BEEN INTRODUCED?

Explain to children how to introduce themselves and their book to a group.

• First, they should say their full name.

• Second, if they have a prop, they should share it with the audience. Now, for novice storytellers, I do not encourage the use of props during the telling as they can be clumsy and distracting, but used in the introduction they can get the audience geared up for what is to follow. For instance, if a child is going to tell THE CHINESE MIRROR by Mirra Ginsburg, the child can say, "What do you see when you look in this mirror?" and hold the mirror up to the audience. After they answer, the teller can say, "When I look into it, I see

[describes self], but when a merchant from China looked into it, he saw something different, as you'll find out when I tell you the amazing story of THE CHINESE MIRROR by Mirra Ginsburg." Another example would be if the teller held up a lemon and said, "This is the very fruit that almost caused unimaginable shame to the town of Alto, Ohio, but for the quick thinking of LENTIL, by Robert McCloskey." Or, a child may hold out a broom. "Think this is for sweeping? Then you need to meet a friend of mine. TILLY WITCH, by Don Freeman."

• Lastly, the child should give credit where credit is due by holding up the cover of the book and saying the book's title and author.

Fight Stagefright

I feel that I'm afraid that I'm gonna forget my lines once I see all the kids or grown-ups there. I'm afraid that I'm not gonna speak loud enough and they will think I'm boring. Other than that I feel fine.

—from the journal of Lauren, third-grader

Here are questions children have asked me about telling stories in front of an unfamiliar audience, and answers you can offer them. Frank discussions go far to allay concerns about performing and to instill public-speaking strategies that could last a lifetime.

WHAT IF I FORGET THE STORY?

The best insurance you have against forgetting is practice. If you have been practicing, if you memorized first and last lines, did picture maps and character maps, the worst that can happen is you will blank out for a moment. In this case, the story is still there, somewhere in your brain's attic. Just take a deep breath, pause a moment to think, smile, and you will find the story again. If you are really stuck, just try to repeat the last thing you said; that sometimes jars the memory.

WHAT IF I MAKE A MISTAKE?

Don't apologize. Most likely, the audience didn't even notice. If you accidentally skip over something important and realize it later, just throw it in: "Oh, yes, and did I mention," or "You should also know . . ."

WHAT IF MY AUDIENCE ISN'T PAYING ATTENTION TO ME?

They *will* pay attention if you make eye contact and speak loudly and expressively. Is there a part in the story where you can invite the audience to join with you? A funny name they can call out? A refrain they can repeat? Can they clap to the rhythm? Join you in making a scary face or a silly face? Welcome them in to your story whenever you can, and they will pay attention. If for some reason you have a rude person in the audience and you aren't getting the attention you deserve, stare at that person and wait until you do. You worked a long time to share this story and you deserve respect.

WHAT IF I THROW UP OR PEE IN MY PANTS?

You won't throw up. Go to the bathroom before you perform.

WHAT IF I GET STAGE FRIGHT AND IT'S JUST TOO SCARY TO EVEN LOOK UP?

Some people suggest imagining the audience in their underwear to combat stage fright. I find this distracting. Better to remember that people are there to hear a story, and you are there to keep a story alive by doing your best to tell it. So the audience is not your enemy; on the contrary, you and the audience are a team. If you are nervous, open and close your fists a few times. Take a deep breath. Smile so all your teeth show. Relax and shine like the star you are.

Being unprepared may exempt a child from performing, but being afraid should not. If you know a child is prepared, do everything you can to get them to do it, no matter what the complaints. Their training is their parachute, so push them out of that storytelling airplane. It's scary, but it's an exhilarating ride and there's a soft pile of success waiting for them to land on.

a tossing game using old plastic Halloween witch's cauldrons for buckets and an unlucky Beanie Baby frog for throwing; a Magic Fish game, in which children used a magnetized fishing pole and tried to hook the lucky fish; an Ugly Duckling game using floating ducks found in the fabulous Oriental Trading catalog (www.orientaltrading.com, or 1-800-875-8480); and a Three Billy Goats Gruff basketball toss (which didn't make a ton of sense but was enjoyed all the same). The prizes we gave away were mostly bookmarks, which can be purchased inexpensively through Upstart (www.highsmith.com, or 1-800-448-4887) or hand made. Face painting was also popular! I let children who were in the storytelling program but were not performing on festival day run the games and attractions so that they, too, were involved and felt important in making the event special.

Raise funds during the festival by combining it with a book fair. If you are with a school, you can arrange a fun and easy book fair with a company such as Scholastic (1-800-724-6527, my favorite) or Troll (www.troll.com/parents/bookfair/location.html). Bear in mind, you may possibly get a better profit margin by arranging a book fair with your local bookseller; many of them will cater fairs to your group's individual needs. Shop around. Or, coordinate the festival with a used book sale, using library discards and donated items.

I don't think you can call anything a real shindig if there's no food, so we had a bake sale (at our peril, see The Cookie Crumbles, p. 75), in keeping with our literary folktale theme. One little girl dressed as Red Riding Hood and wandered around with basket and napkins, selling her grandmother's cookies and keeping the change in her apron. We dyed frosting green and had Frog-Prince Cupcakes. We also served Giant's Rings (doughnuts), Brownie's Brownies, Gold Bricks from Aladdin's cave (Rice Krispies treats), and washed it all down with Magic Potion (punch).

Storytellers in the Spotlight

When the frenzy has reached fever pitch, ring a bell, flick lights, or give some signal and direct children and families to the performance areas. The average attention span for a crowded grade-school audience watching other children is about a half hour. That means if you have more than five storytellers you want to put on center stage, you need another stage; otherwise, the audience may be squirming or yawning by the end. This is not necessarily a reflection on the storyteller, of course; most children are gifted at squirming and yawning. However, this will be little consolation to the performer. If you have a large group of performers, create two stages, in separate rooms or in areas distant enough from

I am confident about the story because I studied it. I know for sure that I can tell it good. I won't forget because I imagine a picture of the book in my head.

—from the journal of Samera, fifth-grader

READ ALOUD AND STORYTELLING?

During a question-and-answer-session panel discussion about literacy, one father stood up and expressed concern that each night he made up stories for his child. He worried that in view of the benefits of read-aloud, he was doing something wrong by simply making things up that weren't in print anywhere. Was storytelling less valuable than read-aloud? The answer is no. What could be more magical and comforting than listening to someone make up a story just for you? Storytelling and read-aloud are close cousins. Both are about listening and imagining a narrative, and connection with the voice that is implicit in the story. Read-aloud simply plays on different sets of skills—most markedly, exposure to print—and has a different body of hard data supporting its advantages. Read-aloud is also easier for many people. Making up a story takes a particular creative talent, but even if you don't have this gift, you can read aloud.

The oral tradition came before the written one, and the written one preserved and elaborated on the oral one—but to do justice to the written one, we find ourselves talking all over again. It's circular. The main thing is to include your child within that circle *somewhere*, to create memorable experiences that keep alive the tradition of love of story.

I was a little bit unhappy. But then I did my introduction. It felt easier. Then when I was done, I was handed an award. I felt extreemly happy. Next a ton of people asked me for my autograph. I got magic potion and a cookie for free! I had fun!

—from the journal of Lauren, third-grader

each other so the performances don't distract from each other. Call the stages by different names, for example the "sun" stage and the "moon" stage. When audience members enter, alternate giving a picture of a sun or a moon along with each program. When it is time to listen to stories, ask people holding "sun" cards to find a seat near the "sun" stage (decorated accordingly) and folks holding "moon" cards to go to the "moon" stage. This way, the audience will be evenly divided for both groups of performers. On the program, simply indicate who is performing at which stage.

Introduce the program, or better yet, have one of the children from your storytelling program introduce it.

When the performers finish, present roses and certificates to the children who presented. After the ovations, encourage the audience to come get autographs. Storytelling: the glamorous life.

A SELECTION OF GOOD BOOKS FOR STORYTELLING

Aardema, Verna WHY MOSQUITOS BUZZ IN PEOPLE'S EARS
A cumulative *pourquoi* tale in which the lion finds the culprit in a crime against the owls.

Abolafia, Yossi FOX TALE
Fox is out-foxed after trading his tail for half a jar of honey.

Bannerman, Helen THE STORY OF LITTLE BABAJI
In a culturally sensitive retelling of the dreaded Little Black Sambo,
a boy matches wits with some fashion-conscious tigers.

Bishop, Claire Huchet THE FIVE CHINESE BROTHERS
Cunning quintuplets survive unfair punishments.

Bruchac, Joseph THE GREAT BALL GAME
Sporting Native American *pourquoi* tale explains which team little bat is
batting for.

Bryan, Ashley ASHLEY BRYAN'S AFRICAN TALES, UH-HUH
Animal stories, morality tales, funny stories. . . . Pick any one of these,
and you'll have a great storytelling, uh-huh!

Calmenson, Stephanie THE TEENY TINY TEACHER
Sweet and only slightly spooky story of a ghost haunting a classroom,
seeking the bone that the teacher is using for science class.

Cates, Karin A FAR-FETCHED STORY
When Grandma sends family members out to fetch wood, each returns
with nothing but a far-fetched story. How will the family keep warm all
winter?

*I hope I don't fall off the
stage if there's one.*

—from the journal of Dana,
fifth-grader

A SAMPLE INTRODUCTION
TO YOUR STORYTELLING FESTIVAL

Stories.
On the antennae of the smallest insect, they quiver.
In the whine of a dog in the deepest darkest night, they
penetrate our bones.
Across the savannas of Africa,
Under the bridges of China,
Through the traffic of our city streets
They reach us, they find us.
Stories.

The Storyteller's Workshop is proud to present "Story-telling: The Tell-Tale Art." The performances you are
about to see are the results of children who have
worked hard to share stories they have enjoyed. Please
show consideration by using eyes that look and ears
that listen, and by remaining until all performances are
completed.

From long ago and far away
And from close
For you today, and for our children in the future . . .
Stories.

At first I was afraid that I might forget my lines, or maybe my hat might fall off, or people might not listen. By the time I got where Mama Imp squeezed Mama into a green egg I got used to it.

—from the journal of Salena, fifth-grader

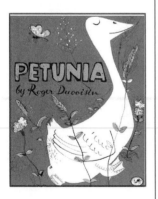

Clements, Andrew **BIG AL**

The biggest, ugliest, scariest fish in the sea finds friends.

Cole, Brock **ALPHA AND THE DIRTY BABY**

When her parents are replaced by wicked trolls, Alpha throws the baby out with the bathwater and cleans up the situation.

Cooney, Barbara **MISS RUMPHIUS**

World-traveling woman seeks to make the world more beautiful, and finds a way.

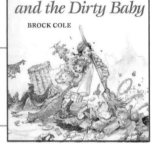

Daugherty, James **ANDY AND THE LION**

After taking out a book about lions from the library, a homespun boy meets the real McCoy.

Davol, Marguerite **THE SNAKE'S TALES**

A snake promises to teach a brother and sister to tell stories in exchange for their berries.

Demi **THE EMPTY POT**

After distributing flower seeds, the emperor offers his kingdom to the child who shows the best effort. Why won't Ping's seed grow?

dePaola, Tomie **THE LEGEND OF THE BLUEBONNET**

A girl sacrifices her most precious possession to stop a drought.

dePaola, Tomie **STREGA NONA**

Spaghetti runs amok when a bumbler forgets a magic spell.

Duvoisin, Roger **PETUNIA**

A silly goose learns the hard way that reading is the first step to being wise and helpful.

Galdone, Paul **THE THREE BILLY GOATS GRUFF**

A bullying toll-keeper meets his comeuppance when three goats cross his bridge.

Gilman, Phoebe **SOMETHING FROM NOTHING**

A talented tailor proves that you can always reuse and recycle. (Also, see the story fitted another way in **JOSEPH HAD A LITTLE OVERCOAT** by Simms Taback.)

Ginsburg, Mirra **THE CHINESE MIRROR**

Silly story of a family who has never seen a mirror before and does not realize it reflects whoever is looking into it.

Ginsburg, Mirra **MUSHROOM IN THE RAIN**

A mushroom mysteriously protects all who hide beneath it.

Goble, Paul **THE GIFT OF THE SACRED DOG**
Story of how horses came to the Native American people.

Haley, Gail **A STORY, A STORY**
Pourquoi tale from Africa explaining how stories came
to earth.

Hurd, Thacher **MAMA DON'T ALLOW**
A saxophone player escapes the crocodile's chomp
with the help of his music.

Keats, Ezra Jack **WHISTLE FOR WILLIE**
Oh, to be able to whistle, every little boy's dream!
With a little frustration and a lot of practice, one little boy makes
this dream come true and calls his dog to boot.

Ketteman, Helen **ARMADILLO TATTLETALE**
A *pourquoi* tale in which a big-mouthed little buddy
needs to learn to run—fast.

Kimmel, Eric **ANANSI AND THE TALKING MELON**
The spider weaves a web of trickery to get some delicious fruit.

Kleven, Elisa **THE PAPER PRINCESS**
A cutout doll, caught in an updraft, works hard to
return to the girl who created her.

Leaf, Munro **THE STORY OF FERDINAND**
Classic story of a peaceful bull who would not fight the
Matador in the big bullfight.

London, Jonathan **FROGGY GETS DRESSED**
Froggy wants to come out of hibernation, but he can't
seem to dress for the weather, despite his mother's help.

Melmed, Laura Krauss **THE RAINBABIES**
A childless couple is magically blessed with a dozen
tiny babies, and cursed with disasters that test their
dedication.

Orgel, Doris **SING, LITTLE SACK!**
A gruesome green guy who has kidnapped a girl is outwitted by her
mother.

Paye, Won-Ldy, and Margaret H. Lippert
HEAD, BODY, LEGS: A STORY FROM LIBERIA
A simple, funny tale of a body that comes together piece by piece.

SHOW AND TALE

You can make a storytelling apron by using a
strong needle and sewing machine to attach
a pocket of clear, durable plastic to any ordinary
apron. Find heavy plastic (the kind that protects
tablecloths) at hardware stores. While you or
children tell a story, the book can be displayed in
the pocket. Or just "wear a book" and be a walking
advertisement. My apron has lettering over the
pocket that asks, "Have you read this?"

You can purchase a "Show-a-Tale" apron
from Book Props, www.bookprops.com, 1-800-
636-5314. It is actually a wearable storyboard,
and *any* object backed with velcro will stick to it.
Book Props also offers a vinyl pocket that functions as a display pouch and can be attached to
the apron.

I felt nervouse. I was a little bit scared. When I started my introduction I felt better. After I was done with my story I felt SPECTACULAR! When I got that certificate and rose I felt so, so happy, like a real storytelling star.

—from the journal of Jarée, fourth-grader

Pinkwater, Daniel Manus THE BIG ORANGE SPLOT
"My house is where I want to be and it looks like all my dreams," explains crazy Plumbean, who soon convinces his neighbors to decorate their homes to match their imaginations.

Polacco, Patricia THUNDERCAKE
With the help of a patient grandmother, a girl learns to be brave during a storm.

Rathmann, Peggy RUBY THE COPYCAT
Imitation is not found flattering to Ruby's classmates and teacher, so she learns to find a style all her own.

Ray, Jane THE TWELVE DANCING PRINCESSES
A dozen party girls magically outwit their father so they can go out dancing every night, but a lucky suitor finds them out.

San Souci, Robert D. THE HOBYAHS
Creepy forest-dwelling goblins plot mischief against a tiny houseful of almost helpless people.

Van Allsburg, Chris TWO BAD ANTS
High adventure found in a day in the life of two exploring insects.

Waber, Bernard IRA SLEEPS OVER
Ira is excited about his first sleep-over, but will his host understand that he just can't sleep without his bear?

Waddell, Martin FARMER DUCK
Quaaaack! Poor duck is overworked and underappreciated by his lazy boss, but not for long in this primary level Orwellian takeoff.

Wood, Audrey HECKEDY PEG
When a witch turns seven children into platters of food, their mother's only hope is to recognize them in their plate state.

Yolen, Jane THE EMPEROR AND THE KITE
A small daughter makes a big rescue when an emperor falls victim to a coup.

PART VII

Inside the Gingerbread House: Fairy Tales, Wonder Tales, and Fantasy

*W*hen they came to the second spring, sister heard how this one too spoke, "Whoever drinks me, whoever drinks me, will be a wolf, will be a wolf," and so she cried, "Dear brother, please don't drink or you will become a wolf and devour me." Brother did not drink and said, "I will wait till we come to the next spring, but then I must drink whatever you may say, I am so very, very thirsty."

—"Brother and Sister," from THE JUNIPER TREE AND OTHER TALES FROM GRIMM

And so it goes. Whoever drinks from the spring of fairy tales will become enchanted, and who knows how our children will be transformed? Will we recognize them after they imbibe of witches baked in ovens, wolves that talk a good talk then devour grandmothers whole, and needles that cause a hundred years' sleep? Politically incorrect, earthy, violent, imaginative, fairy tales can at once frighten children and speak their language.

Fairy tales (and other wonder tales such as fables) are representations of the most organic struggles we experience as humans: brain versus brawn, oldest versus youngest, temptation versus temperance, sloth versus initiative, cowardice versus bravery, jealousy versus admiration, journey versus home, capture versus rescue, loss versus rebirth, punishment versus rewards . . . all pulsating with the driving undercurrent of virtue versus evil. Such simplistic dualities are universal and accessible to children, who, being human first, experience such struggles within the context of their own young lives. Fairy tales introduce conflicts and emotions that are familiar, but disguised in symbols, characters, and plot. Fairy tales are dreams in print. Certainly, our fears are contained in them, and the territory is strange. But for all the risk, would we ever deny our children the chance to dream?

Fairy Tales

A fairy tale is really a particular type of folktale, and a particular type of fantasy, called a "wonder tale." You know you are reading a wonder tale if you notice any of the following:

Giants, ogres, dragons, trolls, and witches
Animals who talk or behave like people
Supernatural helpers, like a fairy godmother
Magic objects or magic powers, like a cloak of invisibility
Magical transformations, like from frog to prince
Sets of three, like three wishes
There is royalty at stake

Don't worry, these won't be on any test! It's simply handy to notice these motifs, because wonder tales have a very formalistic, clear-cut style, from "Once upon a time . . ." all the way to " . . . and they lived happily ever after." It makes these stories very easy to remember and retell. Additionally, children who have been taught to recognize these motifs have a strong framework for creating their own wonder tales based on their own culture and personal style. Wonder tales are great stuff for future writers.

Wonder tales that focus more on the supernatural and its role in the rise or fall of power are more typically what we think of as "fairy tales." Some wonder tales are called "nursery tales" because with simpler motifs and a lot of talking animals, they are geared toward a younger audience. Nursery tales are kind of like the "T-ball" of wonder tales; fairy tales are "coach pitch." "The Gingerbread Man," "Goldilocks and the Three Bears" and "Henny Penny"/"Chicken Little" are some examples of nursery tales that prepare children for the temperament of wonder tales to come. But really the distinctions are not so rigid, and "nursery tale" ends up being just another term for a traditional kind of folklore. As someone sharing books with children, all that's really important to know is that when you share a wonder tale, you are telling a story with a magical quality, you will likely have a child's attention, and you are joining a long tradition of both oral and written storytelling.

Before There Were Beanie Babies

Before there were Beanie Babies or baseball cards, there were people who collected stories. They were called "folklorists." (I believe it's still a job, but I'm not sure you get health benefits or a 401k.) These folklorists went around collecting stories and *they wrote them down.* This is what separated literary fairy tales (which needed authors to put the pen to paper) from the oral folktale tradition (which needed storytellers to remember and say the story out loud). Because of the work of these folklorists, we are still reading and telling the tales hundreds of years later.

Some of the most famous fairy-tale collectors were:

Joseph Jacobs (1854–1916) from Britain. He especially liked stories about lazy folks, and tales with a bit of irony. He brought us "The Three Little Pigs," "The Little Red Hen," and "Jack and the Beanstalk."

Jacob and Wilhelm Grimm (around 1785–1860) from Germany. They were brothers and did not have a very good sense of humor. Over a period of twelve years they bothered old ladies to tell them all the stories they had been passing on to grandchildren. When the brothers had enough material, they compiled it into KINDER UND HAUSMARCHEN (HOUSEHOLD STORIES), which included some of the creepiest and best known wonder tales: "Rumpelstiltskin," "Hansel and Gretel," "Snow White," "Little Red Cap," "Rapunzel," "The Frog Prince," and, I guess in a fit of cheerfulness, "The Shoemaker and the Elves." The closer you get to the Grimms' versions of these tales, the more horrible and violent the stories become, but keep in mind that the Grimms approached their work more anthropologi- 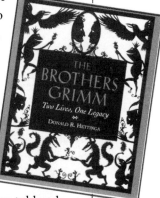 cally. They wanted to preserve the tales in the way they were told and didn't adapt them for children (like Joseph Jacobs did). So if you don't like these stories, blame your German great-great-great-great-grandmother. There's more about these brothers in the children's biography, THE BROTHERS GRIMM: TWO LIVES, ONE LEGACY by Donald R. Hettinga.

Charles Perrault (1628–1703) from France. Oh-la-la! His stories are among the most sexy and romantic, and were all the rage among the court of Louis XIV. He probably snarked them from the governess of his son, Pierre, and added his own literary flair to create "Cinderella," "Sleeping Beauty," "Puss in Boots," "The Twelve Dancing Princesses," and "Beauty and the Beast." Disney owes him big-time.

Aleksandr Afanasyev (1826–1871) from Russia. He transcribed "The Great Big Enormous Turnip," and such complicated and violent tales as "Vasilisa the Beautiful," and "The Fool of the World and the Flying Ship." He introduced the world to Baba Yaga, a colorful folkloric witch who, for my money, makes Snow White's witch look like a Girl Scout.

Peter Christien Asbjørnsen (1812–1885) from Norway. He compiled the celebrated collection EAST OF THE SUN AND WEST OF THE MOON, which includes the marvelous title story as well as the classic "The Three Billy Goats Gruff." Like the Grimm brothers, Asbjørnsen was interested in preserving the voice of the storyteller. Unlike the Grimm brothers, his storytellers were funny and fast-paced and used characters that were a little sharper on the take.

So we see, our classical canon of wonder tales comes from a European tradition and was collected mostly in the eighteenth and nineteenth centuries. The adventure, romance, and violence in the stories reflect folks trying to compensate for a lack of television. Since the wonder-tale epoch, more modern fairy tales have been written. They incorporate a more multicultural perspective and more sensitivity to children. While less sensational, these new narratives still utilize a lot of the traditional wonder-tale drama, motifs, and oral sensibilities (which is why several are mentioned in A Selection of Good Books for Storytelling, p. 244). Three Caldecott Award–winning books, for instance, are modern wonder tales. In William Steig's SYLVESTER AND THE MAGIC PEBBLE, a donkey is transformed into a boulder when he makes a thoughtless wish. In Tomie dePaola's STREGA NONA, a hardworking witch goes on vacation and returns home to find her magic pasta pot gone haywire. And in Arlene Mosel's THE FUNNY LITTLE WOMAN, a giggling granny is kidnapped by a wicked Japanese "oni," a cross between a giant and a troll, and is forced to cook rice with a magic spoon. Additionally, one of my favorite modern wonder tales is Laura Krauss Melmed's THE RAINBABIES, in which an older couple wishes for a child and is given a dozen miniature infants. The man and woman are given tasks to see if they are worthy parents, and in the end, the appearance of both royalty and a supernatural helper determine whether they will be granted their heart's desire. Surely, this story has all the markings of a classic wonder tale, with the addition of glorious full-color, double-page illustrations that simply were not possible during the time of Grimm or Perrault.

In Don and Audrey Wood's moody HECKEDY PEG, seven children, each named for a day of the week, are turned into food by a wicked witch and rescued by a resourceful mama. Another great one to look at is Trina Schart Hyman's RAPUNZEL. While holding faithfully to the Grimms' story, the motifs are enhanced by the use of light and dark in the illustrations and details in the borders framing every picture. Besides adding beauty and information, the borders make it so that the child looks into the story through the safety of a kind of "window," creating distance between the child's tender and curious spirit and the fevered distress of the story. History, art, child psychology, four-color processing—we are such lucky readers. Never before has there been a time when so many elements have joined together to make wonder tales this wonderful.

With such a wealth of diverse, gentle, and satisfying reads available, why would we still subject children to the "old school" wonder tale? Well, you don't have to, but many of us still want to. First of all, wonder-tale folklore is like mythology, in that there are many allusions to it throughout print and the culture at large. It becomes an academic assumption that children will have a familiarity with the plots and characters that comprise fairy tales, and we don't want our children to miss out on any jokes. Psychoanalysis also offers beautiful arguments in defense of fairy tales, spellbindingly articulated in **THE USES OF ENCHANTMENT** by Bruno Bettelheim. It is possible that fantasies are a kind of repressed wish-fulfillment, as Freud's theories suggest, or that the motifs of fairy tales are borne out of a universal "collective unconscious," as Jung's theories submit. But in spite of such expert rationales, a few weeks after you read Bettelheim's treatise, the same uneasiness about selling such surreal stuff as children's fare may creep back. I know it does for me. In which case, do what you should always do when sharing books for children: Trust your instincts, and stay within your comfort zone. Children can smell fear like armpit sweat, and they need the grown-up to remain a fearless protector, or the stories can just be *way* too scary.

Case in point: my mother calmly read me "Hans My Hedgehog" from the Grimms' **THE JUNIPER TREE** when I was eight. Twenty-five years later, I haven't forgotten the character Hans My Hedgehog. I tremble at the thought of Hans My Hedgehog. I am afraid of Hans My Hedgehog. I am *completely creeped out* by Hans My Hedgehog.

I love Hans My Hedgehog.

Now, I have read "Hans My Hedgehog" to over a hundred children. Yes, it is a peculiar story. I don't share it because misery loves company. I share it because company loves misery. There we are together, a family of readers. How close can I get, how long can I go without bringing up the odd old Uncle Hedgehog? We always end up talking about that which is most affecting, strange, or memorable. We are usually forgiven for it. I read "Hans My Hedgehog" to twelve-year-olds, because children younger than that invariably notice my goosebumps. So, share wonder tales with older children or wear long sleeves and read to the goggle-eyed little ones. Don't worry. We can read fairy tales and still live happily ever after.

❧ *Potato Pick:*

THE GIRL WHO SPUN GOLD
*by Virginia Hamilton,
illustrated by Leo and
Diane Dillon*

This book is gorgeous! This book is gorgeous! This book is gorgeous! Did I mention this book is gorgeous? Not only is it gorgeous, but it is an African retelling of the "Rumpelstiltskin" story. When sweet Quashiba's mother lies and tells Big King that her daughter can spin golden thread, Quashiba is first happily wed and then unhappily locked in a room until she can perform this miracle, which she does, with the help of the mysterious and sinister Lit'Mahn. The illustrations are appropriately illuminated in gold ink, and children will love the picture of Lit'Mahn exploding in anger. What I really like about this story is that even after the foe was reckoned with, Quashiba was angry with the king for three long years and would not speak to him for what he put her through. I don't blame her, do you? (7 and up)

THE GOLDEN SHELF: A FAIRY-TALE COLLECTION FOR READ-ALOUD

Doherty, Berlie	• FAIRY TALES
Lang, Andrew, ed.	• THE BLUE FAIRY BOOK
Segal, Lore, and Maurice Sendak, eds.	• THE JUNIPER TREE AND OTHER TALES FROM GRIMM
Sierra, Judy, ed.	• CAN YOU GUESS MY NAME? TRADITIONAL TALES AROUND THE WORLD
Watson, Jane Wener, ed.	• THE GOLDEN BOOKS TREASURY OF ELVES AND FAIRIES: WITH ASSORTED PIXIES, MERMAIDS, BROWNIES, WITCHES, AND LEPRECHAUNS
Wilde, Oscar	• THE HAPPY PRINCE AND OTHER STORIES
Yolen, Jane, ed.	• FAVORITE FOLKTALES FROM AROUND THE WORLD

Single-Title Fairy Tales: Some Notable Illustrators

A good wonder tale collection consists of both anthologies and single tales. In terms of picture books, I have a few favorite contemporary creators; they illustrate and retell, unless otherwise noted.

During his career, **Paul Galdone** illustrated and retold nearly every nursery tale you can imagine, and his bright, expressive, uncluttered pictures are perfect for laptime or for holding up in front of a crowd. In my early twenties I sacrificed almost an entire paycheck to own all of his titles at once, greedy thing! But not having to choose between them was worth hearing the angry complaints of my landlord. Since then, I have worn out the pages of his version of THE GINGERBREAD BOY and CAT GOES FIDDLE-I-FEE. His THREE BILLY GOATS GRUFF is unbeatable, and his PRINCESS AND THE PEA is perfection. When you are looking for a classic title for read-aloud, he is unrivaled. NURSERY CLASSICS: A GALDONE TREASURY makes a lovely gift, but it only includes four stories and I prefer a shelf-full. Also illustrated by Paul Galdone:

The Elves and the Shoemaker
Henny Penny
Three Little Kittens
The Three Little Pigs
Rumpelstiltskin
The Teeny-Tiny Woman: A Ghost Story
The Three Bears

My second favorite artist is **Jane Ray.** Her body of work is not as encompassing as some illustrators', but the work she presents embodies the elegant spirit of classic fairy tales while her contemporary touches make them more accessible to today's children. For instance, in her TWELVE DANCING PRINCESSES, the princesses appear to be from many ethnic backgrounds, and two of the princesses wear glasses. Such additions are included so naturally that they are almost taken for granted. Jane Ray has done a number of religious books, myths, and tales with an environmental undercurrent. She is an artist who is fearless in portraying love between characters. Gilding glimmers on every page, making an illuminated text or a sacred book, and adding to the feeling of found treasure within the pages. Also illustrated by Jane Ray:

> *Fairy Tales* (retold by Berlie Doherty)
> *Hansel and Gretel*
> *The Happy Prince* (by Oscar Wilde)
> *Magical Tales from Many Lands* (retold by Margaret Mayo)

One of the masters of children's-book illustration, **Trina Schart Hyman,** takes a special interest in fairy tales. Hyman uses her artwork to carry authentic tales to new emotional heights. Her paintings convey a depth of mood, beauty, and action that is truly sensory, a world unto itself. Because of their complexity in word and picture, the books have a more intimate feel to them and make for good discussions with your child. Because she holds closely to raw originals, I prefer sharing her retellings with slightly older children. When I read these books to many children at once, I make color transparencies of the illustrations and show them on an overhead projector as I read; otherwise, the details of the pictures are lost. Hyman's painting veers into the realm of fine art. Give it its propers, and children will get more out of fairy tales than you ever would believe. Illustrated by Trina Schart Hyman:

> *Bearskin*
> *Iron John*
> *King Stork*
> *Little Red Riding Hood*
> *Rapunzel*
> *Sleeping Beauty*
> *Snow White*
> *The Water of Life*

K. Y. (or Kinuko) **Craft**'s graphic designs have decorated myths such as CUPID AND PSYCHE, PEGASUS, and KING MIDAS AND THE GOLDEN TOUCH, and may be recognizable from the book jackets of award-winning fantasy novelists Ursula Le Guin, Orson Scott Card, Isaac Asimov, and Patricia A. McKillip. But her oil-over-watercolor interpretations of wonder tales are so especially wondrous that you'll think she paints with a wand instead of a brush. Flowers or foliage are abundant and always in a heady bloom, as if to suggest that while we are reading we're never far from some romantic garden or enchanted wood. Her illustrations seem to be lit by a blazing candelabra. And nobody does princesses like K. Y. Craft. Staring back from the page startled, pale, and doelike, beneath cascading mounds of perfect curls, these beauties are wrapped in billowing gowns. A certain decadence and formality marks her style, and reading her books is a breathtaking experience. Also illustrated by K. Y. Craft:

> *Baba Yaga and Vasilisa the Brave*
> *Cinderella*
> *Sleeping Beauty*
> *The Adventures of Tom Thumb*
> *The Twelve Dancing Princesses*

The Viennese illustrator **Lisbeth Zwerger** has received a great deal of international acclaim, including the Hans Christian Andersen Medal. Her watercolors are part cloud, part dream, and all beauty. Her delicate lines float in an abundance of air and space, and her palette whispers instead of shouts. If there are such things as fairies, I am sure her books are what they have on their shelves. Zwerger has illustrated some of the greatest classics of all time, such as Baum's THE WONDERFUL WIZARD OF OZ, Carroll's ALICE IN WONDERLAND, Wilde's THE CANTERVILLE GHOST, O. Henry's THE GIFT OF THE MAGI, and the King James version of STORIES FROM THE BIBLE, but besides biggies she has brought some lesser known European wonder tales to the forefront. Also illustrated by Lisbeth Zwerger:

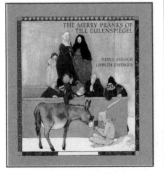

> *Andersen Fairy Tales*
> *Christian Morgenstern: Lullabies, Lyrics, and Gallows Songs*
> *Dwarf Nose*
> *Hansel and Gretel*
> *Little Hobbin*
> *Little Red Cap*

The Merry Pranks of Till Eulenspeigel
The Nightingale
The Nutcracker
The Selfish Giant
The Swineherd
Thumbeline

Unpretentious colored-pencil artwork makes **Bernadette Watts** a hit at storytime. When I am looking for a cheery classic for a primary group, or a bedtime cuddle, I can depend on her big pages, simple text, and jolly portrayals of fairy-tale favorites. Not the fanciest, but definitely the friendliest. Illustrated by Bernadette Watts:

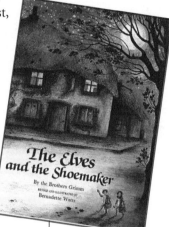

The Bremen Town Musicians
The Elves and the Shoemaker
The Fir Tree
Goldilocks and the Three Bears
The Lion and the Mouse: An Aesop Fable
Mother Holly
Rapunzel
Rumpelstiltskin
The Snow Queen
Snow White and Rose Red
The Town Mouse and the Country Mouse: An Aesop Fable
The Ugly Duckling
The Wind and the Sun: An Aesop Fable
The Wolf and the Seven Little Kids

While classic wonder tales have survived centuries, specific picture-book editions go in and out of print on a revolving-door basis, even within a couple of years. The moral is, get it while it's hot. Loveliness is not a criterion for print longevity. Even the work of legendary artists from the first golden age of children's literature such as Arthur Rackham, Errol LeCain, and Edmund Dulac, who illustrated many of the most recognizable editions from our grandparents' collections, fluctuates in availability. Publishers are constantly trying to make what's old new again. The effect is twofold: Some treasures are buried, but new talents have a chance to seek their fortunes. Take care when ordering wonder tales from bookstores to specify the illustrator you want. I have made suggestions in the next list to help you round out your fairy-tale shelf, but no doubt in the process of looking for them, you will discover other opulent offerings.

CATCH A MAGIC FISH

Catch a magic fish, just like in THE FISHERMAN AND HIS WIFE. Cut about an inch straight down (not across!) into the tip of a plastic drinking straw. You should have two slits. Slide a long piece of yarn into and across the slits, which should hold it securely. This is the fishing pole. Then, decorate a cutout construction-paper fish with glitter, googly eyes, paint, marker—the more embellishments, the merrier. Punch a hole where the mouth should be, and tie the other end of the yarn to it, and you've got a fish on a stick! For a variation, attach a magnet to the end of the yarn and decorate several fish, putting metal paper clips where their mouths would be. How many can your child catch?

BEAUTY AND THE BEAST illustrated by Mercer Mayer or Jan Brett

CINDERELLA, GOLDILOCKS AND THE THREE BEARS, RED RIDING HOOD, and THE THREE LITTLE PIGS illustrated by James Marshall

CINDERELLA illustrated by Marcia Brown

EAST OF THE SUN AND WEST OF THE MOON illustrated by Michael Hague

THE FISHERMAN AND HIS WIFE illustrated by Margot Zemach

THE FOOL OF THE WORLD AND THE FLYING SHIP illustrated by Uri Schulevitz

THE FROG PRINCE illustrated by Jan Ormerod

A HANDFUL OF BEANS illustrated by William Steig

JACK AND THE BEANSTALK by Gennady Spirin

MANY MOONS by James Thurber, illustrated by Louis Slobodkin or Marc Simont

MELISANDE by E. Nesbit, illustrated by P. J. Lynch

PRINCESS FURBALL, illustrated by Anita Lobel

PUSS IN BOOTS, illustrated by Fred Marcellino (Or try THE WHITE CAT, illustrated by Gennady Spirin.)

RAPUNZEL, HANSEL AND GRETEL, and RUMPELSTILTSKIN, each illustrated by Paul O. Zelinsky

SNOW WHITE, illustrated by Charles Santore or Angela Barrett

Popular Fairy-Tale Archetypes

These are all picture books unless otherwise indicated.

Liberated Princesses

Tired of waiting for Prince Charming? Read these books to your child when she requires a rescue from the tower of masculine power . . . or when you just want a great read-aloud. Boys and girls *both* enjoy them!

Princess Smartypants
By Babette Cole

Bateman, Teresa	• THE PRINCESSES HAVE A BALL
Cecil, Laura	• THE FROG PRINCESS
Cole, Babette	• PRINCE CINDERS
	• PRINCESS SMARTYPANTS
Defelice, Cynthia	• THE REAL, TRUE DULCIE CAMPBELL

Gray, Margaret	• THE UGLY PRINCESS AND THE WISE FOOL
Haan, Linda de, and Stern Nijland	• KING & KING (Features gay princes.)
Hoggarth, Janet	• THE PRINCESS PARTY BOOK: FAVORITE HAPPY EVER AFTER STORIES . . . AND MORE! (Includes activities.)
Kaye, M. M.	• THE ORDINARY PRINCESS (Chapter book.)
Kimmel, Eric A.	• THE FOUR GALLANT SISTERS
Levine, Gail Carson	• ELLA ENCHANTED (Chapter book.)
Mack, Todd	• PRINCESS PENELOPE
Martin, Rafe	• THE STORYTELLING PRINCESS
Morgenstern, Susie	• PRINCESSES ARE PEOPLE, TOO
Munsch, Robert	• THE PAPER BAG PRINCESS
Ordal, Stina Langlo	• PRINCESS AASTA
Phelps, Ethel Johnston	• TATTERHOOD AND OTHER TALES (Short story collection.)
Priceman, Marjorie	• PRINCESS PICKY
Scrimger, Richard	• PRINCESS BUN BUN
Shannon, Margaret	• THE RED WOLF
Tchana, Katrin	• THE SERPENT SLAYER AND OTHER STORIES OF STRONG WOMEN
Williams, Jay	• THE PRACTICAL PRINCESS
Zemach, Margot	• THE PRINCESS AND FROGGIE

Great Giants

It's true what they say: Bigger is better! Don't forget, children live in a world of real-life giants who tell them what to do, what to eat, when to go to bed, so the harder the storybook giants fall, the funnier.

Cole, Brock	• THE GIANT'S TOE
Goode, Diane	• DIANE GOODE'S BOOK OF GIANTS & LITTLE PEOPLE (Contains the screamingly funny "How Big-Mouth Wrestled the Giant.")
Grimm Brothers	• THE BRAVE LITTLE TAILOR
Nolen, Jerdine	• BIG JABE
Pomerantz, Charlotte	• MANGABOOM
Prelutsky, Jack	• AWFUL OGRE'S AWFUL DAY

DRAGONS ARE HOT STUFF!

The picture book RAISING DRAGONS by Jerdine Nolen will inspire the laying of many "dragon eggs." Simply make papier-mâché paste (see recipe in Making Puppets, p. 230). Once the paste cools, dip strips of newsprint into the mixture and lay them evenly on a nice, big, blown-up balloon until it is completely covered. Two layers of strips make for a stronger "eggshell." Let the whole thing dry; it takes about two days, depending on the humidity. Pop and remove the balloon by gently pulling it out from the paper shell; then decorate! Lots of children working together can make an amazing dragon's nest. Then continue to flame their interest with these:

Coville, Bruce	• JEREMY THATCHER, DRAGON HATCHER (Chapter book.)
Davol, Marguerite W.	• THE PAPER DRAGON
Deedy, Carmen Agra	• THE LIBRARY DRAGON
Gannett, Ruth Stiles	• MY FATHER'S DRAGON (Superior chapter-book read-aloud series.)

Seeger, Pete	• ABIYOYO • ABIYOYO RETURNS
Thurber, James	• THE GREAT QUILLOW
Walker, Paul Robert	• GIANTS! STORIES FROM AROUND THE WORLD
Wood, Audrey	• RUDE GIANTS

April Fools, Tricksters, and Simpletons

Everybody plays the fool—or the trickster—some time! That's what makes these stories so universal and so much fun to share out loud. Get ready to laugh!

FOOLISH FOOLS

Carey, Valerie Scho	• THE DEVIL AND MOTHER CRUMP
Hamilton, Virginia	• A RING OF TRICKSTERS
Hewitt, Susan	• THE THREE SILLIES
Kellogg, Steven	• THE THREE SILLIES
Ross, Tony	• THE BOY WHO CRIED WOLF
Seuss, Dr.	• THE SNEETCHES
Shulevitz, Uri	• THE GOLDEN GOOSE
Sierra, Judy	• SILLY & SILLIER

ZLATEH THE GOAT
AND OTHER STORIES
by ISAAC BASHEVIS SINGER
Pictures by MAURICE SENDAK

Gibbons, Gail	• BEHOLD . . . THE DRAGONS! (Picture book nonfiction.)
Grahame, Kenneth	• THE RELUCTANT DRAGON
Kent, Jack	• THERE'S NO SUCH THING AS A DRAGON
Pendziwol, Jean	• NO DRAGONS FOR TEA (A book about fire safety!)
Robertson, M. P.	• THE EGG
Rupp, Rebecca	• THE DRAGON OF LONELY ISLAND (Chapter book.)
Shannon, Margaret	• ELVIRA

Sis, Peter	• KOMODO!
Thayer, Jane	• THE POPCORN DRAGON
Thomas, Shelley Moore	• GOOD NIGHT, GOOD NIGHT (Short chapter book.)
Williams, Jay	• EVERYONE KNOWS WHAT A DRAGON LOOKS LIKE
Willis, Val	• THE SECRET IN THE MATCHBOX
Wilson, Gina	• IGNIS
Wrede, Patricia	• DEALING WITH DRAGONS (Another superior chapter-book read-aloud!)

Singer, Isaac Bashevis	• NAFTALI THE STORYTELLER AND HIS HORSE, SUS • WHEN SHLEMIEL WENT TO WARSAW (Short stories.) • ZLATEH THE GOAT AND OTHER STORIES
Walker, Richard	• THE BAREFOOT BOOK OF TRICKSTER TALES

GREEDY FOOLS

Demi	• THE MAGIC GOLDFISH (For a fish craft to go with this book, see Catch a Magic Fish, p. 260.)
Ginsburg, Mirra	• TWO GREEDY BEARS
Kimmel, Eric A.	• ONIONS AND GARLIC: AN OLD TALE
Zemach, Harve and Margot	• A PENNY A LOOK

OUTWITTING WITCHES

Palatini, Margie	• PIGGIE PIE!
Wood, Audrey	• HECKEDY PEG

OUTFOXING FOXES

Galdone, Paul	• WHAT'S IN FOX'S SACK?
McKissack, Patricia C.	• FLOSSIE & THE FOX
Small, Ernest	• BABA YAGA
Steig, William	• DOCTOR DE SOTO

ANANSI: MASTER TRICKSTER

Anansi is the paragon of tricksters, a folkloric spider taking both arachnid and human form as best serves his purposes. These stories have African roots and are good choices for Black History Month, but are just as wonderful for weaving a storytelling web any time of year. Children love writing their own Anansi tales.

Aardema, Verna	• ANANSI DOES THE IMPOSSIBLE! (Anansi in human form.)
	• ANANSI FINDS A FOOL (Anansi in human form.)
Arkhurst, Joyce Cooper	• THE ADVENTURES OF SPIDER: WEST AFRICAN FOLKTALES
Berry, James	• DON'T LEAVE AN ELEPHANT TO GO AND CHASE A BIRD (A kinder, gentler Anansi.)
	• FIRST PALM TREES
Cummings, Pat	• ANANSE AND THE LIZARD
Haley, Gail	• A STORY, A STORY (A classic, a classic!)
Kimmel, Eric A.	• ANANSI AND THE MOSS-COVERED ROCK
	• ANANSI AND THE TALKING MELON
	• ANANSI GOES FISHING
McDermott, Gerald	• ANANSI THE SPIDER: A TALE FROM ASHANTI
Mollel, Tololwa M.	• ANANSE'S FEAST: AN ASHANTI TALE
Temple, Frances	• TIGER SOUP: AN ANANSI STORY FROM JAMAICA

Also, if you are looking for Native American trickster tales, try the **Iktomi** series by Paul Goble. Almost every culture has a trickster. How many can your children discover?

SIMPLE MISUNDERSTANDINGS: NOODLEHEAD STORIES

Allard, Harry	• THE STUPIDS DIE
Ginsburg, Mirra	• THE CHINESE MIRROR
Parish, Peggy	• AMELIA BEDELIA
Salley, Coleen	• EPOSSUMONDAS
Spirn, Michele Sobel	• THE KNOW-NOTHINGS
Stoeke, Janet Morgan	• MINERVA LOUISE AT SCHOOL

FRIENDS TRICKING FRIENDS

Bryan, Ashley	• THE CAT'S PURR
Cronin, Doreen	• GIGGLE, GIGGLE, QUACK
Hoban, Russell	• A BARGAIN FOR FRANCES
MacDonald, Amy	• PLEASE, MALESE! A TRICKSTER TALE FROM HAITI
Marshall, James	• GEORGE AND MARTHA BACK IN TOWN (Try story number three, "The Trick"!)
McKee, David	• ELMER
Stevenson, James	• MUD FLAT APRIL FOOL

FOOLING THE LANDLORD

Cole, Joanna	• DON'T TELL THE WHOLE WORLD!
Hayes, Joe	• JUAN VERDADES: THE MAN WHO COULDN'T TELL A LIE
	• A SPOON FOR EVERY BITE
Lobel, Arnold	• MING LO MOVES A MOUNTAIN
Stadler, John	• THE CATS OF MRS. CALAMARI
Tchana, Katrin	• SENSE PASS KING: A STORY FROM CAMEROON

NOT-SO-FOOLISH FOOLS

Ransome, Arthur	• THE FOOL OF THE WORLD AND THE FLYING SHIP (Outstanding inexpensive video version available from Library Video Service, item #OK9221, call 1-800-843-3620 to order.)
Thurber, James	• MANY MOONS

SURPRISE ENDINGS—FOOLED YA!

Asch, Frank, and Vladimir Vagin	• HERE COMES THE CAT!
Meddaugh, Susan	• TREE OF BIRDS
Shannon, Margaret	• ELVIRA

GERALD MCDERMOTT IS NOBODY'S FOOL!

Make sure your child gets to know terrific trickster-tale-teller (can you say that three times fast?) Gerald McDermott, who has written and illustrated many vibrant volumes. To name a few:

COYOTE: A TRICKSTER TALE FROM THE AMERICAN SOUTHWEST

JABUTÍ THE TORTOISE: A TRICKSTER TALE FROM THE AMAZON

RAVEN: A TRICKSTER TALE FROM THE PACIFIC NORTHWEST

ZOMO THE RABBIT: A TRICKSTER TALE FROM WEST AFRICA

Fairy Tales: A World Tour

Nowadays tales can be told without the fair hair and fair skin, but with at least the same amount of flair. While the wonder tale can be craggy territory in terms of finding books in print that suit your taste, excellent multicultural variants abound giving us an opportunity to celebrate the long-awaited integration of the fairy-tale shelf. For instance, Virginia Hamilton's THE GIRL WHO SPUN GOLD (see Potato Pick, p. 256), is a 24-carat take on Rumpelstiltskin told in a lively West Indian dialect. Laurence Yep's THE DRAGON PRINCE: A CHINESE BEAUTY & THE BEAST TALE, is vibrant with illustrations by Kam Mak that flow from page to page like ribbons and silk. There is Diane Stanley's fetching Neopolitan Rapunzel PETROSINELLA; Ed Young's fearful Red Riding Hood retelling LON PO PO; and Mike Artell's chummy Cajun PETITE ROUGE; Melodye Benson Rosales's African American answer to Goldilocks, LEOLA AND THE HONEYBEARS; and the surprising North African Snow White, RIMONAH OF THE FLASHING SWORD by Eric A. Kimmel.

One princess in particular really gets around. The universally beloved Cinderella has many labels on her suitcase, and if you want to take a fairy-tale trip around the world, just follow her. Read traditional versions illustrated by Marcia Brown and K. Y. Craft, and then meet just a few of Cinderella's international cousins:

Climo, Shirley	• THE EGYPTIAN CINDERELLA • THE IRISH CINDERLAD
Coburn, Jewell Reinhart	• DOMITILA: A CINDERELLA TALE FROM THE MEXICAN TRADITION • JOUANAH: A HMONG CINDERELLA
Daly, Jude	• FAIR, BROWN, & TREMBLING: AN IRISH CINDERELLA STORY
dePaola, Tomie	• ADELITA: A MEXICAN CINDERELLA STORY
Hayes, Joe	• ESTRELLITA DE ORO/LITTLE GOLD STAR: A CINDERELLA CUENTO (Mexico.)
Hickox, Rebecca	• THE GOLDEN SANDAL: A MIDDLE EASTERN CINDERELLA STORY
Jaffe, Nina	• THE WAY MEAT LOVES SALT: A CINDERELLA TALE FROM THE JEWISH TRADITION
Louie, Ai-Ling	• YEH-SHEN: A CINDERELLA STORY FROM CHINA
Martin, Rafe	• THE ROUGH-FACED GIRL (Algonquin Indian.)
Pollock, Penny	• THE TURKEY GIRL: A ZUNI CINDERELLA (With an unhappy ending.)
San Souci, Robert D.	• CENDRILLON: A CARIBBEAN CINDERELLA
Schroeder, Alan	• SMOKY MOUNTAIN ROSE: AN APPALACHIAN CINDERELLA
Sierra, Judy	• THE GIFT OF THE CROCODILE: A CINDERELLA STORY (Indonesia.)
Steptoe, John	• MUFARO'S BEAUTIFUL DAUGHTERS: AN AFRICAN TALE
Wilson, Barbara Ker	• WISHBONES: A FOLKTALE FROM CHINA

Fairy Tales for Your Funny Bone

Parodies comprise a whole neighborhood in fairy-tale land. A parody takes recognizable motifs or points of view and twists them to tell the story in a humorous new way. Parodies are usually more hip, more liberated, funnier—one even might be tempted to read them instead of the traditional tale. That's a mistake, because the intent of a

WANT TO KNOW WHAT A REAL FAIRY CASTLE LOOKS LIKE?

WITHIN THE FAIRY CASTLE by Colleen Moore in cooperation with Chicago's Museum of Science and Industry and Terry Ann R. Neff offers a tour in print of possibly the most priceless dollhouse in the world, specially designed with fairies in mind. While not a read-aloud, it's a definite stare-at-for-hours. Then you and your child can make a dollhouse. It doesn't have to be fancy at all—even a cardboard box sectioned off can carry a child into a world of invented narrative. And don't forget, boys like dollhouses, too, evidenced in THE DOLLHOUSE CAPER by Jean S. O'Connell. Make marvelous miniatures with your kids, using the stuff-around-the-house guide, TINY TREASURES from the American Girl Library, view haute couture for fairy-sized wardrobes in FAIRIE-ALITY: THE FASHION COLLECTION FROM THE HOUSE OF ELLWAND by Eugenie Bird, and go shopping with a fairy in A FAIRY WENT A-MARKETING by Rose Fyleman.

parody is not to replace the original. The whole joke is in the way the story diverts from the traditional tale; so make sure children *know* the original, allowing them to fully appreciate the author's humor. Use parodies to talk about how an author's decisions about setting and point of view can dramatically impact the story. A good parody makes you laugh, and a great parody invents a story and characters that endure on their own.

FOR "GOLDILOCKS AND THE THREE BEARS"

- DEEP IN THE FOREST by Brinton Turkle
- DUSTY LOCKS AND THE THREE BEARS by Susan Lowell
- GOLDILOCKS RETURNS by Lisa Campbell Ernst
- GOLDILOCKS AND THE THREE BEARS: A TALE MODERNE by Steven Guarnaccia (Beatnik bears with very mod furniture!)
- GOLDILOCKS AND THE THREE HARES by Heidi Petach
- MR. WOLF AND THE THREE BEARS by Jan Fearnley
- TACKYLOCKS AND THE THREE BEARS by Helen Lester

FOR "LITTLE RED RIDING HOOD"

- RUBY by Michael Emberley
- LITTLE RED RIDING HOOD: A NEWFANGLED PRAIRIE TALE by Lisa Campbell Ernst (Granny don't take no mess in this version!)
- BRIDGET AND THE GRAY WOLVES by Pija Lindenbaum
- NO DINNER! by Jessica Souhami
- ADVENTURES OF POLLY AND THE WOLF by Catherine Storr

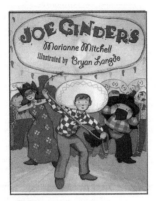

🌸 *Potato Pick:*

JOE CINDERS

By Marianne Mitchell, illustrated by Bryan Langdo

In this story, the tables are turned and it's a cowboy who dreams of two-stepping the fall fiesta at Miss Rosalinda's Rancho Milagro. The illustration of Joe swaying with a pitchfork and dreaming of the dance is one of pure romance. Thanks to a mysterious serape-wrapped señor, Joe scores some red boots and a matching pickup truck, and before long Rosalinda is asking him to marry her on bended knee. The author's surprising twist on traditional roles is believable and refreshing and compromises no one, and the expressive rounded figures make the characters all the more endearing. The sandy palette is perfection, the pictures matching the comical text that hollers to be read aloud. There are many Cinderella retellings available, but this one stands on its own as oh so *sabroso!* Both boys and girls will love it. (6 and up)

FOR "THE LITTLE RED HEN"
- COOK-A-DOODLE-DOO! by Janet Stevens and Susan Stevens Crummel (Great cookbook, too, with a recipe for strawberry shortcake.)
- MR. WOLF'S PANCAKES by Jan Fearnley
- THE LITTLE RED HEN (MAKES A PIZZA) by Philemon Sturges

FOR "CINDERELLA"
- DINORELLA: A PREHISTORIC FAIRYTALE by Pamela Duncan Edwards
- BIGFOOT CINDERRRRRELLA by Tony Johnston
- CINDERELLA'S RAT by Susan Meddaugh
- CINDERELLA PENGUIN, OR, THE LITTLE GLASS FLIPPER by Janet Perlman

FOR "SLEEPING BEAUTY"
- SLEEPING UGLY by Jane Yolen

FOR "THE LITTLE MERMAID"
- PRINCESS FISHTAIL by G. Brian Karas

FOR "THE THREE BILLY GOATS GRUFF"
- THE THREE SILLY GIRLS GRUBB by John and Ann Hassett

FOR "THE THREE LITTLE PIGS"
- WHERE'S THE BIG BAD WOLF? By Eileen Christelow
- PORKENSTEIN by Kathryn Lasky
- THE THREE LITTLE JAVELINAS by Susan Lowell
- THE TRUE STORY OF THE 3 LITTLE PIGS! by Jon Scieszka
- THE THREE LITTLE WOLVES AND THE BIG BAD PIG by Eugene Trivizas
- WAIT! NO PAINT! by Bruce Whatley

FOR "THE PRINCESS AND THE PEA"
- THE PRINCESS AND THE PIZZA by Mary Jane Auch
- THE PRINCESS AND THE PEA by Alain Vaes

FOR "THE EMPEROR'S NEW CLOTHES"
- THE PRINCIPAL'S NEW CLOTHES by Stephanie Calmenson
- THE DINOSAUR'S NEW CLOTHES by Diane Goode
- THE EMPEROR'S OLD CLOTHES by Kathryn Lasky

FOR "THE FROG PRINCE"
- THE FROG PRINCIPAL by Stephanie Calmenson
- PONDLARKER by Fred Gwynne

FOR "JACK AND THE BEANSTALK"

* LOOK OUT, JACK! THE GIANT IS BACK! by Tom Birdseye
* KATE AND THE BEANSTALK by Mary Pope Osborne

FOR "HANSEL AND GRETEL"

* HANSEL AND GRETEL by Dom DeLuise
* THE DIARY OF HANSEL AND GRETEL by Kees Moerbeek

FOR "THE BOY WHO CRIED WOLF"

* THE WOLF WHO CRIED BOY by Bob Hartman
* BETSY WHO CRIED WOLF by Gail Carson Levine

COLLECTIONS OF CHARACTERS IN ONE CRAZY BOOK

* BEWARE OF THE STORYBOOK WOLVES by Lauren Child
* MR. WOLF'S PANCAKES by Jan Fearnley
* ONCE UPON A MARIGOLD by Jean Ferris (Chapter book.)
* IF THE SHOE FITS by Alison Jackson
* ONCE UPON A TIME . . . by Nick Scharratt (Interactive book, use press-out pieces to create a new story each time.)
* THE STINKY CHEESE MAN AND OTHER FAIRLY STUPID TALES by Jon Scieszka
* LITTLE LIT: FOLKLORE & FAIRY TALE FUNNIES edited by Art Spiegelman and Françoise Mouly (Comic-book format.)

A LETTER-PERFECT PARODY

THE JOLLY POSTMAN by Janet and Allan Ahlberg is a story told through letters delivered by a fairy-tale mailman. The actual letters are tucked within the pages of the book, which double as envelopes. Children love to see what colorful treats the Jolly Postman delivers, and adults can appreciate the humor, too. Goldilocks sends a handwritten apology for her recent intrusion upon the three bears, the witch delights in her sale circular from Hobgoblin Supplies, the wolf is issued a subpoena, and Cinderella is delighted to receive the galleys of her upcoming biography. If your children enjoy this, which they surely will, another good fairy-tale book told in letters is YOURS TRULY, GOLDILOCKS by Alma Flor Ada.

ONCE UPON A TIME? YEEEEE-HAH!

If your daughter would sooner see herself sporting a ten-gallon cowboy hat than a diamond tiara, or if your son would rather ride a bucking bronco than a white stallion, stick yer spurs into these fairy tales retold with a Tex-Mex flavor. There's mor'n one way to lasso a story, ahl tell you whut!

Harris, Jim	JACK AND THE GIANT: A STORY FULL OF BEANS
Johnston, Tony	THE COWBOY AND THE BLACK-EYED PEA
Kimmel, Eric	THE RUNAWAY TORTILLA
Lowell, Susan	THE BOOTMAKER AND THE ELVES CINDY ELLEN: A WILD WESTERN CINDERELLA LITTLE RED COWBOY HAT
Mitchell, Marianne	JOE CINDERS

❧ *Potato Pick:*

HARE AND TORTOISE RACE
TO THE MOON

by Oliver J. Corwin

An Aesop's fable is blasted off
into modern times via rocket
ships as two rivals head for the
moon. This book brims with
fabulous sound effects, from
Tortoise's engine's "putt, putt,
putt" to Hare's energetic cries of
"Woo-hoo!" The stellar artwork
is full of fabulous geometric
shapes and patterns and styl-
ized line drawings set against a
black background. The best part
is that Hare and Tortoise start
out their contest as the best of
friends, and thanks to good
sportsmanship, they end that
way, too. (5 and up)

Fables and Fantasy

Aesop was an ancient Greek slave who made up wonder stories to diplomatically advise his masters. His fables, with their clear-cut "moral" or lesson at the end, have a stronghold in American culture, influencing founding fathers such as Ben Franklin and used as a staple in the *McGuffey Readers*, the texts used in pioneer schools. Even in modern times, Aesop's work inspires authors and illustrators to continue reinterpreting his timeless tales. Children respond readily to the insight and swift justice of fables and are often great at writing their own. So hurry and get some fables and their spin-offs; a rolling stone gathers no moss, after all.

Bader, Barbara	• AESOP & COMPANY: WITH SCENES FROM HIS LEGENDARY LIFE
Brown, Marcia	• ONCE A MOUSE
Corwin, Oliver J.	• HARE AND TORTOISE RACE TO THE MOON
Daugherty, James	• ANDY AND THE LION
Lobel, Arnold	• FABLES
Lynch, Tom	• FABLES OF AESOP
Orgel, Doris	• THE LION & THE MOUSE AND OTHER AESOP'S FABLES
Poole, Amy Lowry	• THE ANT AND THE GRASSHOPPER
Scieszka, Jon	• SQUIDS WILL BE SQUIDS
Steig, William	• AMOS & BORIS
Summers, Kate	• MILLY AND TILLY: THE STORY OF A TOWN MOUSE AND A COUNTRY MOUSE
Ward, Helen	• THE HARE AND THE TORTOISE
Wisdom, Jude	• WHATEVER WANDA WANTED
Zwerger, Lisbeth	• AESOP'S FABLES

Like fairy tales, availability of Aesop's fables fluctuates wildly. Look for many excellent out-of-print editions such as **ANNO'S AESOP** by Mitsumasa Anno, **THREE AESOP FOX FABLES** by Paul Galdone, **ONCE IN A WOOD: TEN TALES FROM AESOP** by Eve Rice, and various Aesop's fables illustrated by Janet Stevens at your public library or on-line.

Fantasy Favorites

Through my children's literature Web site (see Cyberspace: The Last(?) Reading Frontier, p. 445), I receive a lot of mail about books people remember from their childhood, the most popular being upper-grade fantasy. You may recognize these classics that the visitors often recommend. They share a lot of the same elements as wonder tales. Magic is memorable.

Babbitt, Natalie	• Tuck Everlasting
Banks, Lynne Reid	• The Indian in the Cupboard
Brown, Jeff	• Flat Stanley
Gannett, Ruth Stiles	• My Father's Dragon
Heide, Florence Parry	• The Shrinking of Treehorn
Jacques, Brian	• The Redwall series
Juster, Norman	• The Phantom Tollbooth
L'Engle, Madeleine	• A Wrinkle in Time
Milne, A. A.	• Winnie-the-Pooh
Norton, Mary	• The Borrowers
Pullman, Philip	• The Golden Compass
Tolkien, J. R. R.	• The Hobbit
White, E. B.	• Stuart Little

Something up Your Sleeve

Pull these picture books out of your hat to please your mini-magician!

Agee, Jon	• Milo's Hat Trick
Fox, Mem	• The Magic Hat
Grindley, Sally	• The Sorcerer's Apprentice (Though Mickey Mouse's performance in the movie *Fantasia* is hard to beat!)
Howe, James	• Rabbit-Cadabra!
Lester, Helen	• The Wizard, the Fairy, and the Magic Chicken
McCully, Emily Arnold	• The Amazing Felix
Meddaugh, Susan	• Lulu's Hat (Short chapter book.)
O'Brien, John	• Poof!
Schneider, Christine M.	• Horace P. Tuttle, Magician Extraordinaire
Seeger, Pete	• Abiyoyo

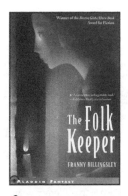

❧ *Potato Pick:*

The Folk Keeper
by Franny Billingsley

Who is Corin? Folk keeper to the mysterious and brutal cellar spirits, clumsy servant to the family at Cliffsend, or Corrina, long-haired seal-maiden with the poetic and potent power of the Last Word? Corin/Corrina has been disguised so long that s/he isn't sure who s/he is anymore, and it takes the power of magic and friendship for the secret to be revealed. Told in page-turning journal form this is fast-paced fantasy with vivid description and exciting characters. (11 and up)

To what do you attribute the success of Harry Potter, and what books are good follow-ups?

Many people believe the magic of Harry Potter lies in . . . *ahem* . . . the *magic* of Harry Potter, and follow the series with fantasy. I disagree that wizardry is where Harry's true literary power resides. What I think children really tune in to is a child hero prevailing over seemingly insurmountable odds, a theme that actually has a long tradition in children's literature (see Roald Dahl Rules!, p. 425). Added to the mix is a certain dark humor and a fast-moving plot, which make the books such entertaining reads. Search out these qualities for follow-up success. Of course, any child will tell you, a bit of magic never hurts, so if your child's just wild about Harry, try these authors: Joan Aiken, Lloyd Alexander, Philip Ardagh, John Bellairs, Eoin Colfer, Bruce Coville, Edward Eager, Debi Gliori, Eva Ibbotson, Diana Wynne Jones, Michael Molloy, Terry Pratchett, Lemony Snicket, Vivian Vandevelde, and Patricia C. Wrede. All of these authors write books that are magical, suspenseful, and oh-so-snarky!

A good title to start with is THE BAD BEGINNING: A SERIES OF UNFORTUNATE EVENTS, BOOK THE FIRST by Lemony Snicket, a book that asks: Who says every cloud has a silver lining? The linings are made of lead for the Baudelaire orphans, who first lost their parents in a fire; and then it's downhill from there. Their parent *in loco* is completely loco, trying to do away with the poor heroes to gain their vast fortune. This book is a tribute to Murphy's Law: Everything that can go wrong, does. "If you have picked up this book with the hope of finding a simple and cheery tale, I'm afraid you have picked up the wrong book altogether," warns the author. "I am bound to record these tragic events, but you are free to put this book back on the shelf and seek something lighter." This series of books has legions of fans and was in fact fervently recommended to me by a fifth-grader. An absolutely miserable story full of wit and exciting vocabulary that is actually defined for readers throughout the text, this is a great pick for preteenagers who have been desensitized by television.

These same readers can dial up a page-turner with DIAL-A-GHOST by Eva Ibbotson. Social workers Miss Pringle and Miss Mannering have taken it upon themselves to find good homes for the Wilkisons, an amiable family lost during a London air raid, as well as a home for the Shriekers, a couple as noxious as a midnight telemarketing call. When the ghosts' home assignments are mixed up, it means a change in fortune to the amiable and asthmatic young heir to Helton Hall. For some reading exorcise . . . I mean, exercise, share this one out loud. Isn't screaming fun now and then?

Selznick, Brian	• THE HOUDINI BOX (Short chapter book.)
Steig, William	• WHICH WOULD YOU RATHER BE?
Van Allsburg, Chris	• THE GARDEN OF ABDUL GASAZI

. . . And older children will enjoy the real-life biography found in **CONJURE TIMES: BLACK MAGICIANS IN AMERICA** by Jim Haskins and Kathleen Benson and **HOUDINI: MASTER OF ILLUSION** by Clinton Cox.

WISHING FOR A GOOD BOOK?

You can be a genie and comply with your child's reading commands using these fantastic books about dreamlike magic powers and wishes come true.

Billingsley, Franny	• WELL WISHED (Chapter book.)
Brittain, Bill	• THE WISH GIVER (Chapter book.)
Brock, Betty	• NO FLYING IN THE HOUSE (Chapter book.)
Clements, Andrew	• THINGS NOT SEEN (Chapter book.)
Craft, Charlotte	• KING MIDAS AND THE GOLDEN TOUCH
Demi	• THE MAGIC GOLDFISH
Eager, Edward	• HALF MAGIC (Chapter book; check out all of Eager's magical books!)
Egan, Tim	• BURNT TOAST ON DAVENPORT STREET
Godden, Rumer	• THE STORY OF HOLLY AND IVY
Heidbreder, Robert	• I WISHED FOR A UNICORN
Howe, James	• I WISH I WERE A BUTTERFLY
Hutchins, Hazel J.	• THE THREE AND MANY WISHES OF JASON REID (Chapter book.)
Jackson, Shirley	• MAGIC WISHES
Jocelyn, Marthe	• THE INVISIBLE DAY
Langton, Jane	• THE FLEDGLING
Levine, Gail Carson	• THE WISH (Chapter book.)
MacDonald, George	• THE LIGHT PRINCESS
McClintock, Barbara	• MOLLY AND THE MAGIC WISHBONE
Taylor, Theodore	• THE BOY WHO COULD FLY WITHOUT A MOTOR (Chapter book.)
Wood, Audrey	• JUBAL'S WISH

🍀 *Potato Pick:*

MOLLY AND THE MAGIC WISHBONE
by Barbara McClintock

When Mama is in bed with a bad cold, helpful Molly goes out to buy fish for the family's dinner and ends up meeting her fairy godmother, who advises her to save the bone she finds in her portion and use it for one magic wish of her choice. Her brothers and sisters have many exciting suggestions. But Molly yields not to temptation. In the days that follow, many occasions arise that warrant a good wish, but Molly prudently solves the problems in other ways. What makes Molly finally use her wish? McClintock deserves more recognition as an illustrator; her style is a cross between the mastery, imagination, and elegance of John Tenniel (**ALICE'S ADVENTURES IN WONDERLAND**) and the sweetness and strong characterization of Ernest H. Shepard (**THE WIND IN THE WILLOWS**). The story is loosely based on the Charles Dickens story "The Magic Fishbone," which is cleverly alluded to in the cover illustration depicting Dickens's fish shop. Definitely fresh! (6 and up)

Got a Light? Sharing the Spirit of Hans Christian Andersen

I once saw a man in a tree. This tree was on Michigan Avenue, Chicago's "Magnificent Mile." The famous tourist and shopping strip is home to the likes of Saks Fifth Avenue, C. D. Peacock's, and Bloomingdale's. The tree was tangled with white Christmas lights that glittered like rhinestones against the gray of the marble building and falling snow. I was working downtown at the time as a salesgirl in a bookstore where many of the customers wore huge fur coats and had sedans waiting for them at the curb. The man in the tree, though, was in tatters. He had just broken the window at Tiffany's and was holding a bracelet. A policeman waited for him patiently at the bottom of the tree. The man wanted to climb down, but he was afraid, so he stayed up there and cried. The noises he made were terrible, loud and howling and sorry. I was on my lunch break. I thought of all the times I passed the window of Tiffany's, I thought of the pretty, sparkling things there, the way they made me feel good and bad at the same time. I looked briefly at the man, his bloody cuts, and I couldn't believe he had done it. I watched him cry in the tree, while the men and women clomped past in leather boots, laden with packages and bags. Oh, just let him have the bracelet, I prayed before going back to work.

Some years later when I was working in a Chicago public-school library, I shared "The Little Match Girl" from **FAVORITE FAIRY TALES** by Hans Christian Andersen. I read aloud:

> *"Poor child," said one of the women in the small crowd that had gathered. "She must have frozen to death."*
>
> *"Yet she looks happy," whispered her friend. "She looks as if she had seen something wonderful before she died."*

I closed the book. Sixty-four eyes stared at me, unblinking. "Well?" a girl finally called out. "What happened next?" "That's it," I shrugged. "The little match girl died."

The children looked at each other, mortified. "She can't *die*," said one girl. "It's a children's book."

"Yeah! Dying's for TV!" a boy reminded us.

"Plus, it's the old days. Kids didn't die in the old days." Some kids laughed at this. "Well, not like *that*, homeless in the street. You said that story's from the 1800s. But she died like it was *now.*"

We discussed what led the match girl to freeze in the streets. The boy who stole her shoes. The father who beat her and made her afraid to go home. The people on the street who passed her, like she was invisible. It wasn't just the cold outside that killed the match girl. It was the cold inside.

I asked the children if the boy or the father or the people on the street knew how they contributed to her fate. Probably not, they agreed. Then I asked the question I always ask, the question the children had come to anticipate from me, my favorite question: Why do you think the author wrote this story?

"To make us sad," one girl pouted.

"He was very cruel, then," I said, "if that's all he wanted to do. Do you think the author was cruel?"

"No, he wanted us to talk about kindness," another girl volunteered.

"Doing nothing is the same as doing something wrong," another child added.

"Don't pass people by."

"People need each other."

"I still say the story is too sad," the pouting girl complained. "Children shouldn't die."

"Would you like her to live again?" I asked. She nodded, all the children nodded. "You're in luck. When the person you care about is a character in a book, that's an easy trick." I turned back to the first page and began reading the story again. "How cold it was! It had been snowing all day—and was still snowing as a little girl made her way along the dark narrow street . . ."

"The Little Match Girl" is perhaps my favorite of all children's stories, because it lights a flame in those who read (or listen to) it. For many visits to the library that followed, the children danced the story; we made a ballet. Some children were wind, some children were food, some children were fire, some children were angels. The match girl dies gracefully, then rises up when the cassette player stops. In that old classroom with radiators clanging and Christmas lights hung, it was a beautiful game, played over and over again. Outside our windows fanned with frost, outside in the real world, the game also played over and over again, with real wind and fire and food and maybe even angels, but less beauty, I think, more pain.

If I were ever rich, I would have a statue built. It would be of a girl, frozen in bronze, holding out a box of matches, all that Andersen wanted us to have by writing that story, all that Andersen wanted us to give. She would be in front of Tiffany's, on Michigan Avenue in Chicago, begging for us to remember that we are our brother's keeper.

Drunk on Hans Christian Andersen Collections

> *He belongs not only to the children, but to all of us; not only to Denmark, but to the world.*
>
> —Eva Le Gallienne, on Hans Christian Andersen in her 1958 Foreword to SEVEN TALES

When I want to share Hans Christian Andersen stories, I find the collections generally superior to the single titles (of course, there are exceptions, Fred Marcellino's heartbreaking rendering of THE STEADFAST TIN SOLDIER and Nadine Westcott's laugh-out-loud EMPEROR'S NEW CLOTHES among them). The translations vary. Some stay with Andersen's occasional religious tone, others are more secular. Some translations are rich and sticky, some are blithe and conversational. The differences are subtle, but be fussy, fussy, fussy. Take for instance, the difference between:

> *Once upon a time there were twenty-five tin soldiers. They were all brothers, for they had all been made of the same old tin spoon. The very first thing they ever heard was "Tin soldiers!" So cried the little boy who opened the box they came in. He clapped for joy and immediately started setting them up on the table.*
>
> —as retold by Tor Seidler

and

> *There were once twenty-five tin soldiers. They were all brothers because they were made from an old tin spoon. They shouldered arms and faced straight ahead, red and blue in their splendid uniforms. The first sound they ever heard in this world, as the lid of their box was removed, was "Tin soldiers!" shouted by a little boy clapping his hands. He had been given them for his birthday and was now arranging them on the table.*
>
> —as retold by Erik Blegvad

Well? Which translation of "The Steadfast Tin Soldier" is better? I cannot say for you. You have to try it on your tongue for size. When you look at them, they are similar, but when you say them, one may leap and one may trip. Which would you rather tell? It's subjective. This is why it is handy to have a few collections, because some are useful for one story and some are right for another. Some retellings benefit from pictures, and some translations are so steady and powerful that the words alone draw forth the images. There's no law that says you can't switch books when you switch stories. Is this a pain? No, it's fun! Just pretend each story in each book is a bottle of fine wine, vintage Andersen, labeled and aged in a particular way. Of course, if you are teaching children about the wine of children's literature you wouldn't stand in front of them and spill it, and heavens, you wouldn't swill it. You would show them how to savor it, take your time and try to notice its Complexity, its Robust Effervescence or it's Dark Woody Flavor, and you would try to detect bitter hints of fermentation. The big difference between wine and Andersen's stories is: One tastes better after you've turned twenty-one, and one tastes better before. Both go well with fish.

Collections

Andersen Fairy Tales illustrated by Arthur Szyk or Lisbeth Zwerger

Elf Hill: Tales from Hans Christian Andersen by Naomi Lewis, illustrated by Emma Chichester Clark (These are cheerful illustrations, very nice for younger children. I have never regretted buying anything illustrated by Clark; every one of her books contains stories with great read-aloud qualities.)

Fairy Tales from Hans Christian Andersen compiled by Russell Ash and Bernard Higton

Little Mermaids and Ugly Ducklings illustrated by Gennady Spirin

Michael Hague's Favourite Hans Christian Andersen Fairy Tales

Seven Tales by H. C. Andersen translated by Eva Le Gallienne, illustrated by Maurice Sendak (Out of print but worth the hunt.)

Twelve Tales by H. C. Andersen, selected, translated, and illustrated by Erik Blegvad (A real Danish person!)

Single Tales

The Emperor's New Clothes illustrated by Nadine Westcott

The Little Mermaid illustrated by Charles Santore

The Nightingale illustrated by Bagram Ibatoulline
(Or try The Emperor and the Nightingale illustrated by Meilo So for a quirky version.)

THE PRINCESS AND THE PEA illustrated by Paul Galdone, Janet Stevens, or Emily Bolam

THE SNOW QUEEN illustrated by Mary Engelbreit

THE STEADFAST TIN SOLDIER illustrated by Fred Marcellino

THUMBELINA illustrated by Susan Jeffers

THE UGLY DUCKLING illustrated by Meilo So, Lorinda Bryan Canley, Jerry Pinkney, or Jonathan Heale (I still like the song sung by Danny Kaye in the MGM movie *Hans Christian Andersen* better than any of the print versions. Frank Loesser, you're my favorite translator!)

Andersen wasn't only gifted at putting pen to paper . . . wait until you see what he could do with a *scissors* and paper! Children can read about the Great Dane's hobby in **THE AMAZING PAPER CUTTINGS OF HANS CHRISTIAN ANDERSEN** by Beth Wagner Brust.

Toys and Games à la Andersen

Celebrate the playfulness of Andersen's stories with these entertainments.

THUMBELINA SCAVENGER HUNT

Who can find ten different things that are smaller than your thumb?

LITTLE MERMAID UNDERWATER SQUISH TOY

Using permanent marker, draw a maze course on the outside of a gallon zip-lock bag. Fill near to full (but not bursting) with blue or green hair gel (Dippity-Do works well), glitter, and one small plastic toy fish. Seal, and tape down with heavy-duty packing tape. Children squish the bag to try to push the fish through the maze.

TIN SOLDIER BOWLING GAME

Using small, empty containers (dishwashing liquid detergent bottles and/or plastic soda bottles work well), draw a soldier and make copies for as many containers as you have. You may want to add a ballerina for the soldiers to have a crush on as well. Color and attach to the containers with glue or tape, and arrange them like bowling pins. Then take a small ball and let the good times roll! A variation is to toss a small hoop and see if it lands around the neck of any of the containers. Ballerina is bonus points.

The Ugly Duckling

From the Samuel Goldwyn Production "Hans Christian Andersen"

By FRANK LOESSER

Lightly with a Waddle

Piano

mp

Voice

G♯dim Am D7-5 G G♯dim Am D7-5 G G♯dim

There once was an ug - ly duck-ling with feath-ers all stub-by and brown   and the

mp

Am D7-5 G F♯7 F♮dim C B7 Em G7

oth - er birds, in so man-y words, said   Get out of town
(Quack like an angry Duck)

C Cm G Em Am D7sus4 D7 G

get out,   get out   get out of town.   And he

went with a quack and a wad-dle and a quack in a flur-ry of Ei-der-down.

That poor lit-tle ug-ly

duck-ling went wan-der-ing far and near but at ev-'ry place they

said to his face now ⊙✗!/ get out of here ⊙✗!/ get out, ⊙✗!/

get out get out of here. And he went with a quack and a

wad-dle and a quack and a ver-y un-hap-py tear.

All thru the win-ter-time he hid him-self a-

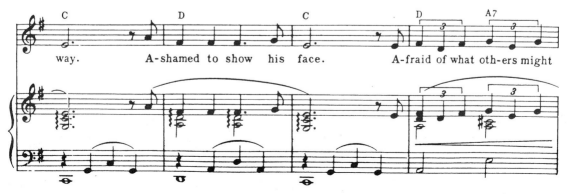

way. A-shamed to show his face. A-fraid of what oth-ers might

say.   All thru the win-ter in his lone-ly clump of

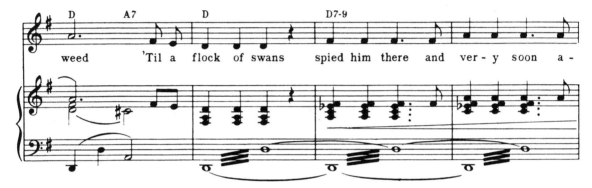

weed   'Til a flock of swans spied him there and ver-y soon a-

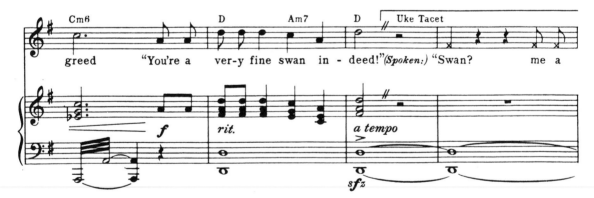

greed   "You're a ver-y fine swan in-deed!" *(Spoken:)* "Swan?   me a

swan?   Aw go on!"   "You're a swan!   Take a look at your-self in the

lake and you'll see!" And he looked and he saw, and he said: "Why it's Me! I *AM* a swan!

Whee! *(Sung:)* I'm not such an ug-ly duck-ling, No feath-ers all stub-by and

brown. For in fact these birds in so man-y words, said Tsk! The best in
(or whistle admiringly)

town Tsk! The best Tsk, Tsk, The best Tsk, Tsk, The best in

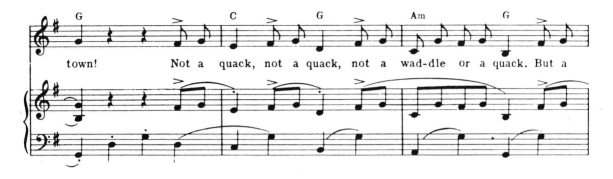

town! Not a quack, not a quack, not a wad-dle or a quack. But a

glide and a whis-tle and a snow-y white back and a head so no-ble and

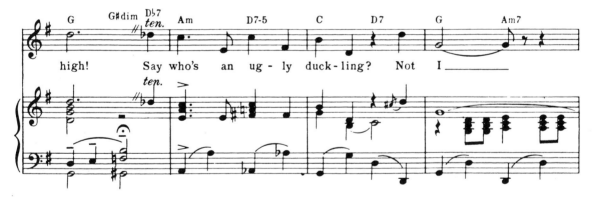

high! Say who's an ug-ly duck-ling? Not I_____

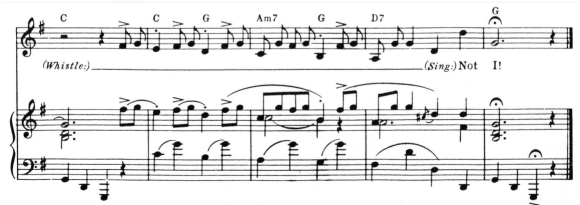

(Whistle:)_____ (Sing:) Not I!

Add Wonder Where You Read: Enchanting Housewares You Can Make

When I worked at the school library, every time the children came through the door I wanted them to remember that reading was sweet. So I redesigned the threshold to bring to mind one of the most enticing places in children's literature: the witch's gingerbread house from the Grimms' "Hansel and Gretel."

We measured the threshold ("we" meaning my husband, because I never measure anything) and then "we" cut a triangle shape out of wood (to resemble a pitched roof). "We" nailed wood to make a tight frame around the triangle, about an inch in depth, so that in the end it resembled a shallow, open-faced, triangular box. "We" attached heavy-duty hooks on the back, so it could eventually be hung. I painted the front of the box and the moldings of the doorway to match the box. Then, I went to the supermarket and collected as many goodies as I could: gumdrops, gumballs, jellies, big swirling lollies, sprinkle-covered cookies, ropes of red licorice, peppermint sticks, and brightly colored hard candies. Don't use anything with chocolate or taffy, because it will melt when summer comes. I laid out the sweets in a pattern on the frame, got out my trusty hot glue-gun, attached all of the sweets in place, and then poured the clearest varnish I could find into the frame, as if I were filling a cake pan with batter. I am telling you I did this because it was the wrong thing to do. The varnish was so thick that it took four months to dry, and got a bit cloudy in places—though it still looked sensational. You, however, will achieve *perfection* if you take the clearest varnish you can find (like Envirotex Lite Pour-On High Gloss Finish) and don't pour, just generously paint all over all the junk you have glued down. This creates a thick veneer that will make it last and, equally important, will coat it so that children and cockroaches can't actually get to it. Make sure you cover every nook and cranny. Do not

AFTER "THEY LIVED HAPPILY EVER AFTER"

*O*nce there was, and once there wasn't . . . So begins an Armenian folktale, a fresh twist on "once upon a time." Over the years, I have collected alternatives to "And they lived happily ever after." How many alternative endings can you and your children find . . . or make up, I wonder.

There's my story. It isn't very long.
If it isn't worth a penny, it's maybe
worth a song.

Thus the story ran.
Tell me a better one if you can.

If they didn't live happily ever after,
That's nothing to do with you or me.

And the lips are still warm on the last person
who told this tale.

Snip, snap, snout. This tale's told out.

If they have not left off their merrymaking
they must be at it still.

involve children in the varnishing. The fumes are too strong and the chemicals can be toxic. It may still take several days to dry, so make sure you have a well-ventilated place to store it away from children. You may want to cover it with a tent of foil as it dries, to keep out dust and unfortunate insects and to resist the temptation to poke it. When it's dry, you will have a masterpiece that will have children wide-eyed and salivating. Hang it wherever you want a magical entrance.

Another item that will add to an enchanted ambience is the "lollipop tree" my mother liked to make when I was a little girl. She would attach lollipops all over a ficus tree, using the little twist ties that you can find at produce departments or in boxes of garbage bags. No matter how many my friends and I would harvest, more lollipops would grow back. If you want to spare a live tree the suffering of being pulled at by children, use a fake ficus and spray the leaves with glitter for added magical effect. Or, you can use fake Christmas trees. The silver, gold or white ones are fun; get them on sale in January. Put a couple of magic lollipop trees in front of your threshold for an entryway fit for a fairy tale.

And finally, no fairy-tale home would be complete without a magic mirror. I took a piece of poster board the size of the mirror hanging in the library and cut out the middle so I had a paper frame. I decorated the frame with colorful drawings of stars and hearts and all variety of romantic sparkly things; at the top, I adorned it with an illustration of an open book and the words, "Mirror, mirror, on the wall . . . who's the best reader of them all?" I covered the frame with clear contact paper to make it last, and attached it to the mirror. If you are a more intrepid artist than I, you can paint directly on the glass. Every time a child looked in that mirror, they could find the magic of reading confidence!

PART VIII

Very, Very Literary: Nurturing Book Lovers and Book Creators

A re bibliophiles made, or born? This section leans toward nurture, with activities and books that will enhance your child's love of language and story and knowledge of the people who make a living using them. Who knows, you may have the next Caldecott or Newbery contender under your roof, or the next Barnes and/or Noble!

Many delightful school enrichment activities can be easily adapted for home schools and unschools, libraries and community centers, and *anywhere* groups of children meet, including your front stoop. Why should schools have all the fun?

And if you know of a school that is not having its fair share of fun, all the more reason to come in wielding these recipes for "potato pedagogy," or working with what you have wherever you have it. The word "enrichment" in schools generally means something extra, activities that require lots of invention and motivation (see The Three *I*s, p. 13). Children who are not labeled as particularly bright do not typically get a lot of "enrichment" at school. Instead, they get "remediation," which is "going over the basics." Yet sometimes the quirkiness of enrichment is just what children need to springboard them over the remediation hump. I have worked with lots of children, and I'll tell you something for free: Enrichment or remediation *alone* never cuts it, but the expectation of participation, creativity, and best efforts from children always makes a difference. Whatever label your child wears at school, you can expect great things from these experiences.

Poetry Readings

A ny one stone on the beach took about a million years to get there. Stones don't have legs and feet, after all. A rock depends on all the forces of the universe to make it what it is and take it where it needs to go. It's the same with a poem. I open a book, and there is a poem, a poem in a book of a hundred poems, a book on a shelf of

"I'M NO ANIMAL"
BY CARLTON MINOR

What's this that came
through the
mail?
A Letter!!! Yes!!! A letter
the school sends
note to my
house like
crazy
They send notes to
my mother
like tickets
to a animal
show
Just because I act up
a bit that not
a ticket to my
performance
I'M NO ANIMAL
I'M NO ANIMAL
I'M NO ANIMAL

"MOTHER'S NERVES"
BY X. J. KENNEDY

*My mother said, "If just
    once more
I hear you slam that old
    screen door,
I'll tear out my hair! I'll
    dive in the stove!"
I gave it a bang and in she
    dove.*

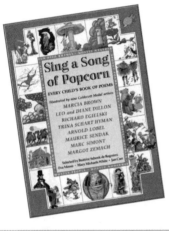

a hundred books, a shelf in a library of a thousand shelves. A poem, like a stone on a shore, is amazing in that it made it there, landed where I, the reader, would pick it up. A poem does not exist to be recognized; it exists because it *must* exist; but from a reader comes the act of examining the poem, admiring the poem, or discarding the poem. When I read a poem, will I carry it with me, will I share it, or will I close the book; and will the poem then drift in on the tides of time into the hands of another reader? A good poem, like a good rock, is a diamond and a miracle in both its creation and its location. I never understand people who say they hate poetry and then turn around and say they love God in any form. It's easy to believe in something big, but when you can believe in something small, that's pretty divine.

Poetry is especially suited to children. Poems are the cousins of songs and are as necessary in the family of joy. Celebrate poetry in daily life by getting to know great poets, anthologists, and their work.

Anthologies

My most dog-eared anthologies (or collections of poems by all different authors) are TALKING TO THE SUN compiled by Kenneth Koch and Kate Farrell, WIDER THAN THE SKY: POEMS TO GROW UP WITH compiled by Scott Elledge, and SING A SONG OF POPCORN: EVERY CHILD'S BOOK OF POEMS selected by Beatrice Schenk

NEED TO START FROM SQUARE ONE?

It's hard to teach children to appreciate poetry or to write their own if you are a little rusty on your rhyme schemes or if you can't tell a sonnet from a limerick. The most valuable titles in this arena are both by Kenneth Koch: ROSE, WHERE DID YOU GET THAT RED: TEACHING GREAT POETRY TO CHILDREN and WISHES, LIES, AND DREAMS: TEACHING CHILDREN TO WRITE POETRY. These outstanding guides will foster a love of the lyrical in both you and your child, no prerequisite knowledge necessary. The following books will also be of interest. Don't be put off by their marketing slants; these are informative and accessible to anyone learning about poetry.

Flynn, Nick	• A NOTE SLIPPED UNDER THE DOOR: TEACHING FROM POEMS WE LOVE
Hirsch, Robin	• FEG: RIDICULOUS POEMS FOR INTELLIGENT CHILDREN
Janeczko, Paul B.	• SEEING THE BLUE BETWEEN: ADVICE AND INSPIRATION FOR YOUNG POETS (Author of several fine poetry guides.)
Kennedy, X. J.	• KNOCK AT A STAR: A CHILD'S INTRODUCTION TO POETRY

de Regniers. Other widely embraced collections are REFLECTIONS ON A GIFT OF WATERMELON PICKLE . . . AND OTHER MODERN VERSE edited by Stephen Dunning, and PIPING DOWN THE VALLEYS WILD: POETRY FOR THE YOUNG OF ALL AGES edited by Nancy Larrick. These books offer general samplings and classic fare, but there are also smorgasbords suited to very specific tastes. Dinosaurs? Sports? Pets? Travel? Loss? There's an anthology, and a poem, for every person, place, and thing; all the themes that exist within children's fiction and nonfiction exist within poetry, as do all the opportunities for interest and integration. I would go so far as to say that if you have only one shelf of children's books in your home, let it be poetry. It is the most versatile of all the genres. Say, for instance, you're going to a dude ranch. Read your child HOME ON THE RANGE: COWBOY POETRY selected by Paul B. Janeczko. (If you live on a ranch, read the poems to the horses.) Or say you're too tired to cook, and you order Chinese food. While awaiting delivery, share a few from MAPLES IN THE MIST: CHILDREN'S POEMS FROM THE TANG DYNASTY collected by Minfong Ho, or CHINESE MOTHER GOOSE RHYMES selected by Robert Wyndham. Here are some more:

SEASONAL POETRY ANTHOLOGIES

GHOSTS AND GOOSE BUMPS . . . POEMS TO CHILL YOUR BONES selected by Bobbi Katz

PIECES: A YEAR IN POEMS & QUILTS by Anna Grossnickle Hines

WINTER POEMS selected by Barbara Rogasky

CULTURAL POEM ANTHOLOGIES

CRICKET NEVER DOES: A COLLECTION OF HAIKU AND TANKA collected by Myra Cohn Livingston

PASS IT ON: AFRICAN-AMERICAN POETRY FOR CHILDREN selected by Wade Hudson

THE SPACE BETWEEN OUR FOOTSTEPS: POEMS AND PAINTINGS FROM THE MIDDLE EAST and THE TREE IS OLDER THAN YOU ARE: BILINGUAL GATHERING OF POEMS & STORIES FROM MEXICO, both edited by Naomi Shihab Nye

WORDS WITH WINGS: A TREASURY OF AFRICAN-AMERICAN POETRY AND ART selected by Belinda Rochelle

ANTHOLOGIES ABOUT THE ENVIRONMENT

THE EARTH IS PAINTED GREEN: A GARDEN OF POEMS ABOUT OUR PLANET selected by Barbara Brenner

EARTHWAYS, EARTHWISE: POEMS ON CONSERVATION selected by Judith Nicholls

"COCOON"
BY DAVID MCCORD

The little caterpillar creeps
Awhile before in silk it
*   sleeps.*
It sleeps awhile before it
*   flies,*
And flies awhile before it
*   dies,*
And that's the end of three
*   good tries.*

ANTHOLOGIES ABOUT FRIENDS

I LIKE YOU, IF YOU LIKE ME: POEMS OF FRIENDSHIP collected by Myra
    Cohn Livingston
VERY BEST (ALMOST) FRIENDS collected by Paul B. Janeczko
YOU AND ME: POEMS OF FRIENDSHIP selected by Salley Mavor

ANTHOLOGIES ABOUT FEELING BETTER

THIS PLACE I KNOW: POEMS OF COMFORT compiled by Georgia Heard
WHAT HAVE YOU LOST? compiled by Naomi Shihab Nye

ANTHOLOGIES JUST FOR BEING A KID

POETRY BY HEART: A CHILD'S BOOK OF POEMS TO REMEMBER compiled by
    Liz Attenborough
TEN-SECOND RAINSHOWERS: POEMS BY YOUNG PEOPLE compiled by
    Sandford Lyne

A Few Great Poetry Anthologists for Children

LEE BENNETT HOPKINS

MARVELOUS MATH: A BOOK OF POEMS; EXTRA INNINGS: BASEBALL POEMS;
DINOSAURS; BLAST-OFF! POEMS ABOUT SPACE; SCHOOL SUPPLIES: A BOOK
OF POEMS; MY AMERICA: A POETRY ATLAS OF THE UNITED STATES . . . With
over seventy anthologies, mostly thematic, it's no wonder this premier

COLLECTING POETRY

Children love to collect trading cards, stuffed toys, key chains, rocks, autographs, chewed bubble-gum specimens . . . So why not poems? Once children have been exposed to both general and thematic anthologies and collections by individual authors, they can simply decorate a box, a large jar, a photo album, or a notebook to keep their favorite findings. Or, they can compile and illustrate their own anthology, creating a volume that reflects their own tastes and that they will want to return to again and again. Explore illustration with your aspiring anthologist by asking questions: Should pictures be colorful, take up a whole page; do such illustrations detract from the poems; are simple line illustrations more complementary? Are photos more suitable; can I take them myself or cut them out of magazines? Explore choice and order: Do I want to alternate long and short poems; what sort of mood do I want to evoke with the first poem, or with the last? There are no right answers, only judgment calls. Children will soon discover that besides the skill needed for writing or reading poetry, there is a certain talent to anthologizing poems.

writer and collector of poetry is a pet among teachers. It is somewhat ironic, though, since as a child Hopkins didn't like school. Perhaps this contributed to his unique flair for finding poetry that speaks to the reluctant reader; in particular, he has the poetry key to little boys' hearts. His collection I share the most is **THROUGH OUR EYES: POEMS AND PICTURES ABOUT GROWING UP.** It contains only sixteen poems, but is a great example of the art of the anthologist, choosing just the right poems that work individually yet create a new whole.

X. J. KENNEDY

Move over, Edward Lear! Kennedy's "X" must stand for eXtra funny. Kennedy's own poetry from **BRATS, FRESH BRATS,** and **DRAT THESE BRATS** is widely anthologized and his recent collection **EXPLODING GRAVY** is no exception to his excellence. He and his wife, Dorothy, demonstrate their own anthology aplomb with their collections **TALKING LIKE THE RAIN: A READ TO ME BOOK OF POEMS** and **KNOCK AT A STAR: A CHILD'S INTRODUCTION TO POETRY.**

BRUCE LANSKY

If you're not sure what poems your child will like, call on Lansky's collections. He works with hundreds of children to rate thousands of poems and compiles the ones that children specifically ask be read over and over again. You'll find these treasures in troves titled **KIDS PICK THE FUNNIEST POEMS; A BAD CASE OF THE GIGGLES; MILES OF SMILES; POETRY PARTY;** and **NO MORE HOMEWORK! NO MORE TESTS! KIDS' FAVORITE FUNNY SCHOOL POEMS.** Even the surliest sixth-graders bare their braces in a smile when presented with Lansky's poetry prescriptions.

IONA AND PETER OPIE

The Opies are renowned folklorists and smarty-pantses who compiled **THE OXFORD DICTIONARY OF NURSERY RHYMES** and a number of scholarly works, but children not yet attending the Ivy Leagues will thank them for collecting the school-yard rhymes found in **I SAW ESAU.** Since Peter's death in 1982, Iona has gathered Mother Goose's finest feathers and nested them in the two-volume set, **MY MOTHER GOOSE LIBRARY.** While there are many lovely editions of Mother Goose available, this is the collection I depend on. And if you need a perfect baby-shower gift, this set is my recommendation (see What's Good for the Goose, p. 44).

"CHOCOLATE MILK"
BY RON PADGETT

Oh God! It's great!
to have someone fix you
chocolate milk
and to appreciate their
*   doing it!*
Even as they stir it
in the kitchen
your mouth is going crazy
for the chocolate milk!
The wonderful chocolate
*   milk!*

RAINDROPS ON ROSES: SHARING YOUR FAVORITE THINGS

Poetry is for those little moments of anticipation and vastness that can overwhelm a child's spirit. If we believe reading is a gift that will help a child to never be lonely, we must give children poems to tuck away and take out as needed: for warmth on a long walk to school across the snow, or for counting the minutes until you return home from work, or for waiting on the stairs in secret for a postman to deliver a package. Poems given as presents, rolled and tied with pretty ribbon, are easy to slip into children's coat pockets and lunch bags. Haiku fit very nicely into fortune cookies (see recipe on p. 300). As a teacher, I also hung a "poem of the week" poster with an attached file filled with copies of that week's poem. This is something a parent can make and can take on as a volunteer task in a classroom. Some children came to look forward to the "poem of the week."

Here are a few famous and favorite ones. You may notice that some were written for children and some were written for adults, but in the end, poems are written for people young and old who are willing to sit still and use their senses, for people willing to imagine, to feel, and to remember. Remember that children can listen at much higher levels than they

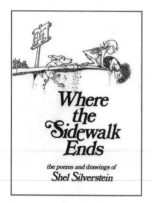

A Few Great Poets for Children

SHEL SILVERSTEIN: THE GRANDADDY OF THEM ALL

All right, perhaps Edward Lear and Ogden Nash may compete for title of Grandaddy, but Silverstein at least wins for Old Offensive Uncle. The author of some of the most popular children's poetry ever written, Silverstein's classic collections are WHERE THE SIDEWALK ENDS, A LIGHT IN THE ATTIC, and, his final book, FALLING UP. Baby boomers may recognize his name from the best-selling parable THE GIVING TREE. With his shrewd and irreverent rhymes that speak to the subversive and silly sides of children and his groundbreaking format of simple line drawings throughout, he set a new standard for children's poetry books. His influence lay the groundwork for bards that followed, such as:

JACK PRELUTSKY

Prelutsky has provided a new generation with fresh collections of verse. Following in Silverstein's footsteps, THE NEW KID ON THE BLOCK, SOMETHING BIG HAS BEEN HERE, and A PIZZA THE SIZE OF THE SUN are generous volumes, sparsely illustrated in pen-and-ink by the gifted cartoonist James Stevenson. Prelutsky, however, is lighter in tone and more prolific than Silverstein. His thematic tomes include NIGHTMARES:

can usually read by themselves. So if a poem is evocative to you, don't hesitate to share it out loud.

"17 Kings and 42 Elephants" by Margaret Mahy

"Bats" by Randall Jarrell

"The Cockroach Who Had Been to Hell" by Don Marquis

"Cynthia in the Snow" by Gwendolyn Brooks

"The 1st" by Lucille Clifton

"From a Childhood" by Rainer Maria Rilke

"Hiawatha's Childhood" by Henry Wadsworth Longfellow

"Homework! Oh, Homework!" by Jack Prelutsky

"I Am Cherry Alive, the Little Girl Sang" by Delmore Schwartz

"If" by Rudyard Kipling

"Incident" by Countee Cullen

"Juke Box Love Song" and "Harlem" by Langston Hughes

"My Heart Leaps Up" by William Wordsworth

"My Papa's Waltz" by Theodore Roethke

"The Night Will Never Stay" by Eleanor Farjeon

"Obedience" by A. A. Milne

"O Captain! My Captain!" by Walt Whitman

"Some Things Don't Make Any Sense at All" by Judith Viorst

"This Is Just to Say" by William Carlos Williams

"Too Many Daves" by Dr. Seuss

"The Tyger" by William Blake

POEMS TO TROUBLE YOUR SLEEP, THE DRAGONS ARE SINGING TONIGHT, THE FROGS WORE RED SUSPENDERS (loosely based on geography), SCRANIMALS, and various holiday collections. His meter is impeccable, if at times repetitive and predictable. His kid-appeal is off the charts. Prelutsky's great and under-recognized strength, though, is as an anthologist. Take, for instance, his collections of anonymous poetry in POEMS OF A. NONNY MOUSE and A. NONNY MOUSE WRITES AGAIN; the lively collection of poems "to tickle your funnybone" FOR LAUGHING OUT LOUD; or the tribute to the animal kingdom, THE BEAUTY OF THE BEAST.

JEFF MOSS, DOUGLAS FLORIAN, AND JAMES PROIMOS

As the lyricist behind *Sesame Street*'s hit song "Rubber Duckie," Jeff Moss was a famous unknown poet before publishing his first best-selling book THE BUTTERFLY JAR. Douglas Florian exploded onto the children's poetry scene with his cymbal-crash-of-a-collection, BING BANG BOING, and then with slimmer self-illustrated animal-themed collections such as BEAST FEAST; MAMMALABILIA; INSECT-LOPEDIA; IN THE SWIM; LIZARDS, FROGS, AND POLLIWOGS; and BOW WOW MEOW MEOW: IT'S RHYMING CATS AND DOGS. Florian's word play and wit are truly original and make for

a nice bridge for children who never tire of "punch-line" poetry yet are ready for a more literary flavor. (I said literary. Not stuffy. Visit his **LAUGH-ETERIA** to see what I mean.) James Proimos has also used the simple art/silly poem formula for his debut, **IF I WERE IN CHARGE THE RULES WOULD BE DIFFERENT!** We are clued in to the sincerity of this statement by the backwards and upside-down writing on the cover.

PAUL FLEISCHMAN

Of course, poets don't necessarily need to follow Silverstein's format to succeed. The world of poetry needs many diverse voices, as Fleischman proves in the winningest way. Fleischman, who began his career as a historical novelist, turned to natural history to earn the coveted 1989 Newbery award for his inventive **JOYFUL NOISE: POEMS FOR TWO VOICES,** a collection of verse from a bugs'-eye view. The poems are carefully scripted so two readers can share them aloud at once, indeed, making a joyful noise. More poems for two voices (bird voices, this time) are found in Fleischman's **I AM PHOENIX,** and a small symphony for four (human) preteens is composed in **BIG TALK.**

MARY ANN HOBERMAN

I was first awed by Hoberman's book-length poem **A HOUSE IS A HOUSE FOR ME** because of the unrelenting brainstorming that occurred within the poem. No, not brainstorm. Brain squall. Brain *typhoon.* The kind of creative thinking that I have really only seen in children and geniuses. Hoberman's poems are each small testaments to the sensory and imaginative life of children, and a hundred of them are collected in **THE LLAMA WHO HAD NO PAJAMA.** Her collection of family poems, **FATHERS, MOTHERS, SISTERS, BROTHERS,** elicits as much spirited recognition and discussion from grade-schoolers as well-written fiction. Some of her single poems comprise the entire text of picture-books, such as in **AND TO THINK THAT WE THOUGHT THAT WE'D NEVER BE FRIENDS, ONE OF EACH,** and **THE SEVEN SILLY EATERS.**

DENNIS LEE

Grab your jump rope! Lee captures all the rhythms of school-yard chants and ties them up in poems. Among his many collections, **ALLIGATOR PIE,** written in 1974, won the Canadian Library Association's Book of the Year and a Hans Christian Andersen honor, and almost thirty years later, Lee proves he's still got rhythm in his picture-book collection **BUBBLEGUM DELICIOUS.** Even Mother Goose herself would find Lee's verse unflappable.

DAVID McCORD

McCord's book **EVERY TIME I CLIMB A TREE** is one of the most personally satisfying books of poetry I have ever read—or shared. It wins the "Poetry Book I Would Take with Me If I Were Trapped on an Island in a *Lord of the Flies*–Type Situation" award, because it has everything needed to keep children poetically engaged. For instance, children love to chorally scream to "Bananas and Cream"; they memorize "The Pickety Fence" with the mania that they memorize rap; and they become increasingly reflective with each line of "This Is My Rock."

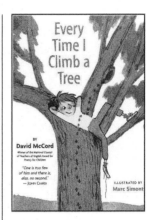

COLIN McNAUGHTON

Perhaps a better name for this poet would be Colin McNaughty; he has Prelutsky's talent with Dennis Rodman's testicles. Only British. (Do they play basketball in England much?) His poetry and zany artwork remind me of the "Wacky Packages" bubble-gum spoof cards of my childhood. Remember them? At once gross and strangely inspired. Children love his poetry as much as they love a poop joke. And that's a lot. His poetry collections include **MAKING FRIENDS WITH FRANKENSTEIN, THERE'S AN AWFUL LOT OF WEIRDOS IN OUR NEIGHBORHOOD,** and **WISH YOU WERE HERE (AND I WASN'T).**

JUDY SIERRA

I have had complete success reading aloud every single one of Judy Sierra's poems. "I Am Looking for My Mother" in Sierra's book of penguin poems, **ANTARCTIC ANTICS,** inspired cheers, laughter, and requests for four encores from second-graders. Equally enjoyed was **THERE'S A ZOO IN ROOM 22,** a collection of class pet poems from A to Z, a feat that for most poets looks good on paper, but in Judy Sierra's case, actually *looks good on paper.*

JAMES STEVENSON

The art of this accomplished cartoonist was made famous in *The New Yorker* magazine, but Stevenson eventually turned his attentions to younger audiences. He created particularly droll picture books, chock full of clever dialogue and situations, often in comic-book form. The big surprise came later in Stevenson's career, when he proved himself to be a formidable children's poet. His collections (all with "corn" in the title), **JUST AROUND THE CORNER, CANDY CORN, SWEET CORN, CORNFLAKES, POPCORN,** and **CORN-FED** are self-illustrated in his signature loose, sketchy style. The poems themselves are humble free-verse observations and go far to show children that (1) poems don't have to rhyme, and (2)

"NOW"
BY PRINCE REDCLOUD

Close the barbecue.
Close the sun.
Close the home-run games
   we won.

Close the picnic.
Close the pool.

Close the summer.

Open school.

❀ *Potato Pick:*

WHEN THE MOON FELL DOWN

by Linda Smith, illustrated by Kathryn Brown

Move over, Edward Lear's "Owl and the Pussycat!" There's a brand new children's rhyming romance in town! This is verse that deserves a place in the classic Mother Goose canon, and was in fact written by a supermom of seven children. At once gentle, funny, and mysterious, this is a definitive bedtime read. Our friend Moon comes down for some adventure and receives a grand tour of the town from a gracious cow. The words are arranged as perfectly as stars in a constellation ("The rye smelled sweet / The night winds whirled / Circling moon in a misty wreath / And he beamed in awe / At this wondrous world— / The stars above and the earth beneath"). Linda Smith died of cancer, and portions of the book's proceeds go to breast cancer research. But you can't purchase this book to be philanthropic, because with every page, you will be receiving much more than you give. I am sure Linda Smith is now delivering readings in heaven, to the delight of A. A. Milne, Robert Louis Stevenson, and Walter de la Mare. We were lucky she left this sliver of shining moon behind before she departed. (3 and up)

poems don't have to be flowery and snooty. Children will look at the world in a new way after reading Stevenson's poems and begin to see that inspiration for their own poetry is in the simple things all around them.

AND MORE . . .

If I were to help you create a guest list for a poetry party, in addition to the talents mentioned above, I would suggest that you invite Arnold Adoff, Hilaire Belloc, Sylvia Cassedy, John Ciardi, William Cole, Walter de la Mare, Kristine O'Connell George, Nikki Giovanni, Eloise Greenfield, Nikki Grimes, Karla Kuskin, Myra Cohn Livingston, Eve Merriam, Lilian Moore, Ogden Nash, Naomi Shihab Nye, Christina G. Rosetti, Judith Viorst, and Clyde Watson. For starters. If you prefer not to entertain such a large crowd in your home, they graciously await your acquaintance at the library.

Poetry Breaks

So much of what we do as adults is with the fervor of religious zealots, pounding on a child's door with a handful of pamphlets. And then we wonder why children sometimes hesitate to answer the door. There is something nice about making poetry available and letting that be the *end* of it, freeing children from the overbearing dreadfulness of adult suggestion. On the other hand, let us not forget that as adults, we are bigger than they are (ha ha) and so we can bang on their doors if we see fit; the trick, I guess, is doing it with panache. Legendary librarian Caroline Feller Bauer suggested knocking softly and carrying a big sign that says "Poetry Break." She interrupts all sorts of mundane activities by holding up the sign and reciting poetry. Bauer generously grants permission for people to reproduce the illustrations from her book THE POETRY BREAK for use in noncommercial, educational activities. You can enlarge the drawings at the copy shop, color them in, put them on poster board, and voilà! Attach a clear pocket to the back of the sign so you can slip a poem in and read it. I often used my poetry-break sign when I was teaching math, so children would think of poetry as an interruption from math drills and therefore be forever enamored with it. As a librarian, I played the wandering poetry minstrel, briefly popping in to classrooms for a poetry break. This is another great school job for a parent volunteer. Keep in mind that poetry breaks work great outside of school, too: Pop in on your child at bathtime, defer dinner, or hop in front of the TV. Poetry breaks are also exciting in the supermarket checkout line, airport, bank, or playground. Too embarrassed? Too shy?

Dear Madame Esmé,

Roses are red, violets are blue,
My kids won't read poems, I'm sick of it, too.
When I say we should read them, they sneer and they scoff.
Silverstein turned them on. Who the hell turned them off?

Dear Gentle Reader,

Violets are blue, roses are red,
Let's not lay blame, let's just fix it instead.
Here are two books that go far to debunk
That poems are frumpy instead of pure funk.

Written in poetic line form and journal style, **LOVE THAT DOG** by Sharon Creech is a very fast intermediate read but has many layers to be explored and enjoyed. The book begins with an entry from Jack's journal: "I don't want to / because boys / don't write poetry. / Girls do." Still, Jack's teacher Miss Stretchberry keeps at it, introducing Jack to worlds of words until he comes across one special, golden poem that speaks to him. This poem connects him with an author and helps him communicate the love and loss that had been weighing in his heart for some time. Besides providing a phenomenal introduction to poetry, Creech offers her signature and surprising character development. The selections Miss Stretchberry shares are included in the back of the book, so you can share them, too. For the over nine set, you could do a lot verse (ouch)!

"Concrete poems are different from regular poems," reads a note from the editor of **A POKE IN THE I: A COLLECTION OF CONCRETE POEMS** selected by Paul B. Janeczko. And how! Not only are the words important, but the way they are arranged on the page, the typeset that is chosen, and the use of blank space make all the difference in the world. A great choice for getting children excited about poetry, concrete poems can be weak, or they can skip rope; they can merge in traffic, drip down a popsicle stick, or fly off in the sky. Wild and highly styled, concrete poems are definitely the "jazz" of poetry, and this volume is aptly illustrated by the jazz king of illustration, Chris Raschka (see Raschka's **CHARLIE PARKER PLAYED BE BOP, MYSTERIOUS THELONIOUS,** or his project with Sharon Creech, **FISHING IN THE AIR,** containing artwork that rivals Chagall). Once children read this book, they will be in good shape to try writing their own concrete poetry, and if your child enjoys **A POKE IN THE I,** find more examples in **SPLISH SPLASH** by Joan Bransford Graham.

HAIKU: SHORT AND SWEET

Haiku is an ancient Japanese poetic form, simply three lines with a 5-7-5 syllabication pattern. Elegant and succinct, these poems are challenging to write and fun to read.

Cassedy, Sylvia, and Suetake Kunihiro, trans.	RED DRAGONFLY ON MY SHOULDER
Chaikin, Miriam	DON'T STEP ON THE SKY: A HANDFUL OF HAIKU
Four Winds Press	DON'T TELL THE SCARECROW
Gollub, Matthew	COOL MELONS—TURN TO FROGS! THE LIFE AND POEMS OF ISSA
Grimes, Nikki	A POCKETFUL OF POEMS
Janeczko, Paul B., ed.	STONE BENCH IN AN EMPTY PARK
Lewis, Richard, ed.	IN A SPRING GARDEN
Livingston, Myra Cohn	CRICKET NEVER DOES: A COLLECTION OF HAIKU AND TANKA
Mannis, Celeste Davidson	ONE LEAF RIDES THE WIND
Spivak, Dawnine	GRASS SANDALS: THE TRAVELS OF BASHO

. . . Also check out the Children's Haiku Garden at www.tecnet.or.jp/~haiku/.

HAIKU FORTUNE COOKIES, ANYONE?

Now in case you have a concern about mixing a Chinese cookie with a Japanese art form, it may interest you to know that the fortune cookie was invented in 1909 by Makota Hagiwara, manager of Golden Gate Park's Japanese Tea Garden. Chinese restaurateurs later appropriated the cookie. So haikus in fortune cookies are perfectly kosher—or the equivalent of "kosher" in Japanese. Try this recipe, adapted from Susan Branch's scrumptious cookbook VINEYARD SEASONS.

Ingredients

3 egg whites	½ cup cake flour
½ cup white sugar	½ teaspoon vanilla
¼ cup brown sugar	

Type or handwrite 24 haiku onto thin strips of paper. Preheat oven to 350°. Put all ingredients (except for the paper) in a food processor and blend for fifteen seconds. Cover cookie sheets with parchment paper and then grease the parchment. Drop the batter by measured table-spoons onto the greased, papered cookie sheet; don't do more than a half-dozen cookies at a time (I *know* that's a pain, but you'll just have to give them to someone *very special*). Bake 10 minutes. Immediately remove with spatula. The rough side should be on the inside of the cookie. Put a fortune in the middle of the cookie and fold it in half quick-quick, like a little paper sandwich, then bring the corners up. Once you've done this with the rest of the batter, let the oven cool to 200°. Put all the finished cookies back on a parchment-covered cookie sheet and bake until toasty brown, about a half hour. Serve with Earl Grey in a pretty pot and you've got yourself some poet-tea.

I think the *idea* of fortune cookies is so exciting, but relative to other cookies I could kill myself making, they taste so bland. They also don't have enough calories, in my opinion, for a self-respecting cookie. This can be fixed. I like to microwave white chocolate with a little butter and mix until smooth, then I dip the end of the finished fortune cookie in the chocolate, and then dip it again in a bowl full of sprinkles. Cool on wax paper.

Sprinkles help every situation.

Worried people will think you rhyme with "crazy"? Let's call "fun" an approximate rhyme for "crazy" and admit that we all could use a poetry break. Your children will love you for it, especially if you do it before they hit puberty. Postpuberty, "Poetry Patrols" can be initiated at the high-school level through literary clubs and volunteer projects. Through the "Poetry Break," verse can serve adolescents as a public attention-getter, hopefully in lieu of a painful body piercing.

Performing Poetry

Less involved and equally as fun as a storytelling festival (see p. 240) is an evening of poetry recitations in which children step up to a microphone in turn to share verse from memory. Many of the same elements of storytelling come into play: pacing, expression, voice projection, body language, eye contact, and text recall. The difference is in the memorization as opposed to the looser interpretations in storytelling. In a poem every word is chosen with care by the author and must be remembered and recited exactly, in order to honor the literary integrity. I've found bed- or trampoline-bouncing or rope-jumping to be helpful when memorizing poetry. Children may bounce or jump as long as they correctly remember the poem (I learned Lewis Carroll's "Jabberwocky" this way when I was eleven, and I still remember it). Just make sure at least some rehearsals are spent with both feet on the ground, because children who continue to bounce as they perform may create a seasick audience.

Children of all ages can memorize and perform poems of varying lengths, and for added support, children can also recite poems together in a group, "choral speaking." Of course, you can cheat and have a poetry *reading*, where the poems aren't memorized. Sometimes this is fine, especially if you have long or erudite poems such as Robert Browning's "Pied Piper of Hamelin," Walt Whitman's "Song of Myself," or Coleridge's "Kubla Khan." Consider a reader's-theater approach (see p. 225) to such ventures in verse. But I still maintain at least some of the presentations should be from memory. Why? It's the difference between margarine and butter. There's something really rich about a child looking you in the eye and hitting you with iambic pentameter. I remember in particular torturing a small class of behaviorally disordered, underachieving, sixth-grade boys by making them memorize a poem every week. But then it started to grow on them, especially after I assigned them the villain's anthem, "The Ballad of Captain Kidd." One morning soon after, one of the boys brought the rest

"My Favorite Word"
by Lucia and
James L. Hymes Jr.
There is one word—
My favorite—
The very, very best.
It isn't No or Maybe.
It's Yes, Yes, Yes, Yes, YES!

"Yes, yes, you may," and
"Yes, of course," and
"Yes, please help yourself."
And when I want a piece of
*   cake,*
"Why, yes. It's on the shelf."

Some candy? "Yes."
A cookie? "Yes."
A movie? "Yes, we'll go."

I love it when they say my
*   word:*
Yes, Yes, YES! (Not no.)

SLAMMING SLAMS?

Another recognized type of poetry performance is a "poetry slam." Poetry slams are basically "open mikes" at which members of the audience are chosen to judge poetry performances. The performances usually consist of original poetry, either read or recited within a set time frame and usually without the embellishments of costumes or props. Poetry slams originated in my home town of Chicago at the fabulous-smoky-finger-snapping Green Mill Lounge in Uptown, and I was actually lucky enough to be in attendance at many of these first slams in which great local poets competed for cash prizes. "Competed" is the operative word here. Although I know slams for young adolescents are increasingly popular, it takes an unusually stalwart ego to handle spontaneous and public judgment of one's work. While grown-up poets sadly may have a hard time making money from their work and see such competitions as a welcome opportunity, children are not in the same position. What we *can* glean from slams for the juvenile end of the spectrum is that reading your own poetry out loud is cool, and audience participation is cool—but children already sort of figured this out, that's why rap music is so popular.

For more information on poetry slams, check out www.poetryslam.com/faq.htm, and children of all ages can get a small taste of the slam spirit in Elizabeth Swados's HEY YOU! C'MERE: A POETRY SLAM.

"A LOST FRIEND"
BY EVAN MARIE OXLEY
You're leaving me.
Please don't go so soon!
I've only begun to know
*   you.*
The flowers die in the rain
*   of me.*

of us to tears with his recitation of "Stopping by Woods on a Snowy Evening" by Robert Frost. I don't remember the boy's real name. After the recitation, he was known as "Miles to Go."

A poetry reading is a lovely program to deliver to older audiences. A local coffee shop might agree to sponsor it, especially if there's media involved; call the community paper a week in advance for coverage. Dress your poets as beatniks for added java flavor, daddy-o. Or, for a great Valentine's Day fund-raiser, invite everyone to get those gowns and tuxes out of mothballs, hang a mirrored ball from the ceiling, and toast love poetry with sparkling white grape juice. Or recite poems by Anonymous wearing mystery masks. And, you don't *need* a theme; for an eclectic program, mix the sad with the funny and the shocking with the sweet, and warn the audience to buckle their seat belts for a ride on and off the track of the rhyming roller coaster. Visit the Poetry Archives (www.emule.com/poetry) to find some classic favorites, Kristine O'Connell George's Poetry Corner (www.kristinegeorge.com) for more recent offerings (and tips for aspiring poets), or, poetry virgins, gather ye children's trade collections while ye may.

Literature Circles

L iterature circles are structured book clubs that, with a little help getting started, children can successfully run with autonomy. Teachers began to use the approach formally in the 1980s, and classrooms all over the country now embrace it. But, in the true spirit of potato pedagogy, it is fun and easy and versatile, and so there is no reason it should be limited to the classroom. Literature circles can exist wherever there is literature and enough independently reading children to form a circle. A square, even.

The widely accepted definition of a "literature circle" comes from Harvey Daniels's comprehensive guide, LITERATURE CIRCLES: VOICE AND CHOICE IN BOOK CLUBS & READING GROUPS:

Literature circles are small, temporary discussion groups who have chosen to read the same story, poem, article or book. While reading each group-determined portion of the text, each member prepares to take specific responsibilities in the upcoming discussion, and everyone comes to the group with the notes needed to help perform that job. The circles have regular meetings, with discussion roles rotating each session. When they finish a book, the circle members plan a way to share highlights of their reading with the wider community; then they trade members with other finishing groups, select more reading, and move into a new cycle. Once members can successfully conduct their own wide-ranging, self-sustaining discussions, formal discussion roles can be dropped.

I love literature circles because they defy ability grouping. Children around eight to twelve years old are at a perfect age for literature circles, though children of all ages are capable of participating. Every child is given an opportunity to contribute in an equally valuable way to the discussion. Since the jobs are broken down, none of the responsibilities are too overwhelming and so nothing detracts from the pleasure of the reading. The idea that a group is depending on and looking forward to an individual's contribution gives the tasks relevance to the child. Most important for schools, literature circles allow trade literature in the classroom. The approach can be used as a supplement or an alternative to textbooks, ensuring vocabulary enrichment and comprehension and all that hoo-ha. But you don't have to worry about any of that hoo-ha; it can be purely recreational. A literature circle is a fun after-school club you can run one day a week, either at school or in your home.

So here's how you do it, if you want to do it the way I learned at a workshop at Loyola University, Chicago. It's worked well when I've done it. Get multiple copies of a wonderful book, one for every child in the circle. (Check out the Must-Reads by the Time You're 13, p. 430 for ideas.) Why not allow the children to participate in the choice of what to read? It may be motivational to set a deadline for the book to be completed. You can give the children a calendar and let them divide up the book into a schedule of reading assignments with specific due dates. Help the children set reasonable goals within the given time frame for these assignments (a hundred pages a night is not reasonable, for instance). Next, give each child a different colored folder. Inside, staple a description of a particular job. I also made homemade bookmarks to match—each had a cute design and the same job description printed on it, to remind children of their mission as they read. The five jobs I have used most successfully are described on the next two pages. The *Discussion Director,* who leads the conversation, the *Literary Luminary,* who picks out passages from the book to read aloud, the *Language Lover,* who looks up the meaning of unfamiliar words, the *Imperial Illustrator,* who draws pictures of pivotal plot points, and the *Practical Predictor,* who looks for cues from the text about what might happen next. You can copy and hand out these descriptions to the children. These are also good questions and ideas for discussing books in any format, such as in a less formal mother-son or mother-daughter book club (see Here Comes the Son!, p. 421).

In the course of the meeting, children presented their material in this order. Then they rotated folders and jobs, so in the end, each folder had the work of many different children, and each child had a chance to do each job and to present at a different point in the book. No one is ever always first or always last, and no children are stuck with a job they find too hard or too easy. If you only have four children in a group, leave out the Imperial Illustrator, because the children can work together to have a creative response at the end of the book. But if you are lucky enough to have a group that is especially enthused about art, the children can rotate the Imperial Illustrator job and have a second job sometimes, or

HELP WANTED

DISCUSSION DIRECTOR

You help everyone be thoughtful about reading!

Your job is to make a list of questions that your group might want to discuss after reading a part of the book. Your questions should have lots of possible answers, not just "yes" and "no." The best questions come from your own reactions and questions that come up while you read!

Some sample questions:

1. Why do you think the author had _____ happen? How would the chapter(s) have changed if _____ had not happened?
2. How does the author make you feel like you are _____?
3. How do you think the character felt about _____? How would you have felt about it?
4. What caused _____ to happen?
5. What would you have done in _____'s situation?
6. How are the characters changing?
7. Did this chapter turn out the way you expected?

On paper:

Write down your own questions to be used for discussion! You don't have to answer them now but jot down what the group has to say when you get together.

LITERARY LUMINARY

You show what is interesting about your book!

Your job is to pick several outstanding passages from the reading and plan for them to be shared in the group. Possible reasons for picking a passage to be shared: Exciting! Scary! Surprising! Funny! Sad! Realistic! Good dialogue! Or choose your own reason.

Different ways your passages can be shared in the group:

1. The Literary Luminary reads the passage out loud.
2. A group member nominated by the Literary Luminary reads out loud.
3. All read silently, then discuss.
4. Your own way!

On paper:

Write down the location of the passages you want to share (page and paragraph number), the reason you picked each passage, and how you want the passage to be shared in a group. Hint: It is easiest to jot down the page and paragraph numbers as you read, rather than having to go back and find them.

LANGUAGE LOVER

You make reading easier by helping everyone understand what the author is trying to say!

Your job is to be on the lookout for new, interesting, powerful, puzzling, or unfamiliar words. Jot down the word while reading, then look up the dictionary definition. You are responsible for helping members find challenging vocabulary and figure out what those words mean.

Different ways to discover word meanings:

1. Have the group locate the word and try to figure out the meaning from context (the sentence it is in) before you share the dictionary definition.
2. Use a thesaurus and look up the word to find a synonym (a word that means the same thing) to substitute in the sentence.

On paper:

Jot down a few of the most challenging words, the pages, paragraph, and line numbers in which the words appear and their dictionary definitions. Also, be prepared to look up any other words that the group suggests, and write down those definitions as well. ▶

▶ **IMPERIAL ILLUSTRATOR**

You create artwork to show main ideas!

Your job is to draw a picture that shows the most important part of the plot, or what is happening. Try to find one scene in the section you just read that really changes the direction of the story, and make some artwork that depicts, or shows, that scene. The more colorful, the better. You can use crayons, markers, paint, collage . . . whatever technique suits your artistic taste!

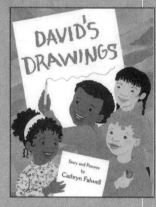

On paper:

Create the artwork. Show it to the group, and explain why you chose this particular scene, why you thought it was an important part of the story.

PRACTICAL PREDICTOR

You show what is possible in your book!

Your job is to think ahead. You are like the circle's fortune-teller, looking for what might be in the future, or the circle's detective, looking for clues that tell how the story might end. Create thoughtful predictions about the story and ask the children in the circle if they agree or disagree with your predictions. Try to find evidence from the book to support what will happen next . . . but NO PEEKING! Do not read ahead in the book, or it isn't a real prediction!

On paper:

Jot down your predictions when you have completed the passage, along with why they might happen. Poll the circle about whether they agree or disagree. Write down any other predictions the group may have.

Or add some jobs that I have heard other teachers use, including the Connector, whose job is to find real-world connections with the reading. For example, how the story relates to the child's own life, similarities or differences to the school or the community, similarities between historical periods, other books, or stories, other writings about the same topic or other writings by the same author. Besides discussing it, the Connector can write a paragraph on this topic for the folder.

Another job is Character Captain. This child's job is to point out traits of individual characters, giving examples of the character's thoughts or behaviors and clues from what other characters say about the character. This can be documented by straight description or by creating character webs

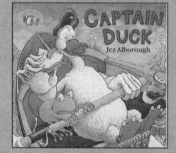

(see "Make Character Webs" in Storytelling: the Tell-Tale Art, p. 238).

Or try having an Essence Extractor, whose job is to remind everyone where in the story they are when the session begins and to summarize what has happened in the story when the session ends. The Essence Extractor writes down the summaries.

everyone can be Imperial Illustrator in addition to their other job. If you have more children in a group, double up on the Discussion Directors or Language Lovers, as these jobs are more time-consuming.

There are many more roles children can play, and many of the same roles go by different names. You can make up your own funny titles for roles. The main thing is that everybody have a job that contributes to a deeper and more thorough understanding of the text. I find smaller groups work better than large groups, if only for the sake of pacing. It's hard for children to wait their turn, and if some are slow in presenting, they may simply run out of time.

To help show children how to do their jobs, initially you can go through a whole book with everyone doing the same jobs at the same time: For instance, everyone reads pages 14–28 and is Discussion Director, and then from pages 29–40 everyone is Literary Luminary, and so forth, with you providing leadership and feedback to make sure everyone understands how to do each job. Especially if the children are younger, this will help to ensure success of the approach. Once they know how to do the jobs, though, you can really hand over the leadership to the children. At that point, you can observe or join the group at your leisure. For five children, I allotted forty minutes for a meeting.

Once, I facilitated six simultaneous literature circles. I was anxious about having so many circles going on at once. Would they just schmooze about what was on TV last night, or would they be on task? Would they argue, would there be put-downs I wouldn't be able to hear and stop? Would one child monopolize the group? Then I recalled something a friend had told me: In some Native American cultures, when there is a meeting and many people are present, a "listening stick" is passed around. Only the person holding the stick may speak; the others silently signal if they want a turn to hold the stick and have the privilege to speak. Adapting this idea, I went to a museum gift store and bought several beautiful rocks, crystals, and minerals, which I kept in a gold box. Every session, the Discussion Director chose a rock. The group that had been most prepared the last time got first pick. Within their circle, the children passed the rock around in the job order and raised their hands when they wanted the privilege to hold the rock and contribute. Then the rock was returned to whoever's turn it was in the job progression. In a room of over thirty children, only five children were quietly speaking at any given time. It was easy to hear whether they were on task and how they were treating each other. The quiet also made it peaceful for the circles who finished early to concentrate on beginning the reading for their next session. You don't need to use a stick or a rock. A listening Beanie Baby, a listening coin, or a listening ball will do the trick as well.

In my class when the children finished their book, each circle worked together to create a project everyone could enjoy. For instance, using clothespins, children hung all the work from the Imperial Illustrator folder on a laundry line that stretched across the room, creating an illustrated time line. The children also enjoyed doing dramatizations of scenes, creating song-and-dance "book commercials" to entice other circles to read their book, making new and improved book covers, writing sequels or "next chapters," designing the ever popular diorama, composing a synopsizing rap, and researching the historical period of the story. They could do anything that could be shared. My only stipulation was that they could not give away the book's ending.

Since I was a teacher, I needed to assess the children to prove that we weren't just reading to enjoy ourselves. The folders made assessments easy. I made a rubric (or checklist) of skills that each job represented, xeroxed the rubric, wrote the child's name at the top, and looked at the work. Since each child had had the opportunity to do every job, I could assess whether they demonstrated comprehension (Discussion Director), prediction skills (Practical Predictor), expanded and commanded their vocabulary, using the dictionary or story context when appropriate (Language Lover), read orally and recognized literary style (Literary Luminary), and located main idea and plot fixtures (Imperial Illustrator). If a child showed a weakness in any one of the jobs, I could assist with a particular skill by offering more individualized attention and extra practice with a short story or poem. I witnessed firsthand what the National Center for Statistics and the U.S. Department of Education reported in *Reading In and Out of School*: Children from classrooms with more book discussions score higher in national reading assessments. Literature circles also helped these children make gains in participation, preparedness, and social skills.

Some groups of children continually enjoy the structure of the jobs. But for others, the tasks that the jobs represent eventually become second nature. After a while, they may not want or need to write everything down, they may just want to informally look up words and predict and ask questions and read aloud cool parts. And that's okay. The circle is still circulating and percolating within them.

LITERATURE CIRCLE ON-LINE SUPPORT

Check out excerpts from Harvey Daniels's best-seller LITERATURE CIRCLES at www.stenhouse.com/0333.htm. You can also find good information at www.literaturecircles.com and the Literature Circles Resource Center at http://fac-staff.seattleu.edu/kschlnoe/LitCircles.

Author/Illustrator Studies: The Best Project Ever

I will never forget one particularly snarly girl whose attitude had me secretly quaking in my shoes. I'd been trying for weeks to teach her eighth-grade class how to evaluate children's literature, and trying for over a year to get this girl to check out a book from the school library. She sat sulking in a corner of the room while we talked about different authors and illustrators and what made them each unique. The day of final projects arrived. I wondered what she had prepared. When it was her turn to present, this intimidating eighth-grade gangsta-wanna-be opened a beautiful display and waxed poetic about the genius of British author Shirley Hughes, whose specialty is books about roly-poly preschoolers who misplace teddy bears, accidentally lock themselves in bathrooms, and cry when their mommies leave them at birthday parties. After her author/illustrator study project, I never looked at that girl quite the same way again, but more important, she didn't look at books the same way. When not planning some mischief with her posse out on the sidewalk, she could be caught in the picture-book section of the school library, using a critical eye in search of other artists of Hughes's caliber. She could also be caught smiling, especially when a new Shirley Hughes title arrived. She always had first dibs.

The goal of author/illustrator studies is to encourage lifelong love of reading through intimate literary and biographical familiarity with a particular author or illustrator (referred to as the "artist"). It is done by moving from a completely guided exploration of artistic work, to a supported exploration, to an independent exploration. While it requires the wearing of the "Teacher Hat" in all its glory, I would be completely remiss if I did not implore you as a parent to take it on. Simply too valuable a process for your children to miss, it helps nine- to twelve-year-olds at many different ability levels come to understand that there are real people behind the books we read, and all books at all levels have artistic voices and styles that ought to be recognized and enjoyed. It ended the "that's a baby book!" syndrome in my library: Suddenly

A FEW GOOD CHOICES FOR AN AUTHOR/ILLUSTRATOR STUDY

PICTURE BOOK ILLUSTRATORS AND AUTHORS

Verna Aardema, Anno, Molly Bang, Quentin Blake, Jan Brett, Margaret Wise Brown, Anthony Browne, Ashley Bryan, Mark Buehner, Janell Cannon, Eric Carle, Henry Cole, Barbara Cooney, Lucy Cousins, Donald Crews, Bruce Degen, Demi, Tomie dePaola, Leo and Diane Dillon, Pamela Duncan Edwards, Lois Ehlert, Ian Falconer, Don Freeman, Paul Galdone, Mordecai Gerstein, Paul Goble, Kevin Henkes, Shirley Hughes, Pat Hutchins, Trina Schart Hyman, Ezra Jack Keats, Steven Kellogg, Elisa Kleven, Leo Lionni, Anita Lobel, Arnold Lobel, James Marshall, Gerald McDermott, Susan Meddaugh, Bernard Most, Bill Peet, Brian Pinkney, Jerry Pinkney, Patricia Polacco, Jack Prelutsky, Marjorie Priceman, Peggy Rathmann, Jane Ray, Margret Rey, Robert D. San Souci, Allen Say, Jon Scieszka, Brian Selznick, David Shannon, Judy Sierra, Shel Silverstein, Peter Sis, David Small, Gennady Spirin, William Steig, Nancy Tafuri, Chris Van Allsburg, Judith Viorst, Bernard Waber, Rosemary Wells, Vera B. Williams, David Wisniewski, Audrey and Don Wood, Jane Yolen, Ed Young . . .

intermediate- and upper-grade children were checking out picture books and experiencing them with a new level of appreciation. When I ran this program in school, three hundred children participated. Of course, you don't need three hundred children. Try it with your own children, maybe adding a few cousins or neighbors. It's a perfect addition to Literature Circles (see p. 303) but equally primo for a parent-run afterschool workshop, home-schooling group, or scout troop (book-loving badge, anyone?), and it's an excellent activity to keep your child out of a summer reading slump. Before you begin, be sure to get a copy of THE AUTHOR STUDIES HANDBOOK, by Laura Kotch and Leslie Zackman. I just love their Venn diagrams!

Study an Artist As a Large Group

Pick a single author or illustrator that you want your group to study, and then seek out and read as much of that artist's work as possible. In our case, we chose Bernard Waber, and over the course of a few days we read aloud IRA SLEEPS OVER; BERNARD; GINA; RICH CAT, POOR CAT; YOU LOOK RIDICULOUS, SAID THE RHINOCEROS TO THE HIPPOPOTAMUS; and LOVABLE LYLE. We also did dramatizations from NOBODY IS PERFICK.

After you have looked at a generous sampling of the author's or illustrator's efforts, work together as a group to chart on a big piece of

NOVELISTS

David Adler, Joan Aiken, Lloyd Alexander, Avi, Natalie Babbitt, John Bellairs, Bill Brittain, Robert Burch, Beverly Cleary, Pam Conrad, Bruce Coville, Sharon Creech, Christopher Paul Curtis, Karen Cushman, Lois Duncan, Paul Fleischman, Jean Craighead George, Patricia Reilly Giff, Rumer Godden, Virginia Hamilton, Kimberly Willis Holt, James Howe, Brian Jacques, Dick King-Smith, E. L. Konisburg, Gail Carson Levine, Myron Levoy, Astrid Lindgren, Lois Lowry, Margaret Mahy, Walter Dean Myers, Mary Norton, Scott O'Dell, Katherine Paterson, Gary Paulsen, Richard Peck, Robert Newton Peck, William Pène du Bois, Mordecai Richler, Ann Rinaldi, Mary Rodgers, Louis Sachar, Marjorie Weinman Sharmat, Zilpha Keatley Snyder, Gary Soto, Jerry Spinelli, Cynthia Voigt, Laura Ingalls Wilder, Patricia Wrede, Laurence Yep . . .

NONFICTION AUTHORS

Aliki, Stephen Biesty, Christina Bjork, Joanna Cole, Ingri and Edgar Parin D'Aulaire, Russell Freedman, Jean Fritz, Gail Gibbons, Ruth Heller, Tana Hoban, Kathryn Lasky, Deborah Nourse Lattimore, Patricia Lauber, Loreen Leedy, David Macaulay, Bruce McMillan, Milton Meltzer, Ann Morris, Lila Perl, Laurence Pringle, Alice Provensen, Doreen Rappaport, Seymour Simon, Diane Stanley, Lisl Weil . . .

newsprint all the attributes of the work, such as characters, setting, conflict, resolution, illustration style, and writing style (see Appendix C1). When you finish with the chart, ask the children: What do all these books share? What does that tell you about the artist? What statements can you make about the artist's style that are consistently true?

Find an Artist

Explain to the children that they are now going to find information about an artist of their own choosing in order to create a display to honor her. Visit the library so that they can decide who that lucky artist will be. Remind older children that it is perfectly acceptable to choose a picture-book artist, as long as they end up analyzing the books in a thoughtful way. Advise them that picture-book authors are not any "easier." Also suggest that they think twice about choosing J. K. Rowling, Marc Brown, Dr. Seuss, or another artist who is already familiar, because part of the excitement is discovering someone whose work is new to them.

Ask the reference librarian to help you and the children locate the mind-blowing SOMETHING ABOUT THE AUTHOR, with over seventy volumes about nearly every children's book artist who ever put a pen (or brush, or crayon) to paper. Go to the index volume to find where the artists of interest are located, and allow the children to photocopy

FAN-LETTER PROTOTYPE

(CHILDREN CAN FILL IN THE BLANKS WITH THEIR INDIVIDUAL INFORMATION)

Your First, Last Name

Your Home or School Street

City, State, Zip Code

Hello, _____!

My name is _____. I am in the _____ grade at _____ Elementary School. I am studying outstanding authors and illustrators. Some of the things we do are _____. Right now we are writing letters to our favorite writers and illustrators, and I thought I had to write to you, because I love what you have done.

The books I read of yours are _____. My favorite part of _____ is _____, because _____. Another thing I like about your books is _____. I have always wanted to ask you _____.

My (mother, father, teacher) says people who make books are more fabulous than movie stars. We are collecting autographed pictures of our favorite book people. I would go crazy if you sent me one for the author/illustrator "Wall of Fame" we are creating, if it is not too much trouble. I hope you keep (writing, illustrating) books and enjoy continued success in your career.

Your Fan,

_____

background information about their chosen artist. Another outstanding resource is the single-volume THE ESSENTIAL GUIDE TO CHILDREN'S BOOKS AND THEIR CREATORS, edited by Anita Silvey, which can be found at the library but is also an affordable and fascinating addition to the bookshelves of any book-loving family.

Get in Touch

Encourage children to write a letter to their artist. Besides being fun, it requires the children to start reading the books so that they have something to say in the letter. Discuss appropriate and inappropriate questions for the artist. You can display a sample letter (see Fan-Letter Prototype, above) on an overhead projector, if you have access to one, or have copies available for children who need to take home an example. Personalize this fan-letter prototype to suit your needs.

You can help children address artist fan mail in care of the publisher, whose address is usually in fine print on the book's copyright page (the page preceding or following the title page). As the letter suggests, children can collect autographed pictures and make an artist "Wall of Fame." I started mine when I was twelve. My first autograph was from Roald Dahl and I still treasure it.

Sometimes the artist is dead. If you prefer not to hold a séance, letters may be modified and sent to members of the artist's family or to her estate (often listed in SOMETHING ABOUT THE AUTHOR, or care of the publisher). Children also can write fictional letters to a character in one of the artist's books. These letters make for a sweet bulletin board (see A Helpful Tack, p. 31), especially when combined with book covers.

Publishers often have all sorts of photos, press kits, bookmarks, and posters that they are happy to unload in the good name of book promotion. Have children call for author/illustrator information. (See How to Call a Publisher for Author/Illustrator Information, below, for sample dialogue you can distribute to children.)

HOW TO CALL A PUBLISHER
FOR AUTHOR/ILLUSTRATOR INFORMATION

(CHILDREN CAN FOLLOW THESE INSTRUCTIONS)

First, look on the copyright page of some of your artists' books to see who publishes most of them. Then, call 1-800-555-1212 to ask for the number of that publisher. Or you can look up the number in BOOKS IN PRINT found in the library.

Say: "May I please be connected to your children's-book publicity department." (If there isn't one, ask for customer service.)
    Wait to be connected.
    Say: "Hello, my name is _____ and I am a _____-grade student at _____ Elementary School in _____. I am doing an author/illustrator study about _____, whose books I know you publish. I was wondering if you have any promotional materials or biographical information you could send me that I could use for my report."
    Listen to answer. You may be asked to give your name and address. Speak slowly.
    If the person says she will send you something, say: "My report is due very soon, I appreciate your sending out anything you can share. Thank you for your time."
    If she says she has nothing to send you, just say: "Oh, well. Thank you for your time."

Use Technology to Research Authors

To model how to do Internet research, read aloud books by an author with a Web site and go through the process with the children. For example, read aloud Rodney Alan Greenblat's UNCLE WIZZMO'S NEW USED CAR, AUNT IPPY'S MUSEUM OF JUNK, and SLOMBO THE GROSS, and compare. Once you have really explored Rodney Alan Greenblat's work, look up his Web site on the Internet, www.whimsyload.com. Then, read Jan Brett's THE MITTEN, GINGERBREAD BABY, TROUBLE WITH TROLLS, DAISY COMES HOME, or any other books illustrated by Jan Brett, compare, and go to www.janbrett.com on the Internet. Ask the children: How do you hunt for author information on the Internet? Do you find different information when you hunt through a search engine and when you look at information given on the publisher's Web site? What do you find out about the author on-line? How does this background information change the way you look at the books?

You don't have to necessarily explore the sites of Rodney Alan Greenblat and Jan Brett. Many artists have great sites. For this modeling-research portion of the author/illustrator study, it makes sense to choose picture-book artists because their books take less time to read. Here are a few picture-book artists' Web sites:

Catherine and Laurence Anholt
www.anholt.co.uk

Peggy Rathmann
www.peggyrathmann.com

David Carter
www.popupbooks.com

Nicole Rubel
www.nicolerubel.com

G. Brian Karas
www.gbriankaras.com

Rosemary Wells
www.rosemarywells.com

Robert Munsch
www.robertmunsch.com

Audrey Wood
www.audreywood.com

Children can find many more artist sites (including authors of novels and nonfiction) for their research at:

www.childrenslit.com/f_mai.htm

www.acs.ucalgary.ca/~dkbrown/authors.html

www.carolhurst.com/authors/authors.html

www.ipl.org/youth/AskAuthor

www.fairrosa.info/cl.authors.html

Between the material found in SOMETHING ABOUT THE AUTHOR, online resources, and promotional materials arriving from the publisher, the children should be able to answer most, if not all, of these questions:

PROFESSIONAL

• What are the names of all the books your artist has completed? How many were there?

• Which was the first? Have any of the books won awards? Which books? Which awards? When?

• What qualities or themes do most of your artist's books share?

• If your artist is an illustrator, which art materials or techniques are typically used?

• Where did your artist attend school? Does he or she hold any degrees?

• What other kinds of jobs did your artist have?

• What book do you know (or believe) is your artist's favorite, and why?

• Which part of creating books comes easily to your artist? Which parts are difficult?

• Is there anything that is a special inspiration to your artist?

PERSONAL

• When was your artist born (year, date)? How old is your artist? If dead, when did your artist die? How old was she or he?

• Where does your artist live?

• Does your artist have any children?

• Does your artist have any pets?

• Does your artist have any special interests outside of creating books?

• Can you give examples of the artist's family, pets, personal experience, or interests appearing in or affecting his or her work?

And finally

• If you had to say in a *few sentences* what your artist does in books that makes him or her different from any other artist, what would you say? (In other words, be able to describe the artist's *style* and favorite *themes*.)

Give a copy of these questions to the children, but explain that they don't have to write the answers out yet; it's not an assignment to turn in. They should just try to learn the answers to as many of the questions as possible, try to become *expert*. They should think of it like knowing all the stats about sports figures. This is the kind of information that would be on the back of an author's baseball card.

Study an Artist in a Small Group

Set up a table or tables, each with a box containing at least four titles from a single artist. On our table we had books by Aliki, Jan Brett, Eric Carle, Demi, Trina Schart Hyman, Elisa Kleven, James Marshall, Bill Peet, William Steig, Vera Williams, and Ed Young. Here are some examples:

Books by Bill Peet

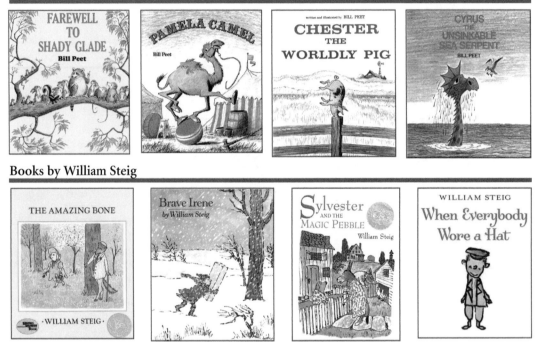

Books by William Steig

Books by Vera B. Williams

In small groups of three or four at the max, children will read to themselves all the books on the table, a quiet time. Next time they meet, they can get noisy as they discuss and list the attributes of the particular artist on the table, giving specific examples. What do all the books have in common? (You have modeled this procedure and given sample questions in the beginning when the large group studied the artist.)

Tell children to use their list to come up with a "style statement" about their artist. In other words, if they were that artist's agent on a trip to New York, how could they describe that artist to an editor in just a few lines so that the artist would be set apart from the thousands of other artists? Do words such as "pretty" or "nice" set an artist apart, or is it more effective to talk about artist materials or recurrent themes? Children will share the style statements they came up with as a group about the artist, and then privately come up with style statements for the artist they are researching on their own. They will save this style statement for their display and oral presentation.

Ask the children how they can incorporate the artist's style into the visual display. For instance: If you were doing Eric Carle, could you decorate it with bugs (a recurrent theme in his books) or perhaps a hungry caterpillar across the top eating holes in your display? If you were doing Jan Brett, would borders be attractive, or hedgehogs be sensible, since she uses them so frequently? Would bubble-shaped lettering be appropriate if you were doing James Marshall?

Plan the Shrine

Although I explain to children early on that we will be making displays, I don't give them the actual guidelines for the displays until we are well into our author/illustrator study. Otherwise they get all caught up in making pretty-pretty and lose focus on the content. But once they have some background knowledge under their wing, we can start talking turkey.

Show children the display protoypes (see Appendix C2). Remind them that these are samples; they can create displays in any arrangements, as long as they include pertinent information.

MEET A REAL LIVE AUTHOR

Planning an author visit is a parent volunteer activity that can reach large numbers of children and create a lasting impression. Connect with Children's Book Authors Who Visit Schools, www.snowcrest.net/kidpower/authors2.html, to see if talent from your area might be willing to call in, log in, stop by, or even fly in! The site's FAQ section also includes lots of helpful hints about how to be a good host.

BOOKS ABOUT AUTHOR VISITS

Borden, Louise	THE DAY EDDIE MET THE AUTHOR
Buzzeo, Toni, and Jane Kurtz	TERRIFIC CONNECTIONS WITH AUTHORS, ILLUSTRATORS, AND STORYTELLERS: REAL SPACE AND VIRTUAL LINKS (Parent/teacher resource.)
Cleary, Beverly	DEAR MR. HENSHAW
Creech, Sharon	LOVE THAT DOG
Melton, David	HOW TO CAPTURE LIVE AUTHORS AND BRING THEM TO YOUR SCHOOLS (Parent/teacher resource.)
Pinkwater, Daniel	AUTHOR'S DAY

The Big Finish

As the grand finale, children set up displays and present everything they have discovered about the artist. Of course, if you are working with children who are not your own, be sure to invite their parents. Presentations should include a five- to ten-minute read-aloud (the works of longer fiction or nonfiction may be excerpted) and should be prefaced or concluded by biographical and professional information about the artist. Allow plenty of Q&A after the presentations, and watch the children show off their knowledge. Don't forget the video camera!

The Full Monty (Not)

If you are daunted by the idea of an author/illustrator study, feel free to pick and choose the parts that seem most doable. You can always help your child request materials from publishers and look at several books by a single artist, and you can casually discuss the artist's style together and get the skinny on a favorite artist in SOMETHING ABOUT THE AUTHOR or by surfing the Internet. Any of these activities will serve to strengthen your child's connection to artists—and to you!

Nurturing the Artist Within

One day when my son was six years old, we went on our regular jaunt to the local bookstore. I noticed he was hunting through the shelves, obviously looking for a very specific title. "Do you need help finding something?" I asked him.

"Where's my book?" he demanded.

The book he was referring to was the one he wrote, *A Championship Race,* which we had bound and submitted to his classroom's author contest and which had received some acclaim.

"We're not going to find it here," I unfortunately had to admit.

"Well, let's ask the salesman to order it," he said, starting for the desk. "They should have it. It won an award."

I had to sit him down with a cookie and explain the rudiments of, well, *distribution.* He listened carefully, obviously vexed but not discouraged, each point I was making merely an exasperating mile he would have to tread before crossing the intended finish line of a book on the shelf. It is a schlep, after all. But I can't begin to tell you how delighted I was that he would consider taking the journey.

Part of creating artists is helping children to recognize two opposing ideas at the same time: (1) nothing is as easy as it looks and (2) anything is possible. It is this combination of work and imagination that powers the creative process.

Great Books for Future Authors and Illustrators

The pen, marker, and crayon prove mightier than the sword. Use these lists to encourage the next generation of book creators.

What Do Illustrators Do?

Written and Illustrated by
Eileen Christelow

NonFiction	
Aliki	• How a Book Is Made
Christelow, Eileen	• What Do Authors Do? • What Do Illustrators Do?
Cummings, Pat, ed.	• Talking with Artists (Volumes I, II, and III)
Fletcher, Ralph	• A Writer's Notebook: Unlocking the Writer Within You
Kehret, Peg	• Five Pages a Day: A Writer's Journey (Biography for older readers.)
Lester, Helen	• Author: A True Story
Marcus, Leonard S., ed.	• A Caldecott Celebration: Six Artists and Their Paths to the Caldecott Medal • Author Talk
Nixon, Joan Lowery	• If You Were a Writer
Silvey, Anita, ed.	• The Essential Guide To Children's Books and Their Creators (A must-have for author/illustrator studies.)
Stevens, Carla	• A Book of Your Own: Keeping a Diary or Journal
Stevens, Janet	• From Pictures to Words: A Book About Making a Book

PERIODICAL POWER!

If you have a talented writer in your home, her best chance at seeing her work in print is through periodicals. One that publishes wonderful stories and artwork by children around the world is *Stone Soup*, at www.stonesoup.com, or snail mail at P.O. Box 83, Santa Cruz, CA 95063. Teens can get published through *Merlyn's Pen*, www.merlynspen.com, or snail mail at P.O. Box 910, East Greenwich, RI 02818.

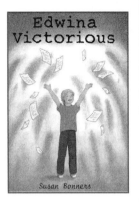

Fiction for Future Writers

Anderson, Laurie Halse	• THANK YOU, SARAH! THE WOMAN WHO SAVED THANSKGIVING
Bonners, Susan	• EDWINA VICTORIOUS
Bunin, Sherry	• DEAR GREAT AMERICAN WRITERS SCHOOL (Mature readers.)
Burch, Robert	• KING KONG AND OTHER POETS
Cleary, Beverly	• DEAR MR. HENSHAW
Clements, Andrew	• FRINDLE • THE SCHOOL STORY
Creech, Sharon	• LOVE THAT DOG
Fanelli, Sara	• DEAR DIARY
Feiffer, Jules	• MEANWHILE . . .
Fitzhugh, Louise	• HARRIET THE SPY
Fuqua, Jonathon Scott	• DARBY
Gantos, Jack	• HEADS OR TAILS: STORIES FROM THE SIXTH GRADE
Giff, Patricia Reilly	• FOURTH-GRADE CELEBRITY
Hesse, Karen	• LETTERS FROM RIFKA
Holmes, Barbara Ware	• CHARLOTTE THE STARLET
Hurwitz, Johanna	• DEAR EMMA
Joseph, Lynn	• THE COLOR OF MY WORDS
Kehret, Peg	• MY BROTHER MADE ME DO IT
Klise, Kate	• REGARDING THE FOUNTAIN
Lisle, Janet Taylor	• HOW I BECAME A WRITER & OGGIE LEARNED TO DRIVE
Little, Jean	• HEY WORLD, HERE I AM!
Lowry, Lois	• GOONEY BIRD GREENE (About a girl who loves storytelling!)
Moss, Marissa	• AMELIA'S NOTEBOOK
Myers, Walter Dean	• BAD BOY • MONSTER (For mature readers. Written in screenplay form; ties in well with Cinema Club, p. 211.)
Nagda, Ann Whitehead	• DEAR WHISKERS
Olsson, Sören, and Anders Jacobsson	• IN NED'S HEAD

Philbrick, Rodman	• THE LAST BOOK IN THE UNIVERSE (Mature readers.)
Ray, Karen	• THE T. F. LETTERS
Skolsky, Mindy Warshaw	• LOVE FROM YOUR FRIEND, HANNAH (An especially wonderful book; great read-aloud.)
Smith, Betty	• A TREE GROWS IN BROOKLYN (Mature readers.)
Spurr, Elizabeth	• THE LONG, LONG LETTER
Teague, Mark	• DEAR MRS. LARUE: LETTERS FROM OBEDIENCE SCHOOL
Townsend, Sue	• THE SECRET DIARY OF ADRIAN MOLE, AGED 13¾ (Mature readers.)
Ure, Jean	• SKINNY MELON AND ME
Webster, Jean	• DADDY-LONG-LEGS
Whiteley, Opal	• ONLY OPAL
Wiles, Deborah	• LOVE, RUBY LAVENDER
Williams, Carol Lynch	• MY ANGELICA (Mature readers.)
Williams, Vera B.	• SCOOTER
Ylvisaker, Anne	• DEAR PAPA

AND SPEAKING OF SNAIL MAIL . . .

Having an old-fashioned "pen pal" is a great way for children to practice writing. Pen pals from one hundred countries are available to children ten and up from International Youth Service (IYS), and order forms may be requested at www.iys.fi or snail mail at PB 125, Fin-20101, Turku, Finland (don't forget, two stamps for every half-ounce of overseas mail). There are other services available, but this is the one I trust. In fact, when I was fourteen I was hooked up by IYS with a pen pal in India, and now she lives in San Diego and is my son's godmother. Never under-estimate the power of the post! (You can pass the time waiting for replies by reading GLUEY, A SNAIL TALE by Vivian Walsh and J. Otto Seibold.)

Fiction for Aspiring Illustrators

Avi	• CITY OF LIGHT, CITY OF DARK: A COMIC BOOK NOVEL
Baker, Keith	• LITTLE GREEN
Banyai, Istvan	• ZOOM
Belton, Sandra	• PICTURES FOR MISS JOSIE
Bloom, Becky	• MICE MAKE TROUBLE
Bulla, Clyde Robert	• THE CHALK BOX KID (Short chapter book.)
Catalanotto, Peter	• EMILY'S ART
Davol, Marguerite W.	• THE PAPER DRAGON
dePaola, Tomie	• THE ART LESSON
Drescher, Henrik	• SIMON'S BOOK
Estes, Eleanor	• THE HUNDRED DRESSES (Short chapter book.)
Falwell, Cathryn	• DAVID'S DRAWINGS
Feiffer, Jules	• THE MAN IN THE CEILING (Chapter Book.)

OPAL WHITELEY
GENIUS IN THE WOODS

When I feel sad inside
I talk things over with my tree.
I call him Michael Raphael.
When I go off the barn roof
it is a long jump into his arms.
I might get my leg or my neck broken
and I'd have to keep still for a long time.
So I always say a little prayer
and do jump in a careful way.
It is such a comfort
to nestle up to Michael Raphael.
He is a grand tree.
He has an understanding soul.

I guess Opal is really more of a writing hero than a reading hero. Opal Whiteley was a gifted diarist who kept a journal during the early 1900s, starting from the age of five. She grew up in nineteen different lumber camps, accompanying her foster family. She meticulously recorded her unique and mysterious observations of the natural world in a style that closely resembles poetry, with a regard for her environment that was well ahead of her time. Unfortunately, when Opal was twelve a foster sister tore the diary in pieces, which Opal then collected and stored in a hidden box.

When Opal was twenty years old and living in poverty, she attempted to sell a nature book to the editor

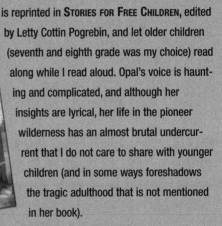

of the Atlantic Monthly Press. While the editor did not sign up that book, she was intrigued with the author enough to ask if Opal had perhaps kept a diary of her life. Of course, Opal burst out crying . . . and then began the painstaking nine-month process of putting back together the thousands of pieces that became the masterpiece we can read today as OPAL: THE JOURNAL OF AN UNDERSTANDING HEART, adapted by Jane Boulton, or the picture-book version, ONLY OPAL. You and your children can also read her diary on-line at http://intersect.uoregon.edu/opal.

While the picture book is lovely, illustrated by the legendary and award-winning Barbara Cooney, my own preference is to make copies of "The Story of Opal" that is reprinted in STORIES FOR FREE CHILDREN, edited by Letty Cottin Pogrebin, and let older children (seventh and eighth grade was my choice) read along while I read aloud. Opal's voice is haunting and complicated, and although her insights are lyrical, her life in the pioneer wilderness has an almost brutal undercurrent that I do not care to share with younger children (and in some ways foreshadows the tragic adulthood that is not mentioned in her book).

Like the work of young WWII diarist Anne Frank (DIARY OF A YOUNG GIRL), the written word contributed to survival both on a personal level and in the annals of history. Both young women gave voice to the profundity and gravity of childhood experience, and gave value to the personal anecdote.

Freeman, Don	• NORMAN THE DOORMAN
Geoghegan, Adrienne	• ALL YOUR OWN TEETH
Gilliland, Judith Heide	• NOT IN THE HOUSE, NEWTON!
Hurd, Thacher	• ART DOG
Johnson, Crockett	• HAROLD AND THE PURPLE CRAYON
Karas, G. Brian	• THE CLASS ARTIST
Katz, Karen	• THE COLORS OF US
Kelleher, D. V.	• DEFENDERS OF THE UNIVERSE (Chapter book.)
Kesselman, Wendy	• EMMA
LaMarche, Jim	• THE RAFT
Levine, Arthur A.	• THE BOY WHO DREW CATS
McClintock, Barbara	• THE FANTASTIC DRAWINGS OF DANIELLE
McPhail, David	• DRAWING LESSONS FROM A BEAR
Nikola-Lisa, W.	• CAN YOU TOP THAT?
Pilkey, Dav	• THE ADVENTURES OF CAPTAIN UNDERPANTS
Pittman, Helena Clare	• STILL-LIFE STEW
Ross, Tom	• EGGBERT: THE SLIGHTLY CRACKED EGG
Saint-Exupéry, Antoine de	• THE LITTLE PRINCE (Chapter book; mature readers.)
Schaefer, Carole Lexa	• THE SQUIGGLE
Williams, Karen Lynn	• PAINTED DREAMS
Williams, Vera B.	• CHERRIES AND CHERRY PITS
Ziefert, Harriet	• ELEMENOPEO

Yes, Kids Get Published, Too!

Filipovic, Zlata	• ZLATA'S DIARY
Frank, Anne	• THE DIARY OF A YOUNG GIRL (Mature readers.)
Hunter, Latoya	• THE DIARY OF LATOYA HUNTER: MY FIRST YEAR IN JUNIOR HIGH
Kallok, Emma	• THE DIARY OF CHICKABIDDY BABY
Lyne, Sandford, comp.	• TEN-SECOND RAINSHOWERS: POEMS BY YOUNG PEOPLE
Nye, Naomi Shihab, ed.	• SALTING THE OCEAN: 100 POEMS BY YOUNG POETS
Pratt, Kristen Joy	• A WALK IN THE RAINFOREST
Vizzini, Ned	• TEEN ANGST? NAAAH . . . A QUASI-AUTOBIOGRAPHY
Watson, Esther Pearl, and Mark Todd, comps.	• THE PAIN TREE AND OTHER TEENAGE ANGST-RIDDEN POETRY

Story Starters

Story starters? Ink impetus? Writing workouts? Jumper cables? Whatever you want to call them, I use them all the time when children complain, "I can't think of anything to write about!" Surely, as a parent, you have heard the same complaint during homework. Copy these story starters and put them on index cards, and let children pick them at random. These are also very helpful for children who are keeping creative writing journals, or who want to start a writers group. Encourage a writer's exercise regime and see the benefits of improved grades along with a broadened appreciation for other people's prose.

- Write a diary entry for a famous person in history.

- Write a story from the point of view of someone with a very difficult job.

- The title is "The kids on my block."

- What an awful bully! Describe how you will escape his (or her) clutches.

- Sometimes people are so silly. Write a "things to do" list for a very silly person.

- Write about someone you met one day on the street.

- Write from the point of view of a raindrop.

- Bring nature to life. For example: "The wind is like a girl turning somersaults." "The trees are old men waiting for a bus."

- Write a diet plan for a hippopotamus.

- Go outside and look at a tree. Write that tree's life story.

- Why do leaves fall? Why does snow fall? Why are there rainbows? Write a fantasy story explaining something in nature.

- What is the view from the top of the Eiffel Tower? From the bottom of Niagara Falls? From the middle of Mount Fuji? Describe how you imagine it would be.

- Write a speech about something you feel is important.

- Write a note of excuse to your teacher.

- Write a note of excuse from your teacher.

• Start at your toes, end at your hair . . . Describe how it feels to be happy.

• Describe giving a speech at a school assembly from the point of view of your stomach.

• Write a will.

• Write a love letter.

• Write a letter to the child you might have in the future.

• Make a list of fifteen questions your parents would answer "no" to.

• Make a list of fifteen questions your parents would answer "yes" to.

• Make a list of compliments. Then make a list of the things another person would say in response to the compliments.

• Make a list of insults. Then make a list of the things another person would say in response to the insults.

• If you were a skywriter, what would you write for everyone to see?

• Write a script for a puppet show.

• Write a school song.

• Write a list of things for an elephant to remember.

• Choose a brief, interesting article from the newspaper, and rewrite the story from the point of view of somebody involved in the incident.

• Describe how it feels to dance.

• Describe your worst fear.

• Some people are unusual. Make up an unusual person. What unusual thing happens to this unusual person?

• Superpower for a day! What will it be?

• Pretend you are a ghost, haunting a house or apartment. Describe the people who live there, and how you haunt them.

• What do you think somebody who just won $10 million would be thinking? Would a person change after acquiring so much wealth? Write a story about change due to a loss or gain of money.

• Write the lesson plan of a very mean teacher.

• You are the last dinosaur before extinction. Describe what you feel and see.

• Describe something blowing in the wind. What is it?

• Look down from the Ferris wheel. Describe what you see, how you feel.

• Describe the first time you crossed the street alone.

• Pretend you are a painter. What will you paint? Why do you choose the colors that you choose? How do you feel as you paint this picture?

• Some people talk to themselves. What do they say?

• Sometimes people say things that you remember all your life. Write down such a conversation.

• Write a good-bye conversation.

• Listen to other people's conversations. Write down what you hear, word for word.

• Write a jump-rope rhyme.

• Make up ten modern superstitions.

• Write a horoscope for each sign in the zodiac.

• Write the rules to a new game.

• Write a pretend advice column. Use your own problems.

• Write a script for a soap opera.

• If you could say something over the school intercom, what would it be?

• What is the difference between a person and a robot? Express this difference by imagining you are a robot turning into a person, or a person turning into a robot.

• Does everybody have something special about them? Pick a character from ordinary, everyday life and show how special that person can be.

• Write a story. At the start, make the character very likeable. By the end, make the character a real stinker (or, vice versa)!

• Look out your window. Write your first impression of each passerby.

• Who is the funniest person you ever met? Why?

• Imagine somebody absolutely rich and absolutely famous. Follow on the heels of that person from the time she wakes up to the time she goes to bed.

• Santa Claus, the Tooth Fairy, the Easter Bunny—invent someone new.

• Write about a group of friends. Do they all get along? Are they all from the same background? How are their personalities different, or the same?

• It was an unforgettable field trip! Write about it.

• Write a fable, with a moral at the end.

• Write how somebody very scared would sound over the telephone.

• Write a poem from the point of view of a musical instrument.

• Write about a conversation going on between the librarian and someone very, very loud.

• Somebody is whispering a secret in your ear. What's it about?

• Write about the peasant who is having a conversation with the queen.

• Pretend you are sorry. Write an apology. What are you sorry about?

• Write a conversation between a brother and a sister, or a sister and a sister, or a brother and a brother.

• Write about how it feels to fly.

• Write words to a song for someone who feels left out.

• Do not write, "I was surprised," but make it clear to the reader that you were surprised. What was the big surprise?

• Write about what a liar would say.

• Describe how things look when you're confused.

• Write something using exclamation points as your only punctuation.

• Write a poem about being tickled.

• Look through the eyes of a fish, and describe what you see.

• Describe somebody blowing a very big bubble.

• Go to a public place such as a library, restaurant, or park. Pick someone you've never met before as a subject, and describe that person.

• Look up from the dentist's chair, and describe what you see.

• Imagine your family at a party. Describe what you see.

• Sit at the kitchen table and choose three foods to eat. Describe how each one tastes.

• Write a crazy *TV Guide.*

• Look in a mirror. Write everything you see.

• Hey, you were a baby once! Look up from your crib. What do you see?

• Describe what it would be like to be in jail.

• Describe the school of your dreams!

• Write a dictionary for words in any subject area you choose: math, sports, dance, rocks, cooking, travel . . .

• Write an advertisement for a new invention.

• What makes a person ugly? Describe a very ugly person, without using the word "ugly."

• What makes a person beautiful? Describe a very beautiful person, without using the word "beautiful."

• Hold something in your hand. Compare it to other things. Make a list: "This thing is like . . ."

• The title is "I'm someplace I do not want to be."

• A Martian has come to visit. Describe this planet, Earthling!

• Describe a room in your home.

• Describe your neighborhood on a summer evening.

• Make it happen again! Describe a memory you have.

• Write a script for the master of ceremonies of a funny fashion show.

• Write a pamphlet about how to give a theme party. Include an invitation, menu, and party games.

• Describe something very sharp. Describe something very smooth. Describe something very rough.

• You are a stray cat in the park. Describe things through a cat's eyes.

• Describe somebody you admire.

• The time machine works! What adventure is ahead?

- It was a case of mistaken identity! What happened?

- Sneaky, sneaky! Write a mischievous plan.

- Write about any of the following:
  a town at the bottom of the sea
  an upside-down town
  a city at the end of a rainbow
  a land at the center of the earth

- Spend the day as a balloon, and describe your experience.

- Grown-ups can be so unfair! Describe an incident in which you were treated unfairly because of your age.

- Something mysterious has happened to your whole class! Only you can change things back to the way they were. Describe how you do this.

- Run away and join the circus. Describe your new life.

- How did you ever end up on the Moon? How will you ever get back to Earth?

- Write a romance between an unusual pair of lovers.

- Pretend you are one hundred years old, and write a time line of your life's highlights.

- You have just met a fortune-teller. What does he or she tell you? Does it come true?

- Write a story about being on your own in the city or the countryside.

- It was a great money-making scheme! Explain it.

- Tell a story about a pet you own, or imagine an incident with a pet you would like to own.

- Describe a walk down the street from the point of view of a ninety-year-old person.

- Write and illustrate a comic strip.

- Write a story about a big contest.

- Write a story about how two lonely people meet.

A Few Pearls of Wisdom for Children Who Write

• Write what you know about. Your own real life is interesting.

• If you don't have something nice to write about someone, change his or her name.

• Try not to begin with "the alarm clock rang" and don't end with "then she woke up. It was all a dream." Also, try not to end stories by killing people. That's trite.

• Avoid too many four-letter words: nice, good, bad, pretty (all right, "pretty" isn't four letters, and I guess "bad" falls a little short). Your writing will be better as soon as you remove adjectives that don't describe things in a specific way.

• Let your readers know about the characters by what they say, what they do, and what other characters say about them.

• Try to make all the characters important to the story. If they aren't important, don't spend a lot of time describing them.

• Have something you want to say before you write, something that you would want to say even if only one person read what you wrote. Being published is not the most important thing.

• Most stories are either about a new person coming into the picture or a journey in life.

• Choose your words carefully. Make every word count. Say things in your own way, not in the way others have said things before.

• The answer to "how long does it have to be?" is always "as long as it takes to tell readers what they need to know."

• People talking in stories is fun. Listen to the way people talk.

• Read a lot. Reading is what will teach you to write more than anything.

• Change a fairy tale around your way.

• Review three restaurants.

• Have a conversation with an angel.

• Outsmart a devil in your own trickster tale.

• Make up interview questions for a teacher, a movie star, a president, a neighbor. Then seek answers.

• Make a list of things to say to a person who is having an awful day.

• Pretend you are a basketball. Write about being in a basketball game.

It Is Important to Know How to Draw (At Least a Little)

When my son started grade school, I was surprised at how important it was for him to know how to draw. It seemed to be taken for granted that he would know how to deftly take his crayons and conjure up people and houses and fish and cars and what-all. My son's fine motor skills weren't quite up to the what-all. Luckily, what-all is all what author Ed Emberley is about. He creates books that show step by step, using the simplest of shapes, how to draw practically everything in the world! As a child, I learned to draw using these books, and years later, my seven-year-old was smiling as well. These titles give young artists confidence.

ED EMBERLEY'S BIG GREEN DRAWING BOOK

ED EMBERLEY'S BIG ORANGE DRAWING BOOK

ED EMBERLEY'S BIG PURPLE DRAWING BOOK

ED EMBERLEY'S BIG RED DRAWING BOOK

ED EMBERLEY'S DRAWING BOOK: MAKE A WORLD

ED EMBERLEY'S DRAWING BOOK OF ANIMALS

ED EMBERLEY'S DRAWING BOOK OF FACES

ED EMBERLEY'S DRAWING BOOK OF TRUCKS AND TRAINS

ED EMBERLEY'S DRAWING BOOK OF WEIRDOS

ED EMBERLEY'S FINGERPRINT DRAWING BOOK

ED EMBERLEY'S GREAT THUMBPRINT DRAWING BOOK

ED EMBERLEY'S HALLOWEEN DRAWING BOOK

ED EMBERLEY'S PICTURE PIE: A CIRCLE DRAWING BOOK

For older children, Lee J. Ames is the Charles Atlas of drawing, turning awkward seventh- and eighth-grade boys (and yes, a few girls) into heroes whom everyone crowds around. With a few thoughtful strokes they are able to create zombies, motorcycles, and cartoon characters. I always found the instructions a little difficult, unable to quite understand how a few circles suddenly turn into a steam engine, but the children seem to manage, if only out of sheer force of will. I have seen boys actually fight over copies of these books in the library (if that's a good thing?). These titles are excellent preparation for a future career with Marvel Comics.

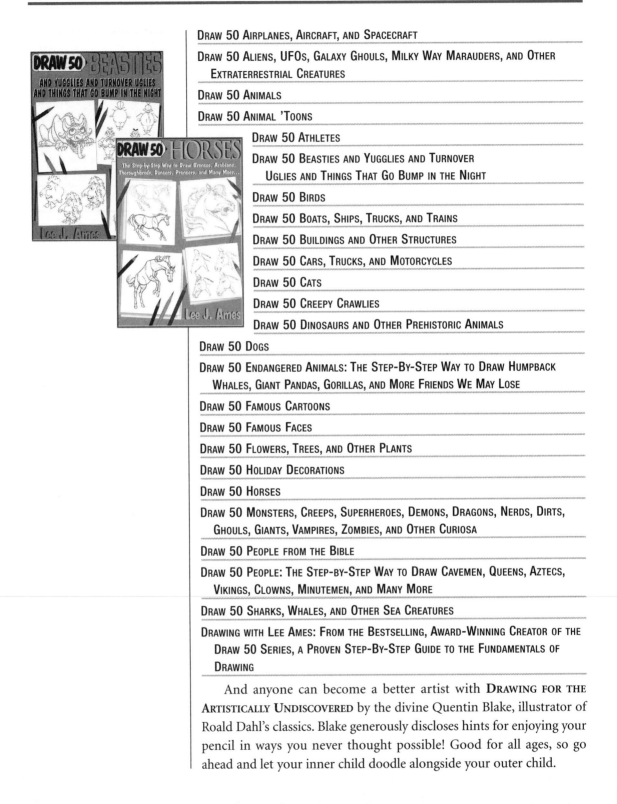

Draw 50 Airplanes, Aircraft, and Spacecraft

Draw 50 Aliens, UFOs, Galaxy Ghouls, Milky Way Marauders, and Other Extraterrestrial Creatures

Draw 50 Animals

Draw 50 Animal 'Toons

Draw 50 Athletes

Draw 50 Beasties and Yugglies and Turnover Uglies and Things That Go Bump in the Night

Draw 50 Birds

Draw 50 Boats, Ships, Trucks, and Trains

Draw 50 Buildings and Other Structures

Draw 50 Cars, Trucks, and Motorcycles

Draw 50 Cats

Draw 50 Creepy Crawlies

Draw 50 Dinosaurs and Other Prehistoric Animals

Draw 50 Dogs

Draw 50 Endangered Animals: The Step-By-Step Way to Draw Humpback Whales, Giant Pandas, Gorillas, and More Friends We May Lose

Draw 50 Famous Cartoons

Draw 50 Famous Faces

Draw 50 Flowers, Trees, and Other Plants

Draw 50 Holiday Decorations

Draw 50 Horses

Draw 50 Monsters, Creeps, Superheroes, Demons, Dragons, Nerds, Dirts, Ghouls, Giants, Vampires, Zombies, and Other Curiosa

Draw 50 People from the Bible

Draw 50 People: The Step-by-Step Way to Draw Cavemen, Queens, Aztecs, Vikings, Clowns, Minutemen, and Many More

Draw 50 Sharks, Whales, and Other Sea Creatures

Drawing with Lee Ames: From the Bestselling, Award-Winning Creator of the Draw 50 Series, a Proven Step-By-Step Guide to the Fundamentals of Drawing

And anyone can become a better artist with **Drawing for the Artistically Undiscovered** by the divine Quentin Blake, illustrator of Roald Dahl's classics. Blake generously discloses hints for enjoying your pencil in ways you never thought possible! Good for all ages, so go ahead and let your inner child doodle alongside your outer child.

Artist Models: Kindred Spirits for Creative Kids

There are all kinds of artists. In a time when arts education is sadly and foolishly undermined, your children can still turn to literature to see their artistic aspirations mirrored back brightly. Help them become familiar with the valuable cultural contributions of virtuosos and the valuable contributions they are poised to make themselves.

Fine Art

Browne, Anthony	• WILLY'S PICTURES
Laden, Nina	• ROBERTO: THE INSECT ARCHITECT
Littlesugar, Amy, and Ian Schoenherr	• MARIE IN FOURTH POSITION: THE STORY OF DEGAS' "THE LITTLE DANCER"
Mayhew, James	• KATIE AND THE SUNFLOWERS
Park, Linda Sue	• A SINGLE SHARD (Chapter book about pottery.)
Pieńkowski, Jan	• BOTTICELLI'S BED AND BREAKFAST
Vande Griek, Susan, Pascal Milelli	• THE ART ROOM (About artist and art teacher Emily Carr.)
Watts, Leander	• STONECUTTER (Chapter book.)
Weitzman, Jacqueline Preiss, and Robin Glasser	• YOU CAN'T TAKE A BALLOON INTO THE METROPOLITAN MUSEUM

. . . Also, see Great Books for Future Authors and Illustrators, p. 319.

STONE-CUTTER
A NOVEL BY
LEANDER
WATTS

Musical Notes

Culter, Jane	• THE CELLO OF MR. O
Dodds, Dayle Ann	• SING, SOPHIE! (Country music.)
Doucet, Sharon Arms	• FIDDLE FEVER (Chapter book.)
Dutton, Sandra	• CAPP STREET CARNIVAL (Chapter book about an aspiring bluegrass singer.)
Fleming, Candace	• WESTWARD HO, CARLOTTA!
Gollub, Matthew	• THE JAZZ FLY

✿ *Potato Pick:*

EMILY'S ART
by Peter Catalanotto

My husband is an artist. When I ask him what his favorite color is, he always says, "All of them." When I ask him what his favorite picture at the museum is, he says, "All of them." This book helped me understand why he is not judgmental! Emily is a talented young artist, though perhaps not as conventional as her classmates. When Emily's art is put in the school art contest, will it be judged fairly, and more important, will Emily be true to herself no matter what the judges may say? The pictures contain imaginative undertones as well; Emily's figure fades slightly as her identity as an artist wavers. When it comes to showing what we can do to support the artist in every child, Emily wins hands down. (6 and up)

Hammerstein, Oscar, and Richard Rodgers	• GETTING TO KNOW YOU! RODGERS AND HAMMERSTEIN FAVORITES
Hill, Elizabeth Starr	• CHANG AND THE BAMBOO FLUTE (Chapter book.)
Hoff, Syd	• ARTURO'S BATON
Hopkinson, Deborah	• A BAND OF ANGELS: A STORY INSPIRED BY THE JUBILEE SINGERS
Howe, James	• MORRIS AND HORACE JOIN THE CHORUS
Hurd, Thacher	• MAMA DON'T ALLOW
Karlins, Mark	• MUSIC OVER MANHATTAN
Koscielniak, Bruce	• THE STORY OF THE INCREDIBLE ORCHESTRA (Lots of history.)
Kuskin, Karla	• THE PHILHARMONIC GETS DRESSED
Lakin, Patricia	• SUBWAY SONATA
Levine, Robert	• THE STORY OF THE ORCHESTRA
Lithgow, John	• THE REMARKABLE FARKLE MCBRIDE
McCloskey, Robert	• LENTIL
McCully, Emily Arnold	• THE ORPHAN SINGER
McPhail, David	• MOLE MUSIC
Medearis, Angela Shelf	• THE SINGING MAN
Meyrick, Catherine	• THE MUSICAL LIFE OF GUSTAV MOLE
Miller, William	• THE PIANO
Moss, Lloyd	• ZIN! ZIN! ZIN! A VIOLIN
Namioka, Lensey	• YANG THE YOUNGEST AND HIS TERRIBLE EAR (Chapter book.)
Pinkney, Brian	• MAX FOUND TWO STICKS
Purdy, Carol	• MRS. MERRIWETHER'S MUSICAL CAT
Raschka, Chris	• MYSTERIOUS THELONIOUS • CHARLIE PARKER PLAYED BE BOP
Ray, Mary Lyn	• PIANNA
Rodowski, Colby	• JASON RAT-A-TAT (Chapter book.)
Romanelli, Serena	• LITTLE BOBO
Rosenberg, Jane	• SING ME A STORY: THE METROPOLITAN OPERA'S BOOK OF OPERA STORIES FOR CHILDREN
Waddell, Martin	• THE HAPPY HEDGEHOG BAND
Walter, Mildred Pitts	• TY'S ONE-MAN BAND

Weaver, Tess	• OPERA CAT
Weik, Mary Hays	• THE JAZZ MAN
Williams, Vera B.	• MUSIC, MUSIC FOR EVERYONE

Dance

Barber, Antonia	• SHOES OF SATIN, RIBBONS OF SILK
Crimi, Carolyn	• TESSA'S TIP-TAPPING TOES
Daly, Niki	• PAPA LUCKY'S SHADOW
Dillon, Leo and Diane	• RAP A TAP TAP: THINK OF THAT! (About dancer Bill "Bojangles" Robinson.)
Dorros, Arthur	• TEN GO TANGO
Edwards, Pamela Duncan	• HONK! THE STORY OF A PRIMA SWANERINA
Fonteyn, Margot	• COPPELIA • SWAN LAKE
Gray, Libba Moore	• MY MAMA HAD A DANCING HEART
Hest, Amy	• MABEL DANCING
Holabird, Katherine	• ANGELINA BALLERINA
Ichikawa, Satomi	• DANCE, TANYA
Isadora, Rachel	• LILI AT BALLET • MAX
Jacobson, Jennifer Richard	• WINNIE DANCING ON HER OWN
Komaiko, Leah	• AUNT ELAINE DOES THE DANCE FROM SPAIN
Mathers, Petra	• SOPHIE AND LOU
Mayer, Marianna	• THE TWELVE DANCING PRINCESSES
Newsome, Jill	• DREAM DANCER
Porter, Tracey	• A DANCE OF SISTERS (Mature readers.)
Sis, Peter	• BALLERINA
Staples, Suzanne Fisher	• SHIVA'S FIRE (Mature readers.)
Streatfeild, Noel	• BALLET SHOES (Classic chapter book for hard-core ballet fans.)
Walton, Rick	• HOW CAN YOU DANCE?

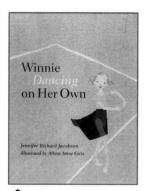

❀ *Potato Pick:*

WINNIE DANCING ON HER OWN

by Jennifer Richard Jacobson, illustrated by Alissa Imre Geis

A friendship triangle threatens to collapse when Winnie bumbles at ballet. This realistic story about staying true to yourself is a terrific chapter-book pick for those tricky second- and third-grade years, but *any* little girl would love this. The delicate line illustrations by Alissa Imre Geis make for a charming pas de deux and a stunning debut for both author and artist. Readers who enjoy books by Beverly Cleary and Eleanor Estes will find a friend in Winnie. (7 and up)

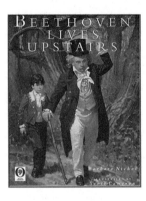

Biography

Anderson, M. T.	• HANDEL: WHO KNEW WHAT HE LIKED
Bjork, Christina	• LINNEA IN MONET'S GARDEN
Brenner, Barbara	• THE BOY WHO LOVED TO DRAW: BENJAMIN WEST
Celenza, Anna Harwell	• THE FAREWELL SYMPHONY (With CD.)
Christensen, Bonnie	• WOODY GUTHRIE: POET OF THE PEOPLE
Darrow, Sharon	• THROUGH THE TEMPESTS DARK AND WILD: A STORY OF MARY SHELLEY
Duggleby, John	• ARTIST IN OVERALLS: THE LIFE OF GRANT WOOD • STORY PAINTER: THE LIFE OF JACOB LAWRENCE
Freedman, Russell	• MARTHA GRAHAM: A DANCER'S LIFE
Gerstein, Mordicai	• WHAT CHARLIE HEARD (About composer Charles Ives.)
Gherman, Beverly	• ANSEL ADAMS: AMERICA'S PHOTOGRAPHER
Glover, Savion	• SAVION: MY LIFE IN TAP
Gollub, Matthew	• COOL MELONS—TURN TO FROGS! THE LIFE AND POEMS OF ISSA
Greenberg, Jan, and Sandra Jordan	• CHUCK CLOSE UP CLOSE
Isadora, Rachel	• ISADORA DANCES (About dancer Isadora Duncan.)
Isom, Joan Shaddox	• THE FIRST STARRY NIGHT (About painter Vincent van Gogh.)
Lasky, Kathryn	• A VOICE OF HER OWN: THE STORY OF PHILLIS WHEATLEY, SLAVE POET
Lester, Julius	• THE BLUES SINGERS: TEN WHO ROCKED THE WORLD
Medina, Tony	• LOVE TO LANGSTON (About poet Langston Hughes.)
Miller, William	• ZORA HURSTON AND THE CHINABERRY TREE
Nichol, Barbara	• BEETHOVEN LIVES UPSTAIRS
O'Connor, Barbara	• KATHERINE DUNHAM: PIONEER OF BLACK DANCE
Orgill, Roxane	• IF I ONLY HAD A HORN: YOUNG LOUIS ARMSTRONG • MAHALIA: A LIFE IN GOSPEL MUSIC • SHOUT, SISTER, SHOUT! (Ten girl singers who shaped a century; great selections from Ethel Merman to Madonna.)
Parker, Robert Andrew	• ACTION JACKSON (About painter Jackson Pollock.)
Patridge, Elizabeth	• RESTLESS SPIRIT: THE LIFE AND WORK OF DORTHEA LANGE

Pavlova, Anna	• I Dreamed I Was a Ballerina
Perdomo, Willie	• Visiting Langston (About poet Langston Hughes.)
Pinkney, Andrea Davis	• Alvin Ailey • Duke Ellington: The Piano Prince and His Orchestra • Ella Fitzgerald: The Tale of a Vocal Virtuosa
Ray, Deborah Kogan	• Hokusai: The Man Who Painted a Mountain
Reef, Catherine	• Walt Whitman
Ryan, Pam Muñoz	• When Marian Sang (About singer Marian Anderson.)
Schroeder, Alan	• Ragtime Tumpie (About dancer Josephine Baker.) • Satchmo's Blues (About trumpeter Louis Armstrong.)
Shafer, Anders C.	• The Fantastic Journey of Pieter Brueghel
Stanley, Diane	• Michelangelo
Sweeney, Joan	• Suzette and the Puppy: A Story about Mary Cassatt
Tallchief, Maria	• Tallchief: America's Prima Ballerina
Warhola, James	• Uncle Andy's: A Faabbbulous Visit with Andy Warhol
Winter, Jeanette	• Beatrix (About Beatrix Potter.) • Emily Dickinson's Letters to the World • Josefina (About clay artist Josefina Aguilar.) • My Name Is Georgia (About painter Georgia O'Keeffe.) • Sebastian: A Book About Bach
Winter, Jonah	• Diego (About painter Diego Rivera.) • Frida (About painter Frida Kahlo.) • Once upon a Time in Chicago: The Story of Benny Goodman

THE FINE ART OF MUSEUM HUNTING

When I was a fifth-grader and went on a field trip to the Art Institute of Chicago, my wise and art-loving teacher Mrs. Schultz had us stop at the gift shop *first*.

We each picked out a postcard of some artwork that appealed to us, and then we hunted for it in the museum, seeing lots of different pieces along the way. It made our visit *so* much more exciting. Now, when I take children to museums, I still love to match art treasures to postcards. Another ploy is to follow the lead of Museum ABC by the Metropolitan Museum of Art and try to find paintings with objects that begin with each letter of the alphabet. Pass on a museum-hunt tradition!

Also, check out the inspired **Getting to Know the World's Greatest Artists** series by Mike Venezia. Cartoons and straightforward language mixed with fine art will make a connoisseur out of your child. These are excellent for reader's theater "talk show" spots, too (see Yackety-Yack to Yesterday and Back, p. 229). The series includes biographies of all these masters:

BOTTICELLI	EL GRECO	MATISSE	TOULOUSE-
BRUEGHEL	GAUGUIN	MONET	L'AUTREC
CALDER	GIOTTO	O'KEEFFE	VAN GOGH
CASSATT	GOYA	PICASSO	WARHOL
CÉZANNE	HOPPER	POLLOCK	WOOD
CHAGALL	KAHLO	REMBRANDT	
DA VINCI	KLEE	RENOIR	
DALÍ	LANGE	ROCKWELL	
DEGAS	LAWRENCE		

Parade of Books

A "Parade of Books" is a special event that is surprisingly easy to plan for your school or community. Children, dressed up in homemade costumes as their favorite book character, march while carrying the corresponding book. Three friends (two of them in the fourth grade) and I planned a cheerful school parade for over four hundred marchers and it became an annual tradition. Here are our rules:

• No bloody, gory costumes . . . this is not a Halloween parade! (Note: Our Book Parades ran during the last week of September or the first week of October, so we were able to beat Halloween to the punch. Many children ended up using their literature-based costumes for Halloween.)

• No comic-book superheroes or trademarked characters (sorry, Rugrats and Pokemon). The rule of thumb was that children had to have read about their character in a book before they saw it on a TV show.

• No elaborate face makeup; children should be able to put on their own costumes.

Start planning about a month in advance. I was concerned that working parents would have a problem with the demands of helping their child make a costume, but instead, they really responded favorably to the time spent with their child deciding on and creating a costume in a noncompetitive atmosphere. Teachers will be more receptive to the event the less you ask them to do, so be organized. Here's a checklist of steps that will get you marching:

❑ Convince administration. Helpful buzzwords: "school spirit," "team-work," "parent involvement," "literature based," "library promotion," "affective reading goals."

❑ Set a date and time.

❑ Send out letters to parents about the parade (see Appendix D1) along with costume suggestions (Appendix D2).

❑ Visit classrooms to verbally explain expectations and costume guide-lines to children. I demonstrated easy costume-making techniques, like cat ears cut from construction paper and taped to a headband, making a Red Riding Hood out of a scarf, and construction paper crowns with scarf tied around the neck as a cape for Prince Charming. Emphasize creativity and do-it-yourself spirit, which is also helpful for those chil-dren who may end up making their own costumes.

❑ Inform teachers (see Appendix D3 for letter prototype).

❑ Optional: Rent costumed characters. If you are planning the parade at a school with available funds, contact Costume Specialists, 1-800-596-9357, to contract for splendid full-body and head costumes for delivery anywhere in the country. At one of our parades, we rented two: one to march at the start (Eric Hill's "Spot") and one at the end (Maurice Sendak's "Wild Thing"). These are always enormous crowd pleasers! Find a strong teenage or adult volunteer to wear the heavy rented costume, which is *extremely* hot. Make sure to have an icy drink available to hydrate the good sport. Additional tips for storybook char-acter costume bookings can be found at www.ssdesign.com/librarypr/content/p121697a.shtml.

❑ Buy long wooden dowel rods (available at hardware stores) so classes can make banners with their room numbers behind which to walk. The banners may be made of felt, or wide butcher or bulletin-board paper.

❑ Decorate a beautiful fancy banner that will start the parade. Ours stated simply, "Parade of Books."

❑ For our parade, children had to be costumed in order to march.

Make arrangements for those who come without costumes to sit and watch with another class. (Sometimes the upper grades elect to sit out the parade in a fit of sullen preteen isolationism, but pre-K up through even fifth grade can be counted on for enthusiastic participation.)

❏ Write a press release, and inform local media. Remember to tell them the five *w*'s: who, what, where, when, why, and they will come if they are able. Add the buzz words "photo op" and "human interest."

❏ Make a cassette of marching music. Get hold of a "boom box" radio. Buy batteries.

❏ Read parade books to get the littlest children excited: **PARADE** by Donald Crews, **THE BEST BUG PARADE** by Stuart J. Murphy, **AND TO THINK THAT I SAW IT ON MULBERRY STREET** by Dr. Seuss, and **THE LITTLE BAND** by James Sage. Older children can read aloud to younger ones.

❏ Make a map of the parade route. We marched on the inside and around the school. Distribute maps to teachers the day before the parade, along with reminders to have their dowel banners ready, and their students ready ten minutes before scheduled marching time. Have a "plan B" in case of rain!

❏ Send home reminders the week before.

❏ Verbally remind children of the parade the day before (use the school intercom if you can) and ask everyone to bring the book that inspired their costume, if it's available. Books can be carried during the march.

❏ Remind participating teachers the day before in writing, giving details on what they are expected to do.

On parade day, pick up the classes about fifteen minutes before scheduled marching and line them up. Turn on the march tape and go! Everybody wave and smile!

Once you do it one year, the parade will be a piece of cake for the next, which is a good thing, because this kind of fun has to be annual!

Storytime Central

Parades. Recipes. Festivals. Parties. Time machines. Performances. These are all wonderful and joyful and splendid, but you don't need to make a big production to be a reading hero. Simply round up the children and read to them. Pick a theme that will rouse your children's interest, choose a few books from the corresponding list, and read aloud. That's it. You're an instant hit and you are doing something for children that is not only fun, but essential, important, and lasting.

These booklists are designed with pre-K through second grade (approximately ages 4 through 7) in mind, with some chapter books and exceptions noted. In the course of creating the thematic lists, I have made no attempt to catalog every title that falls under the theme. Instead, the books recommended are all titles that I have personally read and *used*. Each title has been teacher tested, kid approved. But many, many more themes and books exist to be discovered by you! Children's librarians are still my favorite expedition team, but when you're spelunking solo, there are four incredible print references that will aid you in your search for storytime gold:

• Cobb, Jane, comp. I'M A LITTLE TEAPOT! PRESENTING PRESCHOOL STORYTIME (This book also has fingerplays and activities to go along with themes, and great songs for opening and closing storytime routines with young children.)

• Freeman, Judy. MORE BOOKS KIDS WILL SIT STILL FOR: A READ-ALOUD GUIDE (available at www.bowker.com)

• Lima, Carolyn W. and John A. A TO ZOO: SUBJECT ACCESS TO CHILDREN'S PICTURE BOOKS, Sixth Edition. (available at www.greenwood.com)

• R. R. Bowker. SUBJECT GUIDE TO CHILDREN'S BOOKS IN PRINT

Any time you have an idea for a theme (or anytime your child comes home from school with a subject to research for a report), look up the topic in any of these books, and you and your child will likely find a related book list as long as both your arms. If you become a family of

hard-core children's-book lovers, I recommend the first three reference books for your home collection. I use mine as often as I use the dictionary (which is a lot). They can usually be special-ordered through bookstores, or you can visit the site URLs where provided. Of course, you can always use them at the library.

Another ploy in big-game thematic book hunting is to visit a behemoth on-line bookstore such as www.amazon.com or www.barnesand noble.com, and do a search. One of the best ways to start the search is by finding just one title that is along the lines of what you had in mind and looking it up. Then scroll all the way down to the "Related Titles" or "More on This Subject" check-boxes, and initiate a search from there. You are more likely to hit the jackpot this way, because you are using categories that the search engine recognizes. I usually look to Judy Freeman's and Carolyn W. and John A. Lima's books before doing on-line searches. Because children's literature specialists created them, the lists are more credible and succinct. However, on-line searches can yield very current recommendations, so mix 'em up. And though big bookstores are great for searches, don't forget your local independent bookseller (www.booksense.com). These folks work hard to sell sleepers, and they are another helpful source for recommendations.

While these lists are great sources for books to read aloud with your own child, once you catch the storytime bug you will want to try reading aloud to a group of children. Start with your child's friends or volunteer to read your child's current favorite book to her school class. You can facilitate a group read-aloud in your house. Or in your backyard, front stoop, or garage. In a pet shop, in a supermarket, in a Laundromat, at a bowling alley, at the hairdresser's. At the zoo, in the park, at the pool. In a church, synagogue, or mosque. On an elevated train, in a subway. In a mall. In a doctor's office. I guess you might even be able to pull it off in a library. You can do this anywhere. *If you can read, you can do this.*

WHEN GIVING A STORYTIME TO A GROUP, REMEMBER TO KISS!

That is, **K**eep **I**t **S**imple, **S**marty.

1. Start with a clear welcome.

2. Share a few good books with a cohesive theme (using the Hints for Reading Out Loud, p. 11).

3. Finish with a closing routine.

Most of the storytimes I give consist of three to five titles, which amounts to about a half hour of reading, discussion, and looking at pictures. Don't strain young children's patience, if you know what's good for you. Less is often more. If you find a lot of books you like on a given theme, have more than one storytime, or lay them out for independent perusal after the storytime. I've included a quick activity or two (Creative Cues) within these lists for hard-core overachieving storytime hosts. Allow an extra fifteen minutes for crafts. And if you enjoy these kinds of creative extensions, be sure to try the **Story S-t-r-e-t-c-h-e-r-s** series by Shirley C. Raines and Robert J. Canady, and look for more ideas at The Best Kids Book Site, www.the bestkidsbooksite.com (a site that lives up to its name).

Picture Books Worth a Thousand Words

I have not included descriptions of the titles in these lists, because, in fact, many of the books can be described the same way when grouped by topic. LITTLE ELEPHANT by Miela Ford is about . . guess what? . . . a little elephant, but so is LITTLE BULL: GROWING UP IN AFRICA'S ELEPHANT KINGDOM by Ellen Foley James. The difference is, as always, what the author has to say, and how the book is executed. With picture books, illustrations are a major part of the story's treatment, and no amount of description can do this justice. The emotional impact of this artwork is subjective, but I'm completely confident you'll find that the titles listed here have qualities that are better than good. Find the ones that most appeal to you and your children. I have also included a few simple chapter books (books with fewer pictures and from which you can excerpt or read in their entirety) to help children learn that they are capable of enjoying books with less visual stimulation.

While these lists focus on picture books, these are not storytimes just for little children. Older children can participate in a different role—one similar to yours. They can think up themes. They can find books that go with that theme. They can become proficient at the Hints for Reading Out Loud (p. 11), and before long, they can actually deliver. So include older children in your storytimes. Let them watch as you share books, with the expectation that at some point they, too, will initiate and lead such happy gatherings.

HELLO, GOOD-BYE

GREET YOUR GROUP
Traditional storytime greeting song:
> Hello, hello, hello and how are you?
> I'm fine, I'm fine, and I hope that you are, too!

BID A FOND FARE-THEE-WELL
Storytime parting finger play:
> We all shared a story time!
> Eyes that look, (Point to eyes)
> Ears that listen, (Point to ears)
> Pictures all around. (Put hands together facing out, like pages in a book, and show them all around)
> Finger plays (Wiggle fingers) and clapping games, (Clap)
> Singing makes a lovely sound! (Touch throat)
> Sitting in a circle, what a lovely time.
> Wave good-bye until next week, (Wave)
> But read more books at home! (Hold palms of hands out in lap, like an open book)

ANDY LATIES
THE BOSS OF STORYTELLING

My storytelling mentor was my boss at The Children's Bookstore where I worked in Chicago. Andy Laties announced his daily storytelling sessions by blowing into a garden hose. Then he introduced himself to each of the children, who introduced themselves in turn. While he read, he was without ego. He simply channeled the book, complete with roars, car honks, and duck quacks. If a plot wasn't going in favor of the sympathetic character, he would slam the book shut and cry, "This is a horrible book for children!" and only reluctantly continue when the children begged and assured him that if there was an unhappy ending, they would help him wipe his nose. He seemed to have an endless repertoire of stories he knew by heart, and I mean *by heart*—a visceral enthusiasm permeated all his interactions with children, and in this way he was a great inspiration to me, and to many families for whom he modeled his effervescent technique. He taught me that when you are going to give a performance to children, give it up and give it all!

Andy was among the first booksellers to offer teacher discounts and rebates, and to encourage school field trips. While his store closed at the onset of the superstore takeovers, his pioneering model of bookstores taking an active role in community literacy is still replicated. He now helps run the Web site www.povertyfighters.com and works at the Eric Carle Museum of Picture Book Art in Amherst, Massachusetts, www.picturebookart.org.

Find heroic independent children's booksellers in your own backyard by visiting www.booksense.com, or go cyber-shopping at a few of my bookmarks: www.chinaberry.com, www.littlereader.com, or www.wildrumpus.com.

It has always amazed me that read-aloud is not more widely employed as part of the language arts curriculum in intermediate and upper grades. As a teacher, I always tried to make sure the students could read aloud or tell a story. I consider it a basic skill. In a program I ran from the school library, seventh- and eighth-graders were prepared to be proactive literates, or "reading renegades." They read the introduction and "Why Read Aloud?" chapter from Jim Trelease's **READ-ALOUD HANDBOOK,** which points out that people who are literate are less likely to do time in jail, and that literacy is tied to a higher standard of living. Then, the students read aloud as public service. Good deeds aside, I figured that most of the children were destined to become parents someday and would make use of their read-aloud skills. In fact, a goodly number turned out to be parents much sooner than I expected. When the children I taught made decisions that made their own lives more challenging, it was a comfort to know that they possessed a skill that would give their own "at-risk" children an edge, as well as some quality family time, if they chose to take advantage.

Young or old, everyone can begin a legacy of literacy in their own families and communities. It all starts with reading aloud.

Stories for a Rainy Day

Aardema, Verna	• BRINGING THE RAIN TO KAPITI PLAIN
Barrett, Judi	• CLOUDY WITH A CHANCE OF MEATBALLS
Blegvad, Lenore	• RAINY DAY KATE
Carle, Eric	• LITTLE CLOUD
Germein, Katrina	• BIG RAIN COMING
Ginsburg, Mirra	• MUSHROOM IN THE RAIN
Gorbachev, Valeri	• ONE RAINY DAY
Hesse, Karen	• COME ON, RAIN!
Kleven, Elisa	• THE PUDDLE PAIL
McPhail, David	• THE PUDDLE

Melmed, Laura Krauss	• THE RAINBABIES
Meyers, Odette	• THE ENCHANTED UMBRELLA
Polacco, Patricia	• THUNDERCAKE
Pomerantz, Charlotte	• THE PIGGY IN THE PUDDLE
Ray, Mary Lyn	• RED RUBBER BOOT DAY
Scheer, Julian	• RAIN MAKES APPLESAUCE
Seuss, Dr.	• THE CAT IN THE HAT
Shannon, David	• THE RAIN CAME DOWN
Spier, Peter	• PETER SPIER'S RAIN
Stojic, Manya	• RAIN
Yashima, Taro	• UMBRELLA

Family Stories

GRANDPARENT STORIES

Ackerman, Karen	• SONG AND DANCE MAN
Aliki	• THE TWO OF THEM
Arkin, Alan	• SOME FINE GRAMPA!
Cooney, Barbara	• MISS RUMPHIUS
Dorros, Arthur	• ABUELA
Dugan, Barbara	• LOOP THE LOOP
Farber, Norma	• HOW DOES IT FEEL TO BE OLD?
Fleischman, Paul	• LOST! A STORY IN STRING
Fox, Mem	• WILFRED GORDON MCDONALD PARTRIDGE
Hurwitz, Johanna	• "Chinese Dinner" from RIP-ROARING RUSSELL
James, Simon	• THE BIRDWATCHERS
Khalsa, Dayal Kaur	• HOW PIZZA CAME TO QUEENS
Marshall, James	• RED RIDING HOOD
Mathis, Sharon Bell	• THE HUNDRED PENNY BOX
McCully, Emily Arnold	• THE GRANDMA MIX-UP
	• GRANDMAS AT BAT
	• GRANDMAS AT THE LAKE
Mills, Claudia	• GUS AND GRANDPA AND SHOW-AND-TELL
Muten, Burleigh	• GRANDMOTHERS' STORIES: WISE WOMAN TALES FROM MANY CULTURES

✿ *Potato Pick:*
THE HICKORY CHAIR
by Lisa Rowe Fraustino,
illustrated by Benny Andrews

Gran had a good "alive smell": lilacs, with a whiff of bleach. Louis loves that smell and her molasses voice as she reads to him out loud. And he loves playing hide-and-seek with her. When the sad day comes and Gran dies, it turns out she has left one last game of hide-and-seek. She has bequeathed her favorite things to her favorite people in secret spots. Can Louis use his "blind sight" to find Grandma's keepsakes for his family and for himself? The descriptions from the point of view of the boy who is, in fact, blind are incredibly rich and sensitive. Benny Andrews's paintings have been displayed in museums throughout the world. His long, solid figures add both grace and gravity to the story. Don't let your child miss a chance to climb into Gran's hickory chair and experience what is bittersweet. (7 and up)

CAROL DIGGORY SHIELDS • Illustrated by HIROE NAKATA

✿ *Potato Pick:*

LUCKY PENNIES AND HOT CHOCOLATE

by Carol Diggory Shields, illustrated by Hiroe Nakata

"My favorite person in the world is coming to visit," begins this cozy story of a boy and his grandfather. There are so many things to share and do: telling knock-knock jokes, watching a movie (as long as it's not too talky or kissy), inventing a new pancake recipe, playing ball. The list of things they like to do, and don't like to do, is told in an authentic voice that is as fresh as a snowflake on the tongue. The illustrations are bouncy and bright and convey the love between these special friends. Children will find that the best part of all, though, is the surprise ending. A perfect lap book for two of your favorite guys. (4 and up)

... And for the official Grandparent's Day Web site, visit www.grandparentsday.com.

Dear Madame Esmé,

We are divorced with joint custody. Please recommend a book our young child can enjoy on both Daddy Days and Mommy Days.

Dear Gentle Reader,

Reading is a great way for divorced parents to work together in a child's interests. Bravo to you! Though I don't usually go in much for "bibliotherapy" or "issue" books, TWO HOMES by Claire Masurel is done with such grace that it reaches way beyond being a book about divorce. It's about a child feeling loved, secure, and happy in two places. Alex gives us a tour of both his homes: his Dad's at the lake, and his Mom's city apartment. "I have two kitchens," he explains. "I have two bathrooms." And in the end, Alex has two parents, whose voices are heard in the final pages. "We love you wherever we are. And we love you wherever you are." The book is never maudlin; in fact, it is genuinely cheerful and interesting to see Alex's homes. This is in no small part due to illustrator Kady MacDonald Denton's absolutely masterful artistic treatment, full of sunny details such as Alex's watercolor paintings of his parents and the generous sampling of smiles throughout. The pictures carry such an unspoken emotional depth that you and your listener will find yourselves lingering in the moments portrayed. I wouldn't hesitate to give this to any child four or older, regardless of family situation. While children whose parents have separated will find a calming sense of normalcy within the pages, it is actually a great introduction for young children who have friends whose parents are divorced and don't understand the deal.

Mommy Stories

Adler, David A.	• Mama Played Baseball
Banks, Kate	• Mama's Coming Home
Brami, Élisabeth	• Mommy Time
Bridges, Margaret Park	• Will You Take Care of Me?
Day, Nancy Raines	• The Lion's Whiskers (Kind stepmother!)
Eastman, P. D.	• Are You My Mother?
Evetts-Secker, Josephine	• The Barefoot Book of Mother and Son Tales • Mother and Daughter Tales
Goode, Diane	• Where's Our Mama?
Hazen, Barbara Shook	• Even If I Did Something Awful
Ho, Minfong	• Hush! A Thai Lullaby
Jonell, Lynne	• Mom Pie
Joosse, Barbara M.	• Mama, Do You Love Me?
Kasza, Keiko	• Mother for Choco
Leuck, Laura	• My Monster Mama Loves Me So
MacLachlan, Patricia	• Sarah, Plain and Tall (Stepmother; short chapter book.)
Minarik, Else Holmelund	• Am I Beautiful?
Polushkin, Maria	• Mother, Mother, I Want Another
Scott, Ann Herbert	• On Mother's Lap
Ungerer, Tomi	• No Kiss for Mother
Waddell, Martin	• Owl Babies
Weeks, Sarah	• Angel Face
Wells, Rosemary	• Hazel's Amazing Mother
Zolotow, Charlotte	• The Quiet Mother and the Noisy Little Boy • This Quiet Lady

Daddy Stories

Berenstain, Stanley and Janice	• The Big Honey Hunt
Brown, Margaret Wise	• The Little Scarecrow Boy
Browne, Anthony	• My Dad
Carle, Eric	• Papa, Please Get the Moon for Me
Creech, Sharon	• Fishing in the Air

✿ *Potato Pick:*

Little Oh

by Laura Krauss Melmed, illustrated by Jim LaMarche

One of the most popular books in school libraries is always The Rainbabies by Laura Krauss Melmed, illustrated by Jim LaMarche, so I was very excited when the dynamic team joined forces again to create this magical original folktale. A daughter is constructed out of origami by a lonely woman, and through a series of adventures, the daughter is separated from her beloved creator, only to be reunited in a surprise ending. I also like this book because it portrays stepparents in a tender light. (6 and up)

THIS QUIET LADY

Charlotte Zolotow · Anita Lobel

Mother's Day, Father's Day, Grandparent's Day . . .

What mom, dad, or grandparent wouldn't appreciate a basket of books just perfect for reading aloud to the tykes that made everyone a family? Throw in some homemade coupons for cuddles and stories on demand, with no expiration date!

❀ *Potato Pick:*

THE PAPER PRINCESS
by Elisa Kleven

A celebration of the life that creative projects take on and of the bond between brother and sister, this story centers on a little girl who draws her own princess out of paper, only to have it carried away by the wind. The Paper Princess is returned home after a blow through town. The collage illustrations are like watching a fireworks show or looking over a crazy quilt—you see something new every time you look. (5 and up)

Degen, Bruce	• DADDY IS A DOODLEBUG
Demi	• THE GREATEST TREASURE
DiTerlizzi, Tony	• TED
Evetts-Secker, Josephine	• THE BAREFOOT BOOK OF FATHER AND SON TALES
Guettier, Benedicte	• THE FATHER WHO HAD 10 CHILDREN
Hines, Anna Grossnickle	• DADDY MAKES THE BEST SPAGHETTI
Hoban, Russell	• THE MOUSE AND HIS CHILD (Chapter book.)
Jenkins, Martin	• THE EMPEROR'S EGG
Kirk, Daniel	• HUSH, LITTLE ALIEN
McCleery, William	• WOLF STORY (Chapter book.)
McMullan, Kate and Jim	• PAPA'S SONG
Numeroff, Laura	• WHAT MOMMIES DO BEST/WHAT DADDIES DO BEST
Seeger, Pete	• ABIYOYO
Steptoe, Javaka	• IN DADDY'S ARMS I AM TALL: AFRICAN AMERICANS CELEBRATING FATHERS
Wells, Philip	• DADDY ISLAND
Wood, Douglas	• WHAT DADS CAN'T DO
Yolen, Jane	• THE EMPEROR AND THE KITE

SIBLING STORIES

Alborough, Jez	• WATCH OUT! BIG BRO'S COMING!
Bartone, Elisa	• PEPPE THE LAMPLIGHTER
Berenstain, Stan and Jan	• THE BERENSTAIN BEARS' NEW BABY
Bishop, Claire Huchet	• THE FIVE CHINESE BROTHERS
Blume, Judy	• THE PAIN AND THE GREAT ONE
	• SUPERFUDGE (Chapter book series.)
	• TALES OF A FOURTH GRADE NOTHING (Chapter book.)
Byars, Betsy	• HOORAY FOR THE GOLLY SISTERS!
	• THE GOLLY SISTERS GO WEST

Cameron, Ann	• THE STORIES JULIAN TELLS
Cleary, Beverly	• BEEZUS AND RAMONA (Chapter book series.)
Ericsson, Jennifer A.	• SHE DID IT!
Grimm Brothers	• HANSEL AND GRETEL • LITTLE BROTHER AND LITTLE SISTER
Havill, Juanita	• JAMAICA TAG-ALONG
Hayes, Sarah	• EAT UP, GEMMA
Henkes, Kevin	• JULIUS: THE BABY OF THE WORLD • SHEILA RAE, THE BRAVE
Hindley, Judy	• THE PERFECT LITTLE MONSTER
Hoban, Russell	• A BABY SISTER FOR FRANCES (All the **Frances** series is full of family.)
Hughes, Shirley	• THE BIG ALFIE AND ANNIE ROSE STORYBOOK (Any **Alfie** books are great family fare.) • DOGGER
Hurwitz, Johanna	• RUSSELL AND ELISA (Chapter book; tons of great brother-sister play throughout the **Riverside Kids** series.)
Hutchins, Pat	• SILLY BILLY! • THE VERY WORST MONSTER
Kleven, Elisa	• THE PAPER PRINCESS
Kvasnosky, Laura McGee	• ZELDA AND IVY
McClintock, Barbara	• MOLLY AND THE MAGIC WISHBONE (Adapted from a story by Charles Dickens . . . lovely!)
Melmed, Laura Krauss	• LITTLE OH
Mosel, Arlene	• TIKKI TIKKI TEMBO
Polacco, Patricia	• MY ROTTEN RED-HEADED OLDER BROTHER
Richler, Mordecai	• JACOB TWO-TWO MEETS THE HOODED FANG (Chapter book.)
Robinson, Barbara	• THE BEST CHRISTMAS PAGEANT EVER (Chapter book.)
Samuels, Barbara	• DUNCAN & DOLORES
Segal, Lore	• TELL ME A MITZI
Sidney, Margaret	• THE FIVE LITTLE PEPPERS AND HOW THEY GREW (Chapter book.)
Silverman, Erica	• FOLLOW THE LEADER

🌸 *Potato Pick:*

MIMMY & SOPHIE
by Miriam Cohen, illustrated by Thomas F. Yezerski

Dedicated "to Brooklyn and the Little Mimmy I once was," this book offers four memories from the Depression, featuring two sisters, told with lots of heart and little schmaltz. Besides being sensitive studies in sibling relationships, an undercurrent of appreciation for the small joys in life runs through all the stories. Generously illustrated with sketchy pen-and-ink drawings in the style of old-time etchings, the book produces the same satisfying comfort one feels watching an old black-and-white movie on a rainy Sunday afternoon. (5 and up)

VINTAGE FAMILY FARE

Call the kinfolk 'round to meet some old-fashioned families! The Cleavers and the Brady Bunch have nothing on these chapter-book clans.

Enright, Elizabeth	THE SATURDAYS
Estes, Eleanor	THE MOFFATS
Gilbreth Jr., Frank, and Ernestine Gilbreth Carey	CHEAPER BY THE DOZEN
Lovelace, Maud Hart	BETSY-TACY
Sidney, Margaret	THE FIVE LITTLE PEPPERS AND HOW THEY GREW
Taylor, Sydney	ALL-OF-A-KIND FAMILY

Snicket, Lemony	• THE BAD BEGINNING (Chapter book, mature readers.)
Steig, William	• THE TOY BROTHER
Van Allsburg, Chris	• JUMANJI • ZATHURA
Warner, Gertrude Chandler	• THE BOXCAR CHILDREN (Chapter book series.)
Wells, Rosemary	• BUNNY CAKES • BUNNY MONEY • MAX'S DRAGON SHIRT (All of Wells's **Max** books contain spectacular sibling stuff.)
Weninger, Brigitte	• WHAT HAVE YOU DONE, DAVY?
Wheeler, Lisa	• TURK AND RUNT
Wishinsky, Frieda	• OONGA BOONGA
Wolff, Ashley	• STELLA & ROY
Yezerski, Thomas F.	• QUEEN OF THE WORLD

BOOKS THAT CELEBRATE ADOPTION

Curtis, Jamie Lee	• TELL ME AGAIN ABOUT THE NIGHT I WAS BORN
Kasza, Keiko	• A MOTHER FOR CHOCO
Katz, Karen	• OVER THE MOON
Keller, Holly	• HORACE
Koehler, Phoebe	• THE DAY WE MET YOU (Acknowledges open adoption.)
Lewis, Rose	• I LOVE YOU LIKE CRAZY CAKES

McCutcheon, John	• HAPPY ADOPTION DAY!
Okimoto, Jean Davies, and Elaine Aoki	• THE WHITE SWAN EXPRESS
Reiser, Lynn	• THE SURPRISE FAMILY
Steptoe, John	• STEVIE (Foster parenting.)

AND THE WHOLE FAMILY WILL ENJOY . . .

Anholt, Catherine and Laurence	• BIG BOOK OF FAMILIES
dePaola, Tomie	• 26 FAIRMOUNT AVENUE (Chapter book series.)
Heide, Florence Parry	• OH, GROW UP! POEMS TO HELP YOU SURVIVE PARENTS, CHORES, SCHOOL, AND OTHER AFFLICTIONS
Hoberman, Mary Ann	• FATHERS, MOTHERS, SISTERS, BROTHERS: A COLLECTION OF FAMILY POEMS
Horvath, Polly	• THE TROLLS (Chapter book.)

The Finer Points of Making (and Keeping) Friends

Aliki	• FEELINGS
	• MANNERS
Carlson, Nancy	• HOW TO LOSE ALL YOUR FRIENDS
Clements, Andrew	• BIG AL
Cohen, Miriam	• WILL I HAVE A FRIEND?
Cooper, Helen	• PUMPKIN SOUP
Crimi, Carolyn	• DON'T NEED FRIENDS
Dugan, Barbara	• LOOP THE LOOP
Elliot, Laura	• HUNTER'S BEST FRIEND AT SCHOOL
Freeman, Don	• DANDELION
Freymann, Saxton, and Joost Elffers	• ONE LONELY SEA HORSE
Heine, Helme	• FRIENDS
Hobbie, Holly	• TOOT & PUDDLE: TOP OF THE WORLD
Howe, James	• HORACE AND MORRIS AND MOSTLY DOLORES
Keats, Ezra Jack	• A LETTER TO AMY
Krasny, Laurie, and Marc Brown	• HOW TO BE A FRIEND: A GUIDE TO MAKING FRIENDS AND KEEPING THEM

CREATIVE CUE

For a **RAINBOW FISH** *read-aloud, cut "scales" out of prismatic paper to give away at the end of the story!*

CREATIVE CUE

Throw a Teddy Bear Picnic! Play the classic song "The Teddy Bears' Picnic" (sung very nicely by Michael Feinstein on his audio **Pure Imagination** *but easy to find on lots of children's audio collections) while you have a beary friendly storytime on a picnic blanket. Honey graham crackers and apple juice make a fine snack, or if you're feeling ambitious, make sandwiches cut out with bear-shaped cookie cutters. A roll of wide red ribbon will allow you to make dressy bow-ties for all your guests' furry friends.*

Lobel, Arnold	• FROG AND TOAD ARE FRIENDS (And the whole **Frog and Toad** series.)
Marshall, James	• GEORGE AND MARTHA: THE COMPLETE STORIES OF TWO BEST FRIENDS
	• THE CUT-UPS (Series.)
Mathers, Petra	• LOTTIE'S NEW FRIEND
Monson, A. M.	• WANTED: BEST FRIEND
Munson, Derek	• ENEMY PIE
Murphy, Jill	• ALL FOR ONE
Parr, Todd	• IT'S OKAY TO BE DIFFERENT
Pfister, Marcus	• THE RAINBOW FISH
Raschka, Chris	• YO! YES?
Rohmann, Eric	• MY FRIEND RABBIT
Schwartz, Amy	• THE BOYS TEAM
Stewart, Paul	• THE BIRTHDAY PRESENTS
Udry, Janice May	• LET'S BE ENEMIES
Viorst, Judith	• I'LL FIX ANTHONY
	• ROSIE AND MICHAEL
Waber, Bernard	• IRA SLEEPS OVER
Weninger, Brigitte	• WHY ARE YOU FIGHTING, DAVY?

The Animal Kingdom

THE BEAR NECESSITIES

Alborough, Jez	• WHERE'S MY TEDDY?
Asch, Frank	• MOONGAME (Lots of good bear books by this author.)
Brown, Margaret Wise	• THE LITTLE FUR FAMILY
Candlewick Press	• THE CANDLEWICK BOOK OF BEAR STORIES
Dalgliesh, Alice	• THE BEARS ON HEMLOCK MOUNTAIN
Dyer, Jane	• LITTLE BROWN BEAR WON'T TAKE A NAP!
Falk, Barbara Bustetter	• GRUSHA
Freeman, Don	• CORDUROY
Ginsburg, Mirra	• TWO GREEDY BEARS
Gipson, Morrell	• MR. BEAR SQUASH-YOU-ALL-FLAT
Hissey, Jane	• OLD BEAR TALES (Sweet *Old Bear* videos available from Library Video Company, 1-800-843-3620.)

Kennedy, Jimmy	• TEDDY BEARS' PICNIC (I like the version illustrated by Alexandra Day.)
Kuiper, Nannie	• BAILEY AND THE BEAR CUB
Marshall, Janet	• A HONEY OF A DAY
McCloskey, Robert	• BLUEBERRIES FOR SAL
Minarik, Else Homelund	• A KISS FOR LITTLE BEAR
Rosen, Michael	• WE'RE GOING ON A BEAR HUNT
Ryder, Joanne	• BIG BEAR BALL
Traditional	• THE THREE BEARS (I prefer the edition illustrated by Feodor Rojankovsky.)

. . . More teddy bears in Toyland Friends, p. 402.

MONKEY BUSINESS

Alborough, Jez	• HUG
Anholt, Catherine and Laurence	• CHIMP AND ZEE
Bornstein, Ruth	• LITTLE GORILLA
Browne, Anthony	• GORILLA • WILLY THE WIMP
Buehner, Caralyn and Mark	• THE ESCAPE OF MARVIN THE APE
Bynum, Janie	• ALTOONA BABOONA
Christelow, Eileen	• DON'T WAKE UP MAMA! A FIVE LITTLE MONKEYS STORY • FIVE LITTLE MONKEYS JUMPING ON THE BED • FIVE LITTLE MONKEYS SITTING IN A TREE • FIVE LITTLE MONKEYS WITH NOTHING TO DO
Gelman, Rita Golden	• MORE SPAGHETTI, I SAY! • WHY CAN'T I FLY?
Goode, Diane	• MONKEY MO GOES TO SEA
Morozumi, Atsuko	• MY FRIEND GORILLA • ONE GORILLA
Perkins, Al	• HAND, HAND, FINGERS, THUMB
Rathmann, Peggy	• GOOD NIGHT, GORILLA
Rey, Margret and H. A.	• THE COMPLETE ADVENTURES OF CURIOUS GEORGE
Sierra, Judy	• COUNTING CROCODILES
Slobodkina, Esphyr	• CAPS FOR SALE

YES, WE HAVE NO BANANAS TODAY!

A great deal of trouble was taken to deliver the primate prince of children's literature to the throne. Legend has it that while the Nazis were pouring into Paris in 1940, Hans and Margret Rey were making their getaway by homemade bicycle. Bouncing along in the handlebar basket was the original manuscript for CURIOUS GEORGE. The Reys rode their bikes for four days until they reached the French-Spanish border, where they sold their bicycles for train fare to Lisbon. From Lisbon they went to Brazil, and then onward to New York City, and into the annals of publishing history.

The **Curious George** series, mirroring the marvelous mischief of children with unrivaled empathy, deserves every bit of the attention it has received over the years. In spots, the books are somewhat dated and almost bizarre. And I'm sure anyone aligned with animal rights is irked by the abduction from the jungle that begins the series. George smokes cigars, swallows puzzle pieces, paints on walls, sniffs ether, and jumps from fire escapes. Children, of course, love every minute of this, because they are a safe distance from the consequences of such naughtiness.

I myself become visibly chagrined every time I read aloud how The Man with the Yellow Hat flippantly leaves George in the hospital. "Then he left. George just sat there and cried." Oh, I get so mad. What sort of Monkey's Uncle is this Man with the Yellow Hat, any-

way, leaving him all alone? Why, if he had been supervising George like he was supposed to, George would have never ended up in the hospital in the first place! And now, he's rushing off. Where does he have to go that's so important? That's it! I'm reporting this to social services! But no, it is only a story . . . and that's easy to forget. The stories so abound with familiar foibles that everyone can find themselves in the fiction. And the crux of every adventure is the childlike virtue of curiosity—while it may have killed the cat, it certainly hasn't done the monkey any harm, with over twenty-five million readers and not a day out of print.

I like to read every one of the original series out loud to first-graders:

CURIOUS GEORGE

CURIOUS GEORGE FLIES A KITE

CURIOUS GEORGE GETS A MEDAL

CURIOUS GEORGE GOES TO THE HOSPITAL

CURIOUS GEORGE LEARNS THE ALPHABET

CURIOUS GEORGE RIDES A BIKE

CURIOUS GEORGE TAKES A JOB

(These are also available in a single volume, THE COMPLETE ADVENTURES OF CURIOUS GEORGE, which is kind of heavy for holding up for read-aloud with large groups but is fine for laptime or for a special gift.)

You can also make available the more recently conceived **New Adventures Featuring Curious George**, which are not written or illustrated by the Reys but "illustrated in the style" by Vipah Interactive. This could have easily been a deplorable marketing ploy to thinly stretch the monkey menu, but the series isn't sleazy, and actually succeeds. The adventures continue to be exciting and detailed, and while the artistic compositions are arguably not as sophisticated as the originals, it is clear that great efforts were made to maintain the integrity of the Rey's style. For children who are going ape for more, this is a perfectly charming bunch.

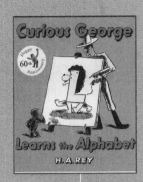

CURIOUS GEORGE AND THE DUMP TRUCK

CURIOUS GEORGE AND THE HOT AIR BALLOON

CURIOUS GEORGE AND THE PUPPIES

CURIOUS GEORGE AT THE PARADE

CURIOUS GEORGE FEEDS THE ANIMALS

CURIOUS GEORGE GOES CAMPING

CURIOUS GEORGE GOES TO A CHOCOLATE FACTORY

CURIOUS GEORGE GOES TO A COSTUME PARTY

CURIOUS GEORGE GOES TO A MOVIE

CURIOUS GEORGE GOES TO THE BEACH

CURIOUS GEORGE IN THE BIG CITY

CURIOUS GEORGE IN THE SNOW

CURIOUS GEORGE MAKES PANCAKES

CURIOUS GEORGE'S DREAM

CURIOUS CHILDREN MAKE A BOOK!

Once children are familiar with the series, they can dictate and illustrate their own Curious George stories. This is easy because the books follow a very

clearly defined formula for adventure, in which curiosity drives the decisions that direct the plot; very well-trodden and logical territory for a school-aged child. By creating their own stories, children can generate their own mischief fantasies in the context of their own life experience. I particularly enjoyed, for example, "Curious George Goes to the Basketball Game" and "Curious George Bombs the Computer," written by young friends of mine. If you have a lot of little children who want to make George books, enlist the help of older children to take dictation.

When I taught, after we had read all the original George books and written our own, I made a medal for each child featuring the final illustration from CURIOUS GEORGE GETS A MEDAL, in which George is looking in the mirror admiring his own achievement. I copied the illustration and added some encouraging words. Then I cut it out in a circle shape, glued gold glitter around the edge, added a blue ribbon and a safety pin, and voilà, reading achievement was recognized. Of course, we ate lots of bananas to mark the occasion as well.

MICE ARE NICE!

Asch, Frank, and Vladimir Vagin	• HERE COMES THE CAT!
Aylesworth, Jim	• THE COMPLETED HICKORY DICKORY DOCK
Brown, Ruth	• A DARK, DARK TALE
Cleary, Beverly	• THE MOUSE AND THE MOTORCYCLE (Chapter book.)
Cousins, Lucy	• MAISY SERIES
Freeman, Don	• NORMAN THE DOORMAN
Godden, Rumer	• MOUSE HOUSE
Hoberman, Mary Ann	• THE MARVELOUS MOUSE MAN
King-Smith, Dick	• THE SCHOOL MOUSE (Chapter book.)
Kraus, Robert	• WHOSE MOUSE ARE YOU?
Lionni, Leo	• FREDERICK
Numeroff, Laura Joffe	• IF YOU GIVE A MOUSE A COOKIE
Pfister, Marcus	• MILO AND THE MAGICAL STONES
Riley, Linnea	• MOUSE MESS
Sabuda, Robert	• COOKIE COUNT
Seidler, Tor	• A RAT'S TALE (Chapter book; good serial read-aloud.)
Steptoe, John	• THE STORY OF JUMPING MOUSE
Waber, Bernard	• THE MOUSE THAT SNORED
Wilbur, Richard	• LOUDMOUSE
Wood, Don and Audrey	• THE LITTLE MOUSE, THE RED RIPE STRAWBERRY, AND THE BIG HUNGRY BEAR

SOMETHING FISHY

Carle, Eric	• A HOUSE FOR HERMIT CRAB
Clements, Andrew	• BIG AL
Davies, Nicola	• BIG BLUE WHALE
Demi	• THE MAGIC GOLDFISH
Freymann, Saxton, and Joost Elffers	• ONE LONELY SEA HORSE
Grimm Brothers	• THE FISHERMAN AND HIS WIFE (I like the version translated by Randall Jarrell, illustrated by Margot Zemach.)

Andrew Clements Yoshi BIG AL

Lionni, Leo	• SWIMMY
Mahy, Margaret	• THE GREAT WHITE MAN-EATING SHARK: A CAUTIONARY TALE
Mayo, Margaret	• "The Kingdom Under the Sea" from MAGICAL TALES FROM MANY LANDS
McKissack, Patricia	• A MILLION FISH . . . MORE OR LESS
Osborne, Mary Pope	• MERMAID TALES FROM AROUND THE WORLD
Palmer, Helen	• A FISH OUT OF WATER
Pfister, Marcus	• THE RAINBOW FISH
Rose, Deborah Lee	• INTO THE A, B, SEA
San Souci, Robert D.	• NICHOLAS PIPE • SUKEY AND THE MERMAID
Spohn, Kate	• THE MERMAIDS' LULLABY
Toft, Kim Michelle, and Allan Sheather	• NEPTUNE'S NURSERY
Troll, Ray	• SHARKABET: A SEA OF SHARKS FROM A TO Z
Van Laan, Nancy	• LITTLE FISH, LOST
Wallace, Karen	• GENTLE GIANT OCTOPUS
Wu, Norbert	• FISH FACES
Yorinks, Arthur	• LOUIS THE FISH

CREATIVE CUE

Make underwater relief scenes to go along with any fishy storytime. Using wax crayons, children can draw colorful scenes of what they know and imagine to live beneath the waves. Then, cover the drawings completely with blue and green watercolor paints to make the pictures wonderfully watery.

WHO'S AFRAID OF THE BIG BAD WOLF (OR FOX)?

Aylesworth, Jim	• THE TALE OF TRICKY FOX
Bloom, Becky	• WOLF!
Bodnar, Judit Z.	• TALE OF A TAIL
Christelow, Eileen	• WHERE'S THE BIG BAD WOLF?
Dahl, Roald	• FANTASTIC MR. FOX (Chapter book.)
Denslow, Sharon Phillips	• BIG WOLF AND LITTLE WOLF
Galdone, Paul	• THE GINGERBREAD BOY • THE THREE LITTLE PIGS • WHAT'S IN FOX'S SACK?
Harper, Wilhelmina	• THE GUNNIWOLF
Hutchins, Pat	• ROSIE'S WALK
Hyman, Trina Schart	• LITTLE RED RIDING HOOD (Also try the versions illustrated by James Marshall and Marjorie Priceman.)

CREATIVE CUE

Let read-aloud lead into a clever research activity. Before reading stories about foxes or wolves, discuss and list everything already believed to be known about these animals. After reading the stories, do all the beliefs still hold true? Children can pick other animals and explore facts and fallacies through nonfiction and folk literature. Are owls really wise? Are pigs really dirty? Are lions really the kings of the jungle?

🥔 *Potato Pick:*

MAX: THE STUBBORN LITTLE WOLF

by Marie-Odile Judes, illustrated by Martine Bourre

Max's father is a real he-man. Or rather, he-wolf. "Wolf fathers and sons are hunters, have always been hunters, and always will be hunters . . . and that is that!" But that *isn't* that, because Max is a vegetarian who cheerfully proclaims his lifelong dream: to become a florist. Max's father's chagrin is hilariously portrayed. My favorite illustration is Max running ahead to warn a vulnerable rabbit of his father's approach, while Papa looks on in shock. The tension in the story is very real as Max's father employs a series of schemes to change Max's tune. While father's frustration is never completely resolved, Max is still the victorious hero, proving that a seed still grows into its own tree, or wolf, or child, no matter who plants it. (4 and up)

Judes, Marie-Odile	• MAX: THE STUBBORN LITTLE WOLF
Kasza, Keiko	• THE WOLF'S CHICKEN STEW
Keizaburo, Tejima	• FOX'S DREAM
Marshall, James	• WINGS: A TALE OF TWO CHICKENS
Masurel, Claire	• BIG BAD WOLF
McCleery, William	• WOLF STORY (Chapter book.)
McKissack, Patricia	• FLOSSIE & THE FOX
Meddaugh, Susan	• THE BEST PLACE
Nickl, Peter	• THE STORY OF THE KIND WOLF
Prokofiev, Sergei	• PETER AND THE WOLF (Try the pop-up illustrated version by Barbara Cooney. Also be sure to listen to the symphony by Prokofiev.)
Scieszka, Jon	• THE TRUE STORY OF THE 3 LITTLE PIGS!
Silverman, Erica	• DON'T FIDGET A FEATHER!
Simon, Seymour	• WOLVES
Steig, William	• DOCTOR DE SOTO
Storr, Catherine	• CLEVER POLLY AND THE STUPID WOLF (Chapter book.)
Watson, Clyde	• FATHER FOX'S PENNYRHYMES
Watson, Wendy	• FOX WENT OUT ON A CHILLY NIGHT
Williams, Sue	• DINNERTIME!

FROG STORIES TO MAKE YOU HOPPY

Ada, Alma Flor	• FRIEND FROG
Arnold, Tedd	• GREEN WILMA
Brown, Ruth	• TOAD
Cain, Sheridan	• LOOK OUT FOR THE BIG BAD FISH!
Cecil, Laura	• THE FROG PRINCESS
Faulkner, Keith, and Jonathan Lambert	• THE WIDE-MOUTHED FROG: A POP-UP BOOK
French, Vivan	• GROWING FROGS
Gwynne, Fred	• PONDLARKER
Kalan, Robert	• JUMP, FROG, JUMP!
Kilborne, Sarah S.	• PEACH & BLUE

GREEN WILMA
Tedd Arnold

Growing Frogs
Vivian French

Langstaff, John	• FROG WENT A-COURTIN'
Lobel, Arnold	• FROG AND TOAD ALL YEAR
	• FROG AND TOAD ARE FRIENDS
	• FROG AND TOAD TOGETHER
London, Jonathan	• FROGGY GETS DRESSED (And the whole **Froggy** series!)
Ormerod, Jan	• THE FROG PRINCE
Steig, William	• GORKY RISES
Walsh, Ellen Stoll	• HOP JUMP
Zemach, Harve and Kaethe	• THE PRINCESS AND FROGGIE

SQUIRRELY FOR BOOKS

Drummond, V. H.	• PHEWTUS THE SQUIRREL
Ehlert, Lois	• NUTS TO YOU!
Ernst, Lisa Campbell	• SQUIRREL PARK
Hurwitz, Johanna	• PEE-WEE'S TALE (Chapter book series.)
Stevenson, James	• THE FLYING ACORNS
Wildsmith, Brian	• SQUIRRELS
Young, Miriam	• MISS SUZY

TALES FROM THE BARNYARD

Arquette, Kerry	• WHAT DID YOU DO TODAY?
Aymé, Marcel	• THE WONDERFUL FARM
Barton, Byron	• THE WEE LITTLE WOMAN
Brown, Craig	• BARN RAISING
	• TRACTOR
Brown, Margaret Wise	• BIG RED BARN
Chitwood, Suzanne Tanner	• WAKE UP, BIG BARN!
Conrad, Pam	• THE ROOSTER'S GIFT
Cronin, Doreen	• CLICK, CLACK, MOO: COWS THAT TYPE
Duffy, Dee Dee	• BARNYARD TRACKS
Ericsson, Jennifer	• NO MILK!
Galdone, Paul	• CAT GOES FIDDLE-I-FEE
Gibbons, Gail	• THE MILK MAKERS
Hale, Sarah Josepha	• MARY HAD A LITTLE LAMB (Illustrated by Salley Mavor.)

🍀 *Potato Pick:*

JUBAL'S WISH
by Audrey Wood, illustrated by Don Wood

The team that brought us such stunning works as THE NAPPING HOUSE, HECKEDY PEG, and KING BIDGOOD'S IN THE BATHTUB has delivered more eye candy with the story of a smiling little frog who finds his friends are down in the dumps. Jubal's merry mood will be contagious to readers, but unfortunately, Jubal's buddies can't seem to catch his case of the cheeries. When a twist of fate offers Jubal a wish to be granted, he selflessly wishes for his friends to be as happy as he is. But his request is answered with a ravaging flood. This isn't at all what Jubal asked for. Or is it? If a dazzling oversized book perfect for reading to children is what *you* have been wishing for, today is your lucky day. (5 and up)

Dear Madame Esmé,

We're preparing for a trip to the farm but tiring quickly of a moo-moo-here and a cluck-cluck-there. Do you have some books that will expand our barnyard banter?

Dear Gentle Reader,

Make a joyful noise with **WAKE UP, BIG BARN!** by Suzanne Tanner Chitwood. Clap-along rhythms will have young children rejoicing in the sounds and sights of a day in the life of a busy barnyard, but what makes this book notable is the torn paper collage artwork. Created from discarded catalogs and magazines, these pictures left me shaking my head wondering, "How does she do it?" You and your children will be inspired to give her method a try. The day on the farm winds down pleasantly into a wish for a good night, making it a lovely bedtime story. And when you wake up to cock's crow (or your children's way-too-early-morning risings), you can read it again.

There's an unexpected noise on the farm in **CLICK, CLACK, MOO: COWS THAT TYPE** by Doreen Cronin. Farmer Brown's none too happy when the cows get hold of a typewriter and join forces with the hens. They are listing their demands: It's no milk and no eggs until they get some electric blankets. Can a deal be negotiated between the farmer and his livestock? This wacky story has a very level-headed theme about the power of communication.

For more realistic fare, **ONCE UPON A FARM** by Marie Bradby lovingly portrays life working the good earth through the eyes of an African American boy and his family. Ted Rand's homey, sprawling watercolors bleed into airy double-page spreads, alternating with smaller visual vignettes. All the elements in the book fit together magnificently to capture a culture of well-balanced work and play, and an overall appreciation of nature. In the end, it is insinuated that the farm itself is plowed over to make way for highways and malls. This book is as significant as Virginia Lee Burton's classic **THE LITTLE HOUSE**, but is more accessible to modern readers. A personal, moving story that goes beyond the typical farm fare, asking children to consider (and adults to reconsider) the real meaning of "progress."

Jackson, Ellen	• Brown Cow, Green Grass, Yellow Mellow Sun
Kinsey-Warnock, Natalie	• From Dawn till Dusk
Krinsley, Jeanette	• The Cow Went over the Mountain
Lasky, Kathryn	• The Emperor's Old Clothes
Morton, Christine	• Picnic Farm
Murphy, Mary	• How Kind!
Nimmo, Jenny	• Something Wonderful
Nolen, Jerdine	• Harvey Potter's Balloon Farm
Ray, Mary Lyn	• Alvah and Arvilla
Root, Phyllis	• Kiss the Cow!
Sawyer, Ruth	• Journey Cake, Ho!
Schertle, Alice	• How Now, Brown Cow? • Poems about Cows
Shannon, David	• Duck on a Bike
Slobodkina, Esphyr	• The Wonderful Feast
Speed, Toby	• Two Cool Cows
Stoeke, Janet Morgan	• Minerva Louise at School (All Minerva Louise books are grade A.)
Van Laan, Nancy	• The Tiny, Tiny Boy and Big, Big Cow
Waddell, Martin	• Farmer Duck
Widman, Christine	• Cornfield Hide-and-Seek
Wormell, Mary	• Hilda Hen's Happy Birthday • Why Not?

CREATIVE CUE

Sarah Josepha Hale's Mary Had a Little Lamb, with historical background on the classic rhyme and unique illustrations by Salley Mavor, is a must for any collection. After reading the book, think up alternative rhymes with children, filling in personal names and dream pets: "Vincent had a little anaconda, its skin was scaly as my grandmother's elbow . . ." and "Sarah had a little shark, its teeth were sharp as pins . . ." Draw pictures to go with the rhymes. If you do alternative rhymes with your child's class, the results make an attractive bulletin board (see A Helpful Tack, p. 31).

And your children can read about the life of Sarah Josepha Hale in Thank You, Sarah! by Laurie Halse Anderson

Rural Reading

Finding the best children's chapter books is much easier than finding a needle in a haystack if you know where to look: the country. Your whole family will enjoy read-alouds from these beautiful and hilarious stories.

Fisher, Dorothy Canfield	• Understood Betsy
Montgomery, Lucy Maud	• The Anne of Green Gables series
Paulsen, Gary	• Harris and Me
Peck, Richard	• A Long Way from Chicago
Peck, Robert Newton	• The Soup series
Wiles, Deborah	• Love, Ruby Lavender

URBANE BOOKS FOR CITY SLICKERS

PICTURE BOOKS

Ahrens, Robin Isabel	• MY BUILDING
Barracca, Debra and Sal	• THE ADVENTURES OF TAXI DOG
Barrett, Judi	• OLD MACDONALD HAD AN APARTMENT HOUSE
Cummins, Julie	• COUNTRY KID, CITY KID
Derby, Sally	• MY STEPS
Johnson, Stephen T.	• ALPHABET CITY
Joosse, Barbara	• STARS IN THE DARKNESS
Keats, Ezra Jack	• WHISTLE FOR WILLIE (All of his books are great city books.)
Medina, Tony	• DESHAWN DAYS
Nikola-Lisa, W.	• BEIN' WITH YOU THIS WAY
Ringgold, Faith	• TAR BEACH
Santoro, Scott	• THE LITTLE SKYSCRAPER
Sayre, April Pulley	• IT'S MY CITY! A SINGING MAP
Stewart, Sarah	• THE JOURNEY
Summers, Kate	• MILLY AND TILLY: THE STORY OF A TOWN MOUSE AND COUNTRY MOUSE

CHAPTER BOOKS

Mead, Alice	• JUNEBUG
Myers, Walter Dean	• SCORPIONS
Selden, George	• THE CRICKET IN TIMES SQUARE
Spinelli, Jerry	• MANIAC MAGEE
Williams, Vera B.	• SCOOTER

HORSE FANCY

Anderson, C. W.	• BILLY AND BLAZE
Byars, Betsy	• LITTLE HORSE
Cooper, Helen	• SANDMARE
Farley, Walter	• The Black Stallion series (Chapter books.)
Fritz, Jean	• LEONARDO'S HORSE
Goble, Paul	• THE GIRL WHO LOVED WILD HORSES
Haas, Jessie	• RUNAWAY RADISH (Short chapter book.)
Henry, Marguerite	• The Misty series (Chapter books.)
Lester, Alison	• THE SNOW PONY
London, Jonathan	• MUSTANG CANYON
Van Camp, Richard	• WHAT'S THE MOST BEAUTIFUL THING YOU KNOW ABOUT HORSES?

HERE, PIG, PIG, PIG!

Aylesworth, Jim	• AUNT PITTY PATTY'S PIGGY
Beaton, Clare	• HOW BIG IS A PIG?
Branford, Henrietta	• LITTLE PIG FIGWORT CAN'T GET TO SLEEP
Brooks, Walter R.	• FREDDIE THE PIG (Chapter book series.)
Browne, Anthony	• PIGGYBOOK
Bynum, Janie	• OTIS
Christelow, Eileen	• THE GREAT PIG ESCAPE
Cresp, Gael	• THE TALE OF GILBERT ALEXANDER PIG
Falconer, Ian	• The Olivia Series
Fries, Claudia	• A PIG IS MOVING IN!
Galdone, Paul	• THE THREE LITTLE PIGS (James Marshall's version is also excellent.)
Hobbie, Holly	• TOOT & PUDDLE
Jeschke, Susan	• PERFECT THE PIG
King-Smith, Dick	• ALL PIGS ARE BEAUTIFUL
	• LADY LOLLIPOP (Short chapter book.)
Lindgren, Barbro	• BENNY'S HAD ENOUGH!
Magnier, Thierry	• ISABELLE AND THE ANGEL
Martin, David	• FIVE LITTLE PIGGIES
Palatini, Margie	• PIGGIE PIE!
Pomerantz, Charlotte	• THE PIGGY IN THE PUDDLE
Rand, Gloria	• LITTLE FLOWER
Richardson, John	• GRUNT
Scarry, Richard	• PIG WILL AND PIG WON'T (Small illustrations but great for discussion.)
Spurr, Elizabeth	• A PIG NAMED PERRIER
White, E. B.	• CHARLOTTE'S WEB
Winthrop, Elizabeth	• DUMPY LA RUE
Wood, Audrey and Don	• PIGGIES

🥔 *Potato Pick:*

LADY LOLLIPOP

by Dick King-Smith, illustrated by Jill Barton

"Each time I sit down to write an animal story, I say to myself, 'What sort of animal?' and I answer, 'Pig!' Then I say, 'No, no, you've just done a pig story.' So I have to wait. And I have waited. And then along came *Lady Lollipop!*" Well, after reading King-Simth's **BABE: THE GALLANT PIG** and now this one, I say, *let the man pen his pig stories!* When the heavily indulged Princess Penelope announces she wants a pig for her birthday, all the peasants present their most precocious porkers for her approval. She chooses the scruffiest one in the lot, but the pig refuses to be separated from her orphan trainer. So Johnny Skinner comes to stay at the castle, too, and ends up training a lot more than his pig. The round, jovial pencil illustrations add folksy humor to the text. I don't know about pig stories, but I certainly never get sick of spoiled princess stories, and this one is especially fast-paced and jolly. Even the chapter titles are fun to read: "Chapter Six: You always want to get your own way," and "Chapter Eight: If the pig comes in, Mommy goes out." Perfect for read-aloud or independent endeavors. (6 and up)

E. B. White's Charlotte's Web . . . Some Fine Book!

One of the most enduring and beloved children's books of the last century is also one of the best read-alouds. The ending is so sad, so don't let it end! Extend the farmyard fantasy with these activities:

• Encourage children to catch a live spider (readily found in my basement, laundry room, etc., and probably yours too!) in a jar. They'll probably find one or two within a few days. Warn them not to try to catch especially big, colorful ones (sometimes their bites can cause illness) but a little gray house spider shouldn't do any harm. Prepare a terrarium with two mounds of clay (Play-Doh is fine) a few inches apart with a stick standing upright from each clay mound. Fill the bottom of the terrarium with water, so you've got two little islands. Release the spider on one of the islands. If you're lucky, the children can watch as the spider spins a web between the two sticks. Make a separate set of islands for each spider you catch. When I worked with schoolchildren we had two spiders. Although mesmerizing to observe, release the spiders after a day, since their chances of catching food are slim. Actually, we only released one. The other one escaped. His name was, fittingly, Marco Polo. (You might want to put wire mesh on the top of your terrarium.)

Background information about spiders can be found in Margery Facklam's SPIDERS AND THEIR WEB SITES.

• Help children design their own webs using white school glue on wax paper. Allow to dry. With the glue, spell out an encouraging word of each child's choosing in the middle, and sprinkle on silver glitter. Let it dry again. Meanwhile, take Polaroid pictures of the children, cut out heads, attach spider legs made of construction paper or pipe cleaners. Peel off dried web from wax paper, attach picture à la spider and hang from thread near a window for decoration (or, make a classroom bulletin board with webs from all the students in your child's class; see A Helpful Tack, p. 31). If the children's attention is caught, read aloud "Invasion of the Cobwebs" from Suzy Kline's HORRIBLE HARRY AND THE GREEN SLIME.

• I've always liked the "fair" section of CHARLOTTE'S WEB. Have your own neighborhood county fair, with homemade pies and a pet show. Let everyone win a blue ribbon! Children can research where county fairs take place and map them. They can graph favorite fair rides, or design their own county fair games. Older children can research the history of the Ferris wheel and build their own models from straws or sticks. Are the children intrigued? If so, read aloud FAIR WEATHER by Richard Peck.

• Follow the lead of Charlotte's friend Templeton, the rat, and suggest children collect "found words" from packages and papers. Make a big collage, or two collages: nice adjectives and not-so-nice adjectives. A fitting follow-up for children who like collecting words is DONAVAN'S WORD JAR by Monalisa DeGross.

• Children can adopt a farm animal and save it from slaughter. Visit www.farmsanctuary.org to learn more.

• Share the picture-book read-alouds about spiders from Buggy for Books, p. 406.

As Charlotte would have spun: *Terrific!*

BOOKS FOR THE BIRDS

Baker, Keith	• LITTLE GREEN
Bang, Molly	• THE PAPER CRANE
Brown, Alan	• HOOT AND HOLLER
DeFelice, Cynthia	• CLEVER CROW
Duvoisin, Roger	• PETUNIA
Eastman, P. D.	• THE BEST NEST
Ehlert, Lois	• CUCKOO
Flack, Marjorie	• THE STORY ABOUT PING
Fleming, Candace	• WHEN AGNES CAWS
Florian, Douglas	• ON THE WING
Gates, Frieda	• OWL EYES
Gerstein, Mordicai	• SPARROW JACK
Ginsburg, Mirra	• THE CHICK AND THE DUCKLING
Hissey, Jane	• HOOT
Hutchins, Pat	• GOOD-NIGHT, OWL!
James, Simon	• THE BIRDWATCHERS
Johnston, Tony	• BARN OWLS
Kraus, Robert	• OWLIVER
Lear, Edward	• THE OWL AND THE PUSSYCAT (Illustrated by Jan Brett.)
Lionni, Leo	• SIX CROWS
Lupton, Hugh	• THE SONGS OF BIRDS: STORIES AND POEMS FROM MANY CULTURES
McCloskey, Robert	• MAKE WAY FOR DUCKLINGS
Meddaugh, Susan	• TREE OF BIRDS
Peet, Bill	• THE SPOOKY TAIL OF PREWITT PEACOCK
Peters, Lisa Westberg	• COLD LITTLE DUCK, DUCK, DUCK
Piven, Hanoch	• THE PERFECT PURPLE FEATHER
Seuss, Dr.	• "Gertrude McFuzz" from YERTLE THE TURTLE
Silverman, Erica	• DON'T FIDGET A FEATHER!
Simmons, Jane	• COME ALONG, DAISY!
Simont, Marc	• THE GOOSE THAT ALMOST GOT COOKED
So, Meilo	• THE EMPEROR AND THE NIGHTINGALE
Sturges, Philemon	• THE LITTLE RED HEN (MAKES A PIZZA)

The Best Nest by P. D. Eastman

CREATIVE CUE

You and your family can make a whole treeful of bird finger puppets. Cut out a small bird shape from construction paper. Keep it simple, with just a head, wings, and tail. Glue on googly eyes. Cut a tiny diamond shape and fold it in half, gluing only the bottom half to your bird for a beak that opens and closes. Glue on a feather at the tail and put tape loops on the back of the wings. Insert index finger and thumb into the loops to make the wings flap. (Adapted from the excellent idea book I CAN MAKE THAT *by Mary Wallace.) Your child can also make sensational peacocks, pigeons, and owls this way.*

Cold Little Duck, Duck, Duck by Lisa Westberg Peters, Pictures by Sam Williams

Come Along, Daisy! by Jane Simmons

Taravant, Jacques	• THE LITTLE WING GIVER
Tomlinson, Jill	• THE OWL WHO WAS AFRAID OF THE DARK
Waddell, Martin	• FARMER DUCK • OWL BABIES
Yashima, Taro	• CROW BOY
Yolen, Jane	• OWL MOON

. . . Also see penguin suggestions in Chilly Willy: Stories from Antarctica and Other Cool Places, p. 141.

READING WITH RABBITS

Bowden, Joan	• THE BOUNCY BABY BUNNY
Dunbar, Joyce	• LOLLOPY
Greenblat, Rodney Alan	• THUNDER BUNNY
Jarrell, Randall	• THE GINGERBREAD RABBIT
Leuck, Laura	• SUN IS FALLING, NIGHT IS CALLING
McCarty, Peter	• LITTLE BUNNY ON THE MOVE
Pfister, Marcus	• HOPPER'S TREETOP ADVENTURE
Potter, Beatrix	• THE TALE OF PETER RABBIT
Rey, Margret and H. A.	• CURIOUS GEORGE FLIES A KITE
Rohmann, Eric	• MY FRIEND RABBIT
Ward, Helen	• THE HARE AND THE TORTOISE
Watts, Bernadette	• HARVEY HARE, POSTMAN EXTRAORDINAIRE
Williams, Margery	• THE VELVETEEN RABBIT
Zolotow, Charlotte	• MR. RABBIT AND THE LOVELY PRESENT

ELEPHANT BOOKS ARE BIG FUN

Brown, Ken	• NELLIE'S KNOT
Ford, Miela	• LITTLE ELEPHANT
Helfer, Ralph	• MOSEY: THE REMARKABLE FRIENDSHIP OF A BOY AND HIS ELEPHANT (Short chapter book; true story.)
Jackson, K. and B.	• THE SAGGY, BAGGY ELEPHANT
James, Ellen Foley	• LITTLE BULL: GROWING UP IN AFRICA'S ELEPHANT KINGDOM
Kennedy, X. J.	• ELYMPICS

Mahy, Margaret	• 17 Kings and 42 Elephants
McKee, David	• Elmer (Picture book series.)
Pearce, Philippa	• Emily's Own Elephant
Seuss, Dr.	• Horton Hatches the Egg
	• Horton Hears a Who!
Vipont, Elfrida	• The Elephant and the Bad Baby
Young, Ed	• Seven Blind Mice

Hooves and Antlers

Foreman, Michael	• The Little Reindeer
Greene, Stephanie	• Not Just Another Moose
Guthrie, Arlo	• Mooses Come Walking
Kleven, Elisa	• The Dancing Deer and the Foolish Hunter
Numeroff, Laura Joffe	• If You Give a Moose a Muffin
Ryder, Joanne	• A Fawn in the Grass
Seibold, J. Otto, and Vivian Walsh	• Olive, the Other Reindeer
Seuss, Dr.	• Thidwick, the Big-Hearted Moose
Small, David	• Imogene's Antlers

Crocodiles and Alligators

Aruego, Jose	• A Crocodile's Tale
Calmenson, Stephanie	• The Gator Girls (Short chapter book, series.)
Cutler, Jane	• 'Gator Aid (Short chapter book.)
Dahl, Roald	• The Enormous Crocodile
Eastman, P. D.	• Flap Your Wings
Hurd, Thacher	• Mama Don't Allow
Marcellino, Fred	• I, Crocodile
Minarik, Else Holmelund	• No Fighting, No Biting!
Sayre, April Pulley	• Crocodile Listens
Sierra, Judy	• Counting Crocodiles
Thomassie, Tynia	• Feliciana Feydra LeRoux
Waber, Bernard	• The House on East 88th Street
Waring, Richard	• Alberto the Dancing Alligator
Westcott, Nadine Bernard	• The Lady with the Alligator Purse (Bad taste, I know!)
Ziefert, Harriet	• Egad Alligator!

✿ *Potato Pick:*

THE VERY KIND RICH LADY AND HER ONE HUNDRED DOGS

by Chinlun Lee

A lovely woman happens to own a hundred dogs, and we get to enjoy them along with her—but without any of the paper training. Once your child is done laughing over some of the dog names (such as "Tinkle" and "Yum Yum") there's great material for discussion. What would you name a dog? Which is your favorite of the hundred dogs? It will be hard to choose because the cheerful watercolor illustrations are absolutely endearing, and each canine is more cunning than the next. A child can only look at the double-page spread with envy, as one hundred dogs come running to play, play, play! And the last page, with the Very Kind Rich Lady in her jammies, curled up with a hundred dogs, well, could anything be cozier? Even after repeated readings this book remains purebred fun! (5 and up)

Pet Store

DOGS

Barracca, Debra and Sal	• ADVENTURES OF A TAXI DOG
Barton, Byron	• WHERE'S AL?
Bemelmans, Ludwig	• MADELINE'S RESCUE
Boase, Susan	• LUCKY BOY
Bottner, Barbara	• BE BROWN!
Burningham, John	• CANNONBALL SIMP
Byars, Betsy, Betsy Duffey, and Laurie Myers	• MY DOG, MY HERO (Short stories.)
Calmenson, Stephanie	• PERFECT PUPPY
Chekov, Anton	• KASHTANKA (Illustrated by Gennady Spirin.)
Clements, Andrew	• CIRCUS FAMILY DOG
Day, Alexandra	• The Carl series (Wordless wonders!)
Duncan, Lois	• HOTEL FOR DOGS (Chapter book.)
Eastman, P. D.	• GO, DOG. GO!
Feiffer, Jules	• BARK, GEORGE
Flack, Marjorie	• ANGUS AND THE CAT (Check out the whole **Angus** series.)
Freymann, Saxton, and Joost Elffers	• DOG FOOD
George, Kristine O'Connell	• LITTLE DOG POEMS
Graeber, Charlotte	• NOBODY'S DOG
Harper, Dan	• SIT, TRUMAN!
Harper, Jessica	• I'M NOT GOING TO CHASE THE CAT TODAY!
Harvey, Amanda	• DOG EARED
Hassett, John and Ann	• CHARLES OF THE WILD
Johnston, Tony	• IT'S ABOUT DOGS (Poems.)
Khalsa, Dayal Kaur	• I WANT A DOG
Lee, Chinlun	• THE VERY KIND RICH LADY AND HER ONE HUNDRED DOGS
L'Engle, Madeleine	• THE OTHER DOG
Lerman, Rory S.	• CHARLIE'S CHECKLIST
Mahy, Margaret	• DASHING DOG!

Little Dog Poems

by Kristine O'Connell George
Illustrated by June Otani

A Boy's Best Friend . . .

I don't know what it is, but something about a good canine chapter book gets a guy right *here*. Give your intermediate reader any of these classics and he'll be wagging his tail, at least until the last chapter. Box of Kleenex optional. Just something in his eye, that's all.

Armstrong, William Howard	SOUNDER
Cleary, Beverly	RIBSY
DiCamillo, Kate	BECAUSE OF WINN-DIXIE (Rare dog story featuring a girl owner.)
Gardiner, John Reynolds	STONE FOX
Gipson, Frank	OLD YELLER
London, Jack	CALL OF THE WILD
Naylor, Phyllis Reynolds	SHILOH
Rawls, Wilson	WHERE THE RED FERN GROWS
Rodowsky, Colby	NOT MY DOG
Wells, Rosemary	LASSIE COME-HOME (I like this edition, illustrated by Susan Jeffers.)

Malachy, Doyle	SLEEPY PENDOODLE
Masurel, Claire	A CAT AND A DOG
	TEN DOGS IN THE WINDOW
McFarland, Lyn Rossiter	WIDGET
Meddaugh, Susan	MARTHA WALKS THE DOG (And the whole **Martha the Talking Dog** series.)
Resier, Lynn	ANY KIND OF DOG
Schneider, Howie	CHEWY LOUIE
Sendak, Maurice, and Matthew Margolis	SOME SWELL PUP: OR ARE YOU SURE YOU WANT A DOG? (Not a great read-aloud in comic-book form, but a fun book for any pet-theme collection.)
Simont, Marc	THE STRAY DOG
Singer, Marilyn	CHESTER, THE OUT-OF-WORK DOG
Sklansky, Amy E.	FROM THE DOGHOUSE: POEMS TO CHEW ON
Tagg, Christine	METAL MUTZ
Walton, Rick	BERTIE WAS A WATCHDOG
Wegman, William	I WANT A DOG
Zolotow, Charlotte	THE POODLE WHO BARKED AT THE WIND

HEAVY PETTING

I'm allergic to cats, and dogs aren't allowed in our building, so it seems like I'm always being the disappointing mom, saying "no" to my son's requests for pets. Fortunately, there are several books I can say "yes" to.

PURRFECTLY PURRFECT: LIFE AT THE ACATEMY by Patricia Lauber is an animal story that's nothing to sneeze at. "As any cat owner knows, cats are born purrfect," but the Acatemy, a school for cats, serves the purrpuss of making sure. After all, cats are purrfectionsists. The purriculum consists of cats in history, cats in geography, eticat, mewsic, and, of course, Spanish (all good schools teach foreign language, you know). Underlying the unrelenting punnery is an engaging story of Dudley, who is too little even for kittengarten, but insists on attending the Acatemy. He is about to fail everything,

and the head of the school is desperately seeking a way to include him in graducation and save the honor of the institution. When I read this book aloud, the children just adored hearing the "what I did over summer vacation" essays the cat students wrote, being privy to their report cards, and learning all the cat facts (which actually were very educational). Generously illustrated with witty pen-and-ink cartoons, this extraordinary cat-alogue of feline fun is a purr-fect pick for both boys and girls in the new chapter-book clique but makes a great read-aloud for younger children, too.

Cat-happy children ages five on up will also be mee-wowed by the expressive studies of a cat in action

in THE GRANNYMAN by Judith Byron Schachner. Rivaling the sensitivity of Robert McCloskey's classic MAKE WAY FOR DUCKLINGS, this is the story of old Simon, blind and deaf and bones creaking, but very much a member of the family and very much an important help when it comes to teaching a kitten the ways of the world. The book celebrates the value of all life while simultaneously celebrating the genre of the picture book itself.

While some children find it a consolation prize to read a good book about a pet when they can't have one themselves, others may find it frustrating. Children who love pets but live where they are not allowed (or desired) might enjoy volunteering at an animal shelter, "adopting" animals at a local zoo, or reading books about children in the same boat. I WANT A DOG by Dayal Kaur Khalsa, TIGHT TIMES by Barbara Shook Hazen, and PET SHOW! by Ezra Jack Keats all have surprise endings that show how children ingeniously cope with their petless situations. Children might also be interested to know that there are pets out there who long for owners, such as THAT PESKY RAT by Lauren Child; some pets carelessly acquired and abandoned, as in PEE-WEE'S TALE by Johanna Hurwitz; and that some children have to wait until they're grown-ups and then can have all the pets they want, as comfortingly stated at the end of Stephanie Calmenson's SHAGGY, WAGGY DOGS.

CATS

Asher, Sandy	• STELLA'S DANCING DAYS
Bechtold, Lisze	• EDNA'S TALE
Edwards, Julie Andrews	• LITTLE BO
Fischer, Hans	• PITSCHI
Gantos, Jack	• Rotten Ralph (Series.)
Geras, Adele	• THE CATS OF CUCKOO SQUARE (Chapter book series.)
Harjo, Joy	• THE GOOD LUCK CAT
Howard, Arthur	• HOODWINKED
Kerri, Judith	• MOG THE FORGETFUL CAT
Kitamura, Satoshi	• ME AND MY CAT?
Lakin, Pat	• CLARENCE THE COPY CAT
Lauber, Patricia	• PURRFECTLY PURRFECT: LIFE AT THE ACATEMY (Short chapter book.)
Le Guin, Ursula	• Catwings (Short chapter-book series.)
McCully, Emily Arnold	• FOUR HUNGRY KITTENS (Wordless picture book.)
McLaren, Chesley	• ZAT CAT!
Moore, Inga	• SIX-DINNER SID
Sachs, Marilyn	• THE FOUR UGLY CATS IN APARTMENT 3D (Short chapter book.)
Schachner, Judith Byron	• THE GRANNYMAN
Segal, Lore	• THE STORY OF MRS. LOVEWRIGHT AND PURRLESS HER CAT
Smith, Maggie	• DESSER THE BEST EVER CAT (Includes loss of pet.)
Spires, Elizabeth	• THE BIG MEOW
Voake, Charlotte	• GINGER
Waber, Bernard	• RICH CAT, POOR CAT
Woelfle, Gretchen	• KATJE THE WINDMILL CAT

OTHER PETS

Cecil, Laura, ed.	• "The Voracious Vacuum Cleaner" from STUFF AND NONSENSE!
Child, Lauren	• THAT PESKY RAT
Davies, Andrew	• POONAM'S PETS
Dodds, Dayle Ann	• PET WASH
Duke, Kate	• ONE GUINEA PIG IS NOT ENOUGH

FOR ALL READERS, GREAT AND SMALL

Does your child have a soft spot for animals? Check out the winners of the ASPCA Henry Bergh Children's Book Award, established to promote the humane ethic of compassion and respect for all living things at www.aspca.org/bookaward.

George, Jean Craighead	• THE TARANTULA IN MY PURSE (Chapter book.)
Hazen, Barbara Shook	• TIGHT TIMES
Hoff, Syd	• DANNY AND THE DINOSAUR
Hull, Rod	• MR. BETTS AND MR. POTTS
Joyce, William	• DINOSAUR BOB
Keats, Ezra Jack	• PET SHOW!
King-Smith, Dick	• I LOVE GUINEA PIGS
Mowat, Farley	• OWLS IN THE FAMILY (Chapter book.)
Noble, Trinka Hakes	• THE DAY JIMMY'S BOA ATE THE WASH
Rathmann, Peggy	• TEN MINUTES TILL BEDTIME
Rylant, Cynthia	• LITTLE WHISTLE
Sierra, Judy	• THERE'S A ZOO IN ROOM 22
Ungerer, Tomi	• CRICTOR (Snake lovers may also enjoy the closeups in THE SNAKE BOOK photographed by Frank Greenaway and Dave King.)

Stories for All Seasons

SPRING

Bunting, Eve	• FLOWER GARDEN
Carle, Eric	• THE TINY SEED
Clifton, Lucille	• THE BOY WHO DIDN'T BELIEVE IN SPRING
Climo, Shirley	• A MATCH BETWEEN THE WINDS
Eastman, P. D.	• THE BEST NEST
Keats, Ezra Jack	• JENNIE'S HAT
Minarik, Else Holmelund	• IT'S SPRING!
Mockford, Caroline	• WHAT'S THIS?
Ray, Mary Lyn	• RED RUBBER BOOT DAY
San Souci, Robert D.	• THE TALKING EGGS
Van Laan, Nancy	• THE BIG FAT WORM

CREATIVE CUE

Your child can spring into reading—literally. Decorate a pogo stick with faux flowers and a banner across the handlebars that says "Spring into Reading!" When I was a school librarian during "Spring Reading" week, any child caught reading for pleasure received a coupon redeemable at recess for a turn on the pogo stick. Organize a "Spring into Reading" read-a-thon at your child's school with a pogo-stick prize. (Slinky toys make inexpensive prizes for runners-up, as does a pasta party with springy fusilli pasta for the class that reads the most.) Or, just decorate any pogo stick and let your child hop on over to the public library for a silly and pleasant afternoon!

. . . Also, to help April showers bring May flowers, see Stories for a Rainy Day, p. 346. For a spring bunny-themed storytime go to Animal Kingdom, "Reading with Rabbits," p. 368, or create an "It's Not Easy Being Green" storytime (fun around St. Patrick's Day) using "Frog Stories to Make You Hoppy," also in Animal Kingdom, p. 360.

SPRING CLEANING, ANYONE?

Put a shine on your shelf with these titles:

Anderson, Peggy Perry	• LET'S CLEAN UP!
Brown, Margaret Wise	• THE DIRTY LITTLE BOY
Cole, Brock	• ALPHA AND THE DIRTY BABY
Daniels, Teri	• THE FEET IN THE GYM
Hutchins, Pat	• TIDY TITCH
Krasilovsky, Phyllis	• THE MAN WHO DIDN'T WASH HIS DISHES
Parish, Peggy	• AMELIA BEDELIA
Sharmat, Marjorie Weinman	• NATE THE GREAT AND THE MONSTER MESS
Slangerup, Erik Jon	• DIRT BOY
Viorst, Judith	• SUPER-COMPLETELY AND TOTALLY THE MESSIEST
Weeks, Sarah	• MRS. MCNOSH HANGS UP HER WASH
Wells, Rosemary	• MAX CLEANS UP
Zion, Gene	• HARRY THE DIRTY DOG

SUMMER

Armstrong, Jennifer	• WAN HU IS IN THE STARS
Bang-Campbell, Monika	• LITTLE RAT SETS SAIL
Carle, Eric	• THE VERY LONELY FIREFLY
Chorao, Kay	• GRAYBOY
Cousins, Lucy	• MAISY GOES SWIMMING • MAISY MAKES LEMONADE
Cowan, Catherine, and Mark Buehner	• MY LIFE WITH THE WAVE (Based on the story by Octavio Paz.)
Crews, Donald	• NIGHT AT THE FAIR
Crews, Nina	• ONE HOT SUMMER DAY
Ehrlich, H. M.	• LOUIE'S GOOSE
Flora, James	• THE FABULOUS FIREWORK FAMILY
Florian, Douglas	• SUMMERSAULTS (Poetry.)
Hoffman, Alice	• AQUAMARINE (Chapter book.)
Hurwitz, Johanna	• SUMMER WITH ELISA (Short chapter book.)
London, Jonathan	• FROGGY LEARNS TO SWIM • SUN DANCE, WATER DANCE
Luciani, Brigitte	• HOW WILL WE GET TO THE BEACH? A GUESSING GAME STORY

SUMMER IS THE PERFECT TIME TO SURF . . . THE INTERNET!

Don't let your child go into a summer slump. Keep reading "in" even when school's "out!"; www.bookadventure. com is an amazing site that offers exciting reading incentives and will help your family set reading goals any time of year. The site also recommends books that will help your child achieve those goals and even allows you to track his progress.

Lunn, Janet	• THE UMBRELLA PARTY
Mahy, Margaret	• THE GREAT WHITE MAN-EATING SHARK
Mathers, Petra	• LOTTIE'S NEW BEACH TOWEL
Murphy, Stuart J.	• LEMONADE FOR SALE • SUPER SAND CASTLE SATURDAY
Nesbit, E.	• FIVE CHILDREN AND IT (Chapter book.)
Riddell, Chris	• PLATYPUS
Roosa, Karen	• BEACH DAY
Santoro, Scott	• ISAAC THE ICE CREAM TRUCK
Schnur, Steven	• SUMMER: AN ALPHABET ACROSTIC
Stevenson, James	• HEAT WAVE AT MUD FLAT
Ziefert, Harriet	• HATS OFF FOR THE FOURTH OF JULY!
Zion, Gene	• THE SUMMER SNOWMAN

PICKS FOR SUMMER CAMP

Arro, Lena	• GOOD NIGHT, ANIMALS (First camp-out.)
Carlson, Laurie	• KIDS CAMP! (Nonfiction idea book.)
deGroat, Diane	• GOOD NIGHT, SLEEP TIGHT, DON'T LET THE BEDBUGS BITE!
George, Kristine O'Connell	• TOASTING MARSHMALLOWS: CAMPING POEMS
Henkes, Kevin	• BAILEY GOES CAMPING (Good for children too young for overnight camp but who have siblings attending.)
Klise, Kate	• LETTERS FROM CAMP: A MYSTERY (For older, independent readers.)
McCully, Emily Arnold	• MONK CAMPS OUT
Willliams, Vera B.	• THREE DAYS ON A RIVER IN A RED CANOE
Wojciechowski, Susan	• BEANY GOES TO CAMP (Short chapter book.)
Wolff, Ashley	• STELLA & ROY GO CAMPING

. . . Also, for spooky books for around the campfire or by flashlight in the bunk, see Chapter Book Bone-Rattlers, p. 80.

AUTUMN

Bunting, Eve	• PUMPKIN FAIR
Cohen, Barbara	• MOLLY'S PILGRIM
Cooper, Helen	• PUMPKIN SOUP
Ehlert, Lois	• RED LEAF, YELLOW LEAF

TALKING TURKEY

Please pass that book, along with the stuffing. Start a Thanksgiving tradition by choosing a title both grown-ups and children can enjoy, and take turns around the table reading aloud. These stories and collections of prayers and poetry are multicultural, with something for any guest at your table. After reading MAY THERE ALWAYS BE SUNSHINE, children can finish the sentence, "May there always be . . ." in their own way.

Anderson, Laurie Halse	THANK YOU, SARAH! THE WOMAN WHO SAVED THANKSGIVING
Bateman, Teresa	A PLUMP AND PERKY TURKEY (Great for vegetarians.)
Bauer, Caroline Feller	THANKSGIVING: STORIES AND POEMS
Chorao, Kay	BOOK OF GIVING: POEMS OF THANKS, PRAISE, AND CELEBRATION
Corey, Shana	MILLY AND THE MACY'S PARADE
Gill, Jim	MAY THERE ALWAYS BE SUNSHINE
Hennessy, B. G.	MY BOOK OF THANKS (Slightly sectarian.)
Jackson, Alison	I KNOW AN OLD LADY WHO SWALLOWED A PIE
Koller, Jackie French	NICKOMMOH! A THANKSGIVING CELEBRATION
Lindbergh, Reeve	IN EVERY TINY GRAIN OF SAND: A CHILD'S BOOK OF PRAYERS AND PRAISE
Pilkey, Dav	'TWAS THE NIGHT BEFORE THANKSGIVING
Rael, Elsa Okon	RIVKA'S FIRST THANKSGIVING
Swamp, Jake	GIVING THANKS: A NATIVE AMERICAN GOOD MORNING MESSAGE
Wheeler, Lisa	TURK AND RUNT (Also great for vegetarians.)

Hall, Zoe	FALL LEAVES FALL!
Jones, Jennifer Berry	HEETUNKA'S HARVEST
Kelley, Marty	FALL IS NOT EASY
Levine, Abby	THIS IS THE PUMPKIN
Pomeranc, Marion Hess	THE CAN-DO THANKSGIVING
Ray, David	PUMPKIN LIGHT
Robbins, Ken	AUTUMN LEAVES (Nonfiction fit for read-aloud.)
Rogasky, Barbara, ed.	LEAF BY LEAF: AUTUMN POEMS (For older listeners.)
Root, Phyllis	OLIVER FINDS HIS WAY
Serfozo, Mary	PLUMPLY, DUMPLY PUMPKIN
Sohi, Morteza E.	LOOK WHAT I DID WITH A LEAF! (Nonfiction; great craft ideas.)
Stevens, Janet	TOPS & BOTTOMS

Fall Is Not Easy

written & illustrated by Marty Kelley

CREATIVE CUE

In FALL IS NOT EASY by Marty Kelley, a tree tries to change color, and ends up looking like a rainbow, a hamburger, a smiley face and more! Your child will love drawing her own trees in the midst of changes.

. . . Also, see Johnny Appleseed Anniversary, p. 80.

CREATIVE CUE

After reading Margaret Wise Brown's THE LITTLE SCARECROW BOY, *make paper plate masks of Scarecrow Boy's increasingly ferocious faces to use while telling the story. Adapts well to a puppet show format, too.*

STORIES ABOUT SCARECROWS

If the Wizard of Oz was *really* a wizard, when the Scarecrow asked for a brain, he would have handed him one of these books.

Brown, Ken	• THE SCARECROW'S HAT
Brown, Margaret Wise	• THE LITTLE SCARECROW BOY
Dillon, Jana	• JEB SCARECROW'S PUMPKIN PATCH
Fleischman, Sid	• THE SCAREBIRD
Kimmel, Eric A.	• PUMPKINHEAD
Preston, Tim	• THE LONELY SCARECROW
Watts, Bernadette	• TATTERCOATS
Williams, Linda	• THE LITTLE OLD LADY WHO WAS NOT AFRAID OF ANYTHING

SCHOOL STORIES

For a child, school encompasses both work and social life. So many childhood struggles for identity and acceptance take place at school, which is why it's such a recurring setting in children's literature.

Aliki	• MARIANTHE'S STORY: PAINTED WORDS/SPOKEN MEMORIES (About a little girl who does not speak English.)
Allard, Harry	• MISS NELSON IS MISSING!
Brandt, Amy	• WHEN KATIE WAS OUR TEACHER (In English and Spanish.)
Brisson, Pat	• BERTIE'S PICTURE DAY
Calmenson, Stephanie	• THE FROG PRINCIPAL • THE TEENY TINY TEACHER
Caudill, Rebecca	• A POCKETFUL OF CRICKET
Clements, Andrew	• FRINDLE (Short chapter read-aloud; Clements writes lots of school stories.)
Cohen, Miriam	• WHEN WILL I READ?
Cole, Joanna	• The Magic School Bus series (Start with MAGIC SCHOOL BUS INSIDE THE EARTH; tricky read-alouds, but very informative.)
Creech, Sharon	• A FINE, FINE SCHOOL
Crews, Donald	• SCHOOL BUS
Daniels, Teri	• THE FEET IN THE GYM

CREATIVE CUE

Stop after page 24 of MISS NELSON IS MISSING! *by Harry Allard and talk about what could have happened to poor Miss Nelson. Your child can write and illustrate her answers, and if you are reading this book with her whole class, use the children's artwork to make a dramatic bulletin board (see A Helpful Tack, p. 31).*

Dorros, Arthur	• THE FUNGUS THAT ATE MY SCHOOL
Dunn, Opal	• ACKA BACKA BOO! PLAYGROUND GAMES FROM AROUND THE WORLD (Nonfiction.)
Fraser, Mary Ann	• I.Q. GOES TO SCHOOL
Frasier, Debra	• MISS ALAINEUS: A VOCABULARY DISASTER
Hale, Sarah Josepha	• MARY HAD A LITTLE LAMB (Illustrated by Salley Mavor.)
Henkes, Kevin	• JESSICA (Also great for preschoolers.)
Hill, Kirkpatrick	• THE YEAR OF MISS AGNES (Lovely short chapter read-aloud.)
Howe, James	• THE DAY THE TEACHER WENT BANANAS
Johnson, Doug	• SUBSTITUTE TEACHER PLANS
Kline, Suzy	• HORRIBLE HARRY IN ROOM 2B (Chapter book series.)
Lasky, Kathryn	• LUNCH BUNNIES
Lester, Helen	• HOOWAY FOR WODNEY WAT • SCORE ONE FOR THE SLOTHS
Leverich, Kathleen	• BEST ENEMIES (Excellent short chapter read-aloud series.)
Lillegard, Dee	• HELLO SCHOOL! A CLASSROOM FULL OF POEMS
Lindgren, Astrid	• PIPPI GOES TO SCHOOL
Lovell, Patty	• STAND TALL, MOLLY LOU MELON
Maguire, Jack	• HOPSCOTCH, HANGMAN, HOT POTATO, & HA HA HA (Nonfiction; more playground games—can't have enough!)
Millman, Isaac	• MOSES GOES TO SCHOOL (Your child can learn to sign "Take Me Out to the Ballgame" with Moses at his school for the deaf.)
Munsch, Robert	• WE SHARE EVERYTHING!
Numeroff, Laura	• IF YOU TAKE A MOUSE TO SCHOOL
Ormerod, Jan	• MS. MACDONALD HAS A CLASS
Parish, Peggy	• TEACH US, AMELIA BEDELIA
Penn, Audrey	• THE KISSING HAND (Great for preschoolers.)
Pilkey, Dav	• THE ADVENTURES OF CAPTAIN UNDERPANTS (Short chapter book series.)

SHOW AND TELL!

Follow up school stories with some old-fashioned show-and-tell.

Cleary, Beverly	• RAMONA THE PEST, chapter 2, "Show and Tell"
Kirk, Daniel	• BUS STOP, BUS GO!
Lasky, Kathryn	• SHOW AND TELL BUNNIES
Rockwell, Anne	• SHOW & TELL DAY
Simms, Laura	• ROTTEN TEETH

🥔 *Potato Pick:*

THE FEET IN THE GYM

by Teri Daniels, illustrated by Travis Foster

This book celebrates the great underdog of the school, the custodian! Handy Bob takes great pride in his job, wiping and washing and scraping and scrubbing until the school shines. But Bob begins to feel a little "walked on" as he wrangles with the footprints of everyone from the shuffling kindergartners, to a troupe of ballet-dancing kids, to a soccer team, to (gasp!) the art class, to (my goodness!) the marching band! How will poor Bob ever get the floor clean? The hilarious story is a perfect rhyming read-aloud, with an underlying message of persistence and pride in a job well done. The book production is outstanding, with superglossy parts to the pages that actually make the footprints look wet. Other read-alouds may very well "pail" in comparison. (6 and up)

If you visit your child's classroom to read aloud this story, let the children make their own paint footprints. (Clean up fast using baby wipes.) Create a bulletin board featuring Handy Bob, or let them follow the footsteps to the school library.

Polacco, Patricia	• MR. LINCOLN'S WAY
	• THANK YOU, MR. FALKER (Great picture book to read aloud to older children; a true story of the author's struggle with a learning disability.)
Pulver, Robin	• MRS. TOGGLE'S ZIPPER (Try all the Mrs. Toggle stories.)
Rathmann, Peggy	• RUBY THE COPYCAT
Rosenberry, Vera	• VERA'S FIRST DAY OF SCHOOL
Roth, Carol	• THE LITTLE SCHOOL BUS
Shannon, David	• DAVID GOES TO SCHOOL
Sierra, Judy	• THERE'S A ZOO IN ROOM 22 (A to Z class pet poems.)

Dear Madame Esmé,

My daughter is a member of a family on the move. Is there a book that will bring smiles to someone who has to change schools frequently and is often the new kid on the block?

Dear Gentle Reader,

STAND TALL, MOLLY LOU MELON *by Patty Lovell will help your daughter feel at home wherever you move. Molly Lou, the shortest girl in first grade, has a voice like a boa constrictor, buck teeth like a beaver, and the grace of a left-handed gorilla. But Molly Lou also has a secret weapon that helps her when she moves to a new location and even when she attends a new school: her loving grandmother's good advice. Alongside a formalistically flawless story, David Catrow's illustrations are hilarious and imaginative. Molly emanates a cuteness that is first cousin to Dr. Seuss's Cindy Lou Who. The illustration of Molly Lou standing in the middle of a paper snowflake that is exponentially larger than her is breathtaking, the image of Molly Lou barreling past the school bully to make a touchdown will elicit cheers, and the close-up of Molly Lou's smile is completely contagious. On the last page, Molly Lou writes a letter to her grandma telling her how it's going, and wait until your child sees Grandma! Children six and over will laugh out loud and cherish this book until they have grandchildren of their own.*

ALTERNATIVE SCHOOLING

Many parents have told me that their children still try the old thermometer-on-the-radiator trick to get out of going to school. Can you blame them? Sometimes it's hard to find your child under all the work sheets teachers send home. Luckily, there are books that will help boys and girls through the daily grind. In SCHOOL TRIP by Tjibbe Veldkamp, little redheaded Davy is supposed to go to his first day of school, but en route, he changes his mind. After all, there might be mean teachers and homework and bullies. So he wanders off into the world and builds his own school, and what an amazing school it is! The text is sparse and the illustrations are loose and expressive, very much in the style of children's literature in the Netherlands, where this book was originally published. The depictions of Davy's unassuming mother and of his teacher Mr. Stern are hilarious. Children five and over can share in one little boy's fantasy, and victory. An especially apropos addition to home-schooling collections as well.

Kirkpatrick Hill, the author of THE YEAR OF MISS AGNES, was a schoolteacher for more than thirty years in the Alaskan "bush." She used her experiences to create vivid and authentic voices in this short chapter book about a one-room schoolhouse. So many teachers in the book's Athabascan community have fled, sickened by the smell of fish and the old ways that permeate the little town. But Miss Agnes comes, bearing beautiful art supplies, opera, and, heaven bless her, children's literature! When Miss Agnes grows homesick for her native England, the children, who have come to love her, try to convince her to stay. This is a great read-aloud and can be integrated into social studies, but its greatest strength is the author's power to include the reader in the experience of being a student in Miss Agnes's school.

THE SECRETS OF MS. SNICKLE'S CLASS by Laurie Miller Hornik has all the stuff children like: gum chewing, homework-free evenings, tooth fairies, and secrets, secrets, secrets. In fact, everyone in Ms. Snickle's class has a secret, but her class has only one rule: No telling secrets. This turns out to be harder than it sounds, especially when the girl who tells everyone else's secret has the biggest secret of all. Children will enjoy the magic button Ms. Snickle presses to turn her classroom into her living room, and the visits to the school nurse by the student who is allergic to secrets. I personally liked the principal, who suspends a child for seven years for swallowing his gum (after all, gum takes seven years to digest). With absolutely outlandish logic reminiscent of Betty MacDonald's classic **Mrs. Piggle-Wiggle** series, this book will tickle the silly bone of the most discerning second- and third-graders.

And finally, leave it to Avi, the master of the serial cliffhanger, to school readers in old-fashioned suspense in his intermediate chapter book THE SECRET SCHOOL. It's 1925, and when the only teacher in Ida's remote Colorado one-room school has to leave and tend to her ailing mother, it seems impossible that Ida will be able to pass her high-school entrance exam. But the children agree to continue secretly attending school. That is, if Ida is willing to teach. This satisfying read-aloud also gives children some sympathetic insights into life on the other side of the teacher's desk.

Polish That Apple! Teacher Gifts

I have never met a teacher who didn't turn her own pockets inside out to subsidize her classroom library—or who didn't appreciate a book as a gift. My favorites to give for holidays and end-of-school:

Aylesworth, Jim	• The Tale of Tricky Fox
Finchler, Judy	• Testing Miss Malarkey
Morgenstern, Susie	• A Book of Coupons (Nice for teacher retirement.)
Pattou, Edith	• Mrs. Spitzer's Garden (Great for kindergarten teachers.)

. . . And don't forget, a gift certificate to a book-store is always a perfect choice.

Simon, Francesca	• Spider School
Slate, Joseph	• The Miss Bindergarten series
Stoeke, Janet Morgan	• Minerva Louise at School
Thaler, Mike	• The Teacher from the Black Lagoon (Librarian, principal, school nurse, and gym teacher from the Black Lagoon also available.)
Veldkamp, Tjibbe	• School Trip
Weeks, Sarah	• My Somebody Special (For preschoolers.)
Wells, Rosemary	• Yoko
Winters, Kay	• Did You See What I Saw? (Poetry.)
Wiseman, Bernard	• Morris the Moose Goes to School (Outstanding, inexpensive video version available from Library Video Company, 1-800-843-3620.)
Wood, Audrey	• Alphabet Adventure
Yashima, Taro	• Crow Boy
Zalben, Jane Breskin	• Don't Go! (Great for preschoolers.)

Not TOO Scary Stories

Babbitt, Natalie	• The Something
Boxall, Ed	• Francis the Scaredy Cat
Calmenson, Stephanie	• The Teeny Tiny Teacher
Cannon, Janell	• Stellaluna (Especially fun when prefaced with photos from Extremely Weird: Bats by Sarah Lovett.)
Carey, Valerie Scho	• The Devil and Mother Crump
Cecil, Laura, ed.	• Boo! Stories to Make You Jump
Cleary, Beverly	• "The Baddest Witch in the World" from Ramona the Pest
Cuyler, Margery	• Skeleton Hiccups
Donaldson, Julia	• Room on the Broom
Duquennoy, Jacques	• The Ghost's Dinner

Dear Madame Esmé,

Any children's books featuring home-schooled heroes?

Dear Gentle Reader,

I've got a stellar one to recommend: STARGIRL *by Jerry Spinelli. A mysterious girl, home-schooled for most of her life, now enters public school wearing long prairie skirts, playing her ukelele and singing "happy birthday" to children in the lunchroom, carrying a pet rat in her knapsack, and leaving cookies on the desks of her classmates. Is she an alien or something? Leo Borlock is no different from everyone else at Mica High: he can't quite believe Stargirl is real, or that he, such an ordinary guy, is falling for her. Then Stargirl cheers for both teams during the basketball championship and the tide turns viciously against her. The undertow of peer pressure threatens to drag her down. The question is whether Leo is trying to save Stargirl from the slings and arrows of outrageous high-school fortune, or whether he is part of the problem. This amazing novel tackles the theme of individuality and asks why we might be intimidated and angered by those who are different. It is a joy and inspiration to read about Stargirl's good deeds and resilience, her innocence of spirit; she is one of those strong fictional figures who will warrant imitation by her readers. Author Spinelli carries us from laughter to heartbreak with his usual panache (à la* MANIAC MAGEE*). Whether read aloud or read alone, don't let children eleven and older enter high school without first having a date with* STARGIRL. *(The home-schooled hero in* SURVIVING THE APPLEWHITES *by Stephanie S. Tolan is also an unforgettable character who goes against the grain.)*

Based on the author's real childhood, THE YEAR I DIDN'T GO TO SCHOOL *by Giselle Potter is told through the journal entries of a little girl who foregoes second grade to traipse around Italy with her family's puppet troupe. Zany illustrations and insightful writing keep readers in on what she learns along the way. Captivating for children six and up who are home-schooled, living abroad, or dreaming of a life without borders.*

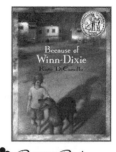

🥔 *Potato Pick:*

BECAUSE OF WINN-DIXIE
by Kate DiCamillo

"Oh, no! Not another dog book!" was my shortsighted response when this little treasure arrived in the mail. And in a sense, I was correct, this is *not* another dog book. Since her mother had left when she was three, India Opal Buloni had lived with her father, a soft-spoken preacher, in a lonely little trailer. Thanks to the help of a smiling stray she meets, she is able to befriend the people in her small town: Otis, working in a pet shop with an arrest record and a special talent for soothing the savage beast; Miss Franny Block, bear-fighting librarian; the mysterious Gloria Dump, possible witch with a penchant for egg salad; and many more original and engaging characters who will resonate with the reader like a sweet-sounding bell long after the book is closed. "We appreciate the complicated and wonderful gifts you give us in each other," prays the preacher, and indeed, the author has offered a complicated and wonderful story, not so much about a dog as it is about friendship and "loving what you got while you got it." (10 and up)

THE HAUNTED HOUSE CONTEST

The school library was everybody's favorite haunt in October, thanks to our wildly popular Haunted House contest. I would ask students to make their own haunted houses out of cardboard boxes and bring them to the library during the weeks preceding Halloween. The children came up with some pretty creepy and elaborate creations (one haunted skyscraper came complete with an elevator!) and the library would grow spookier and spookier every day. Then, all the children who entered were invited to a storytelling party— where I would fill a jack-'o-lantern with dry ice and water so it smoked like witches' brew, share some eerie stories, and announce the grand-prize winners, who received beautiful scary story books! The annual tradition grew increasingly popular: The first year, we had sixteen entries, and two years later, we had seventy-five haunted houses in the library. This event is a sensational way to get involved in your child's classroom, make your branch or school library frighteningly festive, or even bring your apartment building together (haunt the laundry room, if it's not creepy enough already).

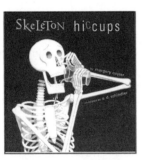

Emberley, Ed	• GO AWAY, BIG GREEN MONSTER!
Fleming, Denise	• PUMPKIN EYE
Glassman, Miriam	• HALLOWEENA
Heide, Florence Parry	• SOME THINGS ARE SCARY
Hendra, Sue	• SCARY PARTY
Horton, Joan	• HALLOWEEN HOOTS AND HOWLS
Howard, Arthur	• HOODWINKED
Katz, Bobbi, ed.	• GHOSTS AND GOOSE BUMPS
Keller, Holly	• BRAVE HORACE
Larrañaga, Ana Martín	• WOO! THE NOT-SO-SCARY GHOST
Lodge, Bernard	• HOW SCARY! (A counting book.)
Martin Jr., Bill	• OLD DEVIL WIND (Great for choral speaking!)
Mayer, Mercer	• THERE'S A NIGHTMARE IN MY CLOSET
Numeroff, Laura	• LAURA NUMEROFF'S 10-STEP GUIDE TO LIVING WITH YOUR MONSTER
O'Malley, Kevin	• VELCOME
Passen, Lisa	• ATTACK OF THE 50-FOOT TEACHER
Pieńkowski, Jan	• HAUNTED HOUSE (Pop-up.) • LITTLE MONSTERS (Pop-up.)
Rex, Michael	• BROOMS ARE FOR FLYING!

Rocklin, Joanne   • THIS BOOK IS HAUNTED

Rosenberg, Liz   • MONSTER MAMA

Schwartz, Alvin   • GHOSTS!
  • IN A DARK, DARK ROOM

Sendak, Maurice   • WHERE THE WILD THINGS ARE

Seuss, Dr.   • "What Was I Scared Of?" from THE SNEETCHES

Shaw, Nancy   • SHEEP TRICK OR TREAT

Steig, William   • WIZZIL

Stridh, Kicki   • THE HORRIBLE SPOOKHOUSE

Turkle, Brinton   • DO NOT OPEN!

Walsh, Melanie   • MONSTER, MONSTER

Williams, Linda   • THE LITTLE OLD LADY WHO WAS NOT AFRAID OF ANYTHING

Winthrop, Elizabeth   • HALLOWEEN HATS

Wisniewski, David   • HALLOWEENIES

. . . Scary stories for older children can be found in Chapter Book Bone-Rattlers, p. 80.

WINTER

Barber, Antonia   • THE MOUSEHOLE CAT

Bateson-Hill, Margaret   • LAO LAO OF DRAGON MOUNTAIN

Brett, Jan   • THE MITTEN
  • TROUBLE WITH TROLLS

Briggs, Raymond   • THE SNOWMAN (Look for the award-winning video.)

Christiana, David   • THE FIRST SNOW

Crews, Nina   • SNOWBALL

Cuyler, Margery   • THE BIGGEST, BEST SNOWMAN

Ehlert, Lois   • SNOWBALLS

Gammell, Stephen   • IS THAT YOU, WINTER?

Gay, Marie-Louise   • STELLA: QUEEN OF THE SNOW

Gershator, Phillis   • WHEN IT STARTS TO SNOW

Keats, Ezra Jack   • THE SNOWY DAY

Keller, Holly   • GERALDINE'S BIG SNOW

Kessler, Ethel and Leonard   • STAN THE HOT DOG MAN (Great storm story.)

Nancy Shaw
Sheep Trick or Treat
illustrated by Margot Apple

CREATIVE CUE

Have a "wild rumpus" march during the double-page spreads in Sendak's classic story WHERE THE WILD THINGS ARE. *Pots and pans make for monstrous musical accompaniment.*

CREATIVE CUE

Be ready with a pair of pale green pants to pull out at the climactic moment of "What Was I Scared Of?" from THE SNEETCHES *by Dr. Seuss*

BEVERLY CLEARY
TIMELESS TALENT

Little Beverly Bunn was the only first-grade girl assigned to the lowest reading group. She dreamed that someday she would write the kind of books that she longed to read, books about the funny adventures of familiar children. Beverly Bunn would grow up to become Beverly Cleary, one of the most beloved and acclaimed children's authors of all time.

I don't think it's the Newbery accolades or the Hans Christian Andersen–award recognition that really sets her apart. What makes Cleary different from other beloved authors is sheer consistency. No other children's author can claim a bestseller in each of the past five *decades*. Cleary manages to gracefully bridge the generation gap between herself and her readers again and again and *again*, creating compulsively readable (and re-readable) realistic fiction that brims with clarity, humor, and her greatest strength: insight.

The depictions of students and teachers that are closest to my heart are contained in Beverly Cleary's **Ramona** books. The classroom is an important and recurring setting in Cleary's books, as it is in the day-to-day of most of

her readers. Cleary is the master of capturing the gravity of a child's emotional life and depicts the teacher's competency as a scale upon which that life is willingly laid. Because of this, there is a tremendous amount at stake as the child seeks approval and trust. In RAMONA THE PEST, when Ramona's well-meaning but inexperienced kindergarten teacher asks Ramona to sit here "for the present," Ramona can hardly wait, expecting a special gift . . . but all the little girl unwraps is disappointment over the misunderstanding. And it's only the beginning of great minds not exactly thinking alike. After all, Ramona can't really be expected to not pull Susan's boing-boing curls . . . or can she?

When the bell rang, Miss Binney opened the door to see her class out, and said to Ramona, "I hope you'll decide you can stop pulling Susan's hair so you can come back to kindergarten."

Ramona did not answer. Her feet, no longer light with joy, carried her slowly toward home. She could never go to kindergarten, because Miss Binney did not love her any more. She would never get to show-and-tell or play Gray Duck again. She wouldn't get to work on the paper turkey Miss Binney was going to teach the class to make for Thanksgiving. Ramona sniffed and wiped the sleeve of her sweater across her eyes. She did love kindergarten, but it was all over now. Cross out Ramona.

Oh, the humanity! So much of the tension in Cleary's work hinges on whether or not grown-ups will be sympathetic. Will the teacher understand Ramona's feelings when Susan copies Ramona's design for a paper owl, or when Ramona wears her pajamas under her school clothes, or when she throws up in class? The teachers in Cleary's books play their roles genuinely, if imperfectly; they are often overheard, flippant, confused, but also apologetic, self-correcting, well-meaning. It almost seems that the teachers are as tentative at being adults as the children are at growing up, and we, as readers, end up rooting for them as much as for their charges.

Cleary won the Newbery Medal in 1984 for DEAR MR. HENSHAW. THE MOUSE AND THE MOTORCYCLE made her a big cheese in the world of intermediate fantasy. But for my coin, nothing beats Klikitat Street—the home of Ramona, Henry, and their friends—as the place to start getting to know Beverly Cleary's work. And once your child falls in love with these characters, you might decide to make the pilgrimage to Portland, Oregon, where bronze figures of Ramona and friends are forever at play in a park just a few blocks from the *real* Klikitat Street. (You can also pay a cyberspace visit at www.mult nomah.ib.or.us/lib/kids/cleary.html.)

RAMONA AND HER FRIENDS CAN BE FOUND IN:

HENRY HUGGINS, 1950

HENRY AND BEEZUS, 1952

HENRY AND RIBSY, 1954

BEEZUS AND RAMONA, 1955

HENRY AND THE PAPER ROUTE, 1957

HENRY AND THE CLUBHOUSE, 1962

RIBSY, 1964

RAMONA THE PEST, 1968

RAMONA THE BRAVE, 1975

RAMONA AND HER FATHER, 1977 (Newbery Honor.)

RAMONA AND HER MOTHER, 1979

RAMONA QUIMBY, AGE 8, 1981 (Newbery Honor.)

RAMONA FOREVER, 1984

RAMONA'S WORLD, 1999

ALSO FROM THE NEIGHBORHOOD . . .

ELLEN TEBBITS, 1951

OTIS SPOFFORD, 1953

You can also read Cleary's autobiography A GIRL FROM YAMHILL.

Lee, Huy Voun	• IN THE SNOW
London, Jonathan	• FROGGY GETS DRESSED
Martin, Jacqueline Briggs	• SNOWFLAKE BENTLEY
Matthews, Caitlin	• WHILE THE BEAR SLEEPS: WINTER TALES AND TRADITIONS
Plourde, Lynn	• SNOW DAY
Poydar, Nancy	• SNIP, SNIP . . . SNOW!
Pulver, Robin	• AXLE ANNIE
Root, Phyllis	• GRANDMOTHER WINTER
Shulevitz, Uri	• SNOW
Sierra, Judy	• ANTARCTIC ANTICS: A BOOK OF PENGUIN POEMS (More polar stories in Chilly Willy, p. 141.)
Steig, William	• BRAVE IRENE
Zolotow, Charlotte	• SOMETHING IS GOING TO HAPPEN

DECEMBER HOLIDAYS

Andersen, Hans Christian	• THE LITTLE MATCH GIRL (Illustrated by Rachel Isadora or Jerry Pinkney, both lovely editions.)
Augustin, Barbara	• ANTONELLA AND HER SANTA CLAUS
Bailey, Mary Bryant	• JEOFFRY'S CHRISTMAS
Barry, Robert	• MR. WILLOWBY'S CHRISTMAS TREE
Bodkin, Odds	• THE CHRISTMAS COBWEBS (Great story, but family's house burns down in the beginning; not for sensitive or fearful listeners.)
Bronson, Linda	• SLEIGH BELLS AND SNOWFLAKES: A CELEBRATION OF CHRISTMAS
Carle, Eric	• DREAM SNOW
Climo, Shirley	• COBWEB CHRISTMAS: THE TRADITION OF TINSEL
cummings, e. e.	• LITTLE TREE
Currey, Anna	• TRUFFLE'S CHRISTMAS
Daly, Niki	• WHAT'S COOKING, JAMELA?
David, Lawrence	• PETER CLAUS AND THE NAUGHTY LIST
Derby, Sally	• HANNAH'S BOOKMOBILE CHRISTMAS
Dunrea, Olivier	• BEAR NOEL
Falwell, Cathryn	• CHRISTMAS FOR 10

SPECIAL WINTER CELEBRATION: THE HUNDRETH DAY OF SCHOOL

If you are only able to visit your child's school once a year, why not come on the hundredth day? The Hundredth Day of School is a holiday that was invented by primary teacher Lynn Taylor and is now celebrated in schools nationwide. The day usually falls in late January or early February. Great ideas abound in the picture book MISS BINDERGARTEN CELEBRATES THE 100TH DAY OF KINDERGARTEN by Joseph Slate. Among them: Draw yourself when you are 100 years old, make a 100-bead necklace, and cook up some "100 Day Hash"! Other recommended books for the 100th day:

Cuyler, Margery	• 100TH DAY WORRIES
Harris, Trudy	• 100 DAYS OF SCHOOL
Kasza, Keiko	• THE WOLF'S CHICKEN STEW
Pinczes, Elinor J.	• ONE HUNDRED HUNGRY ANTS
Rockwell, Anne	• 100 SCHOOL DAYS
Wells, Rosemary	• EMILY'S FIRST 100 DAYS OF SCHOOL

Children who read chapter books will enjoy THE HUNDRED DRESSES by Eleanor Estes or THE HUNDRED PENNY BOX by Sharon Bell Mathis, which both encourage the start of collections (see Activity and Special Interest Books in the Battle Against "B," p. 204 for more collecting ideas). Children of all ages can have fun trying to remember a hundred exciting things that happened since September. Bet you get a hundred different answers!

Foreman, Michael	• THE LITTLE REINDEER
Garland, Michael	• CHRISTMAS MAGIC
Glaser, Linda	• THE BORROWED HANUKKAH LATKES
Godden, Rumer	• THE STORY OF HOLLY & IVY
Jaffe, Nina	• IN THE MONTH OF KISLEV: A STORY FOR HANUKKAH
Johnson, Crockett	• HAROLD AT THE NORTH POLE
Jones, Elizabeth Orton	• BIG SUSAN
Joosse, Barbara	• A HOUSEFUL OF CHRISTMAS
Kastner, Jill	• MERRY CHRISTMAS, PRINCESS DINOSAUR
Kimmel, Eric	• THE CHANUKKAH GUEST
	• HERSHEL AND THE HANUKKAH GOBLINS
	• THE JAR OF FOOLS: EIGHT HANUKKAH STORIES FROM CHELM
	• THE MAGIC DREIDELS: A HANUKKAH STORY
	• WHEN MINDY SAVED HANUKKAH
	• ZIGAZAK! A MAGICAL HANUKKAH NIGHT
Krensky, Stephen	• HOW SANTA GOT HIS JOB
	• HOW SANTA LOST HIS JOB

GIVE THEM SHELTER

Since security is a basic tenet for child development, homelessness may be a concept that is particularly difficult for children to imagine, or observe, let alone experience. These picture books offer some thoughtful and age-appropriate insight into this situation.

Bartoletti, Susan	•	THE CHRISTMAS PROMISE
Bunting, Eve	•	FLY AWAY HOME
Disalvo-Ryan, DyAnne	•	UNCLE WILLIE AND THE SOUP KITCHEN
McGovern, Ann	•	THE LADY IN THE BOX

🌸 *Potato Pick:*

SNOWFLAKE BENTLEY

by Jacqueline Briggs Martin, illustrated by Mary Azarian

I read this out loud to first through eighth grades with tremendous success; following one's dream is a universal theme fit for any age. The book chronicles the real life of William Bentley, whose great passion is snow. Though his neighbors scoff at his fascination with such an ordinary phenomenon, his parents, hardworking Vermont farmers, spend all their savings on a camera so that Bentley can photograph snowflakes and eventually publish a book of these images, his "gift to the world." Patience, perseverance, and appreciation for the wonder all around us are just a few of the virtues touted in this outstanding volume. A Caldecott winner, and a definite "don't miss!" (All ages)

Mathers, Petra	•	HERBIE'S SECRET SANTA
McPhail, David	•	SANTA'S BOOK OF NAMES
Medearis, Angela Shelf	•	SEVEN SPOOLS OF THREAD: A KWANZAA STORY
Mendez, Phil	•	THE BLACK SNOWMAN
Newman, Lesléa	•	RUNAWAY DREIDEL!
Palatini, Margie	•	MOOSELTOE
Pinkney, Andrea Davis	•	SEVEN CANDLES FOR KWANZAA
Pinkwater, Daniel	•	IRVING AND MUKTUK: TWO BAD BEARS (New Year's Eve.)
Polacco, Patricia	•	WELCOME COMFORT
Price, Moe	•	THE REINDEER CHRISTMAS
Primavera, Elise	•	The Auntie Claus series
Reiss, Mike	•	SANTA CLAUSTROPHOBIA
Rosen, Michael	•	CHANUKAH LIGHTS EVERYWHERE
Saint James, Synthia	•	IT'S KWANZAA TIME!
Say, Allen	•	TREE OF CRANES
Seibold, J. Otto	•	OLIVE, THE OTHER REINDEER
Sloat, Teri	•	PIECES OF CHRISTMAS
Stevenson, James	•	THE OLDEST ELF
Van Allsburg, Chris	•	THE POLAR EXPRESS
Wood, Don and Audrey	•	MERRY CHRISTMAS, BIG HUNGRY BEAR!
Yorinks, Arthur	•	THE FLYING LATKE

DAN DAILEY
REMEMBER NOT TO FORGET

I can't help but cover my eyes with both hands when riding shotgun alongside Dan Dailey, the energetic, enigmatic publisher of *The Five Owls* magazine. Dan likes to live life in the fast lane when he can, but memory lane is where he really gets his drive. Even if some of those memories are pretty heartbreaking.

When Dan's wife, Holly Ramsey, a twenty-six-year-old designer and mother of their six-year-old, was stricken with multiple sclerosis, she wanted to find meaningful work she could do from home. Creating a literary magazine about children's books came to Holly in a dream and *Five Owls* was born. The original five owls were part of a weather vane at a children's library on Long Island. In 1924 the owls had inspired Anne Carroll Moore of the *New York Herald Tribune* to call her weekly children's book column "The Three Owls," representing author, illustrator, and critic. When Holly founded her magazine she brought the remaining two owls home to roost, designating them as book editor and designer. She managed the magazine for seven years from her home, before succumbing to ovarian cancer in 1993. That could have been the end of *The Five Owls,* too, but it wasn't.

Dan Dailey *likes* children's books, but I would not say he *loves* children's books. I've never seen him sniff one or squeeze one—behaviors, I have noticed, common to bibliophiles. What Dan Dailey loves is remembering. Besides continuing the legacy of an outstanding literary magazine in honor of Holly (www.fiveowls.com), he worked hard to help create an amazing nature preserve in remembrance of his departed father. Dan also motivates others to create living memorials, which honor people by preserving their memory. Through *The Five Owls,* he set up a fund for memorial donations used to buy outstanding new children's books for underfunded libraries, or gift-wrapped and distributed (from the trunk of his beloved convertible) by "Santa" throughout needy neighborhoods during the holidays.

Dan once quoted to me Madame du Deffands's observation, "The distance is nothing; it is only the first step that is difficult." Using his "remembrances of things past" as an impetus, Dan takes that first step over and over again, living by example and using what has gone before to clear a path for what could come next.

CHARACTERS FOR CHARACTER EDUCATION

Bullying and put-downs are prevalent on the playground at many schools, despite efforts to stop them, but there are books that encourage the character education schools espouse. Read-aloud is shown to develop empathy in children, so replace fights with flights by reading with your child.

WINGS by Christopher Myers is one of those books that many readers will still be thinking of many days later. Your child will remember the stark paper-cut image of Ikarus Jackson, the boy with wings— long, strong, proud wings. He swoops and dives throughout a collage city landscape, slam-dunking a basketball, and then on to school where his wide and wonderful

wings block the blackboard. But not everyone finds his wings wonderful, and soon Ikarus becomes the object of ridicule. One girl notices the lonely drooping of his wings and must find the strength to love what is different in another person to help Ikarus fly again. This book, told in a few well-chosen words, performs the soaring feat of addressing the power of friendship and the need in all children to be appreciated for who they are. Unlike the Icharus of Greek mythology, Ikarus's wings do not melt away, and children will find their own spirits soaring as they see in themselves the ability to help others fly.

Alex turns to karate to protect himself from the bully in Laurie Myers's great realistic chapter book SURVIVING BRICK JOHNSON. Alex's younger brother has a very different perception of the big brute, and little by little Alex discovers that knowing thine enemy can mean making a friend. This book tunes in to the special stresses of little boys, and the allusions to baseball-card trades are an added bonus.

In HOOWAY FOR WODNEY WAT by Helen Lester, poor Rodney Rat can't pronounce his "R"s, which is a problem if you're a wodent . . . I mean rodent. But when big bully Camilla Capybera comes to class, it's wonderful Wodney's wit that puts her in her place. What a great wead-aloud! Illustrator Lynn Munsinger illustrated this and many other books about winning friends and influencing critters: Check out HUNTER'S BEST FRIEND AT SCHOOL by Laura Malone Elliot, in which a raccoon has to decide whether the peer pressure is at a boiling point, and WANTED: BEST FRIEND by A. M. Monson, in which Cat advertises for a new amigo and learns the hard way that new friends may be silver, but old friends are gold. Munsinger's animal illustrations are at once hilarious and sensitive, putting her in the ranks of Caldecott winner Kevin Henkes. Children will love creating their own advertisements, considering what qualities they look for in a friend and what qualities make them a good friend in return.

And finally, MARTHA WALKS THE DOG by Susan Meddaugh is a great picture book about the tremendous power of words, especially kind ones. The villain of the story, a vicious neighborhood dog, gets a mental makeover once his master puts a muzzle on the meanness and decides to give compliments instead. If you want to stop put-downs in your child's school or at home, give this book a read-aloud spin. Or your child can lend it to the critics in her life. Maybe they'll get the hint!

Katz, Karen	• TWELVE HATS FOR LENA: A BOOK OF MONTHS
Lionni, Leo	• FREDERICK
Muller, Gerda	• CIRCLE OF SEASONS
Schulman, Janet	• A BUNNY FOR ALL SEASONS
Sendak, Maurice	• CHICKEN SOUP WITH RICE
Spinelli, Eileen	• HERE COMES THE YEAR
Tafuri, Nancy	• SNOWY FLOWY BLOWY
Updike, John	• A CHILD'S CALENDAR
Wood, Audrey	• WHEN THE ROOT CHILDREN WAKE UP

Unlovable Love Stories

Kissing! Hugging! UUUGGGHHH! What self-respecting kid goes in for the smoochy slop of Valentine's Day? So I offer these love stories for children that slip in affection as surreptitiously as a letter from a secret admirer. Since the authors aimed their bows and arrows at such a wide range of children's ages/developmental stages, recommendations are included here to make sure you hit the target.

Adoff, Arnold LOVE LETTERS

What's Valentine's Day without some billet-doux? Bittersweet as a box of chocolates, these out-of-the-ordinary odes celebrate affection for parents, pets, teachers, friends. There's even a little love poem to oneself. My personal favorite is the love poem run off on a copy machine to warm the hearts of many of the girls in the class. (9 and up)

Clark, Emma Chichester NO MORE KISSING!

"Why does there have to be so much kissing?" a little monkey wonders in earnest, watching his primate family peck away. Even when he tells them in plain monkey-ese that he's had his fill, they still can't seem to resist giving him lip service. When a new baby arrives in the tree house, no one but his big brother can see that the baby is crying because he obviously hates kissing, too. This is a rare and honest sibling love story, and you'll go bananas over Clark's illustrations. (4 and up)

Craft, M. Charlotte CUPID AND PSYCHE

The illustrations by K. Y. Craft in this classic Greek myth—among the greatest love stories of all time—could not be more lush and golden if Midas had touched them himself. Your child will thrill to the vanquishing of Psyche's dreadfully jealous sisters, the discovery and betrayal of Psyche's invisible lover, and the victory of love over all, even death. (9 and up)

deGroat, Diane ROSES ARE PINK, YOUR FEET REALLY STINK

A must-read before your child starts making valentines. Friends have a terrible misunderstanding, resulting in some poignant and heart-piercing poetry being written on cards. This cast of animal classmates has to stop seeing red so that they can enjoy the holiday. (6 and up)

Devlin, Wende and Harry A KISS FOR A WARTHOG

Competition rears its ugly head when the Oldwick Zoo tries to outdo the Quimby Zoo with an addition of a warthog named Allegra, sent special delivery by sea from Africa. But Allegra, upon seeing all the kissing between Oldwick residents refuses to leave the gangplank until she gets hers. Who will step up and kiss the warthog? Even if you don't want a smooch, you will want to read this book about neighborly love again and again. (5 and up)

Friedman, Ina R. HOW MY PARENTS LEARNED TO EAT

A daughter recounts how her American soldier father and Japanese student mother met and secretly tried to learn how to use each other's eating utensils in order to impress the other. Suspenseful and realistic, this story proves that love has no boundaries, and will have your family sharing stories of how Mommy and Daddy first met. (7 and up)

Shannon, David NO, DAVID!

Inspired by a book he wrote when the only words he could write were "no" and "David," Shannon portrays unbridled naughtiness and unconditional love in its finest rendering since Sendak's WHERE THE WILD THINGS ARE. David runs pantless down the street, chews with his mouth open, picks his nose, breaks a vase, and receives a firm time-out in the corner. But ultimately he receives a hug and consolation: "Yes, David, I love you." Boys and girls will delight in David's destruction of social mores and be moved by Mommy's forgiveness. More mischief can be found in DAVID GOES TO SCHOOL and DAVID GETS IN TROUBLE, in which David learns to apologize. (4 and up)

Steig, William SHREK!

"Your nose is so hairy, / Oh, let us not tarry, / Your look is so scary, / I think we should marry." So sings the princess to the monster Shrek, uglier than both his parents put together, blowing flames by the time he toddled, and able to vent smoke from either ear. Your child will love following this hideous character on his quest past dragons, knights, and witches to find his true love. Steig's vibrant, action-packed illustrations make for a perfect marriage of text and art. Even better than the movie, for my buck. Also, by the same author: POTCH & POLLY, SYLVESTER AND THE MAGIC PEBBLE, and CALEB & KATE, all abounding with . . . ugh! . . . love. (6 and up)

Waber, Bernard **LOVABLE LYLE**

Everybody loves Lyle the Crocodile. Or do they? Notes signed "Your Enemy" keep appearing. The Primm family wonders who could possibly hate Lyle, and why? The mystery is solved in this story about not judging a book by its cover. (4 and up)

Williams, Carol Lynch **MY ANGELICA**

Angelica is sure she is going to be a best-selling romance novelist just like her mother. Unfortunately, writing skills are not genetic. Confident Angelica, however, is totally oblivious to the fact that her love stories are lacking. It's up to her faithful boyfriend, who truly loves her, to save Angelica from embarrassment in the school writing contest. A hilarious Valentine's Day read that explodes the clichés of romance while celebrating the love to be found readily all around us. (11 and up)

Have these books brought out the hopeless romantics in your family? Then try other pretty-in-pink picture books for Valentine's Day, or any day you love to read aloud.

Blos, Joan W.	• ONE VERY BEST VALENTINE'S DAY
Bond, Felicia	• FOUR VALENTINES IN A RAINSTORM
Capucilli, Alyssa Satin	• WHAT KIND OF KISS?
Cole, Babette	• TRUELOVE
Greenwald, Sheila	• IT ALL BEGAN WITH JANE EYRE: OR, THE SECRET LIFE OF FRANNY DILLMAN (Mature readers.)
Halperin, Wendy Anderson	• LOVE IS (from Corinthians 13)
Hurd, Thacher	• LITTLE MOUSE'S BIG VALENTINE
Maitland, Barbara	• THE BOOKSTORE VALENTINE
Matthis, Nina	• THE GRANDMA HUNT
Melmed, Laura Krauss	• A HUG GOES AROUND
Minarik, Else Homelund	• A KISS FOR LITTLE BEAR
Modell, Frank	• ONE ZILLION VALENTINES
Radunsky, Vladimir	• TEN
Rockwell, Anne	• VALENTINE'S DAY
Ross, David	• A BOOK OF HUGS • A BOOK OF KISSES
Spinelli, Eileen	• SOMEBODY LOVES YOU, MR. HATCH

🥔 *Potato Pick:*

BUTTONS
by Brock Cole

Buttons, buttons, who's got the buttons? When an old man's buttons burst, three valiant daughters devise clever and not-so-clever plans to replace the valuable buttons. With the language and romance of a fairy tale, and with lovely, sketchy illustrations, this book is destined to be a classic. The double-page wedding spread at the end is a feast for the eyes. There are no holes in **BUTTONS,** and no bookshelf should be without this splendid and satisfying volume. (7 and up)

OTHER GOOD BUTTON BOOKS:

Freeman, Don	• CORDUROY
Reid, Margarette S.	• THE BUTTON BOX
Sierra, Judy	• TASTY BABY BELLY BUTTONS

Stevenson, James	• A VILLAGE FULL OF VALENTINES
Wheeler, Lisa	• PORCUPINING: A PRICKLY LOVE STORY
Winthrop, Elizabeth	• SLOPPY KISSES

Case Clothed!

Andersen, Hans Christian	• THE EMPEROR'S NEW CLOTHES (I like the version illustrated by Nadine Bernard Westcott.)
Barrett, Judi	• ANIMALS SHOULD DEFINITELY NOT WEAR CLOTHING
Blackaby, Susan	• REMBRANDT'S HAT
Brett, Jan	• THE HAT • THE MITTEN
Cocca-Leffler, Maryann	• MR. TANEN'S TIES
Cullen, Catherine Ann	• THE MAGICAL, MYSTICAL, MARVELOUS COAT
Daly, Niki	• JAMELA'S DRESS
Dixon, Ann	• BLUEBERRY SHOE
Dodds, Dayle Ann	• THE KETTLES GET NEW CLOTHES
Dorrie, Doris	• LOTTIE'S PRINCESS DRESS
Estes, Eleanor	• THE HUNDRED DRESSES (Short chapter book.)
Geringer, Laura	• A THREE HAT DAY
Hearson, Ruth	• KNITTED BY GRANDMA
Hest, Amy	• THE PURPLE COAT
Huck, Charlotte	• PRINCESS FURBALL
Jocelyn, Marthe	• HANNAH AND THE SEVEN DRESSES
Kuskin, Karla	• THE PHILHARMONIC GETS DRESSED
Landström, Olof and Lena	• WILL'S NEW CAP
London, Jonathan	• FROGGY GETS DRESSED
Marsden, Carolyn	• THE GOLD-THREADED DRESS (Short chapter book.)
Mills, Lauren	• THE RAG COAT
Munsch, Robert	• THOMAS' SNOWSUIT
Slobodkina, Esphyr	• CAPS FOR SALE
Taback, Simms	• JOSEPH HAD A LITTLE OVERCOAT
Wells, Rosemary	• MAX'S DRAGON SHIRT
Weston, Carrie	• LUCKY SOCKS
Ziefert, Harriet	• A NEW COAT FOR ANNA

A THREE HAT DAY

LAURA GERINGER
PICTURES BY
ARNOLD LOBEL

HANNAH and the Seven Dresses

MARTHE JOCELYN

Dear Madame Esmé,

Winter update: My child has lost one hat, one boot, three scarves, and has four left gloves. Please recommend something to keep me from losing my temper.

Dear Gentle Reader,

At least your child remembered to remove his extremities before losing the articles. Find your sense of humor with THE MISSING MITTEN MYSTERY by Steven Kellogg. Maybe mittens don't grow on trees . . . but they do in this extremely imaginative romp. When a little girl loses her fifth mitten, she tries hard to track it down, leading to a series of scenarios. First she imagines an eagle carrying it off, then she fantasizes that the mitten got tired of being a mitten and hopped away. Perhaps a mouse is using the mitten for a sleeping bag. Consider giving this book to a teacher during the holidays, to be enjoyed well past winter, or pair it with Jan Brett's THE MITTEN for a great storytime for children five and up.

CREATIVE CUE

Children can trace their own mittens on paper, then color and hang them from a branch to make their own mitten tree like the one in Steven Kellogg's THE MISSING MITTEN MYSTERY.

Books, in Living Color!

Brown, Margaret Wise	• THE COLOR KITTENS
Cabrera, Jane	• CAT'S COLORS
Ehlert, Lois	• COLOR FARM
	• COLOR ZOO
Hooper, Patricia	• HOW THE SKY'S HOUSEKEEPER WORE HER SCARVES
Hubbard, Patricia	• MY CRAYONS TALK
Johnson, Crockett	• HAROLD AND THE PURPLE CRAYON
Jonas, Ann	• COLOR DANCE
Kleven, Elisa	• THE LION AND THE LITTLE RED BIRD
Lionni, Leo	• A COLOR OF HIS OWN
Lobel, Arnold	• THE GREAT BLUENESS AND OTHER PREDICAMENTS
Martin Jr., Bill	• BROWN BEAR, BROWN BEAR, WHAT DO YOU SEE?
Peek, Merle	• MARY WORE HER RED DRESS AND HENRY WORE HIS GREEN SNEAKERS

CREATIVE CUE

Harold's crayon takes him anyplace and every place. After children draw themselves in the midst of a purple-crayoned adventure, they will be eager to hear the rest of the **Harold** series of books by Crockett Johnson.

A PICTURE FOR HAROLD'S ROOM

HAROLD AT THE NORTH POLE

HAROLD'S ABC

HAROLD'S CIRCUS

HAROLD'S FAIRY TALE

HAROLD'S TRIP TO THE SKY

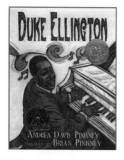

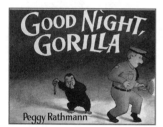

Pinkney, Andrea Davis	• DUKE ELLINGTON: THE PIANO PRINCE AND HIS ORCHESTRA
Pinkney, Sandra L.	• A RAINBOW ALL AROUND ME
Rathmann, Peggy	• GOOD NIGHT, GORILLA
Serfozo, Mary	• WHO SAID RED?
Seuss, Dr.	• MY MANY COLORED DAYS
Stinson, Kathy	• RED IS BEST
Tabor, Nancy Maria Grande	• SOMOS UN ARCO IRIS: WE ARE A RAINBOW
Walsh, Ellen Stoll	• MOUSE PAINT
Weiss, George David, and Bob Thiele	• WHAT A WONDERFUL WORLD

Big-Top Reading

Armstrong, Jennifer	• PIERRE'S DREAM
Bemelmans, Ludwig	• MADELINE AND THE GYPSIES
Bogacki, Tomek	• CIRCUS GIRL
Bronson, Linda	• THE CIRCUS ALPHABET
Burningham, John	• CANNONBALL SIMP
Clements, Andrew	• CIRCUS FAMILY DOG
Damjan, Mischa	• THE CLOWN SAID NO
Daugherty, James	• ANDY AND THE LION
Davenport, Meg	• CIRCUS! A POP-UP ADVENTURE
Duncan, Lois	• SONG OF THE CIRCUS
Ehlert, Lois	• CIRCUS
Ernst, Lisa Campbell	• GINGER JUMPS
Falconer, Ian	• OLIVIA SAVES THE CIRCUS
Freeman, Don	• BEARYMORE
Gottfried, Maya	• LAST NIGHT I DREAMED A CIRCUS
Laden, Nina	• CLOWNS ON VACATION
Martin Jr., Bill	• CHICKEN CHUCK
McCully, Emily Arnold	• MIRETTE ON THE HIGH WIRE
Nimmo, Jenny	• ESMERALDA AND THE CHILDREN NEXT DOOR
Paul, Ann Whitford	• LITTLE MONKEY SAYS GOOD NIGHT
Piumini, Roberto	• THE SAINT AND THE CIRCUS
Priceman, Majorie	• EMELINE AT THE CIRCUS

IN THE CENTER RING

Most children love the imaginative play of the circus, so follow up any circus storytime with a silly circus game, craft, or treat. My favorite circus ideas come from a reading ringmaster who shared these on-line.

Monkey, Monkey Clown Play this instead of "Duck, Duck Goose."

King of the Clowns One child is named King or Queen of the Clowns. One at a time, the children kneel before the royalty and say, "King (or Queen) of the Clowns, I am your loyal subject. Never shall I laugh or smile." Meanwhile, the Royal Highness can make any funny face or expression he or she wants. If the child can go one minute without laughing or smiling, she or he takes the throne and the game continues with the next child.

Lion Tamers Let the children pretend that they are animal trainers and are teaching their animals to jump through a hoop. Children take turns throwing stuffed animals through a hula hoop or other large ring.

Tightrope Walker Lay a rope on the floor, and walk it! Show the children how to use arms for balance. How about a parasol for effect?

Paper Plate Clowns Let the children make everything except the nose. Use pre-cut triangles for hats, and use yarn hair, facial features cut from magazines, crepe paper streamers, and anything else you can think up. Cut a small hole in the center of the plate. Stick in a small balloon and blow up partially as the red clown nose. (Take care to help; balloons present a choking hazard for children.) Or, make paper plate elephants. Let children paint paper plates with gray poster paint, then add construction-paper ears and big wiggly eyes. Cut out a circle from the center of the plate—this is where children stick their arms through to make the trunk!

Circus Train The children may draw any animal they wish. Paste the animal onto a clean Styrofoam meat tray (get them unused from your butcher). Make the bars of the cage with pipe cleaners. Add black construction paper circles for wheels. The animals in their cages can be displayed on a wall, as if they were in a circus train. Or, for a going-home treat, draw stripes with permanent markers on a Ziploc bag, and glue circles for wheels at the bottom. You can put animal crackers in the bag.

Old-Fashioned Cracker Jacks Pop four quarts of popcorn. Melt a $\frac{1}{2}$ cup butter in a heavy pan. Add to this 1 tablespoon of molasses and $\frac{1}{3}$ cup honey. Mix into the popcorn. Add peanuts. Spread mixture in a greased pan and bake for 12 minutes at 350 degrees. Stir once. Let the Cracker Jacks cool and serve in paper cups. Don't forget to add a small prize to each cup.

Music, Maestro! "Did You Ever See a Clown?" (Sung to "Did You Ever See a Lassie?") Have children form a circle. One child in the middle should perform actions. Take turns.

> Did you ever see a clown,
> A clown, a clown
> Did you ever see a clown,
> Move this way and that?
> Move this way and that way
> And that way and this way
> Did you ever see a clown
> Move this way and that?

THE ART OF THE PAPER CUT: POP-UP BOOKS

And now for some insight into that eccentric genius of the children's bookshelf, every child's antidote to reading atrophy: the pop-up book. For insider info, I sought out two of America's great illustrators and paper engineers, David A. Carter (with over fifty books to his credit, among them HOW MANY BUGS IN A BOX?) and the innovator Robert Sabuda (THE NIGHT BEFORE CHRISTMAS and COOKIE COUNT: A TASTY POP-UP).

David Carter doesn't just work with paper. He works with curiosity. It started when he was a little boy in Utah, "playing in fields, lifting up rocks and boards, looking for bugs. That's exactly what my bug books are."

Robert Sabuda, too, was a curious child. "I liked to take things apart to see how they worked . . . not that I could put them back together," he laughs. Now, both Sabuda and Carter are heavily involved in putting things together, creating pop-up prototypes to be hand assembled in factories. Large machines die-cut parts into four-foot jigsaw puzzles whose tiny pieces are hammered out with a rubber mallet in a choreography befitting Willie Wonka's chocolate factory, and with results just as tantalizing.

"I love to watch children's eyes get big," Carter says. "I had a hard time reading as a child. But if I had had these books, I promise you, I'd have been looking at them."

Sabuda agrees. "These books cover a cross section of humanity. People, aged four or eighty-four, open a pop-up book and wonder, 'How does this happen? How can I make it happen? If I can make *this* happen, I can make *anything* happen.' You have magic in your hands. Pop-ups broaden a person's horizons of what a book can be."

These affirmations make me wonder why pop-ups aren't celebrated more in schools, libraries, and academic circles. There is no Newbery or Caldecott for these books. "It's like the way comedies are dealt with in the movie world," Carter muses. "Everybody likes them, but they are less recognized as an art form." This may be changing. The Movable Book Society offers a fascinating history and gallery of the pop-up, and is linked from Carter's home page, www.popupbooks.com. I've included pop-ups throughout my booklists, and they hold their own. Just as no movie collection is complete without comedies, no book collection should be without these works of art and engineering that move children into a lifelong love of reading with the pull of a tab or a lift of a flap.

You may also be happily surprised at how pop-ups encourage careful book handling (though they are often much more durable than they appear). When I worked as a librarian, I placed them in oversized clear plastic bags with a note taped to the front: "If you like this book, return it in the same condition in which you borrowed it, and then we'll buy more." After fifty circula-

tions with books returned in pristine condition, it was clear the children wanted more. And more. And *more*. Expensive? Yes, perhaps. But we all got a Fourth of July's worth of bang for the library's buck.

Every genre seems represented in the movable feast that is pop-up: Classics come to life, as demonstrated in Barbara Cooney's artful rendition of Prokofiev's PETER AND THE WOLF, Marjorie Priceman's LITTLE RED RIDING HOOD, and in Sabuda's project honoring the 100th anniversary of L. Frank Baum's THE WONDERFUL WIZARD OF OZ, done in block prints, requiring over 350 carved blocks to create. The nonfiction is also formidable, from Jonathan Miller and David Pelham's masterpiece THE HUMAN BODY, to Sabuda's YOUNG NATURALIST POP-UP HANDBOOKS, to Robert Crowther's AMAZING POP-UP HOUSE OF INVENTIONS, to Ron Van Der Meer's comprehensive KIDS ART PACK, and ARCHITECTURE PACK, and the lively contributions of Jennie Maizels and Kate Petty's AMAZING POP-UP GRAMMAR BOOK, AMAZING POP-UP MULTIPLICATON BOOK, and AMAZING POP-UP MUSIC BOOK. Concept books such as CHUCK MURPHY'S COLOR SURPRISES and Lucy Cousins's bold Maisy series are perfect for inclusion in primary storytimes. And, of course, there

is a strong picture-book showing, including paper engineer extraordinaire Jan Pieńkowski's HAUNTED HOUSE and Meg Davenport's CIRCUS! Some books even incorporate sound, such as Carter's CURIOUS CRITTERS and Jonathan Allen's DON'T WAKE THE BABY!

And if your child wants to hop on pop-up, offer her a chance to make her own 3-D books with POP-O-MANIA: HOW TO CREATE YOUR OWN POP-UPS by Barbara Valenta and HOW TO MAKE SUPER POP-UPS by Joan Irvine; and adults and older children can use David A. Carter and James Diaz's sophisticated guide, THE ELEMENTS OF POP-UP: A POP-UP BOOK FOR ASPIRING PAPER ENGINEERS.

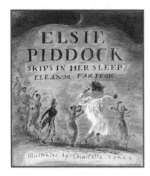

🍀 *Potato Pick:*

ELSIE PIDDOCK
SKIPS IN HER SLEEP

*by Eleanor Farjeon, illustrated
by Charlotte Voake*

I'd hazard to say that Eleanor
Farjeon was one of the greatest
children's authors of all time (do
you know the hymn "Morning
Has Broken" sung by Cat
Stevens? She wrote that!). The
master Edward Ardizzone often
illustrated her work during her
life, which ended in 1965. Then
Charlotte Voake came along to
foot the bill, and here we are,
with a big, gorgeous reissue of
the 1937 story about a little girl
who can do the High Skip, the
Slow Skip, the Skip Double,
Strong Skip, and the Skip Against
Trouble. Born to skip, even when
she's an old, old woman, heroine
Elsie manages to save the skipping ground from the greedy
new Lord so children and fairies
can skip there forever more.
Break out the ropes and skip
along, but whatever you do, don't
skip this book! (6 and up)

Sampson, Michael and Mary Beth	• STAR OF THE CIRCUS
Sendak, Jack	• CIRCUS GIRL
Seuss, Dr.	• IF I RAN THE CIRCUS
Slate, Joseph	• MISS BINDERGARTEN PLANS A CIRCUS WITH KINDERGARTEN
Slobodkina, Esphyr	• CIRCUS CAPS FOR SALE
Smith, Jos. A.	• CIRCUS TRAIN
Spier, Peter	• PETER SPIER'S CIRCUS (Small illustrations; better for lap or small group.)

Toyland Friends

Alborough, Jez	• MY FRIEND BEAR
Bart, Kathleen	• A TALE OF TWO TEDDIES
Beck, Ian	• HOME BEFORE DARK
Blake, Quentin	• CLOWN
Bliss, Corinne Demas	• THE LITTLEST MATRYOSHKA
Butler, Dorothy	• MY BROWN BEAR BARNEY
Caudill, Rebecca	• THE BEST-LOVED DOLL
Cecil, Laura	• KINGFISHER BOOK OF TOY STORIES
Clark, Emma Chichester	• WHERE ARE YOU, BLUE KANGAROO?
Cooper, Helen	• TATTY RATTY
Daly, Niki	• OLD BOB'S BROWN BEAR
Egielski, Richard	• SLIM AND JIM (Yo-yos!)
Feiffer, Jules	• I LOST MY BEAR
Fine, Anne	• THE JAMIE AND ANGUS STORIES (Short stories.)
Freeman, Don	• CORDUROY
Godden, Rumer	• THE STORY OF HOLLY & IVY
Gruelle, Johnny	• MARCELLA: A RAGGEDY ANN STORY
Heap, Sue	• WHAT SHALL WE PLAY?
Hissey, Jane	• OLD BEAR TALES
Hoban, Russell	• THE MOUSE AND HIS CHILD (Chapter book.)

Hughes, Shirley	• DOGGER
Hutchins, Pat	• TIDY TITCH
Kastner, Jill	• PRINCESS DINOSAUR
Kennedy, Jimmy	• THE TEDDY BEARS' PICNIC (I like the version illustrated by Alexandra Day.)
Lewis, Naomi (comp.)	• ROCKING HORSE LAND AND OTHER CLASSIC TALES OF DOLLS AND TOYS
Lindgren, Astrid	• MIRABELL
Martin, Ann M., and Laura Godwin	• THE DOLL PEOPLE (Chapter book.)
McClintock, Barbara	• DAHLIA
McPhail, David	• THE TEDDY BEAR
Milne, A. A.	• THE COMPLETE TALES & POEMS OF WINNIE-THE-POOH (Chapter book.)
Murphy, Frank	• LEGEND OF THE TEDDY BEAR
O'Connell, Jean S.	• THE DOLLHOUSE CAPER (Boys and dolls!)
Paraskevas, Betty	• THE TANGERINE BEAR
Russo, Marisabina	• THE LINE-UP BOOK
Rylant, Cynthia	• THE TICKY-TACKY DOLL
Scott, Steve	• TEDDY BEAR, TEDDY BEAR
Stephens, Helen	• BLUE HORSE
Tudor, Tasha	• A IS FOR ANNABELLE: A DOLL'S ALPHABET
Vulliamy, Clara	• SMALL
Waugh, Sylvia	• THE MENNYMS (Chapter book.)
Wells, Rosemary	• RACHEL FIELD'S HITTY: HER FIRST HUNDRED YEARS
Williams, Karen Lynn	• GALIMOTO
Williams, Marjorie	• THE VELVETEEN RABBIT
Williams, Ursula Moray	• ADVENTURES OF THE LITTLE WOODEN HORSE (Chapter book.)
Winslow, Marjorie	• MUD PIES AND OTHER RECIPES: A COOKBOOK FOR DOLLS
Wood, Audrey	• THE RED RACER
Zolotow, Charlotte	• WILLIAM'S DOLL (Great musical version with Marlo Thomas and friends on the audio *Free to Be . . . You and Me.*)

❀ *Potato Pick:*
ROCKING HORSE LAND AND OTHER CLASSIC TALES OF DOLLS AND TOYS
compiled by Naomi Lewis, illustrated by Angela Barrett

The tales in this anthology were originally collected in a book titled THE SILENT PLAYMATE: A COLLECTION OF DOLL STORIES. I remember taking it out of the library and renewing it until the librarian wouldn't let me renew it anymore. I couldn't buy it; it was out of print. So imagine my shock and delight to find stories

such as the deliciously creepy "Rag Bag," in which a wicked and persistent fairy child kidnaps a favorite doll, and the inventive "Town in the Library" written by the mannered master E. Nesbit. If you want a smile sewn on your child's face, read these stories aloud. (7 and up)

OH, YOU BEAUTIFUL DOLL!

There are plenty of plush pals available through the Merry Hearts catalog, 1-800-675-1766, www.merryhearts.com. Your child's favorite book characters will be found in ready-to-cuddle versions, and these toys are also great gifts for libraries or classrooms.

LOST AND FOUND

If you find a pink rubber Cadillac about the length of a thumb, missing the right front wheel, will you let me know? I lost it about twenty-seven years ago when I brought it on a school field trip. If you don't find it, that's okay, I've *almost* gotten over it.

Children constantly deal with lost and found: Teeth fall out, growth is so intense that it can be measured monthly in pencil marks along the molding of a doorway, teachers come and go with the passing of every year. Mix in friends that move away, siblings arriving as suddenly as UPS packages, deaths of grandparents or pets, and the marital relations of parents . . . really, it's a bit much, when you think about it.

Enter toys. They don't move away or grow away, and inasmuch as children can keep track of them, they can be depended upon for comfort in the face of life's many mutations. In this way, toys are very much like books in that they provide a necessary and expansive chance to escape into imagination unalone. I suppose "unalone" isn't really a word, but in the case of toys and books, it ought to be. In books, it is through authors that children find themselves unalone; through toys, children find friendship, and often worlds of their own invention.

Perhaps this is why books *about* toys are among the most evocative and successful works in children's literature. Such books suggest that the ability to love is more powerful than the changes and challenges we face, and the security that comes from this lesson is never lost on children. In WHEN I WAS YOUR AGE: ORIGINAL STORIES ABOUT GROWING UP, Mary Pope Osborne generously and candidly describes her great childhood love affair with "All-Ball," a bouncing *bon ami* whose presence helped the author navigate the fearful weeks before her father left to fight in the Korean War.

And Johnny Gruelle actually channeled the grief of the real-life loss of his thirteen-year-old daughter Marcella to create the beloved **Raggedy Ann** series, thereby keeping her memory very much alive.

Merrily, many toys in books are as much about finding as losing. Shirley Hughes's DOGGER is recovered at a junk sale to the reader's relief, and in Johanna Hurwitz's RUSSELL AND ELISA, a doll named "Airmail" survives an inadvertent sleepover at the public library. ADVENTURES OF THE LITTLE WOODEN HORSE by Ursula Moray Williams features an unassuming hero made brave through his unconditional love for his maker. After traveling the world, he reassuringly returns home again. The reunion that concludes Margery Williams's VELVETEEN RABBIT is more bittersweet, "He never knew that it was really his own Bunny, come back to look at the child who had first helped him to be real." Perhaps most poignant is the ending to A. A. Milne's classic THE HOUSE AT POOH CORNER, with its foreshadowing of the putting away of childish things: "Pooh," said Christopher Robin quite earnestly, "If I—if I'm not quite—" he stopped and tried again. "Pooh, whatever happens, you will understand, won't you?"

Before children are ready to put away their toys, make sure they've read a few good toy tales.

Far Out Space Stories

Armstrong, Jennifer	• WAN HU IS IN THE STARS
Barttram, Simon	• MAN ON THE MOON (A DAY IN THE LIFE OF BOB)
Baumgart, Klaus	• LAURA'S STAR
Berger, Barbara Helen	• A LOT OF OTTERS
Brown, Don	• ONE GIANT LEAP: THE STORY OF NEIL ARMSTRONG (Read-aloud biography.)
Butterworth, Nick	• Q POOTLE 5
Carle, Eric	• PAPA, PLEASE GET THE MOON FOR ME
Cecil, Laura	• NOAH AND THE SPACE ARK
Conly, Jane Leslie	• THE RUDEST ALIEN ON EARTH (Chapter book.)
Conrad, Pam	• CALL ME AHNIGHITO
D'Aulaire, Ingri, and Edgar Parin	• Greek myths about Helios and Selene from the D'AULAIRES' BOOK OF GREEK MYTHS
Esbensen, Barbara Juster	• THE STAR MAIDEN
Getz, David	• FLOATING HOME
Gollub, Matthew	• THE MOON WAS AT A FIESTA
Hirst, Robin and Sally	• MY PLACE IN SPACE
Kitamura, Satoshi	• UFO DIARY
Levy, Elizabeth	• SOMETHING QUEER IN OUTER SPACE
Livingston, Myra Cohn	• SPACE SONGS
Marshall, Edward	• SPACE CASE
Mayo, Margaret	• "The King Who Wanted to Touch the Moon" from MAGICAL TALES FROM MANY LANDS
Pinkwater, Daniel	• GUYS FROM SPACE
Raschka, Chris	• CAN'T SLEEP
Ripley, Catherine	• WHY DO STARS TWINKLE? AND OTHER NIGHTTIME QUESTIONS (Nonfiction.)
Sadler, Marilyn	• ALISTAIR IN OUTER SPACE
Scieszka, Jon, and Lane Smith	• BALONEY (HENRY P.) (Your child will learn to speak alien-ese!)
Seibold, J. Otto, and Vivian Walsh	• MONKEY BUSINESS

CREATIVE CUE

Let children design their own aliens, cut them out, and add to a mural of a visiting spaceship; also makes a far-out poster to put over a science fiction bookshelf.

NIGHT AND DAY

Ask a group of children who they would rather be, the sun or the moon, and why? Then separate the "suns" from the "moons" and have them draw their suns with bright crayons and glitter, or moons with white crayons and blue watercolor. When I did this with one group, we drew pictures on the top and wrote the reasons for our choices on the bottom. Copy the poem "The Sun and the Moon" by Elaine Laron from FREE TO BE YOU AND ME and center it on a bulletin board, then decorate with the "moon" artwork on one side and the "sun" artwork on the other.

Service, Pamela F.	• STINKER FROM SPACE (Chapter book.)
Ungerer, Tomi	• MOON MAN
Waugh, Sylvia	• SPACE RACE (Chapter book.)
Wethered, Peggy	• TOUCHDOWN MARS! AN ABC ADVENTURE
Yaccarino, Dan	• ZOOM! ZOOM! ZOOM! I'M OFF TO THE MOON!
Yorinks, Arthur	• COMPANY'S COMING

Buggy for Books

Aardema, Verna	• WHY MOSQUITOS BUZZ IN PEOPLE'S EARS
Aylesworth, Jim	• OLD BLACK FLY
Banks, Lynne Reid	• HARRY THE POISONOUS CENTIPEDE (Chapter book.)
Barton, Byron	• BUZZ BUZZ BUZZ
Berenstain, Stan and Jan	• THE BIG HONEY HUNT
Bono, Mary	• UGH! A BUG
Carle, Eric	• THE GROUCHY LADYBUG
	• THE HONEYBEE AND THE ROBBER
	• THE VERY BUSY SPIDER
	• THE VERY CLUMSY CLICK BEETLE
	• THE VERY HUNGRY CATERPILLAR
	• THE VERY LONELY FIREFLY
	• THE VERY QUIET CRICKET
Carter, David A.	• HOW MANY BUGS IN A BOX? (Try all of David Carter's buggy books.)

Collicott, Sharleen	• TOESTOMPER AND THE CATERPILLARS
Dubowski, Cathy East	• SNUG BUG
Edwards, Pamela Duncan	• ED & FRED FLEA
Egielski, Richard	• BUZ
	• JAZPER
Ehlert, Lois	• WAITING FOR WINGS
Fleischman, Paul	• JOYFUL NOISE: POEMS FOR TWO VOICES
Florian, Douglas	• INSECTLOPEDIA
Greenberg, David	• BUGS!
Howe, James	• I WISH I WERE A BUTTERFLY
Howitt, Mary	• THE SPIDER AND THE FLY (Classic poem illustrated by Tony DiTerlizzi.)
Joyce, William	• THE LEAF MEN AND THE BRAVE GOOD BUGS
Kennedy, Kim	• MR. BUMBLE
Kirk, David	• MISS SPIDER'S TEA PARTY (Try the whole **Miss Spider** series.)
Lindgren, Barbro	• A WORM'S TALE
Lobel, Arnold	• GRASSHOPPER ON THE ROAD
Martin Jr., Bill	• THE LITTLE SQUEEGY BUG
Maxner, Joyce	• LADY BUGATTI
McBratney, Sam	• THE CATERPILLOW FIGHT
McDonald, Megan	• INSECTS ARE MY LIFE
Murphy, Kelly	• THE BOLL WEEVIL BALL
Murphy, Mary	• CATERPILLAR'S WISH
Murphy, Stuart J.	• THE BEST BUG PARADE
Nadler, Ellis	• THE BEE'S SNEEZE
Nickle, John	• THE ANT BULLY
Pinczes, Elinor J.	• A REMAINDER OF ONE
Sandved, Kjell B.	• THE BUTTERFLY ALPHABET
Selden, George	• THE CRICKET IN TIMES SQUARE (Chapter book.)
Shields, Carol Diggory	• THE BUGLIEST BUG
Spinelli, Eileen	• SOPHIE'S MASTERPIECE: A SPIDER'S TALE
Swope, Sam	• GOTTA GO! GOTTA GO!
Van Laan, Nancy	• THE BIG FAT WORM
Waber, Bernard	• A FIREFLY NAMED TORCHY
Wolkstein, Diane	• STEP BY STEP

CREATIVE CUE

Play Cocoon Wrap! You will need at least six children to play the game. Buy rolls of toilet paper. Two children will wrap the third child, the chrysalis. Set a timer. Who can wrap the chrysalis most completely in three minutes? Then, which chrysalis can emerge from the cocoon the fastest? Reward all players by making wings out of poster board. Attach the wings around children's arms with extra large rubber bands. For cool antennae make crowns out of corrugated "Bordette" bulletin-board border, stick pipe cleaners into the corrugation, and attach small Styrofoam balls to the ends. You'll have a room full of children who will be bugging you in no time!

Gesundheit! Stories for Sick Children

When you can't keep the doctor away, try a book a day. These should help spirits rise higher than your child's temperature. If you have a relative who is a pediatrician, these would make good gifts for the waiting room. Or how about a gift basket for the children's ward at your local hospital?

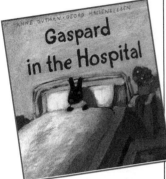

Bemelmans, Ludwig	• MADELINE
Cherry, Lynne	• WHO'S SICK TODAY?
Dealey, Erin	• GOLDIE LOCKS HAS CHICKEN POX
Duquennoy, Jacques	• OPERATION GHOST
Edwards, Pamela Duncan	• ED & FRED FLEA
Gutman, Anne	• GASPARD IN THE HOSPITAL
Hershenhorn, Esther	• CHICKEN SOUP BY HEART
Hest, Amy	• DON'T YOU FEEL WELL, SAM?
Karim, Roberta	• THIS IS A HOSPITAL, NOT A ZOO!
Loomis, Christine	• ONE COW COUGHS: A COUNTING BOOK FOR THE SICK AND MISERABLE
MacLachlan, Patricia	• THE SICK DAY
Marshall, James	• TAKING CARE OF CARRUTHERS
Moss, Miriam	• SCRITCH SCRATCH (Head lice.)
Parish, Herman	• CALLING DOCTOR AMELIA BEDELIA
Perkins, Lynne Rae	• THE BROKEN CAT
Piumini, Roberto	• DOCTOR ME DI CIN
Rey, Margret and H. A.	• CURIOUS GEORGE GOES TO THE HOSPITAL
Rosa-Casanova, Sylvia	• MAMA PROVI AND THE POT OF RICE
Rosenberry, Vera	• WHEN VERA WAS SICK
Rylant, Cynthia	• LITTLE WHISTLE'S MEDICINE
Shannon, David	• A BAD CASE OF STRIPES
Slate, Joseph	• MISS BINDERGARTEN STAYS HOME FROM KINDERGARTEN
Smith, Maggie	• DEAR DAISY, GET WELL SOON
Thomas, Patricia	• "STAND BACK," SAID THE ELEPHANT, "I'M GOING TO SNEEZE!"
Thurber, James	• MANY MOONS
Wells, Rosemary	• FELIX FEELS BETTER

Dear Madame Esmé,

My child has had the hiccups for two straight days. I think he is doing it on purpose. Does children's literature have a cure for the hiccups?

Dear Gentle Reader,

Laughter is almost always the best medicine. Fill this preschool prescription promptly by sharing HICCUP SNICKUP by Melinda Long, in which a little girl asks, How, how, HOW do you cure the hiccups? Put a paper bag over your head? Let your brother scare you? Drink from the wrong side of a cup? Book-lovers will be laughing to the point of hiccups, burps, and other bodily functions trying to sing the "hiccup snickup" song three times fast, and doing the dazzling dance daringly demonstrated in these noodle-y, doodle-y illustrations by Thor Wickstrom. Have (hic!) fun . . . and be sure to (hic!) share . . . this book, the more the mer(hic!)rier.

Hiccup, in HICCUP: THE SEASICK VIKING by Cressida Cowell, doesn't actually have hiccups. He has other problems. Sweet and tiny, he isn't much of a Viking, especially next to his burly dad, Stoick the Vast. Hiccup fears going to sea. When Hiccup goes to see Old Wrinkly and asks, "Do Vikings ever get frightened?" the old man doesn't laugh at his fears, but encourages Hiccup to find the answer himself. And his dad, green with seasickness, learns the hard way that the real meaning of bravery isn't living without fear, but rather, not letting fears stand in one's way. Don't miss the great Viking song in the book, the best sea chanty since "Yo Ho Ho and a Bottle of Rum!"

The last line of hiccup defense is DON'T MAKE ME LAUGH by James Stevenson. We are warned early on, "Do not laugh. Do not even smile. If you laugh or smile, you will have to go back to the front of the book." But who could ever resist a chuckle as Pierre, the excellent waiter, is tickled by the reader's finger and drops an enormous plate of food? Or a guffaw as the reader's gentle breathing causes an elephant to sneeze? Or a howl as a little of the reader's humming causes a hippopotamus to dance through a fancy glass store? Illustrated in a relaxed cartoon style, this book is a great study of cause and effect and of vaudeville.

✿ Potato Pick:

MISS BINDERGARTEN STAYS HOME FROM KINDERGARTEN
by Joseph Slate, illustrated by Ashley Wolff

Miss Bindergarten is out of commission due to the flu, and her class gets four-star substitute Mr. Tusky. Children who are new to this classroom experience are gently and reassuringly introduced to the new situation of teacher absence. I can't decide which gorgeous, bold illustration is my favorite: turtles playing "Chutes and Ladders," a hippo tucked in bed playing with plastic dinosaurs, or Miss Bindergarten's trusty cockatiel cooking and feeding her vegetable soup. If your child has already read MISS BINDERGARTEN GETS READY FOR KINDERGARTEN and MISS BINDERGARTEN CELEBRATES THE 100TH DAY OF KINDERGARTEN, he knows Miss Bindergarten doesn't just get well, she gets better and better and better!

Got an Issue? Here's a Tissue!
Books and Bibliotherapy

"My child has a learning disability," a mother once said to me. "What should he read?" My answer: "How about a good book?" Learning-disabled children are separated enough and it is unnecessary to segregate them further in terms of reading material. Like all children, children who have academic challenges need to be motivated to read, even more so, because it may take more effort to decode language in written form. Picture books and comic books (see Comic Books, p. 59) offer visual cues that contribute toward more successful experiences and minimize frustration, and I have observed that nonfiction that directly relates to an area of interest can be very motivating for children with challenges. But there's no single magic phonetic arrangement of words on a page that can reverse a reading challenge (though some marketers would have you believe otherwise). I do know that children with learning differences still respond to narratives that are exciting. So the question is not *what* should you read but *how*. *All* children benefit from books thoughtfully selected with individual motivations in mind. Read patiently, out loud, and often.

Of course, there are some books with characters that children with learning differences may identify with, but these are not just for children who have been "identified"; they are quality books for anyone.

Betancourt, Jeanne	My Name Is Brain Brian
Bruchac, Joseph	A Boy Called Slow: The True Story of Sitting Bull
Daly, Niki	Once Upon a Time
Gantos, Jack	Joey Pigza Swallowed the Key
Giff, Patricia Reilly	The Beast in Ms. Rooney's Room (Part of the **Kids of Polk Street School** series; great short realistic chapter books for reluctant readers.)
King-Smith, Dick	Spider Sparrow (Mature readers.)
Levy, Elizabeth	Keep Ms. Sugarman in the Fourth Grade
Philbrick, Rodman	Freak the Mighty (Mature readers.)
Polacco, Patricia	Thank You, Mr. Falker
Severance, John B.	Einstein: Visionary Scientist
Spinelli, Jerry	Loser

In particular, for children ten and up, Joey Pigza Swallowed the Key offers a long-overdue insight into the spinning-blender world that so many children experience. Although surrounded by loving, supportive, or well-intentioned adults, Joey cannot find it within himself to make good choices. Whether running to the school nurse after swallowing his own house key (and bringing it up again), running amuck during a field trip to an Amish farm, or running with scissors, Joey is running out of chances. When he is finally deemed dangerous to himself and others, he is sent to the scary "special ed" school downtown. Told from the rare first-person perspective of a boy with a severe behavioral disorder, the book's well-developed characters, humor, and guts earned it a National Book Award.

"Learning disability" is just one in a list of issues with which your child may have to contend. The question I am most commonly asked is what book is best for a child facing a particular challenge in life. Such recommendations can be helpful to young children for whom the world is new, and so need constant reassurances about the dark, moving, visits to the doctor, and the like. But generally, the well-intentioned practice of "bibliotherapy," or prescribing literature specifically to help children deal with challenges, is thin ice. Nine times out of ten, locating bibliotherapeutic books is the adult's idea, not the child's. Usually, if you ask a child what she'd like to read, she'll say something like "a book about sports" or "scary stories" or "a joke book," not "a book about head lice" or "something on sibling rivalry." It is nice to have topical books available, but not assigned.

Bibliotherapy can feel intrusive if it comes unrequested, especially as a child grows older, more self-aware and more self-conscious. The grown-up is acknowledging, "I know this about you: Your parents are getting a divorce/you're different/you can't control yourself/you're not good at school." Do you have a relationship with the child in which he has volunteered this information and you are confident he wants you to know this? Then you must be very close. Otherwise, it's just rude. As author Jill Paton Walsh noted in

CELEBRATING CHILDREN'S BOOKS, "I think it's possible to learn from works of fiction; I don't think it's possible to teach from them. . . . One does not rush to give ANNA KARENINA to friends who are committing adultery. Such impertinence is limited to dealings with children."

There is some value in being able to identify with a character or situation, but I don't think identifying with a challenge is usually enough to warrant a book recommendation. Both in quality children's literature and real life, people and characters are multifaceted, and challenges are only a part of the whole person. The litmus test of whether the book is worth sharing is if it has redeeming qualities *even if you don't have the challenge addressed*. THE BALANCING GIRL by Berniece Rabe is suspenseful, even if you're not in a wheelchair. I HAVE A SISTER, MY SISTER IS DEAF by Jeanne Whitehouse Peterson is provocative and has lovely illustrations, even if your sister can hear you loud and clear. ONE MORE WEDNESDAY by Malika Doray is comforting and honest, even if you haven't lost a grandparent. The transport of reading a good book is always the best prescription for *whatever* ails you . . . or your child. If you do find yourself in a position in which bibliotherapeutic material for children will be welcomed, check out www.acpl.lib.in.us/Childrens_Services/primer.html.

🍀 *Potato Pick:*

IT'S OKAY TO BE DIFFERENT
by Todd Parr

Bet your child didn't know that it's okay to eat macaroni and cheese in the bathtub. (My son was very excited to learn this.) It's okay to dance by yourself. It's okay to have different kinds of friends. With its bibliotherapeutic title, I was worried the book would beat us over the head with dogma but it won both me and my audience over with its genuine cheerfulness and truth. For instance, "It's okay to need help" depicts a sunny smiling person being led by an equally sunny and smiling guide dog. The skin tones and hair come in every color in this book. . . . I do mean *every* color. Even the zebra has taken a run through the rainbow! Great for discussion at all age levels— it's okay to love this book, along with Todd Parr's other zany offerings such as **THE FEEL GOOD BOOK** and **ZOO DO'S AND DON'TS**. (All ages)

Dear Madame Esmé,

I don't understand it. I tell my child that the cars won't hit us if we look both ways, that if we are careful to chew our food twenty-five times we won't choke, and that the monsters will not get us if we simply lock all the doors and lean chairs up against them. And yet, I still seem to have a nervous child. What book might calm my child's concerns?

Dear Gentle Reader,

There is nothing to fear but lack of reading material. **UNDERSTOOD BETSY** by Dorothy Canfield Fisher is much cheaper than therapy, and faster, too. Elizabeth Ann has grown up under the frenetic care of a neurotic aunt who has instilled in the pale and fragile girl a fear of dogs, coughs, and exertion. When the aunt is no longer able to care for her, Elizabeth Ann is sent to live with "those horrid Putney cousins!" in the Vermont countryside. Then, it is page after page of great ordinary-days-turned-adventure stories, as chores, friends, and outdoor life turn Elizabeth Ann into a healthy and happy Betsy. Fisher does a great job of drawing her readers into the thoughts and feelings of her little heroine, making for a very droll and memorable read for ages eight and up. Written originally in 1917 by Fisher to promote the Montessori method of teaching and learning, **UNDERSTOOD BETSY** still holds up as a testament to the potential of all children. The new pencil illustrations by Kimberly Bulcken Root have a country charm well suited to this story. These picture books about venturing and gaining are courageous choices, too:

Bottner, Barbara	• THE SCAREDY CATS
Edwards, Pamela Duncan	• THE WORRYWARTS
Gorbachev, Valeri	• CHICKEN CHICKENS
Henkes, Kevin	• WEMBERLY WORRIED
Marshall, James	• PORTLY MCSWINE
McCourt, Lisa	• I LOVE YOU, STINKY FACE
	• I MISS YOU, STINKY FACE
	• IT'S TIME FOR SCHOOL, STINKY FACE
Roche, Denis	• LITTLE PIG IS CAPABLE
Thomas, Frances	• ONE DAY, DADDY

Plant the Seed to Read: Garden Books

A book is like a garden in your pocket. —Anonymous

Ahlberg, Allan	• THE SNAIL HOUSE
Anderson, Janet S.	• SUNFLOWER SAL
Azarian, Mary	• A GARDENER'S ALPHABET
Barker, Cicely Mary	• THE FLOWER FAIRY SERIES
Bogacki, Tomek	• MY FIRST GARDEN (Very inspiring for novice gardeners.)
Bunting, Eve	• FLOWER GARDEN
Carle, Eric	• THE TINY SEED
Cherry, Lynne	• HOW GROUNDHOG'S GARDEN GREW
Cooney, Barbara	• MISS RUMPHIUS
Demi	• THE EMPTY POT
Dixon, Ann	• BLUEBERRY SHOE
Ehlert, Lois	• GROWING VEGETABLE SOUP • PLANTING A RAINBOW
Ernst, Lisa Campbell	• MISS PENNY AND MR. GRUBBS
Fleischman, Paul	• WESLANDIA
Fleming, Candace	• MUNCHA! MUNCHA! MUNCHA!
Ford, Miela	• MY DAY IN THE GARDEN
Gibbons, Gail	• FROM SEED TO PLANT
Glaser, Omri	• ROUND THE GARDEN
Harness, Cheryl	• THE QUEEN WITH BEES IN HER HAIR
Heller, Ruth	• THE REASON FOR A FLOWER
Krauss, Ruth	• THE CARROT SEED
Lobel, Arnold	• "The Garden" from FROG AND TOAD TOGETHER
Nolen, Jerdine	• PLANTZILLA
Pacovska, Kveta	• THE LITTLE FLOWER KING
Pallotta, Jerry	• THE FLOWER ALPHABET BOOK
Posada, Mia	• DANDELIONS: STARS IN THE GRASS
Roberts, Bethany	• THE WIND'S GARDEN

Sunflower Sal
Janet S. Anderson

Blueberry Shoe

Candace Fleming   G. Brian Karas
Muncha! Muncha! Muncha!

A NOSEGAY OF FLOWER FICTION FOR INTERMEDIATE READERS

Anderson, Lena, and Christina Bjork	• LINNEA IN MONET'S GARDEN
Burnett, Frances Hodgson	• THE SECRET GARDEN (Of course!)
Edwards, Julie Andrews	• MANDY
Gardiner, John Reynolds	• TOP SECRET (Great read-aloud.)
Mahy, Margaret	• THE GIRL WITH THE GREEN EAR

🌼 *Potato Pick:*

BOOK! BOOK! BOOK!

by Deborah Bruss, illustrated by Tiphanie Beeke

When the children go back to school, the animals on the farm are left with nothing to do. The hen takes the initiative to lead the livestock to the library, and they each take a turn approaching the librarian who, alas, can't decode their discourse. The question is whether they'll find a way to get the goods. This chummy story has a punch line that is all sweet corn, and the watercolor and acrylic illustrations are folksy and bright. Look for the wide-smiling frog on every page. (4 and up)

Rockwell, Anne	• BUMBLEBEE, BUMBLEBEE, DO YOU KNOW ME? A GARDEN GUESSING GAME
Rubel, Nicole	• NO MORE VEGETABLES
Smith, Maggie	• THIS IS YOUR GARDEN
Stevens, Janet	• TOPS & BOTTOMS
Stewart, Sarah	• THE GARDENER
Traditional	• JACK AND THE BEANSTALK (My favorite edition is illustrated by Gennady Spirin.)
Waddell, Martin	• THE HOLLYHOCK WALL
Winslow, Marjorie	• MUD PIES AND OTHER RECIPES: A COOKBOOK FOR DOLLS
Zion, Gene	• THE PLANT SITTER (Out-of print, but look for it used or at the library.)

. . . Don't forget more flowery favorites under "Spring" in Stories for All Seasons, p. 374, and find pals to pollinate with in Buggy for Books, p. 406, or For the Birds, p. 367. Also, see Johnny Appleseed Anniversary, p. 80, and Reading for Your Great-Great-Great-Grandchildren: Children's Books about the Environment, p. 177, for more leafy greens.

Books about Books

Bloom, Becky	• WOLF! (Great for teaching children to read with expression.)
Blos, Joan W.	• "At the Library" from BROOKLYN DOESN'T RHYME
Bradby, Marie	• MORE THAN ANYTHING ELSE
Brown, Don	• ACROSS A DARK AND WILD SEA
Bruss, Deborah	• BOOK! BOOK! BOOK!
Brutschy, Jennifer	• JUST ONE MORE STORY (Great book about family storytelling.)
Bunting, Eve	• THE WEDNESDAY SURPRISE
Cleary, Beverly	• "Beezus and Her Little Sister" from BEEZUS AND RAMONA
Cohen, Miriam	• WHEN WILL I READ?
Conover, Chris	• THE LION'S SHARE
DeFelice, Cynthia	• THE REAL, TRUE DULCIE CAMPBELL
Duvoisin, Roger	• PETUNIA
Estes, Eleanor	• "Rufus M." from RUFUS M.

George, Kristine O'Connell	• Book!
Gile, John	• Oh, How I Wished I Could Read!
Haseley, Dennis	• A Story for Bear
Lamm, C. Drew	• Pirates (Fine for fans of spooky stories.)
Léonard, Marie	• Tibili: The Little Boy Who Didn't Want to Go to School
Lyon, George Ella	• Book
Mahoney, Daniel J.	• The Saturday Escape
Mora, Pat	• Tomas and the Library Lady
Pawagi, Manjusha	• The Girl Who Hated Books
Sanvoisin, Eric	• The Ink Drinker
Spanyol, Jessica	• Carlo Likes Reading
Spinelli, Jerry	• The Library Card (Chapter book.)
Stadler, Alexander	• Beverly Billingsly Borrows a Book
Stanley, Diane	• Raising Sweetness
Stewart, Sarah	• The Library
Townley, Roderick	• The Great Good Thing (Chapter book.)
Williams, Suzanne	• Library Lil
Winters, Kay	• Abe Lincoln: The Boy Who Loved Books

. . . And for some nonfiction and fiction books about books, see Great Books for Future Authors and Illustrators, p. 319.

Gender Benders: Books for Both Boys and Girls

One of my responsibilities in the school library was weeding outdated books from the collection. This was like going on an archaeological dig, because I never knew what historical curiosities I would find. One title was something along the lines of *When I Grow Up I Want to Be,* featuring a grinning young girl speculating about her future. She could be . . . a mommy! A nurse! A secretary! A teacher! Ummm . . . that about covered it. While all of those options are perfectly helpful and meaningful callings, it was interesting to think how within the passing of such a short span of time, that same grinning girl might more readily consider options like Supreme Court justice, astronaut, or basketball player. While girls in children's literature have been notoriously spunky, it is inspiring and significant to see that recent

❁ *Potato Pick:*
The Lion's Share
by Chris Conover

This is a book fit for a king . . . or a prince or princess, as the case may be. When Prince Leo II, a lion, is born with wings on his back, King Leo Golden Mane proclaims, "He will go far!" In fact, little Leo flies *too* far. He finds himself lost in the fabled land of the polar bear King Otto, who teaches him to read and sends him back to his own land to deliver leadership through literacy and peace. The oversized illustrations are realistic in detail and whimsical in spirit; my favorite is the spread of Prince Leo dreaming of Noah's Ark, animals marching two by two out of the pages of Leo's book. The endpapers are a whole alphabet of classics from children's literature. Ask your child to guess what each letter stands for. Whether shared on a lap or in a large group, children of all ages will love this book executed with the highest standards in mind. (5 and up)

children's books focus on possibility rather than limitation for *both* genders (even suggesting in places that boys *do* cry, enjoy an occasional hug, and can successfully grow a flower or bake a cake). Both boys and girls can choose books that feature problem-solvers, risk-takers, trend-setters, and unconventional legendary figures. Honest portrayals and inclusive thematic literature have liberated the children's section (and also explain why that other book had not been checked out since 1972).

Girl Power

Little ladies and gentlemen can step right up; there's something for everyone! Fact and fiction so fantastic that it doesn't even matter whether you were dressed in pink or blue as a baby! The girl who rescues the prince! The girl with the untamed tantrum! The girl who gets dirty and just doesn't care! It's the marvel of the modern age: a level playing field with a co-ed team. Here are a few of the star attractions.

Girl Power Picture Books	
Bang, Molly	• Dawn
Bemelmans, Ludwig	• The Madeline series
Brett, Jan	• The Trouble with Trolls
Byars, Betsy	• The Golly Sisters Go West • Hooray for the Golly Sisters!
Cooney, Barbara	• Miss Rumphius
Cooper, Susan	• Tam Lin
DeFelice, Cynthia	• The Real, True Dulcie Campbell
Demi	• A Grain of Rice
dePaola, Tomie	• Legend of the Bluebonnet
Fleming, Candace	• Westward Ho, Carlotta!
Graves, Keith	• Loretta: Ace Pinky Scout
Harper, Charise Mericle	• There Was a Bold Lady Who Wanted a Star
Hearne, Betsy	• Seven Brave Women
Henkes, Kevin	• Lilly's Purple Plastic Purse
Hoffman, Mary	• Amazing Grace
Hopkinson, Deborah	• Birdie's Lighthouse
Huck, Charlotte	• Princess Furball
Kleven, Elisa	• The Paper Princess

Lattimore, Deborah Nourse	• PUNGA: GODDESS OF UGLY
Lovell, Patty	• STAND TALL, MOLLY LOU MELON
Lowell, Susan	• LITTLE RED COWBOY HAT
Martin Jr., Bill, and Michael Sampson	• SWISH!
Masini, Beatrice	• A BRAVE LITTLE PRINCESS
McClintock, Barbara	• HEARTACHES OF A FRENCH CAT
McCully, Emily Arnold	• BEAUTIFUL WARRIOR: THE LEGEND OF NUN'S KUNG FU • THE BOBBIN GIRL • LITTLE KIT, OR, THE INDUSTRIOUS FLEA CIRCUS GIRL • MIRETTE ON THE HIGH WIRE
Munsch, Robert	• MAKEUP MESS • THE PAPER BAG PRINCESS
Narahashi, Keiko	• TWO GIRLS CAN!
O'Neill, Alexis	• LOUD EMILY • THE RECESS QUEEN
Osborne, Mary Pope	• KATE AND THE BEANSTALK
Pomerantz, Charlotte	• MANGABOOM
Resier, Lynn	• CHERRY PIES AND LULLABIES
Sage, James	• SASSY GRACIE
San Souci, Robert D.	• CUT FROM THE SAME CLOTH: AMERICAN WOMEN OF MYTH, LEGEND, AND TALL TALE • FA MULAN: THE STORY OF A WOMAN WARRIOR • SUKEY AND THE MERMAID • THE TALKING EGGS • A WEAVE OF WORDS • YOUNG GUINEVERE
Small, David	• IMOGENE'S ANTLERS
Stamm, Claus	• THREE STRONG WOMEN
Steig, William	• BRAVE IRENE
Stewart, Sarah	• THE GARDENER
Theroux, Phyllis	• SEREFINA UNDER THE CIRCUMSTANCES
Thompson, Kay	• The Eloise Series
Williams, Suzanne	• LIBRARY LIL
Willis, Jeanne	• I WANT TO BE A COWGIRL
Yolen, Jane	• THE EMPEROR AND THE KITE
Zolotow, Charlotte	• THIS QUIET LADY

Our Only May Amelia
by Jennifer L. Holm

❀ *Potato Pick:*

OUR ONLY MAY AMELIA
by Jennifer L. Holm

"Ladies and princesses don't get to have adventures because they get left behind," observes May Amelia, and being left behind is the last thing she wants to happen. But "no kind of young lady" is May Amelia to her teacher, father, and cruel and cantankerous grandma. The only girl born to a Finnish American family at the turn of the century on the Nasel River, she secretly longs for the baby growing in her Mama's belly to be a girl. Will her dream come true? While she's waiting to find out, May Amelia joins her seven lively brothers on adventures at the logging camp, battling against cougars, and uncovering secrets of shanghaied sailors. This historical fiction based on the diaries of the author's grandaunt is told in present tense, giving it a rare sense of immediacy and life. (Mature readers, 11 and up)

Girl Power Fiction

Adler, David A.	• The Cam Jansen mystery series
Aiken, Joan	• THE WOLVES OF WILLOUGHBY CHASE
Alcott, Louisa May	• LITTLE WOMEN
Avi	• THE TRUE CONFESSIONS OF CHARLOTTE DOYLE
Billingsley, Franny	• THE FOLK KEEPER
Brashares, Ann	• SISTERHOOD OF THE TRAVELING PANTS
Brink, Carol Ryrie	• CADDIE WOODLAWN
Calhoun, Mary	• KATIE JOHN
Cameron, Ann	• THE SECRET LIFE OF AMANDA K. WOODS
Carroll, Lewis	• ALICE'S ADVENTURES IN WONDERLAND • THROUGH THE LOOKING GLASS
Cleary, Beverly	• BEEZUS AND RAMONA (Try all the **Ramona** series books for a high-energy girl. See Beverly Cleary, Timeless Talent, p. 386)
Cushman, Karen	• THE BALLAD OF LUCY WHIPPLE • CATHERINE, CALLED BIRDY • MATILDA BONE • THE MIDWIFE'S APPRENTICE
Dahl, Roald	• MATILDA
Danziger, Paula	• AMBER BROWN IS NOT A CRAYON (First in a series.)
DeFelice, Cynthia	• THE GHOST OF FOSSIL GLEN (Mature readers.)
Dietz, Heather, ed.	• NEWBERY GIRLS
Edwards, Julie Andrews	• MANDY
Farmer, Nancy	• A GIRL NAMED DISASTER (Mature readers.)
Greene, Bette	• PHILIP HALL LIKES ME. I RECKON, MAYBE
Holm, Jennifer L.	• OUR ONLY MAY AMELIA (Mature readers.)
Leverich, Kathleen	• BEST ENEMIES
Levine, Gail Carson	• ELLA ENCHANTED
Lindgren, Astrid	• PIPPI LONGSTOCKING
Lord, Bette Bao	• IN THE YEAR OF THE BOAR AND JACKIE ROBINSON
Lowell, Susan	• I AM LAVINA CUMMING
Lowry, Lois	• NUMBER THE STARS
McDonald, Megan	• The Judy Moody Series
McGraw, Eloise	• THE MOORCHILD

BEECH TREE CHAPTER BOOKS

BEST ENEMIES

Kathleen Leverich

with friends like Felicity, who needs enemies?

Montgomery, Lucy Maud	• ANNE OF GREEN GABLES (Beloved classic.)
Moss, Marissa	• AMELIA'S NOTEBOOK. (The whole **Amelia** series is spectacular.) • RACHEL'S JOURNAL
Naylor, Phyllis Reynolds	• The Alice series (Mature readers.)
O'Dell, Scott	• ISLAND OF THE BLUE DOLPHINS
Orgel, Doris	• THE DEVIL IN VIENNA
Phelps, Ethel Johnston, ed.	• TATTERHOOD AND OTHER TALES
Pleasant Company	• The American Girl book series, various authors (MEET ADDY is especially affecting.)
Pullman, Philip	• THE FIREWORK-MAKER'S DAUGHTER
Skolsky, Mindy Warshaw	• LOVE FROM YOUR FRIEND, HANNAH
Staples, Suzanne Fisher	• SHABANU (Mature readers.)
Tarnowska, Wafa	• THE SEVEN WISE PRINCESSES: A MEDIEVAL PERSIAN EPIC
Tchana, Katrin	• THE SERPENT SLAYER AND OTHER STORIES OF STRONG WOMEN
Testa, Maria	• SOME KIND OF PRIDE
Williams, Vera B.	• SCOOTER
Wolff, Virginia Euwer	• BAT 6
Wrede, Patricia C.	• DEALING WITH DRAGONS
Yolen, Jane	• NOT ONE DAMSEL IN DISTRESS: WORLD FOLKTALES FOR STRONG GIRLS

Girl Power Nonfiction

Adler, David A.	• AMERICA'S CHAMPION SWIMMER: GERTRUDE EDERLE
Adronik, Catherine M.	• HATSHEPSUT (Biography of Egypt's successful female pharaoh.)
Appelt, Kathi, and Jeanne Cannella Schmitzer	• DOWN CUT SHIN CREEK: THE PACK HORSE LIBRARIANS OF KENTUCKY
Atkins, Jeannine	• WINGS AND ROCKETS: THE STORY OF WOMEN IN AIR AND SPACE

SICK OF SEVENTEEN?

If you want your young daughter to stop poring over articles about what lip gloss to wear for her first kiss, subscribe to these instead. They may not have pictures of cute guys to hang in lockers, but they're still pretty good.

American Girl Magazine
Spunky and splashy, definitely with a finger on the pulse of active preteen girls.
www.americangirlstore.com/subscribe_ecomm.html

New Moon Magazine
Very intelligent, but what else would you expect when the editorial board is run by girls 9–14? Young Gloria Steinem might have subscribed.
www.newmoon.org

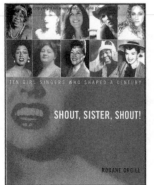

Brewster, Hugh, and Laurie Coulter	• To Be a Princess: The Fascinating Lives of Real Princesses
Brown, Don	• Uncommon Traveler: Mary Kingsley in Africa • A Voice from the Wilderness: The Story of Anna Howard Shaw
Bridges, Ruby	• Through My Eyes
Colman, Penny	• Girls: A History of Growing Up Female in America
Freedman, Russell	• Eleanor Roosevelt
Gilliland, Judith Heide	• Steamboat! The Story of Captain Blanche Leathers
Harness, Cheryl	• Remember the Ladies: 100 Great American Women
High, Linda Oatman	• The High-Diving Horse
Hoobler, Dorothy and Thomas	• Real American Girls Tell Their Own Stories
Hopkinson, Deborah	• Fannie in the Kitchen
Keenan, Sheila	• Maria's Comet (About Maria Mitchell, first American woman to discover a comet.) • Scholastic Encyclopedia of Women in the United States
Krull, Kathleen	• Lives of Extraordinary Women: Rulers, Rebels (and What the Neighbors Thought) • Wilma Unlimited
Lasky, Kathryn	• Vision of Beauty: The Story of Sarah Breedlove Walker
Lindbergh, Reeve	• Nobody Owns the Sky
Macy, Sue	• Bull's-Eye: A Photobiography of Annie Oakley • Girls Got Game
Mayer, Marianna	• Women Warriors: Myths and Legends of Heroic Women
Meltzer, Milton	• Ten Queens
Morrison, Lillian	• More Spice than Sugar: Poems about Feisty Females
Myers, Walter Dean	• At Her Majesty's Request: An African Princess in Victorian England
Orgill, Roxane	• Shout, Sister, Shout!

Here Comes the Son! Mother-Daughter Book Clubs Meet Their Male Counterparts

I remember reading my *Little Lulu* comic books and feeling delicious outrage every time I came upon the illustration of Tubby's clubhouse, in which a large sign was posted, in all capital letters: NO GIRLS ALLOWED. *How dare he! Well, I never! Of all the . . . !*

Twenty-some years later, I am surprised to find myself feeling similar pangs of indignation as I come across signs posted in bookstores and libraries, announcing meetings for mother-daughter book clubs, in which revived Ophelias and their mommies congregate to you-go-girl their way through wonderful children's literature. Sound like sour grapes? You bet your boots it is. I am the mother of a son.

The mother-daughter book club phenomenon was initiated by Shireen Dodson, assistant director of the Center for African American History and Culture at the Smithsonian Institution. She is a lovely woman

❀ *Potato Pick:*

YOU FORGOT YOUR SKIRT, AMELIA BLOOMER!

by Shana Corey, illustrated by Chesley McLaren

What's proper about fainting from corsets and getting stuck in doorways? What's proper about wearing a dress that weighs as much as a dozen bricks? Nothing, decides Amelia Bloomer, the real-life lady from the late 1800s. After meeting Elizabeth Cady Stanton's cousin, who was not wearing the fashion of the day, Bloomer popularized pants by publishing patterns in her own newspaper. Ahead of her time, Bloomer made a prime contribution to the convenience of women. The book's illustrator has designed windows for Saks Fifth Avenue and Henri Bendel, and her flirtatious fashion savvy shines with all the colors and sweeping brushstrokes of a makeup counter. The story is full of facts but reads like fiction, bouncing along and perfectly suited to a curlicue-type style. This book hangs well, with styles and smiles on every page. (6 and up)

GUYS READ!
Check out the "Guys Read" initiative at www.guysread.com.

CREATIVE CUE
For a pirate storytime, create treats using THE PIRATE COOKBOOK by Mary Ling. Follow the storytime with a treasure hunt using maps of the children's own design. Let the children hide prizes and then create maps on crumpled brown paper. More activities, including hoisting a pirate flag, can be found in THE PIRATE'S HANDBOOK by Margarette Lincoln.

who wrote a popular book, **HOW TEN BUSY MOTHERS AND DAUGHTERS CAME TOGETHER TO TALK, LAUGH, AND LEARN THROUGH THEIR LOVE OF READING.** *Well, isn't that special,* I thought ruefully, as I turned page after page of insightful recommendations. I can't find a thing wrong with the idea or the book. Except that my son and I were not invited.

One day, as I peered over the top of my copy of **DAVE AT NIGHT** by Gail Carson Levine, watching my then four-year-old son light-saber to and fro, defeating some invisible enemy and occasionally blocking the view of the ever-looping *Toy Story* video, I thought, Hey, *I* would like to Talk, Laugh, and Learn through My Love of Reading with my son. Am I going to have to dress him up like Christopher Robin to get him into one of these clubs?

The answer, of course, is not to beat them, but join them. Whether designed for boys or girls, storytimes and book clubs hone listening skills and attention spans, preparing children for the day when novels can be discussed and larger themes explored. So start young. The mothers of boys four to seven years old can take turns designing and hosting thematic storytimes based on the boys' interests. (Dads, you can do this, too, and be reading role models for sons *or* daughters!) In a fit of "So there!" a mother of a son might explore some of these stereotypical subjects (knowing in her heart that boys, just like girls, have varied interests and ultimately any of the themes of any of the booklists may be enjoyed):

Pirate Storytime

Cox, Judy	• **RABBIT PIRATES: A TALE OF THE SPINACH MAIN**
Fox, Mem	• **TOUGH BORIS**
Gorbachev, Valeri	• **ARNIE THE BRAVE**
Mahy, Margaret	• **THE GREAT PIRATICAL RUMBUSTIFICATION** • **THE MAN WHOSE MOTHER WAS A PIRATE**
McNaughton, Colin	• **CAPTAIN ABDUL'S PIRATE SCHOOL**
Tucker, Kathy	• **DO PIRATES TAKE BATHS?**

Transportation Storytime

Barton, Byron	• **AIRPORT**
Booth, Philip	• **CROSSING**
Brown, Margaret Wise	• **TWO LITTLE TRAINS**
Burton, Virginia Lee	• **MIKE MULLIGAN AND HIS STEAM SHOVEL** (Rather long but beloved read-aloud.)

Cassedy, Sylvia	• ZOOMRIMES: POEMS ABOUT THINGS THAT GO
Cecil, Laura	• NOAH AND THE SPACE ARK
Collicutt, Paul	• THIS TRAIN
Crews, Donald	• FREIGHT TRAIN • SCHOOL BUS
Cuetara, Mittie	• THE CRAZY CRAWLER CRANE AND OTHER VERY SHORT TRUCK STORIES
Drummond, Allan	• CASEY JONES
Eastman, P. D.	• GO, DOG. GO!
Gutman, Anne, and Geoig Hallensleben	• LISA'S AIRPLANE TRIP
Hillenbrand, Will	• DOWN BY THE STATION
Kalman, Maira	• FIREBOAT: THE HEROIC ADVENTURES OF THE JOHN J. HARVEY (Contains reference to September 11.)
Kirk, Daniel	• GO!
Meister, Cari	• BUSY BUSY CITY STREET
Selgin, Peter	• "S.S." GIGANTIC ACROSS THE ATLANTIC
Steen, Sandra	• CAR WASH
Sturges, Philemon	• I LOVE TRAINS!
Zelinsky, Paul O.	• THE WHEELS ON THE BUS

CREATIVE CUE

Follow a transportation storytime by helping children make tempera-paint decorations of cardboard-box "vehicles": Use paper plates and brass fasteners for wheels. Take pictures; make fake "reading on the road" licenses. Every child can also be given his own copy of Richard Scarry's CARS AND TRUCKS AND THINGS THAT GO. See if the children can find Goldbug in each picture. Then, take a field trip through the car wash!

Baseball Storytime

Blackstone, Margaret	• THIS IS BASEBALL
Burleigh, Robert	• HOME RUN: THE STORY OF BABE RUTH
Chabon, Michael	• SUMMERLAND (Chapter book.)
Curtis, Gavin	• THE BAT BOY AND HIS VIOLIN
Giff, Patricia Reilly	• RONALD MORGAN GOES TO BAT
Golenbock, Peter	• TEAMMATES
Gutman, Dan	• Baseball Card Adventure series (Chapter books.)
Isadora, Rachel	• NICK PLAYS BASEBALL
Mandel, Peter	• SAY HEY! A SONG OF WILLIE MAYS
Mochizuki, Ken	• BASEBALL SAVED US

🥔 *Potato Pick:*

CASEY AT THE BAT

by Ernest Lawrence Thayer,
illustrated by Christopher Bing

Get yer hotdogs! Peanuts! Caldecott winner here! Open the faux leather scrapbook cover to reveal the faithful retelling of the antihero of Mudville, the Mighty Casey who comes to bat at the bottom of the ninth, and on the last pitch he . . . well, read and see! Each page is adorned with newspaper clippings, standings, advertisements, tickets, letters, cards, coins, and confetti. This is the most loving offering to the game seen in children's literature since the novel IN THE YEAR OF THE BOAR AND JACKIE ROBINSON by Bette Bao Lord. (6 and up, and a great Father's Day gift)

CREATIVE CUE

For children who enjoy baseball books, start a reading home-run derby by letting children advance a base on a diamond-shaped "scorecard" for every book they read in a week. How many runs can the children read in? Then take a field trip: Have children bring their favorite sports book to a sports event and ask the athletes to autograph the endpapers before or after the game!

Norworth, Jack	• TAKE ME OUT TO THE BALLGAME (The version by Maryann Kovalski also swings.)
Parish, Peggy	• PLAY BALL, AMELIA BEDELIA
Park, Barbara	• SKINNYBONES (Short chapter book.)
Shannon, David	• HOW GEORGIE RADBOURN SAVED BASEBALL
Slote, Alfred	• FINDING BUCK McHENRY (Great chapter book.)
Tavares, Matt	• ZACHARY'S BALL
Testa, Maria	• BECOMING JOE DiMAGGIO (Short novel told in verse.)
Thayer, Ernest Lawrence, and Christopher Bing	• CASEY AT THE BAT
Welch, Willy	• PLAYING RIGHT FIELD

BOOK CLUBS FOR OLDER BOYS

When considering what would engage intermediate male readers 8–12, I think more in terms of authors than of particular books. The "back of the baseball card" approach serves well here: What are the particulars of the people behind the books? What in Gary Paulsen's own life would compel him to write such graphic survival stories as HATCHET and HOW ANGEL PETERSON GOT HIS NAME? What in Louis Sachar's life could allow him to travel from such a comic setting as that found in SIDEWAYS STORIES FROM WAYSIDE SCHOOL to the tragic and haunting desert of HOLES? Roald Dahl treats his readers to remarkable heroes, but there is a darker, more misogynous side to some of Dahl's books (and his life)—books such as GEORGE'S MARVELOUS MEDICINE and THE WITCHES. I want

to be there when my son reads these, to help him navigate this difficult terrain, to ponder together that most important question, *why did the author write this book?* You can do some research into the author's background before the book club meets (see Author/Illustrator Studies, p. 309 for helpful references).

Besides strengthening the author/reader connection, a boys book group allows for talking about feelings and issues. For example, I want to support my son through the dangerous reads of Jerry Spinelli's

MANIAC MAGEE, which tells a tale as tall as the Empire State and just as full of humanity, and I want to offer the superglue to mend my son's broken heart as he reads about the broken necks in **WRINGER,** also by Spinelli. I want to be his booster in the shadow of a bully in Laurie Myers's **SURVIVING BRICK JOHNSON.** I want to give him the key that unlocks **THE INDIAN IN THE CUPBOARD** by Lynne Reid Banks. I want to belly-laugh with my son over Robert Newton Peck's memoirs, his **Soup** series, and then cry over the tribute to his father, **A DAY NO PIGS WOULD DIE.** I want to watch my son recognize his many moods in Judith Viorst's collection of stories, **ABSOLUTELY, POSITIVELY ALEXANDER.** I want to ask my son, What do you always want to remember? What do you hold dear? What do you want to win? What are you afraid of losing? Who do you want to be? Who are you? Sure, we can make this journey on our own, but it is nice for both of us to have the option of accessing a greater circle of support in this endeavor of self-discovery, and the diverse perspectives add to our reading experience. The scheduling of book club meetings also serves as motivation to read regularly, which is part of helping children to improve as readers.

All right, having a boy often means no pink frilly dresses, but I'll be darned if I miss out on any more than that. When the daughters of the mother-daughter clubs grow up, they'll thank us mother-son club leaders for having nurtured the strong and not-so-silent types: men who love to read and know how to share that love.

ROALD DAHL RULES!

In Roald Dahl's garden in England, one of the paving stones reads: "Those who don't believe in magic will never find it." I disagree. Anyone who reads a book by Roald Dahl is sure to find it, and then, they will believe. I can't think of an author who is more compulsively readable or more notoriously naughty than Roald Dahl. His books have drawn continuous admiration and controversy since the publication of his **JAMES AND THE GIANT PEACH** in 1961. Even my younger brother who professed to being in the "Hate Books" rather than "Great Books" program at school was very pleased with the first few pages of Dahl's original masterwork, in which James's parents

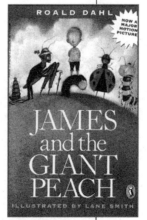

MATT CHRISTOPHER: A GOOD SPORT

After an injury halted his career as a semiprofessional baseball player, Matt Christopher scored big by using his creative talents to write dozens of sports stories. Although he started writing in 1954, children today still fill the stands, ignoring some of the more dated material and instead choosing to cheer over his straightforward, action-packed books. Intermediate jocks, who may not have shown an interest in reading, will go into double page-turning overtime with his most popular series. The stories are peppered with that secret lingo only sports enthusiasts can really appreciate. Matt Christopher was extremely prolific, and thank goodness, because like ballpark peanuts, it's hard to stop at just one. Your child can also join the Matt Christopher fan club at www.mattchristopher.com.

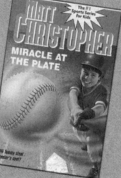

BASEBALL

Baseball Flyhawk	Miracle at the Plate
Baseball Pals	No Arm in Left Field
Baseball Turnaround	Pressure Play
Catcher with a Glass Arm	Prime-Time Pitcher
Challenge at Second Base	The Reluctant Pitcher
The Diamond Champs	Return of the Home Run Kid
Double Play at Short	Shortstop from Tokyo
The Fox Steals Home	The Submarine Pitch
The Kid Who Only Hit Homers	Windmill Windup
Look Who's Playing First Base	The Year Mom Won the Pennant

BASKETBALL

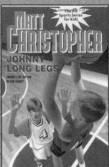

This Basket Counts
Center Court Sting
Johnny Long Legs
Long Shot for Paul
Red-Hot Hightops
Shoot for the Hoop
Wheel Wizards

CYCLING

Dirt Bike Racer
Dirt Bike Runaway
Mountain Bike Mania

DIVING

Dive Right In

FOOTBALL

Catch That Pass!	Long-Arm Quarterback
Crackerjack Halfback	The Team That Couldn't Lose
Football Fugitive	Tight End
Football Nightmare	Touchdown for Tommy
The Great Quarterback Switch	Tough to Tackle

GOLF

Fairway Phenom

HOCKEY

Cool As Ice
Face-Off
The Hockey Machine
Ice Magic
Penalty Shot
Wingman on Ice

ROLLER HOCKEY

INLINE SKATER

ROLLER HOCKEY RADICALS

SKATEBOARD

SKATEBOARD RENEGADE

SKATEBOARD TOUGH

SNOWBOARDING

SNOWBOARD MAVERICK

SNOWBOARD SHOWDOWN

SOCCER

THE COMEBACK CHALLENGE

GOALKEEPER IN CHARGE

SOCCER DUEL

SOCCER HALFBACK

SOCCER SCOOP

TOP WING

TENNIS

TENNIS ACE

TRACK

RUN, BILLY, RUN

RUN FOR IT

VOLLEYBALL

SPIKE IT!

Later in his career, Christopher turned his attention to his sports biographies series, a more coed endeavor that really underscored his strength as a researcher as well as his general admiration of athletes, which many young readers share.

	On the Field with . . .
At the Plate with . . .	. . . Alex Rodriguez
. . . Ichiro	. . . Derek Jeter
. . . Ken Griffey Jr.	. . . Julie Foudy
. . . Mark McGwire	. . . Mia Hamm
. . . Samy Sosa	. . . Terrell Davis

In the Goal with . . .	On the Halfpipe with . . .
. . . Briana Scurry	. . . Tony Hawk
In the Huddle with . . .	On the Ice with . . .
. . . John Elway	. . . Mario Lemieux
On the Bike with . . .	. . . Tara Lipinski
. . . Lance Armstrong	On the Mound with . . .
On the Course with . . .	. . . Greg Maddux
. . . Tiger Woods	. . . Randy Johnson
On the Court with . . .	On the Track with . . .
. . . Grant Hill	. . . Jeff Gordon
. . . Hakeem Olajuwon	
. . . Kobe Bryant	
. . . Lisa Leslie	
. . . Michael Jordan	
. . . Venus and Serena Williams	

. . . If for some reason Matt Christopher doesn't score well for the home team, there are several other authors warming up in the bullpen. Dan Gutman is an outstanding sportswriter for intermediate children, and he has a special gift for tackling fact and fiction. His **Baseball Card Adventure** series, in which the legends on baseball cards come to life to share a bit of sports history with the card collector, is imaginative and well researched. Intermediate and older children can also scout out John R. Tunis, Robert Lipsyte, Bruce Brooks, and Chris Crutcher for novels. Sue Macy is the author who can coach girls or boys looking for a little sports history. Periodicals count as reading, too, so encourage your young sports enthusiast to check out the daily sports standings in the newspaper, or subscribe to *Sports Illustrated for Kids* at www.sikids.com (sorry, no swimsuit issue for the little ones). Novels, history, biography, trivia . . . no matter what your game plan, sports can bring a reluctant child onto the winning team of readers.

are devoured by an angry rhino and Aunts Sponge and Spiker are flattened. There is no shortage of action and imagination in a Roald Dahl book. Dark humor and cynicism, histrionic banter punctuated by nonsensical vocabulary, and the consummate battle between good and evil all characterize Dahl's work. Dahl is not without his detractors. I knew my own childhood was over when I read THE WITCHES and began to see the rationale behind his critics' rankling, but luckily at that point nothing could really make me recoil from Roald. True, when he is bad, he is horrid: arguably sexist, racist, ageist, violent, crude, and rude. But when he is good, he is very *very* good, both in his unwavering voice and pacing, and because, although he paints a dark sky, a star of justice always brightly shines. From a child's point of view, his writing is utterly empathetic. Dahl places a young character in a ring with a powerful opponent, but by the last round that child emerges a winner, a hero, and the young reader's spirit is invariably elevated by this portrayal. Because of this, Dahl will always be the champion of reluctant readers and children in general, influencing and inspiring (but never quite surpassed by) popular authors such as J. K. Rowling and Lemony Snicket.

When introducing Roald Dahl to a group of children, I always start by reading THE TWITS because it's short and sweet . . . well, maybe "sweet" is not the best word choice. It is basically an anti-love story in which two dreadful people play nasty tricks on each other, only to find in the end that the tables have turned—literally. I like to put a fake eyeball (available at www.orientaltrading.com) in the bottom of a beverage, drink up, then pretend to discover it at the bottom of my glass, staring up at me. This is one of the pranks Mrs. Twit plays on Mr. Twit, his terror met with the glib remark, "I've got my eye on you." I make enlarged copies of Quentin Blake's illustration of filthy Mr. Twit, and children decorate his beard by gluing on the goopiest, grossest bric-a-brac they can find. Inspired by scenes in the book, we eat plenty of "wormy spaghetti" and make elegant Roly-Poly Bird masks with feathers and paper plates.

We then move on to THE ENORMOUS CROCODILE—an enormous read-aloud hit every time, and we make simple crocodile marionettes by putting together construction-paper parts of a crocodile and attaching them with yarn to a long, horizontal wooden rod. I usually make a prototype and cut out the construction paper parts ahead of time, but I don't give tons of direction outside of presenting a finished example; it's a good chance for children to cooperate and problem-solve.

MATILDA, starring Mara Wilson and Danny DeVito, is an entertaining opportunity to compare movie to book. I don't think Roald Dahl would mind this media crossover; he was an accomplished screenwriter (ever see *Chitty Chitty Bang Bang*?). CHARLIE AND THE CHOCOLATE FACTORY in print form is an imaginative tour de force, but the movie *Willy Wonka & the Chocolate Factory* starring Gene Wilder is equally delicious; read the book and compare. After Charlie has found his golden ticket that allows him to enter the factory, I pause the video and pass out chocolate bars with a homemade foil "golden ticket" tucked inside one. The lucky child who finds it gets . . . what else? . . . a copy of a book by Roald Dahl. We also make "Oompa Loompa Lesson Books," in which children illustrate each page with a different heading:

> If you're not greedy, you will go far.
> If you have manners, you will go far.
> If you're not spoiled, you will go far.
> If you like reading, you will go far.
> If you _____, you will go far.

If Charlie sets off a craving for cocoa, you can segue into some sweet treats by other authors, such as CHOCOLATE FEVER by Robert Kimmel Smith and THE CHOCOLATE TOUCH by Patrick Skene Catling.

Allow children to savor Dahl's other classic titles in Literature Circles (see p. 303). I like to combine group activities and read-aloud to help children gain interest and confidence, and then give them the opportunity to enjoy Dahl's wicked works more privately. You can also enjoy a smorgasbord in THE ROALD DAHL TREASURY. Some of the tamer and more tasteful books are Dahl's earlier tomes, but I wouldn't bother being too choosy, because most likely the child who reads one Roald Dahl book will end up reading them all.

BOOKS BY ROALD DAHL

- THE BFG
- BOY
- CHARLIE AND THE CHOCOLATE FACTORY
- CHARLIE AND THE GREAT GLASS ELEVATOR
- DANNY, THE CHAMPION OF THE WORLD
- DIRTY BEASTS
  - THE ENORMOUS CROCODILE
  - ESIO TROT
  - FANTASTIC MR. FOX
  - GEORGE'S MARVELOUS MEDICINE
  - GIRAFFE AND THE PELLY AND ME
  - GOING SOLO
  - JAMES AND THE GIANT PEACH
  - THE MAGIC FINGER
  - MATILDA
- THE MINPINS
- ROALD DAHL'S REVOLTING RHYMES
- THE VICAR OF NIBBLESWICKE
- THE WONDERFUL STORY OF HENRY SUGAR AND SIX MORE
- THE WITCHES

You can also hear the author read his works on Caedmon's *The Roald Dahl Audio Collection*. Visit www.roalddahl.com for further activities, biographical information, and all things scrumdiddlyumptious.

Must-Reads by the Time You're Thirteen

Big children need love and literature, too. Just as Russell's Book Basket (p. 40) can carry a family through the primary stage when an interest in books is on the rise, this is the list of books I have come to count on to resuscitate reading with intermediate children, who are at calculated risk of faltering in their reading motivation. I chose titles with lasting value, with themes and styles that will speak to both genders. I have to trust that the titles will promote a love of reading and cultivate a sensitive, intelligent, good-humored, and brave spirit. I'm not sure exactly what statewide goal that addresses, and I haven't bothered to check if any of these match objectives on a standardized test, but regardless, they seem mighty important. So, academically, the list is always the priority when I teach intermediate children. This is the list that answers the question, "If they were my own children about to leave grade school, what would I hope they would have in their hearts?"

As a teacher, I always felt a sense of urgency to read aloud as many titles as possible within the school year, but as parents, we have the luxury of pacing ourselves, delivering positive read-aloud experiences as our children grow from one stage to the next. If you read aloud to your child, you will create a bond that can never be broken, a source of joy for both you and your child and an example that will echo through generations. Maybe "must read" is a tricky mandate given the will and tastes of the individual child, but these are at least "must try." For helpful hints about reading out loud, see p. 11.

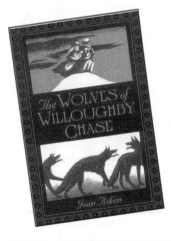

Must-Reads by Thirteen

Aardema, Verna WHAT'S SO FUNNY, KETU?

African folktale about a man who believes he must keep a secret in order to stay alive. Picture book.

Aiken, Joan THE WOLVES OF WILLOUGHBY CHASE

Two children cooperate to overcome the trickery of an avaricious governess in this chilling, thrilling nod to Dickens. Chapter book fiction.

Ardizzone, Edward TIM ALL ALONE

Tim, separated from his parents at sea, must be brave until he can find them again. Picture book.

Banks, Lynne Reid THE INDIAN IN THE CUPBOARD

Omri gets more responsibility than he bargains for when his plastic toy comes to life. Chapter book fantasy.

Bellairs, John THE HOUSE WITH A CLOCK IN ITS WALLS

A mystery waits to be solved within the walls and corridors of the mansion of an eccentric uncle, but the clock is ticking. Chapter book fiction, mystery.

Brittain, Bill THE WISH GIVER

Four wishes are granted to four small-town folk, no trade-backs, no-nothing-backs. Chapter book fantasy.

Brown, Jeff FLAT STANLEY

Crushed by a bulletin board, Stanley makes use of his new shape. Short story.

Brumbeau, Jeff THE QUILTMAKER'S GIFT

A quiltmaker designs a beautiful blanky to cover a greedy king's behind. Picture book.

Burch, Robert IDA EARLY COMES OVER THE MOUNTAIN

Like an Appalachian Mary Poppins, this energetic young woman comes to help run a home in Depression-era Georgia. Chapter book fiction.

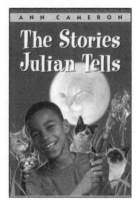

Cameron, Ann THE STORIES JULIAN TELLS

Three vignettes about life in a lively African-American family. Short stories.

Carey, Valerie Scho THE DEVIL & MOTHER CRUMP

Folktale about a woman "mean as the devil" who *almost* meets her match. Picture book folktale.

Cleary, Beverly BEEZUS AND RAMONA

An older sister seeks to find redeeming qualities in her bratty little sister, and in herself. One of the very first in the Ramona series. Chapter book fiction.

Clements, Andrew FRINDLE

A boy invents a new word and makes an adversary of his dictionary-devout teacher. Chapter book fiction.

Creech, Sharon LOVE THAT DOG

Jack's opinion of poetry changes after connecting with an author. Fiction told in verse.

Curtis, Christopher Paul THE WATSONS GO TO BIRMINGHAM, 1963
A turbulent time told through the cross-eyes of little brother Kenny. Chapter book, historical fiction.

Dahl, Roald CHARLIE AND THE CHOCOLATE FACTORY
Willy Wonka opens his door and reveals his candy-making secrets to five children, of which four are near-fatally flawed. Chapter book fantasy.

Dahl, Roald THE TWITS
A monkey family makes a creative escape from the clutches of the world's most repulsive couple. Chapter book fantasy.

D'Aulaire, Ingri and Edgar D'AULAIRES' BOOK OF GREEK MYTHS
The definitive guide to Greek mythology for children. Mythology/short stories.

DeJong, Meindert THE HOUSE OF SIXTY FATHERS
Tien Pao is caught in the crossfire of war when his sampan is swept into Japanese territory, separating him from his family. Chapter book, historical fiction.

DeJong, Meindert THE WHEEL ON THE SCHOOL
Students try to bring storks to nest in a small Dutch village. Chapter book fiction.

Demi THE EMPTY POT
An emperor announces a gardening contest to find his successor. Picture book folktale.

DiCamillo, Kate BECAUSE OF WINN-DIXIE
With the help of a stray dog, a lonely girl makes unconventional friends in her southern town. Chapter book fiction.

Edwards, Julie Andrews THE LAST OF THE REALLY GREAT WHANGDOODLES
A professor takes children on a magical hunt for an endangered species. Chapter book fantasy.

Erdrich, Louise THE BIRCHBARK HOUSE
Adventures on the frontier from the perspective of an Ojibwa girl. Chapter book, historical fiction.

Estes, Eleanor THE HUNDRED DRESSES
Teasing takes an especially unfashionable turn when a poor girl is targeted. Chapter book fiction.

Farber, Norma **HOW DOES IT FEEL TO BE OLD?**
A grandma gives the straight dope, in free verse. Poetry.

Farjeon, Eleanor **A LITTLE BOOKROOM**
A wide variety of both realistic and wonder tales that speak
straight to the heart of a child. Short stories.

Fisher, Dorothy Canfield **UNDERSTOOD BETSY**
A timid city girl learns to take life by the reins in the
countryside. Chapter book fiction.

Fitzgerald, John D. **THE GREAT BRAIN**
A young schemer turns a buck in turn-of-the-century Utah.
Chapter book fiction/memoir.

Fleischman, Paul **HALF-A-MOON INN**
A chiller about a mute boy who is held captive in a hellatious bed-
and-breakfast. Chapter book fiction.

Gardiner, John Reynolds **STONE FOX**
A boy needs to win a bobsled race to save his grandfather's farm.
Chapter book fiction.

Glass, Tom **EVEN A LITTLE IS SOMETHING**
Vignettes from a little girl's life in modern Thailand. Short stories.

Hughes, Ted **THE IRON GIANT**
A postmodern monster comes to Earth in an ecological parable.
Chapter book fantasy.

Jarrell, Randall **THE BAT-POET**
A bat who stays awake during the day gains the
insight he needs to make him an artist. Chapter
book wonder tale.

Kipling, Rudyard **MOWGLI'S BROTHERS** (Illustrated by
Christopher Wormell.)
Coming-of-age story about a boy raised by jungle
animals. Wonder tale/legend.

Koch, Kenneth, and Kate Farrell **TALKING TO THE SUN:
AN ILLUSTRATED ANTHOLOGY OF POEMS FOR YOUNG PEOPLE**
An introductory collection spanning time, culture, and style, illustrated
with fine art. Poetry.

JANUSZ KORCZAK
THE FATHER FIGURE

Janusz Korczak was an outstanding and sometimes controversial pediatrician, teacher, and, starting in 1912, fundraiser and director of an orphanage for Jewish children in Warsaw, Poland. He wrote what I consider to be the greatest read-aloud of all time, KING MATT THE FIRST, for the children in that orphanage. This book, as popular and celebrated as PETER PAN in some parts of Europe, is almost unknown in America. The hero in the story is a boy-king who tries to issue reforms for his nation and form a parliament of children. The book is a sort of biographical fantasy, in which Korczak reinvents himself as a boy to communicate his vision of the active role children could play in creating a better world. In his orphanage, his ideas were made flesh; the children actually did largely govern themselves with a children's court, a children's parliament, and their own newspaper.

Throughout his life, Korczak advocated tirelessly for the respectful treatment of all children. Given several chances by friends to escape to freedom, Korczak refused to abandon the children of his orphanage. Holding the two youngest by the hand, he walked with two hundred children to the train station, with the oldest child holding a green flag, a symbol of children's freedom. On August 6, 1942, Korczak and the children were gassed at Treblinka. While his life was cut short by the Nazi occupation of Warsaw, his hope for a better quality of life for children lives on.

Korczak is a hero to me, no less for the way he lived than the way he died. Psychologist Bruno Bettelheim suggests that Korczak believed the only way to reform the world is to change our manner of raising children. An intrinsic part of the way he brought up the children in his orphanage was through literature. He wrote books for children with the intent of reading them aloud, to *all* ages. Because of this, I believe read-aloud was part of his utopian vision; and as such, it does honor to his memory to read aloud to both older and younger children.

Konigsburg, E. L. FROM THE MIXED-UP FILES OF MRS. BASIL E. FRANKWEILER
A brother and sister run away from home and hide out in New York's Metropolitan Museum of Art. Chapter book fiction/mystery.

Korczak, Janusz KING MATT THE FIRST
Masterpiece about a country run by a child. Chapter book fiction.

Kotzwinkle, William TROUBLE IN BUGLAND
It's entomological, my dear Watson! Sherlock-style mysteries solved by a mantis sleuth. Mystery/short stories.

Levine, Gail Carson **ELLA ENCHANTED**

The gift of obedience feels like a curse in this compelling Cinderella takeoff. Chapter book fantasy.

Lewis, C. S. **THE LION, THE WITCH, AND THE WARDROBE**

Siblings go into a closet and discover Narnia, where good and evil clash. Chapter book fantasy.

Lindgren, Astrid **PIPPI LONGSTOCKING**

An impish girl makes life very interesting for her neighbors. Chapter book fiction.

Lisle, Janet Taylor **AFTERNOON OF THE ELVES**

A popular girl is drawn into the imaginative world of an outcast neighbor, learning her family secrets and struggling to understand the pain that is happening right next door. Chapter book historical fiction.

Lord, Bette Bao **IN THE YEAR OF THE BOAR AND JACKIE ROBINSON**

A Chinese immigrant girl finds her place in the States through baseball. Chapter book, historical fiction.

Lowry, Lois **NUMBER THE STARS**

The Danish resistance helps a family escape capture by the Nazis. Chapter book, historical fiction.

Martin, Jacqueline Briggs **SNOWFLAKE BENTLEY**

One man uses his dream of photographing snowflakes to create a gift for the world. Picture book biography.

McCaughrean, Geraldine, trans. **ONE THOUSAND AND ONE ARABIAN NIGHTS**

If Queen Shahrazad wants to keep her head, she has to tell the king a cliffhanger every night. Short stories/legend.

Naylor, Phyllis Reynolds **SHILOH**

Marty is faced with huge ethical dilemmas when he tries to shelter a mistreated dog. Chapter book fiction.

Nhuong, Huynh Quang **THE LAND I LOST**

Memories of a boyhood in Vietnam. Chapter book memoir.

Paulsen, Gary **HATCHET**

Left for dead in the Canadian wilderness after a plane crash, Brian must become self-reliant to survive. Chapter book fiction.

What to Do When Your Child Doesn't Want You to Read Aloud

*O*kay, it happens. Children get old and grouchy, as early as age seven. They don't want to do the things they did when they were little—they can read them*selves,* they've moved *on,* don't you *get* it? Well, don't get it, or they won't get it. Try these strategies instead:

Communicate honestly. Tell your child in plain English (or Spanish or Japanese or Pig-Latin) that you *know* he is a great reader; this is simply very important to you. Explain that reading out loud is part of who you are as a parent, and what you love to do, that you look forward to it and would miss it if you didn't. Explain that reading out loud is a present you are trying to give and it will change his life in amazing ways, and ask if he could just trust you on that now. Explain that read-aloud is something you do in this family no matter how old he is and you hope that he will grow up and do it for his children as well. Your child may allow you to begin reading just to get you to stop talking like this!

Wheedle a little. "Did I not do for you all day? So now do this one thing for me." Effectiveness of guilt trips may vary according to cultural tendencies ingrained for generations. Some children have developed an immunity.

Go to bed a little earlier. Sometimes children are just plain tired at the end of the day and konk out as you begin reading, or are simply too cranky to listen. Go to bed about twenty minutes earlier to improve read-aloud mood and attention span.

Go to bed a little later. This is a good bargaining chip for older children. Offer that they might stay up an extra half hour if you can spend it reading together. If they are old enough to give attitude about it, suggest you try it for just a week and serialize a novel. They'll be hooked.

Change the schedule. Bedtime seems to be the reading time of choice, but be versatile when your family's needs demand it. If your schedule doesn't allow you to read aloud before bed, try reading aloud during breakfast instead. Or during carpool. Or before homework (believe me, there's nothing going on in the homework that read-

Peck, Richard **A Long Way from Chicago**
Grandma Dowdel is kicking behind and taking names for each of the seven summers Joey and Mary Alice come up for a visit. Chapter book fiction.

Peck, Robert Newton **Soup and Me**
Two mischievous boys frolic in the Vermont countryside. Chapter book fiction.

aloud won't help). Just try to be consistent in whatever time you decide on; *regular* read-aloud impacts academic achievement more dramatically.

Turn the TV or computer games off. Match time spent staring at screens with time spent reading aloud. Rule of thumb: Use your library card at least as often as your Blockbuster card.

Make it a reward. Extra help with the housework or good grades can mean an extra story or chapter at the end of the day.

Let someone else read aloud. Have a guest reader, such as a grandparent, the spouse who doesn't usually read aloud, a family friend, or an older sibling. Or get a book on tape (see Fast Forward to Listening Fun, p. 200), but get the book as well, and follow along so your child still gets the exposure to print.

Make a list. Sometimes just keeping track of what you're reading inspires children to read more. It's fun to watch the list get longer and longer! You can even jot titles and dates on the door, by the growth chart.

Go to the library or bookstore more often. New titles can jumpstart interest.

Take turns reading aloud. You read a page, your child reads a page. Or, take parts in dialogue. Praise generously!

Read aloud what you never thought you would. Give in to your children's desires. Let them pick anything, *anything* they want. So, it's the five-hundred-page *Technical Encyclopedia of All-You-Never-Wanted-to-Know About Race Cars/Video Games/Arachnids.* So, it's a magazine article from *Teen-Beat-Me-over-the-Head-with-Makeup Tips.* You learn something new every day! Your willingness to share in your children's interests not only improves their self esteem, it makes you look cool and (almost?) worth talking to. Besides, if your children are interested in it, how bad can it be? (Don't answer that.) If it's more than you can bear, negotiate: "One thing *you* pick, one thing *I* pick."

Give in, but read alongside. If you've tried these strategies but read-aloud is still a battle, ease up. Fighting is counterproductive. If your child won't come around and join you, you can still model read-aloud with your spouse or partner. You can also compromise by getting book lights and reading silently alongside your child. Remark on notable passages you come across, and ask sporadic questions that encourage your child to do the same with you.

Pène du Bois, William **The Twenty-One Balloons**
Professor William Waterman Sherman plans to spend his retirement crossing the Pacific in his hot-air balloon, but instead comes down on a volcanic island inhabited by inventors and gourmets. Chapter book fantasy.

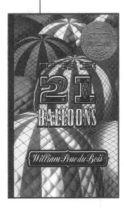

Pinkwater, Daniel **The Big Orange Splot**
Mr. Plumbean's house is where he wants to be, and it looks like all his dreams in this tribute to nonconformity. Picture book.

GOOD BOOKS ABOUT GOOD KIDS DOING GOOD DEEDS

If I had my way, these books would be included in every middle- and upper-grade curriculum. Not only do they show older children in a positive light, they celebrate the power of one.

Bonners, Susan	• EDWINA VICTORIOUS
Buchanan, Jane	• THE BERRY-PICKING MAN
Howe, Norma	• THE ADVENTURES OF BLUE AVENGER (For mature readers.)
Klise, Kate	• REGARDING THE FOUNTAIN
McGovern, Ann	• THE LADY IN THE BOX

Spinelli, Jerry	• LOSER
	• STARGIRL
Wittlinger, Ellen	• GRACIE'S GIRL

Polacco, Patricia PINK AND SAY
Two Union soldiers, one black, one white, meet against the backdrop of the Civil War. Picture book/historical fiction.

Richler, Mordecai JACOB TWO-TWO MEETS THE HOODED FANG
Imprisoned for insulting a grown-up, Jacob Two-Two (who says everything twice to be heard over his brothers and sisters) must depend on Kid Power to free him from the clutches of his pro-wrestling jailer. Chapter book fantasy.

Robinson, Barbara THE BEST CHRISTMAS PAGEANT EVER
The Herdmans, aka "the worst kids in the entire history of the world," are cast in some unlikely roles. Chapter book fiction.

Rowling, J. K. HARRY POTTER AND THE SORCERER'S STONE
Hogwarts School will never be the same after the arrival of this wizard-in-training. Chapter book fantasy.

Sachar, Louis HOLES
Unlucky underdog Stanley Yelnats has to do hard time in a Texas juvenile detention facility. Chapter book fiction.

Sachar, Louis SIDEWAYS STORIES FROM WAYSIDE SCHOOL
A Zen guide to elementary education in the schoolhouse that was built thirty stories high. Short stories.

Saint-Exupéry, Antoine de THE LITTLE PRINCE
Lost in the desert, a pilot finds an oasis in the insights of an intergalactic boy. Chapter book fiction.

Segal, Lore, trans. THE JUNIPER TREE AND OTHER TALES FROM GRIMM
A collection of classic fairy tales in all their gory glory. Short stories.

Sendak, Jack THE HAPPY RAIN
When the sun starts to shine, a town that has only known gray skies is thrown into a panic, leaving children to research solutions. Picture book.

Seuss, Dr. THE SNEETCHES AND OTHER STORIES
A collection on the theme of prejudice and tolerance. Picture book/short stories/poems.

Silverstein, Shel THE GIVING TREE
A tree gives more than it receives and a man receives more than he gives in a resonating parable. Picture book.

Singer, Isaac Bashevis ZLATEH THE GOAT AND OTHER STORIES
Sometimes zany, often poignant stories of fools and wise men translated from the Yiddish. Short stories/folktales.

Spinelli, Jerry MANIAC MAGEE
A larger-than-life hero confronts racism while living on the street. Chapter book fiction.

Steig, William SHREK!
Even putrid monsters can find romance in this unlikely love story. Picture book.

Stockton, Frank R. THE GRIFFIN AND THE MINOR CANON
When a hungry beast invades a small town, a civic-minded church subordinate is sent to handle the problem. Short story.

Storr, Catherine THE ADVENTURES OF POLLY AND THE WOLF
Wolf sets out to write a memoir to prove "Polly is the stupid one," but the facts speak for themselves. Short stories; sequel to **CLEVER POLLY AND THE STUPID WOLF,** which is also hilarious.

Van Allsburg, Chris THE POLAR EXPRESS

Modern classic of one boy's midnight trip to the North Pole on Christmas Eve. Picture book.

Van Allsburg, Chris THE WRETCHED STONE

The crew of the *Rita Anne* undergoes a dastardly metamorphosis upon the arrival of a strange, glowing rock. Picture book.

Van Meter, Vicki TAKING FLIGHT

True account from a twelve-year-old girl who piloted a plane over the Atlantic. Memoir.

White, E. B. CHARLOTTE'S WEB

"Some Pig" Wilbur meets world and conquers world with the help of an A+ arachnid. Chapter book wonder tale.

Wilder, Laura Ingalls LITTLE HOUSE IN THE BIG WOODS

First in a series of books depicting the hardscrabble life of a pioneer family. Chapter book fiction/memoir.

Williams, Ursula Moray THE ADVENTURES OF THE LITTLE WOODEN HORSE

A toy ventures out in the wide world to seek his fortune and help the man who made him. Chapter book wonder tale.

Zemach, Harve and Margot A PENNY A LOOK

A schemer gets a bright idea to capture a one-eyed man with the help of his less ambitious brother. Picture book.

For additional fiction titles that have earned a consensus for excellence by librarians, check out the Newbery winners in Appendix A1.

Teen Angst: The Classic Young Adult Problem

"I can't wait to be done with high school so I can start reading again!" one of my former students confessed to me in a recent e-mail. I, too, remember the burden of CRIME AND PUNISHMENT, in which the punishment did not seem to fit the crime of my freshman year. So imagine my shock when I found it being taught in a seventh-grade classroom at the school where I worked. It was explained to me that "they're advanced," but when I saw the way the children were experiencing the book, it seemed merely an exercise in moving eyes across words and checking off page numbers. As children pass through the threshold of adulthood, many schools and parents are eager to inflict the most ambitious literary works on these young readers. It appears that the purpose is twofold: Having children read material that is meant for adults makes parents and principals feel as though their children are smarter, and it helps separate the wheat from the chaff as far as future intellectuals. Why such harsh words? Funny, out of the sixty children who read CRIME AND PUNISHMENT, not a single one of them came into the library and asked me if Dostoyevsky or his countrymen had written anything else. The experience did nothing to motivate future reading, and why would it? I can't imagine that Dostoyevsky had a seventh-grade audience in mind when he composed his masterpiece. Timing is everything. You don't serve babies caviar, force them to eat it, and then call them connoisseurs.

Still, I'm not opposed to mixing in a fish egg now and again. My favorite book in eighth grade happened to be THE HOUSE OF THE SEVEN GABLES by Nathaniel Hawthorne, an acquired taste that was initially force-fed to us by poor Mrs. Smith, who had to contend with a class mutiny by the fourth chapter. She persevered, because *she* loved THE HOUSE OF THE SEVEN GABLES. She wanted us to read it not because of test scores or other impressions we might make, but because she felt this really hard book happened to be a really good book. For her to deal with the whining and profanity of my classmates, she must have deeply believed that if she didn't share this novel with us, nobody else would. She was probably right. The classics can be difficult, the language is sometimes archaic, and it is very helpful to have a teacher (particularly a teacher who understands and likes the book) as a guide. The rules for sharing classics should essentially be the same as for sharing children's literature: Consider what the author is trying to say, and whether the audience can be properly motivated to receive it.

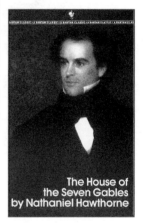

The House of
the Seven Gables
by Nathaniel Hawthorne

For some young audiences, the literature most readily received is the literature written with them in mind, loosely referred to in literary circles as "young adult literature," or "YAs" (an acronym pronounced *why-ay,* not *yah*). The difference between intermediate and YA literature is the difference between the earnest last-ditch attempts at control parents have on their children around age eleven and the throwing-hands-up-in-the-air that occurs around age twelve. Scenes in YA literature may contain swearing, sexuality, drug use, violence, alternative lifestyles, diseases, and a general cynicism that make very busy beavers out of censors and critics. In fact, the content and intensity of YAs is not to every young person's taste. Some teen readers are sustained by sticking to fantasy and mystery series. Others may go through high school preferring intermediate literature or adult literature, or fluctuating between the two with no interest in the 'tween scene, which is perfectly fine. If YAs don't appeal to, or offend, your family's values, the best revenge is simply to ignore them. The First Amendment is on YA literature's side, and furthermore, giving books negative attention tends to increase sales.

Still, it is worth noting that YA literature has come a long way since the breatkthrough novels of the 1960s and 1970s, such as Louise Fitzhugh's **THE LONG SECRET** and Judy Blume's **ARE YOU THERE, GOD? IT'S ME, MARGARET.** Now that bras and menstrual cycles are rather a given, mild profanity is part of the American vernacular, and Hollywood has shown our children more freak shows than P. T. Barnum could ever have dreamed up, YAs don't startle as much. The writing seems less gratuitous, with authors directing more formalistic attention to their books. Sometimes the results are beautiful and moving portrayals of this brief but highly charged time of life. While many YA books are still fraught with overwhelming conflicts, the writing style can be sophisticated enough to warrant mature literary discussion. "Questionable" material is frequently authentic to those conflicts and the characters experiencing them, and unlike most explicit movies, the reader is privy to the inner workings of the characters and sees consequences of actions fully carried out. YAs also tend to contain very timely sensibilities, with references to technology, politics, and modern mores presented in a personalized and thoughtful way that is hard for teens to find anywhere else. In addition, I have observed that YA literature does a particularly sympathetic job in speaking to boys. If you have a guy who is turned off by high school English, you may be surprised to find him turned right back on to reading with a few well-chosen YAs placed conveniently at his bedside, alongside a cereal bowl or maybe even in the bathroom.

YA literature can be readily compared to contemporary adult fiction, only with younger characters and situations. Many popular adult books, particularly those popular with book clubs, have young adult corollaries that are perfect for parallel reading circles with the teens from book-club member's families. For instance, Rebecca Wells's

DIVINE SECRETS OF THE YA-YA SISTERHOOD finds a younger sibling in Ann Brashares's **SISTERHOOD OF THE TRAVELING PANTS,** and Helen Fielding's **BRIDGET JONES'S DIARY** finds its junior in Louise Rennison's YA novel **ANGUS, THONGS, AND FULL-FRONTAL SNOGGING.** There are also YA corollaries for the typical high school reading list: **MONSTER** by Walter Dean Myers is a nice match for **NATIVE SON** by Richard Wright. **THE ENDLESS STEPPE: GROWING UP IN SIBERIA** by Esther Hautzig is better than Cliffs Notes for understanding the backdrop of Alexander Solzhenitsyn's **A DAY IN THE LIFE OF IVAN DENISOVICH.** East Coaster Holden Caulfield in J. D. Salinger's **THE CATCHER IN THE RYE** might have mentored West Coaster Steve York in Rob Thomas's **RATS SAW GOD.** Joanne Greenberg's **I NEVER PROMISED YOU A ROSE GARDEN** gets freshly cut perspective in Sonya Sones's **STOP PRETENDING: WHAT HAPPENED WHEN MY BIG SISTER WENT CRAZY.** Rodman Philbrick's **FREAK THE MIGHTY** is a nice complement to John Steinbeck's **OF MICE AND MEN,** as is Francisco Jiménez's **THE CIRCUIT** to Steinbeck's **GRAPES OF WRATH.**

Should young people read Sharon M. Draper's cyber-romance **ROMIETTE AND JULIO** *instead* of Shakespeare's **ROMEO AND JULIET?** Of course not. I am not recommending these books in lieu of the classics, but why not in addition to? We should make this literature available, offer it, suggest it, and when the work merits it, ask that teachers consider assigning it alongside the classical canon. A few YA standards have snuck into high school curricula over the years, based on their own virtues, such as Paul Zindel's **THE PIGMAN** and Robert Cormier's **I AM THE CHEESE,** but there is room and occasion for many more. While a few children respond to the classics easily, many young adults really appreciate seeing that books are being written *now* that they can enjoy and understand. If they can experience both, they can compare and make observations about quality and accessibility, choices that they will continue to make as lifelong readers. If your child's school does not facilitate this, you as a parent still can.

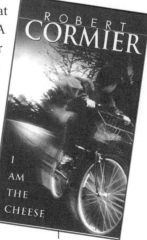

YA encompasses all the subheadings of children's literature: fiction, fantasy, mystery, poetry, biography. . . . An entire book could be written recommending such titles, and this is not that book. The offerings below, however, will give your family a taste of notable YA fiction for precocious upper-grade readers and teens, and many more exciting recommendations may be found at the following Web sites:

Internet Public Library
www.ipl.org/teen/

Hennepin County Library TeenLinks
www.hclib.org/teens/

Books for the Teen Age from the New York Public Library
www2.nypl.org/home/branch/teen/

Teen Edition from the Chicago PublicLibrary
www.chipublib.org/008subject/003cya/teened/teintro.html

The Michael L. Printz Award for Excellence in Young Adult Literature (given by the American Library Association)
www.ala.org/yalsa/printz/index.html

YA LITERATURE:

Almond, David	• SKELLIG
Anderson, Laurie Halse	• SPEAK
Anderson, M. T.	• BURGER WUSS
Avi	• NOTHING BUT THE TRUTH
Block, Francesca Lia	• WEETZIE BAT
Bloor, Edward	• TANGERINE
Brooks, Bruce	• THE MOVES MAKE THE MAN
Calhoun, Dia	• FIREGOLD
Card, Orson Scott	• ENDER'S GAME
Creech, Sharon	• WALK TWO MOONS
Farmer, Nancy	• THE HOUSE OF THE SCORPION
Fleischman, Paul	• WHIRLIGIG
Flinn, Alex	• BREATHING UNDERWATER
Fritz, April Young	• WAITING TO DISAPPEAR
Fuqua, Jonathon Scott	• THE REAPPEARANCE OF SAM WEBBER

Holt, Kimberly Willis	• WHEN ZACHARY BEAVER CAME TO TOWN
Mosher, Richard	• ZAZOO
Powell, Randy	• TRIBUTE TO ANOTHER DEAD ROCK STAR
Sachar, Louis	• HOLES
Sheldon, Dyan	• CONFESSIONS OF A TEENAGE DRAMA QUEEN
Spinelli, Jerry	• STARGIRL
Staples, Suzanne Fisher	• SHABANU
Tashjian, Janet	• THE GOSPEL ACCORDING TO LARRY
Wolff, Virginia Euwer	• MAKE LEMONADE

. . . Also check out the historical fiction in the Once upon a Time Line (p. 100) and Survival Stories (p. 143) lists, which contain many titles young adults in particular will enjoy.

Cyberspace: The Last(?) Reading Frontier

I like computers. I think of them as glorified pencils, just another tool that when used correctly can be very helpful and creative, and when used incorrectly simply means someone's being a schnook. The Internet goes far to connect book-lovers with needed information and with other book-lovers. While some children's books are downloadable, until they make a computer that can comfortably join in a lap-time cuddle or can be easily held up in front of a group of children, I don't think fans of children's books in traditional print have anything to worry about.

For me the joy of children's literature is in the sharing, and I wondered how technology could help me to do it. When I began to think about creating a Web site devoted to children's literature, I turned to—what else?—a children's book. HOME PAGE: AN INTRODUCTION TO WEB PAGE DESIGN by Christopher Lampton was very helpful, along with the more grown-up but extremely readable guide, HTML FOR THE WORLD WIDE WEB by Elizabeth Castro, for learning Web design language. Inadvertently, my students helped me name my site.

It started with a new child, a fourth-grader, just transferred to our school, homesick and full of noisy complaints. I overheard his conversation.

COMPUTER CHAPTER BOOKS

Cooper, Susan	THE BOGGART
Danziger, Paula, and Ann M. Martin	SNAIL MAIL NO MORE
Gliori, Debi	PURE DEAD MAGIC
Keller, Holly	ANGELA'S TOP-SECRET COMPUTER CLUB
Regan, Dian Curtis	MONSTERS IN CYBERSPACE
Rosen, Michael	CHASER (Mature readers.)
Tashjian, Janet	THE GOSPEL ACCORDING TO LARRY (Mature readers.)
Vandevelde, Vivian	CURSES, INC.

"How come the library teacher here gives so much work?" He groused. "Teachers at my *old* school didn't make us do such big projects. Teachers at my *old* school didn't read out loud to us big kids. Teachers at my *old* school weren't always talking about books, books, books."

The boy sitting next to him sighed. "Well, you're not *at* your old school, are you? You're on Planet Esmé now."

PlanetEsme.com: A Wonderful World of Children's Literature was designed to talk about books, books, books. I wanted to make sure that every title that appeared on the site had been a successful shared experience between a grown-up and a child. The site accepted no advertising, no banners or pop-up windows. Other excellent children's-literature sites existed, of course. What I hoped to create was a site where preschool through sixth-grade teachers could go for unparalleled credibility, titles that they could trust would be well received by children. The motto became "teacher tested, kid approved," and the goal was to put great books in the hands of great children. Because of this, standards were high, and the site grew to be a kind of FDA for children's literature.

Books couldn't just be good to appear on the highly trafficked "Don't Miss" page, they had to be *reeeally* good, laugh-out-loud good, please-keep-reading good, cry-at-the-end good, think-about-the-next-day good, nine-out-of-ten teachers-and-ten-out-of-ten-students-agree *good*. I soon found out that many of my visitors were parents, grandparents, homeschooling families, religious leaders, and community builders. Potato pedagogues everywhere were logging on to find out the latest and greatest in children's literature. Best of all, people were sending back mail to confirm that the recommended titles were indeed kid approved where they lived, too. Within two years, with advertising primarily by word of mouth, the site was averaging 90,000 hits and 5,000 new visitors a month. Several of the books recommended on the site went on months later to win national awards, and I was proud to have predicted a Newbery winner and a Caldecott Honor. The Web site has become one of my most personally gratifying projects. With the computer, all the walls fell away. Everybody really could come and visit me, on my little cyber planet. We could connect.

Last Lines: Connecting Readers

And it is with the thought of connections that I close, because it relates to what you remember is the Most Important Question when you read a book: Why did the author write this? In order to answer, I have to think about another question, this one from my editor. "Why do you write *'children'* when you are talking about read-aloud and literacy initiatives?" she asked me as she was reading this book. "Isn't your book about reading to one's *own* child? When you talk about reading to a group of children, it's intimidating."

And I thought to myself, we're here on earth with so many, many children. Who is so exonerated as to claim simply one child?

Especially when talking about sharing something as plentiful as potatoes?

Philosophy and fifty cents will get you a cup of coffee. My editor operates with my best interests and those of my publishing house in mind, and I recognize that as usual, she is right. These ideas and recommendations are applicable and can be modified to any single child, the child you diaper and feed and schlep to lessons and play dates, the child whose report card you sign and whose college fund you are custodian to. This book is for *your child,* singular, and that is wonderful, and that was my intent. Daily read-aloud fulfills an emotional need of your child's, to be close and to feel safe, and gives him the chance to discuss concerns with you. In stories, your child can see conflicts resolved and be reassured that even the biggest fear or foe can be overcome through love, contemplation, and bravery. Through reading, your child can also find comfort and escape and the opportunity to mature. Your child deserves all that. Your one child *is* precious, your one child *is* worthy.

But.

As I wrote, I had another intent, a private agenda, a bigger thought. It was my secret ambition that this book would build community around the power of literacy. It was my hope that if people could see how easy and fun and rewarding shared reading really is, they would do it, and they would be empowered and enthused enough that it wouldn't be a big deal to do it for other people, too. In this way, more children would be served, would see *how* to serve, and would grow up to value what was given to them. More children would have the critical thinking, interest, information, tolerance, and empathy fostered by literacy. And then, going back to the singular child, the one, my son could live among such people. Do you dream this likewise for your son or daughter? Is there room in our dream for all sons and daughters?

It doesn't happen unless we regard all children as family. Is this a tall order? In a speech given in 1993 for Children's Literature New England, author Katherine Paterson observed:

Plowshares demand more of us than swords. The work of peace is infinitely more difficult than the waging of war. For one thing we've had so little practice—not only little practice in peacemaking, but also so little practice in imagining it.

I hope this book has helped you to imagine it and has given you the power to practice it. If children's literature is the potato, the thing that nourishes, then we are the plowshares that ready the land for planting. Our greatest strength is each other.

Appendices

A1: Newbery Award Winners

2003

Winner: *Crispin: The Cross of Lead*, Avi
Honor Books:
The House of the Scorpion, Nancy Farmer
Pictures of Hollis Woods, Patricia Reilly Giff
Hoot, Carl Hiassen
A Corner of the Universe, Ann M. Martin
Surviving the Applewhites, Stephanie S. Tolan

2002

Winner: *A Single Shard*, Linda Sue Park
Honor Books:
Everything on a Waffle, Polly Hovarth
Carver: A Life in Poems, Marilyn Nelson

2001

Winner: *A Year Down Yonder*, Richard Peck
Honor Books:
Because of Winn-Dixie, Kate DiCamillo
Hope Was Here, Joan Bauer
Joey Pigza Loses Control, Jack Gantos
The Wanderer, Sharon Creech

2000

Winner: *Bud, Not Buddy*, Christopher Paul Curtis
Honor Books:
Getting Near to Baby, Audrey Couloumbis
Our Only May Amelia, Jennifer L. Holm
26 Fairmount Avenue, Tomie dePaola

1999

Winner: *Holes*, Louis Sachar
Honor Book:
A Long Way from Chicago, Richard Peck

1998

Winner: *Out of the Dust*, Karen Hesse
Honor Books:
Ella Enchanted, Gail Carson Levine
Lily's Crossing, Patricia Reilly Giff
Wringer, Jerry Spinelli

1997

Winner: *The View from Saturday*, E. L. Konigsburg
Honor Books:
A Girl Named Disaster, Nancy Farmer
The Moorchild, Eloise Jarvis McGraw
The Thief, Megan Whalen Turner
Belle Prater's Boy, Ruth White

1996

Winner: *The Midwife's Apprentice*, Karen Cushman

Honor Books:
What Jamie Saw, Carolyn Coman
The Watsons Go to Birmingham—1963, Christopher Paul Curtis
Yolonda's Genius, Carol Fenner
The Great Fire, Jim Murphy

1995

Winner: *Walk Two Moons*, Sharon Creech
Honor Books:
Catherine, Called Birdy, Karen Cushman
The Ear, the Eye, and the Arm, Nancy Farmer

1994

Winner: *The Giver*, Lois Lowry
Honor Books:
Crazy Lady! Jane Leslie Conly
Dragon's Gate, Laurence Yep
Eleanor Roosevelt: A Life of Discovery, Russell Freedman

1993

Winner: *Missing May*, Cynthia Rylant
Honor Books:
What Hearts, Bruce Brooks
The Dark-Thirty: Southern Tales of the Supernatural, Patricia C. McKissack
Somewhere in the Darkness, Walter Dean Myers

1992

Winner: *Shiloh*, Phyllis Reynolds Naylor
Honor Books:
Nothing but the Truth: A Documentary Novel, Avi
The Wright Brothers: How They Invented the Airplane, Russell Freedman

1991
Winner: *Maniac Magee*, Jerry Spinelli
Honor Book:
The True Confessions of Charlotte Doyle, Avi

1990
Winner: *Number the Stars*, Lois Lowry
Honor Books:
Afternoon of the Elves, Janet Taylor Lisle
Shabanu: Daughter of the Wind, Suzanne Fisher Staples
The Winter Room, Gary Paulsen

1989
Winner: *Joyful Noise: Poems for Two Voices*, Paul Fleischman
Honor Books:
In the Beginning: Creation Stories from Around the World, Virginia Hamilton
Scorpions, Walter Dean Myers

1988
Winner: *Lincoln: A Photobiography*, Russell Freedman
Honor Books:
After the Rain, Norma Fox Mazer
Hatchet, Gary Paulsen

1987
Winner: *The Whipping Boy*, Sid Fleischman
Honor Books:
A Fine White Dust, Cynthia Rylant
On My Honor, Marion Dane Bauer
Volcano: The Eruption and Healing of Mount St. Helens, Patricia Lauber

1986
Winner: *Sarah, Plain and Tall*, Patricia MacLachlan
Honor Books:
Commodore Perry in the Land of the Shogun, Rhoda Blumberg
Dogsong, Gary Paulsen

1985
Winner: *The Hero and the Crown*, Robin McKinley
Honor Books:
Like Jake and Me, Mavis Jukes
The Moves Make the Man, Bruce Brooks
One-Eyed Cat, Paula Fox

1984
Winner: *Dear Mr. Henshaw*, Beverly Cleary
Honor Books:
The Sign of the Beaver, Elizabeth George Speare
A Solitary Blue, Cynthia Voigt
Sugaring Time, Kathryn Lasky
The Wish Giver: Three Tales of Coven Tree, Bill Brittain

1983
Winner: *Dicey's Song*, Cynthia Voigt
Honor Books:
The Blue Sword, Robin McKinley
Doctor De Soto, William Steig
Graven Images, Paul Fleischman
Homesick: My Own Story, Jean Fritz
Sweet Whispers, Brother Rush, Virginia Hamilton

1982
Winner: *A Visit to William Blake's Inn: Poems for Innocent and Experienced Travelers*, Nancy Willard
Honor Books:
Ramona Quimby, Age 8, Beverly Cleary

Upon the Head of the Goat: A Childhood in Hungary 1939–1944, Aranka Siegal

1981
Winner: *Jacob Have I Loved*, Katherine Paterson
Honor Books:
The Fledgling, Jane Langton
A Ring of Endless Light, Madeleine L'Engle

1980
Winner: *A Gathering of Days: A New England Girl's Journal, 1830–32*, Joan W. Blos
Honor Book:
The Road from Home: The Story of an Armenian Girl, David Kherdian

1979
Winner: *The Westing Game*, Ellen Raskin
Honor Book:
The Great Gilly Hopkins, Katherine Paterson

1978
Winner: *Bridge to Terabithia*, Katherine Paterson
Honor Books:
Ramona and Her Father, Beverly Cleary
Anpao: An American Indian Odyssey, Jamake Highwater

1977
Winner: *Roll of Thunder, Hear My Cry*, Mildred D. Taylor
Honor Books:
Abel's Island, William Steig
A String in the Harp, Nancy Bond

1976
Winner: *The Grey King*, Susan Cooper
Honor Books:
The Hundred Penny Box, Sharon Bell Mathis
Dragonwings, Laurence Yep

1975
Winner: *M. C. Higgins, the Great*, Virginia Hamilton
Honor Books:
Figgs & Phantoms, Ellen Raskin
My Brother Sam Is Dead, James Lincoln Collier and Christopher Collier
The Perilous Gard, Elizabeth Marie Pope
Philip Hall Likes Me, I Reckon Maybe, Bette Green

1974
Winner: *The Slave Dancer*, Paula Fox
Honor Book:
The Dark Is Rising, Susan Cooper

1973
Winner: *Julie of the Wolves*, Jean Craighead George
Honor Books:
Frog and Toad Together, Arnold Lobel
The Upstairs Room, Johanna Weiss
The Witches of Worm, Zilpha Keatley Snyder

1972
Winner: *Mrs. Frisby and the Rats of NIMH*, Robert C. O'Brien
Honor Books:
Incident at Hawk's Hill, Allan W. Eckert
The Planet of Junior Brown, Virginia Hamilton
The Tombs of Atuan, Ursula K. Le Guin

Annie and the Old One, Miska Miles
The Headless Cupid, Zilpha Keatley Snyder

1971
Winner: *The Summer of the Swans*, Betsy Byars
Honor Books:
Knee Knock Rise, Natalie Babbitt
Enchantress from the Stars, Sylvia Louise Engdahl
Sing Down the Moon, Scott O'Dell

1970
Winner: *Sounder*, William H. Armstrong
Honor Books:
Our Eddie, Sulamith Ish-Kishor
The Many Ways of Seeing: An Introduction to the Pleasures of Art, Janet Moore
Journey Outside, Mary Q. Steele

1969
Winner: *The High King*, Lloyd Alexander
Honor Books:
To Be a Slave, Julius Lester
When Shlemiel Went to Warsaw and Other Stories, Isaac Bashevis Singer

1968
Winner: *From the Mixed-Up Files of Mrs. Basil E. Frankweiler*, E. L. Konigsburg
Honor Books:
Jennifer, Hecate, Macbeth, William McKinley, and Me, Elizabeth, E. L. Konigsburg
The Black Pearl, Scott O'Dell
The Fearsome Inn, Isaac Bashevis Singer
The Egypt Game, Zilpha Keatley Snyder

1967
Winner: *Up a Road Slowly*, Irene Hunt
Honor Books:
The King's Fifth, Scott O'Dell
Zlateh the Goat and Other Stories, Isaac Bashevis Singer
The Jazz Man, Mary H. Weik

1966
Winner: *I, Juan de Pareja*, Elizabeth Borton de Treviño
Honor Books:
The Black Cauldron, Lloyd Alexander
The Animal Family, Randall Jarrell
The Noonday Friends, Mary Stolz

1965
Winner: *Shadow of a Bull*, Maia Wojciechowska
Honor Book:
Across Five Aprils, Irene Hunt

1964
Winner: *It's Like This, Cat*, Emily Cheney Neville
Honor Books:
Rascal: A Memoir of a Better Era, Sterling North
The Loner, Ester Weir

1963
Winner: *A Wrinkle in Time*, Madeleine L'Engle
Honor Books:
Thistle and Thyme: Tales and Legends from Scotland, Sorche Nic Leodhas
Men of Athens, Olivia Coolidge

1962
Winner: *The Bronze Bow*, Elizabeth George Speare
Honor Books:
Frontier Living, Edwin Tunis
The Golden Goblet, Eloise Jarvis McGraw
Belling the Tiger, Mary Stolz

1961
Winner: *Island of the Blue Dolphins*, Scott O'Dell
Honor Books:
America Moves Forward: A History for Peter, Gerald W. Johnson
Old Ramon, Jack Schaefer
The Cricket in Times Square, George Selden

1960
Winner: *Onion John*, Joseph Krumgold
Honor Books:
My Side of the Mountain, Jean Craighead George
America Is Born: A History for Peter, Gerald W. Johnson
The Gammage Cup, Carol Kendall

1959
Winner: *The Witch of Blackbird Pond*, Elizabeth George Speare
Honor Books:
The Family Under the Bridge, Natalie Savage Carlson
Along Came a Dog, Meindert DeJong
Chúcaro: Wild Pony of the Pampa, Francis Kalnay
The Perilous Road, William O. Steele

1958
Winner: *Rifles for Watie*, Harold V. Keith
Honor Books:
The Horsecatcher, Mari Sandoz
Gone-Away Lake, Elizabeth Enright
The Great Wheel, Robert Lawson
Tom Paine, Freedom's Apostle, Leo Gurko

1957
Winner: *Miracles on Maple Hill*, Virginia Sorensen
Honor Books:
Old Yeller, Fred Gipson
The House of Sixty Fathers, Meindert DeJong
Mr. Justice Holmes, Clara Ingram Judson
The Corn Grows Ripe, Dorothy Rhoads
Black Fox of Lorne, Marguerite de Angeli

1956
Winner: *Carry On, Mr. Bowditch*, Jean Lee Latham
Honor Books:
The Secret River, Marjorie Kinnan Rawlings
The Golden Name Day, Jennie Lindquist
Men, Microscopes, and Living Things, Katherine Shippen

1955
Winner: *The Wheel on the School*, Meindert DeJong
Honor Books:
The Courage of Sarah Noble, Alice Dalgliesh
Banner in the Sky, James Ullman

1954
Winner: *. . . And Now Miguel*, Joseph Krumgold

Honor Books:
All Alone, Claire Huchet Bishop
Shadrach, Meindert DeJong
Hurry Home, Candy, Meindert DeJong
Theodore Roosevelt, Fighting Patriot, Clara Ingram Judson
Magic Maize, Mary and Conrad Buff

1953
Winner: *Secret of the Andes*, Ann Nolan Clark
Honor Books:
Charlotte's Web, E. B. White
Moccasin Trail, Eloise Jarvis McGraw
Red Sails to Capri, Ann Weil
The Bears on Hemlock Mountain, Alice Dalgliesh
Birthdays of Freedom, vol. 1, Genevieve Foster

1952
Winner: *Ginger Pye*, Eleanor Estes
Honor Books:
Americans Before Columbus, Elizabeth Baity
Minn of the Mississippi, Holling C. Holling
The Defender, Nicholas Kalashnikoff
The Light at Tern Rock, Julia Sauer
The Apple and the Arrow, Mary and Conrad Buff

1951
Winner: *Amos Fortune, Free Man*, Elizabeth Yates
Honor Books:
Better Known As Johnny Appleseed, Mabel Leigh Hunt
Gandhi, Fighter Without a Sword, Jeanette Eaton
Abraham Lincoln, Friend of the People, Clara Ingram Judson

The Story of Appleby Capple,
Anne Parrish

1950
Winner: *The Door in the Wall,*
Marguerite de Angeli
Honor Books:
Tree of Freedom, Rebecca Caudill
The Blue Cat of Castle Town,
Catherine Coblentz
Kildee House, Rutherford
Montgomery
George Washington, Genevieve
Foster
*Song of the Pines: A Story of
Norwegian Lumbering in
Wisconsin,* Walter and Marion
Havighurst

1949
Winner: *King of the Wind,*
Marguerite Henry
Honor Books:
Seabird, Holling C. Holling
Daughter of the Mountains,
Louise Rankin
My Father's Dragon, Ruth S.
Gannett
Story of the Negro, Arna
Bontemps

1948
Winner: *The Twenty-One
Balloons,* William Pène du Bois
Honor Books:
Pancakes-Paris, Claire Huchet
Bishop
Li Lun, Lad of Courage, Carolyn
Treffinger
*The Quaint and Curious Quest of
Johnny Longfoot,* Catherine
Besterman
*The Cow-Tail Switch and Other
West African Stories,* Harold
Courlander
Misty of Chincoteague,
Marguerite Henry

1947
Winner: *Miss Hickory,* Carolyn
Sherwin Bailey
Honor Books:
Wonderful Year, Nancy Barnes
Big Tree, Mary and Conrad Buff
The Heavenly Tenants, William
Maxwell
The Avion My Uncle Flew, Cyrus
Fisher
The Hidden Treasure of Glaston,
Eleanore Jewett

1946
Winner: *Strawberry Girl,* Lois
Lenski
Honor Books:
Justin Morgan Had a Horse,
Marguerite Henry
The Moved-Outers, Florence
Crannell Means
Bhimsa, the Dancing Bear,
Christine Weston
New Found World, Katherine
Shippen

1945
Winner: *Rabbit Hill,* Robert
Lawson
Honor Books:
The Hundred Dresses, Eleanor
Estes
The Silver Pencil, Alice Dalgliesh
Abraham Lincoln's World,
Genevieve Foster
*Lone Journey: The Life of Roger
Williams,* Jeanette Eaton

1944
Winner: *Johnny Tremain,* Esther
Forbes
Honor Books:
These Happy Golden Years, Laura
Ingalls Wilder
Fog Magic, Julia Sauer
Rufus M., Eleanor Estes
Mountain Born, Elizabeth Yates

1943
Winner: *Adam of
the Road,*
Elizabeth Janet
Gray (Elizabeth
Gray Vining)
Honor Books:
*The Middle
Moffat,* Eleanor Estes
Have You Seen Tom Thumb?,
Mabel Leigh Hunt

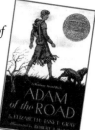

1942
Winner: *The Matchlock Gun,*
Walter D. Edmonds
Honor Books:
Little Town on the Prairie, Laura
Ingalls Wilder
George Washington's World,
Genevieve Foster
*Indian Captive: The Story of Mary
Jemison,* Lois Lenski
Down Ryton Water, Eva Roe
Gaggin

1941
Winner: *Call It Courage,*
Armstrong Sperry
Honor Books:
Blue Willow, Doris Gates
Young Mac of Fort Vancouver,
Mary Jane Carr
The Long Winter, Laura Ingalls
Wilder
Nansen, Anna Gertrude Hall

1940
Winner: *Daniel Boone,* James
Daugherty
Honor Books:
The Singing Tree, Kate Seredy
*Runner of the Mountain Tops: The
Life of Louis Agassiz,* Mabel
Robinson
By the Shores of Silver Lake, Laura
Ingalls Wilder
Boy with A Pack, Stephen W.
Meader

1939
Winner: *Thimble Summer*,
Elizabeth Enright
Honor Books:
Nino, Valenti Angelo
Mr. Popper's Penguins, Richard
and Florence Atwater
Hello the Boat! Phyllis Crawford
*Leader by Destiny: George
Washington, Man and Patriot*,
Jeanette Eaton
Penn, Elizabeth Janet Gray
(Elizabeth Gray Vining)

1938
Winner: *The White Stag*, Kate
Seredy
Honor Books:
Pecos Bill, James Cloyd Bowman
Bright Island, Mabel Robinson
On the Banks of Plum Creek,
Laura Ingalls Wilder

1937
Winner: *Roller Skates*, Ruth
Sawyer
Honor Books:
Phebe Fairchild: Her Book, Lois
Lenski
Whistler's Van, Idwal Jones
The Golden Basket, Ludwig
Bemelmans
Winterbound, Margery Williams
Bianco
The Codfish Musket, Agnes Hewes
Audubon, Constance Rourke

1936
Winner: *Caddie Woodlawn*,
Carol Ryrie Brink
Honor Books:
Honk, the Moose, Phil Stong
The Good Master, Kate Seredy
Young Walter Scott, Elizabeth Janet
Gray (Elizabeth Gray Vining)
*All Sail Set: A Romance of the
Flying Cloud*, Armstrong Sperry

1935
Winner: *Dobry*, Monica
Shannon
Honor Books:
The Pageant of Chinese History,
Elizabeth Seeger
Davy Crockett, Constance Rourke
*A Day on Skates: The Story of a
Dutch Picnic*, Hilda Von Stockum

1934
Winner: *Invincible Louisa: The
Story of the Author of Little
Women*, Cornelia Meigs
Honor Books:
The Forgotten Daughter, Caroline
Snedeker
*Swords of Steel: The Story of a
Gettysburg Boy*, Elsie Singmaster
The ABC Bunny, Wanda Gág
The Winged Girl of Knossos, Erick
Berry
New Land, Sarah Schmidt
*Big Tree of Bunlahy: Stories of My
Own Countryside*, Padraic Colum
Glory of the Seas, Agnes Hewes
The Apprentice of Florence, Ann
Kyle

1933
Winner: *Young Fu of the Upper
Yangtze*, Elizabeth Foreman Lewis
Honor Books:
Swift Rivers, Cornelia Meigs
*The Railroad to Freedom: A Story
of the Civil War*, Hildegarde Swift
*Children of the Soil: A Story of
Scandinavia*, Nora Burglon

1932
Winner: *Waterless Mountain*,
Laura Adams Armer
Honor Books:
The Fairy Circus, Dorothy P.
Lathrop
Calico Bush, Rachel Field
Boy of the South Seas, Eunice
Tietjens

Out of the Flame, Eloise
Lownsbery
Jane's Island, Marjorie Allee
*The Truce of the Wolf and Other
Tales of Old Italy*, Mary Gould
Davis

1931
Winner:
*The Cat Who
Went to Heaven*,
Elizabeth
Coatsworth
Honor Books:
Floating Island,
Anne Parrish
*The Dark Star of Itza: The Story of
a Pagan Princess*, Alida Malkus
Queer Person, Ralph Hubbard
Mountains Are Free, Julia Davis
(Julia Davis Adams)
Spice and the Devil's Cave, Agnes
Hewes
Meggy MacIntosh, Elizabeth Janet
Gray (Elizabeth Gray Vining)
*Garram the Hunter: A Boy of the
Hill Tribes*, Herbert Best
Ood-le-uk the Wanderer, Alice
Lide and Margaret Johansen

1930
Winner: *Hitty, Her First Hundred
Years*, Rachel Field
Honor Books:
*A Daughter of the Seine: The Life
of Madame Roland*, Jeanette
Eaton
Pran of Albania, Elizabeth Miller
The Jumping-off Place, Marian
Hurd McNeely
*The Tangle-Coated Horse and
Other Tales: Episodes from the
Fionn Saga*, Ella Young
Vaino, a Boy of New Finland, Julia
Davis (Julia Davis Adams)
*Little Blacknose: The Story of a
Pioneer*, Hildegarde Hoyt Swift

1929

Winner: *The Trumpeter of Krakow: A Tale of the Fifteenth Century*, Eric P. Kelly
Honor Books:
The Pigtail of Ah Lee Ben Loo, with Seventeen Other Laughable Tales & 200 Comical Silhouettes, John Bennett
Millions of Cats, Wanda Gág
The Boy Who Was, Grace Hallock
Clearing Weather, Cornelia Meigs
The Runaway Papoose, Grace Purdie Moon
Tod, of the Fens, Elinor Whitney

1928

Winner: *Gay-Neck, the Story of a Pigeon*, Dhan Gopal Mukerji
Honor Books:
The Wonder Smith and His Son: A Tale from the Golden Childhood of the World, Ella Young
Downright Dencey, Caroline Snedeker

1927

Winner: *Smoky, the Cow Horse*, Will James
Honor Books:
No Record

1926

Winner: *Shen of the Sea*, Arthur Bowie Chrisman
Honor Book:
The Voyagers: Being Legends and Romances of Atlantic Discovery, Padraic Colum

1925

Winner: *Tales from Silver Lands*, Charles Finger
Honor Books:
Nicholas: A Manhattan Christmas Story, Annie Carroll Moore
The Dream Coach, Anne Parrish

1924

Winner: *The Dark Frigate*, Charles Boardman Hawes
Honor Books:
No Record

1923

Winner: *The Voyages of Doctor Dolittle*, Hugh Lofting
Honor Books:
No Record

1922

Winner: *The Story of Mankind*, Hendrik Willem van Loon
Honor Books:
The Great Quest: A Romance of 1826, Charles Boardman Hawes
Cedric, the Forester, Bernard Marshall
The Old Tobacco Shop: A True Account of What Befell a Little Boy in Search of Adventure, William Bowen
The Golden Fleece and the Heroes Who Lived Before Achilles, Padraic Colum
The Windy Hill, Cornelia Meigs

A2: Caldecott Award Winners

2003

Winner:
My Friend Rabbit, illustrated and written by Eric Rohmann
Honor Books: *The Spider and the Fly*, illustrated by Tony DiTerlizzi (text: Mary Howitt)
Hondo & Fabian, illustrated and written by Peter McCarty
Noah's Ark, illustrated and written by Jerry Pinkney

2002

Winner: *The Three Pigs*, David Weisner
Honor Books:
The Dinosaurs of Waterhouse Hawkins, illustrated by Brian Selznick (text: Barbara Kerley)
Martin's Big Words: The Life of Dr. Martin Luther King, Jr., illustrated by Bryan Collier (text: Doreen Rappaport)
The Stray Dog, Marc Simont

2001

Winner: *So You Want to Be President?* illustrated by David Small (text: Judith St. George)
Honor Books:
Casey at the Bat, illustrated by Christopher Bing (text: Ernest Lawrence Thayer)

Click, Clack, Moo: Cows That Type, illustrated by Betsy Lewin (text: Doreen Cronin)
Olivia, Ian Falconer

2000

Winner: *Joseph Had a Little Overcoat*, Simms Taback
Honor Books:
A Child's Calendar, illustrated by Trina Schart Hyman (text: John Updike)
Sector 7, David Wiesner
When Sophie Gets Angry—Really, Really Angry, Molly Bang
The Ugly Duckling, illustrated by Jerry Pinkney (text: Hans Christian Andersen)

1999

Winner: *Snowflake Bentley*, illustrated by Mary Azarian (text: Jacqueline Briggs Martin)
Honor Books:
Duke Ellington: The Piano Prince and His Orchestra, illustrated by Brian Pinkney (text: Andrea Davis Pinkney)
No, David! David Shannon
Snow, Uri Shulevitz
Tibet Through the Red Box, Peter Sís

1998

Winner: *Rapunzel*, retold and illustrated by Paul O. Zelinsky
Honor Books:
The Gardener, illustrated by David Small (text: Sarah Stewart)
Harlem, illustrated by Christopher Myers (poem: Walter Dean Myers)
There Was an Old Lady Who Swallowed a Fly, Simms Taback

1997

Winner: *Golem*, David Wisniewski
Honor Books:
Hush! A Thai Lullaby, illustrated by Holly Meade (text: Minfong Ho)
The Graphic Alphabet, David Pelletier, edited, Neal Porter
The Paperboy, Dav Pilkey
Starry Messenger, Peter Sís

1996

Winner: *Officer Buckle and Gloria*, Peggy Rathmann
Honor Books:
Alphabet City, Stephen T. Johnson
The Faithful Friend, illustrated by Brian Pinkney (text: Robert D. San Souci)
Tops & Bottoms, Janet Stevens

Zin! Zin! Zin! A Violin, illustrated by Marjorie Priceman (text: Lloyd Moss)

1995

Winner: *Smoky Night*, illustrated by David Diaz (text: Eve Bunting)
Honor Books:
John Henry, illustrated by Jerry Pinkney (text: Julius Lester)
Swamp Angel, illustrated by Paul O. Zelinksy (text: Anne Isaacs)
Time Flies, Eric Rohmann

1994

Winner: *Grandfather's Journey*, Allen Say
Honor Books:
Peppe the Lamplighter, illustrated by Ted Lewin (text: Elisa Bartone)
In the Small Small Pond, Denise Fleming
Raven: A Trickster Tale from the Pacific Northwest, Gerald McDermott
Yo! Yes?, Chris Raschka
Owen, Kevin Henkes

1993

Winner: *Mirette on the High Wire*, Emily Arnold McCully
Honor Books:
The Stinky Cheese Man and Other Fairly Stupid Tales, illustrated by Lane Smith (text: Jon Scieszka)
Seven Blind Mice, Ed Young
Working Cotton, illustrated by Carol Byard (text: Sherley Anne Williams)

1992

Winner: *Tuesday*, David Wiesner
Honor Book:
Tar Beach, Faith Ringgold

1991

Winner: *Black and White*, David Macaulay
Honor Books:
Puss in Boots, illustrated by Fred Marcellino (text: Charles Perrault; translated by Malcolm Arthur)
More More More, Said the Baby: Three Love Stories, Vera B. Williams

1990

Winner: *Lon Po Po: A Red-Riding Hood Story from China*, Ed Young
Honor Books:
Bill Peet: An Autobiography, Bill Peet
Color Zoo, Lois Ehlert
The Talking Eggs: A Folktale from the American South, illustrated by Jerry Pinkney (text: Robert D. San Souci)
Hershel and the Hanukkah Goblins, illustrated by Trina Schart Hyman (text: Eric Kimmel)

1989

Winner: *Song and Dance Man*, illustrated by Stephen Gammell (text: Karen Ackerman)
Honor Books:
The Boy of the Three-Year Nap, Allen Say (text: Dianne Snyder)
Free Fall, David Wiesner
Goldilocks and the Three Bears, James Marshall
Mirandy and Brother Wind, illustrated by Jerry Pinkney (text: Patricia C. McKissack)

1988

Winner: *Owl Moon*, illustrated by John Schoenherr (text: Jane Yolen)

Honor Book:

Mufaro's Beautiful Daughters: An African Tale, John Steptoe

1987

Winner: *Hey, Al*, illustrated by Richard Egielski (text: Arthur Yorinks)

Honor Books:

The Village of Round and Square Houses, Ann Grifalconi

Alphabatics, Suse MacDonald

Rumpelstiltskin, Paul O. Zelinsky

1986

Winner: *The Polar Express*, Chris Van Allsburg

Honor Books:

The Relatives Came, illustrated by Stephen Gammell (text: Cynthia Rylant)

King Bidgood's in the Bathtub, illustrated by Don Wood (text: Audrey Wood)

1985

Winner: *Saint George and the Dragon*, illustrated by Trina Schart Hyman (text: Margaret Hodges)

Honor Books:

Hansel and Gretel, illustrated by Paul O. Zelinsky (text: Rika Lesser)

Have You Seen My Duckling? Nancy Tafuri

The Story of Jumping Mouse: A Native American Legend, John Steptoe

1984

Winner: *The Glorious Flight: Across the Channel with Louis Blériot*, Alice and Martin Provensen

Honor Books:

Little Red Riding Hood, Trina Schart Hyman

Ten, Nine, Eight, Molly Bang

1983

Winner: *Shadow*, illustrated by Marcia Brown (text: Blaise Cendrar; translated by Marcia Brown)

Honor Books:

A Chair for My Mother, Vera B. Williams

When I Was Young in the Mountains, illustrated by Diane Goode (text: Cynthia Rylant)

1982

Winner: *Jumanji*, Chris Van Allsburg

Honor Books:

Where the Buffaloes Begin, illustrated by Stephen Gammell (text: Olaf Baker)

On Market Street, illustrated by Anita Lobel (text: Arnold Lobel)

Outside over There, Maurice Sendak

A Visit to William Blake's Inn: Poems for Innocent and Experienced Travelers, illustrated by Alice and Martin Provensen (text: Nancy Willard)

1981

Winner: *Fables*, Arnold Lobel

Honor Books:

The Bremen-Town Musicians, Ilse Plume

The Grey Lady and the Strawberry Snatcher, Molly Bang

Mice Twice, Joseph Low

Truck, Donald Crews

1980

Winner: *Ox-Cart Man*, illustrated by Barbara Cooney (text: Donald Hall)

Honor Books:

Ben's Trumpet, Rachel Isadora

The Garden of Abdul Gasazi, Chris Van Allsburg

The Treasure, Uri Shulevitz

1979

Winner: *The Girl Who Loved Wild Horses*, Paul Goble

Honor Books:

Freight Train, Donald Crews

The Way to Start a Day, illustrated by Peter Parnall (text: Byrd Baylor)

1978

Winner: *Noah's Ark*, Peter Spier

Honor Books:

Castle, David Macaulay

It Could Always Be Worse, Margot Zemach

1977

Winner: *Ashanti to Zulu: African Traditions*, illustrated by Leo and Diane Dillon (text: Margaret Musgrove)

Honor Books:

The Amazing Bone, William Steig

The Contest, Nonny Hogrogian

Fish for Supper, M. B. Goffstein

The Golem: A Jewish Legend, Beverly Brodsky McDermott

Hawk, I'm Your Brother, illustrated by Peter Parnall (text: Byrd Baylor)

1976
Winner: *Why Mosquitoes Buzz in People's Ears: A West African Tale*, illustrated by Leo and Diane Dillon (text: Verna Aardema)
Honor Books:
The Desert Is Theirs, illustrated by Peter Parnall (text: Byrd Baylor)
Strega Nona, Tomie dePaola

1975
Winner: *Arrow to the Sun: A Pueblo Indian Tale*, Gerald McDermott
Honor Book:
Jambo Means Hello: A Swahili Alphabet Book, illustrated by Tom Feelings (text: Muriel Feelings)

1974
Winner: *Duffy and the Devil,* illustrated by Margot Zemach (text: Harve Zemach)
Honor Books:
Three Jovial Huntsmen, Susan Jeffers
Cathedral, David Macaulay

1973
Winner: *The Funny Little Woman*, illustrated by Blair Lent (text: Arlene Mosel)
Honor Books:
Anansi the Spider, adapted and illustrated by Gerald McDermott
Hosie's Alphabet, illustrated by Leonard Baskin (text: Hosea, Tobias, and Lisa Baskin)
Snow-White and the Seven Dwarfs, illustrated by Nancy Ekholm Burkert (text: translated by Randall Jarrell)
When Clay Sings, illustrated by Tom Bahti (text: Byrd Baylor)

1972
Winner: *One Fine Day*, Nonny Hogrogian
Honor Books:
Hildilid's Night, illustrated by Arnold Lobel (text: Cheli Durán Ryan)
If All the Seas Were One Sea, Janina Domanska
Moja Means One, illustrated by Tom Feelings (text: Muriel Feelings)

1971
Winner: *A Story, a Story*, Gail E. Haley
Honor Books:
The Angry Moon, illustrated by Blair Lent (text: William Sleator)
Frog and Toad Are Friends, Arnold Lobel
In the Night Kitchen, Maurice Sendak

1970
Winner: *Sylvester and the Magic Pebble*, William Steig
Honor Books:
Goggles, Ezra Jack Keats
Alexander and the Wind-Up Mouse, Lio Lionni
Pop Corn & Ma Goodness, illustrated by Robert Andrew Parker (text: Edna Mitchell Preston)
Thy Friend, Obadiah, Brinton Turkle
The Judge, illustrated by Margot Zemach (text: Harve Zemach)

1969
Winner: *The Fool of the World and the Flying Ship*, illustrated by Uri Shulevitz (text: Arthur Ransome)
Honor Book:
Why the Sun and the Moon Live in the Sky, illustrated by Blair Lent (Text: Elphinstone Dayrell)

1968
Winner: *Drummer Hoff,* illustrated by Ed Emberley (text: Barbara Emberley)
Honor Books:
Frederick, Leo Lionni
Seashore Story, Taro Yashima
The Emperor and the Kite, illustrated by Ed Young (text: Jane Yolen)

1967
Winner: *Sam, Bangs, & Moonshine*, Evaline Ness
Honor Book:
One Wide River to Cross, illustrated by Ed Emberley (text: Barbara Emberley)

1966
Winner: *Always Room for One More*, illustrated by Nonny Hogrogian (text: Sorche Nic Leodhas)
Honor Books:
Hide and Seek Fog, illustrated by Roger Duvoisin (text: Alvin Tresselt)
Just Me, Marie Hall Ets
Tom Tit Tot, Evaline Ness

1965
Winner: *May I Bring a Friend?* illustrated by Beni Montresor (text: Beatrice Schenk de Regniers)
Honor Books:
Rain Makes Applesauce, illustrated by Marvin Bilek (text: Julian Scheer)
The Wave, illustrated by Blair Lent (text: Margaret Hodges)
A Pocketful of Cricket, illustrated by Evaline Ness (text: Rebecca Caudill)

1964

Winner: *Where the Wild Things Are*, Maurice Sendak
Honor Books:
Swimmy, Leo Lionni
All in the Morning Early, illustrated by Evaline Ness (text: Sorche Nic Leodhas)
Mother Goose and Nursery Rhymes, illustrated by Philip Reed

1963

Winner: *The Snowy Day*, Ezra Jack Keats
Honor Books:

The Sun Is a Golden Earring, illustrated by Bernarda Bryson (text: Natalia M. Belting)
Mr. Rabbit and the Lovely Present, illustrated by Maurice Sendak (text: Charlotte Zolotow)

1962

Winner: *Once a Mouse . . .*, Marcia Brown
Honor Books:
Fox Went Out on a Chilly Night, Peter Spier
Little Bear's Visit, illustrated by Maurice Sendak (text: Else Holmelund Minarik)
The Day We Saw the Sun Come Up, illustrated by Adrienne Adams (text: Alice E. Goudey)

1961

Winner: *Baboushka and the Three Kings*, illustrated by Nicholas Sidjakov (text: Ruth Robbins)
Honor Book:
Inch by Inch, Leo Lionni

1960

Winner: *Nine Days to Christmas*, illustrated by Marie Hall Ets (text: Marie Hall Ets and Aurora Labastida)
Honor Books:
Houses from the Sea, illustrated by Adrienne Adams (text: Alice E. Goudey)
The Moon Jumpers, illustrated by Maurice Sendak (text: Janice May Udry)

1959

Winner: *Chanticleer and the Fox*, illustrated by Barbara Cooney (text: adapted from Geoffrey Chaucer)
Honor Books:
The House That Jack Built, Antonio Frasconi
What Do You Say, Dear? illustrated by Maurice Sendak (text: Sesyle Joslin)
Umbrella, Taro Yashima

1958

Winner: *Time of Wonder*, Robert McCloskey
Honor Books:
Fly High, Fly Low, Don Freeman
Anatole and the Cat, illustrated by Paul Galdone (text: Eve Titus)

1957

Winner: *A Tree Is Nice*, illustrated by Marc Simont (text: Janice May Udry)
Honor Books:
Mr. Penny's Race Horse, Marie Hall Ets
1 is One, Tasha Tudor
Anatole, illustrated by Paul Galdone (text: Eve Titus)
Gillespie and the Guards, illustrated by James Daugherty (text: Benjamin Elkin)
Lion, William Pène du Bois

1956

Winner: *Frog Went A-Courtin'*, illustrated by Feodor Rojankovsky (text: John Langstaff)
Honor Books:
Play with Me, Marie Hall Ets
Crow Boy, Taro Yashima

1955

Winner: *Cinderella, or, The Little Glass Slipper*, illustrated by Marcia Brown (text: Charles Perrault; translated by Marcia Brown)
Honor Books:
Book of Nursery and Mother Goose Rhymes, illustrated by Marguerite de Angeli
Wheel on the Chimney, illustrated by Tibor Gergely (text: Margaret Wise Brown)
The Thanksgiving Story, illustrated by Helen Sewell (text: Alice Dalgliesh)

1954

Winner: *Madeline's Rescue*, Ludwig Bemelmans
Honor Books:
Journey Cake, Ho! illustrated by Robert McCloskey (text: Ruth Sawyer)
When Will the World Be Mine? illustrated by Jean Charlot (text: Miriam Schlein)
The Steadfast Tin Soldier, illustrated by Marcia Brown (text: Hans Christian Andersen; translated by M. R. James)
A Very Special House, illustrated by Maurice Sendak (text: Ruth Krauss)
Green Eyes, A. Birnbaum

1953

Winner: *The Biggest Bear*, Lynd Ward
Honor Books:
Puss in Boots, illustrated by Marcia Brown (text: Charles Perrault; translated by Marcia Brown)
One Morning in Maine, Robert McCloskey
Ape in a Cape, Fritz Eichenberg
The Storm Book, illustrated by Margaret Bloy Graham (text: Charlotte Zolotow)
Five Little Monkeys, Juliet Kepes

1952

Winner: *Finders Keepers,* illustrated by Nicolas Mordvinoff (text: Will Lipkind)
Honor Books:
Mr. T. W. Anthony Woo, Marie Hall Ets
Skipper John's Cook, Marcia Brown
All Falling Down, illustrated by Margaret Bloy Graham (text: Gene Zion)
Bear Party, William Pène du Bois
Feather Mountain, Elizabeth Olds

1951

Winner: *The Egg Tree*, Katherine Milhous
Honor Books:
Dick Whittington and His Cat, Marcia Brown
The Two Reds, illustrated by Nicolas Mordvinoff (text: Will Lipkind)
If I Ran the Zoo, Dr. Seuss
The Most Wonderful Doll in the World, illustrated by Helen Stone (text: Phyllis McGinley)
T-Bone, the Baby Sitter, Clare Newberry

1950

Winner: *Song of the Swallows*, Leo Politi
Honor Books:
America's Ethan Allen, illustrated by Lynd Ward (text: Stewart Holbrook)
The Wild Birthday Cake, illustrated by Hildegard Woodward (text: Lavinia R. Davis)
The Happy Day, illustrated by Marc Simont (text: Ruth Krauss)
Bartholomew and the Oobleck, Dr. Seuss
Henry Fisherman, Marcia Brown

1949

Winner: *The Big Snow,* Berta and Elmer Hader
Honor Books:
Blueberries for Sal, Robert McCloskey
All Around the Town, illustrated by Helen Stone (text: Phyllis McGinley)
Juanita, Leo Politi
Fish in the Air, Kurt Wiese

1948

Winner: *White Snow, Bright Snow,* illustrated by Roger Duvoisin (text: Alvin Tresselt)
Honor Books:
Stone Soup, Marcia Brown
McElligot's Pool, Dr. Seuss
Bambino the Clown, Georges Schreiber
Roger and the Fox, illustrated by Hildegard Woodward (text: Lavinia Davis)
Song of Robin Hood, illustrated by Virginia Lee Burton (text: edited, Anne Malcolmson)

1947

Winner: *The Little Island*, illustrated by Leonard Weisgard (text: Golden MacDonald [Margaret Wise Brown])
Honor Books:
Rain Drop Splash, illustrated by Leonard Weisgard (text: Alvin Tresselt)
Boats on the River, illustrated by Jay Hyde Barnum (text: Marjorie Flack)
Timothy Turtle, illustrated by Tony Palazzo (text: Al Graham)
Pedro, the Angel of Olvera Street, Leo Politi
Sing in Praise: A Collection of the Best Loved Hymns, illustrated by Marjorie Torrey (text: selected, Opal Wheeler)

1946

Winner:
The Rooster Crows, illustrated by Maud and Miska Petersham
Honor Books:
Little Lost Lamb, illustrated by Leonard Weisgard (text: Golden MacDonald [Margaret Wise Brown])
Sing Mother Goose, illustrated by Marjorie Torrey (text: Opal Wheeler)
My Mother Is the Most Beautiful Woman in the World, illustrated by Ruth C. Gannett (text: Becky Reyher)
You Can Write Chinese, Kurt Wiese

1945
Winner: *Prayer for a Child*, illustrated by Elizabeth Orton Jones (text: Rachel Field)
Honor Books:
Mother Goose, illustrated by Tasha Tudor
In the Forest, Marie Hall Ets
Yonie Wondernose, Marguerite de Angeli
The Christmas Anna Angel, illustrated by Kate Seredy (text: Ruth Sawyer)

1944
Winner: *Many Moons*, illustrated by Louis Slobodkin (text: James Thurber)
Honor Books:
Small Rain: Verses from the Bible, illustrated by Elizabeth Orton Jones (text: selected, Jessie Orton Jones)
Pierre Pigeon, illustrated by Arnold E. Bare (text: Lee Kingman)
The Mighty Hunter, Berta and Elmer Hader
A Child's Good Night Book, illustrated by Jean Charlot (text: Margaret Wise Brown)
Good Luck Horse, illustrated by Plao Chan (text: Chin-Yi Chan)

1943
Winner: *The Little House*, Virginia Lee Burton
Honor Books:
Dash and Dart, Mary and Conrad Buff
Marshmallow, Clare Newberry

1942
Winner: *Make Way for Ducklings*, Robert McCloskey
Honor Books:
An American ABC, Maud and Miska Petersham
In My Mother's House, illustrated by Velino Herrera (text: Ann Nolan Clark)
Paddle-to-the-Sea, Holling C. Holling
Nothing at All, Wanda Gág

1941
Winner: *They Were Strong and Good*, Robert Lawson
Honor Book:
April's Kittens, Clare Newberry

1940
Winner: *Abraham Lincoln*, Ingri and Edgar Parin d'Aulaire
Honor Books:
Cock-a-Doodle Doo, Berta and Elmer Hader
Madeline, Louis Bemelmans
The Ageless Story, Lauren Ford

1939
Winner: *Mei Li*, Thomas Handforth
Honor Books:
Andy and the Lion, James Daugherty
Barkis, Clare Newberry
The Forest Pool, Laura Adams Armer
Snow White and the Seven Dwarfs, Wanda Gág
Wee Gillis, illustrated by Robert Lawson (text: Munro Leaf)

1938
Winner:
Animals of the Bible, illustrated by Dorothy P. Lathrop (text: Helen Dean Fish)
Honor Books:
Four and Twenty Blackbirds, illustrated by Robert Lawson (text: Helen Dean Fish)
Seven Simeons, Boris Artzybasheff

B1: BIRTHDAY CLUB FORM, PAGE ONE

Join the Birthday Club!

Celebrate your child's birthday with a gift all of the children at school can enjoy!

For a contribution of $10 or more, your child will have a brand new book dedicated in his/her name in the school library. A permanent label will be affixed to the book to honor your child's growth and contribution, and your child will receive a happy-birthday certificate as well. Half birthdays celebrated for the summer-born!

Fill out and return the form on the back of this sheet by _____ to include your child in birthday fun!

Birthday Club Form

Please print. Please use a separate form for each child.

Child's information:

- Child's name: _____

- Birthday: _____

- How old will your child be turning on this birthday? _____

- Home room in the current school year: _____

(Note: birthdays that fall within summer break will have half birthdays recognized.)

Parent's information:

- Parent's name: _____

- Home Phone: _____

- Our family is making a $_____ contribution to the school library ($10 minimum per child). Checks are to be made payable to the _____ School Library.

Please return this form and contribution to the school office. All ages are encouraged to join. Books will be selected based on library need, but efforts will be made to make birthday books extra fun and interesting. Thank you for your support and participation!

For library use only:

Book Purchased: _____

Shelf location: _____

B2: BIRTHDAY CLUB SAMPLE CERTIFICATES

Happy Birthday
Wishes to

_____!

A new book has been donated to

the _____ Library

in honor of your _____ birthday!

Have a wonderful year!

Happy Half-Birthday
Wishes to

_____!

A new book has been donated to

the _____ Library

in honor of your special day!

You're doing a great
job growing up!

THIS BOOK
HAS BEEN DONATED
IN HONOR OF
_____'S

_____ BIRTHDAY

THIS BOOK
HAS BEEN DONATED
IN HONOR OF
_____'S

_____ BIRTHDAY

THIS BOOK
HAS BEEN DONATED
IN HONOR OF
_____'S

HALF BIRTHDAY

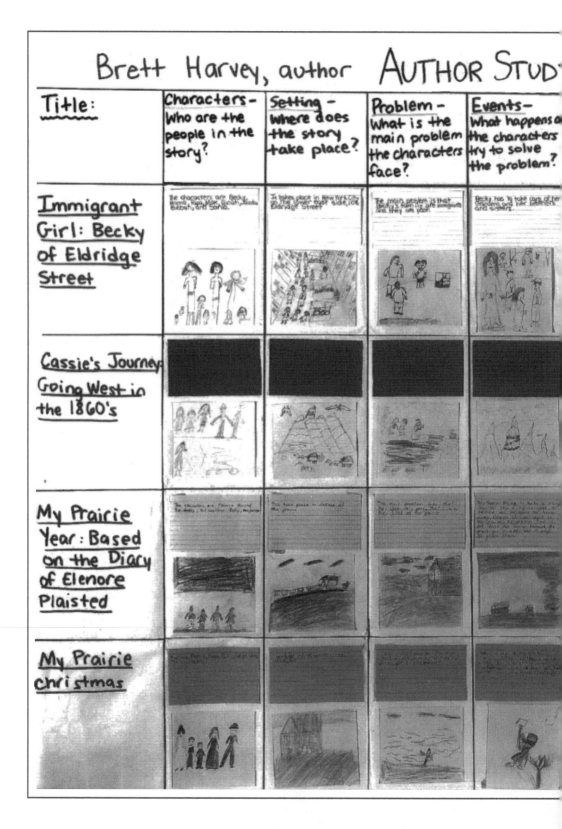

Brett Harvey, author   AUTHOR STUDY

Title:	Characters – Who are the people in the story?	Setting – Where does the story take place?	Problem – What is the main problem the characters face?	Events – What happens as the characters try to solve the problem?
Immigrant Girl: Becky of Eldridge Street				
Cassie's Journey: Going West in the 1860's				
My Prairie Year: Based on the Diary of Elenore Plaisted				
My Prairie Christmas				

Deborah Kogan Ray, illustrator

Solution— How does the problem get solved?	Illustrations— How do the pictures tell the story?	Research— How did Brett Harvey get the information for the story?	Other observations— What else did you notice about the book? Try comparing it to another book.

C1: SAMPLE ATTRIBUTE CHART FROM *THE AUTHOR STUDIES HANDBOOK* BY LAURA KOTCH AND LESLIE ZACKMAN

C2: DISPLAY PROTOTYPES

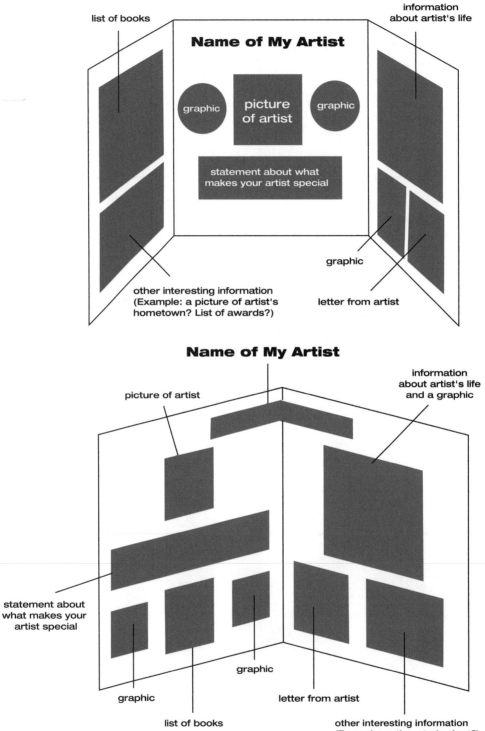

list of books

information about artist's life

Name of My Artist

graphic

picture of artist

graphic

statement about what makes your artist special

graphic

other interesting information (Example: a picture of artist's hometown? List of awards?)

letter from artist

Name of My Artist

picture of artist

information about artist's life and a graphic

statement about what makes your artist special

graphic

graphic

list of books

letter from artist

other interesting information (Example: author study chart?)

MARK YOUR CALENDAR FOR OUR

Parade of Books!

Children from _____ through _____ grades

are invited and encouraged to dress up

in a homemade costume

as their favorite storybook character

to march in and around our school!

Time: _____

Date: _____

BRING THE FAMILY TO CHEER YOUR CHILD,

YOUR CHILD'S CLASS, AND THE JOY OF READING!

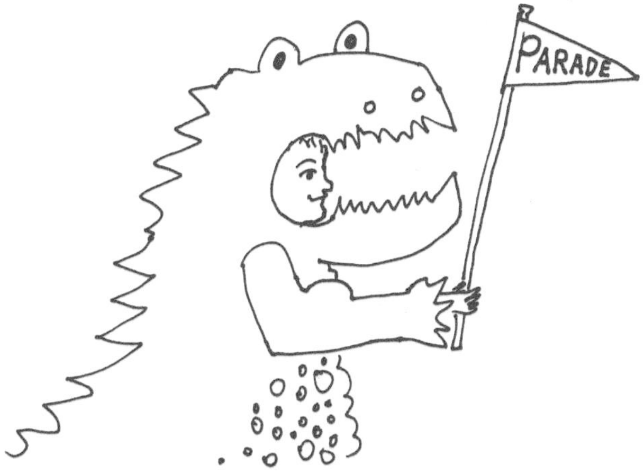

D2: COSTUME SHEET, PAGE ONE

Parade of Books Costume Ideas!

Children are marching together on _____, dressed as favorite storybook characters, rallying for a love of reading!

Please help by working with your child to make something to wear that fits our theme. (Please, let's avoid superheroes, cartoon characters, or horror-related costumes.)

Children are encouraged to bring a copy of their character's book on that day.

You are welcome to watch the parade outside at _____. Bring little brothers and sisters to cheer! Bring a camera!

Hope this idea sheet helps get creative juices flowing!

Use household items to make a fun costume in less than an hour!

EASY EARS

Cut "ears" out of construction paper (either triangles or half-moons), leaving a little extra length at the bottom of each ear. Fold a "flap" at the bottom of the ear and tape to a plastic headband. Great for mice (IF YOU GIVE A MOUSE A COOKIE by Laura Joffe Numeroff), bears (CORDUROY by Don Freeman), pigs (OLIVIA by Ian Falconer), or even aardvarks (ARTHUR by Marc Brown).

PAPER BAGS

Design a gown from one, as in THE PAPER BAG PRINCESS by Robert Munsch, or cut out a cowboy vest and don a cowboy hat like those in PECOS BILL by Steven Kellogg! More ideas in WHAT CAN YOU DO WITH A PAPER BAG? by the Metropolitan Museum of Art.

GOOGLY EYES

Make googly eyes for FROG AND TOAD by Arnold Lobel or LYLE, LYLE CROCODILE by Bernard Waber from egg cartons. Attach to half of a paper plate, colored green, and tie around the forehead. Wear green turtleneck, pants, or tights. Add green felt spikes for dinosaur or dragon characters.

FAIRY-TALE COSTUMES

Construction-paper crowns sparkling with glitter for kings and queens . . . scarf capes for princes . . . construction-paper hats (roll in a cone shape) with a scarf at the top for princesses or decorated with silver moons for wizards. Aluminum-foil stars on foil-covered sticks make excellent wands.

OR MAKE A PLACARD INSTEAD OF A COSTUME

Take two pieces of poster board, punch two holes at the top of each piece and tie yarn to attach the boards, leaving about 3 to 5 inches of "give" on the yarn. Your child can slip the boards over his or her head, carrying the boards on his or her shoulders. Your child can then decorate the poster board as a favorite book cover. A walking advertisement for a great book!

Need more inspiration and how-tos?
Visit www.planetesme.com/parade.html
and your public library.

D3: Parade of Books "Letter to Teacher" Sample

Hello, Wonderful Teachers!

IMPORTANT INFORMATION! The principal has approved our PARADE OF BOOKS, which will include grades _____ through _____. We welcome upper-graders as well, either as participants or audience members. Here's the deal:

The children get to dress up as their favorite storybook character toward the end of the day on _____ and march around the inside and (weather permitting) outside of the school. Families will be invited to cheer for their children outside. An apple juice reception will follow in the library. We need to stress to the children that this is NOT A HALLOWEEN PARADE, and costumes that are not related to children's books or are store-bought, trademarked character costumes are discouraged. Let's encourage the children to create their own costumes using items from their closets, construction paper, and recyclables. I am happy to come and demonstrate at your request. Teachers are welcome to wear costumes also, but of course this is your choice. Children should carry the book that inspired their costume in the parade.

Students will march as a class, and you will soon receive a dowel on which to hang a banner with your room number on it. Your class will march behind it. Thank you so much for doing this. While we ask that you and your class create the banner, anything else is optional: boom-box marching music or homemade instruments, character-name sashes, etc. You might want to have children present an oral "book share" in class about the book from which their costume is derived. Do whatever makes participation fun and exciting for you, not what interferes with any other classroom priorities.

Announcements for parents are being prepared and copied and will be ready for distribution early next week.

If you need help before the parade day, please ask, and feel free to share any questions, comments, or concerns with me. I'll keep you posted with any new information.

Sincerely,

p. 290. "My Mother's Nerves" copyright © 1975 by X. J. Kennedy. First appeared in *One Winter in August and Other Nonsense Jingles*, published by Margaret K. McElderry Books. Reprinted by permission of Curtis Brown, Ltd.

p. 291. From *Every Time I Climb a Tree* by David McCord. Copyright © 1949 by David McCord; first appeared in *The New Yorker*. By permission of Little, Brown and Company, Inc.

p. 293. "Chocolate Milk" from *New & Selected Poems*, 1963–1992 by Ron Padgett. Reprinted by permission of David R. Godine, Publisher, Inc. Copyright © 1995 by Ron Padgett.

p. 297. "Now" copyright © 1983 by Lee Bennett Hopkins. First appeared in *The Sky is Full of Song*, published by Harper & Row. Reprinted by permission of Curtis Brown, Ltd.

p. 300. From *Vineyard Seasons* by Susan Branch. Copyright © 1988 by Susan Stewart Branch. By permission of Little, Brown and Company, Inc.

p. 301. Hymes Jr, poem "My Favorite Word" from book *Oodles of Noodles*, copyright © 1964 by Lucia and James Hymes Jr. Reprinted by permission of Pearson Education, Inc.

p. 302. "A Lost Friend" from *Ten-Second Rainshowers: Poems by Young People*, compiled by Sandford Lyne. Reprinted with permission from Evan Marie Oxley.

p. 303. From *Literature Circles: Voice and Choice in the Student Centered Classroom* by Harvey Daniels. Copyright © 1994. Reprinted with permission from Stenhouse Publishers.

p. 334. "Singing Time" copyright © 1923 by George H. Doran Co., from *The Fairy Green* by Rose Fyleman. Used by permission of Doubleday, a division of Random House, Inc.

p. 367. From *I Can Make That*. Reprinted by permission of the publisher, Maple Tree Press, Inc.

p. 386. From *Ramona the Pest* by Beverly Cleary. Text Copyright © 1968 by Beverly Cleary.

pp. 468–69. From *The Author Studies Handbook* by Laura Kotch and Leslie Zackman. Published by Scholastic Professional Books, a division of Scholastic Inc. Copyright © 1995 by Laura Kotch and Leslie Zackman. Reprinted by permission.

Indices

Q

Esmé Raji Codell runs the popular children's literature Web site PlanetEsme.com. She is the author of the best-selling *Educating Esmé*, which won *ForeWord* magazine's Memoir of the Year and the distinguished Alex Award for Outstanding Book for Young Adult Readers, and *Sahara Special*, a novel for children. Her public-radio reading earned first place for national education reporting from the Education Writers Association. She has been a classroom teacher, school librarian, and children's bookseller. She lives in Chicago with her husband and son.